WILLIAM SMITH O'BRIEN
AND THE YOUNG IRELAND REBELLION OF 1848

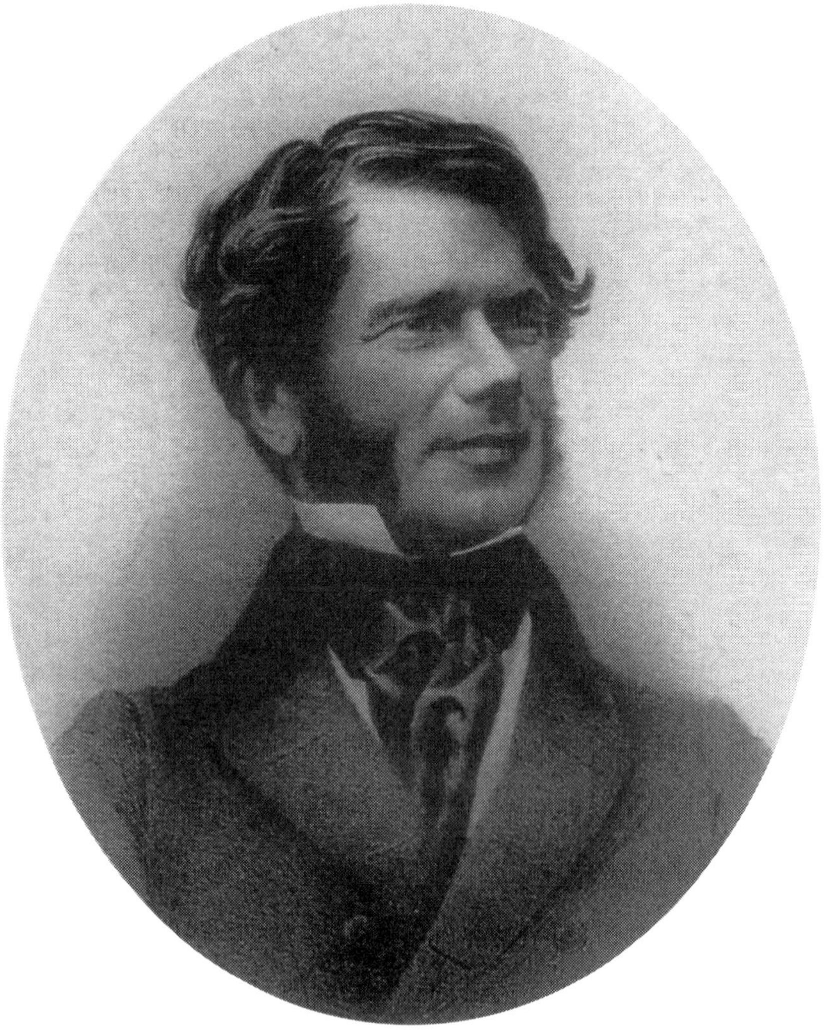

William Smith O'Brien
and the
Young Ireland Rebellion of 1848

Robert Sloan

FOUR COURTS PRESS

Set in 10 on 12 point Ehrhardt for
FOUR COURTS PRESS LTD
Fumbally Lane, Dublin 8, Ireland
e-mail: info@four-courts-press.ie
http:\\www.four-courts-press.ie
and in North America
FOUR COURTS PRESS
c/o ISBS, 5804 N.E. Hassalo Street, Portland, OR 97213.

© Robert Sloan 2000

A catalogue record for this title
is available from the British Library.

ISBN 1-85182-524-x hbk
ISBN 1-85182-589-4 pbk

All rights reserved. No part of this publication may be reproduced, stored in or introduced into a retrieval system, or transmitted, in any form or by any means (electronic, mechanical, photocopying, recording or otherwise), without the prior written permission of both the copyright owner and the publisher of this book.

Printed in Great Britain
by MPG Books, Bodmin, Cornwall

Contents

LIST OF ILLUSTRATIONS		7
PREFACE		9
1	Young Exile	11
2	New Directions	24
3	The Independent Member	43
4	Repeal	72
5	The Living Treasure	105
6	The Road to Secession	133
7	Hard Times	165
8	Springtime of Nations	197
9	Ballingarry	238
EPILOGUE		291
BIBLIOGRAPHY		304
INDEX		312

List of Illustrations

	O'Brien, from Gluckman's daguerreotype of 1848	*frontispiece*
1	O'Brien's prison quarters	151
2	The battle of Limerick	223
3	The geography of the Rebellion	251
4	Ballingarry	263
5	The affray at Widow McCormack's	277
6	Arrest of O'Brien at Thurles	282
7	O'Brien and Meagher in Kilmainham Gaol	292
8	O'Brien on trial at Clonmel	293
9	Pottery figures of O'Brien and his wife Lucy	299

CREDITS

1, 4, 5, 6, 8 *Illustrated London News*; 9 Maurice Denham Jephson, *An Anglo-Irish Miscellany. Some Records of the Jephsons of Mallow* (Dublin, 1964); 7 National Library of Ireland; 2 *Punch*; 3 Matthew Stout

Preface

On 30 July 1998, Taoiseach Bertie Ahern visited a derelict house near Ballingarry in Tipperary to commemorate a failed revolution. The revolution of 1848 has no proud place in the history of Irish nationalism, and the leader of the doomed enterprise, William Smith O'Brien, is not a celebrated hero of Ireland's struggle for independence. He stands very much in the shadow of Tone, Emmet, O'Connell and Davis. In many respects, the court of history has judged well, for O'Brien's revolt was a sorry affair with barely a redeeming feature. Nevertheless, the O'Brien story is an important one. As a young man, he conformed to the Tory principles of his family. Then, from 1835, he was the liberal Member of Parliament for Limerick. The epitome of the independent Member, his courageous opposition to Daniel O'Connell is the most striking feature of his conduct in the 1830s. In January 1837 and again in May 1839, O'Connell tried to turn the Limerick constituency against O'Brien, but the latter's spirited response marked him out as a man of principle and resolve. At this time, O'Brien believed in the British Parliament's capacity to give good government in Ireland. His attempts to secure liberal reform were largely unsuccessful, however, and he entered the 1840s with a growing conviction that he and the other Irish Members were wasting their time at Westminster. In 1843, his extraordinary Commons campaign for 'justice' for Ireland prefigured the tactics of Parnell, but the effort ended in disappointment and O'Brien joined the Repeal Association in October 1843. For the next five years he was a major political figure, first as O'Connell's loyal deputy, then as his critic and rival, and finally, in 1848, as the leader of the revolt in Tipperary. O'Brien was an exceptionally brave politician whose sense of honour and duty sent him into the lion's den time and time again. However, there is no disputing the incompetence of his management of affairs in 1848. His ignominious failure meant that he could be despised by men who were not his betters – by British leaders who failed to govern well, and by Irish politicians, including many who called themselves nationalists, who did not share his attachment to the idea that they should govern themselves.

This book was written with the assistance of many people. John Wigley and David Cooper read the manuscript and made extremely useful comments. Carol Allison did the typing, and David King guided me through the mysteries of computing. Arnold Hunt, then at Trinity College, Cambridge, and the staffs of the

Bodleian Library in Oxford, the British Library, Liverpool Record Office, the Royal Irish Academy, Trinity College, Dublin, and the National Library of Ireland were immensely tolerant and helpful. Anthony O'Brien welcomed me into his home in Dublin and permitted full access to the papers in his possession. The governors and Headmaster of Haberdashers' Aske's School, Elstree, kindly granted the sabbatical term in which much of the research was undertaken. Finally, a special debt of thanks is owed to Peter Forde, whose hospitality in Dublin was inexhaustible.

I

Young Exile

O'Brien was born at Dromoland in Clare on 17 October 1803, less than three months after Robert Emmet led the century's first and most celebrated armed revolt against British rule. The young O'Brien was to be influenced far less by contemporary politics than by his extraordinary family history. The O'Briens had claimed the kingship of Thomond (Clare) for 1,000 years until 1543. One of them, Brian Boru, was high king of Ireland and the warrior who defeated the Vikings at the great battle of Clontarf in 1014. Brian Boru's successors contested the high kingship for another century after his death at Clontarf, and later O'Briens scored notable victories against Norman and English invaders. In 1543, Murrough O'Brien, the 57th king of Thomond, relinquished his royal title and acknowledged Henry VIII as king of Ireland; he also accepted the royal supremacy and the family duly became Protestant. The Dromoland O'Briens, who were descended from Murrough's third son, Donough, represented county Clare in the Irish parliament during much of the 18th century. Sir Lucius, O'Brien's grandfather, was a member of that parliament for over 30 years and a leading supporter of Henry Grattan and the cause of Ireland's legislative independence. O'Brien's father, Sir Edward, was one of the defiant minority who voted against the Union in 1800.[1]

This was a history that made O'Brien a proud aristocrat. Later in life, he proclaimed that Murrough O'Brien, in renouncing the kingship of Thomond and accepting an English title (Inchiquin), had 'submitted to a derogation of dignity ... The lapse of more than three hundred years which has taken place since that humiliation was inflicted upon our family does not reconcile me to it.'[2] O'Brien's consciousness of being 'a child of its [Ireland's] most ancient race'[3] and a scion of 'one of the oldest and most distinguished families in Europe'[4] gave him a sense of station, and of duty to Ireland, that is the key to understanding his political career. He secured a different form of legacy on his mother's side. In 1799, Sir Edward

---

[1] Ivar O'Brien, *O'Brien of Thomond: The O'Briens in Irish History, 1500-1865* (Chichester, 1986). Donough O'Brien, *History of the O'Briens from Brian Boroimhe, AD 1000 to AD 1945* (London, 1949). Grania R. O'Brien, *These My Friends and Forebears: The O'Briens of Dromoland* (Whitegate, Co. Clare, 1991). [2] *Munster News*, 1 October 1862. Smith O'Brien Papers, MS 3375. [3] Ibid., MS 464, Draft Address of William Smith O'Brien, 1848, 15. [4] *Munster News*, 1 October 1862. Smith O'Brien Papers, MS 3375.

had married Charlotte, the daughter of a rich attorney, William Smith. Smith agreed to waive the mortgages he held on Dromoland, and his large estate at Cahirmoyle in west Limerick was bequeathed in the first instance to his daughters and in the second to William. Cahirmoyle did not come into O'Brien's possession until the 1830s, but his debt to his mother's father was acknowledged by his assumption of the middle name of Smith upon the old man's death in 1809.

O'Brien came to know well the severe and censorious side of his parents. However, his early childhood saw Sir Edward fond and proud of his 'quick & intelligent' boy, who at four years old was 'forwarder at his books than most boys at six or seven'.[5] Like his elder brother, he was sent away to be educated entirely in England – at a prep school in Welling (Kent), Harrow for three years, the Reverend Percy Scott's school at Great Harborough in Warwickshire, and Trinity College, Cambridge. It has been suggested that his English schooling bred in him the mannered reserve that subsequently made him seem cold and aloof to the Irish.[6] Sir Edward, seeing his sons when in London to attend Parliament, noted the contrast between elder brother Lucius, who was 'most amiable & lovable', and William who at nine was 'a little more of a Prickle'.[7] O'Brien certainly acquired an English accent and probably appeared and acted much like the young English gentlemen who were his companions. However, his pride in being an O'Brien meant that his education in England did nothing to shake his sense of being Irish. The ideal of service to country, meaning Ireland, was a constant refrain in a series of letters he wrote from England to his parents in 1819 and 1820, at the age of 15-16.

> ... my ambition is to serve and do good to my country; my desire is to prove myself not unworthy such [sic] a father as you, nor of the honourable name of O'Brien, of that family which has always been the defender and guardian of its country. I hope to imitate the example of a grandfather whose sole aim was to benefit his country. I shall be satisfied if I can show myself to be a faithful tho unprofitable servant of my God, the friend of Ireland, and a blessing to mankind ... At present there is but one thing that makes me wish to live, which is, the hope that I may some day be useful to my country.[8]

The weight of family history could hardly be more clearly visible. These letters reveal a rather prim and opinionated young man. He also showed an anxiety to please his mother that suggests an unhappy boarding school boy who craved the affection of absent parents. His mother was an evangelical Protestant and O'Brien's desire for her approval took the form of an unctuous piety:

---

5 Inchiquin Papers, T20/2961, Sir Edward O'Brien to Lady O'Brien, 29 June 1808.   6 Sir Charles Gavan Duffy, *Young Ireland: A Fragment of Irish History, 1840-1845* (Dublin, 1884), 141.   7 Inchiquin Papers, T22/2966, Sir Edward O'Brien to Lady O'Brien, 15 February 1813.   8 Smith O'Brien Papers, MS 8655 (3), O'Brien to Sir Edward and Lady O'Brien, 18 —— 1820; O'Brien to Lady O'Brien [March 1819]. See also ibid., O'Brien to Lady O'Brien, 10 March, 6 June 1819.

> I know you are very cautious about believing that a sinner has been awakened ... pray earnestly for me that I can have grace to keep me in the right way and may not fall a victim to the temptations of this sinful world ... pride reigns in my heart, and self-conceit ... I have another difficulty to contend with which makes me distrust myself as much as any thing – this is my excessive want of attention to family prayer and very often in the church ... I must confess ... there are many times when I go down on my knees and rise up again without having listened to one word ... I am ... thankful that I am not left to my own wicked nature.[9]

He earnestly hoped 'that we may all be led to seek our happiness in religion *for in that alone true happiness is to be found*'. Explaining his decision to abandon an ambition to join the Royal Navy, he wrote that 'God has directed me to give it up' and apprehended the 'vices and temptations' that made a sailor's cockpit 'very little better than a second hell'.[10] It is difficult to see here the O'Brien who would later challenge the privileges of the established Church and prove a less than avid church-goer. On a lighter note, O'Brien's priggishness was nowhere more evident than in his laboured comments on various recreational activities. His view that fishing 'accustoms a person to think slightly of giving his fellow creatures pain' shows a certain sensitivity, but he added: 'I have laid it down as a principle never to do anything which I do not think right, merely because other people do it, even if it should be my dearest friend or nearest relation.' Hunting earned severe censure as a diversion which could 'lessen the spirituality of the mind'. He could 'easily conceive of *doing nothing* lessening the spirituality of the mind, as when the mind is not employed in doing what is good it will invariably be employed in doing what is not right ... Riding is a fine amusement certainly but I can neither ride nor walk without an object in view'.[11] Perhaps O'Brien's notorious stiffness went deeper than anything even the English public school system could instil!

His decision against a naval career followed advice from Mr James O'Brien that Britain's naval supremacy – no other country's fleet 'would not be beaten in a minute by a few of our ships' – meant that he 'should have nothing to do'. Above all, he decided that, given his 'love of reading and getting knowledge', he would 'be able to serve my country much better in some other pursuit'. This studiousness was demonstrated, rather impressively, in his asking his parents to supply him with books by Cicero, Livy, Horace, Virgil and other classical authors, and he urged them to 'ask Mr Scott to let me study in my own room, for the other boys make such a noise sometimes ... Do ask Mr Scott for this. I have many reasons for asking which perhaps I do not like to say.'[12] The last may be a reference to bullying. He

---

9 Ibid., O'Brien to Lady O'Brien, 6 June 1819.   10 Ibid., O'Brien to Lady O'Brien [March 1819], 10 March 1819. See also ibid., O'Brien to Lady O'Brien, 18 March 1819.   11 Ibid., O'Brien to Lady O'Brien, 26 September 1819.   12 Ibid., MS 426, f1, James O'Brien to O'Brien, 27 February 1819; ibid., MS 8655 (3), O'Brien to Lady O'Brien, 10 March 1819. James O'Brien, an army officer, was not a relative; in his youth he 'had been taken under the wing of Sir Lucius O'Brien'. Grania O'Brien, *These*

was modest about his abilities: 'my talents are moderate, they are certainly not brilliant, but they are such as may with the assistance of application and a *good* education raise me to eminence in my profession. As to application, ... I think I am very far from being deficient in it. I possess an enthusiasm ... of the highest earthly kind.' He opted for a career at the bar, as his parents had 'long wished, and often urged'. He had been sent to the Reverend Scott's to improve his mathematical and scientific education (in preparation, presumably, for the Navy). In now faulting Scott's 'exclusively scientific knowledge' and inability to teach the classics, O'Brien was aware of how, even with Cahirmoyle, his situation differed from that of Lucius, the Dromoland heir: 'it is *really* more *necessary* that I should have a suitable education than that he should. For his fortune will make him independent, whereas I shall have to depend on my own industry.'[13]

In March 1821, he followed Lucius up to Trinity College, an institution then entering a golden age of scholarship that saw it produce Macaulay and Tennyson. O'Brien's university career was less than glorious, and it brought the development of some ominous traits. He appeared to lose his way, in that he spent five years taking a three-year degree, not least because there were at least two long interruptions in his studies, in 1824 and 1825, and a natural 'indolence' was noted by his sister Grace and Sir Edward.[14] He lost sufficient of his religious faith to make his sister warn that 'you are not fit to die & this ought to make you reflect very seriously on your state'.[15] In 1826 he claimed a 'view of religion' by which 'in this world, what is called vice brings with it its own punishment and virtue its own reward'.[16] His correspondence never again bore the sort of religious references that characterised the evangelical wing of the Church, a fact which possibly pleased Sir Edward and dismayed Lady Charlotte in equal measure.[17] In 1824, he planned to register at the King's Inns in Dublin to train as a barrister; instead, in April 1825 he registered at Lincoln's Inn in London, for the English bar, after his father told him he could 'see no prospect of my Low Politics getting him any situation' in Ireland and pressed him therefore 'to do something for himself'.[18]

One curious aspect of O'Brien's Cambridge career was his membership of the Apostles. This group was established in 1820, and O'Brien was elected (co-opted) as its 38th member in November 1824. The 12 Apostles met every Saturday evening to discuss the topic – usually political or literary – chosen by the member whose turn it was to present a paper (and act as host). According to one member from the 1820s, J.M. Kemble, 'No society ever existed in which more freedom of thought

---

My Friends and Forebears, 106. 13 Smith O'Brien Papers, MS 8655 (3), O'Brien to Sir Edward and Lady O'Brien, 18 — 1820. 14 O'Brien Papers in possession of Anthony O'Brien (AO), Letter Box, Bundle 3, Grace O'Brien to O'Brien, November 1824. Inchiquin Papers, T24/3626, Sir Edward O'Brien to Lady O'Brien, 19 April 1825. 15 O'Brien Papers (AO), Letter Box, Bundle 3, Grace O'Brien to O'Brien, 28 August 1821. 16 Ibid., Birthday Reflections of William Smith O'Brien, 17 October 1826. 17 On Sir Edward's not sharing his wife's religious zeal, see Aubrey de Vere, *Recollections of Aubrey de Vere* (New York, London, 1897), 78. 18 Inchiquin Papers, T24/2978, 3625, Sir Edward O'Brien to Lady O'Brien, 22 May 1824, 25 February 1825.

was found, consistent with the most perfect affection between the members ... Temper, moral conduct and good feeling were quite as essential as brilliant acquirements'. Sir Arthur Helps, another member, recorded that, 'Rank neither told for a man, nor against him. The same with learning', and even with 'goodness'; instead the Apostle had above all to be 'open-minded'.[19] One cannot be sure that O'Brien was a typical Apostle. His political and personal conduct during the years after Cambridge suggests he was in some degree the sort of free spirit described by Kemble and Helps. Whether there was much similarity between the man of 1848 and the nest of traitors in the Apostles of the 1930s is more questionable. Richard Deacon has argued, with 1848 in mind, that he demonstrated the 'passionate idealism' of the Apostles, and for Peter Allen he 'exemplifies, in an extreme form, the intense, enthusiastic political commitment then shared by ... most of the Apostles'. Perhaps so, but it is difficult to see in O'Brien's act of desperation in 1848 the intellectual iconoclasm and insidious treachery of the later Apostles.[20]

In October 1824, O'Brien received a letter from his uncle Lucius in which the young man's 'heart' and 'ability' and possession of 'whatever ennobles the human mind' received fulsome tribute.[21] His father, too, found him 'an amiable man with good principles' and 'a very good companion', with whom he 'got on very well' when they holidayed together in Paris in March-April 1825.[22] Whatever qualities O'Brien displayed to his family, or to the Apostles, they were not in the end sufficient to make him a successful student. Most of the undergraduates left after three years with an unexamined Pass (Ordinary) degree. A small number tried for the examined Mathematics and Classical Tripos, the Honours degree. O'Brien finally sat these exams in 1826 and was 'gulphed' – that is, he failed and was consigned to the ranks of the Pass men, the 'hoi polloi'. This seems the likely explanation of a letter that Sir Edward sent his wife in May 1926; disappointed and unimpressed, he feared that his son's 'unfortunate Cambridge affair will drive all idea [*sic*] of his going to the Bar out of his Head. If he ever was suited, to so laborious a profession, which I much doubt. I have better hopes of Edward.'[23] Of course, he still left Cambridge with the same degree as the great majority of students, and his brothers Lucius and (in 1829) Edward did no better.

From May 1826, O'Brien kept a rough diary in which his principal activities were noted briefly each day.[24] It suggests that he did not try seriously for the bar at Lincoln's Inn, where, as noted above, he had enrolled back in April 1825. He left

---

[19] Both quoted in Peter Allen, *The Cambridge Apostles: The Early Years* (Cambridge, 1978), 7-8. [20] Richard Deacon, *The Cambridge Apostles* (London, 1985), 30. Peter Allen, *The Cambridge Apostles: The Early Years*, 32. Allen, for whom 1848 proved O'Brien's 'unremitting dedication to the absurd', thought O'Brien a 'curious', unrepresentative choice as an Apostle. [21] Smith O'Brien Papers, MS 426, f2, Lucius O'Brien to O'Brien, 19 October 1824. [22] Inchiquin Papers, T24/2979, 3625, 3626, Sir Edward O'Brien to Lady O'Brien, 25 February, 26 March, 19 April 1825. [23] Ibid., T25/3627, Sir Edward O'Brien to Lady O'Brien, 2 May 1826. [24] O'Brien Papers (AO), Rough Diary, 1826-39.

London for Ireland in May 1826 and did not return until the following February, and there was another long absence between October 1827 and his going into Parliament in April 1828. He attended infrequently the obligatory Lincoln's Inn dinners: five in February 1827, four in May, three in June-July, and none at all thereafter.[25] Much later, in January 1834, he cancelled his registration 'having given up the intention of being called to the bar'.[26] The diary suggests a well-read young man, with an interest in history and in practical matters like poor laws and currency reform (but not the law). On 17 October 1826, on his 23rd birthday, he wrote lengthy 'Birthday Reflections' in which he admitted to feeling 'disappointed' with not having become 'engaged in active life'. He was pleased 'that good nature, benevolence & a desire to make others happy are qualities of my disposition. That I am neither sordid nor ungenerous. That I am incapable of envy.' He was more modest about his 'limited' acquirements, his tendency to 'languish' in 'ease and retirement', and his 'rather solid than brilliant' understanding. 'Judgement predominates over imagination. Wit and invention I have none. Discrimination is the faculty in which I most excel.' He aspired to 'a life of publick usefulness', reminiscent of the idea of service to his country that he preached as an adolescent. To be 'loved and respected in one's own generation and revered by posterity' was a worthy goal. Possessing a vain 'love of praise' and a desire for 'power', he proclaimed 'ambition' to be his 'master failing ... the element of my existence' – but it was ambition tempered and made virtuous by the ideal of service, what he called 'usefulness'. This motive 'consecrates and sanctifies' ambition. He would 'endeavour to establish a good moral character' and, hinting at political aspirations, work to improve beyond the 'indifferent speaker' and 'slow writer' he still was. All in all, it was a revealing portrait. Some aspects, notably his modesty and the emphasis on virtue and public service, will feature again in O'Brien's story, but the idea that he sought popularity and power is less easy to find in his subsequent conduct as a politician.[27]

In a letter O'Brien wrote in January 1826 to the editor of the *Clare Journal*, he suggested Tory views, endorsing the country's political institutions and expressing confidence that 'the germ of amendment' was correcting any imperfections. His claim that county Clare was 'untainted by the animosity of party' makes interesting reading in view of the extraordinary events to come. The letter proclaimed the merits of a canal project to make the river Fergus navigable as far as Ennis.[28] Though sincere in his advocacy (the idea was to be pursued for several years), the letter smacks of an attempt to advertise his merits to the borough's electors, perhaps in the knowledge that Lucius was about to succeed Sir Edward to the county seat and that the second son might aspire to the lesser position of Member for Ennis. On returning to Clare in May 1826, he became involved with the new Ennis Mechanics Institute, part of a general movement to advance the education of arti-

25 Ibid., Rough Diary, 1826-8.   26 *Records of the Hon. Society of Lincoln's Inn*, ii, Admissions 1800-1893, 113. *Lincoln's Inn Black Book*, xxii, 288.   27 O'Brien Papers (AO), Birthday Reflections of William Smith O'Brien, 17 October 1826.   28 Smith O'Brien Papers, MS 426, f4, O'Brien to the Editor of the *Clare Journal*, 9 January 1826. The letter was not sent.

sans. The sudden appearance in their midst of what must have seemed an exotic (and very English) creature did not fail to have an impact on the people of Ennis. In the general election in June, a group of inhabitants petitioned in his favour, citing his 'patriotic exertion' in relation to the Institute. His brother heard in Cambridge that O'Brien was 'to be returned for the Borough'. However, as Sheedy has noted, 'an agreement seems to have been made between the O'Brien and Fitzgerald families to alternate the right to appoint the Borough members', and so Vesey Fitzgerald nominated an English 'stranger', Franklyn Lewis. O'Brien spoke at the subsequent county election in favour of his brother, Lucius, who was elected in place of his father.[29]

For the 18 months after this, O'Brien's rough diary suggests a leisurely existence: lots of reading when at home and an active social life – dinners, balls, the opera – during the nine months he spent in London in 1827 and his three months in Dublin in February-April 1828. In February 1828, on arriving in Dublin, he joined the Catholic Association.[30] Its campaign for Emancipation – the right of Catholics to full civil equality, meaning access to Parliament and public office – was then in full swing. Like a growing number of Irish MPs, his father, as a liberal Tory, had been an active supporter of Emancipation (hence the reference to his low politics), 'one of the earliest of the advocates,' O'Brien wrote, of the 'good & glorious cause'.[31] O'Brien's conduct was only unusual in that he formally joined Daniel O'Connell's organisation. As he later explained, 'Though, myself, a Protestant I have felt as acutely as any Roman Catholic – more acutely than many – the injustice to which the Roman Catholics of this country have been habitually subjected. Under the influence of these impressions I became a member of the Catholic Association before I entered public life and have never ceased to vindicate their claim to be placed in all respects upon a perfect equality with Protestants.'[32]

In April 1828, aged 24, O'Brien entered Parliament. He did so under privileged circumstances that left him not at all embarrassed before his radical allies of the 1840s: 'I was brought into parliament by my father as member for the borough of Ennis, a close borough' – it had a maximum of only 13 electors – 'to which our family possessed an alternating nomination' with Vesey Fitzgerald.[33] The private correspondence reveals a little more about the nature of the election and about Sir Edward's dissatisfaction with O'Brien's purposeless existence. Sir Edward had to make a 'considerable sacrifice' which he could 'ill afford' – meaning he had to bribe the electors, or perhaps to purchase the seat from Fitzgerald. In a grudging letter

---

29 O'Brien Papers (AO), Letter Box, Bundle 2, Edward O'Brien to O'Brien, 2 June 1826. Kieran Sheedy, *The Clare Elections* (Dublin, 1993), 136-9. 30 O'Brien Papers (AO), Rough Diary, 16, 22 February 1828. 31 Smith O'Brien Papers, MS 18310 (1), O'Brien to Anne O'Brien, 21 February 1829. 32 Ibid., MS 464, Draft Address of William Smith O'Brien, 1848, 15. By 1829, 1400 of the Association's 14,000 members were Protestants. Thomas Wyse, *Historical Sketch of the Late Catholic Association of Ireland* (London, 1829), ii, 83. 33 Smith O'Brien Papers, MS 10515 (4), Smith O'Brien's sketch of his political life, 25 September 1844. See also ibid., MS 449, f3399, Smith O'Brien's account of his entry into Parliament, n.d. The vacancy arose on Lewis's retirement.

to his son, he wrote that, 'tho dissatisfied with you', he did not 'seriously think of passing you by, at the most important & perhaps critical period of your life'. His 'hope [that] you will justify the confidence I place in you' implies a distinct *lack* of confidence. He finished with an interesting comment on the nature of the process: 'The election will be held on Wednesday, & *I by no means wish* you to be there, as it is not a popular election, & it is not usual to take any notice of the event.'[34] To Lady Charlotte he doubted if either Lucius or William would be 'able to distinguish themselves', but he believed that it was 'of great importance' that William should have 'an object to give his mind full occupation, and if he does not succeed in exerting himself he shall have nobody to blame but himself'. Warming to this theme a few days later, he wrote that, 'Active employment in legitimate & honourable pursuits is the secure foundation of happiness, & I hope & believe that we shall both have reason to congratulate ourselves on William's getting into Parliament. It will at once place him in the best class of society & raise his mind to a higher standard.'[35]

O'Brien replied to his father with a 'most satisfactory letter', in which he promised to resume his studies for the bar at Lincoln's Inn.[36] He did not do so. However, O'Brien's maiden speech (in favour of a paper currency) was greeted by a father who seemed relieved that his son had found his vocation: 'You will see by the Morning Post which I send that William does not intend to be a silent Member of the House & I have great satisfaction in hearing that he acquitted himself reasonably well. He is very attentive to the business of the House & I hope ... it will give him that occupation which his mind seemed to want ...'[37] His first-ever recorded vote was cast in favour of Catholic Emancipation, after the major debate initiated by Sir Francis Burdett in May 1828. In July, he said the Tory government's Irish policy had provoked 'the scorn of Ireland and the derision of Europe' and declared that 'whatever influence his name and character could command should be used to promote the cause of the Catholics'.[38] Because of the Catholic issue, in 1828 he 'gave no regular support to the Tory Ministry although my father was one of the class called Liberal Conservatives'.[39]

The political newcomer unexpectedly found himself caught up in national affairs with the advent of the Clare by-election of July 1828. Tom Steele, O'Connell's loyal supporter in Clare, at first urged O'Brien to stand, promising that the Clare liberals and the Association would 'support you to the utmost of our power'.[40] O'Brien

---

[34] O'Brien Papers (AO), Letter Box, Bundle 2, Sir Edward O'Brien to O'Brien, 19 April 1828. [35] Inchiquin Papers, T26/2983, Sir Edward O'Brien to Lady O'Brien, 28 April, 2 May 1828. [36] Ibid., Sir Edward O'Brien to Lady O'Brien, 1 May 1828. [37] Ibid., Sir Edward O'Brien to Lady O'Brien, 2 June 1828. *Hansard*, New Series, xix, 1014, 3 June 1828, O'Brien. [38] *Hansard*, xix, 675-80, 12 May 1828, Division; xix, 1613-14, 3 July 1828, O'Brien. Lucius also voted for Emancipation in the May division. [39] Smith O'Brien Papers, MS 10515 (4), Smith O'Brien's sketch of his political life, 25 September 1844. [40] Ibid., MS 426, f9, Steele to O'Brien, 19 June 1828.

had to reject the offer; Sir Edward had 'promised his support to Mr Fitzgerald', and the latter was 'a supporter of Catholic Emancipation'.[41] He also revealed his fundamental conservatism when he told Steele 'that the kindly relations subsisting between landlord and tenant ought not upon light grounds to be torn asunder'. This became the central feature of the famous Clare by-election, when the landlords, including Sir Edward, found their influence challenged and broken by Catholic priests who persuaded the tenantry to elect an outsider from Kerry, Daniel O'Connell. Ironically, given the political enmity that the contest would begin, O'Connell's election address included a fulsome tribute to O'Brien, the 'excellent' young man who 'has paid the Catholic rent and is a member of the Association'.[42] O'Brien warmly supported the Emancipation bill that followed O'Connell's victory – 'I feel like a slave who has shaken off his chains,' he told his sister – and he (and Lucius) duly voted for the measure in March 1829.[43] However, this did not diminish his resentment over the way in which the Clare tenants had been induced to rebel. He supported the two political securities attached to Emancipation. Firstly, on the bill to suppress the Association, O'Brien 'expressed his concurrence in any act which would put an end to the ascendancy of a faction, which already revelled in the anticipated triumph of civil war' – this despite his own membership of the Association. Secondly, the bill to deprive the 40-shilling freeholders of the vote – now seen as 'a weapon fatal to the authority of the landlord', in Peel's words – had his 'hearty concurrence, as a measure most salutary for Ireland. It would put an end to the political strife between landlord and tenant.'[44] These events initiated the prolonged state of hostility between O'Brien and O'Connell which was to show many times that political courage was not one of the qualities lacking in O'Brien.

In June 1829, another form of courage was called for when the animosity generated by the Clare election led to O'Brien's fighting a duel with Tom Steele. The Commons had voted in May 1829 against permitting O'Connell to remain in Parliament without another, post-Emancipation election. In a hustings speech on 9 June 1829, O'Connell denounced Lucius's duplicity in this matter. At Christmas 1828 Lucius had told an intermediary (Pierce Mahony), and subsequently said to O'Connell himself, that he 'recognised me as his colleague' (as Member for Clare) and that 'whatever support he could give I may fully calculate on when we met in London' – and then in the May division Lucius and 'his worthy brother' walked out of the House without voting. O'Connell threatened to 'bring the [rotten] state of the Borough of Ennis' before the Commons and asked the Clare voters, 'What has Mr Lucius O'Brien done for you?' This led to an angry letter from Donough

---

41 Ibid., f11, O'Brien to Steele, n.d. The two letters were published in July 1829. *Clare Journal*, 6 July 1829.   42 Thomas Wyse, *Historical Sketch of the Late Catholic Association*, i, 371-90. Sheedy, *Clare Elections*, 142-53.   43 Smith O'Brien Papers, MS 18310 (1), O'Brien to Anne O'Brien, 21 February 1829. Hansard, xx, 892-6, 1633-8, 6, 30 March 1829, Divisions.   44 Hansard, xx, 212, 1348-9, 10 February, 19 March 1829, O'Brien. The measure reduced the number of county voters from 216,000 to only 37,000; see K.T. Hoppen, *Elections, Politics and Society in Ireland, 1832-1885* (Oxford, 1984), 1. Peel is quoted in R.F. Foster, *Modern Ireland, 1600-1972* (London, 1988), 301.

O'Brien, Lucius's uncle, apparently designed to provoke a duel. O'Connell privately poured scorn on 'the house of Dromoland' and on Lucius's performance as a 'useless' supporter of Emancipation and a Member who had 'done nothing for the County of Clare'. He refused to consider a duel: 'My principles are well known. There is blood – human blood – on my hand and nothing can tempt me to commit that crime again.'[45]

O'Brien, however, obviously infuriated by O'Connell's questioning of his brother's integrity, blundered into a duel. He sent a letter to the *Clare Journal* in which he condemned O'Connell's 'grossest falsehoods' about the O'Briens and the 'pernicious designs' of a man bent on instigating 'rancour and anarchy'. But he also claimed that the gentry of Clare had been 'unanimous' in their opposition to O'Connell in 1828. He apparently underlined the word 'unanimous' for it was printed in italics.[46] Tom Steele and O'Gorman Mahon, Clare landlords who had backed O'Connell, were angered by the suggestion they 'had ceased to be reckoned among the "gentry" of County Clare'.[47] Steele sent a letter to the *Globe and Traveller* newspaper in London charging that 'the assertion of Mr O'Brien is a lie and that he knew it to be so', and denouncing O'Brien's 'blackguardism' and 'personal impertinence, audacious falsehood, and political baseness and ingratitude'.[48] Though the editor substituted asterisks for these defamatory expressions, O'Brien insisted on a public apology from Steele and, on not getting one, demanded 'the reparation used among gentlemen in such cases'.[49] This was hardly surprising in the circumstances: although Irish opinion, led by O'Connell, began to turn against duelling in the 1820s, it remained a common occurrence and, provocatively insulted as he was, O'Brien's response was to be expected from the son of an aristocratic (and for long a duelling) family.[50]

The duel took place at Kilburn Meadows, outside London, at seven o'clock on the evening of 30 June 1829. From 12 paces each man fired once and missed. Both Steele and Woronzow Greig, O'Brien's second, subsequently paid tribute to O'Brien's 'gallantry' and 'courage'.[51] In fact, however, O'Brien emerged from the affair with his reputation only just intact. Just before the duel he had effectively apologised to Steele for his initial error – 'In using the term unanimous I merely intended to repeat what was notorious, ... that the overwhelming majority of the landowners and gentlemen of Clare supported Mr Fitzgerald but by no means meaning to cast any reflection upon the individuals who opposed him.' He subsequently

---

45 *Dublin Evening Post*, 13 June 1829, O'Connell. Maurice R. O'Connell (ed.), *The Correspondence of Daniel O'Connell* (Dublin, 1972-80), iv, 1581, 1593, 1594, 1599, O'Connell to Mahony, 4 June, 29, 31 July, 10 August 1829; 1595, Mahony to O'Connell, 1 August 1829. O'Connell swore that he would never fight again after he killed John D'Esterre in a duel in 1815.   **46** *Clare Journal*, 22 June 1829, O'Brien to the Freeholders of the County of Clare, 17 June 1829.   **47** Denis Gwynn, *The O'Gorman Mahon: Duellist, Adventurer and Politician* (London, 1934), 86.   **48** Smith O'Brien Papers, MS 426, f18, Steele to Greig, 29 June 1829.   **49** Gwynn, *The O'Gorman Mahon*, 93, O'Brien to Steele, 30 June 1829.   **50** James Kelly, *That Damned Thing Called Honour: Duelling in Ireland, 1570-1860* (Cork, 1995), 253-71.   **51** Smith O'Brien Papers, MS 426, f15, Shawe to O'Brien, 3 July 1829; f36, Memorandum of Woronzow Greig, July 1829.

Young Exile

wrote again to the *Clare Journal* 'disclaiming all intention of offering any insult to those gentlemen who supported O'Connell'.[52] His young brother felt he had been 'incautious' in his words, while his exasperated father scolded him for misusing the word 'unanimous' and told him that the slighted gentry of Clare were 'all in arms against you'.[53] At Kilburn, after the two men had fired, Greig intervened as Steele reached for his other pistol, declaring the affair terminated. Then O'Gorman Mahon, Steele's second and a famous duellist, demanded 'satisfaction on his part and that of his brothers for the same supposed insult which was the cause of the meeting with Mr Steele'. Greig rejected this 'very improper method of proceeding' and persuaded Mahon to desist.[54] However, the Mahon-inspired account that was published in the newspapers implied that O'Brien had been withdrawn prematurely from the duel with Steele and had been unwilling to fight Mahon. A false rumour went round that Greig, on stepping forward after the first shots, had shouted, 'Good God, my friend is shot'. Much embarrassment ensued, as O'Brien and Greig tried to publish an account that safeguarded O'Brien's good name and complained privately about the 'ruffianly and ungentlemanlike' conduct of Mahon.[55] All in all, O'Brien appears a political innocent who was wrong footed from the beginning.

Although the fact that a duel occurred was not especially remarkable, O'Brien's conduct perhaps sheds some light on his later political career. The latter saw him driven forwards, time and again, by a compelling sense of 'duty', often in apparent disregard of the practical consequences. It is fanciful to speak of the politics of the duellist, but one can certainly discern the politics of aristocratic pride. O'Brien's background made him a man for whom the merits of expediency and compromise ranked far below duty, honour and reputation.

O'Brien's diary entry for 3 April 1830 was 'Son born'. The mother was Mary Ann Wilton, the sister of a male servant of Lucius O'Brien. It is not clear when O'Brien's relationship with Mary began. He frequently dined at her mother's London residence from April 1827, with such frequency indeed (thrice in April, five times in May, and so on) that it is possible his relationship with the daughter of the house began in 1827. On 24 January 1829, he wrote to his sister, Anne, 'Tell Grace [another sister] that I have written to the idol of my heart ... I hope it will do no harm. If she still loves me it cannot, & if absence has rendered her indifferent, which I do not believe, it can do no harm either. One thing is certain, that if she fails me I shall mourn for ever.'[56] The language of the letter from brother Edward three weeks later suggests that their parents may have objected to the liaison; Edward wrote of his prayers 'that the hearts of those who have your happiness in their power

---

52 Ibid., f25, Note by Smith O'Brien, n.d.; f32, O'Brien to Greig, July 1829. *Clare Journal*, 6 July 1829.
53 Smith O'Brien Papers, MS 426, f29, Sir Edward O'Brien to O'Brien, 11 July 1829; f34, Edward O'Brien to Greig, July 1829.   54 Ibid., f36, Memorandum of Woronzow Greig, July 1829.   55 Ibid., ff28, 32, O'Brien to Greig, July 1829; ff31, 33, 34, Edward O'Brien to Greig, July 1829. *Clare Journal*, 9 and 13 July 1829.   56 Smith O'Brien Papers, MS 18310 (1), O'Brien to Anne O'Brien, 24 January 1829.

might be softened towards you. I have perceived much lately to shew that little is wanting to complete the work of reconciliation.' He hoped that God would give O'Brien 'strength to overcome' the 'fretful anxiety for the future which I daresay you have suffered from', as a result, possibly, of parental disapproval so strong that his inheritance was endangered.[57] O'Brien initially gave way, or was rejected; writing to his sister some days later, he pined over the thought that 'that full confidence in the affection of one for whom no trial, no length of absence, could have altered my attachment is no more. I am pretty secure indeed against any alteration in my feelings for in all probability I shall never desire to unite myself with any other – but I have lost that consoling reliance ... which sustained me through so many hours of wounded affection & blighted hope.'[58] Then, on 4 January 1830, O'Brien recorded: 'Wrote to my father about MW', in all likelihood about the pregnancy. Sir Edward's reply is not extant – the diary entry merely reads 'Letter from Sir E.' (11 January) – but his response was probably hostile. Two weeks after the birth, Lucius arrived in London to help his brother deal with the repercussions of his folly. On 28 April, Lucius wrote to Mary Wilton:

> I hereby promise in the event of the death of my brother William Smith O'Brien, during our joint lives to continue to you during your life the annuity of Fifty pounds granted and secured to you by his bond of even date herewith ... with this Proviso that if ever at any time this affair be brought before the Public & Mr William Smith O'Brien's name or my own name appear but once in a Public paper as connected with this transaction so long as the annuity be paid my promise shall be void. It is made solely with a view to my Brother's convenience & not from any kind of regard to yourself with whom I am not acquainted ...

The rest was deleted but, still legible, it says much about Lucius's view of the situation:

> or your mother who ought to have taken better care of you. On this day too I shall discharge your brother though I value him as a good and faithful servant and am very sorry to do so and consider every kind of transaction ended between me and any of the members of your Family except in the event which this letter contemplates.[59]

The matter did not end there. O'Brien and Mary Wilton had a second child, this time a daughter, on 3 July 1831. By this stage, the relationship was over. O'Brien went to Ireland in April 1831 and did not return for either his daughter's

---

[57] O'Brien Papers (AO), Letter Box, Bundle 2, Edward O'Brien to O'Brien, 16 February 1829. [58] Smith O'Brien Papers, MS 18310 (1), O'Brien to Anne O'Brien, 21 February 1829. [59] Inchiquin Papers, T28/4649, Lucius O'Brien to Mary Wilton, 28 April 1830. O'Brien's diary entry for 27 April read 'Pd Mrs W. £14'.

Young Exile

birth or the joint baptism of the two children at St Margaret's Church, Westminster, on 6 January 1832. The boy was called William O'Brien and the girl Mary Wilton O'Brien, and William Smith O'Brien was given as their father. In 1989, a Madame Brignot from Paris, who was staying at Dromoland (now a luxury hotel), made enquiries about her ancestor, William Smith O'Brien. This led to the discovery of the later history of O'Brien's secret family. Mary Wilton, passing off as a 'widow', married a man called Henry (his surname), according to a Boulogne-sur-Mer record of 1846. William O'Brien became an engineer but died of paraplegia and rheumatic fever in 1874. Daughter Mary Wilton O'Brien married a Frenchman, Eugene Bourgain, on 17 March 1857 in London; the marriage certificate gave William Smith O'Brien as her father but described him, wrongly, as 'deceased'. In 1995, Ivar O'Brien and Hugh Weir, present-day members of the O'Brien family, met 93-year-old Madame Bourgain, Mary's granddaughter.[60]

This was not yet the age of Victorian morality and any judgement of O'Brien's relationship with Mary Wilton must recognise that such behaviour was unusual rather than unknown. Indeed, Lady Charlotte's father, William Smith, had kept a mistress at Cahirmoyle for many years and produced two illegitimate children (see below), so it was not unheard of even within the family. Whether O'Brien acknowledged and made provision for (or even knew of) his daughter is uncertain. His calling his second legitimate son William (1839), when he already had a child of that name, appears insensitive, but he may not have known how Mary christened their son, and his eventual wife's possible ignorance of the earlier affair may have complicated matters. It may be that his letter to Sir Edward in January 1830 expressed a desire to marry Mary; of course, O'Brien's financial dependence was such that he could not have married her in defiance of his parents.

Whatever the rights and wrongs of O'Brien's conduct, its importance in identifying his true nature cannot be underestimated. Taken with the evidence of his aimless existence as a young man and the fact he fought two duels (there would be a second in 1831), the Mary Wilton affair shows that he was not the staid and predictable individual some have described. If it is accepted that there was an impulsive and headstrong side to him, it is easier to comprehend the twists and turns of O'Brien's subsequent political career. In a sense, however, these excitements and troubles belonged to a period in the young man's life that was drawing to a close. Around this time, O'Brien began to take politics seriously and in the process seemed almost to recreate himself, eventually to become a respected, industrious and liberal Member of Parliament. It is to O'Brien's political development that one must now turn.

---

60 Hugh W.L. Weir, 'William Smith O'Brien's Secret Family', in *The Other Clare*, xx (April 1996), 55-6.

2

New Directions

Sir Edward was right in thinking that his son applied himself well to Parliamentary business. O'Brien told his sister he would 'attend with the utmost assiduity to the business of the House' and forswear the temptations of 'society', and, according to the rough diary, his attendance record in the Commons was indeed immaculate.[1] His contribution to debate, however, was minimal: for example, between April 1829 and the dissolution of July 1830 he spoke only twice. (O'Connell, by way of contrast, was heard 90 times in three months (March-June) in 1830.) He did write a pamphlet on the monopoly of the East India Company, and it was with obvious pride that Sir Edward distributed it among friends and acquaintances.[2] In the pamphlet, O'Brien came out as a moderate reformer, wanting some liberalisation of the Company's economic monopoly and its system of government in India. For a future nationalist he entertained some interesting ideas, identifying completely with the views of the English upper class: 'the great mass of the [Indian] people yield an obedience founded upon gratitude for the blessings of our rule', which was 'mild, beneficent, and humane'. He predicted that the 'debasing creed' of Hinduism would 'give place to the pure morality and exalted spirit of Christianity' and urged that 'we must teach them to feel as British citizens ... In learning our language, and reading our books, the natives of India will imbibe their spirit, and exchange the feelings and ideas of Asia for the juster notions and more elevated principles of Europe.'[3] Such sentiments give some indication of the distance O'Brien would later travel from his intellectual and political roots. He also secured a place (having requested one of Peel) on the Commons select committees appointed in 1830 and 1831 to inquire into the Company's affairs.[4] His father was pleased to hear that the committee's work had 'given new life to the energies of William's mind & he is delighted at coming almost daily in collision with men of superior minds ... I have

---

[1] Smith O'Brien Papers, MS 18310 (1), O'Brien to Anne O'Brien, 21 February 1829. See also O'Brien Papers (AO), Letter Box, Bundle 3, Anne O'Brien to O'Brien, 18 February 1829. [2] Inchiquin Papers, T26/3031, Sir Edward O'Brien to Lady O'Brien, 22, 25 February 1830. [3] William Smith O'Brien, *Considerations relative to the renewal of the East-India Company's Charter* (London, 1830), 33-5. [4] Smith O'Brien Papers, MS 426, f41, Peel to O'Brien, 8 January 1830. *Journals of the House of Commons*, lxxxv, 23, 9 February 1830; ibid., lxxxvi, 214, 4 February 1831.

no doubt that both he and his brother [Lucius] will get into the very best society of London.'⁵ Remarkably, Sir Edward wrote in these fond and optimistic terms in the month after hearing of Mary Wilton's pregnancy; he would always be quick to forgive.

At this time, O'Brien was a loyal, if silent, Tory, as he subsequently acknowledged when he wrote that 'after the Duke of Wellington carried Emancipation and lost the support of the Ultra Tories I became an adherent of his administration'.⁶ Because Emancipation had cost Wellington the backing of the ultras, he felt that the Duke 'had a fair claim to the generous support of such of the advocates of Catholic Emancipation as, like myself, were unpledged to any other party. Under these circumstances I voted with the ministry upon all motions which appeared to me to be brought forward for the purpose of harassing what was, at that time [1829-30], a very weak administration.' In supporting Wellington, he was also 'acceding to the wishes of my father', as he told his Limerick constituents in 1837.⁷ In fact, on the numerous occasions in 1830 when liberals and Whigs divided the House, O'Brien did not once vote against the Tory ministry; in the (relatively few) divisions for which *Hansard* recorded both majority and minority votes, O'Brien either sided with the government or did not vote. His later claim that he voted 'against the Government ... upon some questions which involved great constitutional principles'⁸ is not borne out by the available evidence. In January 1830, Peel thanked O'Brien for his 'approbation, confidence and support'.⁹ The famous civil list division of 15 November 1830 saw O'Brien siding with the defeated Tory ministry, going on to send Peel 'assurances of esteem and friendship' in the wake of Wellington's resignation.¹⁰ He 'dined with Sir R. Peel' on 15 December 1830.¹¹

O'Brien did not relax his hostility to O'Connell, in July 1830 accusing him of 'sowing dissensions and of alienating the affections of the people from the institutions of the country and impeaching all Irish members who did not choose to enlist under his incendiary banner'.¹² They naturally differed on the great issue of the period, Parliamentary Reform. O'Brien's views were flagged up by his support for the disfranchisement of the 40s. freeholders in 1829 and his voting record in some of the preliminary skirmishes of 1830.¹³ In May 1830, he opposed O'Connell's universal suffrage bill – 'The multitudes have always been the dupes of the wicked and designing, the instruments of tyranny, the enemies of freedom' – and, significantly, added 'a few words in favour of the borough system, against which so many and such violent attacks had been made'. He argued that members of noble families who

---

5 Inchiquin Papers, T26/3031, Sir Edward O'Brien to Lady O'Brien, 27 February 1830.   6 Smith O'Brien Papers, MS 10515 (4), Smith O'Brien's sketch of his political life, 25 September 1844.   7 *DEP*, 23 December 1834. *Limerick Chronicle*, 28 January 1837.   8 Smith O'Brien Papers, MS 10515 (4), Smith O'Brien's sketch of his political life, 25 September 1844.   9 Ibid., MS 426, f41, Peel to O'Brien, 8 January 1830.   10 *Hansard*, Third Series, i, 549-556, 15 November 1830, Division. Smith O'Brien Papers, MS 426, f45, Peel to O'Brien, 20 November 1830.   11 O'Brien Papers (AO), Rough Diary, 15 December 1830.   12 *Clare Journal*, 30 June 1830. Sheedy, *Clare Elections*, 159-60.   13 *Hansard*, New Series, xxii, 360-1, 724-6, 11, 18 February 1830, Divisions; xxiv, 1255, 28 May 1830, Division.

represented boroughs in the Commons later brought to the Lords some experience 'as advocates of popular rights'.[14] In March 1831, the Whigs revealed a Reform Bill that stunned moderate opinion and made one of O'Brien's supporters wonder 'what broguemaker, chandler or shoemaker may be elected for Ennis'.[15] O'Brien was involved in the Tory scheming that preceded the second reading: Lord Chandos thanked him for his 'very important opinion' and promised that if a Whig victory seemed likely 'I shall deem it to be my duty to collect together several influential friends to suggest to them the propriety and the policy of some such measure as you have lucidly favoured me with. There are two parties to be consulted ... the Ex Ministers and the Ultra Tories. I hope to have the pleasure of seeing you in the House today when we can talk over the subject.'[16] Neither O'Brien nor Chandos spoke in the debate, so the nature of the strategem is not known. Astonishingly, O'Brien was absent for the division and this allowed the second reading to be carried by one vote, 302 to 301; he had returned home to support his father in another by-election for Clare.[17]

There were indications that O'Brien was now moving away from Toryism. It is possible that his hedging prompted Peel's post-resignation 'earnest request that no consideration of personal confidence in me may prevent you from taking any part in political affairs or forming any political connection which may best suit your views of the public interest'.[18] On 2 January 1831, O'Brien initiated what became a cordial and prolonged correspondence with the Whig Chief Secretary, Lord Stanley, complimenting him on his 'able and vigorous' response to the upsurge of 'revolutionary spirit' in the forms of agrarian violence and agitation for repeal of the Union. He pledged his 'readiness ... to cooperate with the Government in the preservation of the Public Peace & of the security of the Empire'. O'Brien warned that 'the Antiunion feeling is nearly *universal* among the lower and middling classes in the south of Ireland'. His solution – what he deemed the 'decisive action [that] will save the empire from dismemberment or civil war' – was rather more Whiggish than Tory: 'This is therefore the moment for bringing into combined action the two principles of government – Firmness and Conciliation.'[19] On 8 February, when Lord Althorp (the Whig Leader of the Commons) spoke against repeal of the Union but in favour of 'measures of conciliation and kindness' for Ireland, O'Brien congratulated the minister on his 'manly declaration' and 'exhorted the Ministers to continue to show that they were not indifferent to the real interests of Ireland; "to be just and fear not", and he was sure they might rely on the national gratitude and on certain success'.[20] Increasingly, O'Brien was presenting his own ideas on

---

14 Ibid., xxiv, 1234-5, 28 May 1830, O'Brien. Sheedy, *Clare Elections*, 159. **15** Smith O'Brien Papers, MS 426, f97, Fitzgerald to O'Brien, 5 March 1831. **16** Ibid., f56, Chandos to O'Brien [12 March 1831]. Dated from O'Brien's rough diary. **17** *Hansard*, Third Series, iii, 805-24, 22 March 1831, Division. O'Brien Papers (AO), Rough Diary, 14 March 1831. *Clare Journal*, 21 March 1831. **18** Smith O'Brien Papers, MS 426, f45, Peel to O'Brien, 20 November 1830. O'Brien's 1830-31 letters to Peel do not survive in the Peel Papers. **19** Derby Papers, 920/DER (14), 122/5, O'Brien to Stanley, 2 January 1831. Smith O'Brien Papers, MS 426, f59, Stanley to O'Brien, 6 January 1831. **20** *Hansard*, Third Series,

'just' measures for Ireland, and they were not Tory ideas. His principal recommendation to Stanley – the 'expedient' by which 'the Antiunion cry could be most effectually suppressed' – was that the state should make 'a provision for the Catholic Clergy ... you will never have any guarantee for the security of British connexion as long as so influential a body remain wholly unattached to the state.' He proceeded to give the Commons notice of his intention to propose state payment of the Catholic clergy. This was to advocate what most Irish Tories regarded as endowment of popish error.[21] His support for an Irish poor law, with a published pamphlet, interventions in Parliament, and the introduction in 1831 of his own poor relief bill, brought him into alliance with Irish liberal Members like James Grattan, Villiers Stuart, his seconder, and Nicholas Philpot Leader, and put him in a small minority among Irish Tories, who tended to be concerned about the tax burden on their property.[22] When O'Connell challenged the education grant to the Kildare Place Society, a Protestant organisation that Catholics regarded with suspicion, O'Brien's response – that 'under proper regulations the grant might be most beneficial; at present it was misapplied' – was not that of an Irish Tory.[23]

All of these measures will be examined below, for – and this bears out the point – they made up much of the legislative programme of the indisputably liberal MP for Limerick that O'Brien would become. He later described his disillusionment with the Tories' 'blind and obstinate resistance to all reform'.[24] There was a developing accommodation with Whiggery and the prospect of beneficial reforms – albeit one that was probably shaken by the excesses of the Reform Bill and what it might mean for the likes of Ennis and its nominee Member. It is possible that his absence for that second reading division reflected O'Brien's political ambivalence as well as his father's electoral circumstances. On 26 March 1831, just after his visit home, O'Brien was admitted as a member of the new Ennis Independent Club that the local liberals had established to fight the next election on an extended franchise.[25] Then, 'as an Irishman', he opposed the Tories on General Gascoyne's motion to 'prevent Ireland getting those additional Members which Ministers had proposed to give to that country' (O'Brien), so finding himself voting with the Whig government in the defeat that prompted the dissolution of Parliament.[26] It must be acknowledged that the paucity of evidence on O'Brien's frame of mind at this crucial time makes it difficult to follow and explain the precise course of his political development.

---

ii, 323-5, 331, 8 February 1831, Althorp, O'Brien. All *Hansard* references below are Third Series.   **21** Derby Papers, 920/DER (14), 122/5, O'Brien to Stanley, 2 January 1831. *Clare Journal*, 7 April 1831. **22** William Smith O'Brien, *Plan for the Relief of the Poor in Ireland, with observations on the English and Scotch Poor Laws, addressed to the landed proprietors of Ireland* (London, 1830). *Parliamentary Papers*, 1830-1, ii, 163. *Hansard*, i, 415-6, 11 November 1830, O'Brien; ii, 246, 8 February 1831, O'Brien; iii, 1222-3, 30 March 1831, O'Brien.   **23** *Hansard*, iii, 403, 14 March 1831, O'Brien.   **24** *DEP*, 23 December 1834. *Limerick Chronicle*, 28 January 1837.   **25** Smith O'Brien Papers, MS 426, f99, Cullinan to O'Brien, 26 March 1831.   **26** *Hansard*, iii, 1236, 1689-1700, 1734, 12, 19, 20 April 1831, O'Brien, Division, O'Brien.

In March 1831, O'Brien fought his second duel, suggesting he still had some of the impetuosity of the young aristocrat. In the general election of August 1830, Lucius had lost Clare to O'Gorman Mahon after a bitter contest in which the latter's brother, William Mahon, took a part in opposing and denigrating the House of Dromoland. O'Gorman Mahon was accused of 'bribery and corruption' and unseated on petition, causing the by-election in which Sir Edward tried to return to Parliament. On the first day, at Ennis court-house, William Mahon publicly denounced Sir Edward's political record and accused Lucius of deliberate complicity in the 'perjurious means' used to unseat O'Gorman. Smith O'Brien replied that if Mahon meant to accuse any member of his family of being 'connected with such men and measures as he describes, otherwise than as honourable men should be, I tell him, he lies most foully (great uproar)'. Because 'a disagreeable result was anticipated', O'Brien was bound over to keep the peace. However, William Mahon sent him 'a message' and, later in the day, the two men fought a duel outside Ennis. Mahon fired and missed, but O'Brien's pistol had not been cocked by his second and so failed to discharge; the seconds agreed that both had 'acted as men of honour' and there the matter ended.[27]

The election produced a miserable outcome, with the venerable Sir Edward losing to the first of four sons O'Connell was to visit on constituencies all over southern Ireland. The O'Brien domination of Clare was ended even before Reform in 1832. And it was under – indeed because of – the old system that O'Brien gave up his seat at Ennis, in the general election of May 1831. Woronzow Greig, O'Brien's friend, later gave his opinion that Vesey Fitzgerald was returned 'I believe on account of Sir Edward O'Brien's dissatisfaction at W. O'Brien's vote in favour of the reform Bill and his preposition [sic] in favour of the Catholics'.[28] This is unlikely. Only on Gascoyne's anti-Irish motion did O'Brien vote with the Whigs on Parliamentary Reform. Sir Edward was an old campaigner for the Catholic cause, and he himself told the Ennis crowd that 'the question of Reform must be carried'.[29] It seems that the O'Briens simply honoured their obligation to Fitzgerald under the system of 'alternating nomination', with Sir Edward appearing in person at the hustings to propose Fitzgerald. Expecting that this would be the last Ennis election before Reform, an undertaker made a coffin in which 'the rotten Charter of the Corporation', which had so restricted the franchise, was deposited for interment. About 2,000 people attended the mock funeral through the streets of Ennis, with a dead rat nailed to the lid of the coffin. The town band played a solemn dirge, a mock priest gave the funeral oration, and the crowd sang a 'requiem to departed rottenness'. Finally the coffin was despatched into the river Fergus.[30]

For O'Brien the result of this election was of major importance: an interruption of almost four years in his Parliamentary career and, in the event, the perma-

---

[27] *Clare Journal*, 21, 24 March 1831. *Limerick Evening Post and Clare Sentinel*, 22 March 1831. O'Brien Papers (AO), Rough Diary, 20 March 1831. See also Grania O'Brien, *These My Friends and Forebears*, 120, for a somewhat fanciful account of how 'the two duelling Williams took themselves to the race course at Ennis' and fought 'in front of a large crowd'.   [28] Smith O'Brien Papers, MS 449, f3398, W. Greig's Annals.   [29] *Clare Journal*, 12 May 1831.   [30] Ibid.

nent end of his political dependence on Sir Edward and Dromoland. He foresaw none of this. He did not envisage a lengthy disconnection from Ennis, for he planned to contest the borough in the first post-Reform election. In June 1831, he canvassed support from men expected to gain the franchise.[31] Of course, Reform and the next election were delayed until, respectively, the middle and end of 1832. O'Brien busied himself (unavailingly) with constituency projects – the Clare-Ennis canal and getting a branch of the Provincial Bank in Ennis – of the sort candidates-in-waiting know well.[32] One thing he probably did *not* do was become president of the Cambridge Union; he is recorded as such in several works, but not only is it inherently unlikely but his rough diary shows he did not return to Cambridge at any time in 1831.[33]

In his correspondence with Stanley, resumed in May 1831, O'Brien continued to move away from his early Toryism. In mid-June he welcomed the Chief Secretary's assurances that the Whig government did 'not look to measures of coercion alone for preserving the peace of this country, but that something will be done towards improving its social condition without which it is vain to expect permanent security'. On this occasion he drew particular attention to the need for a poor law in Ireland. In August, he warned that 'England holds this country only by a thread ... the Repeal Question is only *deferred* until the Reform Bill passes ... A provision for the Catholic Clergy, a firm hand and good measures (not excepting my favourite Poor Laws) may avert the crisis.' In September, he adopted an entirely Whig/liberal position when he welcomed Stanley's establishment of the National Education System. This promised a mixed, non-denominational system of primary education, funded by Parliament and run by a central board of commissioners. Education would be more easily available to Catholics who had previously feared proselytism in the schools run by the Kildare Place Society and other Protestant institutions, and the mixed education promised was regarded as a means of mitigating religious conflict. O'Brien had reason to be more aware than most of the difficulties of the question: his mother had tried to set up schools in Clare and encountered Catholic suspicion of her evangelical zeal.[34] Now he wrote to Stanley observing 'with the greatest satisfaction that national education in this country is at last to be placed upon a rational and statesmanlike footing ... Ireland must feel much indebted' for a reform that would end the 'eternal heartburnings and jealousies' that had characterised the issue. 'As a healing measure,' he went on, 'I doubt whether the settlement of this question will not be more effective than even Catholic Emancipation

---

31 O'Brien Papers (AO), Rough Diary, 6-11 June 1831. Smith O'Brien Papers, MS 426, f110, Greene to O'Brien, 14 June 1831; f111, Scott to O'Brien, 15 June 1831.   32 Ibid., f112, McGrath to O'Brien, 2 July 1831; f115, Killaly to Gosset, 29 July 1831; ff117, 122, Grantham to O'Brien, 22 August, 25 October 1831; ibid., MS 449, f3424, Dawson to O'Brien, 22 December 1831. On the bank, see ibid., MS 426, f123, Sullivan to O'Brien, 22 December 1831; f125, Fitzgerald to O'Brien, 25 December 1831; f127, Hunter to O'Brien, 28 December 1831.   33 Percy Cradock, *Recollections of the Cambridge Union, 1815-1939* (Cambridge, 1953), 171. *Alumni Cantabrigienses* (Cambridge, 1951), pt. 2, iv, 579.   34 Grania O'Brien, *These My Friends and Forebears*, 109-10.

itself & it may go far to calm that unquiet feeling which has given a popularity to the cry for a Repeal of the Union.' This would prove to be an overoptimistic view. On Parliamentary Reform his liberalism was more questionable. He told Stanley he wanted the Irish bill to have an equivalent of the Chandos clause that gave £50 tenants-at-will the right to vote in the English counties. This ultra Tory amendment was favoured by landlords because, not possessing leases, these tenants were expected to be relatively compliant. He was untroubled by the fact that such dependence would feed the (radical) demand for voting by secret ballot, for it was 'inevitable' anyway and would produce 'little change except perhaps for the better'; this position suggests his later opposition to O'Connell on the ballot was not deep-rooted. O'Brien seemed rather proud of becoming the correspondent of an important minister, telling Stanley how it pleased him 'to communicate with one who has the power and, as I believe, the disposition to be useful to the country, which needs, above all others [sic], the fostering care & the judicious management of an intelligent & philanthropic statesman'.[35]

O'Brien dined with the Ennis Club in October 1831. In December, he began what would become an important association with Thomas Wyse on education and wrote a public letter to Stanley about Grand Jury reform.[36] His most striking foray into politics came with a public letter to O'Connell on 19 January 1832. The occasion was the Whigs' proposal to increase Ireland's representation by only five members, to 105, when O'Brien believed that a figure of 'at least 123' was appropriate to the combination of her population, territory, wealth and tax burden. The small county of Wiltshire in England was to have four members, but vast and populous county Cork was given only two. He thought that Ireland had been treated badly by the Act of the Union, with 100 members, but now 'a national insult [was] superadded to a national wrong'. O'Brien simultaneously denounced and appealed to O'Connell. He deprecated the 'constant appeals to the worst passions of the multitude' and the 'denouncing as a traitor every man who has not become the abject slave of your will'. A united Irish opposition was needed – 'the determined and unanimous resistance of the Irish Members' – yet O'Connell continued to assail the Orangemen, 'not the only occasion upon which the unmeasured violence of your public conduct has proved prejudicial to the interests of your country'. He concluded with an unconvincing declaration that he was writing 'in a spirit of remonstrance, not of hostility'. (In fact, O'Connell also called for a united front against the Irish Reform Bill, arguing, in terms O'Brien might have used, that, 'It is an Irish question, not a sectarian one'.) O'Brien's courage was again impressive: no longer an immune, nominee Member of Parliament, he would shortly be seeking the support of Catholic electors who regarded O'Connell as their political leader, yet he was entirely unafraid of the Great Dan and did not hesitate to express his

---

35 Derby Papers, 920/DER (14), 122/5, O'Brien to Stanley, 15 June, 17 August, 18 September 1831.
36 O'Brien Papers (AO), Rough Diary, 6 October 1831. Smith O'Brien Papers, MS 426, f124, Wyse to O'Brien, 24 December 1831 (reply to O'Brien's of 5 December). *DEP*, 8 December 1831, O'Brien to Stanley, n.d.

disdain in the strongest terms. To Wyse he wrote, 'What a pity it is that O'Connell is taking such a furious course [on repeal]. Every body is afraid to unite with him & this is a moment when Irishmen of all Parties should unite to save Ireland from an act of injustice which will be severely felt another day. I am glad to see that you have denounced in proper terms the insult which is offered to us as a nation ... It is almost enough to make one a Repealer, & will do more to bring about a repeal than all O'Connell's haranguing. Who can doubt that if we had twenty additional active members in the House – to say nothing of their weight in voting – that the interests of Ireland would be better attended to and its demands & claims more respected?'[37] This was the first of many occasions when O'Brien raised the possibility of becoming a repealer.

Suggesting a sense of O'Connell's electoral threat, the Whigs carried an ungenerous, conservative Irish Reform. The representation was the 105 against which O'Brien and O'Connell had railed. The number of county voters rose from 37,000 to 60,957, one voter in every 116 inhabitants, against one in 24 in England and Wales. Greater equality was effected in the boroughs, with one voter in every 26 inhabitants, against one in 17 in England.[38] In Ennis, the 13 Protestant freemen who traditionally held the franchise were swamped by the new £10 householders, giving 222 mostly Catholic voters (in a population of almost 10,000).[39] Though by no means extensive, the new franchise meant that the era of the close borough, of O'Brien-Fitzgerald domination, was well and truly over and that O'Brien now had to think in terms of securing support from men who were mostly liberal in politics and Catholic in religion. Not every Ennis liberal was convinced that O'Brien should be supported for the seat. His name was included on the list of those invited to a political dinner organised in April 1832 by the Ennis Club, but, he was told by an ally, the proposal that he should be described as 'being identified with the "Independence of Ennis"' was 'negatived by a majority of *two*' in the club.[40] This opposition to O'Brien probably owed something to his public hostility to O'Connell. But it emanated on this occasion from the club's support for repeal of the Union. Preached by O'Connell from January 1830, repeal – that is, the restoration to Dublin of an Irish parliament under the Crown – finally caught the popular imagination in 1832. Those who opposed repeal believed it would lead, especially if O'Connell became dominant in the Irish parliament, to conflict between Dublin and London and in the end to Ireland's separation from Britain. The Act of Emancipation had demonstrated, it was argued, Westminster's capacity to give Ireland good government. For all his occasional doubts (and threats), O'Brien shared these views, remaining an opponent of repeal until his dramatic conversion in 1843. Now the

---

[37] *Clare Journal*, 26 January 1832, O'Brien to Daniel O'Connell, 19 January 1832; ibid., 2 February 1832, O'Connell to the Political Union of Ireland, 24 January 1832. Wyse Papers, MS 15025 (1), O'Brien to Wyse, 16 January 1832. [38] Hoppen, *Elections, Politics and Society in Ireland*, 1-2. Angus MacIntyre, *The Liberator: Daniel O'Connell and the Irish Party, 1830-1847* (London, 1965), 29-36. [39] Charles R Dod, *Electoral Facts, from 1832 to 1852* (London, 1852), 107. [40] Smith O'Brien Papers, MS 449, f3426, D'Arcy to O'Brien [April 1832].

O'Connell-inspired practice of requiring a 'repeal pledge' from candidates threatened his political future. His response was admirably defiant:

> ... as an independent man I must say that if my return for the Borough of Ennis is to depend upon my attendance or non-attendance at a Club dinner at which the Repeal of the Union is one of the Toasts which I should be called upon to drink, I am afraid I must give up all hopes of enjoying that honour. It will however be a consolation to me to think that the promises which were made to me freely & without condition have not been forfeited by any act of mine which can fairly be considered as a breach of our mutual agreement.
>
> Upon the question of the Repeal of the Union, or indeed on any other question, it is not my intention to give any *Pledge*, although if I again get into Parliament my vote shall be determined by the disposition which I find in the Government to do justice to my country.[41]

Given O'Brien's subsequent conduct, the closing remark is interesting, but it was entirely typical of anti-repeal candidates to defuse opposition in this way; Lucius, at the previous year's Clare by-election, had declared that Sir Edward would support repeal if 'convinced by argument in the House Of Commons'.[42] The extent of O'Brien's concern – and something of his humanity – is indicated by his closing remarks to his correspondent, Burton D'Arcy: 'One word to yourself personally. You are in a situation to be the leader of a large party in Ennis as long as you go with the Public feeling. No one would regret so much as myself to see you lose that position – so that if you find the Tide turning against me do not set yourself to oppose it ...'[43]

Despite these signs of trouble ahead, O'Brien continued to present the public face of an aspiring candidate, pressing for state funding of the Fergus canal project and proposing that the landed proprietors of Clare should form an organisation that would guard against the inherent corruptions of the Grand Jury system.[44] He spent June and July in northern Ireland and Scotland, exhaustively touring the latter, before returning to Clare in August. On 9 September 1832, O'Brien suddenly announced that, though 'promised the support of at least five sixths' of the electors, 'circumstances wholly unforeseen' by him meant he would not be standing in the coming election.[45] His assertion in relation to 'five-sixths' of the electors was supported by the *Clare Journal* – 'he was so well received upon his canvass that a contest was unlikely' – and by local backers who informed him his return had been cer-

---

[41] Ibid., f3427, O'Brien to D'Arcy [April 1832]. [42] *Clare Journal*, 21 March 1831. [43] Smith O'Brien Papers, MS 449, f3427, O'Brien to D'Arcy [April 1832]. [44] *Clare Journal*, 28 May 1832, O'Brien to D'Arcy, 22 May 1832; ibid., 23 July 1832, O'Brien to Burgoyne, 27 May 1832; ibid., 30 August 1832, O'Brien to the Landed Proprietors of the County of Clare, n.d. [45] Ibid., 13 September 1832, To such of the Future Electors of Ennis as have promised their support at the ensuing election to Mr W.S. O'Brien, 9 September 1832.

tain.⁴⁶ Such assessments were notoriously unreliable – wild claims littered the election contests of the 1830s – and it is possible that the repeal-inspired opposition within the Ennis Club meant the picture had changed since O'Brien's successful canvass in June 1831. O'Brien had felt the need to ask his father to provide funds, including 'a Hundred a year to give to the charities of the town'. Sir Edward, who had spent much of his fortune on elections and would later refuse financial support to Lucius, a good Tory, in the county, turned him down: 'I shall be happy to see you returned by the voices of the people of Ennis. But I shall never again spend any money in a pursuit which if it does not flow freely from the wishes of the people is not worth having.'⁴⁷ There is a suggestion that the refusal annoyed O'Brien and influenced his decision: Sir Edward had to point out that O'Brien's 'retiring from Ennis was altogether your own act, in which I had no part whatever'.⁴⁸

Such factors – the possibility of opposition and Sir Edward's refusal to fund a campaign – may have played a role, but it is quite likely that O'Brien withdrew mainly for the reason he publicised in September 1832, gave to his parents, and proclaimed again in 1837 and 1844: the 'wholly unforeseen' circumstance of his marriage and the resultant move from Clare.⁴⁹ On 11 August, he had 'met Miss G. at the Currah'.⁵⁰ This was Lucy Gabbett, the daughter of Joseph Gabbett of Highpark, Limerick, whom he married six weeks later. O'Brien could look forward to establishing his own family home in a different county, for his mother now allowed him to take possession of Cahirmoyle in Limerick. The role of second son cannot have been entirely comfortable and it is possibly significant that from October 1831 he had lived not at Dromoland but at Inchiquin Cottage in nearby Corofin. The desire to move away can only have been increased by his father's disapproval of the marriage. He stated this, and his general view of O'Brien's 'character', in a letter written shortly after O'Brien's one-day visit to Dromoland on 22 August – probably the occasion on which, 11 days after he and Lucy had met, he informed his parents of his marriage plans.

> Dromoland
> August 27, 1832
>
> My dear William
> Having already expressed a very decided opinion on the connection you are about to form, I have only to regret that you are proceeding with your usual precipitation, & without any attempt to conciliate my feelings on the most important step of your life.

---

46 Ibid., 13 September 1832. Smith O'Brien Papers, MS 427, f175, McGrath to O'Brien, 15 September 1832; f181, Gore to O'Brien, 25 September 1832. 47 O'Brien Papers (AO), Letter Box, Bundle 2, Sir Edward O'Brien to O'Brien, 15 August 1832. 48 Ibid., Sir Edward O'Brien to O'Brien, 25 January 1833. 49 Ibid., Lady O'Brien to O'Brien, 13 August 1838. Smith O'Brien Papers, MS 10515 (4), Smith O'Brien's sketch of his political life, 25 September 1844. *Limerick Chronicle*, 28 January 1837. 50 O'Brien Papers (AO), Rough Diary, 11 August 1832. Perhaps he referred here to Curragh Chase, the neighbouring home of the de Vere family, but it is also possible that they met at a racecourse.

> Your mother & I have decided to give you Six Hundred Pounds a year in land in the County of Limerick, which will include the House & Domain of Carmoyhill [*Cahirmoyle*] ... You will also receive Fifty Pounds a year ... during my life.
>
> Robert will pay up the Balance of your [*Investors?*] Allowance the first of October & as this closes our money transactions I request to hear no more on the subject.
>
> I hope most sincerely that I have been mistaken in the estimation I have formed of your character – & that you are forming a match that will ensure both your present and future happiness. I can have no wish beyond this object, and shall as soon as you are married receive your wife with all courtesy and treat her with the kindness of a daughter.
>
> I am your affectionate
> Father
> Edward O'Brien[51]

It is not clear if it was to the Gabbetts' status as minor gentry or to the haste ('precipitation') of O'Brien's decision that Sir Edward objected. At any rate, it is notable that even in the most sensible and stabilising decision of O'Brien's life, marrying Lucy, he was wilful and impulsive.

Significantly, it was Lucius, not Sir Edward, who served as a party to the marriage agreement that O'Brien signed with Joseph Gabbett on 17 September 1832, and the marriage took place on 19 September not at Dromoland but in the parish church of Milltown Malbay, west Clare.[52] Lucy's nature will become evident in the role she was to play as O'Brien's loyal and long-suffering wife. That the O'Brien family, including Sir Edward, quickly became attached to her is apparent from the obvious affection in their references to her in letters to O'Brien. Of the Cahirmoyle estate – which was valued in September 1832 at £4,016 a year – Sir Edward and Lady Charlotte now gave O'Brien only 318 acres, worth £600 a year.[53] The house at Cahirmoyle was badly run down and, in Lady Charlotte's opinion, more like a farmhouse than a gentleman's seat.[54] The £2,000 'marriage portion' payable by Joseph Gabbett was not realisable – it was to fund an insurance on O'Brien's life – but he did receive £1,111 as his share of £10,000 left by old William Smith for Lady Charlotte's children.[55] So, O'Brien entered his new existence comfortably well off but by no means rich. He left the impression in Clare that he had 'given up public life' in order 'to live as a country gentleman' at Cahirmoyle.[56] Marriage in

---

51 Papers relating to William Smith O'Brien, Trinity College, Dublin, MS 10612/1, Sir Edward O'Brien to O'Brien, 27 August 1832. O'Brien's rough diary is the source for his Dromoland visit of 22 August. 52 Smith O'Brien Papers, MS D9798, Marriage settlement of William Smith O'Brien and Lucy Gabbett, 17 September 1832. 53 O'Brien Papers (AO), Conveyance of Cahirmoyle to William Smith O'Brien, 18 September 1832. Smith O'Brien Papers, MS 427, f169, Furlong to O'Brien, 1 September 1832; f173, Arthur to O'Brien, 8 September 1832. 54 O'Brien Papers (AO), Letter Box, Bundle 2, Lady O'Brien to O'Brien, 13 August 1838. 55 Inchiquin Papers, T32/3066, Receipt dated 28 May 1833. 56 Smith

itself was possibly a factor in the decision to leave politics; to one friend, O'Brien appeared 'not anxious' to sacrifice his home life 'for late hours and bad company in St Stephen's' at Westminster.[57] O'Brien and his new wife moved to Limerick at the end of October 1832 and lived in her father's house at 78 George's Street (now O'Connell Street) in the city; they did not take up residence at Cahirmoyle until October 1834.

In Limerick, O'Brien immediately conducted himself in ways which showed a continuing interest in politics. He joined the local liberal club on 11 November 1832.[58] He wrote to Lord Dunraven, a moderate Tory who had wielded considerable electoral influence in Limerick before Reform; he apparently criticised the sitting Whig MPs for the county, Richard Fitzgibbon and Standish O'Grady, and urged Dunraven to present his son as a candidate. Quite possibly this was intended to stimulate Dunraven's interest in backing O'Brien himself. Dunraven duly encouraged O'Brien to try: 'The co. is so open that if no country gentleman will come forward we shall have some Agitator appearing at the eleventh hour. It is perhaps presumptuous in me [sic] to give an opinion, but are you acting advisedly in giving up Parliament? Canvass this county, and if you then see your way, well and good. If not, don't stand. If the O'Grady family support you Fitzgibbon can't stand and they probably will support you if they think a contest *inevitable*.'[59] There is no evidence that O'Brien initiated such a canvass. Also at this time, he resumed his interest in an Irish poor law, pressing in particular for the setting up of 'a Central Committee in Dublin as a nucleus for the supporters of the measure in the Provinces to rally round'. Villiers Stuart and bishop James Doyle, allies in the cause, rightly apprehended O'Connell's opposition and doubted the Whig government's resolve.[60] Continuing an interest he had already voiced in Parliament, he founded and became honorary secretary of a Limerick emigration society, with Canada envisaged as a potential home for those who wished to begin new lives overseas.[61]

Above all, in January 1833, O'Brien contributed his views on the question that dwarfed all other Irish matters in importance in the 1830s, that of the established Protestant Church of Ireland. It was the issue which more than any other defined party allegiance, and it was probably his view of the Church question that finally divorced O'Brien from his Tory beginnings. By 1830 the Church, with some assistance and pressure from Parliament, had done much to purge itself of the worst

---

O'Brien Papers, MS 427, f175, McGrath to O'Brien, 15 September 1832; f176, Vandeleur to O'Brien, 17 September 1832. **57** Ibid., f178, Cassidy to O'Brien, 24 September 1832. Cassidy also wrote that, 'The sacrifice of time and money is great, but some one must go to London. The rich can afford it better than others.' Ibid., f179, Cassidy to O'Brien, 19 September 1832. **58** O'Brien Papers (AO), Rough Diary, 11 November 1832. **59** Smith O'Brien Papers, MS 427, f185, Dunraven to O'Brien, 6 November 1832. **60** Ibid., f186, Doyle to O'Brien, 6 November 1832; f188, Stuart to O'Brien, 18 November 1832. **61** O'Brien Papers (AO), Rough Diary, 25 November 1832, 16 January 1833. Smith O'Brien Papers, MS 449, ff3418, 3433, O'Brien to Howick, n.d.

excesses of absenteeism, pluralism and churchless parishes.[62] However, with 22 bishops and about 2,000 inferior clergymen, the Church still assumed proportions that reflected an expectation that the mass of the Irish people would adhere to it. In fact, according to a Parliamentary report in 1835, only 852,064 belonged to the Church, while there were 6,427,712 Catholics and 642,356 Presbyterians. What made the Church issue so contentious was the fact that the people in general, Catholics and Presbyterians included, were taxed to support the church of only a tenth of the population. The principal form of such taxation was tithe, the charge that farmers of all denominations paid for the maintenance of the Church of Ireland clergy. From 1830, Catholic resistance to tithe reached new heights in many parts of Ireland. Bishop James Doyle played the major role in initiating this; his denunciation of the charge encouraged the priesthood to lead their flocks in a general refusal to pay. To Doyle's dismay, violence quickly ensued, as peasants clashed with the forces sent to seize the goods of defaulters. In Wexford in June 1831, the Protestant yeomanry killed 12 people in an affray over tithe, and in Kilkenny in December 17 constables were killed by a 2,000-strong mob of protesters. There was a resurgence of the agrarian secret societies, which spread violence and intimidation through much of rural Ireland.[63]

By January 1832, such was the disturbed state of Ireland, one leading Irish Whig foresaw 'all the horrors of revolutionary war' if the existing Church system was retained.[64] On 14 February 1832, Chief Secretary Stanley made his famous declaration that the government intended 'the extinction of the present system of tithes'. The complete 'extinction' of tithes became the rallying call of Irish liberals. As Thomas Wyse noted, Stanley's words were *'ambiguous,* but we will make use of them and now make them go the entire way, however reluctantly ... We may expect to see the whole followed up by a reduction of the Church.'[65] Wyse was confident that Parliament would have to 'ratify the decision of the country' which had 'virtually extinguished' tithe. Church reform was also inevitable: 'Churches must have Pastors and Pastors must have Churches'.[66] Stanley's measure to collect tithe arrears was rejected as an act of coercion without relief. What Edward Littleton called a 'stout little phalanx' of Irish Members – half-a-dozen repealers and more than twice that number of liberal-unionists – took part in the first significant revolt against the Whigs' handling of the question.[67] They advocated 'appropriation' of surplus Church

---

62 E.P. Brynn, 'A Political History of the Church of Ireland, 1801-1845' (M. Litt., Trinity College Dublin, 1968), 37-271. D.H. Akenson, *The Church of Ireland: Ecclesiastical Reform and Revolution, 1800-1885* (New Haven, London, 1971), 111-32.   63 MacIntyre, *The Liberator,* 175-83. G. Broeker, *Rural Disorder and Police Reform in Ireland, 1812-36* (London, 1970), 202-17.   64 Monteagle Papers, MS 13372 (3), Newport to Spring Rice, 3, 7 January 1832.   65 *Hansard,* x, 322, 14 February 1832, Stanley. Wyse Papers, MS 15019 (5), Wyse to George Wyse, 15 February 1832. See also Personal Journals ... by James Grattan, MS 14147, 14 February 1832.   66 Wyse Papers, MS 15019 (5), Wyse to George Wyse, 20, 27, 28 February, 2 March 1832; ibid. (6), Wyse to George Wyse, 26, 31 May, 18, 25, 30 June 1832.   67 A. Aspinall (ed.), *Three Early Nineteenth Century Diaries* (London, 1952), 206, Littleton, 8 March 1832. See also ibid., 210-11, Le Marchant [8 March 1832]. Personal Journals ... by James Grattan, MS 14147, 8 March 1832.

income to non-ecclesiastical purposes, particularly relief of the poor, leaving the clergy an amount compatible with 'the simplicity of a Christian Church' and the number of Anglicans in Ireland. Whether they were motivated like Wyse by a sense of the injustice of forcing Catholics to sustain a Protestant Church, afraid as landlords that tithe resistance would spread to rents and add 'the ruin of the landed proprietor to that of the Established Church',[68] or speaking with fear of the hustings before their eyes, Irish liberals were pressing as never before for radical reform and reduction of the Church.

In January 1833, with a private letter to Stanley and publication of a pamphlet, O'Brien belatedly entered the fray. He told Stanley of his 'strong sense of the impending crisis' created by the question. He lived 'in a part of Ireland which is almost wholly Catholic' and he could 'see the abuses of the Church'. A member of the landed class, he had 'a great deal too much to lose by revolutionary change to desire to sap the foundations of property', but he was aware of how the failure to reform the Church had worsened popular discontent: 'The opportunity was lost – feelings became exasperated, and almost every post ... has brought an account of the effusion of blood.' He urged a 'compromise' settlement:

> Let them [the government] provide with the utmost liberality for the full & adequate performance of all the spiritual duties which the wants of the Protestant population require in the estimation of the most zealous Protestant. If no surplus remains, they ought not to take a guinea from the Church. But if as I believe would be the case there shd be a large surplus, let it be applied to purposes in which Catholic & Protestant have a common interest.
>
> I have I am aware taken an unwarranted liberty in writing in so candid a manner. But with the views which I entertain of the present prospects of Ireland, you will find some apology in my belief that every thing which I value most, property, friends, even life itself, is dependent upon the course which the government takes during the next two years. If you make a provision for the Catholic Clergy – if you introduce a fair, equitable and searching Church Reform – if you give us a well regulated Poor Law – and an amended Grand Jury system – during this session – you will hear very little of Repeal next year. If on the contrary things are left on their present footing for a year or two longer, the Gentry will no longer be able to remain at variance with the People upon this question – and a separation or a civil war will probably be the alternative.[69]

O'Brien would effect moderate reform in order to end hostility to the Church, kill off repeal, and preclude conflict between landlords and peasantry. In his pamphlet, introducing himself as 'an individual who belongs to no party', he claimed that there were 'few examples in the history of a free nation of an anomaly such as

---

68 Monteagle Papers, MS 13372 (3), Newport to Spring Rice, 7 January 1832.   69 Smith O'Brien Papers, MS 427, f217, O'Brien to Stanley, 29 January 1833.

... the Established Church of Ireland', sustained as it was on a prodigious scale by a majority who 'desire no benefit from its ministrations'; in Clare, there were fewer than 5,000 Protestants in a population of 258,262. The result was 'discontent, assassination and rebellion ... the country reeks with blood'. The government's policy had been 'an alternate series of delusive professions and inconsistent severity' which produced exasperation and 'swelled the ranks of Repeal'. Church property, far from inviolate, was 'given in trust for the benefit of the community at large' and Parliament had a right to redistribute it accordingly. After reducing the number of Protestant clergy (including the bishops, from 22 to only four) and paying them on a modest scale, there would be a surplus Church income of about £500,000. This should be devoted to 'useful purposes in which Catholics and Protestants have a common interest – whether it be the relief of the poor, or the support of hospitals, schools, colleges, public works, etc., etc.' In other words, on appropriation of surplus Church property, the issue that was to dominate the debate for many years, O'Brien took an impeccably liberal view.

However, O'Brien did not advocate extinction of tithe. Like many English critics of Irish landlordism, he believed that extinction would merely benefit the landlord, who could raise rents. A third of the tithe would continue and it would be supplemented by a new tax; out of this he proposed to pay the Anglican clergy, the Presbyterian ministers and the Catholic priests – all on 'a similar scale of allowance'. Payment of the priests had numerous advocates among Protestant liberals, but O'Brien was the only one who openly campaigned on the subject, regardless of O'Connell's strong opposition. His rationale, perhaps influenced by memories of Clare in 1828, naively fuelled Catholic fears of loss of independence: 'The Ministers of every religion being among the most influential classes of society, ought to be so far attached to the State as to have no immediate interest in disturbing the existing order of things ... To receive a stipend from the State in no way militates with [sic] their independence, provided it is not left in the power of government to withhold it, but at the same time it gives them something to lose by the subversion of order.' Equally, his hostile depiction of the priests' current reliance on the voluntary support of the laity – 'a servile dependence upon the people' – did nothing to lessen the other main Catholic objection to state payment, that it would sever the bonds of affection created by mutual dependence between priest and people. O'Brien showed here a mixture of courage and political ineptitude, for this was an issue that later (and predictably) caused him considerable difficulty.[70]

For the moment, the pamphlet produced problems closer to home, for it drove another wedge between O'Brien and his father. The latter called it *'far too radical for my taste*, savouring of the O'Connell school' and 'too much in accordance with Doctor Doyle'. By conciliating the tithe resisters, he was 'making Physical Force a ground on which ministers & statesmen are to regulate the affairs of the country ... On the whole I consider it more of an inflammatory production than what ought

---

70 William Smith O'Brien, *Thoughts upon Ecclesiastical Reform and Suggestions for the Conciliatory Adjustment to the Tithe Question* (Limerick, 1833).

to come from the pen of *a statesman* & my regret for you not being in Parliament arises from thinking that a freer intercourse *with superior men* would correct the evident tendency of your mind to adopt *the feelings & sentiments of the Democracy* ... & while you spoliate your own church you shut your eyes to the exorbitant & increasing exactions of the Catholic Priesthood.' In another, undated letter, Sir Edward wrote, '*Your mother disapproves of your Pamphlet* & you certainly would destroy the Protestant religion altogether *in Clare* ... I regret you threw away the representation of Ennis when you might have taken a part in settling the question' in Parliament.[71] Of course, events on the ground showed that O'Brien was right in seeing that Catholics would not resume payments towards an inflated and alien church and that resistance could not simply be defeated by coercive means. The refusal of the Tory House of Lords to acknowledge this meant that the Irish Church question would still be alive long after O'Brien's return to Parliament in 1835.

In the first half of 1833 and in 1834, O'Brien established himself as a prominent and useful member of Limerick society, involved in the promotion of bridge-building, emigration, farming improvement, poor laws and education. In June 1833, he took Lucy on an extended tour of western Europe – principally France and Switzerland – and then spent four months in various parts of England, returning to Ireland in March 1834.[72] A dispute over the future of King's Island, 60 acres of corporation-owned land that the Tory leader, Lord Gort, refused to acknowledge might revert to public use on the expiration of his life-interest, enabled O'Brien to proclaim his determination to be of service to the people of Limerick. That he virtually accused Gort of 'short-sighted selfishness' and looked forward to 'a total revolution in the dynastics of Corporate towns' (that is, municipal reform) can only have attracted the favourable attention of local liberals.[73] Sir Edward had tried to dissuade him from settling at Cahirmoyle – 'neither the society nor the farming of that remote country hold out much inducement to a young couple to be set down permanently on small reserves' – and proposed that, instead, they could have 'a set of rooms' in newly rebuilt Dromoland.[74] Perhaps fortunately, in view of the family row that soon followed, O'Brien resisted the temptation and moved into Cahirmoyle in October 1834.

O'Brien's early return to politics can have surprised nobody, given his active role in public affairs. On 15 December 1834, he sent in his application for membership of the Anti-Tory Association, the body that O'Connell had established to oppose the Tory ministry which took power in November 1834. In his letter, O'Brien deprecated the 'great national calamity' of a Tory victory and hoped that the coming election would give Ireland MPs who were 'devoted to the advance-

---

71 O'Brien Papers (AO), Letter Box, Bundle 2, Sir Edward O'Brien to O'Brien, n.d., 25 January 1833. 72 Ibid., Rough Diary, 1833 and 1834. 73 *Limerick Chronicle*, 7 June 1834, O'Brien to the Editor, 31 May 1834; ibid., 5 July 1834, O'Brien to Gort, 3 July 1834. 74 O'Brien Papers (AO), Letter Box, Bundle 2, Sir Edward O'Brien to O'Brien, 28 December 1833.

ment of liberal measures'. He specified a 'total alteration of the present tithe system', a tax on absentee landlords, a poor law, and other reforms, all of them to be presented to Parliament as 'the bill of rights of the Irish nation'. On tithe, he showed no regard for Protestant (or his father's) sensitivities when he wrote, 'I call this a national object because the Irish are in the aggregate a Catholic people, and as such this question ought to be viewed', and he presumably counted himself among 'those Protestants who love equal justice better than the ascendancy of their own sect'. One Association member, Dominick Ronayne, sensibly noted the difference between 'total alteration' and the 'total extinction' of tithe that most liberals advocated. O'Connell welcomed O'Brien's adhesion but strongly disapproved of his advocacy (repeated in the letter) of state payment of the priests.[75]

Sir Edward, apparently unprepared to respect O'Brien's liberal views as genuine principles, was outraged by what he regarded as demagogic pandering to the masses. He warned,

> You are at a critical period of your life & not now a young man. If you aspire to the character of a statesman, let your conduct be marked by *caution, prudence* and *foresight*.
>
> Beware of the temptation of Popularity & be not lured from the situation you ought to hold in society by allowing yourself to become a tool in the hands of the Democracy. Take a lead ... but *cautiously* ... no demagogue *ever succeeded*. You may be of great use to your country by taking a middle course.
>
> Beware of the County of Limerick where you could only succeed by separating the ties of landlord & tenant. The same objection would *not* lie to [*sic*] the City ...[76]

On 21 December, he wrote that he and Lady Charlotte felt so 'exasperated' he hoped O'Brien would 'defer your visit here till a more favourable period. When time shall have more reconciled us to the course you are pursuing in your mad career of Politics. I wish to have my family in happiness & harmony about me, which I am sorry to say your presence at the present moment would not increase.' In other words, he cancelled O'Brien's and Lucy's invitation to spend Christmas at Dromoland, something Lady Charlotte was to do again in 1843. Sir Edward signed off with 'your affectionate tho much annoyed father, Edward O'Brien'.[77] In early January 1835, his language was still unrestrained, his state of mind worsened by the bitterness (and futility) of Lucius's contest for Clare:

> You have taken your line, a fatal one in my opinion to you ... , in joining the O'Connell school & submitting to be a degraded member in his Tail.

---

75 *DEP*, 23 December 1834.   76 O'Brien Papers (AO), Letter Box, Bundle 2, Sir Edward O'Brien to O'Brien, 18 December 1834.   77 Smith O'Brien Papers, MS 8656 (5), Sir Edward O'Brien to O'Brien, 21 December 1834.

> That was the step I deprecated. With regard [to] your general politics, I never wish to interfere ... Do not answer this. I am easily agitated & sometimes irritable, but soon recover my equilibrium tho my health suffers. Temporising with adversaries is weakness. The straight-forward, direct course is the only sure one.
>
> I am too old to turn Democrat ...[78]

It is possible to admire O'Brien for adhering to his 'line' despite this sort of emotional pressure, which must have pained him, while at the same time deprecating his insensitivity towards an aged and uncomprehending father. His brother Edward, who was also critical of his political decision, probably had a point when he urged O'Brien to 'be cautious what you write home. Why unnecessarily wound the feelings of parents for the want of a little perhaps you will call it *jesuitical* caution?'[79] Fortunately, by mid January, Sir Edward and Lady Charlotte were prepared again to forgive their errant son and to rebuild 'good feeling and friendship on all sides'.[80]

In the general election of January 1835, O'Connell advocated a united effort against the Tory ministry, and so in Limerick he initially favoured the re-election of Colonel Standish O'Grady and Colonel Richard Fitzgibbon, the sitting Whig Members, Protestants with family landed interests in the county that were much more substantial and longstanding than O'Brien's. However, O'Grady and Fitzgibbon had angered their liberal constituents when they voted for the Whig coercion bill of 1833. They were accused, moreover, of inadequate Commons attendance; O'Grady, in particular, gave offence on this score, voting only six times in 132 divisions in 1833 (and three of these votes were for coercion). Their unpopularity with local liberals led the County Club (on 6 January) to invite O'Brien to challenge for the seat. The club's leading figure, Michael O'Shaughnessy, went to Dublin to argue for O'Brien in the committee of the Anti-Tory Association, prevailing despite O'Connell's doubts.[81] O'Shaughnessy succeeded in uniting behind O'Brien both the County Club and the more radical Limerick Political Union, campaigning against the colonels and what the *Limerick Star* called 'the overbearing incubus of family nomination and monopoly'.[82] In a series of speeches, O'Brien offered his 'decided hostility' to a Tory ministry that had been 'the consistent and unrelenting enemies' of Ireland and its Catholics. His election address referred to two specific issues: he would 'abolish' tithes – this time the words were unequivocal – and 'reduce the endowment of the Protestant Church', and, secondly, he would 'remove from our [municipal] Corporations their present character of exclusion and monopoly'. Ironically, given his position in 1828, he sought and gained the support

---

78 O'Brien Papers (AO), Letter Box, Bundle 2, Sir Edward O'Brien to O'Brien, 3 January 1835. 79 Ibid., Edward O'Brien to O'Brien, 24 December 1824. See also ibid., Edward O'Brien to O'Brien, 9 January 1835: 'A House that is divided cannot stand.' 80 Ibid., Sir Edward O'Brien to O'Brien, 14 January 1835, with supplementary note from Lady O'Brien. 81 *Limerick Star*, 13, 20 January 1835. O'Brien Papers (AO), Rough Diary, 6 January 1835. Smith O'Brien Papers, MS 429, f461, Edward O'Connell to O'Brien, 1 August 1837. 82 *Limerick Star*, 9 January 1835.

of the local Catholic clergy in order to counter the hostility of the landlords; indeed, his election campaign resembled an extended round of visits to the priests in their parishes. He avoided the question of repeal – a feature of elections all over Ireland as liberals focused on defeating the Tories. O'Brien was sufficiently at ease to risk a slightly dangerous joke, telling the Political Union he 'did not deny that a Parliamentary life was most gratifying to him. In fact, it was his hobby.' O'Grady eventually withdrew and gave O'Brien and Fitzgibbon an uncontested victory.[83] Thus O'Brien began his long and fateful career as the liberal Member for Limerick.

---

83 Ibid., 9, 13, 16, 20 January 1835.

3

The Independent Member

Irish politics at the time of O'Brien's return to Parliament were still dominated by the man, Daniel O'Connell, whose success in achieving Emancipation gave him an extraordinary pre-eminence among Irish Catholics. The Liberator's influence was such that in most of southern Ireland his opponents could survive as MPs only with great difficulty, a fact first clearly demonstrated in the 1832 election, when about 30 liberal-unionists (anti-repeal liberals) were defeated by repealers. Some acknowledged O'Connell's power as a political reality and avoided open conflict with him. However, others were alienated by his encouragement of electoral revolts against the landed élite and repudiated his 'wholly impracticable' ideas on repeal. Thirty Irish liberal MPs voted against the repeal motion of April 1834, and many would not go as far as O'Brien did in joining O'Connell's Anti-Tory Association in December 1834. James Grattan, for example, thought his brother Henry's adhesion 'most injudicious'; he 'could not act with O'Connell'. Louis Perrin, soon to become the liberal-unionist Member for Cashel, refused to join the Association because he feared being considered 'an O'Connellite'. When O'Connell endorsed his candidacy in Waterford, Thomas Wyse almost withdrew rather than give the impression that he came in as O'Connell's 'nominee or protégé'.[1] In fact, the majority of liberal-unionists stayed aloof from the Association, though some of these, as much as O'Brien, still owed their seats to O'Connell's acceptance of them as anti-Tories. O'Brien was one of 33 liberal-unionist Members in the new Parliament, while the Great Dan's notorious 'tail' of repealers numbered 32. O'Connell's support for the Whig government that replaced Peel in 1835 brought better relations between O'Connell and the liberal-unionists as they united behind the liberal measures with which the Whigs sought to conciliate the Catholic majority in Ireland. However, differences would continue to arise, with many as averse to O'Connell's embrace as they had been alienated by his hostility. It was O'Brien who defied O'Connell more than any other Irish politician between 1835 and 1843. None was to match the persistence with which he asserted a principled independence as the Member for Limerick.

---

1 Notebooks of James Grattan, MS 3853, December 1834, January 1835. Hatherton Papers, D260/M/01/14, ff453, 473, 565, Craig to Littleton, 30 November, 1, 15 December 1834 (on Perrin). Wyse Papers, MS 15025 (3), Wyse to Abraham [December 1834].

Initially, O'Brien was a quietly conscientious Member whose endeavours won him friends in Limerick and, for the most part, produced barely a ripple of interest in the wider political world. He arrived in London on 12 February 1835 and took lodgings at 1 Wilton Street, the first of many temporary residences he was to occupy in the capital during the next decade. On 18 February, the day before the new Parliament opened, he attended the Lichfield House meeting at which O'Connell agreed to help the Whigs to defeat the government. O'Brien voted for the Whig candidate for Speaker on 19 February and for the Whig amendment to the Address a week later. After attending another opposition meeting on 23 March, he voted for the appropriation of surplus Irish Church revenues in the three great divisions which finally ended Peel's government.[2] In fact, he gave loyal support to the Whigs throughout the session. He was the most industrious of Members, attending either the House or one of several select committees on almost every weekday.[3] He also spoke frequently, mostly pursuing his existing interests. He defended the annual grant to the non-denominational National Education System against its Tory critics (who objected to the exclusion of the Bible from the classrooms during ordinary school hours), and he seconded the bill whereby Thomas Wyse hoped to improve the workings of the National System and to establish 32 secondary 'academies' and four 'provincial colleges'. He was appointed to Wyse's select committee to inquire into Irish education and spent much of the summer assisting in taking evidence.[4] He pressed again for additional seats for Ireland, deprecating the 'injustice' of the Reform Act and the 'absurdity' of declaring it a final settlement.[5] He supported the Whigs' tithe bill by which the traditional tithe would be abolished and, instead, landlords would pay the Church 70% of the old charge, which they could recover through increased rents. The surplus created by suppressing 860 parishes in which there were under 50 Protestants would be 'appropriated' to the education of all denominations in the National System. Like almost all liberals, O'Brien welcomed this 'compromise' whereby non-Catholics would continue to support the Church but surplus revenue would go 'for the general benefit of the community'. The Lords removed the appropriation clause, causing the bill to be given up until the following year.[6]

O'Brien also resumed his campaign for an Irish poor law. From the 1820s, pamphleteers and MPs had commented on the fact that, while in relatively prosperous England there was a system of compulsory poor relief, in Ireland the destitute had to rely on a level of provision – from Grand Jury presentments, Parliamentary grants and voluntary contributions – that was hardly commensurate with the scale of Irish poverty. A native of one of the poorer counties, O'Brien had argued in his 1830 pamphlet that 'no kingdom in Europe exhibits such a mass of wretchedness and

---

2 O'Brien Papers (AO), Rough Diary, February-March 1835. *Hansard*, xxvi, 56-61, 410-415, 19, 26 February; xxvii, 772-7, 861-4, 969-74, 2, 7 (x2) April 1835, Divisions.   3 O'Brien Papers (AO), Rough Diary, February-August 1835.   4 *Hansard*, xxvii, 1199-1228, 19 May 1835, Wyse, O'Brien; xxix, 484, 13 July 1835, O'Brien. O'Brien Papers (AO), Rough Diary, June-August 1835.   5 *Hansard*, xxix, 775-80, 20 July 1835, O'Brien. See also O'Brien Papers, MS 428, f340, Circular on the Representation of County Limerick, n.d.   6 *Hansard*, xxix, 1067-72, 23 July 1835, Division; xxix, 1200, 29 July 1835, O'Brien.

destitution' as Ireland. This led him to a sense of obligation based on a view of the responsibilities of his class. 'The most important duty which attaches to the possession of property,' he wrote, was a 'paternal regard for those classes by whose labours that property is rendered valuable.' Adequate provision would disarm 'jealousy and cupidity' and give property 'that security upon which the happiness and existence of society depend'; he was happy to acknowledge 'the double motive of benevolence and self-interest'. The popular English idea of a poor law that would bring to account a greedy and neglectful Irish landlord class he held only in relation to one sort of owner, the absentees, men who exacted rents but fulfilled none of the paternal duties of the landlord. What O'Brien envisaged was standard fare among Irish poor law enthusiasts: a system of outdoor relief for the 'feeble and infirm', that is for those physically unable to work, and it was such a bill that he seconded on its introduction by Sir Richard Musgrave in July 1835. The measure was directly opposed by O'Connell, who believed that a poor law would discourage individual effort and destroy the bonds of charity and family obligation by which the Irish peasantry survived their sometimes desperate condition.[7]

Even more dangerously, in May 1835 O'Brien gave notice of a motion for state payment of the Catholic clergy, just weeks after O'Connell had restated his opposition to it in the House. When it caused 'some animadversions in Dublin' (it was denounced in a public meeting), he sent his constituents a full explanation of his views, which were unchanged since his earlier pamphlet. The *Limerick Star* declared, 'Let not Mr O'Brien be tempted to endanger the solid popularity which he, at present, enjoys with his constituents'. The leading Limerick liberals whose advice he sought informed him that his supporters were hostile to the pensioning of the Catholic clergy. He was told by Father Thomas O'Brien Costelloe, secretary of the County Club and soon to be O'Brien's bitter adversary, that 'the peculiar circumstances of religious difference existing between your family and the R.C. Clergy would contribute to render any interference on your part, in their revenues, very suspicious, and to weaken the enthusiasm manifested by them in your favour at the late Elections'. When trusted confidants like Robert Potter and Michael O'Shaughnessy issued similar warnings, the latter despite his personal opinion in favour of the measure, O'Brien withdrew the motion. As on the poor law, however, he had demonstrated his readiness to act against the known wishes of O'Connell.[8]

On 4 September, O'Brien wrote to E.J. Stanley, patronage secretary to the Treasury, giving notice that, as their 'Whig representative', he would be seeking favours on behalf of constituents. He disclaimed any interest in benefiting person-

---

[7] O'Brien, *Plan for the Relief of the Poor in Ireland. Hansard*, xxvi, 1206-11, 1214, 19 March 1835, O'Brien, O'Connell; xxvii, 203, 24 March 1835, O'Brien; xxix, 331-8, 8 July 1835, O'Brien, O'Connell. MacIntyre, *The Liberator*, 209-11, 217-18.   [8] *Limerick Star*, 19 May 1835, O'Brien to the Constituency of the County of Limerick, 13 May 1835. Smith O'Brien Papers, MS 428, f302, Geary to O'Brien, 15 May 1835; f303, Griffin to O'Brien, 19 May 1835; f304, Potter to O'Brien, 23 May 1835; ff305, 310, Costelloe to O'Brien, 24 May, 4 July 1835; f306, O'Shaughnessy to O'Brien, 24 May 1835; f312, Hogan to O'Brien, 1 August 1835. *Hansard*, xxvii, 728, 2 April 1835, O'Connell.

ally from patronage – in 1844 he would claim that, 'During the seven years that they [the Whigs] held office I sought no favor from them for myself or family' – and he made it clear that he would remain entirely independent in his political conduct: 'I do not wish in the smallest degree to involve myself in any implied pledge of *future* support to the present government. My support will be hereafter as it has already been, entirely governed by my sense of the merit or demerit of the course of policy which they pursue.'[9] He was not another of the 'jobbing' Irish Members that the English press (and later nationalists) so despised. Virtually all MPs would have used similar language in this age of the independent Member, but O'Brien would live out that ideal more fully than most. He returned to Ireland on 8 September and wrote the first of his annual reports to his constituents on the Parliamentary session. This report, which was not usual practice, again showed an independent support of the Whig administration. His strongest words were used to castigate the Tories for their opposition to appropriation, and he thought most of the Whig measures 'entitled to praise'. But he regretted the fact that no Irishman had been appointed to one of the principal Irish posts and, with the tithe bill rejected in the Lords and municipal reform and a poor law delayed, he complained of 'fruitless labours and wasted hours' in the House of Commons and expressed 'sincere disappointment that I can present you with nothing but a catalogue of measures defeated or postponed'. On payment of priests, he said he 'yielded to what I believed to be the general wish of the Catholics of Ireland, in postponing the discussion of the subject, but my own convictions are unchanged'.[10]

This determination to be his own man was confirmed by his decision in October 1835 to refuse involvement in a Limerick dinner for O'Connell. Whilst Thomas Wyse congratulated him on not being one of 'the idolators', one of the organisers apparently warned him that he risked alienating his supporters. O'Brien's reply reveals much about his character and his approach to politics:

> As I would not willingly say any thing which would hurt the feelings of others I do not think it necessary to state in detail the reasons which prevent me from joining in this invitation.
>
> With reference to the effect alluded to in your letter, which my taking this course may have upon the future conduct of some of my supporters in the County, I can only say that I did not accept the representation on the condition of yielding homage to any man, so neither do I desire to hold it on such terms. The attachment and esteem of my fellow countrymen I greatly covet, but if I fail to obtain them by own personal character and public conduct, I have no desire to seek them by any other means or through any other influence.[11]

---

9 Smith O'Brien Papers, MS 428, f325, O'Brien to Stanley, 4 September 1835; ibid., MS 10515 (4), Smith O'Brien's sketch of his political life, 25 September 1844.   10 *Limerick Star*, 25 September 1835, O'Brien to the Constituency of the County of Limerick, 24 September 1835.   11 Smith O'Brien Papers, MS 428, f327, Wyse to O'Brien, 14 October 1835; f328, O'Brien to Edward O'Connell, 15 October 1835.

O'Brien had deeply-held convictions about the need for an MP to pursue the dictates of his conscience and to resist any suggestion of outside influence. He prized 'that independence of mind which ought to be one of the qualifications of an useful and upright public man'.[12] He would later show, and in this respect he was not typical, a willingness to resign his seat if his views could not be reconciled with those of his electors: he was to ask on several occasions if his constituents wished 'to restore me to private life'. But he refused to allow that any person not a constituent should determine his conduct, and the fact that it was his old adversary, O'Connell, who might wield such influence can only have increased his determination. The dinner in Limerick took place on 19 October, without the presence (or any mention) of O'Brien.[13]

O'Brien passed much of his time after September planting and repairing (and entertaining) at Cahirmoyle, and he spent Christmas there before going to Dromoland for a week in January 1836. On the day before he left Limerick for London, he gave some indication of his priorities for the new session with a letter pressing his poor law ideas on the Chief Secretary, Lord Morpeth.[14] He introduced his own poor law bill in February and expressed frustration at the government's slowness to act despite the new Royal Commission report's assertion that over 2.3 million Irish people lived much of the year in destitution.[15] He warmly supported the government, however, on its measure to reform Ireland's municipal corporations. These institutions were riddled with abuse and anomaly, with functions often neglected, property mismanaged, and Catholics largely excluded by the Protestant patrons who nominated most of the governing bodies. Peel, responding to the bill, adopted Stanley's drastic proposal to prevent control falling into Catholic hands by abolishing the corporations altogether; their duties could be performed by appointed officials and elected boards with specific, limited functions. Given that in England in 1835, the Municipal Corporations Reform Act had created a system of borough councils elected by all male ratepayers, the issue became one on which Irish liberals demanded 'equal justice' for Ireland. O'Brien described as 'miserable and contemptible' the Tory mistrust of Catholics and, when the Lords mutilated the bill by adopting the abolitionist course, he furiously denounced the idea 'that Irishmen were unfitted to enjoy the same rights and privileges' as the English and Scots. He wrote to the inhabitants of Limerick to say they had been 'wronged, disparaged, insulted' by the course taken in the Lords. If Ireland was treated as 'a subordinate province', and its people as 'an inferior race', he would 'seek an independent legislature...as the only means of preserving it from oppression, contempt, and disgrace'. It was an extremely angry letter that had more passion and indignation in it than anything he had ever written before.[16]

12 *Limerick Chronicle*, 11 January 1837, O'Brien to Costelloe, 17 December 1836. 13 *Limerick Star*, 20 October 1835. 14 O'Brien Papers (AO), Rough Diary, 24 January 1836. Larcom Papers, MS 7698, O'Brien to Morpeth, 23 January 1836. 15 *Hansard*, xxxi, 229-30, 9 February; 33, 598-602, 4 May; 33, 833, 11 May 1836, O'Brien. 16 *Hansard*, xxxii, 1-7, 8 March; 32, 439-40, 21 March; xxxiv, 250-4, 9

O'Brien supported the Irish tithe bill on second reading in June. The knowledge that the Lords would defeat the bill again on the appropriation clause subsequently led him to describe the lower House's deliberations as 'a complete farce... Except for the pleasure of hearing themselves talk, he knew not for what purpose they were there at all'.[17] The Lords did precisely as he (and everyone else) expected. O'Brien's bill to regulate Ireland's medical charities was given up before second reading.[18] His only success – and it was a limited one – in the session came when he questioned the workings of the Royal Dublin Society. This body, created in the 18th century to promote the arts and sciences in Ireland, had degenerated, claimed O'Brien, into a social club for the convenience of the Dublin-based members. There was controversy when the learned and widely respected Catholic archbishop of Dublin, Daniel Murray, was 'black-beaned' (denied membership) in 1835. The fact that it received a Parliamentary grant left the society open to Commons scrutiny and so O'Brien secured (and became chairman of) a select committee to inquire into its administration. The report proposed the institution of fully developed lecture programmes and a system of entry whereby a candidate was rejected only if one third of the members present voted against him. This began the process of reform – the secretary assured O'Brien in 1839 that all of his recommendations had been acted upon – but the government, seeing 'imperfect fulfilment' of the committee's proposals, withdrew the grant in 1840.[19] When O'Brien himself was elected a member in February 1844, he commented that he was not 'blackballed' as he could have been.[20]

In May 1836, O'Brien complained bitterly to Morpeth that 'no one situation of any kind has thru my instrumentality been bestowed upon any person connected with the County of Limerick by the Irish Government ... For myself I have no personal favour to ask ... [but] I do regret that my countrymen in general, and those whom I represent in particular, obtain so small a share of the favour and attention of a government to which they give such an efficient support'. He subsequently made this complaint in his annual address to the electors and in a private letter to the Prime Minister. Again, however, he could not offer blind loyalty in exchange for favour, telling Melbourne that, 'My support will be given to the measures of Government as long as I approve of them – without reference to patronage ...' Melbourne acknowledged the 'conscientious & disinterested ground upon which your support has been given'.[21] In fact, most Irish liberals warmly approved of the

---

June; xxxiv, 1281, 5 July 1836, O'Brien. *Limerick Chronicle*, 28 May 1836, O'Brien to the Constituency and Inhabitants of the County of Limerick, 20 May 1836.   **17** *Hansard*, xxxiii, 1348-51, 2 June; xxxiv, 1148, 1152, 1158-9, 1 July 1836, O'Brien.   **18** *Hansard*, xxxiii, 1207-8, 31 May 1836, O'Brien.   **19** *Hansard*, xxxii, 523-5, 23 March 1836, O'Brien. *Journal of the House of Commons*, lxxxxi, 660-1, 14 July 1836, Resolutions. Smith O'Brien Papers, MS 430, f602, Henderson to O'Brien, 22 February 1839. Terence de Vere White, *The Story of the Royal Dublin Society* (Tralee, 1955), 97-103, 107-13.   **20** Smith O'Brien Papers, MS 8653 (20), O'Brien to Lucy O'Brien, 29 February 1844. Duffy, on the other hand, described a normal election, with O'Brien admitted by 105 votes to 5. Duffy, *Young Ireland, 1840-1845*, 166.   **21** Smith O'Brien Papers, MS 428, f380, O'Brien to Morpeth, 16 May 1836; f417, O'Brien to Melbourne, 20 October 1836; f418, Melbourne to O'Brien, 31 October 1836. *Limerick Star*, 13 September

Whig government's appointments policy, which broke with the tradition of preference for Protestants. It was the failure to achieve reforming legislation, with the refusal of the Lords to pass the government's tithe and municipal corporations bills, that produced most disappointment. In July 1836, O'Connell formed a major new organisation, the General Association, to agitate for these measures. 16 liberal-unionist Members joined the Association. O'Brien was one of the (small) majority of those who stayed aloof. He did join another body that was not led by O'Connell; this was the Reform Registry Association, established in January 1836 to promote the registration of liberal voters.[22]

O'Brien returned to Limerick at the end of July and at a county meeting on 8 August expressed 'perfect confidence' in the Whig Lord Lieutenant, Lord Mulgrave. He said that for the first time in centuries the Irish government ruled 'honestly and impartially for the benefit of the majority of its people'. However, in his annual report the frustration evident in some of his Commons contributions was clearly expressed. The 'repeated evasions' in relation to a poor law and the Lords' rejection of appropriation came in for criticism, but it was the denial of municipal reform, with its blatantly anti-Catholic motive, that he denounced most vigorously, not least because the Tory Lord Lyndhurst had called the Irish 'aliens' who could not be treated in the same way as Englishmen. He argued that the Union must be based on 'perfect equality', and if this were denied 'the sooner the connection is dissolved the better'; he would seek in these circumstances to restore an 'independent legislature'. Overall, little good had been effected, thanks mainly to the Lords, leaving him 'truly disheartened'.[23] O'Brien's raising the possibility of becoming a repealer is notable, of course. What happened in 1843 did not require a complete, unheralded reversal of political direction. However, the chronology of his development – the simple fact that he did not take the step for many years – lends some perspective. Many liberal politicians insisted on a genuine Union that would serve Irish interests. O'Brien's language in 1836 went little further; he had not yet gone near still less crossed over the watershed that would make him a repealer.

At the end of 1836, the earnest young politician ruffled O'Connell's feathers and found himself involved in the sort of (political) duel that would have driven less resolute men into silence if not submission. In November, William Sharman Crawford, the MP for Dundalk, had induced the General Association to adopt voluntarist resolutions on the Irish Church, that is an opposition to any form of compulsory assessment to support the clergy. In two public letters, O'Brien's response was to reject a voluntary principle that would involve 'constant bidding for popularity' by the clergy and 'servile dependence upon the caprices of the people'. He would support the Whig

---

1836. See also Smith O'Brien Papers, MS 428, f410, O'Brien to Morpeth, 21 August 1836. *Hansard*, xxxii, 439-40, 21 March 1836, O'Brien. **22** *Pilot*, 13, 18, 20 January 1836. Smith O'Brien Papers, MS 428, f368, Lalor to O'Brien, 18 April 1836 **23** *Limerick Star*, 9 August, 13 September 1836, O'Brien to the Constituency of the County of Limerick, 8 September 1836.

tithe bill – reforming rather than ending compulsory assessment – and would secure equality between the religions by paying the Catholic clergy (and increasing the allowances received by Presbyterian ministers). His intention was to move in 1837 for a committee of inquiry and to persist with the idea of paying the priests unless Catholics were found to be generally opposed. If, however, his constituents 'expect[ed] their representatives to support the voluntary principle', he would resign: 'I invite them to substitute in my place some one whose sincere convictions will allow him consistently to maintain this opinion'.[24] The result was a challenge to his position as Member for Limerick, a venomous assault by O'Connell, and a response from O'Brien that was almost ostentatious in its display of principled courage. Father Costelloe wrote to O'Brien on 16 December to inform him that, as its secretary, he was calling a meeting of the County Club to discuss the future representation of the county. Costelloe cited O'Brien's support for state payment of the Catholic clergy. He also suggested, according to O'Brien, that the Limerick electors were 'discontented because I have not placed myself under the leadership of Mr O'Connell'. O'Brien reminded him that he went into Parliament 'to represent the constituency of Limerick and not to support the views of Mr O'Connell, or any other individual'. He would perform his duties according to his 'conscience' until his constituents willed otherwise; this might occur before the next election, for he was prepared to obey any 'unequivocal manifestation' of a desire that he should resign.[25]

The club duly met on 7 January and opposed payment of the Catholic clergy but expressed confidence in their MP. They opted for 'a lenient course of persuasion' on their differences and O'Shaughnessy, who chaired the meeting (perhaps to O'Brien's advantage), complimented their 'talented and efficient representative'.[26] However, O'Connell, before he could have known about this meeting, issued a public letter to the Limerick electors – in itself a provocative intrusion – in which he criticised O'Brien's support for 'the mischievous scheme of pensioning the Catholic Clergy'. The electors should 'peremptorily direct' him 'to desist from his ill-judged plan'. He also wrote that O'Brien's opposition to voting by secret ballot in elections – he had abstained on Grote's motions in both 1835 and 1836 and argued against the ballot in his annual report in September – constituted 'such an obliquity of judgement – upon at least one political subject – as to render it doubtful whether the man can be fit to be entrusted with the duties of a Representative in the House of Commons'. The ballot would protect tenants from the vengeance of their landlords, from the sort of persecution, he claimed, suffered by the O'Brien tenants who had rebelled in the Clare by-election in 1828.[27]

O'Brien's reply was forceful and defiant. Given Catholic opposition, it would be 'fruitless, and in a Protestant indelicate', to propose state payment of the priest-

---

24 *Limerick Star*, 2 December 1836, O'Brien to the Roman Catholics of the County of Limerick, 30 November 1836; ibid., 30 December 1836, O'Brien to the Editor of the Newry Examiner, 16 December 1836. 25 *Limerick Chronicle*, 11 January 1837, O'Brien to Costelloe, 17 December 1836. 26 *DEP*, 12 January 1837. 27 *Limerick Chronicle*, 11 January 1837, O'Connell to the Electors of the County Limerick, 8 January 1837.

hood at present, but he reserved 'the full power of advocating the measure at a future date'. Against the ballot he contended that the necessity had not been demonstrated – intimidation of voters was not widespread, he believed – and, until it was, free men should proceed with 'manly pride' in 'discharging a sacred trust openly'. This was certainly a principled point of view, for, though a landlord himself, his chances in Limerick would be damaged, not enhanced, by landlord intimidation of voters. He was especially annoyed by O'Connell's 'unfounded' allegations against his father's conduct in 1828. On the general question of O'Connell's influence, he would 'never consent to be the slave or the tool of Mr O'Connell' and would immediately renounce his seat 'if the condition annexed to its possession were subserviency to the views of Mr O'Connell or any other individual'. He warned that if O'Connell 'should again interpose his arrogant dictation between me and my Constituents, I shall assuredly not shrink from the task of freely and searchingly questioning the title upon which he founds that supremacy over the opinion of my countrymen which alone can justify such an interference'. O'Connell then filled two newspaper columns with scathing denunciation of O'Brien's 'overweening vanity', 'bull-frog inflation of self-importance', 'rancour and malignity', and so on, and predicted his 'relapse into his original, and, I now dread, congenital Toryism ... no treasury hack ever voted more uniformly with Peel and his gang of rotten-borough members'. It was an extraordinary attack, but O'Brien, undaunted, issued a vehement (if less colourful) response in which O'Connell's 'capricious dictatorship' was repudiated.[28]

Father Thaddeus O'Malley, attributing O'Connell's enmity to O'Brien's advocacy of a poor law, admired the 'spirit' and 'dignity' of O'Brien's defiance but added a warning that O'Connell's 'hold on the *imagination* of the people' spelt danger: 'You must deal with the masses cautiously'. O'Brien was also congratulated by Denham Jephson, the liberal-unionist Member for Mallow, on his 'very able answer to Mr O'Connell. It is a temperate & manly rebuke for his impertinent interference'. He predicted that O'Brien's 'independent rejection of Mr O'Connell's dictation' would win him support in Limerick.[29] O'Brien considered it 'impossible to say' what lengths the O'Connellites would go to in his constituency but, replying to Jephson, thought his letter 'will do good in this part of Ireland ... I find that the feeling of the reasonable Catholics & liberals is entirely in my favour ... Fortunately I value my seat but lightly indeed compared with my independence. Hitherto I have had nothing to complain of but on the contrary, much to gratify me, & I do not apprehend that it will now be otherwise.'[30] O'Shaughnessy apparently told him that 'opinion is divided amongst the Dublin liberals ... the O'Connellites being against

---

28 Ibid., 14 January 1837, O'Brien to the Electors of the County of Limerick, n.d.; ibid., 25 January 1837, O'Connell to the Electors of the County of Limerick, 22 January 1837; ibid., 28 January 1837, O'Brien to the Electors of the County of Limerick, 25 January 1837. 29 Smith O'Brien Papers, MS 429, f443, Jephson to O'Brien, 17 January 1837; f445, O'Malley to O'Brien, 23 January 1837; ibid., MS 449, f3408, O'Malley to O'Brien, n.d. 30 Maurice Denham Jephson, *An Anglo-Irish Miscellany. Some Records of the Jephsons of Mallow* (Dublin, 1964), 229, O'Brien to Jephson, 17 January 1837.

me, the moderates in my favour. I shall be anxious to see whether the former will make a move in Co. Limerick. The sword is now fairly drawn ...'[31] A 'move' against him in Limerick did not materialise, his opponents perhaps seeing that their decision of 7 January could hardly be undone. When the club met again on 4 February, Costelloe made some muted criticisms, notably of the disrespect shown to O'Connell, but even he said he wished that O'Brien would 'long continue' to represent Limerick.[32] O'Brien was delighted; he was 'off with flying colours ... I am glad to see so good a feeling towards me. I wish our friend Costello[e] was a little more friendly ...' By mid-February he was hopeful 'that the whole O'Connell controversy is now over. Whether I shall feel its effects at the next election is a matter which I cannot at present determine. I do not however fear the result.' Though assuring Lucy that he was 'indifferent' to the approval of others, he was happy to report from London that men of all parties congratulated him on his part in the contest; in a reference to O'Connell's insult, he wondered if 'in the eyes of some my *bullfrog* dimensions have swollen considerably since Mr O'Connell has thought proper to make me the object of his venom'.[33]

O'Brien's was an impressive display from which he emerged as a more substantial political figure. That the affair could have ended very differently was demonstrated by a letter published a few days earlier. Sharman Crawford had been critical of O'Connell's support for the Whigs' tithe bill. They shared a belief in the voluntary principle, but while O'Connell would accept the bill as an 'instalment' Crawford rejected any measure that still required non-Anglicans to pay for the Established Church. His Dundalk constituents had met and passed resolutions in favour of O'Connell's position, and so Crawford wrote to announce that he would not stand in Dundalk at the next election.[34] O'Brien and Crawford were the only Irish liberal Members to confront O'Connell head-on during this Parliament, and only O'Brien survived to do so again in the next. There was no hint of evasion or prevarication in his conduct. Richard Davis has recently presented an O'Brien who was 'balanced on a particularly shaky tightrope. To stay in politics he needed to appear progressive enough to satisfy the bulk of his Catholic constituency' and avoid entanglement with 'the influence of O'Connell'. On the other hand, Davis believes, family pressures, most notably 'the need to obtain funding from the House of Dromoland', pulled him towards conservative positions. The suggestion that he worried about how he might 'appear' and felt the need to 'tread carefully', lest he alienate one side or the other, seems curiously at odds with the evidence. He openly and repeatedly defied O'Connell when anyone concerned to stay in politics would have remained quiet. And, given his liberal and, eventually, revolutionary course, his family obviously had little or no power over him; if Lady O'Brien tried to tie him up with her purse strings (see

---

31 Smith O'Brien Papers, MS 8653 (4), O'Brien to Lucy O'Brien, 29 January 1837.   32 *Limerick Chronicle*, 8 February 1837.   33 Smith O'Brien Papers, MS 8653 (5), O'Brien to Lucy O'Brien, 1, 4, 6, 9, 10 February 1837; ibid. (6), O'Brien to Lucy O'Brien, 13 February 1837. O'Brien Papers (AO), Letter Box, Bundle 4, O'Brien to Lucy O'Brien, 16 February 1837.   34 *Limerick Chronicle*, 1 February 1837, Crawford to the Electors of Dundalk, 25 January 1837.

below), they were remarkably ineffective. O'Brien was not torn between two opposing influences. The truth was much more simple: he was his own master and he pursued the dictates of conscience regardless of the consequences.[35]

Sir Edward endorsed his son's stand against O'Connell and, disapproving of the Whig alliance with the agitator, commented that, 'Whatever may be the merits of the administration, his protection will sink them'.[36] Sir Edward and Lady O'Brien had their own problems at this time, in which O'Brien became peripherally involved. William Smith had had two illegitimate children with Bridget Keevan, the woman he kept at Cahirmoyle. The son, Thomas Smith, died in 1812 at the age of eight, but the daughter, Jane Brew (her married name), insisted from 1828 that her brother was really still alive. She believed he had been inveigled away from school in England and taken to Jamaica. In 1835, her advertisements in the West Indies turned up someone who claimed to be Thomas Smith, and Mrs Brew pressed Sir Edward and Lady Charlotte (the executors of William Smith's will) to ensure that her brother received the substantial property left to him by his father. This came to a head in January 1837 when the story found its way into the newspapers in England and Ireland, appearing under such titillating headings as 'The Lost Heir' and 'Romance in Real Life'. At the end of January, Sir Edward sent a letter to the newspapers to establish the facts of the matter and to show, in particular, that Thomas Smith did die in 1812.[37] O'Brien, concerned about 'the general impression that a portion of the Cahirmoyle estate is affected by Smith's claim', had encouraged this initiative and may have helped his younger brother, Edward, to write their father's letter, and he duly distributed copies to the London papers.[38] O'Brien's research in London in the spring of 1837 uncovered the truth about the impostor who claimed to be Thomas Smith; he was the son of a market-gardener from Ealing.[39] Sir Edward, however, did not live to see the business concluded; he died on 13 March 1837.[40]

In the midst of all these difficulties, Lucy O'Brien gave birth to their first child, a son, Edward, on 24 January 1837. O'Brien missed the opening of Parliament – 'I cannot absent myself from her until the trying moment is over'[41] – but he returned to his duties at the end of the month. He wrote almost daily to Lucy, telling her continually how much he missed his 'little wife' and their son ('Love & a kiss to baby' was a favourite signing off line). It was the beginning of an important ele-

---

35 Richard Davis, *Revolutionary Imperialist: William Smith O'Brien 1803-1864* (Dublin, Darlinghurst, 1998), 86, 100, 113, 147.   36 O'Brien Papers (AO), Letter Box, Bundle 1, Sir Edward O'Brien to O'Brien, 1 February 1837.   37 *Pilot*, 3 February 1837, Sir Edward O'Brien to the Editor, 30 January 1837.   38 Smith O'Brien Papers, MS 8653 (4), O'Brien to Lucy O'Brien, 3, 4 February 1837; ibid., MS 22342, O'Brien to Sir Edward O'Brien, 22, 23 January 1837. Inchiquin Papers, T33/3757, O'Brien to Lady O'Brien, 20 November 1835.   39 Smith O'Brien Papers, MS 8653 (1), O'Brien to Lucy O'Brien [April 1837]; ibid. (8), O'Brien to Lucy O'Brien, 29 April 1837; ibid., MS 8655 (3), O'Brien to Lady O'Brien, 24 April 1837. Inchiquin Papers, T33/3757, O'Brien to Sir Edward O'Brien, 16 February, 5 March 1837; O'Brien to Jane Brew, 23 April 1837; O'Brien to Lady O'Brien, n.d., 20 May 1837. Davis, *Revolutionary Imperialist*, 91-3.   40 For an interesting account of Sir Edward's death, which he predicted would occur that year, see Aubrey de Vere, *Recollections*, 79-80.   41 Jephson, *Anglo-Irish Miscellany*, 229, O'Brien to Jephson, 17 January 1837.

ment of the O'Brien story: the tension between his commitment to work in London and his longing to be with his family at Cahirmoyle. In May 1837, Lucy joined him in London without little Edward and from 1838 she brought her child[ren] across as well. But O'Brien's loneliness, of which he complained endlessly, when Lucy was not with him in London, and the financial problems brought about when she was (see below), blighted his enjoyment of his chosen career and eventually influenced his course in politics. This, however, is to anticipate the events of the 1840s.

O'Brien's first contribution to Parliamentary debate in 1837 came when a Tory drew attention to the formidable body that the General Association had become: O'Brien pointed out that it was the Tory policy of blocking beneficial reforms that caused agitation and would stimulate a renewal of the demand for repeal. He wrote to Lucy, 'I was glad to have an early opportunity of saying a few words to show my friends in Ireland that my course of Parl. conduct will not be in the smallest degree changed in consequence of my recent battle with O'Connell, to disappoint in short the hopes of some of our Conservative friends & to defeat the predictions of some of my Radical *enemies* ...'[42] He deliberately abstained, despite O'Connell, when Grote moved again for the ballot in March, and his support for the grant to the Catholic seminary at Maynooth was expressed in such terms – the priests should have 'the support and protection of the state' – as virtually to restate his views on paying the Catholic clergy.[43] In April, O'Brien abstained when Sir Henry Hardinge moved for the withdrawal from Spain of the British Legion, a volunteer force which was fighting for Queen Isabella against the reactionary Don Carlos. O'Brien told Lucy that his objection was to Palmerston's policy of intervention in Spain. However, the Legion had numerous Irish soldiers and included O'Connell's cousin. O'Connell arranged to have O'Brien (and other defaulters) condemned in the *Pilot* newspaper, instructing the ever-compliant editor, Richard Barrett: 'Mention Smith O'Brien's refusal to vote on the late division respecting the Irish Legion, although his countrymen were violently calumniated by Sir H. Hardinge, and although it was a question which, if carried against the Ministry, must have caused their resignation and deprived Ireland of Lord Mulgrave. Take care that this should not appear to originate from me. Comment upon the absence of every other member who was absent but of course treat the friends lightly ...' The *Pilot* duly denounced O'Brien and the other abstainers as 'betrayers' of the cause of 'freedom and reform' and called on the Limerick constituency to rid themselves of their 'insolent representative'. The affair illustrates the dangers of the independent course that O'Brien pursued, and the fact that everybody suspected the hand of O'Connell in much that the *Pilot* did only increased the possibility that O'Brien's Limerick support would be induced to desert him.[44]

42 *Hansard*, xxxvi, 95, 3 February 1837, O'Brien. Smith O'Brien Papers, MS 8653 (5), O'Brien to Lucy O'Brien, 4 February 1837. 43 *Hansard*, xxxvii, 67-71, 7 March 1837, Division; xxxviii, 1628, 26 June 1837, O'Brien. O'Brien Papers (AO), Rough Diary, 7 March 1837: 'Ballot. Did not vote.' 44 M. O'Connell,

Much of O'Brien's attention was taken up with another measure on which he and O'Connell would differ, the poor law bill of 1837-8. The Royal Commission's report of 1836 recommended drainage and reclamation schemes, emigration and a range of other measures. This interventionist approach proved too radical for a Whig government which wanted a poor law that would incorporate the supposed economies of the new (1834) English system's workhouse test of destitution. Lord John Russell sent George Nicholls, a poor law commissioner in England, to assess the applicability of the English measure to Ireland. After a notoriously brief, six-week tour, in September-October 1836, Nicholls concluded that conditions in Ireland were well suited to the general principles of the English Act, and so it was a version of the latter that Russell brought in in 1837. The King's death and resultant dissolution of Parliament in June caused the loss of all the Irish measures, but the poor law bill was reintroduced in December and passed in 1838. O'Brien welcomed the emergence at last of a poor law, explicitly countering O'Connell's objections; these were 'founded in error', for the extent of poverty in Ireland necessitated effective legislation. However, O'Brien found much to fault in the bill. He thought that the provision of relief to the able-bodied would prove excessively expensive, when alternative measures (emigration, public works) would not only be less burdensome on the ratepayer but also assist in raising people out of poverty. Like most of the Irish poor law enthusiasts, he deprecated the decision to deny outdoor (non-workhouse) relief to the aged and infirm, people who did not deserve the punitive regime required by the workhouse test of destitution. In Committee, he (with O'Connell's backing) moved twice for provision of outdoor relief but found the government and a clear majority of Irish Members insistent that the workhouse test was needed to deter all but the truly destitute. In several respects, he did not act as a typical landlord, proposing, for example, that landlords should pay two-thirds of the poor rate instead of sharing the burden equally with their tenants. On all major points, the government defeated the attempts to amend the bill, O'Brien generally finding himself in the minority. He voted for the third reading in April 1838 but did so in the hope of future amendment, and, rather than satisfying him, the measure established a system which would provoke a string of complaints from him in years to come.[45]

The death of King William IV on 20 June occasioned the general election of July-August 1837. In his address to the electors, written from London, O'Brien pre-

---

Correspondence of Daniel O'Connell, vi, 2397, O'Connell to Burrett, 21 April 1837. Smith O'Brien Papers, MS 8653 (8), O'Brien to Lucy O'Brien [21 April 1837]. *Pilot*, 24 April 1837. See also Smith O'Brien Papers, MS 455, Commonplace Book, 'Spanish Policy: Reasons for disapproving Lord Palmerston's foreign policy as regards his mission of the British Legion to the assistance of the queen of Spain'. Maurice R. O'Connell, 'O'Connell and the Spanish Civil War 1834-39', in Maurice R. O'Connell (ed.), *Education, Church and State* (Dublin, 1992), 35-9. **45** *Hansard*, xxxvi, 478-9, 13 February, O'Brien; xxxviii, 292-402, 28 April, O'Brien; xxxviii, 1165, 2 June 1837, O'Brien; xl, 977-81, 9 February, O'Brien; xli, 73-7, 79-80, 23 February, O'Brien, Division; xli, 976-81, 983-4, 16 March, O'Brien, Division; xlii, 540, 9 April, O'Brien; xlii, 715, 30 April 1838, Division. *The Times*, 5 June 1837, Division.

sented himself as an advocate of equal treatment of Protestants and Catholics and said that it was 'chiefly because this principle has been strenuously maintained by the present Government in their legislative measures, and boldly carried into effect in their exercise of the patronage of the Crown, that they appear to me to have entitled themselves to the support of your Representatives'.[46] He wisely saw Costelloe – 'Breakfasted with the Rev. Mr Costello[e]' was his diary entry for 10 July – soon after returning to Limerick. O'Brien's position as one of the two liberal candidates for the county was never in doubt, given the desire for a united front against the Tories. The O'Connellite *Limerick Star* immediately supported 'the active and excellent' O'Brien (and, 10 days later, gave a somewhat grudging approval of Fitzgibbon).[47] Michael O'Shaughnessy, now the president of the County Club, secured O'Connell's endorsement of O'Brien: in a public letter dated 10 July, O'Connell described O'Brien as 'an efficient, useful member, and, what we want now, a friend to the Queen and thorough anti-Tory', so he advocated his re-election even though 'Mr O'Brien has opinions in which I do not concur'. O'Connell went on to give O'Brien further backing in the General Association and at a meeting in Limerick.[48] However, when a published circular indicated the Liberator's support for O'Brien, the latter protested to the club secretary:

> It has given me much pain to perceive that in a circular which has appeared in print respecting my election ... an attempt has been made to compromise the independence which as a member of Parliament I will never cease to claim for myself, by placing Mr O'Connell's name in such connection with mine as would make it appear that I am acceptable to the county only because it pleases him to tender his support. I can assure you it greatly diminishes the pride and pleasure which I should otherwise feel in appearing as one of the chosen representatives of the people & if this sort of identification were supposed to involve anything like a pledge that my votes or actions were to be in the smallest degree controlled by Mr O'Connell I should not hesitate for a moment to call upon the electors to put some one else in my place ... A general coincidence of views upon questions of public policy exists between his opinions and mine but I will not consent to go into Parliament in any respect subject to his dictation and I wish distinctly that this should be fully understood by the people of this county ...

O'Brien asked (in vain) that this letter should be presented in the County Club, as he would be 'sorry to obtain support from any other quarter upon grounds which are not fully understood'.[49] Very much the man of principle, he objected as much to O'Connell's interference in his favour as he had to the hostile intrusion of six months earlier. The letter was not published – though the (Tory) *Chronicle* did

---

46 *Limerick Star*, 25 July 1837, O'Brien to the Electors of the County of Limerick, 23 June 1837. 47 *Limerick Star*, 4, 7, 14 July 1837. 48 *Limerick Chronicle*, 22, 26 July 1837. *Limerick Star*, 14, 18, 25 July 1837. 49 Smith O'Brien Papers, MS 49, f459, O'Brien to Edward O'Connell, 31 July 1837.

refer briefly to its existence[50] – and so did not influence the election. O'Brien and Fitzgibbon were challenged by a Tory, a distant relative of the former's, Augustus Stafford O'Brien. Again showing that (in a constituency estimated to be five-sixths Catholic) he was aware of the need to court the local priesthood, O'Brien declared that even 'if the whole body of the gentry were leagued against him he should defeat them with the people headed by the Catholic Clergy'.[51] Most striking of all was his reaction to the election-day riot in which his supporters apparently attacked A.S. O'Brien's committee room, injured several men, and caused the Tory to withdraw from the election on the grounds that his people, 'in peril of their lives', could not go to the Court House to vote. The *Chronicle* denounced the 'barbarous outrage' committed by 'sanguinary miscreants whose object was obviously slaughter'. O'Brien, however, called the affray 'a circumstance incidental ... a little casual obstruction', and he congratulated his supporters on 'such an enthusiastic exhibition as you have made of adherence to the cause'. Perhaps the Tories exaggerated the affair in order to justify a petition against the result, and it is even possible that the *Star* was right in its claim that the Tory crowd initiated the brawl.[52] But O'Brien's glib dismissal still surprises. He was now an experienced politician, attuned to certain realities, be they priest-led rebellions against the landlords or the sort of electoral rowdiness that was commonplace in both Britain and Ireland.

O'Brien and Fitzgibbon were re-elected. The fact that the latter topped the poll suggests the continuing strength of landlord influence. As often happened, a period of revenge and recrimination followed. Lord Clare (whom O'Brien duly questioned) was accused of punishing tenants who supported O'Brien, and in another case 'the week after the election twelve of the [disobedient] tenants were distrained and compelled to pay up their rents to the last farthing' (O'Mara). In November, Chidley Coote apparently 'summoned his Tenantry to wait on him at his residence' to sign a petition alleging 'that they were prevented through intimidation from going to the Poll', a 'mere fabrication' according to O'Brien's correspondent.[53] O'Brien gave a general denunciation of the vengeful landlords in a public dinner for the Limerick Members on 2 October.[54] This is interesting in view of O'Brien's refusal (which continued in 1838) to support the ballot. Wyse congratulated O'Brien on his having succeeded in spite of the brushes with O'Connell: '... my fears were quite idle ... This is, "Ireland as it ought to be" and shows we are getting out of the *Congé d'Elire* system and into something like men thinking for themselves. It is one of the best signs of the times I know of and gives me great hopes ...' O'Brien's fellow-enthusiast for emigration, William Hutt of Hull, wrote to say he had 'always considered your seat one particularly honourable to you on account of your unconcealed independence of the governing power in Ireland', meaning O'Connell.[55]

---

50 *Limerick Chronicle*, 5 August 1837. 51 *Limerick Star*, 28 July 1837. *Limerick Chronicle*, 29 July 1837.
52 *Limerick Chronicle*, 12 August 1837. *Limerick Star*, 11 August 1837. 53 Smith O'Brien Papers, MS 429, f465, Clare to O'Brien, 28 August 1837; f470, O'Brien to Maunsell, 2 October 1837; f478, Barrett to O'Brien, 12 November 1837; f496, O'Mara to O'Brien, 13 February 1838; ibid., MS 441, f2296, O'Brien to Clare [26 August 1837]. 54 *Limerick Chronicle*, 4 October 1837. 55 Smith O'Brien Papers,

The Limerick Tories lodged a petition against O'Brien's (and Fitzgibbon's) return. O'Brien's concern was aggravated by his knowledge that he lacked the finances to resist; he wrote to Lucy that 'it is very hard to fight without the munitions of war let a man be as brave as a lion'.[56] The Limerick petition was thought to be supported from a special fund that English Tories had established to help their Irish counterparts to challenge election results. In the House in December 1837, O'Brien led the protest against this so-called 'Spottiswoode conspiracy', by which English Tories who knew nothing about the circumstances of an election could force a Member either to take on the crippling cost of fighting a petition (thousands of pounds, potentially, if he had to bring over witnesses to be heard by the election committee in London) or to withdraw from the contest and surrender the seat. His motion failed, but MacIntyre believed that the publicity 'no doubt made use of the fund more difficult'. O'Connell, who lost more money than most through election petitions (MacIntyre estimated that it cost him about £12,500 to contest the Dublin and Youghal petitions of 1835), supported O'Brien and attacked the system whereby partisan Commons committees considered petitions. He was reprimanded by the House for this affront to its dignity; O'Brien, knowing that O'Connell's accusation was true and therefore setting aside any personal feeling against his adversary, was one of the minority who voted for O'Connell and against the censure motion.[57] The Limerick petition was finally discharged in April 1838 after no party attended to support it. O'Shaughnessy understood that 'the Spottiswoode gang refused the supplies'.[58]

O'Brien returned to Ireland on 19 December 1837 and spent Christmas at Dromoland. In January he had the house at Cahirmoyle and six acres of land conveyed to his mother in return for an annual payment of £120. This was apparently a result of O'Brien's financial difficulties. With rental income from only a small property, 318 acres, he struggled to cope with the expense of running and improving Cahirmoyle and living for half the year in London. He took cheap lodgings for little more than a pound a week when by himself in London, but this rose to over £4 during the several months in which he was joined by Lucy.[59] Back in February 1837, he had asked if she was 'aware that there is a deliberate intention at Dromoland to *starve* me out of parliament'. He reckoned then that he would have 'an increased income' from his parents if he gave up his seat, which would mean his effective

MS 429, f462, Hutt to O'Brien, 5 August 1837; f469, Wyse to O'Brien, 26 September 1837. *Congé d'Elire*: royal permission to elect a bishop. In this context it meant the practice of electing those favoured by O'Connell. **56** Smith O'Brien Papers, MS 8653 (11), O'Brien to Lucy O'Brien, 20 November 1837. See also ibid. (12), O'Brien to Lucy O'Brien, 5, 10 Dec. 1837. *Freeman's Journal*, 8 January 1838. **57** *Hansard*, xxxix, 687-94, 747-55, 6, 7 December 1837, O'Brien; xxxxi, 233-6, 27 February 1838, Division. MacIntyre, *The Liberator*, 124-5. **58** *Journal of the House of Commons*, lxxxxiii, 423, 3 April 1838. Smith O'Brien Papers, MS 429, f514, O'Shaughnessy to O'Brien, 11 March 1838. **59** Ibid., MS 8653 (2), O'Brien to Lucy O'Brien, n.d.; ibid. (4), O'Brien to Lucy O'Brien, 31 January 1837; ibid. (12), O'Brien to Lucy O'Brien, 5 December 1837; ibid. (14), O'Brien to Lucy O'Brien, 14 Feb. 1839.

withdrawal from the liberal politics they deprecated – a 'curious mode,' he commented, 'of [governing?] the opinions of a man of 33 years of age'.[60] In July, his mother sent (through Lucy) a 'solemn protest' against his standing for re-election; she was 'decidedly of [the] opinion that a continuance in parliament must be ruinous to him & render his future life very uncomfortable unless he obtains some lucrative situation, for … it is quite impossible that he can afford to live half the year in this country & the other half in London on any income I could feel it at all right to give him, & I do certainly wish both him & every one of my children to *know* & *remember* that when their dear Father was taken from me, I came to the full & decided determination *never to pay debts for them* …'.[61] O'Brien's solution was to propose 'to let Carmoyle [as Lady O'Brien habitually called Cahirmoyle] even to a stranger that you might spend much of yr time in London'. Instead, his mother took possession of the house but gave O'Brien and his family the use of it whenever they were in Ireland.[62] She told him he could not afford to buy a London house (which he appears to have proposed), expressed frustration over his pestering her for money and lack of gratitude for past assistance, and inquired accusingly about what he had done with the money he received after his marriage. She could 'remember your peculiar tendency to let your thoughts fly more rapidly than human powers are capable of moving'. A reference to the 'points on which we so widely differ' probably reflected her hostility to his politics.[63] Lady O'Brien did continue to assist O'Brien financially, but she was never generous and his worries over money persisted.

His mother might not have agreed, but O'Brien's politics in 1838 suggested a new maturity as he joined the Whigs (and O'Connell) in seeking a compromise settlement of the Irish tithe and corporations questions. The Lords' mutilation of the Irish corporations bill in 1836 had led to criticism of the unelected chamber's defiance of the will of the Commons and to abuse of the Tories for refusing equal treatment to Ireland. Peel, under pressure from moderate Tories, came to doubt if the policy of 'unqualified resistance' could be permanently maintained in view of opinion in both Ireland and England; by spring 1837, he seriously contemplated giving up the abolitionist course and conceding a moderate reform. The latter would require, as Sergeant Jackson put it, 'a *bona fide* qualification which whilst it would admit Roman Catholics to a just share in Municipal Government should not give them a monopoly'.[64] With the passing of the poor law in 1838, such a safe and reli-

---

60 Ibid. (6), O'Brien to Lucy O'Brien [February 1837]. 61 Ibid. (10), Lady O'Brien to Lucy O'Brien, 3 July 1837. 62 O'Brien Papers (NLI), Letter Box, Bundle 2, Lady O'Brien to O'Brien, 13 August 1838; ibid., Rough Diary, 1, 31 January 1838; ibid., Conveyance of Cahirmoyle from W.S. O'Brien to Dame Charlotte O'Brien, 29 January 1838. 63 Smith O'Brien Papers, MS 8653 (13), O'Brien to Lucy O'Brien, 24 July 1838; ibid., MS 429, f566, Lady O'Brien to O'Brien, 13 November 1838. 64 Peel Papers, Add MSS 40,423, f76, Clerk to Peel, n.d.; f160, Purport of Peel's communications with Stanley and Graham; ff176, 301, Papers by Peel, 23 April, 4 July 1837; ibid., Add MSS 40,424, f113, Jackson to Peel, 31 August 1836. Graham Papers, 33, Peel to Graham, 28 March 1837. Wellington Papers, Port. 42, f88, Peel to Wellington, 4 September 1836; ibid., Port. 45, ff94, 110, Peel to Wellington, 9, 15 April 1837.

able qualification was realisable, using the national valuation that was to be undertaken as the basis of the poor rate. On 19 May 1838, about 30 Tory Members met at Peel's house and resolved to seek a settlement of the question by amending the government's re-introduced bill.[65] The resultant proposal, to establish 11 corporations with a £10 franchise under the poor law valuation, was presented by Peel as an offer that matched the Whigs' concession in omitting appropriation from the tithe bill (see below). Following Russell, who gave Peel's speech a cautious welcome, O'Brien said he 'thought that, in the present balanced state of parties, it would be wise to accede to a compromise, which they could do without dishonour. The one wished to appropriate part of the Irish Church revenues to the purpose of education, the other to abolish corporations, but neither could carry their object exclusively. Therefore, to do anything they must coalesce ...' He saw in Peel's words 'much that was satisfactory' and an opportunity for 'peace and improvement of the country'.[66]

This was realistic and courageous politics from all concerned, including O'Brien. Such a compromise could have been (and later was) attacked from both sides, yet it was a necessity if a settlement was to be achieved before the Tories returned to office (as the close-run thing in 1837 suggested they might soon do). This is not to say that all was plain sailing thereafter. The government proposed a £5 qualification and on 1 June 1838 carried this in the House against Peel's £10 amendment. O'Brien voted with the government, but James Grattan privately recorded the true state of liberal opinion:

> I am getting what I asked in the Government Bill, what we all asked ... We must not lose the bill. I told Sheil & Wyse so on the 2nd. They say we will not but Sheil says we must talk big ... I do not think we have a right to complain now after having listened to & approved of Peel's offer the night he first made it. Sheil approved of it next day at Brooks. So did others of the Catholicks even, & the importance of the Corporation Bill is greatly magnified. It is only in the large towns it is of moment. If we complain in the House they will complain & be dissatisfied in the Country & thus we will diminish the benefit of the Bill as O'Connell has done that of the Poor Bill, & I will not be a party to this ... I have spoken to O'Brien, Stuart, &c about the Corps. bill. They agree with me but are not ready to take any steps ... I will not support Lord John in his 5.00.[67]

Wyse also doubted if the £10 figure was 'too high. Is it really so? This was faintly affirmed & faintly denied on both sides'. He felt that 'compromise' was 'certain'.[68] Russell privately suggested an £8 qualification, but he was beaten out of it by

---

65 Graham Papers, 35, Graham to Stanley, 20 May 1838. 66 *Hansard*, xliii, 448-72, 29 May 1838, Peel, Russell, O'Brien. 67 Personal Journals ... by James Grattan, MS 14149, 30 May, 1, 6, 8 June 1838. *Hansard*, xliii, 540-2, 1 June 1838, Division. 68 Wyse Papers, MS 15018 (2), Diary of Thomas Wyse, 1 June 1838.

O'Connell and went on to secure majorities (which included O'Brien) for the £5 franchise and the third reading.[69] The Lords substituted a £10 franchise. The Irish liberal members, meeting on 19 July in the Reform Club, 'all agreed' to reject this but 'then differed about the 8.00'. Grattan, anxious not to 'delay the pacification of Ireland' over 'trifling' differences, favoured £8, 'O'Brien also', and the latter's diary entry for 21 July was, 'Spoke to Lascelles about Corp. Bill. Wrote to Ld Melbourne'. At a second meeting on 31 July, Russell overruled O'Connell's objections, leading O'Brien to tell Grattan that 'it went off well'. The £8 figure was carried in the Commons on 2 August, with O'Brien, O'Connell and Grattan all on board, but the Lords rejected it and the measure was lost for another year.[70]

A tithe measure, however, was passed in 1838. The Lords showed in 1835 and 1836 that they would never accept a bill that appropriated Church revenues for other purposes. O'Connell therefore indicated his readiness to give up appropriation as early as December 1836.[71] Ministers came to the conclusion that it should be omitted in order to reach a settlement. On 15 May 1838, a Commons majority (including O'Brien) rejected a Tory attempt formally to expunge the appropriation resolution of April 1835. However, Russell announced the abandonment of appropriation on 18 May and O'Brien probably spoke for most liberals when he said some days later that they should now give way. An English radical attempt to add an appropriation clause was easily defeated by a broad alliance that included O'Connell, O'Brien and most of the Irish liberals; and a small revolt against the third reading met the same fate.[72] Grattan, who on this front as well was desperate for a settlement, admitted that the measure contrived merely to 'give a new title to Tythe'.[73] Landlords were made 'tithe proctors' for the clergy. They had to pay the clergy 75% of the old tithe and recover the charge (plus 25%) from their tenants. So, with people of all denominations still made to support the clergy of a minority, the anomaly at the heart of the question remained unresolved. Appropriation would have been a partial remedy – and state payment of the Catholic clergy, as O'Brien had urged, could have brought something akin to full equality of treatment. The Catholic refusal to consider such payment, and the hopelessness of the appropriation clause, meant that by 1838 O'Brien no longer showed much interest in the Church question. In this he was like most politicians, but the very limited reform effected by the Whigs meant that the Church grievance would be fertile ground for O'Connell's return to agitation in the 1840s.

---

69 M. O'Connell, *Correspondence of Daniel O'Connell*, vi, 2543, O'Connell to Morpeth, 10 June 1838, Personal Journals ... by James Grattan, MS 14149, 15 June 1838. *Hansard*, xliii, 652-6, 1070-5, 11, 25 June 1838, Divisions. 70 Personal Journals ... by James Grattan, MS 14149, 15 June, 19, 31 July (also 2, 9 August) 1838. Broadlands MSS, MEL/RU/51, Russell to Melbourne, 20 July 1838. Russell Papers, PRO 30/22/38, f215, Russell to Normanby, 27 July 1838; f225, Tavistock to Russell, 29 July 1838. O'Brien Papers (AO), Rough Diary, 21 July 1838. *Hansard*, xliv, 922-4, 2 August 1838, Division. 71 Russell Papers, PRO 30/22/2D, f268, O'Connell to Warburton, 29 December 1836 (also in M. O'Connell, *Correspondence of Daniel O'Connell*, v, 369). 72 *Hansard*, xlii, 1353-8, 15 May, Division; xlii, 1364-5, 18 May, Russell; xliii, 471-2, 29 May, O'Brien; xliii, 1202-5, 2 July, Division; xliv, 693-5, 26 July 1838, Division. 73 Personal Journals ... by James Grattan, MS 14149, 30 May 1838.

After the poor law passed through the Commons, O'Brien concentrated most of his efforts in 1838 on education. He regularly attended the Central Society of Education and the Society for the Diffusion of Useful Knowledge in London and he seconded a Wyse motion for the establishment of a central board of education in England.[74] However, Irish education was his particular interest. He protested in the House in July 1838 about the 'partial distribution of the grant' to the National System, which left some districts without adequate schooling; he proposed that the grant should be increased and the localities given power 'to raise money by assessment' in order that there should be a school in every parish. Grattan joined in with criticism of the quality of education provided in the National System and noted in his journal that his outburst was 'a good hint to the Board, who will job as all such do ... I am right about the schools. In Roscommon, the national Schools are ridiculous.'[75] Spring Rice, the Chancellor of the Exchequer, was stung by these criticisms – 'we were more bitterly attacked by our friends than our foes' – into a thoroughgoing reform of the system's 'loose & imperfect' procedures, while archbishop Whately, fearing that the Board (of which he was the working head) had lost the confidence of Parliament, contemplated resignation.[76] It was a revealing indication of the impact that independent Members could make through a few pointed remarks in the House of Commons.

O'Brien was again a member of Wyse's select committee – appointed for the fourth time in December 1837 – on Irish education. Wyse wrote the first draft of the report; he later commented to O'Brien, 'I know how little I should have been enabled to work out without your co-operation, especially in our Committee ... You remember my *never ending* Report. It is a matter of doubt whether it would have ever had a *blue cover* but for *you*.' He also referred to their 'thorough identity of opinion' on the subject.[77] The final report, submitted on 9 August 1838, suggested many administrative changes in the National System, including examination of teachers, an expanded programme of school building, and O'Brien's proposal on local assessment (taxes) for education. Wyse observed a year later that 'many of our suggestions ... either had been or were about to be adopted'.[78] Few of the National schools were mixed (comprised of both Protestants and Catholics) – owing to the continuing Protestant objections about unscriptural education and to the more recent insistence of some Catholics (archbishop MacHale of Tuam, and the Christian Brothers) on separate schooling. This was acknowledged briefly in the report's concession that if religious differences were such as to prevent co-operation the Board

---

74 O'Brien Papers (AO), Rough Diary, 2 December 1837 *et seq. Hansard*, xliii, 733, 14 June 1838, O'Brien.   75 *Hansard*, xliv, 811-2, 30 July 1838, O'Brien, Grattan. Personal Journals ... by James Grattan, MS 14149, 30 July, 1 August 1838.   76 Monteagle Papers, MS 533, f133, Rice to Morpeth, 29 November 1838; f139, Rice to Leinster, 29 November 1838; ibid., MS 543, f123, Rice to Whately, 14 December 1838; ibid., MS 13370 (11), Whately to Rice, 4 December 1838.   77 Smith O'Brien Papers, MS 429, f486, Wyse to O'Brien, 4 January 1839; ibid., MS 430, f599, Wyse to O'Brien, 26 January 1839. O'Brien Papers (AO), Rough Diary, 14 May 1838. See also William Smith O'Brien, *Education in Ireland* (London, 1839), 141.   78 Smith O'Brien Papers, MS 430, f671, Wyse to O'Brien, 10 September 1839.

should be prepared to endow separate, exclusive schools.[79] In an article on Irish education written for the Central Society of Education, O'Brien showed regard for both Protestant and Catholic scruples. While he wanted to persist with mixed education where possible, the system should 'exclude no portion of the people' and this meant running separate schools where the 'deep-rooted and conscientious convictions' of local clergy and laity demanded them.[80] Again, as with the tithes and corporations questions, O'Brien showed a capacity to adjust to circumstances. He was a more realistic politician than some of his more publicised actions seemed to suggest. More to the point, he brought greater flexibility and sensitivity to measures than he managed to deploy when his personal integrity and honour were thought to be at stake.

O'Brien and Lucy (who was with him again in London) returned to Cahirmoyle in the autumn of 1838 and he issued his annual report to his constituents early in September. He restated his support for the new poor law, which, though by no means 'a perfect measure', did not justify the 'present extravagant alarm' about its likely cost. He defended the tithe bill as the best that could be achieved, albeit 'not a final and satisfactory adjustment', and he felt that the government had 'judged wisely' in opting for the £8 compromise in the corporations question.[81] In November and December, O'Brien wrote the education pamphlet that was published in 1839. But his contribution to one aspect of the education debate, that on post-secondary colleges, was to be more substantial. Ireland had only one university, the University of Dublin, of which Trinity was the only college. Catholics were admitted from 1794 and by the late 1830s made up over 100 of the 1500 students, but non-Anglicans were excluded from the fellowships and scholarships. In addition, there was a lack of colleges of general higher education to cater to Ireland's growing middle class. From 1829, bishop James Doyle and, above all, Thomas Wyse advocated an extension of higher education, sometimes seeking reform of Trinity and 'a second university', on occasion suggesting 'provincial colleges' that would operate at a lower, more intermediary level than a university.[82] In 1834, O'Brien backed a proposed college in Limerick to give 'the best university education' to 4-500 'children of the middling classes'.[83] In October 1837, a meeting was held in Cork to promote the founding of a university there; it was 'respectably, though not numerously, attended'.[84] The select committee report that Wyse wrote with O'Brien's assistance in 1838 highlighted the dearth of provision (outside Belfast) for the middle classes; it proposed that Parliament should assist in the establishment of 'provin-

---

[79] Parliamentary Papers, 1837-8, vii, 315 [80] O'Brien, *Education in Ireland*, 147-52, 158-9. [81] *Limerick Chronicle*, 8 September 1838, Review of Proceedings in Parliament, during the last session, by Mr William Smith O'Brien, addressed to his constituents, 5 September 1838. [82] Thomas Wyse, *Historical Sketch of the Late Catholic Association*, ii, 110. W. J. Fitzpatrick, *The Life, Times, and Correspondence of the Right Rev. Dr Doyle, Bishop of Kildare and Leighlin* (Dublin, 1890), ii, 139-43. Winifrede M. Wyse, *Notes on Education Reform in Ireland* (Waterford, 1901), 14, Slattery to Wyse, 28 November 1830; 17-10, Wyse to Doyle, 11 December 1830. *DEP*, 17 December 1831, Wyse to Stanley, 9 December 1831. [83] Smith O'Brien Papers, MS 427, f260, O'Brien to Fitzgerald, 17 April 1834. [84] *DEP*, 4 November 1837. M. O'Connell, *Correspondence of Daniel O'Connell*, vi, 2471, Roche to O'Connell, 18 November 1837.

cial colleges', one 'at least' in each province, to provide 'a high degree of education', and that a central board might be empowered to confer degrees on their students.[85] Wyse then initiated a public meeting in Cork, held on 15 November 1838, to petition for a provincial college in Munster.[86]

There was some criticism from Tories who apprehended a Catholic rival to Trinity, but it was the alienation of Smith O'Brien and the Limerick interest that cast the principal cloud over proceedings. O'Brien's response to the Cork invitation was to argue (publicly) that the college should be sited at Limerick; he intended 'to stimulate the enlightened minds' of Limerick to urge that city's claims, and he could not co-operate with those who favoured Cork.[87] The 'unworthy selfishness' of this view was criticised at the Cork meeting and one of its organisers (James Roche) urged that 'Mr Wyse's own declaration on the subject should almost be decisive'.[88] That O'Brien put his perception of public duty before loyalty to his closest friend in politics comes as no surprise. He organised a public meeting in Limerick on 5 January 1839 and insisted there that its centrality and the superiority of its existing educational institutions made Limerick's claims preferable to those of the much larger Cork. His preferred option, however, was that each of the two cities should have a college.[89] This proposal (which suggests that the 'at least' one college reference in the select committee report was O'Brien's doing) was followed up in O'Brien's 1839 pamphlet with a plan for colleges in Cork, Limerick, Kilkenny, Belfast, Londonderry, and other large towns.[90] Wyse pointed out that O'Brien was actually undermining the entire endeavour as he conceived it:

> I am desirous to see secured as high a standard of classical, scientific and industrial education as can well be obtained, with the hope of seeing the four Colleges afterwards aggregated into a '*Corps Academique*' or University ... This can scarcely be attained by multiplying at the outset these establishments. They cannot have the same efficiency or pursue the same high standards as if few.[91]

He subsequently told O'Brien that his view was 'only reasonable ... If we *can* bear so many *Colleges* well and good, but I am for *Colleges* remember and not institutions *between* Colleges & [secondary] Academies'.[92] There was indeed a consider-

---

85 *Parliamentary Papers*, 1837-8, vii, 408-21.   86 Wyse Papers, MS 15025 (4), Bullen to Wyse, 2 September 1838. *DEP*, 2 October, 20 November 1838. Winifrede M. Wyse, *Notes on Education Reform*, 55-7, Wyse to George Wyse, 17 November 1838.   87 *Cork Standard*, 5 November 1838, O'Brien to Roche, 27 October 1838.   88 *DEP*, 20 November, 1838, M.J. O'Connell. Smith O'Brien Papers, MS 329, ff556, 562, 564, Bullen to O'Brien, 19, 26, 27 November 1838; f563, Roche to O'Brien, 26 November 1838, ibid., MS 430, f571, Rice to O'Brien, 18 December 1838; f585, M. J. O'Connell to O'Brien, 25 December 1838.   89 *Limerick Standard*, 8 January 1839. Wyse Papers, MS 15025 (6), Circular of Prospectus (Limerick). Thomas Wyse, *Speech on the extension and improvement ... education in Ireland ... 1844* (Cork, 1845), 128-31.   90 O'Brien, *Education in Ireland*, 170-4.   91 Smith O'Brien Papers, MS 429, f486, Wyse to O'Brien, 4 January [1839].   92 Ibid., MS 430, f599, Wyse to O'Brien, 26 January 1839.

able gap between their respective objects. While Wyse envisaged the system of university colleges which was later conceded, O'Brien spoke at Limerick of a college which youths would enter at 14 years of age and leave at 17, when they could go on to Trinity.[93] Given all this, and the opposition O'Brien would offer to Peel's measure in 1845, the proposal in 1948 to celebrate O'Brien's role as 'one of the founders' of University College Cork, by establishing an O'Brien Library of Irish History, was hardly justified.[94] The other point of interest was the response to O'Brien's proposal that the education in the new colleges should be entirely secular. This was criticised not by Limerick's Catholics but by Tories who had had their opinions forged during the bitter opposition to the National System's 'unscriptural course'. They caused the Limerick meeting to degenerate into what an angry O'Brien called 'a scene of turbulent uproar'. Thus the affair foreshadowed the controversy of 1845 over 'Godless education'.[95]

Eighteen thirty-nine was to bring the crisis that came close to ending O'Brien's political career. He returned to London at the end of January, missing the birth of his second son, William, who turned out to be virtually deaf, in February 1839. O'Brien complained soon after of 'the despondency of my solitude' in London, a familiar refrain.[96] His first contributions in the House concerned the poor law. He had already involved himself in its administration, despatching advice to George Nicholls (chosen to head the new Commission), attending poor law meetings in Newcastle (west Limerick) in November 1838, and, as a magistrate, becoming an *ex officio* member of the Newcastle board of guardians that was elected in January. In Parliament, he denied Tory claims of sectarianism in the Limerick elections, regretted the slowness in applying the poor law, and argued again that state-assisted emigration was needed to relieve poverty.[97] In mid-March, O'Brien was 'much annoyed to perceive in the papers today that O'Connell called me his honourable "friend". However, as I endeavour to follow Shakespeare's advice, "Even in thy right hand carry gentle Peace", I must not quarrel with the consequences', meaning that his avoidance of dissent was bound to attract O'Connell's blessing, much though it was unwanted.[98] In fact, a renewal of hostilities was not far distant. O'Brien brought in two bills in March, one on registration of voters, the second to regulate polling. The former was a measure he first prepared in late 1837, when the Limerick

[93] *Limerick Standard*, 8 January 1839. [94] O'Brien Papers (AO), Box 2, Prospectus of the O'Brien Library of Irish History, University College Cork. This library was never established. [95] Smith O'Brien Papers, MS 429, f568, Stoddart to O'Brien, 16 December 1838; ibid., MS 430, f578, MacDonnell to O'Brien, 21 December 1838; f588, Dunraven to O'Brien, 29 December 1838; f590, O'Brien to Raleigh, 7 January 1839. *Limerick Standard*, 8, 11 January 1839. [96] Smith O'Brien Papers, MS 8653 (15), O'Brien to Lucy O'Brien, 4 March 1839. [97] O'Brien Papers (AO), Rough Diary, 21, 23 November 1838, 19 January, 27 March 1839. Smith O'Brien Papers, MS 429, ff551, 582, Nicholls to O'Brien, 25, 29 October 1838. *Hansard*, xlv, 347, 371, 12, 14 February 1939, O'Brien. Also on emigration, see ibid., xlviii, 917, 25 June 1839, O'Brien. [98] Smith O'Brien Papers, MS 8653 (15), O'Brien to Lucy O'Brien, 19 March 1839.

petition led him to think that a more reliable system of registration would preclude 'the evil of opening registries before committees of the H. of Commons'. He was warned by O'Shaughnessy that his proposal of yearly revision would cause 'an annual contest between landlords and tenants in which the latter must ultimately yield ... such a bill would be fatal to the liberal interest in Ireland'.[99] Most notably, in April 1839 O'Connell wrote his first-ever letter to O'Brien, an indication of his concern; he showed a keen awareness of O'Brien's sensitivities:

> Your *Registry Bills* are down for an early day next week before the Irish members can arrive in London. I wish I could persuade you to let them drop altogether convinced as I am that if they pass they annihilate the liberal interest in Ireland – and you will become unconsciously the worker out of the greatest mischief that could possibly be done in this country. I know that I have no influence nor any right to have any influence over you but surely you can not doubt that I am thoroughly acquainted with the working of the present system and competent to form a just opinion of the result of your alterations and in that point of view – and in that alone – entitled to be listened to by you with some attention. Allow me to tell you that the most virulent of the Orange Tories could not desire a more fatal measure to us their opponents than your registry bill or your polling bill – the registry bill especially ... we all deeply deplore that these fatal blows are aimed at us by a friendly hand ... You will perceive that I will feel it my duty to divide the house upon every stage of these bills. You have no prospect of carrying them except with and by the votes of the worst enemies of Ireland. The Irish Government are decidedly hostile to them ...[100]

When it emerged that 'the government were not disposed to support' the bill, O'Brien 'could scarcely hope to carry it'; he postponed the second reading several times and then gave up.[101] It was the liberal failure to bite the bullet and carry a measure – probably not O'Brien's, which was surely misguided – that gave Stanley the chance to damage the Whigs with his registration bill in 1840. O'Brien and O'Connell also differed on the corn laws. In February, a Limerick meeting in favour of repealing these laws resolved 'to withdraw our countenance at future elections from any representative who shall refuse to support the prayer of our petition'. This occasioned a predictable response from O'Brien: 'If such a menace was intended to serve as a notice, to govern the conduct of the Members for the County, I can only say, that so far as I am concerned, it is wholly inoperative. The opinion of my

---

99 O'Brien Papers (AO), Rough Diary, 27 November, 28, 29 December 1837. Smith O'Brien Papers, MS 429, f514, O'Shaughnessy to O'Brien, 11 March 1838; ibid., MS 430, f614, O'Shaughnessy to O'Brien, 13 April 1839. *Limerick Chronicle*, 8 September 1838, Review of Session by O'Brien. 100 Smith O'Brien Papers, MS 430, f611, O'Connell to O'Brien, 5 April 1839 (also in M. O'Connell, *Correspondence of Daniel O'Connell*, vi, 2601). 101 *Limerick Chronicle*, 26 October 1839, O'Brien to the Constituency of the County of Limerick, 14 October 1839.

Constituents will at all times command my deepest respect ... but I trust that the time will never arrive when either the desire of obtaining, or the fear of forfeiting, a seat in Parliament, will induce me to support measures which I do not conscientiously believe to be conducive to the interests of my country.'[102] In the first great Commons debate on the subject, in March 1839, O'Brien spoke and voted with the majority against repeal. He regarded the question entirely from an Irish point of view: Ireland was an agricultural country whose farming required protection, irrespective of the needs of England's manufacturing classes.[103] He would still be a protectionist in 1846. In mid-April, he backed the government in a major debate on Ireland. Lord Roden, the Irish Tory leader, had persuaded the Lords to establish a committee of inquiry into 'the state of Ireland since 1835 in respect of Crime and Outrage', and Russell's immediate response was to ask the Commons for a vote of confidence in the Irish government. James Grattan considered Russell's decision 'ridiculous, uncalled for, promoting division between the two Houses and disturbing Ireland ...'[104] But all of the Irish liberal Members rallied in defence of the government, which prevailed in the division. O'Brien's speech was a strong argument for the administration's record of appointing Catholics to public office and against the Tories' 'exaggerated charges' on crime, and he attacked bad landlords (citing Lord Lorton, who had evicted 45 Catholic families from his estate in Longford) whose conduct provoked outrages.[105]

In May 1839 came the climactic event of the session, the government's resignation, after O'Brien was one of the ten liberals (or radicals, as most of them were) who voted against the Jamaica bill on 6 May.[106] Liberal Members often voted against the government – there was nothing like rigid discipline – and O'Connell's revolts on the poor law, corn laws and the ballot did not damage his alliance with the Whigs. O'Brien's record also included dissent, notably when he voted for an elective legislature for Canada (March 1837) and for an end to the system of negro apprenticeship (forced labour) in the West Indies (May 1838).[107] The Jamaica bill was designed to suspend the constitution of Jamaica after the island's assembly had refused to adopt the Prisons Act passed at Westminster and obstructed the abolition of negro apprenticeship. By a strange twist of fate, the Jamaica affair involved (and set against one another) the principles behind the two earlier revolts: O'Brien felt 'unable to support an attempt to substitute arbitrary power for an elected assembly', albeit a planter-elected assembly that excluded and mistreated the negro majority. The bill, he argued, established 'as a precedent the suspension of constitutional

---

102 Ibid., 13, 20 February 1839, O'Brien to J.D. Lyons, 15 February 1839. 103 *Hansard*, xlvi, 809-11, 859-64, 18 March 1839, O'Brien, Division. 104 Personal Journals ... by James Grattan, MS 14149, 26 March 1839. 105 *Hansard*, xlvii, 119-22, 447-56, 16, 19 April 1839, O'Brien, Division. 106 *Hansard*, xlvii, 967-72, 6 May 1939, Division. 107 *Hansard*, xxxvii, 144-7, 8 March 1837, Division; xliii, 104-7, 123-6, 22 May 1838, O'Brien, Division. Typically he told Lucy the anti-government vote on Canada was 'very much against my own inclination, but in obedience to my strong *convictions* that I was right'. Smith O'Brien Papers, MS 8653 (7), O'Brien to Lucy O'Brien, 9 March 1837. He also opposed the government when he backed Lord Ashley's bill on child labour in factories in June 1838. *Hansard*, xliii, 979-81, 22 June 1838, Division.

rights as a means of escaping from a temporary difficulty'.[108] The rebellion reduced the government majority to only five. This meant it would be difficult if not impossible to carry the measure through Committee. On 7 May, unwilling to accept defeat on a major bill and tired of the burdens of office, Melbourne offered his resignation to the Queen and advised her to send for Peel.

James Grattan's view of the outgoing ministers was typically excited and scornful: 'they are so touchy & hasty & have gone out about nothing ... What a mess for Ireland, for the Queen, who will now fall into the hands of the Tories ... they never should have given up while they had *one* majority ... thus are 294 men sacrificed ... They have ruined their party & disgusted & destroyed their friends ... I fear they want morality & principle ...'[109] O'Brien, equally surprised at the resignation, believed not only that it was unnecessary but also that 'the character of Parliament' would be 'entirely destroyed' if 'the threat of a resignation be continually held out to independent members of Parliament' in order to force their compliance in all measures.[110] O'Connell, by this stage fully committed to the Whigs, was devastated when they went out. His anger was directed against O'Brien and, above all, Joseph Hume, whom O'Connell had installed in Kilkenny in 1837 after he lost his English seat:

> All is over. The Melbourne Ministry have expired ... Tomorrow the Duke of Wellington and the Tories will try. Blessed be God, it is a sad infliction! Principally to be attributed to Joseph Hume. His conduct encouraged Smith O'Brien and others to revolt. O'Brien, though very ill-conditioned, would not have had the courage to behave so badly as he did if he had not been countenanced by Hume ...[111]

O'Connell encouraged the Kilkenny liberals to ditch Hume and, given his pessimism about retaining Dublin, to adopt himself for the borough in the expected elections.[112] But he also moved against O'Brien, even after his delight that the Bedchamber Crisis – when Queen Victoria refused Peel's request for removal of two of her (Whig) Household ladies – meant that Melbourne was restored on 9 May. He sent Father Costelloe a letter that included an interesting analysis of O'Brien's character:

> What are you to do with Smith O'Brien? In asking the question I have no personal feeling to gratify. All I want to know is what do you think best for the county in particular and the country in general? I easily forgive his fool-

---

108 *Limerick Chronicle*, 15 May 1839, O'Brien to the Electors of the County of Limerick, 8 May 1839. Ibid., 12 June 1839, O'Brien in County Club. 109 Personal Journals ... by James Grattan, MS 14149, 7, 8 May 1839. 110 *Limerick Chronicle*, 15 May 1839, O'Brien to the Electors of the County of Limerick, 8 May 1839. 111 M. O'Connell, *Correspondence of Daniel O'Connell*, vi, 2611, O'Connell to Fitzpatrick, 7 May 1839. 112 Ibid., 2613, 2614, 2621a, O'Connell to Smithwick, 7, 8, 14 May 1839; 2615, O'Connell to Sullivan, 8 May 1839.

ish imprudence towards myself. The question remains, what is best done with him? He is an exceedingly weak man, proud and self-conceited and, like almost all weak men, utterly impenetrable to advice. You cannot be sure of him for half an hour. But are you in a condition to get rid of him, and have you a candidate to supply his place? The answer to these two questions ought to be decisive as to the mode of proceeding and to you I apply for such answers and for suggestions as to the steps which ought to be taken. It would be, at all events, most desirable that he should be pledged not to oppose the present ministry.[113]

If pride is a weakness, this judgement is not entirely unfair. O'Brien, of course, had no wish to be a man O'Connell could 'be sure of', a part of the 'tail'. Costelloe never revealed O'Connell's part, but he reacted immediately, 'leaving no stone unturned,' William Griffin reported from Limerick, 'to accomplish what he has been long aiming at'.[114] O'Brien, unwisely in Griffin's opinion, opened the door by writing a public letter to his constituents in which he offered to resign if a majority of them 'pronounced against me ... as I wish to represent you only so long as I possess your confidence'.[115] Costelloe asked the liberal Lord Cloncurry to permit his son, Edward Lawless, to stand for the constituency and apparently received 'a favourable reply' (Griffin). He called a meeting of the County Club for 21 May, at which one member described O'Brien as 'a dangerous politician' who would turn against his own side 'at any moment he got a crotchet in his head'. In four resolutions, carried over the objections of chairman Caleb Powell, O'Brien was effectively called upon to resign: 'as he wishes to represent us only so long as he possesses our confidence, we now declare that he no longer possesses that confidence'.[116]

O'Brien replied, in a letter intended for publication, that, while he felt no self-reproach over a vote dictated by duty and conscience, he would apply for the Chiltern Hundreds (that is, resign from Parliament) on 7 June unless those electors not present at the club meeting gave evidence of their desire that he should remain their MP.[117] It is likely that at this moment O'Brien fully expected he would be resigning; indeed his diary entry reads simply, 'Wrote stating intention to resign'.[118] His long-term mainstay, 'father of the Club' Michael O'Shaughnessy, sent a stinging rebuke of O'Brien's 'inexcusable' conduct that was hardly supportive of his eventual suggestion that 'a strong expression of opinion' in favour of O'Brien might 'remove the necessity of resignation'.[119] However, O'Brien also commanded support. Powell thought 'an error of judgement' in the division lobby 'does

---

113 M. O'Connell, *Correspondence of Daniel O'Connell*, vi, 2623, O'Connell to Costelloe, 16 May 1839. 114 Smith O'Brien Papers, MS 430, f616, Griffin to O'Brien, 18 May 1839. 115 *Limerick Chronicle*, 15 May 1839, O'Brien to the Electors of the County of Limerick, 8 May 1839. 116 Smith O'Brien Papers, MS 430, f619, Powell to O'Brien, 23 May 1839. *Limerick Chronicle*, 25, 29 May 1839. 117 *Limerick Chronicle*, 29 May 1839, O'Brien to Powell, 25 May 1839. 118 O'Brien Papers (AO), Rough Diary, 25 May 1839. 119 *Limerick Chronicle*, 25 May 1839, O'Shaughnessy to Edward O'Connell, 20 May 1839.

not disentitle you to my political confidence', William Griffin acknowledged his 'perfect right to free judgement', and another friend described how most 'respectable' constituents backed him against 'Father Costelloe & the priests' and their lower-class followers.[120] Many of those who wrote in such terms had received letters from O'Brien, so his response to the crisis was more active than the public exchanges seemed to suggest. At the end of May, an address to O'Brien, issued in Limerick, declared for the 'principle of honest and independent representation' and opposed resignation. Electors in the west of the county – particularly in Rathkeale and Newcastle, the towns closest to Cahirmoyle – were urged by O'Brien's friends to attend a second County Club meeting.[121]

As the meeting approached, Griffin predicted that 'you will have a great triumph over Mr O'Connell – who evidently aims at a dictatorship in Irish elections'. The meeting on 1 June brought 'the most strong and violent discussion' (O'Hanlon), including a violent – and rather bizarre – altercation between some of the priests. Costelloe accused a Father Moore of having 'deceived people': 'you said you were sick, while at the time walking about' – which charge Moore denounced as 'downright falsehood'. Costelloe avowed his long-standing opposition to O'Brien ('from the commencement of his parliamentary career') and presented the entire catalogue of his sins, in particular his desire to make the clergy 'pensioners on the state' and his refusal to honour O'Connell. Now he had the effrontery, Costelloe went on, to divide the club from which he had 'emanated'. Edward O'Connell revealed (and gave the newspapers) the private letter by which O'Brien repudiated O'Connell's support in July 1837. From the other side, a member attacked Costelloe's holding 'a correspondence with this Lord or that' to offer the representation of the county, and a series of speakers argued that their confidence in O'Brien was not negated by a single vote, however regrettable. The club was seriously divided and a compromise was reached when it was resolved that a decision should be postponed until the autumn assizes, and 'that our chairman [Powell] do write to Mr O'Brien to request him to retain his seat in the interim'.[122]

Robert Potter's report that 'the persons who sustained the resolutions which passed were chiefly new members' is testimony to the labours of O'Brien's friends, but it was Griffin's opinion that Costelloe again had a majority and held back only because he feared being blamed for causing a by-election by those who did not want 'to be arrayed against their landlords unnecessarily'. The course O'Brien now pursued mirrored very closely advice given by Griffin. In his formal reply to Powell, O'Brien said he was 'wholly unable to comprehend' the 'purport or design' of the

---

120 Smith O'Brien Papers, MS 430, ff616, 621, Griffin to O'Brien, 18, 27 May 1839; f617, Skelton to O'Brien, 22 May 1839; f618, Powell to O'Brien, 22 May 1839.   121 *Limerick Chronicle*, 29 May 1839. Smith O'Brien Papers, MS 430, ff621, 623, Griffin to O'Brien, 27, 29 May 1839; f631, O'Hanlon to O'Brien, 1 June 1839.   122 *Limerick Chronicle*, 5 June 1839. Smith O'Brien Papers, MS 430, ff6223, 630, 641, Griffin to O'Brien, 29 May, 1, 3 June 1839; f631, O'Hanlon to O'Brien, 1 June 1839; ff632, 639, Powell to O'Brien, 1, 2 June 1839; f637, Lyons to O'Brien, 2 June 1839; f640, Edward O'Connell to O'Brien, 3 June 1839.

decision and unwilling 'to appear in the House of Commons in the ridiculous and contemptible character of an "*ad interim*" member – the position in which I am now invited to place myself'. So, he proposed to cross over from London to hold a public meeting at which the electors could inform him if he still possessed their confidence. This was an astute tactic. It would intimidate opponents and exploit personal loyalties, the 'feeling of personal friendship or liking which, although they universally condemn your vote, I [Griffin] perceive weighs with a very great number'.[123] O'Brien's papers contain a number of replies to his letters requesting the attendance of supposed supporters. He arrived in Limerick on 8 June and three days later held the meeting of electors at the court house. He entered with a priest on each arm – Doctors Coll and Hogan of Newcastle and Rathkeale, respectively – a picture his later friends in Young Ireland would have thought more John O'Connell than Smith O'Brien. In a long speech he defended his vote as a matter of principle and conscience and wondered if the voters would prefer 'to catch the most ignorant man you can find in the streets, and command him to vote that black is white at the bidding of the Minister'. It was a powerful performance. His opponents, if they attended at all, remained silent. The meeting unanimously expressed confidence in him – 'we are of opinion that his Parliamentary conduct has been influenced by the strictest integrity, and therefore request he will retain his seat as one of our representatives' – and broke up after giving three cheers 'for Mr O'Brien, the County Club and Daniel O'Connell'.[124]

It was a close run thing, and had he not proved a skilful fighter as well as a redoubtable man of principle the outcome would probably have been less favourable. He left Limerick the following day, to return to his Parliamentary duties in London. He voted for the re-drafted Jamaica bill on 19 June and seems to have rebuilt his bridges with the Whigs, if anything can be read into his presence at Morpeth's fête at Chiswick on 22 June and his dining with Palmerston (not for the first time) on 7 July.[125] He abstained in the June division, a large one, on the ballot, regardless of O'Connell. At the end of the month, in a conciliatory gesture, O'Connell wrote to request 'the favour of your attendance' in the House for a motion he intended; if O'Brien replied (which one doubts), the letter is not extant.[126] A few months later, Robert Potter, a leading attorney and one of his most important Limerick allies, told O'Brien that from 'a recent conversation' he had had with Costelloe, he had 'reason to believe that you will meet with very little further opposition in that quarter'.[127] This turned out to be an accurate forecast, and if O'Brien managed not only to save himself but also to intimidate and silence his critics his victory was truly complete.

---

123 Ibid., f633, Potter to O'Brien, 2 June 1839; f635, Griffin to O'Brien, 2 June 1839. *Limerick Chronicle*, 8 June 1839, O'Brien to Powell, 4 June 1839.   124 *Limerick Chronicle*, 12 June 1839.   125 *Hansard*, xlviii, 524-9, 19 June 1839, Division. Smith O'Brien Papers, MS 454, Rough Diary, 22 June, 7 July 1839.   126 *Hansard*, xlviii, 504-8, 18 June 1839, Division. Smith O'Brien Papers, MS 430, f660, O'Connell to O'Brien, 29 June 1839.   127 Ibid., f675, Potter to O'Brien, 9 October 1839.

4

Repeal

The Whigs limped on for another two years after the May crisis of 1839, achieving little and increasingly demoralised as defeat in the next elections became certain. They were relatively quiet years for O'Brien. In August 1839, he returned to Ireland and spent an uneventful few months with friends and family. Politics featured when, in his annual report to the electors in October, he expressed disappointment that little had been achieved in terms of Irish legislation and was entirely unapologetic about his part in the May crisis.[1] On 1 December, he heard Father Mathew preach a 'charity sermon'. Mathew had launched a remarkably successful temperance campaign, inducing thousands to give up alcohol, and O'Brien was to demonstrate his admiration of the movement on numerous occasions. Above all, O'Brien worked on proposals regarding emigration, which he planned to set before Parliament in the new year; his correspondence for the second half of 1839 was dominated by returns from organisations involved in taking emigrants to the colonies.

On 8 January 1840, O'Brien left Cahirmoyle for London. The rough diary by which his movements are known gives a good idea of the sort of existence O'Brien had during the six months he spent in London each year.[2] The journey to London took two days – more, obviously, if he stopped *en route*. Initially, when the MP for Ennis and again in the mid 1830s, he usually sailed from Cork or Waterford to Bristol, and from there went by coach to London. From the late 1830s, he often travelled through Dublin and Liverpool, doing the English part of the journey by train. His family's joining him, as they did every spring, added greatly to this burden; in March 1840, for example, he crossed to Dublin to bring them over, and in June he accompanied them back to Limerick, arriving there on 7 June and then setting off again for London the next day. It is no wonder he complained of 'the expense & wear & tear' of such journeys.[3] He had no permanent home in London, residing in 'lodgings' and moving from place to place with surprising frequency.

---

1 *Limerick Chronicle*, 26 October 1839, O'Brien to the Constituency of the County of Limerick, 14 October 1839. This was the last of O'Brien's annual reports.   2 The first volume of this diary, covering the years 1826-1839, is in the private papers of Anthony O'Brien. The second volume (1839-1847) is part (MS 454) of the main Smith O'Brien collection in the National Library.   3 Smith O'Brien Papers, MS 432, f932, O'Brien to Lucy O'Brien, 23 March 1843.

During the 1840 session, he lived for six weeks at 14 Lower Belgrave Street (Woronzow Greig's home), three weeks at 6 Wilton Place, 10 weeks at 5 Upper Berkeley Street, and a month at 2 Stafford Street. The fact that he went home every Easter was one reason for this mobility – he gave up his lodgings – but it was also because his family's arrival necessitated a change to larger premises like Upper Berkeley Street. It was hardly the comfortable life enjoyed by wealthy Members with London homes.

O'Brien lived a quiet, even bleak existence in the capital. He did not quite forgo 'almost all the pleasures of society' as he claimed when struggling to impress his rebellious constituents in 1839.[4] He went to opera and the theatre, usually with visiting family. He had a club, the Oxford and Cambridge, where he dined 'every day ... at half past three', getting what he assured Lucy was a good meal for only two or three shillings.[5] But he was also the model of industry. He kept up his almost daily attendance in the House, sometimes serving on committees in the morning and then remaining in the chamber from late afternoon until well past midnight. He once told Lucy that he felt 'so miserable when absent during the sitting of Parlt. under the reproaches of my conscience ...'[6] He frequented societies connected with serious interests, notably the Colonial Society (emigration), the Society for the Diffusion of Useful Knowledge, the Central Society of Education and the Statistical Society. It is noticeable how little contact, outside the House, he had with other MPs. His dining companions (with Greig well to the fore) were rarely Parliamentarians. He was not, it appears, a man who enjoyed the company of his fellow-politicians. Nor did he find – or seek – any sort of companionship through the church; he attended services two or three times a month on average, but he went to many different churches and could have had no sense of belonging to a single community of worshippers.

In Parliament in 1840, O'Brien's first votes involved his approval of the motions to find John Joseph Stockdale guilty of contempt of the House and have him taken into custody by the Sergeant-at-Arms. Stockdale had brought a legal action against *Hansard* for publication of a report ordered by the Commons.[7] Ironically, in 1846 O'Brien would be the one whom the Sergeant-at-Arms imprisoned for contempt of the House. At the end of January he helped the government prevail in a confidence motion. A few days later, reacting to the Newport rising of November 1839, O'Brien seconded a motion for a select committee into the causes of discontent among Britain's working classes. He hoped the inquiry would yield measures 'to improve their moral and physical condition', and he attributed their regrettable 'alienation' from the constitution, as shown by the success of the Chartists, to the fact that the Reform Bill of 1832 empowered the middle classes (he believed) but

---

4 *Limerick Chronicle*, 29 May 1839, O'Brien to Powell, 25 May 1839. 5 O'Brien Papers (AO), Letter Box, Bundle 4, O'Brien to Lucy O'Brien, 16 February 1837. 6 Smith O'Brien Papers, MS 8653 (13), O'Brien to Lucy O'Brien, 20 July 1838. 7 *Hansard*, li, 181-4, 190-2, 17 January 1840, Divisions.

left the workers excluded. The 'only means of allaying those feelings would be by greatly extending the elective franchise'. Such extension, he no doubt took some pleasure in saying, would make the ballot an irrelevance. It was unusual for him to take a leading part on a non-Irish issue, and both his sympathy with the industrial classes and the radicalism of his analysis sounded more like Bronterre O'Brien than Smith O'Brien. The episode is important in that it suggests he had no appreciation of the strength of the Whig-Tory consensus on 'finality', the idea that there would be no further constitutional reform after 1832. This failure to understand the mindset of Britain's political elite would cause repealers, including O'Brien in due course, to have an entirely baseless confidence in their capacity to secure repeal.[8]

The long-running and embittering question of municipal reform was finally concluded in 1840. In 1839, the government (with O'Brien's support) had carried the £8 franchise in the Commons.[9] They decided to give way when the Lords, inevitably, inserted the figure of £10. O'Connell and Wyse accepted this, and so probably did the vast majority of liberals. Then the Speaker dropped a bombshell when he adjudged that a Lords amendment on taxation powers was a breach of Commons privilege, causing the loss of the bill.[10] Eager for a settlement, the Whigs conceded the £10 franchise in their 1840 bill and the only dissent came from a few Tories who worried that even this would deliver corporations into Catholic hands. O'Brien, countering one Tory motion, said that 'no man pretending to the character of a statesman could insist on treating the two countries differently with regard to municipal corporations'. This pointed towards a future of complaints that the measure, with its narrow franchise and restriction to only 10 towns, did not give 'equal justice'. As with the tithe and poor law measures, this was another settlement that did not settle.[11]

Stanley, now a fully fledged Tory, brought in a registration of voters (Ireland) bill in February that he was able to defend by pointing to how its provisions, including annual revision, had featured in the bills of O'Brien and other liberals. O'Brien argued that because there was more emphasis on excluding ineligible voters than facilitating the registration of good ones, the net effect of the bill would be to reduce an Irish franchise that was already smaller than England's. The House had had enough, however, of hearing of the frauds and anomalies of the Irish registers, which the Whigs had failed to remedy, and the government was defeated in five great tests of strength. Although Stanley had to give up the bill in July, for the opposition to every clause meant it would have taken months to carry, the divisions were humil-

---

8 *Hansard*, li, 1073-9, 31 January 1840, Division; li, 1234-6, 4 February 1840, O'Brien. On extending the franchise, see also *Limerick Chronicle*, 26 October 1839, O'Brien to Constituency. Bronterre O'Brien (no relation) was a Chartist leader in England. 9 *Hansard*, xlvi, 199-202, 8 March; xlviii, 1226-7, 4 July; 49, 347-8, 15 July 1839, Divisions. 10 M. O'Connell, *Correspondence of Daniel O'Connell*, vi, 2643-9, O'Connell to Fitzpatrick, 5, 7, 8, 9 August 1839; Ebrington to O'Connell, 6, 10 August 1839; O'Connell to Ebrington, 8 August 1839. Wyse Papers, Diary of Thomas Wyse, 5078, 9 August 1839. *Hansard*, l, 1, 7 August 1839, Speaker. 11 *Hansard*, lii, 273, 14 February, Division; lii, 540, 531-44, 24 February, O'Brien, Divisions; lii, 778-9, 28 February, Division: lii, 1068-70, 9 March 1840, Division.

iating to a government whose days were clearly numbered. O'Connell, O'Brien and the Irish liberals played a full part in resisting the measure, many seeing in it not just a threat to their seats but also evidence that on another question, the extent of the franchise, a majority in the Commons was not prepared to give equal treatment to Ireland. The issue spilled over into the next session, when O'Brien gave his 'hearty support' to the government's (franchise-extending) bill and opposed Stanley's; neither passed. He was thanked by a group of Limerick radicals for 'his valuable services in his place in parliament on all occasions for the benefit of Ireland, more particularly for his manly expression of feeling against the jockeyship of scorpion Stanley on the introduction of his disfranchising bill'.[12]

The greatest disappointment of the session for O'Brien was the fate of his emigration motion of June 1840. He believed that with the poor law coming into effective operation in 1840 an emigration initiative was necessary to prevent its being overwhelmed by the able-bodied poor. In his Commons speech, he discussed his advocacy of emigration from the time of his membership of the National Colonisation Society in 1830 and his belief in the 'principle of self-supporting emigration'.[13] By selling land in the colonies – he focused mainly on Australia, Canada, and the Cape – the government could raise the funds necessary to give free passage to emigrants. The emigrants (rescued from destitution), the home community (relieved of the burden of the able-bodied poor), and the colonies (provided with people to help develop their economies) would all be beneficiaries. It would 'extend the resources and promote the aggrandisement of our colonial empire' and give British people a sense of pride 'in viewing our country as the parent of many nations'. In the key resolution, he moved that free passage should be provided by the state. He had some support. However, several speakers referred to the empty benches, the 'scanty attendance', in the House (an 1841 motion, not by O'Brien, would be counted out). Above all, many Members, among them both Russell and Peel, feared that the project would involve massive expense and taxation, and the motion was negatived without a division.[14] The congratulations of many like-minded people – including a tribute from E.G. Wakefield, the doyen of the movement, to 'the most complete and valuable statement of the present condition of the subject' – may have stiffened his resolve and, typically, he later announced 'his intention to bring forward a motion every session for the promotion of emigration.'[15]

---

12 *Hansard*, lii, 33-5, 25 March, O'Brien; liii, 157-62, 26 March; liv, 233-7, 454-9, 1073-8, 18, 20 May, 11 June; lv, 154-8, 26 June 1840, Division; lvi, 241, 242-5, 2 February, O'Brien, Division, lvi, 867-9, 23 February, O'Brien; lvi, 1126-31, 25 February 1841, Division. Smith O'Brien Papers, MS 431, f769, Resolution of the Limerick Citizens Club, 8 February 1841.   13 On the history of his involvement, see also ibid., MS 430, f718, Hutt to O'Brien, 27 March 1840.   14 *Hansard*, liv, 832-67, 885-91, 2 June 1840, O'Brien, Russell, Peel. W.S. O'Brien, *Emigration. Speech by Mr William Smith O'Brien, M.P., on moving resolutions relative to emigration in the House of Commons on Tuesday the 2d of June 1840* (London, 1840). See also Smith O'Brien Papers, MS 449, f3430, Evans to O'Brien, 17 July [1840].   15 Ibid., MS 431, f742, Wakefield to O'Brien, 6 July 1840. *Hansard*, lvi, 527, 11 February 1841, O'Brien. See also Davis, *Revolutionary Imperialist*, 131-5.

In the middle of the session, on 21 May, he heard of the death of his young brother Edward, whose wedding O'Brien had attended only nine months earlier. He wrote to Lucy that, 'I did not know how much I loved and valued him till now'. On a happier note, he arrived back at Cahirmoyle in July just in time to be with Lucy for the birth of their first daughter, Lucy, an event he celebrated with an elaborate set of stars around the entry in his diary.[16] His routine at home now included frequent attendance at the Board of Guardians in Newcastle. As always when at Cahirmoyle, he read widely, his September 1840 reading including Rousseau's *Social Contract*, Romilly's *Life*, and works by Bentham, Guizot and Thucydides. In politics, the question of repeal re-emerged to separate him again from O'Connell. In April 1840, anticipating the Tories' return to government, O'Connell had formed the Repeal Association to campaign for repeal of the Union. A new pro-repeal Citizens Club was formed in Limerick in September. In the following month, O'Connell attended a repeal dinner in Limerick. O'Brien refused to attend; one of the speakers read out 'a concise letter' from O'Brien 'declining the invitation in rather a decided manner'.[17]

The first Parliamentary session of 1841 saw an embattled ministry whose most reliable defenders were the Irish liberals, a reflection of the view that a Tory government would transform the political condition of Ireland (by ruling through the Protestant minority) to a degree unimaginable in England. In March 1841, O'Brien did turn his attention elsewhere when, in a surprising intervention, he came close to urging war against the United States. In 1837, Canadian soldiers had crossed the border and, after a skirmish in which an American was killed, seized and burned the *Caroline*, an American steamer used for carrying supplies to rebels in Canada. The result was a series of violent exchanges between Americans and Canadians. Then, in November 1840, a Canadian deputy sheriff, Colonel Alexander McLeod, boasted in an American tavern of his role in the *Caroline* seizure; he was arrested by the New York authorities and charged with murder and arson. At the same time, a long running boundary quarrel led to the military occupation of the disputed area of Canada by the Maine militiamen and an uncompromising territorial claim by the Maine legislature. O'Brien thought these acts amounted to 'nothing short of a declaration of war against this country' and he called on Foreign Minister Palmerston to show some of the 'vigour' recently displayed against Mehemet Ali 'in a case of a more doubtful character'. He believed the House would lend the support necessary 'for the maintenance of the honour and character of Great Britain in every part of the world' and opined that Britain could not 'maintain her rank as the greatest nation of the world if she allowed herself to be insulted'. Similarly imperialistic language had featured in the emigration speech of 1840 and in earlier (1838) comments

16 Smith O'Brien Papers, MS 454, Rough Diary, 20, 21, 23 May, 23 July 1840. Ibid., MS 8653(16), O'Brien to Lucy O'Brien, 23 May 1840. Edward's son, Edward Arthur, was born posthumously. 17 Ibid., MS 431, f755, Potter to O'Brien, 21 September 1840. *Limerick Chronicle*, 10 October 1840.

on Canada. What was untypical was his bellicosity; when he said vigour he meant armed force, urging the despatch of a 'strong fleet' and 'a powerful army'. On no other occasion did O'Brien show such enthusiasm for military action. Of course, the episode merely confirmed, albeit in an unexpected way, the fact that O'Brien was a strong-willed politician who spoke his mind. In this case his passion was spent on a cause of dubious worth; McLeod was acquitted when he was exposed as an outrageous liar who had had no role in seizing the *Caroline*.[18]

Much less surprising was O'Brien's major speech seconding William Ewart's motion for the appointment of a minister of education. He believed that, after protection of life and property, the state had 'no higher duty' than the promotion of education and he was clear that voluntary efforts were entirely inadequate; the state must intervene. 'It was truly humiliating to find that this country, the first in commerce and in arms, was nearly the last amongst civilized nations in regard to popular education.' He believed that the state should increase its investment in education until primary schooling was received by every child in Britain and Ireland, a goal that was not to be achieved for another half-century.[19] Perhaps, however, people like O'Brien were merely setting down markers for future reference, for it was clear that the Whigs no longer commanded the confidence of the House of Commons and would not be launching education or any other initiatives for some time. O'Brien supported the ministers on the sugar duties, when they lost heavily, and on the confidence motion – lost by a single vote – which brought the dissolution of Parliament in June 1841.[20]

O'Brien claimed in 1844 that, having attended Parliament 'almost as assiduously as the lamp-post of the House of Commons', by July 1841 he had concluded that it was all 'a waste of time' and he should retire into 'private life'. His language was possibly influenced by the circumstances of 1844, when he was agitating for repeal, but in his election address in June 1841 he said he was 'painfully conscious how disproportionate have been the results obtained to the exertions employed'. It is easy to see why he might have felt disillusioned by 1841. O'Brien's approach to politics was that of the Parliamentarian, the legislator who hoped to pass improving laws. The much-vaunted success of the Whig administration in Ireland involved executive decisions, mainly giving Catholics a share in Crown patronage. The legislative record on poor laws, tithes, and municipal reform did not fulfil O'Brien's expectations, and Parliament's conduct on emigration, Irish representation, registration and the franchise was even worse from his point of view. Add to all this his financial concerns and possibly a wish to spend longer with his growing family, and the desire to quit Parliament becomes entirely understandable. However, the County Club, which only five months earlier had complimented his 'steady adherence to the advocacy of the interests of Ireland', won him round, partly by promising to

---

18 *Hansard*, lvi, 1354, 5 March 1841, O'Brien; see also ibid., lvii, 1496, 6 May 1841, O'Brien. Glyndon G. Van Deusen, *The Jacksonian Era: 1828-1848* (New York, 1959), 138-40, 173. On Canada: *Hansard*, xl, 387-92, 23 January 1838, O'Brien. 19 *Hansard*, lvii, 942-8, 6 April 1841, O'Brien. 20 *Hansard*, lviii, 668-73, 18 May; lviii, 1241-6, 4 June 1841, Divisions.

take on all of the election expenses. He attended the club five times in June–July 1841, when his own endorsement as a candidate was settled and Caleb Powell, an O'Brien ally in the crisis of 1839, was put forward to replace Fitzgibbon, who had annoyed many by being absent for the crucial confidence vote. They were elected without a contest, at a cost to each of £18.[21] The Irish elections as a whole saw the return of 45 liberal-unionists, not least because O'Connell again stressed unity against the Tories and did not press the repeal question; there were 20 nominal repealers (only a dozen of them actively committed) and 40 Tories.

Misfortune overshadowed O'Brien's Limerick success when, later in July, Lucy O'Brien lost a boy in childbirth.[22] Grace, O'Brien's sister, wrote of 'all poor Lucy has gone through ... I was very sorry to hear that you had both lost your poor little baby, though as God has blessed you with other children you will feel its loss less...'[23] O'Brien returned to Parliament in August and sent his wife a letter that reveals both his unhappiness and a warmer side to his nature than was generally evident:

> My Dearest Lucy
> I was beginning to get into very low spirits when your letter ... reached me & has revived my spirits. Truly I was not formed by the *idiosyncrasies* of my nature to be alone. The solitude of London is worse than that of a wilderness. It is true I meet plenty of acquaintances when I go out – all of whom are very kind – but the companion of the domestic House is wanted ... I am at a loss to know what brought me here so much sooner than was needed ... I might have remained at home several days longer without injury to anyone, and with much benefit to myself and satisfaction to others. As for amusement I have ... determined to go to the Haymarket and then has my zeal failed when I bethought of the bore of sitting for three or four morbid hours stewing in a playhouse ... London is excessively empty – not a carriage to be seen – a few struggling MPs looking excessively dismal at being brought up from their homes ...
> ... I am much interested by what you tell me about Edward's little prayer. May it avail! God knows I ought not to be insensible to the value of the prayers of others for I find it very difficult to pray for myself ...[24]

He subsequently wrote that it would be 'such a comfort to get home again, and to see our dear children. I am tired of the wandering life which I have led this year, and shall take measures for it never recurring again. Even though the sacrifice should

---

21 *FJ*, 30 January 1844, O'Brien in Repeal Association. Smith O'Brien Papers, MS 431, f775, Fitzgerald to O'Brien, 26 February 1841; ibid., MS 454, Rough Diary, 23, 26 June, 1, 7, 10 July 1841. *Limerick Chronicle*, 30 June 1841, O'Brien to the Electors of the County of Limerick, n.d.   22 The diary entry was 'Lucy confined of a boy – died'. Smith O'Brien Papers, MS 454, Rough Diary, 23 July 1841.   23 Ibid., MS 431, f796, Grace O'Brien to O'Brien, 3 August 1841.   24 Ibid., f801, O'Brien to Lucy O'Brien, 20 August 1841.

be either the alternative of my going out of Parliament or that of your continuing in London for a longer portion of the year [*sic*]'.[25]

O'Brien attended a meeting of Whig and liberal MPs at the Foreign Office on 23 August and spoke in the debate on the Address that would settle the fate of the Whig government. In a wide-ranging speech, he expressed 'the gratitude of the Irish nation' towards an administration that had tried to put English and Irish, and Protestants and Catholics within Ireland, 'upon a perfectly equal footing'. On the next evening, 27 August, every Irish liberal Member, O'Brien included, stood by the government in the division on the Address, but the Whigs lost by almost 100 votes (360-269) and gave up the reins of power to Peel and the Tories.[26] O'Brien immediately left for Ireland, travelling through Belfast to Londonderry, where he visited the new workhouse and attended a Presbyterian church service; he went on to Dublin for a dinner in honour of the former Chief Secretary, Lord Morpeth, on 14 September. He then returned home, where he would remain for the rest of the year. The Board of Guardians in Newcastle again took up much of his time. He corresponded with Sir Robert Ferguson (his host in Londonderry) and George Nicholls about workhouse diets (and drew from Nicholls a recognition of the value of 'emigration as an adjunct to our Poor Law'), and his Christmas stay at Dromoland facilitated a visit to the Ennis workhouse. His support for Caleb Powell, when the latter was accused of preventing a Mr Furnell from gaining patronage from the poor law commissioners, produced a response that is testimony to O'Brien's standing at least in his young colleague's eyes: Powell was 'deeply sensible of the active friendship' shown by O'Brien and so appreciative of his 'spirit, taste and sense' he would have accepted his advice regardless of both public opinion and his own judgement.[27] O'Brien also attended a dinner to Father Mathew and a 'temperance soirée', on 14-15 October, welcoming the chance to acknowledge 'this truly good man' and to show 'our sympathy with his labours'.[28]

If most of this suggests that life went on as usual for O'Brien, the wider political picture was transformed by the advent of a Tory administration. For two years not a single Catholic was appointed to a significant political or legal position; patronage went instead to Irish Tories like Lefroy, Jackson, Sugden and Lucas, with some of the recipients (Lefroy especially) noted for a virulent anti-Catholicism that still regretted the Emancipation of 1829. Peel showed every sign of wishing to rule Ireland again through its Protestant garrison. O'Brien, who in the August debate had urged the Tories not to 'thrust into office those who were conspicuous for their

---

25 Ibid., MS 8653 (16), O'Brien to Lucy O'Brien, 30 August 1841. 26 Ibid., MS 454, Rough Diary, 21, 23 August 1841. *Hansard*, lix, 290-3, 26 August, O'Brien; lix, 450-5, 27 August 1841, Division. 27 Smith O'Brien Papers, MS 431, f802, Nicholls to O'Brien, 24 August 1841; f804, Ferguson to O'Brien, 2 October 1841; ff806, 807, Powell to O'Brien, 17, 19 October 1841; ibid., MS 454, Rough Diary, September-December 1841. 28 Ibid., 14, 15 October 1841; ibid., MS 431, f805, O'Brien to Anon., 10 October 1841.

vilification of the people of Ireland', apparently expressed his dissatisfaction to Ferguson – causing the latter, tongue in cheek, to reply, 'I am quite surprised that you are not well pleased with Peel's appointments: depend upon it that the man who gets on the shelf Lord Ellenborough and his notions on corn, Perceval with his Orangeism, Dawson with his wild indiscretion, and rids the House of Commons of Lefroy and Sugden, has either great talent or great luck'.[29]

Irish liberal complaining hardly amounted to effective opposition. O'Connell again campaigned for repeal but met with little enthusiasm; Tories celebrated his 'decline and fall', and Wyse wrote from London that, 'Everyone of any thought here looks with pity and pain on the manner O'Connell is squandering himself'.[30] In January 1842, when Morpeth stood for the vacant City of Dublin seat, the reported reluctance to contribute to his election fund and his eventual defeat by a Tory were symptomatic of the liberal malaise.[31] The financial and economic questions that dominated the Parliamentary debates of 1842 found Irish liberalism divided. They were split on Villiers's motion on repeal of the corn laws, O'Brien siding with the main party leaders against O'Connell. O'Brien found little support from any quarter for his attempts to give better protection to Irish oats and preferential treatment to colonial producers.[32] He (and Ferguson) broke ranks to support Peel's introduction of an income tax, believing that 'the exigencies of the state required it'. His line on this earned striking tributes from his Tory brothers-in-law, Arthur Martineau ('I cannot help saying that in my opinion you fully deserve the praise of all honest men for the upright and high-principled conduct you have shewn ... I agree with you in thinking that party spirit is a sadly blinding and deluding thing') and Stephen de Vere ('I cannot avoid ... letting you know how very much pleased I am with your conduct upon Peel's taxation scheme. It is open, manly, independent and I think perfectly right in principle. You are the only public man that I see determined to act as you think right *coute qui coute*.')[33]

On 22 March, O'Brien raised the extraordinary case of 'the Philipstown murder'. He reported the allegation that a party of gentlemen and English army officers gathered in this King's County town on 11 December 1841 and, as the high point of their revelries, made 'an idiot boy' drunk 'and having besmeared his clothes with turpentine, set fire to them to make him run for their amusement'. The boy died from the injuries after six days of agonising pain. The coroner's jury, largely made up of 'retainers' of the party's host, gave a verdict of accidental death. The *Dublin Monitor*, a liberal newspaper, had campaigned for an inquiry, and it was Chief

---

29 Ibid., f809, Ferguson to O'Brien, 23 December 1841. Lefroy was made a judge, Sugden the Irish Chancellor.   30 Wyse Papers, MS 15019 (9), Wyse to George Wyse, 27 September 1842.   31 Peel Papers, Add MSS 40,480, ff60, 70, Eliot to Peel, 8, 20 January 1842. *Dublin Evening Mail*, 17, 24 January 1842.   32 *Hansard*, lx, 1082-8, 24 February, Division (Villiers); lx, 1204, 1221-'31, 28 February, O'Brien, Divisions; lxi, 579, 14 March 1842, O'Brien.   33 Ibid., lxi, 1142-6, 23 March, O'Brien; lxii, 444-50, 710-3, 1040-3, 13, 18, 22 April 1842, Divisions. Smith O'Brien Papers, MS 431, f839, de Vere to O'Brien, 8 March 1842; f843, Martineau to O'Brien, 28 March 1842. Martineau was the husband of O'Brien's sister, Anne, and Stephen de Vere was the brother of Ellen, wife of O'Brien's brother, Robert.

Secretary Eliot's refusal of this that led to O'Brien's bringing the question to Parliament. Eliot saw no reason to question the decision of the jury, given that those members unconnected to the affair had concurred in the verdict. It is impossible to know if the facts were really as stated by the *Monitor* and O'Brien; the affair may or may not have been the 'tragic commentary on the attitude of the aristocracy' that one recent historian has deplored.[34]

In late April 1842, O'Brien told Costelloe of his intention to quit Parliament. The only extant evidence of this is Costelloe's reply, but it is possible to deduce something of O'Brien's thinking from this. He seemed to contemplate resigning immediately, causing the priest to express concern about the state of the registers. Costelloe wrote of 'the cloud which for the present Peel's barefaced hypocrisy has cast over all Parliamentary proceedings'. But this would assuredly 'bring you at a future day into power, and enable you to serve your country, and perhaps recover your losses. I am sure you would be much happier at Cahirmoyle for a week, or a month, but I think your vocation is Parliament ...' It would appear that O'Brien had cited his desire to be with his family, his financial difficulties (which Costelloe thought might be remedied by a government post, not that O'Brien ever showed an interest in office), and the frustrations of political life under the Tories. He implored O'Brien to reconsider: 'nothing could give more pain to the constituency than your retirement ... [You are] daily acquiring more and more Parliamentary character.'[35] The idea was not pursued, but it is quite possible that the episode gave rise to the decision (mentioned below) to try for just one more year in Parliament. At any rate, doubt and pessimism were clearly evident even before 1843 and that year's momentous decision to quit Westminster and join the repealers in Ireland.

O'Brien returned to Ireland in June and missed the major Irish debate of the Parliament, when Richard Sheil led liberal complaints that 'the old system of [Protestant] ascendancy' had been 'partially restored'. In fact, only 20 Irish liberal Members voted, even Russell found Sheil's argument unconvincing, and the ministers were happy with 'the very triumphant debate'.[36] It was a discouraging end to a demoralising year in opposition. O'Brien again spent much of the recess on administering the poor law in Newcastle. On 13 August Lucy gave birth to their third son, Lucius Henry, welcomed by Greig as 'the little stranger'.[37] In September, O'Brien was again invited to a repeal meeting in Limerick but, 'not satisfied that any advantage can arise from agitating this question, under present circumstances', he declined.[38] O'Brien and his family went to Dromoland at Christmas. There the valet of another guest – John MacDonnell of New Hall, the unfortunate second

---

34 *Hansard*, lxi, 1072-4, 1074-7, 22 March 1842, O'Brien, Eliot. *Dublin Monitor*, 28 December 1841 *et seq*. Patsy Adam-Smith, *Heart of Exile: Ireland, 1848* (Melbourne, 1986), 39-42. 35 Smith O'Brien Papers, MS 431, f852, Costelloe to O'Brien, 1 May 1842. 36 *Hansard*, lxv, 243-64, 313-5, 18 July 1842, Sheil, Division. Broadlands MSS, GC/RU/63, Russell to Palmerston, 23 July 1842. Graham Papers, 1IR, Graham to de Grey, 19 July 1842; de Grey to Graham, 20, 21 July 1842. 37 Smith O'Brien Papers, MS 431, f871, Greig to O'Brien, 25 September 1842. 38 *Limerick Chronicle*, 1 October 1842, O'Brien to Browne, 26 September 1842.

who had failed to prepare O'Brien's pistol in the duel in 1831 – was arrested for stealing Lucy's gold watch from her dressing table. On 3 January, the criminal, Joseph Hodder, was sentenced to be transported for seven years and duly despatched to Van Diemen's Land.[39]

In 1843, asserting the futility of attendance in a British Parliament that was deaf to Irish demands, O'Connell instructed the repeal Members to remain in Ireland to agitate against the Union. In an astonishing political recovery, O'Connell and repeal went on to win the support of millions of Irish Catholics in the course of what he called 'the great Repeal Year'. Grievances about tithes, the poor law, corporations and, prominent for the first time, landlord-tenant relations were, when taken with the Peel government's apparent lack of sympathy, used to argue that a Dublin parliament was needed to remedy Ireland's problems. Thousands flocked to the great 'monster meetings' at which O'Connell demanded legislative independence. It was the first great crisis of the Union. The liberal-unionist Members played a significant part in the story. The absence of the repealers left them as the sole spokesmen of Irish liberalism at Westminster. They were able to fill the role of interpreters of Irish discontent in what became a remarkable Parliamentary campaign. The 40 liberal-unionists were a mixed bag of Protestants and Catholics, Whigs and liberals, and they had as little idea of party unity as the stereotypical independent Member of 19th century fame. That they came to act as a Parliamentary party during 1843 owed much to the pressure of events in Ireland. But it was also attributable to the two men who orchestrated their efforts, Thomas Wyse and, surprisingly given all he had done to assert the independence of the individual Member, O'Brien.

Later in the year, of course, O'Brien abandoned these colleagues and joined the repealers. There was no still indication of this possibility in January 1843; invited to another Limerick dinner for O'Connell, his reply was an abrupt 'I decline for reasons which it is unnecessary to state to be present at the approaching dinner'.[40] When he returned to London, however, he showed he had his own reasons for quitting Parliament. As he reported to Lucy, he sent his mother a letter 'written in one of my fits of *irrevocable* determination to give up Parliament. I entertain this notion so sincerely that I thought it right to let her know that such a matter is under consideration.' He went on to give a clear explanation of the personal and political motives that made him so uncertain of his future course:

> ... If my continuance in Parlt. were a mere question affecting only my own personal happiness I should have little difficulty in deciding in favor of that mode of life which would prevent a separation from my family. But inas-

---

39 Ibid., 7 January 1843. Smith O'Brien Papers, MS 454, Rough Diary, 31 December 1842, 3 January 1843. Davis, *Revolutionary Imperialist*, 145-6.   40 Smith O'Brien Papers, MS 432, f903, Leahy to O'Brien, 12 January 1843; O'Brien to Leahy, 14 January 1843, reply drafted on back of Leahy's letter.

much as the question of public duty is also involved in the decision I continue to hesitate and vacillate, feeling that if without sufficient reason I leave my post I ought to be regarded as a deserter who leaves the army with which he has enlisted merely because he is unwilling to encounter the labours & dangers to which it is exposed. I must confess however that a growing conviction has gradually impressed itself on my mind which has led me to two separate conclusions. The one is that I individually could be more useful out of Parlt. than in it – the other that the British Parlt. is incapable of properly legislating for Ireland, the country with which all my sympathies & interests are for weal or for woe inseparably connected. If I pause before I retire, I do so not only because I contemplate the probability that I may one day regret such a step when the sacrifices imposed upon me by attending Parlt. will be less than they now are – but ...[41]

Unfortunately the rest of this important letter is missing. His 'growing conviction' that Parliament was 'incapable of properly legislating for Ireland' was a significant development. He was already travelling on the tortuous journey that made him a repealer. On 23 March, he sent Lucy a long letter in which he tried, rather awkwardly, to involve himself in her world and her in his, and there was more evidence of his dissatisfaction with the MP's life:

My Dearest Lucy,
I have to thank you for a very long and agreeable letter. Why not tell me the gossip about projected marriages? I am not so philosophical as to be indifferent to all these little matters. They constitute after all the most important part of life and the most amusing part of conversation.

On Thursday last we had a very long and very interesting debate on the Treaty with America so that I failed as I expected to obtain an opportunity of bringing on my motion. Lord Palmerston made an admirable speech. I listened to it for three hours and ten minutes without ever allowing my attention to flag. He spoke without halt or pause, illustrating a very complex subject ... with wonderful clearness & accuracy in language as correct & elegant as if it had been a written composition. All this was done without reference to a single note. Altogether it was a fine intellectual effort, and places Lord Palmerston in a high rank among orators. I remember when he used to speak very indifferently. Is not this very encouraging?

I think it not improbable that I shall return to Ireland next week ... it will be a *bolt* – turning my back upon a variety of Parliamentary questions about which I feel much interest and with respect to which I ought to take a part. But life has other duties except attendance on divisions, &c – & if I can start next week I shall have three clear weeks at home which will greatly contribute D[eo] V[olente] to my happiness & that of others & prepare me

---

[41] Ibid., MS 8653 (17), O'Brien to Lucy O'Brien, 21 February 1843.

for a solitary return to London, whereas if I stay here till the last moment my vacation will be so short as scarcely to justify the expense & wear & tear of a journey to Ireland.

... I went last night with Charles [*Harris*] to the Geological Society and there heard the outpourings of geological eloquence – bonus! bonus! bonus! – from the lips of Lyell, De la Beche, Greenough, Buckland and other celebrities.[42]

Later in the evening of 23 March, O'Brien introduced the motion referred to in this letter, when he moved for a committee to inquire into the operation of the Irish poor law. In a long speech, he argued that defects in the law – notably the system of rating by electoral division (as opposed to a single union rate), the inadequate provision for emigration, and the exclusive insistence on workhouse relief – and the 'vexatious and meddling interference' of the Commission had provoked 'universal condemnation'. O'Brien noted in a hand-written memorandum that 'in the middle of his speech an English member rose and moved that the House be counted. The requisite number of members (40) being present he [O'Brien] proceeded with his speech but first protested in terms of warmest indignation against the attempt made to get rid of a discussion upon a subject which excited much interest in Ireland and stated that if this mode of dealing with Irish affairs were continued he should endeavour to secure their fair discussion in an Irish Parliament.' He told Lucy it was 'an ebullition of indignation on my part such as I never before displayed in public'.[43] O'Brien was not successful in securing the committee – the division was lost by 108 votes to 23 – and his impatience with Parliament's response to Irish concerns could hardly be clearer. The threat to become a repealer was now, given the storm brewing in Ireland, a great more realistic than it had been when he used language almost as strong back in 1836. Further evidence of at least common ground with the repealers came when he (twice) asked Michael Staunton, a journalist, for details of his research into the financial aspects of the Act of Union. Staunton had spoken about these arrangements, alleging that they worked to Ireland's disadvantage and justified repeal of the Act, in the major debate in Dublin corporation at the end of February, the showcase event that sparked off the revival in repeal fortunes. O'Brien did not pursue Staunton's suggestion that he should move for an inquiry into the question, but his interest in it would continue.[44]

O'Brien kept his half-promise to return early for Easter (using the time to attend to local poor law matters as well as seeing his family). On resuming his place in

---

42 Ibid., MS 432, f932, O'Brien to Lucy O'Brien, 23 March 1843.   43 Ibid., MS 8653 (17), O'Brien to Lucy O'Brien, 25 March 1843; ibid., MS 432, f930, Memorandum by O'Brien. O'Brien seems to have written this to accompany the copy of his speech that he had been asked to send to the *Dublin Evening Mail*. Ibid., MS 454, Rough Diary, 23, 24 March 1843. *DEM*, 27 March 1843. *Hansard*, lxvii, 1347-69, 23 March 1843, O'Brien.   44 Smith O'Brien Papers, MS 432, ff951, 966, Staunton to O'Brien, 2, 9 May 1843.

Parliament later in April, he began to work closely with Wyse. The latter was the calculating, even manipulative organiser of their campaign, while it was O'Brien who led from the front. They began in response to the intention of a British Tory, Lane Fox, whom Wyse called 'a sort of anti O'C. fanatic', to move in favour of coercion as the answer to the growing agitation in Ireland. Wyse, in the first of a series of letters to his brother, described the sorry state of Parliamentary liberalism:

> Whigs there are none, at least no Whig party. All our old Treasury arrangements are given up, no circulars, no whipping, anyone speaks, fights, guerrillas as he can ... There is no Opposition, in fact, in the true disciplinarian style of the word. The time is not yet come. Our Irishmen are still more scattered. The '*moderés*' are the only in attendance. All the O'Connellites are still away.[45]

Wyse was clear that coercion could not remedy Ireland's problems and he and O'Brien decided to use Fox's motion to make the point: '[O'Brien] very judiciously thought it was a moment not to be lost to the moderate section in Ireland ... we [Wyse and O'Brien] went over the resolutions he proposes to move in amendments together. The provocation was great, and all admit Lane Fox deserves the answer.'[46]

On 28 April, O'Brien had given notice of three resolutions he would move as an amendment to Fox's motion. They asked the Commons to inquire whether the recent upsurge of repeal was not due to Parliament's failure to tend Ireland's needs and to the 'overbearing, exclusive, anti-national spirit in which the affairs of Ireland have been administered', and called for early consideration of measures for Ireland.[47] Wyse fully appreciated the importance of O'Connell's absence:

> ... We can speak with more weight in our attitude of an independent Irish party than under his wing, and say things which from us will have their effect, tho' from him they would provoke little more than scoff or jeer. O'Brien and others of us are determined to be explicit enough. The Arms Bill will give us another opportunity ... The Bill ... will appear a Bill for disarming the Catholics and leaving the Orangemen armed.[48]

The arms bill (which is considered below) prompted O'Brien to ask Chief Secretary Eliot if the government 'had nothing better to offer Ireland' and to urge measures that would actually 'remedy the cause of discontent'.[49] On 5 May, O'Brien announced his opposition to Eliot's poor law amendment bill, which diminished 'popular control' by increasing the proportion of *ex officio* guardians from one-third

---

45 Wyse Papers, MS 15019 (10), Wyse to George Wyse, 2 May 1843. Richard Davis's rather thin treatment of the Parliamentary campaign of 1843 follows from his surprising decision to ignore almost all of the Wyse letters. Davis, *Revolutionary Imperialist*, 147-55.   46 Wyse Papers, MS 15019 (10), Wyse to George Wyse, 2 May 1843.   47 *Hansard*, lxviii, 1027, 28 April 1843, O'Brien.   48 Wyse Papers, MS 15019 (10), Wyse to George Wyse, 2 May 1843.   49 *Hansard*, lxviii, 1011, 27 April 1843, O'Brien.

to a half and extended the powers of the Commission.[50] His post-bag suggests he was regarded as a major authority on the subject. He told Lucy that the government was bringing in 'a new Coercion Bill under the name of an Arms Bill' and a poor law bill that was 'a complete failure'. Such measures, from a House that was 'profoundly ignorant of the state of feeling in Ireland', were effectively 'in aid of Repeal'.[51] After the poor law debate, he wrote that he was 'greatly surprised at the folly, the madness of the present Govt. This amendment? of the Poor law will call forth universal opposition, and as if there were not a sufficient number of topics of complaint they have brought forward an atrocious Arms Bill. In the meantime nothing is doing [*sic*] for the advantage or improvement of the country. I moved to try to awaken them to the danger of the course which they are pursuing but I fear that my efforts will be unavailing. In the meantime how I wish I was at home with you ...'[52]

In the event, Fox's coercion proposal was abandoned; John Gray of the *Freeman's Journal* gave O'Brien the credit: 'the wholesome dread produced by your judicious amendment has frightened Peel into gagging Lane Fox ...'[53] O'Brien gave notice that he would now move his resolutions as a substantive motion. He informed Lucy that he was 'not sorry for this delay as the progress of events in Ireland will induce the Govt. in the interim to give more attention to Irish concerns and perhaps they may take the opportunity on my motion of indicating some changes of policy which may promise more satisfactory govt. for Ireland'. He was under no illusions about the cause of any such change: 'People here are at last beginning to get a little frightened about Repeal. That is a good sign. There is never any chance of getting anything in the way of conciliatory govt. from England until she becomes alarmed ...' To a Limerick neighbour, General Richard Bourke, he wrote that the Irish knew that the only demands listened to in London were 'those which are coupled with an apprehension of disagreeable consequences', meaning the current 'state of general commotion'.[54]

On 19 May, O'Brien publicly described his disillusionment with the Union. In reply to the Limerick corporation's request that he should advocate repeal, he wrote that had he been in the Irish parliament at the time of the Act of Union in 1800 he would have joined his father in opposing that 'iniquitous measure'. He was deterred from seeking its repeal by a fear that the attempt would bring 'much risk to the peace and security of both countries' and by a hope that there could yet be 'a per-

---

50 Ibid., lxviii, 1340, 5 May 1843, O'Brien.   51 Smith O'Brien Papers, MS 8653 (18), O'Brien to Lucy O'Brien, 2 May 1843.   52 Ibid., MS 432, f959, O'Brien to Lucy O'Brien, 6 May 1843.   53 Ibid., f957, Gray to O'Brien, 6 May 1843.   54 Ibid., ff965, 978, O'Brien to Lucy O'Brien, 9, 22 May 1843. Bourke Papers, MS 8477 (10), O'Brien to Bourke, 25 May 1843. On a more personal note, he revealed a little of his attitude to religion in the first letter to Lucy, telling her he 'went to church both on last Sunday & on the preceding Sunday, so that I am more devotional abroad than at home. God help me if my salvation is to depend on the regularity of such outward attendance upon the forms of religion. I hope I possess a grateful heart for all the blessings I enjoy. I know I entertain a strong sense of my own weakness & often mutter a silent prayer to be kept out of harm, but as for more ostentatious methods of proving religious feeling I fear I stand very low in acceptability. *Any way*, as we say in Ireland, may God bless you & and the children. This prayer will I trust do no harm if it does no good.'

fect union' yielding 'many benefits ... which could not be obtained under separate legislation and government'. He admitted that the post-Union 'system of misgovernment' of Ireland did not augur well for such an outcome. He had been 'induced to doubt' his preference for making the union work when 'every hour's experience continues to prove the futility' of that course. But he felt that the same 'unanimous determination of the Irish people' that would be necessary to secure repeal would be sufficient to compel Westminster to give Ireland better legislation. 'So long, then, as a hope of obtaining good government through other means than a severance of the legislative connexion remains on my mind, I shall adhere to the union. When that hope is extinguished, I shall not fear to contemplate the remaining alternative', repeal.[55] From others this might have been an evasive reply to satisfy constituents, but enough is known of O'Brien's character (and of the future course of events) to appreciate that he meant what he said. He knew Lucy would 'think I have furnished too many arguments for repeal. *N'importe*, it is better that the truth should be known and my warning voice may have some weight at Headquarters.'[56] He subsequently declared, 'Serves them right' when reporting the growing anxiety of Englishmen who always ignored Ireland until she was thrown into 'a Hurricane of popular commotion ... It is too bad that quiet men like myself cannot be allowed to live at home at ease surrounded by a happy & contented population because the Govt. choose to neglect the first principles of constitutional freedom in their management of Ireland. Where it will all end God only knows. Maybe bring good out of evil & secure ... tranquillity & prosperity. As for myself ... I feel as if I could consent to sacrifice everything if by doing so I could place upon a stable foundation the liberties & welfare of my country.'[57] It is likely that he meant becoming a repealer when he wrote of his readiness to 'sacrifice everything'.

O'Brien gave an indication that his old weakness – some would say strength – persisted when he deserted the liberal opposition to speak and vote for the Canada corn bill, 'compelled in spite of my wishes' to back the ministry 'as they have in fact adopted the proposal which I made last year in favour of the colonies'.[58] Legislative issues were eclipsed by the storm that arose when, towards the end of May, the Irish Lord Chancellor (Sir Edward Sugden) began to dismiss magistrates who attended repeal meetings; O'Connell and Lord Ffrench were the first to be 'superseded' for this reason. Liberal-unionist Members questioned Home Secretary Graham on the subject on 26 May, O'Brien asking if he would be deprived of his commissions if he presented a petition for repeal and, on being told that only participation in a repeal meeting would have this consequence, inquiring whether or not these meetings had occasioned breaches of the peace. Graham had to concede

---

55 *DEM*, 31 May 1843, O'Brien to Raleigh, 19 May 1843. **56** Smith O'Brien Papers, MS 8653 (18), O'Brien to Lucy O'Brien, 21 May 1843. **57** Ibid., O'Brien to Lucy O'Brien, 26 May 1843. **58** Ibid., MS 432, f978, O'Brien to Lucy O'Brien, 22 May 1843. This letter ended with, 'What makes you fancy that I think our [son] Lucius ugly? All that I ever said is that he is not sufficiently handsome to justify the trumpeting forth his praise ... Kiss the dear children for me.' *Hansard*, lxix, 698-700, 747-51, 22 May 1843, O'Brien, Division.

that (with one exception) there had been no violence.⁵⁹ The government's position was vulnerable, for Sugden was dismissing magistrates who were taking part in peaceable activity designed to secure repeal of a law. Wyse was angered by the 'outrageous attempt' to suppress the right to discuss 'public measures', but he was also aware of the advantage to be reaped: 'we are consoled by the consideration that the signal imbecility of the proceeding is equal to its injustice, and working far better for us than we could do for ourselves ...'⁶⁰

O'Brien's protest took the form, on 29 May, of submitting his resignation from the magistracies of Clare and Limerick, informing the Chancellor that he could not retain any office that would compel him to 'forego the acknowledged right' of every British subject to seek the repeal of a law, especially one that 'was obtained by the basest means and by the foulest corruption'. Regarding the deprived magistrates, O'Brien said he wished 'to participate in whatever indignities or sufferings may be inflicted upon them by their anti-Irish rulers'.⁶¹ Such language suggests that the affair brought him a significant step closer to repeal. O'Brien's was not the only (or the first) resignation, but O'Connell clearly considered it the most important. He had the Repeal Association send O'Brien 'the grateful thanks of his countrymen' and himself expressed 'a fervent hope that your [O'Brien's] powerful mind may ere long be brought to the conviction that a resident legislature alone can substantially serve Ireland'.⁶² O'Brien's response was complimentary towards the Association – it held 'many of the best and ablest of our land' – and claimed that they shared a common goal, 'to obtain for Ireland good government, to put an end, once and for ever, to the unjust, exclusive, overbearing, and anti-national system of domination by which Ireland has been oppressed for 600 years'. These were strong words, but he again said he still clung to the hope that this could be achieved within the Union.⁶³ O'Brien's praises were sung at repeal meetings all over Ireland; he was now a popular hero, for the first time, as a result of his resignation and public statements that repudiated the existing Union even if he had not yet given up on the possibility of a better one.

O'Brien was caused some embarrassment when the Tory *Dublin Evening Mail* denounced the appointment of Lucius, his brother, to the Lord Lieutenancy of Clare on the grounds that it represented an attempt to conciliate O'Brien. The latter wrote to the *Mail* to state that he had no political connection with his brother, who was a Tory, causing the *Mail* to respond with the accusation that Lucius had betrayed his fellow-Tory, Crofton Vandeleur, in the 1835 election. This was a sore point with Lucius, who believed himself the victim of Vandeleur's underhand dealings.⁶⁴ He wrote privately to O'Brien: 'I do not feel that you are at all responsible for the observations of the Mail. You did what you felt to be right, in sending a

---

59 Ibid., lxix, 982-3, 26 May 1843, O'Brien, Graham.   60 Wyse Papers, MS 15019 (10), Wyse to George Wyse, 6 June 1843.   61 *Limerick Chronicle*, 31 May 1843. Smith O'Brien Papers, MS 432, f988, Henry Sugden to O'Brien, 1 June 1843; f990, O'Brien to Graham, 2 June 1843.   62 Ibid., f993, Ray to O'Brien, 7 June 1843.   63 *DEM*, 14 June 1843, O'Brien to Ray, 9 June 1843.   64 Ibid., 29 May, 5 June 1843, O'Brien to Editor, 1 June 1843; ibid., 7 June 1843, Sir Lucius O'Brien to Editor, 6 June 1843.

letter quite as much about yourself as about me & could not have foreseen the consequences.' O'Brien explained that 'it seemed so strange that I should be running breast-high against the Govt. at the very moment that you [Lucius] were receiving at their hands a sort of favour, that it was necessary for the character of both of us to explain that in politics we stand quite independent of each other. When I saw the very unexpected article in the Mail which was appended to my letter I regretted the step ...' He thanked Lucius and his wife (Mary) for their kindness to Lucy during his absence; he was especially grateful because 'differences of opinion on political matters have a natural & almost unavoidable tendency to produce estrangement – especially amongst members of the same family'.[65] In fact, O'Brien had thought at one stage that the matter would force Lucy to leave Dromoland (where she had stayed from mid-May), lest her presence there might 'connect Lucius in any way with my proceedings in Parliament'. Fearing, moreover, that his mother, as a result of his political activities, would exclude them from Cahirmoyle, he asked Lucy to 'prepare for the worst' by selling one horse to Lucius for £30 and returning the other to his mother. He wanted 'to clear off all debts if possible so as to be prepared for any contingency ... My own expenditure is limited to the lowest point at which I can live as a gentleman in London.' When Lucy complained that he did not 'sufficiently think of wife & children' in his 'political operations', he protested that it was for them that he applied himself 'with zeal to every peaceful & constitutional effort to establish the liberties of the country on a satisfactory basis'.[66]

With O'Connell attracting tens of thousands to the monster meetings, it was widely feared that Ireland was 'on the eve of a Convulsion'.[67] A sense of crisis, of mortal danger, permeated every discussion. A single incident could spark off an uncontrollable riot. The violence of O'Connell's language evoked the danger of civil war; at a dinner after the Kilkenny monster meeting of 8 June, he claimed leadership of a body of men that was 'quite abundant for the conquest of Europe. Wellington never had such an army as we saw today.'[68] In his letter to Ray, O'Brien had reflected the tension of the moment, warning that 'a great national effort originating in the highest and noblest impulses' – his characterisation of the repeal agitation – might 'degenerate into an unsuccessful rebellion, disastrous alike to the victors and the vanquished'.[69] The liberal-unionists sought to induce the government to stave off violence by measures that would assuage anger. O'Brien explained to his wife that his task was to 'open the eyes of the Government to the perils into which they are about to plunge the country if they do not endeavour to govern Ireland with a proper respect to the interests and feelings of *all classes* of the pop-

---

65 Smith O'Brien Papers, MS 432, f998, Sir Lucius O'Brien to O'Brien, 9 June 1843. Inchiquin Papers, U10/3407, O'Brien to Sir Lucius O'Brien, 12 June 1843.   **66** Smith O'Brien Papers, MS 8653 (18), O'Brien to Lucy O'Brien, 31 May 1843; ibid. (19), O'Brien to Lucy O'Brien, 2 June 1843.   **67** Peel Papers, Add MSS 40,448, f290, Graham to Peel, 6 May 1843.   **68** *FJ*, 10 June 1843.   **69** *DEM*, 14 June 1843, O'Brien to Ray, 9 June 1843.

ulation ...' He acted out of 'a strong sense of duty' to 'avert that crisis to which the blindness & folly of rulers is hurrying us'. He did not feel confident in success, however, telling Lucy on 2 June that the present was 'probably my last session in a British Parliament' before giving it up as hopeless and throwing himself 'into the ranks of those who seek for what every day's experience more & more teaches me to believe is the only effective remedy for misgovernment – *an Irish Parliament*. Be perfectly tranquil however on the subject of rebellion. The uplifting of an arm to commit violence would be to me a signal for retreat – but unless such a movement shd originate with the Orangemen in [the] north I have no apprehension of a popular outbreak.'[70]

So, O'Brien was clear from early June that he would 'probably' be driven to seeking repeal. Wyse, always more optimistic than his ally, did not see that Peel had a viable alternative to conciliation. British opinion, he felt, was moving in this direction, with many talking of 'throwing the Church overboard, increasing the Members, lowering the franchise, reorganising the law of landlord & tenant, expanding education, and providing largely for public works in Ireland. I hear them every day – Protestant & Catholic, Tory as well as Whig and Radical.' He described to his brother the means by which the liberal-unionists hoped to maintain the apparent drift towards conciliation, revealing in the process that their famous declaration of August 1843 – the 'Remonstrance' – was envisaged months beforehand by Wyse and O'Brien, as part of a general plan to engineer public opinion:

> These views are constantly present to a small section of us – O'Brien, Ross, Crawford, Reddington. (Denham Norreys to a certain degree). Under all circumstances we adhere to these great reforms, but are not indifferent to any others. Our course is to let the Repeal movement fight our battle – and when the acceptable time shall arise, and the public mind shall be ripe, to be ready with our Ultimatum in set formal terms under the name of Declaration of Rights. (Say nothing of this.) O'Brien and I have had several consultations on it, and we shall not be wanting when the House & Country are ready to receive it.[71]

The reference to 'Declaration of Rights', reminiscent of the French Declaration of the Rights of Man of 1789, shows that Wyse did not lack a sense of the momentousness of the events of 1843. He believed that the liberal-unionists had revived the Whig opposition: 'The Irish members have awakened them – they alone. O'Connell's absence has been fortunate. We [the Irish] ... are now a compact, united, energetic and working body, which the House is beginning to feel and respect. All formerly was attributed to the head showman [O'Connell]. The quieter the man was, the more his words were left ...' It was more than a matter of displacing the Tory ministry; he wanted to expel them 'from the citadel' but also

---

70 Smith O'Brien Papers, MS 8653 (19), O'Brien to Lucy O'Brien, 2 June 1843.   71 Wyse Papers, MS 15019 (10), Wyse to George Wyse, 6 June 1843.

'very considerably to re-fashion the whole concern – a far more important matter than any cheque-mating of parties'. This would require a sustained effort to present an alternative Irish policy:

> Our future action is very obvious. We are determined to let nothing pass, to put forward in one shape or another all our claims. Hence O'Brien's *finance*, and Reddington's *army* and my *education* motions – the Provincial Colleges ... and the University (of which say nothing yet), in readiness for a fitting opportunity. The Whigs *must* follow. They do it reluctantly enough. Lord John excepted, who has spoken out? Many of them think too rarely. But the day *will* come ... there must be a total fusion of the party.[72]

On 8 June, Wyse met the Whig leaders at Russell's house and persuaded them that to avoid giving the campaign 'a party character' the Irish MPs should be allowed to take the lead in presenting a programme of remedies for Ireland's grievances:

> ... This I knew to be the feeling of many of the most moderate and temperate (O'B., Ross & others so confessed themselves to me yesterday), and even for party purposes it was the most expedient course ... I am glad to say that this view was strongly approved by Lord John, and adopted as the course to be pursued ... I went after to the meeting of Irish members, 15 of us, and saw O'B. (to whom I *certainly* mentioned this, which he highly approved), and ... we went into consideration of a letter to the absent members. We opposed anything *public* or *remonstrant* but each engaged to write to those whom he could influence. I threw out hints at a future meeting [*sic*] of coming to some declaration but I find there will be no occasion for this yet ...[73]

His closing remarks suggest that Wyse and O'Brien were not fully open to the others about the intended declaration, a fact not without some relevance to the difficulties that would emerge. On 12 June, Wyse wrote that, 'The document we have in view must be one for which we can stand up before all men, not of declamation only but *sound sense & knowledge*: for we are not addressing a few thousands of shouters at the Curragh but well informed and thoughtful politicians, who have the *power* as well as the *understanding* ...'[74] Two days later, he reported that, 'Much is in agitation. O'B. and I have been active in ascertaining aspects of Irish opinion in & out of the House to be sure before we set down to the work what sort of support we are likely to have ...' He found that many of the others were federalists – supporters of the idea of a Dublin parliament for local matters – but that O'Brien

---

72 Ibid., Wyse to George Wyse, 6 June 1843. 73 Ibid., Wyse to George Wyse, 8 June 1843. 74 Ibid., Wyse to George Wyse, 12 June 1843.

was '*strongly against*. "Repeal", he says, or "Union" – no intermediate house.' Wyse, though long an advocate, believed federalism would be rejected by the English as a surrender to O'Connell and that its denial would merely strengthen O'Connell by showing 'the folly of looking for any minor concession'. They 'must confine to another kind of operation':

> O'Brien and I are decided ... about our declaration & we have been considering ... the various topics. As it is likely to have an important effect & to be a historic document we must take some care ... This briefly is our policy – to have this document approved by the Irish members, *signed* by them and then followed up by the intermediates & moderates in Ireland. We shall have an alternative at the close, which in case of refusal or rejection will leave every subscriber to it hereafter with or against Repeal as he may think fit ... it will (as will really be the case) be seen as the only means left of tempering and staying the existing agitation and warding off the evils which otherwise may follow. It will place us all in our *true* position and will enable us to retain (a most important matter for its liberty & quiet) some control over the feelings and judgement of the country. As to topics – Church, Franchise, Representation, Public Works, Education, Grand Jury Reform, Finance and Patronage will form our head complaints. Tenure of land & Emigration shall not be neglected. In fact we intend a regular manifesto – and such as will give *unity of action* and *opinion* to our section at last, not only now but in all future sessions ... If the matter is well managed we shall I think ultimately succeed and at all costs we shall rally together a party which it is quite obvious only require some such course to bring and keep them together.[75]

The aim, then, was a reform programme for Ireland and a united liberal-unionist party, with the declaration the basis of both. On 13 June, O'Brien sent his wife a letter that expressed hope – perhaps the result of Wyse's contagious enthusiasm – as well as impatience:

> This long separation is very painful; but whatever doubts I might under other circumstances have entertained about the propriety of staying here, I have none in the present crisis of Irish affairs. The post for action on the part of those who like myself feel deeply for the wrongs of the country yet are not prepared to espouse the Repeal cause is evidently the British House of Commons and I have every impression that we shall be able to make some impression [*sic*] for the benefit of Ireland before the end of the session. Such is my view of the duty of a liberal Member at present. It has been for some time my fixed resolve not to return to the British Parliament in case the present session shd pass over without some change of policy towards Ireland.

---

75 Ibid., Wyse to George Wyse, 14 June 1843.

In this event my exertions shall be bestowed in Ireland – in what manner will depend on circumstances. I cannot persuade myself however that the present session will elapse without some important change. At all events it shall not be my fault if the coming crisis is not averted by just & conciliatory measures, & with this view I shall remain here so long as there is hope that I can be useful ...

Pray do not allow your spirits to be depressed. I have no fears but on the contrary great hopes for our country, and at all events whether weal or woe betide we must be prepared for whatever events Providence may ordain, endeavouring to perform our duty as well as we can ...[76]

The arms bill of 1843 was intended to regulate the possession of weapons, amending laws which were due to expire at the end of the session. The liberal-unionists disliked its provisions, including the harsh penalties (up to seven years' transportation) for illegal possession and the increased powers of search given to magistrates. Above all, however, it was thought that remedial legislation, rather than this coercive measure, was needed to stem the repeal tide. It was this train of thought that led to the presentation of the full array of grievances, the bill providing the principal vehicle by which the state of Ireland was presented for debate in the Commons. Opposition was well organised. Wyse's letters of 15 and 16 May were the first of many to refer to meetings of Irish Members 'on the resistance to the Arms Bill'.[77] The second reading debate lasted for three nights, 29-31 May: the liberal-unionist Members led the assault, with O'Brien demanding 'ample, fair and full justice' for Ireland and warning that the bill was creating repealers. He tellered the division, which the government won easily, but O'Brien was privately pleased with the Irish Members' display of 'sharpshooting'.[78] 'O'Brien and I,' wrote Wyse on 14 June, 'think we should fight it at every stage. Lord J[ohn] & O'F[errall] do not, *lest we should have small divisions*. We can't accept *that*. Who cares for divisions now? The point is, the great point, to show that Ireland has in her *representatives* men on whom she *can rely* ...'[79]

Wyse's motion to refer the bill to a select committee led to another three-day debate on 15-16 and 19 June. Graham, the Home Secretary, said that conciliation in Ireland had 'been carried to its utmost limits', a claim that Irish liberals mercilessly exploited as evidence that the Tories had nothing to offer Ireland.[80] O'Brien deprecated Graham's 'perfect recklessness of public opinion' in Ireland, which could only 'increase the excitement' there.[81] However, Wyse was delighted that Graham's

---

76 O'Brien Papers (AO), Letter Box, Bundle 4, O'Brien to Lucy O'Brien, 13 June 1843.   77 Wyse Papers, MS 15019 (10), Wyse to George Wyse, 15, 16 May 1843.   78 Smith O'Brien Papers, MS 8653 (18), O'Brien to Lucy O'Brien, 28, 31 May 1843. *Hansard*, lxix, 1118-20, 1217-20, 30, 31 May 1843, O'Brien, Division.   79 Wyse Papers, MS 15019 (10), Wyse to George Wyse, 14 June 1843. Richard More O'Ferrall was the liberal-unionist Member for Kildare and an office-holder in Melbourne's administration.   80 *Hansard*, lxx, 52, 16 June 1843, Graham. He apologised for the statement in 1845.   81 Smith O'Brien

'immense blunder' had given them 'an opportunity of falling on him sword in hand'. The government was embarrassed – 'I wish you could have seen Peel's face' – and the Irish Members were buoyant. Now they spoke 'with a self reliance and vigor [*sic*] they had not before', and they were listened to not as O'Connell's 'puppets but as interpreters of the feelings of large masses of the country ... It is quite clear we are getting to close quarters on all the great questions and before the end of the session shall have the programme of our future campaign fairly traced out.'[82] In the meantime, they were resolved 'to *fight every inch*' on the arms bill. Only O'Ferrall's half-heartedness – he thought it 'unwise to add by these discussions in the House to the flame in Ireland', but 'he stood quite alone' – clouded the picture for Wyse.[83] O'Brien wrote to Lucy, after another night of combat on 23 June, that 'we have had hard battling in the House of Commons. I do not think that Peel and Co will be in a hurry to bring in measures of coercion for Ireland after the sample which he had of our vigour' in the arms bill debates.[84]

It was at the committee stage, from 23 June until 27 July, that the opposition to the arms bill became truly extraordinary. The Irish forced 51 divisions. *Hansard* listed 25 of them; Viscount Clements of Leitrim led the way with 25 votes against the bill, O'Brien came second with 24. The extent of organisation behind this effort was remarkable. Wyse told his brother on numerous occasions of meetings 'to distribute our *parts* and order of battle man by man' and of how David Pigot of Clonmel acted 'as our Attorney general in bringing our amendments into shape ... Our order of Battle is very good.' On 3 July, he wrote from the front line, 'Another night of fierce fighting on the Arms Bill, now 2 in the morning, just completed at 1 o'clock ... We have not, after 3 nights, allowed them to get beyond 11 clauses, or rather 8 – 3 postponed – and without a single *factious* move.'[85] Graham privately acknowledged that the 'resistance and delay' which had met the arms bill was a 'foretaste of the struggle which a coercion bill would cause'. This was the principal reason for the Cabinet's refusal early in July to propose an extension of the Processions Act to cover the temperance bands, which had become an auxiliary of the repeal agitation.[86] Peel was driven to exasperation:

> There is a certain Lord Clements in the House of Commons, an unparalleled bore and with means of obstructing public business by a combination of ignorance and perseverance unequalled in the annals of Parliament. He took 13 divisions last night on miserable points in the Arms Bill. I was haunted throughout the remainder of the night after the business was over by the sound of his voice.[87]

Papers, MS 8653 (19), O'Brien to Lucy O'Brien, 18 June 1843. 82 Wyse Papers, MS 15019 (10), Wyse to George Wyse, 17 June 1843. 83 Ibid., Wyse to George Wyse, 20 June 1843. 84 Smith O'Brien Papers, MS 432, f1011, O'Brien to Lucy O'Brien, 24 June 1843. 85 Wyse Papers, MS 15019 (10), Wyse to George Wyse, 17, 20, 26 June, 3 July 1843. 86 Graham Papers, 4IR, 9IR, Graham to de Grey, 27 June, 9 July 1843. Peel Papers, Add MSS 40,531, f165, Peel to Farnham, 20 July 1843. 87 Peel Papers, Add MSS 40,531, f264, Peel to Brougham, 21 July 1843. See also ibid., Add MSS 40,478, f119,

Even F.S. Murphy, one of the liberal-unionists, quipped that 'the penalties are bad, but the Clementcy worse'.[88] Wyse proudly boasted that they were sending the bill up from the Commons 'amidst the united execrations of one section of the Irish members'.[89] Their success in securing amendments – for example, the defining of arms as firearms only and the reduction of penalties – was secondary to the creation of an effective Parliamentary party. The *Dublin Evening Post* hailed 'as well disciplined an opposition' as it had ever seen.[90] Angus MacIntyre called it 'the first genuine example of the use of those methods of obstruction by which Parnell and his party later brought Parliamentary government to a standstill'.[91]

O'Brien was an active participant in this opposition, but it was another aspect of the campaign that saw him take the lead. On 4 July 1843, he introduced his motion on the state of Ireland, a shortened version of the resolutions he had drawn up in answer to Lane Fox. It called on the House to 'resolve itself into a committee, for the purpose of taking into consideration the causes of the discontent at present prevailing in Ireland, with a view to the redress of grievances and to the establishment of just and impartial government in that part of the United Kingdom'. The debate monopolised the business of the House for five nights and explored every conceivable Irish question. Both Irish and British liberals assailed the appointments and measures (and, in many cases, lack of measures) of the government. 12 Irish liberal speakers – only one of whom was a confirmed repealer – joined in this assault, and the Irish liberals voted unanimously for the motion.[92] O'Brien's speech provided an exemplary statement of the full range of Irish Catholic grievances and a cogent argument that the agitation in Ireland was attributable to the failure of all administrations, above all the present one, to provide 'just and impartial government'. It was his 'conscientious conviction that Ireland would be at this moment a more happy and more prosperous country than it now is if the Union of 1800 had not taken place ... the cry for Repeal is not the voice of treason, but the language of despair.' He did 'often doubt' if his search for a 'perfect union' was 'consistent with the duty which I owe to the country possessing the first claim upon my devotion'. He made a final appeal that showed he could still turn either way:

> Still, however, I cling to the hope of good government from a British Parliament. When that hope is extinct, I shall not fear to contemplate the remaining alternative; nor, if I should be compelled to espouse the cause of Repeal, shall I be the least earnest of its advocates. I have satisfied myself that it is practicable – I have satisfied myself that it is consistent with the

Peel to de Grey, 24 July 1843. 88 Earl of Ilchester (ed.), *Elizabeth, Lady Holland to her son, 1821-1845* (London, 1946), 209, Holland to son, 3 July 1843. 89 Wyse Papers, MS 15019 (10), Wyse to George Wyse, 31 July 1843. 90 *DEP*, 29 June, 8 July 1843. 91 MacIntyre, *The Liberator*, 273. 92 *Hansard*, lxx, 1088-92, 12 July 1843, Division. Benjamin Chapman voted against the motion but subsequently explained that this was an accident. *DEP*, 15 July 1843.

allegiance which I owe to my Sovereign. Looking to the future, rather than to the past, I am not yet fully satisfied that it is equally advantageous to Ireland as such an union as I have described. Give to us, then, who still cling to the legislative connexion, with the hope of obtaining justice at your hands, but with the determination that if it be withheld, our country shall command our services – give us, by your decision this night, something which we may present to our fellow-countrymen, as a pledge of your disposition to repair the many wrongs which have been inflicted upon Ireland – give us arguments which we may address to them, when they tell us of the many instances which prove that Ireland has lost much and gained little by the Union.[93]

A fortnight earlier, O'Brien had written in similar terms and revealed publicly that he had come to Parliament that session to try for just one more year to secure useful legislation for Ireland. Though disappointed so far, he had not yet given up hope, he claimed, of redress within the Union.[94] He told Lucy, however, that he had 'little doubt' the majority against his motion would be 'very great' and 'that consequently we shall be compelled to fall back upon agitation in Ireland for the redress of Irish grievances'.[95] In private conversation with Wyse, O'Brien showed considerable respect for the repealers. When Wyse doubted O'Connell's determination to withstand coercion, O'Brien assured him that there was 'virtue and resolution enough in Ireland even *without* O'C. to carry on most effectively the moral force system of agitation. Were the Habeas Corpus Act tomorrow suspended he would at once take all risks and march to prison as cheerfully as to dinner. Hundreds he says would do the same ... and this followed generally would render a government however violent comparatively ineffective ... It is possible,' thought Wyse, 'that in the present excited state of Ireland it might be so, but I doubt much whether it would *last* ...'[96]

The great debate on O'Brien's motion produced no conciliatory statements of the sort urged by O'Brien, and the eventual result on 12 July was defeat by 79 votes. However, with some Tories speaking out 'for Ireland and *against* the Church', Wyse celebrated 'the sense of insecurity which it has introduced in the hostile camp, and the divided air it gives to the [Tory] party before the public ... it is amazing how rapidly and thoroughly the Conservatives out of the House at least are coming round ...' Indeed, the emergence of Tory calls for a more conciliatory policy caused Graham to fear the government had 'an uphill battle to fight, if indeed we still retain the confidence of the House of Commons'. Wyse believed that, 'Even the Cabinet is not unanimous'. He had heard that Gladstone and Wellington both opposed the wait-and-see response to the Irish crisis, and, painting a remarkable

---

93 *Hansard*, lxx, 630-77, 4 July 1843, O'Brien.   94 *DEM*, 28 June 1843, O'Brien to Maher, 20 June 1843.   95 Smith O'Brien Papers, MS 8653 (19), O'Brien to Lucy O'Brien, 21 June 1843. See also ibid., MS 22363, O'Brien to Lucy O'Brien, n.d.   96 Wyse Papers, MS 15019 (10), Wyse to George Wyse, 3 July 1843.

picture of disunity, he reported that, 'Last night Stanley was taking notes to answer Graham. Peel took them out of his *hand*. He did not speak, and the debate went off without a single Government speech, except ... the Attorney General's.'[97]

In addition, the stock of the liberal-unionists was raised in Ireland. This was especially true for O'Brien. He received numerous laudatory letters, mostly from repealers, and O'Connell had the Repeal Association congratulate him on his 'able, statesmanlike and manly speech'. O'Brien complied with the request for a copy of his speech and it was duly published by the Association. John O'Connell expressed his 'admiration of your conduct throughout this session'. O'Shaughnessy wrote that 'every Irishman, and above all every Limerick man, is proud of you. Your name is spoken of in terms of praise from one end of the kingdom to the other ...'[98] If O'Brien had been interested solely in popularity and acclamation, he had only to continue the Parliamentary campaign of the summer of 1843. Great progress had been made. O'Brien, Wyse and the liberal-unionists had established themselves as the leaders of a vigorous assault on Peel's Irish policy, contributing to divisions and uncertainty among the Tories and winning respect from many quarters. They had taken admirable advantage of a movement (repeal) whose motives they understood even if they did not subscribe to its conclusions. However, the campaign had not yet achieved a change in the way Ireland was governed. In fact, it was soon evident that the liberal-unionists themselves could not unite behind a simple statement of ideas on the future government of their country. The rhetoric of debate was one thing. The task of formulating a liberal-unionist reform programme was to prove less rewarding, and it was this that finally drove O'Brien to repeal.

In July–August 1843, following up on the success of the debate, the liberal-unionists sought to rouse opinion in Britain on the need to respond to the repeal agitation by removing the grievances on which it fed. They did not attend a 17 July meeting of Marylebone constituents on the state of Ireland; as Wyse wrote, 'it would only look too much like *imploring sympathy* ... We stand and are determined to stand on far higher ground. We speak as the organs of a Nation to a Nation and call not for *favours* but *rights*.'[99] O'Brien approached Russell and proposed that there should be 'meetings in town & country in support of a liberal policy towards Ireland'.[100] Towards this, he and Wyse prepared a requisition for a general meeting of Whig and liberal MPs. This document, Wyse reported, was adopted on 17 July by 'a preliminary meeting of a few Irish MPs' who, Ireland 'having been denied

---

97 Ibid., Wyse to George Wyse, 11 July 1843. Graham Papers, 9IR, Graham to de Grey, 12 July 1843. The Tory dissentients in debate were Rous, Lascelles, Cochrane, Manners and Smythe, and the last three ('Young Englanders') voted against the government in the division. **98** Smith O'Brien Papers, MS 432, f1019, Staunton to O'Brien, 6 July; ff1021, 1029, 1034, Ray to O'Brien, 7, 14, 21 July; f1025, Powell to O'Brien, 9 July; f1030, John O'Connell to O'Brien, 17 July; f1031, O'Shaughnessy to O'Brien, 18 July 1843. **99** Wyse Papers, MS 15019 (10) Wyse to George Wyse [17 July 1843]. **100** Broadlands MSS, GC/RU/74, Russell to Palmerston, 15 July 1843.

justice by Parlt. & Ministers', now wished to appeal to the MPs and electors of Britain. Wyse believed that, 'Most of the English and all the Irish with the exception of O'F[errall] highly approve. Even Lord John thinks it right & expedient.' 19 Irish Members signed the requisition.[101] The meeting at the Reform Club on 18 July was attended by nearly 100 MPs. It did not go well. Palmerston, Wood, Bernal and others argued against the Irish proposal of public meetings in Britain. Russell proved to be 'too cunning to commit himself' when it was suggested that he should declare in Parliament what he would do for Ireland if again in office. The Whigs were happy to denounce Tory policy but reluctant to pledge themselves to specific remedies.[102]

However, it was in preparing the long-intended manifesto of liberal-unionism that the heart-breaking problems would occur. O'Brien and Wyse worked on the 'solemn remonstrance' of the liberal-unionist Members to the British people. All, according to Wyse on 29 July, was 'going on well' when the document was 'concocting still between O'B. and self'.[103] Then, when they held a series of private meetings with other liberal-unionists, the disagreements began: 'O'Brien and I have been indefatigable in preparing the *Remonstrance* – for such we *now* are resolved to call it – and not Address, Appeal, etc. You have little idea of the difficulties we have had to contend with on *all* sides – & the patience and perseverance requisite to overcome them'. Each member of the steering committee of five – Wyse himself, who chaired the meetings, O'Brien, Villiers Stuart, Ross and Morgan John O'Connell – prepared drafts, O'Brien was charged 'to melt them into each other', and there followed lengthy discussions between the five principals and, on 31 July, within a broader circle of liberal-unionist Members. The principal annoyance at first was O'Ferrall's opposition to 'the whole proceeding – [he] thought it could answer no possible purpose, no one would sign it, it would be torn in pieces by O'Connell – finally were we prepared if our party came in to adopt it? ... We laughed openly at his idea of its embarrassing *a future ministry* ... [He is] under the tow of his master instead of *above* it and more *servile* than even what is demanded by his former and future superior', Russell. There is a suggestion here, reinforcing the lesson of the July 18 meeting, that the Whig leaders were wary of any statement that could assume the character of a manifesto they would be expected to fulfil in office. Wyse was imperious and dismissive – '*We at least shall have done our duty*' – but O'Brien slid quickly into disillusionment. Regarding O'Ferrall, Wyse noted, 'Even O'Brien is sometimes disgusted by his paltry, truckling, insidious conduct, and almost tempted to give up'.[104] On 1 August, others raised objections, leaving O'Brien 'quite out of patience, & had he anticipated so much cavil & opposi-

---

101 Wyse Papers, MS 15019 (10), Wyse to George Wyse [17 July 1843]. Smith O'Brien Papers, MS 22352, Requisition, To the Liberal Members of the House of Commons, July 1843. G.P. Gooch (ed.), *The Later Correspondence of Lord John Russell, 1840-1878* (London, 1925), i, 64, Russell to Lansdowne, 19 July 1843. 102 *DEM*, 21 July 1843 (the 'too cunning' line). *DEP*, 25 July 1843. Gooch. *Later Correspondence*, i, 64, Russell to Lansdowne, 19 July 1843. 103 Wyse Papers, MS 15019 (10), Wyse to George Wyse, 29 July 1843. 104 Ibid., Wyse to George Wyse, 31 July 1843.

Repeal 99

tion [he] would never have undertaken it'. Wyse 'laugh[ed] at his want of experience', but even he now doubted 'whether we shall have more than 15 or 20' signatories.[105]

Three days later, Wyse shed more light on their difficulties:

> We are proceeding in our good work, but am sorry to say amidst much disagreement and obstacle. O'Brien was with me early yesterday with the 'Remonstrance' ... Our numerous changes have greatly improved it, and I now think, tho' in many points not so strong as he and I would have desired, yet as strong as we could (to meet others) make it, and on the whole more vigorous than from what early conversations with our party & others we had reason to expect [*sic*]. We had two paragraphs on the *Financial* question, which appeared to O'Brien and me very important if not essential, but after very long discussions on all its bearings, we were left by the Committee in a minority of two (he and I) and obliged to withdraw it. The paragraph also with reference to the Repeal was more precise and energetic. Villiers Stuart proposed an amendment which softened it considerably down, and which, in order to gain general acquiescence, was also conceded. It still stands however a manifesto of which no Irishman not a Tory need be ashamed, and with many points on which even Tories must coincide.
>
> As Chairman, and for the trouble I had taken throughout, O'Brien requested me to take the first place in signing it, and at all hazard of sounding jealous, I thought it right to do so. I fixed my name, and he his – and [*we*] undertook to get the signatures of the other members in the House. We agreed also on a circular to be addressed to absent members for their names on authority to sign ...[106]

O'Brien's papers contain four printed drafts of the Remonstrance, two of them heavily annotated by O'Brien. The changes reported by Wyse were significant. O'Brien deleted (and wrote 'Postponed' beside) a paragraph demanding that Ireland's 'financial relations' with Britain should be 'defined' and 'adjusted' in order that the Irish 'may no longer have reason to believe that their condition in relation to financial interests is less favourable than it would be if the Union were abrogated'. The warning near the end that 'every day's delay' strengthened repeal was initially a more forceful contention that 'the time is fast approaching, if it be not already past, when no alternative except the restoration of their Parliament will satisfy the majority of the Irish nation'.[107] The final version was a clear statement of the grievances advanced in Parliament (and in Ireland) throughout the summer. The privileged position of the Church of Ireland, the restrictive municipal and Parliamentary franchises, the failure to appoint a fair proportion of Catholics to public office and the

---

105 Ibid., Wyse to George Wyse, 1 August 1843. 106 Ibid., Wyse to George Wyse, 4 August 1843.
107 Smith O'Brien Papers, MS 433, ff1048, 1048a, 1048b, 1048c.

state of landlord-tenant relations featured prominently. The poor law was not mentioned, almost certainly because the MPs were hopelessly divided on the issue. There is a suggestion of more agreement on Ireland's grievances than upon remedies, with the latter discussed only briefly and in general terms. However, each remedy was prefaced with a bold 'We demand'; and on several points the document was forthright, albeit vague, notably in requiring 'perfect equality' between the different religions in Ireland.

The hope that the Remonstrance would serve as the manifesto of liberal-unionism and O'Brien's adherence to the latter as a viable option were greatly undermined when Wyse and O'Brien sought the signatures of the other liberal-unionist MPs. As Wyse wrote,

> On going down to the House about 7, I found O'Brien much disappointed. He had been able to procure very *few* names. Even those who had first approved hesitated. V. Stuart, who had been with us in all the discussions, and had drawn up [a draft of] an Address himself, doubted. Lord Clements refused me plump ... saying it was a proceeding he did not approve of, did not like parts ... Somerville ... said he agreed with every word, an excellent document, but it would do no good – it put us in a false position and [ ] would not sign it. O'Connor Don, who had also taken part in our councils, had declined – Repeal out? – (it would be attacked by O'Connell – this the true motive) – and would not sign. Sheil, who had *promised* the *day before* & had *highly* approved the movement to me – as well as O'Brien – 'would sign if O'Brien wished it, to oblige him', but O'Brien purposely and indignantly refused. O'F[errall] of course not only will not, but is laughing and enjoying the refusals. Carew hesitated, but I succeeded in showing him how *innocent* at least the proceeding was – it was not more than each and all had been saying in their speeches and addresses to constituents and would have to say, and much more, again – he signed. Notwithstanding all this, we have succeeded in getting 15 signatures so far, and I think we may hope for 10 more. But this is not what ought to have been the case. The universal representation on our side of the House should have signed it. They will yet have to regret their pusillanimous conduct, to give it no more unkindly or truer name.
>
> I make no comment on the conduct of these men, but I observed to O'B., who was much annoyed and indignant at such tergiversation, that this was too much the case with our Irish politicians & he would not be surprised if he knew them as well as I did. We have every courage but moral courage – that we want. He said, had he anticipated half what he had met or experienced from our own side, he never would have touched the subject. I would – & time will prove me right ... As I often say to O'Brien, '*Fais ce que dois*' ...[108]

---

[108] Wyse Papers, MS 15019 (10), Wyse to George Wyse, 4 August 1843.

Wyse, a veteran of the struggle for Catholic Emancipation, clearly considered himself more experienced and worldly than O'Brien, and it is possible that the latter's personal aloofness had not helped him to come to know his colleagues. Many factors made Members reluctant to sign the Remonstrance. Some apparently felt it was no more than an empty gesture that would achieve nothing in practice. O'Connell's scornful reaction – the likelihood he would 'carve document and signers without mercy'[109] – was feared by MPs who knew the man's power to sway their constituents. The idea of signing a pledge was difficult to reconcile with the desire of independent Members to retain a free hand; Clements, for example, 'did not like to afford his signature to a pledge!!'[110] Finally, to Wyse's disgust, some were afraid of embarrassing and alienating the British Whig leaders, the future 'ministerialists' whose patronage the likes of Sheil and More O'Ferrall wished to cultivate. Wyse, himself a man who might have aspired to another period in office under the Whigs, stood on the high ground: ' ... now is the time to speak out,' he told Sheil, 'and let there be no doubt or question of the matter'. As for O'Connell, 'it is *right* in the face of a thousand O'Connells. But we are not such fools as to leave it in doubt. O'Connor Don has been induced to write to him [O'Connell], in forwarding the circular, and should he not sign request at least his neutrality.'[111]

H.G. Ward, the English radical, tried to revive the question of appropriation of Irish Church revenues, but his motion was counted out on 2 August. Wyse commented, 'We were astounded at the catastrophe'. O'Brien suffered further frustration when he made several futile attempts to amend the (much delayed) poor law amendment bill.[112] But it was the struggle over the Remonstrance that seemed to demoralise him completely. On 8 August, Wyse revealed that O'Brien was almost decided on conversion to repeal:

> O'Brien is *impatient* and can't endure any longer delay. I had him with me three hours on Sunday in Kensington Gardens. We were talking over every bearing of this most momentous subject – and agreeing on all but one. He is *decided* on leaving Parlt. and throwing himself into the Repeal movement in November, if nothing be done in the interval by the Govt ... I have done all I could to change this resolution – but he is more than firm – obstinate. He is sick of begging – and will beg no longer – ten years he has been doing, and without avail, nothing else. He will bring the matter soon to a crisis – though he is sacrificed, and sacrificed he must be, in the attempt.

Wyse counselled against the move. It would damage the credibility of liberal-unionism – they could all be dismissed as 'Repealers in transition' – and 'sow distrust amongst our own body, as you must perceive not by any means subdued – and go far I am afraid to break us up altogether as a party. I shall feel it particularly, for on him and one or two more only can I thoroughly rely.' Wyse failed to shake

---

109 Ibid., Wyse to George Wyse, 4 August 1843 (second letter).   110 Ibid.   111 Ibid.   112 Ibid. *Hansard*, lxxi, 228, 235, 322, 560, 3, 4, 7, 11 August 1843, O'Brien.

O'Brien out of either his pessimism or his sense of obligation, apparent on so many occasions, to do what was 'right':

> I am greatly afraid he [*O'Brien*] has more enthusiasm than experience. I expressed to him the want of *heart* and *soul* and *honesty* and *honour* and *firmness* of the men with whom he was about to unite. His only answer was, 'Is it right? – I have been considering all that and will not be deterred from fixing a course because of its supporters. I have done my duty for *two years now unceasingly* ... We have *no hope* from *anything else.*' I endeavoured to show how much had been gained and how much *more might ere long*. Nothing made [*an*] impression and I am sure you will see his declaration ere long.
>
> Should such be the case, O'F[*errall*] and S[*heil*] and the rest will set the whole down to vanity and interpret all the Remonstrance movement as a mere trick. He and I the workers, the other Irish members the dupes. No matter, they have *no right* to judge him. They cannot understand *such a man*.[113]

The respect Wyse had for O'Brien's unimpeachable integrity could not have been stated more strongly than in those last three words.

As Wyse anticipated, O'Connell did not inveigh against the Remonstrance. The final list of signatures delighted Wyse; 29 liberal members signed, 14 in London, the rest in response to circulars. All but two (Henry Grattan and Sir David Roche) were liberal-unionists. But Wyse now doubted the document's likely impact: 'I am not very anxious on the matter, it is more in the view of a historic document, to which we may hereafter have frequently to recur, both in and out of Parliament, as justification of future proceedings, than as an appeal designed or likely to produce immediate and especially popular effect, that I think it of value.'[114] These remarks, perhaps reflecting the disillusioning effect of all the problems they had faced, seem at odds with earlier hopes that the Remonstrance, as the culmination of the skilful manoeuvres of the liberal-unionists in Parliament, would sway British public opinion. In fact, the reaction of the British and Irish press was disappointing, almost desultory. Charles Gavan Duffy, the editor of the *Nation* newspaper, subsequently wrote that, 'The address was probably as little heeded as the appeals and remonstrances of Hancock and Franklin to the British nation two generations earlier; it was scarcely published in the government organs and found no echo even in the Whig press'[115]

Wyse struggled still with O'Brien:

> ... I strenuously continue to advise him to keep his position and work on for at least another session ... I cautioned him as to the results of his step ... I know *the men* too well; whatever the mass of the people may be, their

---

113 Wyse Papers, MS 15019 (10), Wyse to George Wyse, 8 August 1843.   114 Ibid., Wyse to George Wyse, 15 August 1843.   115 Duffy, *Young Ireland, 1840-1845*, 124.

chiefs are hollowness ... and not a set with whom O'B. can or ought to work. He knows nothing of them and suspects nothing. He has very *little experience* indeed of the vileness and iniquity of these underhand politicians and is of too confiding & frank a spirit not to take every thing they say for granted. He would be their leader & then their victim. Whether my eloquence or his wife's has worked the wonder, he has at last promised he will not only do *nothing* before November, but keep altogether out of the way – and for that purpose is about to set out at once to Germany ... Should Parlt. not meet however in Nov. he means he says to join the Association ... My plan is quite other. I never was less in love with Repeal.[116]

He went on to conjure up a frightful image of 'the hundred-headed tyranny' that would follow repeal. Another liberal-unionist Member, David Pigot, regretted 'the tone of despondency' in O'Brien's letter to him. He opined that the 'suspension of your Parliamentary service would be, indeed, a grievous calamity' given 'the high position in public life which you have acquired ... No, my dear O'Brien, such men as you are not *their own property*, to give to their country or to withhold from it.'[117] O'Brien's standing among his colleagues was clearly considerable. Wyse's comments on his naive appreciation of the repealers seem strange after O'Brien's struggles against O'Connell and such as Costelloe, Steele and Barrett. Until 1843, his principled stand against O'Connell was probably the most notable (and admirable) aspect of his political career. Yet there was percipience in what Wyse wrote. O'Brien would never regret his conversion to repeal but he would eventually despair of the repealers. There is much, even, to be said for the idea that he became 'their leader & then their victim'.

On 18 August, somewhat bizarrely, O'Brien sent Queen Victoria (through the Home Secretary) and Prince Albert copies of his now-published state of Ireland speech.[118] On the same day, he wrote a short but important note to his sister, Anne Martineau, telling her he was about to travel to Germany: 'I am anxious to get out of the way of Politics for a few weeks being tired to death after six months of unavailing toil ... it is not my intention to return to the Brit. Ho. Comm. after the expiration of the present year. I cannot afford to waste my life in fruitless efforts to serve my country & I have long been of opinion that I should be more useful at home.'[119] He duly left for Europe on 20 August. Despite what he told Wyse and his sister, the trip was not merely to 'keep altogether out of the way'; he had attended German lessons twice a week between April and June.[120] He travelled through Belgium and Germany for almost two months. The comments in his journal, focusing as they

---

116 Wyse Papers, MS 15019 (10), Wyse to George Wyse, 15 August 1843.   117 Smith O'Brien Papers, MS 440, f2131, Pigot to O'Brien, 19 August [1843].   118 Ibid., MS 433, f1063, O'Brien to Graham, 18 August 1843; f1064, O'Brien to Prince Albert, 18 August 1843.   119 Ibid., MS 18310 (2), O'Brien to Anne Martineau, 18 August 1843.   120 Ibid., MS 454, Rough Diary, 27 April-22 June 1843.

do on industry, farming, architecture and education, remind the reader of the essentially practical nature of his interests. On 22 September, he visited the Hungarian Diet at Pressburg (now Bratislava) but, as it met only once a year and was far from representative, he found it no model for an Irish legislature.[121]

On 11 October, O'Brien sailed from Hamburg ('At sea. Purgatory' was his diary entry for 12 October) and travelled by Hull and Liverpool to Dublin. There, on 18 October, he called on O'Connell at his town house in Merrion Square – 'I waited upon him at his private residence for the first time in my life' – before proceeding to Cahirmoyle.[122] During his absence the government had struck at O'Connell. It banned the monster meeting planned for Clontarf on 8 October, and O'Connell was arrested and charged with conspiracy. The answer to discontent, it seemed, was to be coercion. On 20 October, three days after his 40th birthday, O'Brien sent in his subscription to the Repeal Association. In his letter to secretary Ray, he cited the 14 years of 'misgovernment' since Emancipation and the 'neglect, ridicule, or defiance' with which the Remonstrance was received as reasons for his conversion, and the Clontarf proclamation as the decisive factor. At public dinners in Limerick in November and December, he claimed that 'it was the proclamation of the Clontarf meeting that made me avow myself a Repealer'.[123] But it is clear from his letters to Lucy (and Wyse's letter of 8 August) that O'Brien was almost decided on joining the repealers long before Clontarf. A factor which O'Brien did not publicise was his disappointment in his own colleagues; he was sickened by the negotiations with the liberal-unionists over the Remonstrance. Of course, it went deeper than this. He had grown tired of seeking measures from a Parliament which had 'little knowledge of Irish wants, and still less disposition to provide' for them.[124] The words he used to his sister on 18 August – 'unavailing toil', 'fruitless efforts' – were to be a constant refrain in his speeches over the next few years. In 1841 and 1842, he had thought of quietly departing the scene. 1843 was different. The sense of crisis created by the extraordinary agitation in Ireland made every Irish politician, as well as Peel and many of the British, think as never before about Ireland's needs. O'Brien, with that inbred sense of duty, could no longer walk away, and having failed to find the answers in London he would now look to a domestic legislature.

---

121 O'Brien Papers (AO), Journal of the Tour of Europe, August-October 1843. See also Smith O'Brien Papers, MS 433, f1081, Greig to O'Brien, 20 November 1843, for Greig's light-hearted comments on O'Brien's 'meteor flight' through Europe. 122 Ibid., MS 454, Rough Diary, 11-19 October 1843. The visit to O'Connell was referred to by O'Brien in a public letter in December 1846. *Nation*, 2 January 1847, O'Brien to Miley, 23 December 1846. 123 *DEP*, 24 October 1843, O'Brien to Ray, 20 October 1843. *FJ*, 6 November, 6 December 1843. 124 *Hansard*, lxx, 675, 4 July 1843, O'Brien.

5

The Living Treasure

O'Brien's accession was warmly welcomed by repealers. There was much rhetoric to the effect that 'the proper place for the descendant of the Hero of Clontarf is at the head of Irishmen'.[1] In the Association, O'Connell read out O'Brien's letter – it was on the occasion of the opening of Conciliation Hall – and talked of 'an event of the utmost importance – an event noting the progress of a cultivated and patriotic public man'. Accepting an invitation to attend a public dinner in Limerick for O'Brien, he wrote that, 'He has done the best possible service, at the fittest possible time ...'; at the dinner, he expressed his 'delight' at the accession of a man of such 'talent and virtue'. He also acknowledged their past differences and said that 'a more independent man I never witnessed in parliament'.[2] John O'Connell, the Liberator's son and political protégé, told O'Brien that 'few events of my life have ever afforded me such sincere delight as your accession to our good cause'.[3]

However, his conversion caused damage elsewhere. In 1843, Wyse and O'Brien had tried to lead an effective Commons opposition of which any ministry would have to take account. This would establish liberal-unionism as the vehicle by which conciliation of Ireland's grievances could be achieved in the British Parliament. Success would both stem the repeal tide and end 'Orange misrule'. Other liberal-unionists clearly shared these aims and pursued them with great determination, notably in the tremendous campaign against the arms bill. The mixed response to the Remonstrance suggests that the hopes for an effective party, for the sort of long-term effort that Parnell and his followers later sustained, were not well founded. But the prospect of another Parliamentary campaign was virtually destroyed when one of its principal figures, O'Brien, effectively pronounced that of 1843 a failure. In 1844-5, liberal-unionists remained active in Parliament, but there was not another attempt to form a cohesive party and such leadership as existed was provided by Russell and the British Whigs. Wyse felt no bitterness about O'Brien's decision, assuring him on 24 November that,

---

[1] Smith O'Brien Papers, MS 433, f1067, Raleigh to O'Brien, 22 October 1843. See also ibid., f1088, Resolutions of the Albany Irish Repeal Association, 23 November 1843. [2] *FJ*, 24 October, 6 December 1843. Smith O'Brien Papers, MS 433, f1084, O'Connell to Raleigh, 25 November 1843. [3] Ibid., f1083, John O'Connell to O'Brien, 22 November 1843. See also ibid., f1073, Ray to O'Brien, 25 October 1843.

however we may differ on the urgency or justice of the grounds which have induced you to it, of this I am as sure as I am of my own life, that it is the result of deepest conviction, noblest self-sacrifice, and thorough love of country – which few in this jobbing, party-humbug age can appreciate, much less practise, and which far from requiring any apology, deserves praise, at least has *mine* and ever will have it.[4]

A few weeks later, Wyse defended O'Brien to one of their mutual friends, Sir Denham Norreys (formerly C.D.O. Jephson), but there was a suggestion that O'Brien's impulsiveness had defeated his own ends:

> I am sorry, with you, our friend O'Brien took the *extrême gauche* course he did, but acquit him of all design on your and my orthodoxy ... don't imagine the *Remonstrance* was a ruse to lure us on in the same path. He is too direct, honest and honourable for that. His faults (errors I should call them) lie in the opposite way. He has not the experience or at least acquaintance we have with his new colleagues, nor weighs well chances, means and above all consequences of the achievement of their projects. Had he continued to fight the battle he had begun so well last Session with patience and endurance, he would have been nearer to the accomplishment of his desires than he can ever be under the banner under which he now serves.[5]

Lord Palmerston displayed his cynicism – and an entire ignorance of the real position – writing, 'I see Smith O'Brien is said to have declared himself a Repealer. These Irish members from the south are obliged to yield to the feelings of their constituents, and such conversions therefore mean just nothing at all, but that the converts wish to keep their seats'. Lord Monteagle, a man whose connections with Limerick should have led to his knowing better, came to a similar conclusion: there were many, he claimed, who supported repeal 'believing it never can be carried' but hoping for some personal advantage, perhaps that they might 'retain their seats in Parliament undisturbed – the latest specimen of this low selfishness is Mr Smith O'Brien'.[6] O'Brien's mother was distressed by his 'selfish & reckless' action in declaring himself 'a Rebel & a supporter of Rebels'. Her long letter on the subject gives an idea of the shock induced by O'Brien's decision. It also shows that O'Brien lacked the sensitivity to deliver the news in an appropriate manner, not that 'C. O'Brien', his 'fondly attached mother', appears an approachable confidante.

> Dromoland. Oct. 24th '43
> My dear William
> Your kind note gave me great pleasure when I received it yesterday & I was beginning to calculate how soon I might have the pleasure of seeing you &

---

4 Ibid., f1085, Wyse to O'Brien, 24 November 1843. 5 Jephson, *Anglo-Irish Miscellany*, 230-1, Wyse to Norreys, 10 January 1844. 6 Russell Papers, PRO 30/22/4C, f89, Palmerston to Russell, 22 October 1843. Monteagle Papers, MS 13394 (5), Monteagle to Napier, 7 December 1843.

Lucy & your dear children at that place [*Cahirmoyle*] in which I so much like to dwell for a little time every year, when the enclosed paragraph from the Times in conjunction with your letter to Lucius dispelled the delusion. And now what can I say to my dear child but to warn him once more as to the course he is pursuing.

I have long seen & felt the great evil of the repeal agitation to my *poor countrymen* & even a child must know that nothing but misery & wretchedness and increased want of employment could follow a separation between Great Britain & Ireland even supposing it to be effected without bloodshed, anarchy & confusion. But the Queen's speech & the late proceedings here put beyond all doubt the light in which the attempt to bring it about is to be regarded, and it is most selfish & reckless & heartless towards your wife & children, to say nothing of yr. mother & brothers, and sisters, to proclaim yourself a Rebel & a supporter of Rebels when up to the present time you were known not to be a repealer. This act of yours my dear William if it be accomplished (which God forbid it is) places all your Friends & especially your affectionately attached mother, in a most painful situation & there is no saying what the consequence of it may be to yourself & to yr. Family. I will not however anticipate evil but simply give this warning – That I never will either directly or indirectly pay a shilling towards the defence of a state prosecution – and must defer signing the settlement I was going to make for your children until a sufficient length of time has passed to give me full assurance that there is no danger your property may be confiscated.

Farewell. If you pursue the course announced in the paper you will bring down my grey head with sorrow to the grave, but however sorrowing I shall never cease to be your fondly attached mother.

C. O'Brien[7]

The evidence is incomplete but it is likely that not a single member of O'Brien's family approved of his becoming a repealer. O'Brien did not always go to Dromoland for Christmas, but on those occasions when he stayed at Cahirmoyle a visit to Dromoland soon followed. This did not happen in 1843, and it is reasonable to assume that his mother wished it so. On Christmas Day, she made 'one effort more to separate my beloved child from the unholy association' he had formed with men who sought 'the destruction of that form of religion which renounces their [Catholic] errors, and teaches us to worship God in spirit & in Truth ... not in forms & ceremonies & vain delusions   This is probably the last time I shall prefer any request on this subject ... May God's peace & blessing rest upon your house at this Holy season – & may He, with the strength of His Holy Arm, deliver you from the grasp of that enemy who desires to take you captive at his will that he may destroy both body & soul'.[8]

---

7 Smith O'Brien Papers, MS 433, f1071, Lady O'Brien to O'Brien, 24 October 1843.   8 Ibid., f1093, Lady O'Brien to O'Brien, 25 December 1843.

It was not an appeal that was likely to succeed with a man who spent the festive season writing about rather different convictions. In a public letter, his first significant contribution to the repeal cause, he outlined his vision of an independent parliament with 'unlimited powers of legislation in regard to the concerns of Ireland', including decisions on trade and war. The Crown would 'retain all its prerogatives', but it would appoint Irish ministers who would be responsible to the parliament in Dublin. Far from involving the 'catastrophe' of full separation, by compelling Britain to regard Ireland with greater 'respect and consideration' the new arrangement would strengthen the ties already implicit in a host of personal connections and mutual interests. Indeed, it would stop them heading towards the fate that befell Belgium and Holland in the previous decade, separated after a revolt by Belgians who believed that the union had failed to honour their interests.[9] It was an informed and well-argued piece, as cogent as anything written on the constitutional implications of repeal, and it suggests that O'Brien acted with head as well as heart when he gave up on the Union.

It was into the business of agitation that O'Brien would now throw all his energies. In 1844 he at last became a politician of first-rank importance. He took a principal role in the Repeal Association from the moment of his first appearance there on 22 January 1844.[10] He 'became by common consent the second man in the movement', and, during the Liberator's imprisonment in May-September 1844, 'by the express desire of O'Connell the leadership was entrusted to Smith O'Brien'.[11] He remained in Ireland throughout, focusing all his efforts on the Association. Thomas Wyse had hoped for a renewal of Parliamentary campaigning and was encouraged by O'Brien's letter of November 1843 proposing a resumption of Wyse's 'old line of operations, with a view to a junction between all'. He informed O'Brien that 'a strong movement might be made, and with effect, for the country ... The arms bill debate revealed to us and the House our real power. If we could only get 60 members, as you say, to work as we did for the last two months of the last session from the *first* day to the *last* of next, we might have some hope of seeing our Remonstrance embodied in useful measures ...' Wyse planned a meeting of all Irish liberal Members, repealers and unionists, in the Reform Club a few days before Parliament re-opened in January 1844. 'It would be out of the shadow of the Conciliation Hall, which some amongst us dread ...'[12] O'Brien, however, envisaged such a meeting in *Dublin*, where agreement on 'practical legislation' could be forged

---

9 William Smith O'Brien, *A Letter of William Smith O'Brien, Esq., M.P., in reply to the Letter of the Rev. T. O'Malley* (Dublin, 1844). Smith O'Brien Papers, MS 454, Rough Diary, 20, 21, 22, 23 December 1843.   10 He was greeted with 'tumultuous enthusiasm', young Thomas Meagher noted. Michael Cavanagh, *Memoirs of Gen. Thomas Francis Meagher* (Worcester, Mass., 1892), 38-43.   11 Sir Charles Gavan Duffy, *Thomas Davis: The Memoirs of an Irish Patriot, 1840-1846* (London, 1890), 188, 213. Duffy, *Young Ireland, 1840-1845*, 175.   12 Wyse Papers MS 15019 (10), Wyse to George Wyse, 17 November 1843. Smith O'Brien Papers, MS 433, f1085, Wyse to O'Brien, 24 November 1843.

and then presented in Parliament not by 'individuals, speaking their own private sentiments', but by representatives of the collected 'public opinion' of Ireland. In an important statement of his views, he explained that he would not cross again to Westminster:

> With regard to myself I must repeat what I told you in London, viz. that it is not my intention to beg any more from the British Legislature. I shall take every opportunity of letting the British Government & Parliament know what we think ought to be done but I will waste no more time in vainly seeking from Parliamentary debate measures which I am sure will only be yielded to fear. Without pledging myself to any irrevocable determination it is my present intention not to go over to the meeting of Parliament ... I am persuaded that our voice will be much more potent when reinforced by the public opinion of Ireland than it would be if spoken in the House of Commons. Experience has taught us that Government will yield nothing to reason & that the Whigs will make no move on behalf of our interests except they fancy that it conduces to their own party interests ...[13]

Only to resist a coercion bill would he go to London. The prospect of a Dublin meeting foundered on Wyse's fear that it would look like an attempt to influence the jury in the coming State Prosecution of O'Connell and his belief that many liberal-unionists were reluctant to unite with the repealers: 'it would end either in wider rupture or a milk & water affair.'[14] Wyse duly circularised the liberal Members to urge attendance at Parliament, but O'Brien wrote to the Association, from Cahirmoyle, that the repeal MPs should adopt 'an attitude of national dignity' at home in Ireland, 'instead of crouching for ever as humble and despised petitioners' at Westminster. This sort of language underlines the impact on O'Brien of the failure of his massive efforts of 1843. O'Connell, Ray informed him, 'entirely' agreed on the stay-away strategy.[15]

O'Brien's first impressions of the Repeal Association were encouraging. He was 'warmly received', the weekly meetings were 'animating' and 'exciting', and he found 'better elements for useful exertion than I expected. There are a vast number of respectable and intelligent men cooperating with this movement who require nothing but opportunities for developing their talents & patriotism. So far as I can perceive every thing is fair & open & I do not anticipate any counteraction from selfishness or jealousy. Ours is indeed a noble mission and if the population abstain from violence it must be productive of the best results to Ireland ...' He 'perceive[d] everywhere a rising spirit of nationality'. All this was written to Lucy, whose scepticism

---

13 Wyse Papers, MS 15019 (10), Smith O'Brien to Wyse, 27 November 1843. See also Jephson, *Anglo-Irish Miscellany*, 230, O'Brien to Norreys, 28 April 1844 (misdated 1841). 14 Smith O'Brien Papers, MS 433, f1102, Wyse to O'Brien, 2 January 1844. See also ibid., f1100, Chapman to O'Brien, January 1844. 15 *FJ*, 16 January 1844, O'Brien to Ray, 12 January 1844. Smith O'Brien Papers, MS 433, f1113, Ray to O'Brien, 17 January 1844.

he tried to drown in a sea of optimism. He even suggested that she should 'thank the Repeal cause' that he was now only a few hours away from Cahirmoyle: 'Is not that consideration enough to make you a Repealer?' It was not. In mid-February, after O'Connell's conviction put her 'in such a fright' and made her 'a trembler for my husband', he had to assure her that while he would use 'bold language' he would not get himself arrested or do anything 'unworthy of a loyal subject'.[16]

Many repeal MPs did not attend the Association regularly (some hardly at all), and both Wyse and John O'Connell had doubted if O'Brien wanted much involvement in its labours.[17] In fact, he was intent on applying himself and became an ever-active man of business. In seven months between January and August 1844, he spoke 30 times in the Association, emerging as its main speaker during O'Connell's absences in England (February-March) and prison. As he admitted to Lucy, however, he did not have 'the touch of eloquence' needed to kindle the 'spirit of patriotism' in the country, so he 'must be content to labour in a humbler vocation, aiding rather than directing'.[18] He attended 28 meetings of the General Committee (the 'cabinet') and chaired the Parliamentary Committee 47 times.[19] He was the embodiment of the idea that industry and constancy were necessary components of a successful political movement. In particular, he was the driving force behind the Parliamentary Committee. On his initiative, it was established by Association resolutions on 5 and 19 February 1844, with a brief to monitor the work of Parliament and suggest measures for legislation. Echoing language used in his November correspondence with Wyse, O'Brien explained that its reports would give weight and form to public opinion and might 'ultimately compel the enactment of a variety of useful measures' – in contrast with the 'contumely' with which (in his experience) Parliament 'treated individual members'. He later held that the reports had 'produced in the minds of the English members an extraordinary effect ... Every intelligent MP says that they are calm, able and most useful.' Thus, 'my notion of making the Repeal Association an introductory legislature has been completely realised'. O'Brien was clear, however, that such success would be limited, for Parliament would generally turn a deaf ear – in which case the repeal cause would be advanced by their 'having proved at once both the hopelessness of expecting useful measures from the imperial parliament and our own capacity to encounter and overcome difficulties of practical legislation'.[20] 33 reports were produced in the next two years, on such topics as fiscal relations between Britain and Ireland, the county franchise, banking and the land question. O'Brien himself wrote none. Instead, he was the Committee's quartermaster, using Wyse and other erstwhile allies to move for returns in Parliament, and the editor of the three general reports by which the Association and the Irish public were made aware of work completed and projects under way.

16 Ibid., MS 8653 (20), O'Brien to Lucy O'Brien, 21, 24, 30 January, 14 February 1844; ibid., MS 8654 (2), Lucy O'Brien to O'Brien, 13 [February 1844].   17 Ibid., MS 432, f1083, John O'Connell to O'Brien, 22 November 1843; f1085, Wyse to O'Brien, 24 November 1843.   18 Ibid., MS 8653 (20), O'Brien to Lucy O'Brien, 21 January 1844.   19 Ibid., MS 454, Rough Diary, 1844.   20 *FJ*, 16 January, 6, 20 February, 5 March 1844. O'Brien to Davis [June-July 1845], in Duffy, *Thomas Davis*, 214.

In all this O'Brien showed the same aptitude for practical matters that had marked his career as a legislator. It is possible that the sense of purpose and pride generated by this activity was of substantial benefit to a movement that, after Clontarf, lacked direction and confidence. It held out the prospect of an efficient political organisation capable of sustaining a long campaign. In May 1844, Caleb Powell complimented O'Brien's 'indefatigable operations, which have unquestionably been of great utility in every respect, & I am persuaded that the Association in its present sober, painstaking organisation is infinitely more formidable than any political body that has existed in Ireland since the extinction of the Irish legislature & it will no doubt while so conducted acquire the confidence & support of the reflecting as well as more ardent patriots'.[21] Duffy later exulted in how by these efforts 'the new leader' (during O'Connell's imprisonment) made the movement 'more vigilant and formidable, more patient and determined after defeat, than it had been at the height of the monster meetings'. Thus O'Brien's 'own character' was 'broadly stamped on the national movement'.[22] However, there was something rather naive about the idea that, as Thomas Davis put it, 'all will be well if we work hard'.[23] Duffy's view that the work reflected O'Brien's long experience as 'an active member of the Society for the Diffusion of Useful Knowledge' begs questions (inadvertently) about the difference between philanthropic projects and political campaigning. The *Freeman's Journal*, in describing and praising the Parliamentary Committee's reports, acknowledged that they were 'comparatively unnoticed' by the Irish public.[24] Political success had more to do with decision-making than with worthy endeavour – with making the right decisions at the right time, in particular where it was possible and necessary to strike the appropriate note with the mass of Irish Catholics, and it was O'Connell who knew best how to succeed in that respect.

O'Connell's imprisonment at the end of May 1844 created such indignation on behalf of the 'martyr' that the repeal movement took on a new lease of life during the following months. O'Brien was in 'high spirits' as he saw 'the cause progressing rapidly, the people behaving nobly', and O'Connell bearing his ordeal 'with fortitude & dignity'. After the Association meeting of 14 June, he told Lucy that, 'Nothing can be more exciting than the enthusiasm which has pervaded all our meetings since the imprisonment of O'Connell. I am very much astounded at the great docility & orderly behaviour of the thousands congregated weekly. The House of Commons might learn some useful lessons from the frequenters of our meetings. It is nevertheless very combustible matter. God grant that it may not be set on fire. If prudence shall regulate our future proceedings I have no doubt that we shall win

---

21 Smith O'Brien Papers, MS 433, f1169, Powell to O'Brien, 18 May 1844. Powell became a repealer in May 1843. 22 Duffy, *Thomas Davis*, 212-3. Thomas Meagher wrote in very similar terms of O'Brien's work. Cavanagh, *Memoirs of Meagher*, 41, 47-8. 23 Smith O'Brien Papers, MS 434, f1294, Davis to O'Brien [October 1844]. 24 Duffy, *Young Ireland, 1840-1845*, 176. *FJ*, 14 June 1844.

the battle without a blow. Every day brings us adherents & replenishes our treasury ...' In fact, the repeal rent soared to over £3,000. O'Brien, as the deputising leader, was not entirely comfortable with his new prominence: 'my position is very peculiar,' he wrote on 12 June, 'certainly it is not what a quiet person such as I have been would have chosen'. The letters sent to the Association contained much by way of 'glorification of your unworthy husband,' he informed Lucy; 'every post brings in from every quarter of the kingdom the most intoxicating draughts. If I were a younger man I should fear their effects upon my head. Perhaps I am not yet beyond reach of their delicious influence.' Ultimately, he claimed, he was impervious to 'the world's praise or censure' and believed that his 'public conduct was quite as deserving of respect on the day on which the Irish journals denounced me for voting against the Jamaica Legislature Suspension Act – but at least I have the pleasure of thinking that neither then when I was universally condemned nor now when extravagantly commended have I been influenced by any unworthy motive. This consciousness is a source of satisfaction of which nothing can deprive me.'[25] Among the 'intoxicating draughts' forsworn by O'Brien were those of the alcoholic kind. On 30 May 1844, the day of O'Connell's imprisonment, he took a temperance pledge, appropriately in view of his admiration of Father Mathew. He decided that he would not drink alcohol again until repeal was achieved, in order to show his 'earnestness' in the cause, and in August he urged that his example should be 'universally followed'. He kept his word until years later, after his return from exile, his doctor prescribed a little claret for medicinal purposes.[26]

If the combination of leader and deputy – of O'Connell's guile and populism with O'Brien's industry and character – represented the Association's 'dream ticket', so to speak, it was undermined by the divisions that weakened and in the end destroyed the movement. O'Brien played a key part in the conflict between O'Connell and the young men who produced the *Nation* newspaper, Young Ireland. In 1844, his relationship with O'Connell was remarkably good. Their past differences were entirely forgotten as O'Brien committed himself to repeal and fully accepted O'Connell's leadership ('our leader'). He shared in the widespread indignation caused by O'Connell's trial, when Catholics were excluded from the jury, and (despite his having had 'so much experience of idle and vain appeals to parliament') he wrote the Association's wordy petition against the 'injustice' of the whole proceeding.[27] (He called it his 'monster' petition in keeping with the monster meetings of 1843 and the 'monstrous' nature of the trial; O'Brien's speeches in the Association showed more humour and rhetorical ability than he has been credited with.) In March 1844, O'Connell, then in London, paid a warm, private tribute to O'Brien:

> I cannot close without offering you my most emphatically cordial thanks for the manner in which you have conducted the Repeal cause since I left

---

25 Smith O'Brien Papers, MS 8653 (20), O'Brien to Lucy O'Brien, 12, 15, 25 June 1844. 26 *Nation*, 10, 31 August 1844, 18 March 1848. Smith O'Brien Papers, MS 434, f1291, Davis to O'Brien, 20 August 1844. Duffy, *Young Ireland, 1840-1845*, 177. 27 *FJ*, 20 February 1844.

> Dublin. I really think your accession quite providential – nothing less. You are by your 'antecedents' and your popular talents and your rank and religion just the *'beau ideal'* of the person wanted to make the cause of repeal keep its course against the stream of persecution on the one hand and of otherwise inevitable desertion on the other. It may perhaps gratify you a little to know that I never felt half so grateful for the exertions of any other political colleague in my long experience.
>
> Even the casual fact of your religion is most useful to the Repeal cause. It is impossible that any Protestant who calmly thinks can imagine that you would be a party to any political movement which could deprive Protestants of their legitimate station and due sway in the state. Politically speaking I am delighted that you are a Protestant.
>
> It looks like affectation to thank you in the name of Ireland by a private letter – yet I venture in the name of Ireland to thank you – and I can promise you that we your colleagues will never prove ourselves unworthy of your cooperation.[28]

Even if O'Brien the landed Protestant was treasured as much for his political value as his personal qualities, O'Connell's delight in his new partner could hardly be more vividly expressed. Just over a week later, O'Connell, back in Ireland, proposed to enter Cork on the following Sunday morning and, as usual, to hold a political meeting after mass. When O'Brien objected that this use of the Sabbath would offend Protestants, O'Connell immediately gave way – 'I am quite sure you are right. The strictness of the Protestant practice in the observance of Sunday is the safer course. You have made me change my plan ...' – and arranged to arrive on Saturday evening, breaking with established practice out of deference to his new ally.[29] After O'Connell was sentenced in May 1844, O'Brien visited him frequently in Richmond Bridewell – not quite the 'almost daily' that Duffy recalled, but a respectful 15 visits between 9 June and 6 September (usually, it must be said, taking advantage of the hospitality that the prison famously lavished on O'Connell; 'Dined in Prison' was often O'Brien's diary entry for these occasions).[30] As effective leader during O'Connell's imprisonment, O'Brien seems to have worked closely and well with Maurice O'Connell, the Liberator's eldest son.[31]

---

28 Smith O'Brien Papers, MS 433, f1152, O'Connell to O'Brien, 23 March 1844 (also, in abbreviated form, in M. O'Connell, *Correspondence of Daniel O'Connell*, vii, 3061). 29 Smith O'Brien Papers, MS 433, f1154, O'Connell to O'Brien, 2 April 1844 (also in M. O'Connell, *Correspondence of Daniel O'Connell*, vii, 3068). O'Brien included a reference to this event in a subsequent, revealing discussion of religion: 'I went to Church on Sunday according to your [Lucy's] expectations. I have scarcely missed a single day since I came to Dublin & have twice refused to attend political meetings on Sunday so my mother has not much to complain of after all. So much for exteriors. Internally I feel of how little value are all such demonstrations. I derive more satisfaction from the acquisition of mastery over one improper desire than in a series of acts which the world [condones].' Smith O'Brien Papers, MS 8653 (20), O'Brien to Lucy O'Brien, 15 June 1844. 30 Duffy, *Thomas Davis*, 213. Smith O'Brien Papers, MS 454, Rough Diary, June-September 1844. 31 'I agree with you that it is well for one or other of us to be on duty at the Corn Exchange'. Ibid., MS 434, f1199, Maurice O'Connell to O'Brien, 30 June 1844.

On the other hand, as Richard Davis has put it, the O'Connells 'cannot have entirely relished the popularity of the Smith O'Brien regime' of the summer of 1844 or the prospect that O'Brien might deny John O'Connell the leadership in succession to the 69-year-old Liberator.[32] Eventually, of course, O'Brien was to break with O'Connell and side with Young Ireland. It comes as no surprise that O'Brien established close relations with Young Ireland. His Protestantism was important here. Young Ireland's vision of a united Irish nation, recalling Wolfe Tone's ambition 'to substitute the common name of Irishman, in place of the denominations of Protestant, Catholic, Dissenter', gave them a particular affinity with a man who shared that aspiration – see, for example, his depiction of a 'union between Orange and Green' as 'the dream of my life'[33] – and who they hoped might induce other Protestant converts to repeal. It was in O'Brien that Thomas Davis of the *Nation* would confide when he deprecated O'Connell's exclusive emphasis on Catholic interests. Also, the Young Irelanders were idealists who lacked confidence in the political integrity of many of O'Connell's acolytes and ultimately in that of O'Connell himself. O'Brien, of course, was the epitome of honour and rectitude and a court of appeal for those who despaired of the 'scoundrels' who surrounded the Liberator. Finally, O'Brien and the Young Irelanders were united as men of business. The Young Irelanders wrote most of the Parliamentary Committee's reports, working closely with a chairman who 'was ready to compete with his juniors in labour' but 'had no jealously of their gifts'.[34] Davis, in particular, though he initially thought O'Brien 'cold in manner', also found him 'true, friendly and laborious. He and I and some others are working up all manner of political information for Association Reports ... These are preparations for self-rule ...'[35] He was soon boasting that, 'Our Parliamentary Committee is working admirably. I have 100 pages of their reports laid by already [in May 1844]. In another week I'll have another 100 ...'[36] He clearly joined with O'Brien in enjoying the quiet industry of the party organiser.[37]

O'Brien exulted in the fact that the Association 'concentrates within itself a great many men of talent & high principle & gentlemanly bearing. Their names are not yet much known to the public but I am persuaded that from amongst the ranks of our fellow-labourers will arise men whose genius will do honor to their country.' After dining with two of the young men, M.J. Barry and Richard O'Gorman, in May 1844, he wrote, 'Nothing is more delightful to me than the fresh enthusiasm of all the younger portion of the Patriot Party. The spirit which prevails amongst them is so much more noble than the miserable soul subduing selfishness which extinguishes the mental independence & dwarfs the intellect of the hacks of English Party [sic] whose proceedings I have for so many years contemplated with disgust. Rely upon it, we have now, with the blessing of Providence, the power to make

---

32 Richard Davis, *The Young Ireland Movement* (Dublin, 1987), 60.   33 Thomas Davis Papers, MS 2644, f341, O'Brien to Davis, 3 August 1845.   34 Duffy, *Thomas Davis*, 212-3.   35 Davis to Pigot, 24 March 1844, *Irish Monthly*, xvi (1888), 265.   36 Davis to Pigot, 8 May 1844, *Irish Monthly*, xvi (1888), 267.   37 John N. Molony, *A Soul Came into Ireland. Thomas Davis, 1814-1845: A Biography* (Dublin, 1995), 242-5.

Ireland a great nation, & under Heaven's guidance she shall be such.'[38] O'Brien developed close personal relations with some of the young men. Certainly, by the second half of 1844 he and Thomas Davis were firm friends. 'Dear O'Brien' and 'Dear Davis' had replaced 'My dear Sir' in their correspondence, and in September there was considerable warmth in Davis's urging, 'Pray write every week ... & argumentatively & at length & not formally alone'.[39] When O'Brien was ill in December 1844, Davis fondly remarked that he was 'more annoyed than anxious about your health. Every one has been sickish & you have an iron frame & a conquering will & Ireland's Angel has care for you.'[40] In the crises of 1844-5, Davis constantly turned to O'Brien as his mentor. Duffy, too, had the highest opinion of O'Brien. His comments on O'Brien's aloofness and lack of oratorical skills are often cited, including his recollection that one of the Young Irelanders, referring to O'Brien's 'formal manners and English accent', said there was 'too much of the Smith and too little of the O'Brien'. But this was only a small part of Duffy's account; the full portrait emphasised O'Brien's 'probity and disinterestedness', industry and devotion, 'firmness of purpose', 'active intellect' and 'generous heart'.[41] It will be seen that he recognised – insisted upon – O'Brien's leadership. It is remarkable that historians who have hailed the vision of Davis and the shrewdness of Duffy have not readily accepted their estimation of the man to whom they deferred.

The conflict that emerged between O'Connell and Young Ireland created perpetual difficulty for O'Brien, who valued the contributions of both and believed that division would be ruinous to the cause. His handling of the problem in 1844 and 1845 was enormously impressive, so much so that one sees in it qualities – patience, sensitivity, realism and adherence to principle – that in other contexts would be considered those of a true statesman. Young Ireland disillusionment with O'Connell began with the Liberator's passive response to Clontarf and his expressed resentment that the *Nation*'s speculations on the use of physical force were deployed against him by the State Prosecutors. There was sharp disagreement when, in February 1844, the young men opposed a proposal to replace the Repeal Association with a new body stripped of its allegedly 'illegal' attributes. O'Brien and O'Connell had acted together on this, seeing the need to forestall a government ban, and it was O'Brien, 'after consultation with Mr O'Connell, and with his concurrence', who drew up and introduced the resolutions in the General Committee. The Young Irelanders 'protested against such a course as false, craven and fatal' (Doheny), and O'Connell and O'Brien gave way.[42] O'Brien disagreed with O'Connell's decision to

---

38 Smith O'Brien Papers, MS 8653 (20), O'Brien to Lucy O'Brien, 14 February, 9 May 1844. 39 Ibid., MS 434, f1292, Davis to O'Brien, 25 September 1844. 40 Ibid., MS 432, f883, Davis to O'Brien [December 1844]. 41 Duffy, *Thomas Davis*, 188, 212-3. Duffy, *Young Ireland, 1840-45*, 141, 175-6, 206. Sir Charles Gavan Duffy, *My Life in Two Hemispheres* (London, 1898), i, 94. 42 *FJ*, 15 May 1847, O'Brien to the *Freeman's Journal* [14/15] May 1847. Later writers produced varying accounts of this affair. See Michael Doheny, *The Felon's Track* (Dublin, 1914), 41. Sir Charles Gavan Duffy, *Young*

go over to Parliament in February 1844. 'O'Connell has vacillated upon the subject,' he informed Lucy, '& has at length yielded to the pressure of friends' advice', and it is possible that he shared Young Ireland disquiet over O'Connell's obvious delight in 'the English [Whig] sympathy humbug' (Davis) during his stay in England.[43] O'Brien did tell O'Connell towards the end of March that he had been 'long enough in London', prompting his return.[44]

In the summer, the government's charitable bequests bill opened a major rift among nationalists. This measure, designed as a part of Peel's new policy of conciliation, took control of charitable bequests from a large, almost exclusively Protestant board and gave it to a smaller body of which almost half the members would be Catholics. Archbishop John MacHale of Tuam led Catholics in denouncing the bill's initial failure to acknowledge the Catholic episcopal titles and the fact that the government and the Protestant commissioners would have roles in administering Catholic bequests. In Parliament most of the small number of Irish Catholic MPs present felt 'bound to respect the scruples of the clergy'[45] and opposed the measure. However, only Dillon Browne of Mayo persisted in this course after the government made numerous amendments to satisfy Catholic objections.[46] Davis, regarding the bill as 'a useful measure' which 'in its final form a majority of the [General] Committee approved', and sensitive to any procedural impropriety, was infuriated by O'Connell's youngest son's moving a vote of thanks to Browne 'without the consent of the Comtee ... I have made up my mind if such conduct be repeated to withdraw silently from the Association. There are higher things than politics & I never will sacrifice my self respect ...'[47] O'Brien's reply, from Cahirmoyle, provides important evidence of his role – and skill – as a mediator:

> I am sorry to perceive that the foundation has been laid for a discussion among the Repealers which will be incalculably mischievous to the Repeal cause if not checked at once.
>
> I am persuaded that R D Brown [sic] would not have made his Chairman speech [*in the Association*] if he had been previously in attendance at the Comm. of the Repeal Association & understood our policy.
>
> Let me entreat you not to allow this quarrel to be exasperated by any recrimination in the next 'Nation'. Above all let me warn you against committing the *Nation* paper to approval of the Charitable Requests Bill. There is much in the act calculated to awaken well-founded fears & jealousies

---

Ireland (London, 1880), 441-5. Duffy, *Young Ireland, 1840-1845*, 165. **43** Smith O'Brien Papers, MS 8653 (20), O'Brien to Lucy O'Brien, 14 February 1844. Davis to Pigot, 24 March 1844, *Irish Monthly*, xvi (1888), 265. Duffy, *Thomas Davis*, 189-91. **44** Smith O'Brien Papers, MS 433, f1152, O'Connell to O'Brien, 23 March 1844 (also in M. O'Connell, *Correspondence of Daniel O'Connell*, vii, 3061). **45** Graham Papers, 16IR, Eliot to Graham, 6 July 1844. **46** For the details and genesis of the bill and a fuller account of Catholic complaints, see Donal A. Kerr, *Peel, Priests and Politics* (Oxford, 1982), 100-24, 129-33. **47** Smith O'Brien Papers, MS 434, f1291, Davis to O'Brien, 20 August 1844. *Nation*, 24 August 1844 (Daniel O'Connell, jnr.).

amongst the R.C. Catholics [sic] of Ireland. If it had not been for the unfortunate Petition which was forced upon the Committee we should have been unanimous in our opposition to it. I trust that in the observations which I shall make upon the subject in my 'second general report' I shall be able to submit such views respecting it as will obtain the concurrence of the whole Committee without compromising the opinions of those who approve of some of its provisions.

'A soft answer turneth away wrath'. We have difficulties enough to contend against in working out the Repeal of the Union without volunteering to raise those which arise from internal discussion.

I rely much upon your prudence, good feelings & self command. At the [same] time I am the last person who would urge any party to sacrifice questions of principle, and as D. Brown opened an attack not sanctioned by the opinion of the Committee it was quite natural that it should have been made a subject of comment.

If my voice can prevail ... let me advise that the dispute be settled *à l'aimable* or *à la Lord Erne* ...[48]

In the event, O'Brien's attempt to find an agreed line in his second general report of the Parliamentary Committee proved problematical. By the end of September, MacHale had induced almost half of the Catholic bishops to sign a protest against the bequests act. Davis, however, argued that O'Brien was wrong to write that the act was 'protested against by the Roman Catholic Clergy', given that some approved of it, and he questioned the wisdom of 'identifying us too much with Lord John of Tuam'.[49] There was a danger, he warned, of the Association's becoming a '*parti pretre*'. At one stage Davis announced that he had 'waived long ago' his views on the measure – that is, accepted defeat – but he later urged O'Brien to omit all references to it from his report on the grounds that 'you & O'Connell & those who think as I do never could agree on the subject'.[50] O'Connell, on the other side, feared that 'as a *layman*' O'Brien had 'not perceived the full nature of the case as a *lawyer* would' and asked 'to be himself the writer of the paragraph on this subject'.[51] The act, he told O'Brien, was 'a subject of high feud between the Catholic Clergy. We *must* not take part with either party. Besides I do assure you that I will satisfy you that the bill would produce none but mischievous results.'[52] O'Brien's 'corrected copy' proved unsatisfactory to O'Connell, who, fearing to 'give offence' through 'our not more emphatically condemning the bill', asked that the report should 'lie over' until the Catholic bishops met in Dublin to decide their

---

48 Thomas Davis Papers, MS 2644, f285, O'Brien to Davis, 29 August 1844. When Lord Erne condemned repeal in an Agricultural Society dinner, O'Brien quietly withdrew and Erne subsequently apologised. *Nation*, 24 August 1844. 49 Smith O'Brien Papers, MS 434, f1263, Davis to O'Brien, 30 October 1844. 50 Ibid., ff1276, 1282, Davis to O'Brien, 13, 30 November 1844. 51 Ibid., f1257, John O'Connell to O'Brien, 25 October 1844. 52 Papers relating to William Smith O'Brien, TCD MS 10613/1, O'Connell to O'Brien, 28 October 1844.

position; 'his feelings,' wrote John O'Connell, 'are so strong on the subject that he could not help acting as he does'.[53] O'Connell condemned Davis as one who had been 'quite led away by his fondness for Church & State connexion & State control'.[54] At their Synod on 12-16 November 1844, a clear majority of bishops opposed the act. O'Brien's report duly acknowledged the 'considerable difference of opinion' on some aspects, but it restated and seemed to endorse the objections that had made 'a large proportion' of both clergy and laity reject the measure.[55] The whole episode suggests O'Brien's sensitivity to Catholic feeling as well as his strong desire to maintain the unity of the Association.

With no desire to repeat the monster meetings campaign of 1843 that had ultimately led to prosecution and imprisonment, O'Connell emerged from Richmond in September 1844 without a clear idea of how the movement should develop. The search for new strategies exposed doubts and differences. O'Connell's first speech back in the Association was so complimentary to the British Whigs who had condemned his imprisonment (and, through three of the five law lords, effected his release), there seemed a prospect of reversion to a Whig alliance and, with it, the abandonment of repeal.[56] The latter possibility was fully brought to the fore by O'Connell's late-autumn dalliance with federalism. Federalists sought not the repealers' independent Irish parliament but a legislature in Dublin to look after domestic matters only, leaving foreign and imperial questions to Westminster, to which Ireland would continue to send representatives. Such a solution, it was believed, would involve less risk (than repeal) of separation of Britain and Ireland. Thomas Wyse and Sharman Crawford had been federalists since the early 1830s. When the repeal agitation revived discussion of the constitutional question, many turned to federalism as a moderate alternative. In June 1843, Wyse counted 17 Irish MPs as federalists.[57] Crawford, Francis Murphy of Cork, John O'Brien of Limerick, D.R. Ross of Belfast and Colonel Henry Caulfield (Lord Charlemont's brother), and the Whiggish Dublin newspaper, the *Monitor*, all declared for federalism in the following months, and Davis found the idea popular with 'the wealthiest citizens of Dublin, Cork and Belfast, many of the leading Whig gentry and barristers and not a few conservatives of rank'.[58]

On 2 October 1844, O'Connell, in an open letter to the Association, announced his 'preference' for federalism over 'simple Repeal'.[59] He hoped that federalism would become 'the rallying point of *all* the Irish Liberals' and force the government 'to canvass the terms on which the Irish legislature should be re-established'.

---

53 Smith O'Brien Papers, MS 434, f1272, John O'Connell to O'Brien, 6 November 1844; f1273, O'Connell to O'Brien, 9 November 1844 (also in M. O'Connell, *Correspondence of Daniel O'Connell*, vii, 3116). 54 Smith O'Brien Papers, MS 434, f1275, John O'Connell to O'Brien, 10 November 1844. 55 Second General Report, *Reports of the Parliamentary Committee of the Loyal National Repeal Association of Ireland* (Dublin 1844), 370-1. 56 *Nation*, 14 September 1844. 57 Wyse Papers, MS 15019 (10), Wyse to George Wyse, 14 June 1843. 58 Duffy, *Thomas Davis*, 256. 59 *DEP*, 15 October 1844.

He persuaded Pierce Mahony to get up a federalist declaration for signature.[60] The idea of courting federalist allies against the Union was not controversial – it was part of a wider ambition to secure Protestant support – with the Young Irelanders at least as keen on it as O'Connell. O'Brien had urged such cooperation in the public letter he wrote in December 1843; moreover, he was unwilling to bind himself 'by any irrevocable pledge against acquiescence in a Federal constitution', for though it was full repeal that he wanted he was sure that a federal system would be an improvement on the existing Union. Davis was angered when an O'Connell proposal to make all Irish MPs take repeal pledges threatened to alienate the federalists.[61] He urged alliance with the federalists as an appropriate strategy for O'Connell to pursue on release from prison, and in October 1844 he went to Belfast to encourage the northern federalists.[62] However, the stated 'preference' for federalism over repeal seemed a betrayal of the fundamental purpose of the movement. O'Connell had abandoned the cause before, in 1835, and this episode revived all the old doubts about his commitment to repeal. O'Brien's letters to his colleagues are not extant and so his view of O'Connell's initiative has to be inferred largely from the words of his correspondents. Though not himself an antagonist, his role was central, consulted as he was by all parties. O'Connell communicated with him throughout and was extravagantly respectful of his opinion. On 1 October, just before the controversial letter to the Association, O'Connell had written to O'Brien that,

> It delights me to tell you that when I left Dublin there was the best prospect of a powerful and influential rally for federative Repeal. It may break off without any effectual assistance to the great cause. The first step will be for the Federalists to display themselves. The second to appoint a committee of arrangement [sic] at which you and my son John should attend to secure us all from any compromise tending to render precarious the right of Ireland to 'legislative self-protection'. I do believe the men who are about to be prominent are sincere and inclined to go the full necessary length with us. Of course our duty is to avoid every delusion. And as to any compromise, *that* is not to be thought of. And indeed I do not hesitate to pledge myself to you most unequivocally not to consent to any arrangement which shall not have your full consent. That is the basis for our future action. Your judgement *must* be satisfied or mine *will* not ...[63]

O'Connell's respect for O'Brien seems more obvious here than the meaning of his objective of 'federative Repeal'. In his next, he deliberately lied about his involve

---

60 M. O'Connell, *Correspondence of Daniel O'Connell*, vii, 3100, O'Connell to Fitzpatrick, 12 October 1844; 3100a, O'Connell to Mahony, 12 October 1844.   61 O'Brien, *Letter to Rev. T. O'Malley*, 15-6. Smith O'Brien Papers, MS 432, f887, Davis to O'Brien, n.d.   62 Duffy, *Thomas Davis*, 224-5, 249-51, 256-9. *Nation*, 14 September 1844. Smith O'Brien Papers, MS 434, f1263, Davis to O'Brien, 30 October 1844.   63 Ibid., f1245, O'Connell to O'Brien, 1 October 1844 (also in M. O'Connell, *Correspondence of Daniel O'Connell*, vii, 3092).

ment with Mahony – 'I had nothing whatsoever directly or indirectly to do with the composition or the material of this document' – and the considerable emphasis on reassurance suggests that O'Brien may have expressed some reservations:

> ... your accession to the repeal cause has been the efficient cause of this advance [*i.e., the rousing of the federalists*], and I do not hesitate to say further, and to *pledge* myself, not to assent to any plan for the restoration of the Irish parliament, or to any details of any such plan, that meets with your disapprobation. We go together, that is, you go with me, because I certainly will not go a single step without you. No man living has been more fortunate than you in the opportunity of showing personal independence. Whatever you do will be the result of your own judgement and, differ with me who may, I will not differ with you. If you were in my opinion so wrong as to violate principle I would retire ... But while I *do* act I will act with you. I am thoroughly convinced that without your accession to the Repeal cause years upon years would elapse before we made any impression upon the general Protestant mind. Ireland owes you an unlimited debt of gratitude, and the popular confidence in you can never be shaken ...
>
> I will not take one single step about it without giving you *previous* intimation and consulting with you fully and deliberately.[64]

O'Connell was a naturally effusive man, and such a show of deference from a leader cannot simply be accepted at face value. Nevertheless, the language of his letters to O'Brien is striking and almost unique. MacHale was the only other man who was addressed in like manner, significantly, for O'Connell could not please both for long and would have to make the choice that religious conscience dictated.

Duffy protested in the *Nation* that O'Connell's declaration would undermine repeal and rejected the Liberator's right effectively to alter the constitution of the Association.[65] Davis told O'Brien that, 'Federalism is not & cannot be a final settlement', and M. J. Barry threatened to resign from the Association rather than have his principles 'made the shuttlecock of any man or body of men'.[66] O'Connell's third letter gave clear evidence of both O'Brien's opposition to federalism and his influence over O'Connell as the latter scuttled for cover. He was 'just in possession' of O'Brien's letter and 'agree[d] with you entirely in your condemnation' of Mahony's federalist document. 'It would never do', the repealers would have to declare their 'total dissent ... [its] details are rather prohibitory of than favourable to rational appeal. To exclude from the Irish parliament financial details and ecclesiastical affairs would be *excision* of the part of the queen as well as of her son Hamlet himself ... At all events nobody can say that there has been wanting the

---

64 Smith O'Brien Papers, MS 434, f1254, O'Connell to O'Brien, 21 October 1844 (also in M. O'Connell, *Correspondence of Daniel O'Connell*, vii, 3103). 65 *Nation*, 19 October 1844. Duffy, *Thomas Davis*, 261-2. 66 Smith O'Brien Papers, MS 434, f1295, Davis to O'Brien, 18 October 1844; f1258, Barry to O'Brien, 27 October 1844.

tone, temper or substance of conciliation on our parts. Indeed the objection is that I have gone too far ...' Somewhat fudging the issue, O'Connell finished with a declaration that it would be 'absurd to submit to any species of 'federalism' which did not take for its basis a *perfectly efficient domestic parliament for all its purposes*'.[67] At the end of October, O'Brien, who 'had scrupulously withheld himself from all party relations and preached forbearance and conciliation on all sides' (Duffy), sent off a public letter on the issue. He acknowledged the federalists as 'friends of Ireland' and fellow-strugglers for 'self-government' and, accordingly, allowed that repealers should 'commune unreservedly' with them. But he stated his own view that 'simple Repeal' was 'both more easily attainable and, when attained, more conducive to the interest of Ireland'. The letter was a superb example of sensitive handling of differences combined with firmness and clarity on the central principle, and John O'Connell thought it 'excellent in manner & matter. Nothing could be more judicious nor better suited to the present time & nothing could be better done.'[68]

With the federalists unwilling to respond to his embrace, and even O'Connellite loyalists like O'Neill Daunt baffled by his preference for federalism, O'Connell retreated. He issued an 'explanatory' letter – 'I do not say my *exculpatory* [letter] because I have no apology to make' – in which he gave up on the federalists and re-dedicated himself to 'simple Repeal'.[69] If Young Ireland secured a victory in this dispute – Barry rejoiced in Young Ireland's display of 'so independent a spirit' and Davis, more bitter than triumphant, was scathing about O'Connell's 'apology for a guilty blunder'[70] – it was their open dissent in the *Nation* that had made a damaging rift out of O'Connell's initial error. O'Brien was the only person to emerge with his reputation fully intact. He did not openly question O'Connell's adherence to repeal and, carefully briefed throughout, he was probably aware that there was more imprecision of language than infidelity in the Liberator's conduct. He was clearly held in high regard by both O'Connell and Young Ireland. He also won the respect of Sharman Crawford, the federalist leader, who contrasted O'Connell's 'vacillating leadership' with O'Brien's 'clear and correct' pursuit of full 'legislative independence'.[71]

O'Brien himself came in for criticism when John O'Connell, though expressing his 'sentiments of regard, on every ground, personal & political', faulted his 'inadvertence' in permitting 'insidious' Young Ireland questioning (in the General Committee) of the Liberator's handling of Association funds; 'men were allowed to state things by which, under cover of reporting gossip, they made unfair, unjust,

---

67 Papers relating to William Smith O'Brien, TCD MS 1063/1, O'Connell to O'Brien, 28 October 1844.   68 *Nation*, 9 November 1844, O'Brien to Crean, 31 October 1844. Smith O'Brien Papers, MS 434, f1272, John O'Connell to O'Brien, 6 November 1844. Duffy, *Young Ireland, 1840-1845*, 218-9.   69 M. O'Connell, *Correspondence of Daniel O'Connell*, vii, 3108, O'Neill Daunt to O'Connell, 29 October 1844; 3110, O'Connell to Fitzpatrick, 31 October 1844. *Nation*, 16 November 1844, O'Connell to Ray, 8 November 1844.   70 Smith O'Brien Papers, MS 434, f1268, Barry to O'Brien, 4 November 1844; f1282, Davis to O'Brien, 30 November 1844.   71 Ibid., f1277, Crawford to O'Brien, 18 November 1844.   72 Ibid., f1240, John O'Connell to O'Connell, 11 September 1844.

ungenerous & utterly unfounded allusions to my father'.[72] The main pressure, however, came from Young Irelanders, who turned constantly to O'Brien, seeking his mediation, Davis in particular frequently urging him to write to O'Connell. There were allegations of jobbery within the Association when one O'Connellite, Richard Nagle, was paid two guineas a week for editorial work; Thomas MacNevin, a *Nation* writer, would 'not allow the people to be *robbed* to aggrandise the small fry, the minnows, the very sprats of the Association'.[73] In November 1844, Davis reacted angrily – almost hysterically – to a Catholic priest's published condemnation of the *Nation's* 'un-Catholic and infidel spirit' after Davis had denounced censorship in the Papal States, praised 'the simplicity of Presbyterian tenets', and argued 'that a man has as good a right to change from Catholicity to Protestantism as from Protestantism to Catholicity'. The last followed the priest's hostile comment on the conversion to Protestantism of Davis's friend, Daniel Owen Madden, and this response from the Protestant Davis suggests that he did not have much sense of how a history of proselytism made Catholics regard such matters. Davis despaired of 'the bigots of the *parti pretre*'. He would 'not be the conscious tool of bigots. I shall not strive to beat down political in order to set up religious ascendancy ... now or never we, Protestants, must ascertain whether we are to have religious liberty ... we will not yield our liberty of opinion, so that unless this onslaught is stopped we shall have an avowed *priest party* including O'C[onnell] face to face with an avowed *liberal party* backed by the Federalists & Conservatives & the lay-minded Repealers.' On the question of religious liberty, Davis expected O'Brien's backing: 'you unless I have quite mistaken you will subscribe to what I now say'.[74]

O'Connell rather amusingly patronised Davis as 'an exceedingly clever fellow' whose 'Protestant monomania' had blinded him to the right of others to state their opinions. When O'Brien requested his intervention to stop the debate, he replied that having 'lost all influence' with Davis he hoped for O'Brien's 'assistance to keep the Association quite disengaged from the controversy'.[75] O'Brien, the mediator, also sent Davis a letter which, as Duffy noted, 'exhibits the just and considerable character of the man'. He said he agreed much more with Davis than the priest but urged the need for Protestants to respect the views of the Catholic majority and above all reminded him that, 'Unity is essential to our success, and therefore division at present would be madness ... I make these observations ... as an uncompromising advocate of civil and religious liberty in its most unlimited sense.'[76] He also stated clearly, in words that must have been intended to cool Davis's passions, that, 'I feel entirely the importance to the cause of Repeal of my maintaining sin-

---

73 Ibid., MS 433, f1096, MacNevin to O'Brien [1844]; ibid., MS 434, f1258, Barry to O'Brien, 27 October 1844.   74 Ibid., MS 432, f895, Davis to O'Brien [November 1844]; ibid., MS 434, ff1276, 1282, 1296, Davis to O'Brien, 13, 30 November, 27 October 1844. Molony, *A Soul Came Into Ireland*, 263-74. Duffy, *Thomas Davis*, 269-81.   75 M. O'Connell, *Correspondence of Daniel O'Connell*, vii, 3109, O'Connell to Davis, 30 October 1844; 3116, O'Connell to O'Brien, 9 November 1844. Smith O'Brien Papers, MS 434, f1273, O'Connell to O'Brien, 9 November 1844.   76 Duffy, *Thomas Davis*, 272-3, O'Brien to Davis, n.d.

cere, unreserved, and friendly co-operation with O'Connell; but I am bound also to add that, under the present circumstances of our relative positions, I would prefer to withdraw for a time from active efforts in the association, rather than appear there as an adversary to his policy.'[77] With O'Brien so insistent, and everyone aware of the damage that religious disputes could do to the movement, the matter was allowed to rest.

After the intense activity of January-September 1844, O'Brien spent almost all of the rest of the year at Cahirmoyle. His fourth son, Robert Donough, was born there on 25 September, inducing O'Connell, endearingly, to send his regards to 'the mother of your sons'.[78] He remained extremely busy, not only mediating the disputes in the movement but also applying himself to the practical projects he enjoyed. He and Davis worked on a 'plan of canvassing a county's patriotism every week at the Conciliation Hall' and on providing members with 'sober earnest practical advice about parish organisation'.[79] O'Brien pressed for more systematic attention ('professional missions') to the registration of electors.[80] He designed an 'Electors Card' – with elaborate artwork and motifs – to be issued to all repealers who had registered to vote; significantly, some 'leading members' allegedly opposed it in the belief that the idea was Davis's.[81] He pressed for the replacement of MPs 'calling themselves repealers who do absolutely nothing for the cause' with 'active, energetic men' and involved himself closely in ensuring that a repeal candidate succeeded to a vacancy in Tipperary. Even here, in a small way, the Association's differences came out, with Davis pouring scorn on the idea of O'Connell's 'ignorant' youngest son standing; O'Brien was the linchpin correspondent with both parties, securing O'Connell's approval of his choice (R.A. Fitzgerald) and, continuing as the mediator, reassuring the distrusting Davis: 'To do O'Connell justice I must say that he is very reluctant to take any part in the occasion which would look like dictation ...'[82]

In October-November 1844, O'Brien wrote the Parliamentary Committee's second general report, 'a very lucid summary,' commented Powell, 'of the useful labours of the Committee it refers to. I am not aware that any legislative proceeding inchoate or complete has escaped the vigilance of the Conciliation Cerberus.'[83] The editor of the *Freeman's Journal* gave due credit to 'the most active, the most

77 Ibid., 308, O'Brien to Davis, 1 December 1844.   78 Smith O'Brien Papers, MS 434, f1245, O'Connell to O'Brien, 1 October 1844.   79 Ibid., f1294, Davis to O'Brien [October 1844].   80 Ibid., ff1244, 1246, Potter to O'Brien, 30 September, 3 October 1844; f1283, Ray to O'Brien, 2 December 1844. Thomas Davis Papers, MS 2644, f293, O'Brien to Davis, 1 October 1844.   81 Ibid., f303, O'Brien to Davis, 11 November 1844. Smith O'Brien Papers, MS 434, ff1276, 1278, Davis to O'Brien, 13, 21 November 1844.   82 Ibid., MS 432, f883, Davis to O'Brien [December 1844]; ibid., MS 433, f1101, O'Connell to O'Brien, 1 January 1845; ibid., MS 434, f1310, O'Connell to O'Brien, 10 January 1845. Thomas Davis Papers, MS 2644, ff281, 293, 299, O'Brien to Davis, 5 January 1845 [misdated 1844 by O'Brien], 1 October, 4 December 1844. M. O'Connell, *Correspondence of Daniel O'Connell*, vii, 3123a, 3124, O'Connell to O'Brien, 1, 10 January 1845.   83 Smith O'Brien Papers, MS 434, f1262, Powell to O'Brien, 30 October 1844.

vigilant, and the most useful' member of the Committee, 'its chairman and instigator, Mr Smith O'Brien'.[84] After a period of illness at the beginning of December, O'Brien went with Lucy to Dromoland for a few days – suggesting some reconciliation a year after the strained relations of 1843 – and then travelled to Dublin for a distinctly unfestive Christmas season of business in Conciliation Hall.[85]

At the start of 1845, as he contemplated returning to Dublin, a buoyant O'Connell addressed O'Brien with '"Aux ordres" as they say in France! I cheerfully obey your commands; for your wish to me is a command.' He acknowledged O'Brien's 'inestimable services. You really are "a living treasure" to the cause.'[86] When Joseph Hume, the English radical, sought in February to persuade the repeal MPs to return to Westminster, he addressed himself to O'Brien as well as O'Connell, recognising the 'great influence' they had in Ireland and O'Brien's standing as 'one of the most ardent & sincere advocates of justice for the Irish People'. Hume's argument was that the Tories had embarked on a policy of conciliation, with a colleges bill and greater assistance for the Catholic seminary at Maynooth known to be on the agenda, and Hume believed that Peel would need the assistance of the Irish to overcome the opposition of his own backbenchers.[87] The prospect of a colleges bill would ordinarily have attracted O'Brien, given his long-standing interest in the issue. It was Wyse's conviction that O'Brien's 'talent, energy and experience' were needed 'now when the "question" is really growing into a "measure"'. From London, in February, Wyse lamented, 'I regret you are not here. Few *feel* or *know* the subject or have the parents' love for it I may fairly say we have.'[88] Even his sister Grace pitched in with a reminder of the attractions of London, regretting 'your voluntary exile from your dear London. I can scarcely understand how you bear the separation ...'[89]

O'Brien, however, remained averse to '"paying the wolf homage", prostrating the dignity of Ireland at the feet' of the English, as he put it in November when he was 'entirely opposed' to a projected O'Connell visit to England.[90] On 3 February, the Association accepted the recommendation of the Parliamentary Committee that the repealers should stay in Ireland, O'Connell admitting that his initial preference for attendance in order to protest about the State Trials had been abandoned in deference to O'Brien's opinion. O'Brien, as well as reciting the familiar mantra of the hopelessness of seeking justice from Parliament, also warned the repeal Members against being used by the Whigs in their self-serving opposition to Peel.[91] Hume's interest was to take a threatening turn a few months later when he gave notice of a 'call of the House' which would require the attendance of all MPs, with those who did not obey guilty of contempt of the House of Commons and therefore liable

---

84 *FJ*, 29 November 1844. 85 Smith O'Brien Papers, MS 454, Rough Diary, October-December 1844. 86 Ibid., MS 434, f1310, O'Connell to O'Brien, 10 January 1845 (also in M. O'Connell, *Correspondence of Daniel O'Connell*, vii, 3124). 87 Smith O'Brien Papers, MS 434, f1314, Hume to O'Brien, 9 February 1845. 88 Ibid., ff1271, 1317, Wyse to O'Brien, 6 November 1844, 14 February 1845. 89 Ibid., f1312, Grace O'Brien to O'Brien, 23 January 1845. 90 Thomas Davis Papers, MS 2644, f303, O'Brien to Davis, 11 November 1844. 91 *FJ*, 4 February 1845.

to arrest by the Sergeant-at-Arms. O'Brien announced that he would not attend and was prepared to 'abide the consequences', a stand which led O'Connell to praise his 'manly and patriotic resolve' and some English papers to accuse him of seeking martyrdom. Contrary to newspaper reports, Peel did not have 'any fear of conflict with Irish Agitators' and considered the declared intention to resist 'a much more powerful motive for enforcing than for abandoning' the call. He did, however, feel that a call needed some 'sufficient cause', which Hume did not offer, and he may have knowingly allowed the House to be counted out on the day, 22 May, appointed for the motion.[92]

The first few months of 1845 were relatively quiet for O'Brien and for the Association, a calm after the storms of 1844. O'Brien attended and spoke in Conciliation Hall almost every week and helped to establish a new '82 Club to commemorate the achievement of legislative independence by the Volunteers in 1782. He also began to study Irish. He regretted his ignorance of 'the most ancient of all the modern languages of Europe' and, prompted by Davis, who was the driving force behind the new class, he decided 'to go to school again'.[93] From 4 February 1845 ('Irish class opened') until the end of May he took Irish lessons; when he was in England in the summer the class 'died away', and the suggestion that if revived 'it must have a new method' implies that the teaching had not been effective.[94] Cordiality reigned. O'Brien had O'Connell to dinner on 1 February and 13 March and dined with John O'Connell on 17 April. Davis gave his friend, John Pigot, a series of optimistic reports: 'We [Young Ireland] and O'C are on better terms than for a long time before'. 'The Land Question is now everything, and O'C. and I very cordial on it and on most things. So far so good ...' 'Repeal is bettering every day, and thank God is less windy than it was', by which he meant there was less empty rhetoric. 'We are working far more cordially in [General] Committee than when you were here.'[95]

An important advance was apparently made in April when the former high sheriff of Fermanagh, John Grey Porter, joined the Association as a federalist. This indication of progress among the northern Protestants was celebrated with enthusiasm by the repealers, and O'Brien's Address to the Electors of Down later in April called on the Down Protestants to rally to repeal and throw off the 'hostile prejudices' between Protestants and Catholics by which 'British supremacy' was maintained. He said he had 'never penned any document with so anxious a desire that it might be successful ... I have all my life felt that an union of Irishmen alone can give security for the rights to which Ireland is entitled.'[96] Unfortunately, Down responded by returning another Tory from the Hill family in the following by-elec-

---

92 *FJ*, 8, 13, 24 May 1845. Peel Papers, Add MSS 40,479, f352, Peel to Heytesbury, 12 May 1845. Duffy, *Young Ireland, 1840-1845*, 240. 93 *Nation*, 3 August 1844, O'Brien in the Repeal Association, 29 July 1844. Duffy, *Young Ireland, 1840-1845*, 207. 94 Smith O'Brien Papers, MS 454, Rough Diary, February-May 1845. Ibid., MS 435, f1366, Hudson to O'Brien, 18 July 1845. O'Brien later resumed his study of Irish; see, for example, his comments in the *Nation*, 22 January 1848. 95 Davis to Pigot, 5, 22, 29 March, 15 April 1845, *Irish Monthly*, xvi (1888), 340-4. 96 *FJ*, 29 April 1845.

tion. The Porter affair also ended unhappily. Finding his new allies hostile to his proposal that the repeal Members should return to Westminster and insistent on the restoration of a fully-fledged Irish parliament, he withdrew from the Association at the beginning of May.[97] O'Brien's (and Young Ireland's) interest in courting the northern Protestants was to continue, with an optimism that persisted despite the most meagre results and the inherent implausibility of the idea that Protestants alienated by government conciliation of Catholics would want Catholic allies. Much of the rhetoric of the repeal movement concerned the heroic efforts of Grattan's Protestant nationalists of the previous century. Few repealers seemed to understand the great change that had occurred since then, how Catholic militancy under O'Connell and northern prosperity within the Union had transformed Protestant opinion.

On the land question, the Devon Commission, set up by Peel in November 1843, produced a report in February 1845 which described the social ills that impoverished much of rural Ireland. Among them, the Commission identified the fact that tenants lacked an incentive to improve holdings of which they could at any time be dispossessed. O'Brien chaired the Parliamentary Committee as it drew up the Association's response, spending 'three or four hours every day' on it for eight weeks, an appreciative O'Connell told the Association.[98] O'Brien, O'Connell and Davis were the main participants, devoting 'much real thought' to it, wrote Davis, 'so that we may be unanimous and practical'.[99] Their reports proposed that all outgoing tenants should be compensated for improvements – effectively extending to the rest of Ireland (and giving legal sanction to) a variant of the Ulster custom of so-called 'tenant-right'.[100] The bill Stanley brought in in June alienated conservatives by giving officials the power to make landlords pay for improvements, while those who took the tenants' part were disappointed that it allowed for compensation only in very limited circumstances. Opposed by all shades of Irish opinion, the bill was referred to a select committee – which step Monteagle called 'the old nursery process of putting a naughty child in the corner' – and abandoned in July.[101] O'Brien remained an advocate of tenant-right for the rest of his political career.

Peel introduced the Maynooth bill on 3 April, describing how the existing grant to the seminary created only 'disgust and discontent at our parsimony' and proposing, therefore, to increase it from £9,000 a year to more than £26,000. The result, he hoped, would be the institution of a priesthood 'better instructed and inspired with more kindly and friendly feelings towards the State', and the 'spirit of kindness' shown by the measure would help to break up the 'formidable confederacy' against the Union.[102] The bill caused Irish liberals no difficulty. There were some rumblings about the insult of this 'bribe', but in general repealers recognised the

---

[97] *FJ*, 6 May 1845. [98] *FJ*, 13 May 1845. [99] Davis to Pigot, 29 March 1845, *Irish Monthly*, xvi (1888), 342. [100] *FJ*, 15 April, 13, 20 May 1845. See also M. O'Connell, *Correspondence of Daniel O'Connell*, vii, 3142, O'Connell to Mahony, 26 April 1845. [101] Bourke Papers, vol. 313, f282, Monteagle to Bourke, 8 July 1845. Hansard, lxxxii, 493, 15 July 1845, Stanley. Duffy, *Young Ireland, 1840-1845*, 264. [102] Hansard, lxxix, 18-38, 1024-42, 3, 18 April 1845, Peel.

measure as a boon and claimed it as one of the fruits of agitation.[103] Irish Protestant hostility was such as to stimulate renewed hopes of Protestant conversions to repeal. Frederick Shaw, an Irish Tory leader and one of the two MPs for the University of Dublin, threatened the government with an 'Irish nation for the first time united, but united in a spirit of general discontent', to which Home Secretary Graham replied that 'the days of Protestant Ascendancy ... are passed'. O'Connell found Graham's speech 'delightful ... The Ministry appear to be really sincere in their determination to do something for Ireland.'[104] O'Brien spoke in the Association of 'language used by Conservatives which might be employed in this hall' and predicted that 'a confederacy' of Irish Tories would soon be negotiating 'the terms on which they would unite with us in seeking the Repeal of the Legislative Union'.[105]

The Maynooth debates produced one incident which showed the passionate and impetuous side of O'Brien's character. The English Whig, T.B. Macaulay, taunted Peel with having promoted repeal by his past policies and pledged that no amount of danger could ever force the Whigs to concede repeal: 'never, till the four quarters of the world have been convulsed by the last struggle of the great English people for their place among the nations'. In the Association on 28 April, O'Brien replied with untypical oratory that brought every man to his feet, conjuring a vision of north and south united, France poised to invade across the Channel, an American fleet offshore carrying 'regiments of Irish emigrants enrolled, armed and disciplined, ready to land on Irish soil to defend the rights of their native land', a million Irishmen in Britain ready to rise, and the Irish third of the British army refusing to shed Irish blood. Then, regardless of the bombast of British politicians, 'the British Empire would be broken up, and thenceforward the history of Ireland would be written as that of a separate and independent country'.[106] The speech was seditious, especially that part which concerned the Irish in the Army; the Lord Lieutenant, Heytesbury, felt it 'approaches so nearly to treason that but for the peculiar circumstances of the moment', the policy of conciliation, 'it might have been a question whether the speaker should not be prosecuted ... the language of Mr O'Connell is much more guarded than that of Mr Smith O'Brien. The best excuse for the latter is that he is hardly sane.'[107] Nobody who actually knew O'Brien made such a suggestion, and it says more about the English estimation and understanding of Irish nationalism, perhaps especially of Protestant nationalism, than about O'Brien.

It was the year's second main item of Irish legislation, the colleges bill, that destroyed the harmony in the Association, and on this occasion O'Brien was involved

---

103 Graham Papers, 21IR, Heytesbury to Graham, 8 April, 4 May 1845. Wyse Papers, 5078, Wyse Diary, 4 October 1845.   104 M. O'Connell, *Correspondence of Daniel O'Connell*, vii, 3140, O'Connell to Mahony [19 April 1845]. *Hansard*, lxxix, 666, 14 April 1845, Shaw; 79, 918, 17 April 1845, Graham.
105 *FJ*, 29 April 1845.   106 Duffy, *Young Ireland, 1840-45*, 239. *Hansard*, lxxix, 1196, 23 April 1845, Macaulay. *FJ*, 29 April 1845.   107 Graham Papers, 21IR, Heytesbury to Graham, 29 April 1845.

more directly than ever before. As with the national schools, religious questions produced sharply divided feelings. O'Brien and the Young Irelanders believed in mixed (Protestant and Catholic) education. However, most Catholics, given the way in which Protestant involvement in Catholic education had been a medium for proselytism, wanted entirely Catholic colleges in the south; as MacHale had already made clear, when Peel raised the subject in July 1844, 'nothing but separate grants for separate education will ever give satisfaction to the Catholics of Ireland'.[108] Bishop Cantwell of Meath predicted that by a mixed system 'the harvest of immorality, irreligion and infidelity among the youth of Catholic Ireland would be quick and abundant'.[109] The government's Queen's Speech announcement of an intention to legislate prompted a brief discussion in the Association on 10 February. R.D. Browne and O'Brien disagreed about mixed education, but O'Brien and O'Connell successfully proposed that any further comment should await presentation of the bill.[110] O'Brien corresponded with Wyse, who approved of the postponement of 'a decision when you could not ensure *decided success*, thus to hazard not only all support in that quarter but sound the signal for a new controversy second only to that of the Bequest Act ... You are right in thinking the Clergy wish such Colleges to be *solely* in *their* hands ... If the objection be deeper and it be to Catholics & Protestants *at all* mixing – until grown up – let us at once understand & pronounce upon it. I know on what side I shall be found ... I regret equally with you the opinion existing on the subject ...'[111] O'Connell warned MacHale against a 'premature movement' – an opposition before they knew 'what these institutions are going to be' – but expressed his belief in 'the education of Catholics being exclusively committed to Catholic authority'.[112] The battle lines were clearly drawn even before the war had begun.

Graham unveiled the government's bill in the Commons on 9 May 1845. It envisaged three provincial colleges, probably at Cork, Belfast and Galway or Limerick. There would be no public endowment of religious instruction, but private funding of such teaching by representatives of each denomination would be facilitated, with lecture rooms made available. In the Association on 12 May, O'Connell gave his 'individual opinion' that the bill was 'fraught with a host of evils' and 'a gross violation of Catholic principle'. The failure to provide for religious instruction led him to support Sir Robert Inglis (an English Ultra Tory) in calling it 'a gigantic scheme of Godless education', and he urged the establishment of a wholly Presbyterian college in Belfast and colleges in Cork and Galway 'for the Catholics'. John O'Connell and several others concurred. Davis, however, welcomed the great expansion of education involved and supported 'the principle of mixed education' as conducive to the 'union of men' that divided Ireland needed.[113] Wyse congratu-

---

108 *DEM*, 26 July 1844, MacHale to Peel, 24 July 1844.   109 M. O'Connell, *Correspondence of Daniel O'Connell*, vii, 3131, Cantwell to O'Connell, 2 February 1845.   110 *FJ*, 11 February 1845.   111 Smith O'Brien Papers, MS 434, f1317, Wyse to O'Brien, 14 February 1845.   112 M. O'Connell, *Correspondence of Daniel O'Connell*, vii, 3134, O'Connell to MacHale, 19 February 1845.   113 *FJ*, 13 May 1845. Duffy, *Thomas Davis*, 287-8.

lated Davis on his 'manly stand'.[114] O'Brien, down at Cahirmoyle from the 10th, sent Ray a letter which expressed his support for mixed education and was directly critical of O'Connell's line:

> The very strong and unqualified language of condemnation applied by the leading speakers at the last Meeting of the Repeal Association to the Plan of the Government for the Establishment of Provincial Colleges in Ireland renders necessary some expression of dissent on the part of those Members of the Association who do not concur in such general condemnation of that measure.
>
> Without at present discussing details, I have no hesitation in saying that I regard the extension of Academical Education as a benefit the value of which to Ireland can scarcely be exaggerated. That I much prefer a system which shall embrace within its operation young persons of different persuasions to one founded upon any principle of Exclusion – and that the project of the Government, if modified in some particulars, would appear to me entirely deserving of public support.
>
> I regret indeed that the principle of United Education on which this measure is founded has not been carried to its legitimate extent by throwing open to Roman Catholics such of the Endowments and Professorships of Trinity College as are not immediately connected with the Ecclesiastical instruction of Ministers of the Church of England.
>
> In conformity with this opinion in favour of the admission of Catholics into the University of Dublin I think that the Protestants of Cork, of Limerick or of Galway would have reason for well founded complaint if they were to find themselves excluded from the advantages of any Collegiate instruction which may be afforded by means of a Parliamentary Grant to Catholics resident in those towns ...[115]

O'Brien regretted this 'difference of opinion' but expected that all would agree on other points: that 'some provision ought to be made for the religious instruction of the students' in their own faiths and that the government's power of appointing the professors gave them 'increased means of Political Corruption'.[116] The letter was intended to be read out in the Association on Monday, 19 May. At a meeting of the Committee of the '82 Club on the previous Saturday, O'Connell and John O'Connell reportedly 'said that "the Protestant sword" had been drawn but they were ready for the encounter & in fact announced that on Monday they would make an onslaught on the friends of mixed education'. Davis informed O'Brien that he was ready 'to make a stand up fight, for nothing could be worse than the unresisted triumph of blind bigotry in a national association'. In the General Committee later that Saturday, O'Brien's 'calm and firm and most timely letter' (Davis) was read,

---

114 Thomas Davis Papers, MS 2644, f467, Wyse to Davis, 19 May 1845. 115 Smith O'Brien Papers, MS 434, f1334, O'Brien to Ray, 15 May 1845. 116 Ibid.

'*on demand*'. Colman O'Loghlen, a pro-repeal lawyer, then opened private negotiations between Davis and O'Connell 'in order to avoid a public and fatal quarrel', and the result was O'Connell's agreement to refrain from comment on the bill on 19 May on the understanding that O'Brien's letter would not be read. Davis duly apologised to O'Brien for 'this very great liberty'. A public reading 'would have led to a violent debate which would almost necessarily have broken up the Association ... Do not think I want to conceal or compromise my opinions on Education, or any one's; I want to prevent a break up of a great party, by an important delay ... we who agreed in your opinions saw no other way of avoiding the shipwreck of the cause.'[117] O'Brien believed (mistakenly) that Davis and O'Loghlen had a 'very much exaggerated' view of the dangers. He thought the 'suppression' of his letter 'exceedingly injurious to my public character' and, if he was right in supposing his opinions influential, likely to be damaging to 'the educational interests of the country'. However, though his language was distinctly sharp, he accepted that Davis had acted for the best of motives and did not press the complaint: 'Having been muzzled so as to prevent me from biting there is but poor satisfaction in indulging in a bark.'[118]

On 19 May, O'Connell kept his promise to refrain from comment on the bill, even silencing Tom Steele on the subject. One incident proved ominous. O'Connell told of how he had been handed a document he was expected to read to the Association. He was shocked to find it was 'a battle song, a warlike song, an incitation to fight'. He said that the author 'totally misconceives our principles' – 'We are not a fighting body, we are a peaceable body' – and would be better out of the Association.[119] The physical force issue was to split the Association in 1846. Its significance in 1845 lay in the fact that the author, J.C. O'Callaghan, was a well known contributor to the *Nation*, and Davis considered O'Connell's response a rebuff for Young Ireland as a whole. Also, the battle song was a commemoration of the battle of Clontarf. What O'Connell saw was a title page bearing both a formal dedication to O'Brien (as the descendant of Brian Boru) and the famous O'Brien crest with its bare arm waving a sword above flames and the Gaelic motto (war cry) of the O'Briens, which O'Connell knew well how to read, 'The strong arm prevails'. It is possible that jealousy exacerbated O'Connell's response. He would certainly have been outraged by O'Brien's private reply to the author of the 'spirited' battle song. After thanking O'Callaghan for the honour of the dedication, he commented in terms that, given O'Connell's hostile outburst, implied dissent from the leader's view: although their policy was 'based upon the employment of Moral Force alone yet it seems to me useful to cherish any historical recollection which is calculated to maintain in the minds of the Irish People a feeling of self reliance & to convince our enemies that if we abstain from the use of physical force [we] take that course

---

117 Ibid., MS 432, ff888, 889, 896, Davis to O'Brien [20, 20, 17 May 1845]; ibid., MS 434, f1339, O'Loghlen to O'Brien, 20 May 1845. 118 Thomas Davis Papers, MS 2644, ff311, 493, O'Brien to Davis, 21 May 1845 (in two parts). Smith O'Brien Papers, MS 434, f1336, O'Brien to Ray, 18 May 1845. Duffy, *Thomas Davis*, 289-90, O'Brien to Davis, 18 May 1845. 119 *FJ*, 20 May 1845.

under the influence of other motives than those arising from want of courage to imitate our warlike predecessors'.[120]

The Catholic bishops produced resolutions on 23 May that did not settle their own or the Association's differences, for they called the measure 'dangerous to the faith and morals of the Catholic pupils' but urged its amendment (not outright rejection) and did not condemn mixed education in principle.[121] O'Brien returned to Dublin on 22 May and spent Sunday 25 May walking in the Wicklow mountains with Davis.[122] It is likely that they discussed the next day's meeting, when the colleges bill would be debated, but they could not have foreseen the traumas of what was arguably the most dramatic encounter in the history of the Association. O'Brien opened with a condemnation of the bill's defects – its leaving Trinity a Protestant bastion, the non-provision of religious instruction, the appointment of professors by the government – but he considered mixed education 'extremely desirable ... , to subdue the animosities of manhood' and rejected 'the principle of separate education'. O'Connell and John O'Connell again condemned the 'execrable bill' and the latter invited the Irish people 'to decide between' the friends and enemies of the church. According to Davis, O'Brien was 'within an ace of leaving the Hall ... during Johnny's speech'.[123] George Conway, a young man Duffy later described as 'destitute of character and veracity' and an agent for John O'Connell, attacked Young Ireland as 'a party' within the Association and suggested that they were tainted with the spirit of Protestant 'ascendancy'. O'Connell 'cheered every offensive sentence, and finally took off his cap and waved it over his head triumphantly'.[124] Davis, in answer to Conway, then initiated the famous exchange:

> Davis – ... my old college friend – my Catholic friend, my very Catholic friend, Mr Conway.
>
> O'Connell – It is no crime to be a Catholic I hope.
>
> Davis – No, surely no, for –
>
> O'Connell – The sneer with which you used the word would lead to the inference.
>
> Davis – No, sir, no. My best friends, my nearest friends, my truest friends are Catholics ...

Davis entered upon an impassioned defence of mixed education. Much of the speech was confused and contradictory – he said 'I do denounce this bill' and 'I do approve of this bill', in quick succession – which might have been the dissembling of a skilled debater. O'Connell returned to attack the bill and also its supporters in the *Nation*

---

[120] Smith O'Brien Papers, MS 434, f1340, O'Brien to O'Callaghan, 28 May 1845; f1349, Davis to O'Brien, 17 June 1845. Thomas Davis Papers, MS 2644, f371, O'Callaghan to Davis, 10 May 1845. [121] *FJ*, 24 May 1845. Kerr, *Peel, Priests and Politics*, 303-8. [122] Smith O'Brien Papers, MS 454, Rough Diary, 22, 25 May 1845. [123] Duffy, *Thomas Davis*, 302, Davis to Lane [June 1845]. [124] Ibid., 293.

– 'a newspaper professing to be the organ of the Roman Catholic people of this country, but which I emphatically pronounce is no such thing. The section of politicians styling themselves the Young Ireland Party, anxious to rule the destinies of this country, start up and support this measure ... I am for Old Ireland ... I shall stand by Old Ireland. And I have some slight notion that Old Ireland will stand by me.' Davis and O'Connell, both 'much affected' and the former in tears, in the end made complimentary remarks about one another and decried the notion of two parties in the Association. O'Brien, who had remained silent during the bitter exchange, joined in the latter sentiment and drew some laughter with his claim to belong to 'middle-aged Ireland'.[125]

At the end of this extraordinary 'blow up', Davis and O'Connell 'were reconciled, and fancy ourselves better friends than ever'.[126] But Davis never forgave the O'Connells, and in Duffy's opinion the collision 'left behind poisonous seeds of distrust and division ... A burning sense of wrong was excited by the foul blow struck at Davis.'[127] For many repealers, however, the look over the abyss of religious schism had a chastening effect. In the following weeks, trust, or at least a working relationship, was slowly rebuilt. In that process a central role was necessarily taken by the one man who commanded the respect of both sides. From May 1845, O'Brien was the essential glue, the last best hope of a movement threatened with ruin.

---

[125] *FJ*, 27 May 1845. Duffy, *Thomas Davis*, 292-7. Duffy, *Young Ireland, 1840-1845*, 254-8. [126] Davis to Pigot, 28 May 1845, *Irish Monthly*, xvi (1888), 344. [127] Duffy, *Young Ireland, 1840-1845*, 258. See also Duffy, *Thomas Davis*, 295.

6

The Road to Secession

On 30 May 1845, the first anniversary of O'Connell's imprisonment, the repealers held a great levée in commemoration of the 'martyrdom' of O'Connell and his co-accused. Organised by Davis and O'Loghlen, it was by all accounts a magnificent affair, with members of the Association, deputations from Ireland's corporations, the trades of Dublin, and the splendidly uniformed volunteers of the '82 Club forming an immense procession to Dublin's Rotundo building to hail the martyrs and rededicate themselves to repeal. O'Brien read the pledge by which all those assembled swore that they would 'never desist from seeking the Repeal of the Legislative Union with England by all peaceable, moral and constitutional means until a parliament be restored to Ireland'. According to Davis, 'The most impressive scene I ever witnessed in a popular assembly was when O'Brien proposed the pledge. He shook like an oak in storm with excitement, and his voice was like the wind through its boughs.'[1] Taken with the imposing meetings at Navan on 22 May and Cork on 8 June, the levée served to highlight the continuing vitality of the repeal movement. The heady days of 1843 were over, but the cause was still more popular than it had been in 1840-2, and the repeal rent (at £642 in the last week of May) remained impressive. Many could recall that the struggle for Catholic Emancipation had involved a long and troubled campaign before the final triumph. Also, Peel's policy had done more to alienate than to win over the Catholic clergy and laity. Whether any British government could ever be brought to concede repeal was a different matter, but it was a still formidable movement that opposed an administration much weakened by the Maynooth storm and nearing self-destruction in the corn laws crisis of 1846. It was formidable, that is, if its disparate elements could remain united behind their leader, a man whose conduct of affairs no longer inspired the confidence of every repealer.

The impulse to unity vied with the animosities that emerged from the disastrous meeting of 26 May. One of the young men, Thomas MacNevin, commented

---

[1] *FJ*, 31 May 1845. Duffy, *Thomas Davis*, 310, Davis to Maddyn, n.d. For a similar account see Davis to Pigot, 2 June 1845, in ibid., 310 and *Irish Monthly*, xvi (1888), 346. See also Journal of O'Neill Daunt, MS 3042, Appendix, f1315, O'Loghlen to Daunt, 6 March 1848, on 'the most remarkable demonstration I ever saw'.

strikingly that O'Connell's attack 'was what I expect from his years & his irritability – the candle stinks as it waxes low in the socket. His retraction was shabby: & his hugging of Davis more like the clumsy pantomime of an ox than any display of manly sincerity.'[2] However, some of those who came up from the provinces for the levée 'urged upon both parties in the late contest that further division would be fatal, and would not be supported or sanctioned by the country'.[3] Davis remained attached to and respectful of O'Connell, but his letters became more than ever strident against John O'Connell and the 'lying, ignorant and lazy clan who surround O'Connell'.[4] When, in the Association on 9 June, John O'Connell again denounced the colleges bill and its supporters, O'Brien forced him to retract the accusation that Protestant nationalists had proselytism as their underlying motive, and in the General Committee John was 'lectured by O'Brien and reproved by all the Catholic bar'. The result was a restoration of the previous practice by which differences were aired in the General Committee and kept out of the public meetings.[5] Down in Cork, at a private dinner, O'Connell described Richard O'Gorman as 'a fine young fellow only that [he] was a little tinctured with unfortunate *Young Irelandism*' and said Young Ireland 'thought that his time was past'; at the public meeting which followed, 'he said something about three cheers for *Old* Ireland, laying a strong emphasis on the world *Old* ...'[6]

Davis was given sound advice by his friend, Denny Lane, that he should allow O'Brien to take the lead in future conflicts: 'if it becomes absolutely necessary to differ from O'Connell, you must get O'Brien, who is a sensible man, and who will do so only in an extreme case, to express in the most temperate manner your dissent. O'Connell would never have dared to treat him as he treated you ...'[7] This was true, even if Davis's reply, that, 'The regard for O'Brien is all assumed' on the part of the O'Connellites, suggests that O'Brien had alienated some through his stand on the colleges and his association with Davis.[8] O'Connell's letter to O'Brien on 9 June gave an indication of his desire to remain on good terms with O'Brien. On the question of whether they should go over to London to press for changes in the colleges bill, he urged:

> Write to me as soon after you receive this as possible. I will [a]wait here [*Cork*] your reply as I yield at once to your reasoning and example. But I see that the bill has already been in committee and at least two clauses adopted. Under *these* circumstances are *we* to go over? Decide for me as well as for yourself and if that decision be in favour of action, I mean, of course, in favour of going over, I will leave this for Dublin immediately after I get

---

2 Smith O'Brien Papers, MS 441, f2288, MacNevin to O'Brien [May 1845].   3 Duffy, *Thomas Davis*, 309-10.   4 Ibid., 302, Davis to Lane [June 1845]; 310, Davis to Maddyn, n.d.   5 Smith O'Brien Papers, MS 432, f893, Davis to O'Brien, 11 June 1845. Duffy, *Thomas Davis*, 302, Davis to Lane [June 1845]. Duffy, *Young Ireland, 1840-1845*, 259. *FJ*, 10 June 1845.   6 Thomas Davis Papers, MS 2644, f145, Lane to Davis, 16 June 1845.   7 Duffy, *Thomas Davis*, 301, Lane to Davis, 11 June 1845.   8 Ibid., 302, Davis to Lane [June 1845].

that answer. I will be all impatience until I get that answer. It will be no small sacrifice to give up my visit to my loved mountains but if you *continue* to think that sacrifice necessary I will readily make it ...[9]

O'Brien told the Association that he could not allow the colleges bill to go through 'without at least recording my parliamentary opposition to the objectionable clauses'. He duly persuaded the General Committee, against Davis's opinion, that the repeal MPs should go over.[10] He wished to improve the bill – to open Trinity by abolishing the religious tests that barred Catholics from scholarships and fellowships, secure adequate provision for religious instruction in the new colleges, and have the appointment of professors taken out of government hands and given to trustees. On these questions all the repealers stood united – another reason, perhaps, for O'Brien's keenness on an effort in Parliament that would focus upon them – even if O'Connell's preference was for 'throwing out the Colleges Bill this session' in order to 'get a better, nay a decidedly good one next year'.[11]

O'Brien left Dublin on 10 June 1845 to make, on the 12th, his first appearance in the Commons in almost two years.[12] He was not well received in the House he had spent so long denouncing as an assembly that cared nothing for Ireland. On 13 June, replying to O'Brien's speech on the 'defective' bill, John Arthur Roebuck, the Radical MP for Bath, accused O'Brien of having produced a stream of 'venom' in the Association and exciting 'groundless discontent, bitter religious animosities, national hatred, and vulgar prejudice'; now he sought to 'insult the Commons' by repeating 'the trash he had picked up in Conciliation Hall'. Another MP (J.C. Colquhoun of Newcastle-under-Lyme) called him a 'deputy dictator' who 'had abandoned his duty in that House'.[13] His old friend in Limerick, William Griffin, commented, 'How abominably W.S. O'Brien has been used by the English Members & indeed by the Irish Liberals who should have supported him.' O'Brien himself was 'a little piqued', and Davis wrote of the 'impertinence' of 'the bitter little gentleman who sits for Bath & snarls, under the privilege of the House, at every man who does not bring him flattery or profit'. Maurice O'Connell lamented 'the unworthy attempt to insult Ireland in yr. person', but he knew, too, that such hostility would be 'useful in showing how little we are to expect of fair play or even common decency ... Roebuck has made *many Repealers* already.'[14]

This sort of righteous indignation was reminiscent of happier times when apparent English hostility to Irish interests won a massive following for the cause. At

---

9 Smith O'Brien Papers, MS 434, f1345, O'Connell to O'Brien, 9 June 1845 (also in M. O'Connell, *Correspondence of Daniel O'Connell*, vii, 3146). 10 Smith O'Brien Papers, MS 432, f884, Davis to O'Brien, 15 June 1845. *FJ*, 10 June 1845. 11 Smith O'Brien Papers, MS 434, f1345, O'Connell to O'Brien, 9 June 1845 (also in M. O'Connell, *Correspondence of Daniel O'Connell*, vii, 3146). 12 Smith O'Brien Papers, MS 454, Rough Diary, 10, 12 June 1845. 13 *Hansard*, lxxxi, 482-4, 485, 488-91, 13 June 1845, O'Brien, Colquhoun, Roebuck. 14 Thomas Davis Papers, MS 2644, f107, Griffin to Davis, 15 June 1845. Smith O'Brien Papers, MS 434, f1348, O'Brien to Davis, 16 June 1845; f1349, Davis to O'Brien, 17 June 1845; ibid., MS 435, ff1353, 1358, Maurice O'Connell to O'Brien, 21 June, 8 July 1845. *FJ*, 1 July 1845, Address of the Repeal Association to William Smith O'Brien.

home in Dublin, however, present reality offered less encouraging prospects. The colleges dispute rumbled on, with Davis's petition in favour of an amended bill effectively countered by a petition 'plump against the bill', organised by John O'Connell for signing 'at the Chapel doors' (Davis). In the General Committee on 14 June, the day before the Liberator left for London, there was what Davis called 'a most serious affair' in which 'all Protestants who interfered in the Education question were denounced in the strongest courteous language [sic] by O'C. & his son, & by other parties in a rougher fashion. O'C. seemed anxious that the supporters of mixed education should secede from the Association; but none of us did so, nor ought we under *any* circumstances short of impending expulsion. We have the same right to be in the Association as any others ... However if there is to be a break up the longer 'tis postponed the better & you [O'Brien] should on no account be absent whenever O'Connell brings the question to such an issue, as he threatens to do on his return from London ...'[15] Davis found all his friends 'firm against secession ... [which] would give Ireland up without a contest to the bigots ... On no account,' he urged O'Brien, 'remain in London after O'C. [returns]'.[16] O'Brien's response to this apparent danger was rather more composed than Davis surely expected. He and O'Connell were now together in London and he probably knew the Liberator's mind (at that moment and in general) better than Davis did. He attempted, with considerable subtlety, to play again the mediator whose job it was to calm his excitable friend.

> I hope no one will *dream* of resigning. The Association is formed for national objects & not to promote the views of any one or more individuals [sic]. I trust however that all the momentary difficulties which embarrass us will be removed & that we shall advance forward with increased rapidity. At the same time these circumstances are *untoward* events which undoubtedly retard the accomplishment of our great aim ...
>
> ... you ought to arrange that two or three of our young speakers should take a part on each Monday [*in the Association*] during O'C.'s absence. It is of the utmost importance that the country should be made to feel that Repeal does not depend on A or B or C but will always have champions bold yet discreet until the end shall be attained. The same reasons ought to induce you all to attend the [*General*] Comm. Why do you not speak often, you will exceed most of us if you practise. I have no doubt that you will find it very easy to get on well with Maurice O'C. and O'Neill Daunt who I suppose are appointed managers ...[17]

15 Thomas Davis Papers, MS 2644, f413, Pigot to Davis, 17 June 1845; f475, Wyse to Davis, 16 June 1845. Smith O'Brien Papers, MS 432, ff884, 893, Davis to O'Brien, 11, 15 June 1845.   16 Ibid., MS 434, f1349, Davis to O'Brien, 17 June 1845. See also ibid., MS 435, f1350, Davis to O'Brien, 19 June 1845. Duffy, *Thomas Davis*, 304, Davis to Lane [June 1845].   17 Thomas Davis Papers, MS 2644, f479, O'Brien to Davis, 20 June 1845.

O'Brien's sympathies were clearly on the side of Davis – not least in the oblique but obvious references to O'Connell ('A or B or C') – but the whole seems a deliberate attempt to defuse the crisis that Davis had described. In the event, as O'Brien probably thought, O'Connell did not try to turn out the Young Irelanders on his return to Ireland. O'Brien's confidence in Maurice O'Connell, a moderate and well regarded figure, was also justified; he 'put an end to a discussion in Committee which was heading fast to mischief' and generally did 'all in my power to prevent the injurious results of the differences on the Colleges bill'.[18] O'Brien did show anger in defending his old ally, Thomas Wyse, against John O'Connell's threat to have the Waterford electors turn him out for his allegedly anti-Catholic vote on the colleges bill. He was not about to forget 'that the cause of education owes more to Mr Wyse than to any one who has laboured in this field for the last fifteen years ... he has been unjustly assailed.'[19]

The efforts of O'Brien, O'Connell and Wyse to have the colleges bill amended were largely unavailing. O'Brien found the ministers 'inflexible', particularly on the appointments issue where they 'evidently are desirous to clutch as much patronage as possible & to bring the Catholic clergy & laity into dependence upon them'. He thought that 'the only course now open to the popular party in Ireland is to denounce the whole bill. The Cath. clergy will do so because it makes no provision for religion. The friends of Irish freedom ought to do so because it gives to the Govt. a powerful engine of corruption ...' He voted against the third reading on 10 July. Thus O'Brien was induced to repudiate and expect 'nothing but evil' from the measure of which he might have been proud to be considered a parent.[20] There was some consolation in his belief that the repealers could now unite in rejecting the measure, albeit for different reasons. Though convinced that 'the tone taken by John O'Connell has done infinite mischief', O'Brien saw 'no practical difference' that would stop 'the friends of mixed education' uniting with 'the *separate* educationists' against the measure.[21] An incidental result of O'Brien's rejection of the colleges bill was his failure to campaign again on behalf of Limerick's claims. The two southern colleges were set up in Cork and Galway, where Catholic Church opposition inhibited their progress, while the college in Belfast thrived. In 1850, the three colleges were aggregated to form the Queen's University.[22]

O'Brien had his opinion of Parliament confirmed once more, commenting that, 'The Irish public will now become fully convinced of the folly of asking Irish members to come here in the vain hope of amending bad legislation'.[23] His alienation from

---

18 Smith O'Brien Papers, MS 435, f1353, Maurice O'Connell to O'Brien, 21 June 1845. 19 Ibid., MS 434, f1348, O'Brien to Davis, 16 June 1845; ibid., MS 435, f1350, Davis to O'Brien, 19 June 1845. *FJ*, 10 June 1845, J. O'Connell. 20 Thomas Davis Papers, MS 2644, f319, O'Brien to Davis, 1 July 1845. 21 Ibid., ff341, 357, O'Brien to Davis, 3, 6 August 1845. Davis, on the other hand, opted to stay aloof from the 'mad bigotry' of the Catholic opposition. Smith O'Brien Papers, MS 432, f880, Davis to O'Brien [4/5 August 1845]. 22 Geraldine Grogan, 'The Colleges Bill 1845-49', in Maurice O'Connell, *Education, Church and State*, 31-4. 23 Thomas Davis Papers, MS 2644, f319, O'Brien to Davis, 1 July 1845.

Parliament brought the first appearance of an issue that was to play a great part in the events of 1846. On 30 June, the secretary of the Commons Committee of Selection informed O'Brien and John O'Connell that their names were on the list from which Members would be chosen to sit on select committees established to examine railway bills. O'Brien replied that he would not serve on any committee that did not concern Irish affairs. There is a suggestion in a letter to Davis that O'Brien wished to pick a fight on the issue: 'I have fairly thrown down the gauntlet on the floor of the House of Commons. My present impression is that neither the Comm[ittee] nor the House will fight. If they are rash enough to accept the challenge we shall have an interesting conflict ...' The end result of his defiance of an order to attend a committee, he knew, might be imprisonment for contempt of the House. It is possible that he sought the martyrdom he had been accused of courting in his earlier responses to Macaulay and Hume. Unlike John O'Connell, who gave the Committee a similar response, O'Brien decided to stay in England to test the legality of the House's power to compel attendance, undeterred even by O'Loghlen's urgent advice that he could indeed be arrested if he remained there. The chairman of the selection committee chose to ignore the defiant letters, and, in the event, neither O'Brien nor John O'Connell was selected (this time) in the ballot.[24]

John O'Connell returned to Dublin and the animosity between him and Young Ireland quickly re-emerged. O'Brien's presence was urged, one ally writing that 'Davis, Sir C. O'Loghlen and the other mixed education men want some help'.[25] Davis remained bitter against 'Johnny', who had 'thrown the agitation two years back' with doctrines that had 'lost our cause some of its best friends'.[26] O'Brien remained in England for some time, spending one week with his mother in Southampton and another at sister Grace's home in Wilton. His intention to pass through Dublin on his return was abandoned when he heard of the death of his sister Catherine's only child, noting in his diary: '*Little Jenny Harris died*'. Also, he was anxious to see a family from which he had been 'absent so long ... having been almost incessantly at work for the public at large since the middle of last December, it is time that I should apply myself to my duties in the country for a short time'. He crossed from Bristol to Waterford on 25 July and went on directly to Limerick.[27]

O'Brien proposed an adjournment of the Association during his and O'Connell's absence in the autumn, but the latter insisted that it should continue under John, probably the thing O'Brien wanted to avoid.[28] Though always more circumspect than Davis, O'Brien showed considerable annoyance when he heard that on 21 July O'Connell had tabled a series of radical proposals – household suffrage, the secret

---

24 Ibid., f319, O'Brien to Davis, 1 July 1845. Smith O'Brien Papers, MS 435, f1357, O'Loghlen to O'Brien, 3 July 1845. *FJ*, 3, 4, 7, 15, 21 July 1845. 25 Smith O'Brien Papers, MS 435, f1361, Fitzgerald to O'Brien, 11 July 1845. 26 Davis to Pigot, July 1845, *Irish Monthly*, xvi (1888), 346. Smith O'Brien Papers, MS 435, f1771, Davis to O'Brien, 26 July 1845. 27 Ibid., MS 454, Rough Diary, July 1845. Thomas Davis Papers, MS 2644, f327, O'Brien to Davis, 23 July 1845. 28 Smith O'Brien Papers, MS 435, f1368, Ray to O'Brien, 20 July 1845.

ballot, the voluntary principle, and abolition of the poor law – for consideration by the Association. He objected to their being proposed without first consulting the General Committee, and he thought nothing could be 'more *fatal* to the success of the cause than that it should be promulgated that those who wish to give to Ireland a domestic Legislature must consider themselves pledged to measures of so extreme a character'. The ballot and household suffrage, in particular, were 'ultra-democratic measures' from which 'great evil' would result.[29] The protest serves as a reminder that O'Brien moved from being a moderate liberal to a repealer without becoming a radical in any other respect; except on repeal, his views on most aspects of public policy were the same after 1843 as before. He expected that the matter would cause a new crisis:

> It will impose upon me the necessity of declaring publicly that I do not assent to these doctrines or rather that I reserve to myself the right of dealing with each question as the circumstances of the country may require & am not prepared to bind myself to these proposals.
>
> After escaping the difficulties connected with the Education Question upon which our differences of opinion very nearly destroyed the present organisation of the Association it is indeed disheartening to find that we are now to be plunged into another controversy. These things discourage me and make me sometimes doubt the possibility of success ...[30]

O'Brien's insistence that he would not be bound by the Association's decisions is reminiscent of the independent Member who made individual conscience his sole guide in the 1830s. Whether such a disposition could make for unity in the party he now helped to lead is questionable. In his comments on the voluntary principle – which he opposed not on religious grounds ('I fear nothing for Protestantism from the deprivation of its endowments') but because it would alienate Protestants from repeal – he was sufficiently angry to use the language of the Tory press, accusing O'Connell of seeking 'to overthrow the Protestant Church'. John O'Connell rebutted this charge and assured O'Brien that the proposals were intended for submission to the Parliamentary Committee in November. He also wrote, however, that there were subjects that involved '*uncompromiseable* principle', and these 'cannot be avoided, no matter how great the difference amongst us'.[31] On this occasion Davis held back. He had just received some sensible advice from John Blake Dillon, another Young Irelander, that not only should the colleges issue be 'let sleep henceforth' but he should also be 'very slow in getting into another row with O'Connell It would be ruinous to yourself [Davis] and to the cause ...'[32] Davis told O'Brien

---

[29] Thomas Davis Papers, MS 2644, f327, O'Brien to Davis, 23 July 1845. *FJ*, 22 July 1845. Smith O'Brien Papers, MS 18295, O'Brien to John O'Connell, 28 July 1845. [30] Thomas Davis Papers, MS 2644, f327, O'Brien to Davis, 23 July 1845. [31] Smith O'Brien Papers, MS 18295, O'Brien to John O'Connell, 28 July 1845; ibid., MS 435, ff1372, 1373, John O'Connell to O'Brien, 27, 30 July 1845. [32] Thomas Davis Papers, MS 2644, f63, Dillon to Davis, 22 July 1845.

that 'after my recent (& successful) strife with him [O'Connell] on the College Bill I thought it wise not to interfere ...' However, he also indulged in a flood of invective against O'Connell – his 'crude & contradictory dogmas & unrelieved stupidity', and so on – and was intent on opposing any attempt 'to pledge the Association to evil resolutions'.[33]

John O'Connell, Davis and even O'Brien, though they wished to avoid another dispute, were all prepared to envisage circumstances in which principled stands would be necessary. Perhaps this could be said for most politicians, but it was ominous that these men now spoke about – and seemed to steel themselves in anticipation of – actions that would destroy the Association. Strangely, despite the fragility of the peace, O'Brien and Davis felt quite optimistic about their prospects. Davis saw a popular movement with an extensive organisation, a 'staff' of young and dedicated men and a 'rising literature', facing a government that had split its own party. As he wrote in the *Nation* on 2 August, he was hopeful that Orangemen alienated by British legislation would turn to repeal.[34] O'Brien was almost ecstatic in response to this 'prospect of an union between Orange and Green', for he had received encouragement in that respect when in London:

> ... Glorious indeed would be the spectacle of an union of the two great contending Irish parties who have been taught to hate each other. From many circumstances which came to my knowledge whilst I was in London but which I do not feel myself at liberty to particularise I am induced to think that the reward of such an union is much nearer than our fondest hopes could lead us to believe, that is, if we do not spoil our own game. This I am afraid that we do at each moment when there is the best ground for hope ...[35]

He earlier told Davis that he had 'received lately intimations of support of the Repeal cause from quarters in which I did not in the least expect to find it', and, warning John O'Connell of the danger of presenting measures which would 'create apprehension amongst those classes of our countrymen who are still adverse to us', he wrote, 'If I were at liberty to mention names and circumstances I think I could convince your father that the *conciliation* policy has succeeded much better than he could have imagined and that the day may not be far distant when we shall secure support in quarters where we had least reason to expect it.'[36] The identity of the Irish Tory in question is suggested by the brief entry in O'Brien's rough diary for 1 July 1845: 'Dined with Frederick Shaw'.[37] Shaw, the leading Irish Tory in the Commons for many years, had been relatively moderate in his politics. For example, he and Peel forged the compromise with the Whigs by which the Irish corporations were reformed in 1840 – producing an attempt by ultras to unseat him in

33 Smith O'Brien Papers, MS 435, f1371, Davis to O'Brien, 26 July 1845.   34 Ibid. *Nation*, 2 August 1845.   35 Thomas Davis Papers, MS 2644, f341, O'Brien to Davis, 3 August 1845.   36 Ibid., f327, O'Brien to Davis, 23 July 1845. Smith O'Brien Papers, MS 18295, O'Brien to John O'Connell, 28 July 1845.   37 Ibid., MS 454, Rough Diary, 1 July 1845.

1841 and a shower of abuse every time 'the Freddy Shaw Act' yielded unwelcome results like O'Connell's becoming Lord Mayor of Dublin in 1841. However, in 1843 he was one of many Irish Tories who denounced Peel's failure to suppress the repeal movement. Maynooth completed his alienation. The Irish Tories, he announced in Parliament, felt 'deserted, abandoned, and betrayed' by a decision which conciliated agitators and endowed Popery. Shaw was one of 29 Irish Tory Members who voted against the bill at either second or third reading. His speech in February about Irish Protestants and Catholics 'united in a spirit of general discontent' is noticed above, and it is reasonable to speculate that O'Brien heard him speak in similar vein when they dined in July. (One indication of their good relations was given in the Commons next day, 2 July. O'Brien's defiance of the Committee of Selection had caused whispered discussion among a group around the Sergeant-at-Arms. Shaw, one of the group, came up behind O'Brien, put a hand on his shoulder, and nodded towards the officer as if to say the latter was preparing to arrest him for contempt. It was intended as a joke!)[38]

In a remarkable outburst at the end of July, the Tory *Dublin Evening Mail* threatened, 'However improbable, it is not impossible that better terms might be made with the Repealers than the Government seem disposed to give. A hundred thousand Orangemen, with their colours flying, might yet meet a hundred thousand Repealers on the banks of the Boyne, and ... sign the Magna Carta of Ireland's independence.'[39] However, nothing like an Irish Tory rally to repeal occurred in 1845. Attempts to browbeat the government – and to win Dublin's bitter circulation war by posing as the Protestant champion – did not constitute a genuine interest in repeal. Irish Protestant hostility to the 'Popish Ministers' did not make them seek unity with Catholics. Lord Lorton, an Irish Tory, launched a 'fierce attack' on government policy and told Graham 'that if Protestant Ascendancy could be re-established by Repeal he would be a Repealer'.[40] This kind of interest in repeal was worse than useless. As Protestant nationalists, O'Brien and Davis may have thought they had a special understanding of the matter, when, in fact, the opposite was true: *because* they were Protestants who became nationalists they were the *least* well qualified to appreciate Protestant antipathies.

O'Brien did not go back to Dublin until November. Davis, who had thought himself 'in iron health' at the beginning of August, died from scarlatina, aged only 30, on 16 September. O'Brien wrote a moving eulogy in which he said that 'love of country' was 'the absorbing passion' of Davis's life. He was 'not at liberty to intrude upon the public my sorrow for the loss of a private friend ... who united a woman's tenderness with the soul of a hero'.[41] He wrote privately to Duffy that he 'could not have said as much *viva voce* for that letter was blurred by many a tear which would have stifled my utterances in a public assembly'. Acting on Duffy's advice, he proposed a national subscription to pay for a bust of Davis; the well

---

38 *FJ*, 4 July 1845. 39 *DEM*, 30 July 1845. 40 Graham Papers, 22IR, Graham to Heytesbury, 6 July 1845. 41 *Nation*, 27 September 1845, O'Brien to Ray, 19 September 1845.

known statue by John Hogan was the result.[42] On 23 September O'Brien entertained O'Connell at Cahirmoyle. On 6 October he attended a 'monster meeting' with O'Connell at Killarney, paying warm tribute in his speech not only to the Liberator but also to John and Maurice O'Connell, and calling on the Irish Protestants to trust in 'the good faith, sense of honour, and regard for religious liberty on the part of the Catholics'. This was followed by a four day visit to O'Connell's home at Derrynane, during which, evidently fit, he 'walked along [the] mountains' to Skague Fort, the great Celtic ruin.[43]

Although the potato disease was detected in Ireland from late August, the first mention in O'Brien's correspondence involved, ironically, a proposal from a resident of an afflicted area of France that Irish farmers might be sent 'to teach' the French 'the way of planting potatoes in Ireland'.[44] October brought confirmation of a major Irish failure and, at the end of the month, Dublin corporation established the Mansion House Committee which, led by O'Connell, pressed the government for measures to stave off the expected shortages. O'Brien's involvement with the problem began in November, when he returned to Dublin despite the imminent birth of his second daughter, Charlotte Grace. In the next four weeks he made the 'impending calamity' the dominant subject of his speeches in the Association. He joined the demand for an immediate recall of Parliament to take the necessary measures, namely to suspend the corn laws (to allow the importation of cheap grain) and to provide employment on railway construction and an extended system of public works. He warned that, although he deprecated violence, the Irish 'will not lie down and die' if the government failed to act. That Parliament was not recalled he termed 'a sin against God' and another demonstration of the necessity of an Irish parliament. He insisted that Ireland had the resources to cope with the emergency, if the right steps were taken, and that no Irishman should 'degrade himself' by appealing for 'English charity'.[45] It is possible to detect the embittering impact that the Famine, even at this stage, had on O'Brien.

The Association was now in a sorry state. John O'Connell, in control during his father's absence in Kerry, had continued in his hostility to all who did not oppose the colleges measure. O'Brien found 'our Repeal friends' in Dublin 'sadly discomfited & disheartened by John O'Connell's ultra Catholicism. If I had not come here,' he wrote to Lucy, 'either a strong party wd have been formed against the Ultra principles or a large number of our associates would have withdrawn in disgust.' It

---

42 Papers of Charles Gavan Duffy, MS 2642, f3435, O'Brien to Duffy, 20 September 1845. Smith O'Brien Papers, MS 435, f1405, John O'Connell to O'Brien, 27 September 1845; ibid., MS 441, Duffy to O'Brien, n.d. Denis Gwynn, *Young Ireland and 1848* (Cork, 1949), 48, 51.   43 *FJ*, 9 October 1845. Smith O'Brien Papers, MS 454, Rough Diary, September-October 1845; ibid., MS 435, ff1398, 1410, O'Connell to O'Brien, 17 September, 1 October 1845 (also in M. O'Connell, *Correspondence of Daniel O'Connell*, vii, 3168, 3170).   44 Smith O'Brien Papers, MS 435, f1407, Bannister to O'Brien, 28 September 1845.   45 *FJ*, 11, 18, 25 November, 2 December 1845.

was 'with the greatest difficulty that I can inspire with hope men who during O'C[onnell]'s imprisonment were zealous & ardent cooperators ... Externally everything is favorable, within there is distrust & dissatisfaction.' He hoped that he had 'set matters right and that future collision may be avoided', but he felt 'the want of Davis beyond description. He possessed that sort of moral courage which it is so difficult to find.'[46] In fact, O'Brien's desire to maintain a united front damaged his own standing. On returning to the Association on 10 November, he not only restated his objections to the new colleges but also condemned those bishops (a minority) who had shown a disposition to accept them; he argued that solidarity in opposition would have forced improving concessions. Duffy wrote to John Pigot in terms that led John O'Hagan, another Young Irelander, who was shown the letter, to comment that, 'What you say about O'B. is very sad but not worse than you hoped for. Pigot forms a much higher estimation of him than either of us.' Pigot, also responding to Duffy, opined that 'your account of O'Brien is very gloomy, but after all I do not participate in your extreme feelings towards him. We mistook his heart, but I think all knew him for a good workman, an honest second rate gentleman, whose factitious position could be turned to most important account. So think I still for one, if he spoke twice more what *we* call contemptibly.'[47] In addition, O'Brien's subscription of only £5 for the Davis statue 'greatly disappointed' Pigot; it was 'ridiculous ... so paltry a sum ... it is hard to know what to believe in this man O'Brien. I hope he has a truer heart than that though.'[48] Pigot and Duffy would have cause to be critical again before coming to a better appreciation of O'Brien's merits.

Another threat to the unity of the movement arose in December 1845. Unbeknown to the Irish, Peel decided in October 1845 that the prospect of famine necessitated a full repeal of the corn laws. Unable to convince his cabinet, he resigned on 6 December and Lord John Russell set about constructing a Whig government. O'Connell's likely response was a matter of concern; in the 1830s, he had abandoned repeal to lend his support to the Whigs and allowed Irish politics to become a degrading quest for patronage. O'Brien, down at Cahirmoyle from 3 December, received a letter from one worried friend, Robert Potter: 'The Whig party here [in Dublin] are wishing to bring round O'Connell to support their interests. It will require your power to keep the influence acquired by the repeal party from being damaged ... I hope you will intimate to O'Connell your views as to the course which the repeal party are bound to adopt.'[49] In fact, O'Brien fired off a letter to the Association on the day, 13 December, he received the news of Peel's going out. The Whigs, he warned, would urge them to waive the agitation for repeal to assist them in 'a struggle for party ascendancy. They will endeavour to effect by corruption' that which their adversaries failed to accomplish by intimidation.' The

---

46 Smith O'Brien Papers, MS 8653 (21), O'Brien to Lucy O'Brien [November 1845], 25 November 1845.   47 *FJ*, 11 November 1845. Papers of Charles Gavan Duffy, MS 5756, f245, O'Hagan to Duffy, 22 November 1845; f247, Pigot to Duffy [22 November 1845].   48 Ibid., f239, Pigot to Duffy, 17 November [1845].   49 Smith O'Brien Papers, MS 435, f1436, Potter to O'Brien, 12 December 1845.

repealers had vowed 'never to desist, never to pause', and he now called on them to rededicate themselves to 'REPEAL AND NO COMPROMISE'.[50] In Dublin, O'Loghlen, who communicated with O'Brien throughout, succeeded in committing the Association to opposing every non-repeal candidate in the expected election.[51]

O'Connell read out O'Brien's letter and gave it his full backing: 'No compromise – no surrender – no postponement – hurrah for Repeal'. But he went on to 'rejoice' in Peel's fall and presented a list of those measures ('I will get all I can for Ireland') that would induce him to support Russell ('I tell Lord John Russell that I will act fairly by him'). O'Connell privately approached David Pigot, a Whig who duly told Russell, with an offer to have the repeal Members attend Parliament to support 'The Anti-Corn Law Ministry'. His dissembling (what Duffy later called 'hybrid language') was in marked contrast to the anti-Whig warning in O'Brien's letter and the *Nation*'s attack on 'the debasing influence of Whiggery ... the mire of corruption'.[52] O'Brien, evidently concerned, wrote privately to O'Connell to express his 'solicitude' about an issue he thought would affect 'not only our chance of witnessing the accomplishment of the Repeal of the Union but also the character of the Irish nation'. He went on:

> If all our exertions, our pledges may I say, our *sacrifices* are to end in placing the Irish nation under the feet of the English Whigs, I own I cannot justify to myself the part which I have acted nor do I think that the repeal agitation will have conferred upon Ireland anything but injury and disgrace.
>
> ... we ought to observe a strict neutrality between the two great English factions, supporting good measures according as they may be proposed by either, but creating for ourselves an Irish national party entirely independent of both. By such a party every question would naturally be considered not with reference to the interests of Lord John Russell and Mr Labouchere, etc. but with a regard to its bearing on the welfare of Ireland and specially on the promotion of the main object which we have in view – the legislative independence of Ireland.

He believed that the O'Loghlen resolutions on elections would create 'such an independent party as I have described. We shall go to the House of Commons or we shall stay at Conciliation Hall. With a phalanx of fifty or sixty men, bold, earnest, resolute men of good character and abilities and with such a body active upon high and independent principles we shall not only command the respect of all parties but we shall hold under our control the destinies of the Empire. I confess I am exceed-

---

50 *FJ*, 16 December 1845, O'Brien to Ray, 13 December 1845. 51 Smith O'Brien Papers, MS 435, ff1436, 1441, 1443, O'Loghlen to O'Brien, 14, 17, 19 December 1845. *FJ*, 23 December 1845. 52 *FJ*, 16 December 1845, O'Connell. *Nation*, 20 December 1845. Russell Papers, PRO 30/22/4E, f159, Pigot to Russell, 15 December 1845. Sir Charles Gavan Duffy, *Young Ireland, Part II: Four Years of Irish History, 1845-1849* (Dublin, 1887), 14. David Pigot, soon to be made Lord Chief Baron, was the father of Young Irelander John Pigot.

ingly careless who may be the minister in England. I believe it to be for the interest of Ireland that administration after administration should be shipwrecked until England shall have learned that it would be wise on her part as well as just to conform to the wish and the determination of Ireland by acceding to our demand for a national parliament. In the meantime we will accept, nay we will insist upon receiving as much useful legislation as we can extort from the British Parliament ...'[53]

O'Brien was advocating here the strategy that Parnell followed some 40 years later. It was, of course, a parliamentary strategy; O'Brien's view that the repeal MPs should stay at home was always conditional on circumstances, unlike that of Sinn Fein in the next century, and the imminent collapse of the Tory majority meant that it now made sense to take up the cudgels at Westminster. O'Connell agreed that they should be neutral between the Whigs and Tories – 'I entirely concur with you that the Repeal members should not give one party vote' – and claimed that if the Jamaica question came up again he would vote as O'Brien did in 1839, 'though it were to turn the Whig minister out of office the next hour'. In a postscript written after Russell failed to put together a ministry, he said, 'If we could have managed to play our cards well in Lord John's Government, we should have *squeezed out* a great deal of good for Ireland without for one moment merging or even postponing Repeal but on the contrary advancing that measure. Every popular concession, as I know, advances the cause of Repeal. I could satisfy you on this point and will when we meet.'[54] This one doubts. O'Brien's own position, with his determination to extract 'useful legislation', was not entirely clear-cut. However, neither logic nor history – the experience of the 1830s – would have encouraged O'Brien to believe that good measures actually advanced repeal, given the implicit demonstration that good government could be achieved without repeal. In the event, Russell's failure meant only that conflict on this question was postponed until the following year.

The correspondence also threw up other potential sources of difference between O'Connell and O'Brien. O'Brien clung to his belief that a fixed duty was preferable to full repeal of the corn laws and would not change merely because Russell had found it 'convenient for party purposes' to 'abandon' his former views. O'Connell, long an advocate of free trade, regretted O'Brien's stand, but he respected it as emanating from 'perfect political integrity and high honour' and fully accepted O'Brien's argument that, given the disagreement, it would have to be 'an open question' in the Association. The Tory *Dublin Evening Mail* had described O'Brien as one who 'has become too much of a hero for Mr O'Connell' and the leader of a separate, Young Ireland faction that would have to be 'put down' to defeat their opposition to a Whig alliance. O'Brien, evidently embarrassed, dismissed the *Mail*'s 'ignoble efforts' to 'raise jealousy' between them. O'Connell graciously assured O'Brien that in 50 years in politics he was 'never jealous of any man' and so he

[53] O'Connell Papers, MS 13649, O'Brien to O'Connell, 18 December 1845 (also in M. O'Connell, *Correspondence of Daniel O'Connell*, vii, 3180).   [54] Smith O'Brien Papers, MS 435, f1445, O'Connell to O'Brien, 20 December 1845 (also in M. O'Connell, *Correspondence of Daniel O'Connell*, vii, 3181).

could 'exult in your present popularity, a popularity most honourably achieved and which I ardently desire to see daily increase and would myself increase it if that were possible'.[55]

O'Connell was a big-hearted man who probably meant these words, and O'Brien might have said the same of O'Connell's popularity with equal sincerity. John O'Connell, however, had less generosity of spirit and proceeded to play the part that made him a key figure in the schism of 1846. January found him insistent that he would no longer hold himself 'bound to silence' on the colleges question. He duly denounced 'the infidel colleges' in the Association, drawing from Young Irelander Richard O'Gorman a strong denial of his claim that they would injure the Catholic faith.[56] In his Third Report of the Parliamentary Committee, O'Brien, in view of the 'difference of opinion' on the measure, simply stated 'the points upon which we have differed, and those upon which we have agreed'. John O'Connell complained that O'Brien did not adequately 'expose its enormities', and at one point threatened 'an appeal to the Association itself'; but when O'Brien held firm he gave way 'rather than seem indisposed to make concessions to you ...'[57] Tensions were exposed by speculations in the *Nation* about the violent methods that repealers might deploy against government forces if the latter used the railways to counter insurrection. O'Connell, adhering to his belief in peaceful agitation and anxious to avoid another prosecution, effectively renounced any connection with the paper when he said that the local repeal wardens would 'utterly disregard' instructions 'from any other quarter'. The column was written by John Mitchel, a young radical from Newry, but it was Duffy, as editor, who received notice of prosecution in January 1846. O'Brien wrote to O'Loghlen to urge 'that the Nation should not be sacrificed and that public sympathy ought to be excited in favour of Duffy'. O'Brien raised the matter on his reappearance in the Association, on 26 January, insisting that the article was 'both morally and legally justifiable' because it was in answer to 'offensive diatribes' in English newspapers. It was an intervention that ran directly counter to O'Connell's known views. Maurice O'Connell, from the chair, prevented his saying more and the next Association meeting brought only a brief protest from O'Brien before he agreed to postpone the question until O'Connell returned from London.[58] The Young Irelanders were disappointed. Duffy later wrote that 'O'Brien, it seemed to me, did just enough to save his self respect – not enough to prevent, or even mitigate, a flagrant injustice'. He admitted to 'a sort of good-natured despair' that O'Brien had permitted the *Nation* to be 'cut off from public sympathy'.[59] In

---

55 O'Connell Papers, MS 13649, O'Brien to O'Connell, 18 December 1845. Smith O'Brien Papers, MS 435, f1445, O'Connell to O'Brien, 20 December 1845. *DEM*, 17 December 1845.   56 Smith O'Brien Papers, MS 435, f1483, John O'Connell to O'Brien, 13 January 1846. *FJ*, 20 January 1846.   57 Smith O'Brien Papers, MS 435, f1512, John O'Connell to O'Brien, 16 February 1846; ibid., MS 440, f2162, John O'Connell to O'Brien, n.d. *FJ*, 17 February 1846. *Third General Report of the Parliamentary Committee of the Loyal National Repeal Association* (Dublin, 1846), 122-8.   58 Smith O'Brien Papers, MS 435, f1485, O'Loghlen to O'Brien, 13 January 1846. *Nation*, 22 November 1845 (Mitchel), 29 November 1845 (O'Connell). *FJ*, 27 January 1846 (O'Brien). Duffy, *Young Ireland: Four Years of Irish History*, 43-5.   59 Ibid., 45.

fact, there was nothing good-natured about the private criticism of O'Brien. The latter seems to have written to Duffy in terms that discouraged opposition to O'Connell, and the response of Duffy and Mitchel may be gauged from the half-hearted defence offered by John Pigot:

> ... O'Brien's letter is no less – no more – than I would have predicted. That he is a cold man – a nervous man – a man of no fire or individual intensity I always knew. That this letter exhibits more than simply the absence of such quality I don't think. On the contrary for a cold & cautious man I think it not blameable: and moreover I entirely believe O'B. a really honest man & inflexibly true to what he says. So there is no word he speaks that I am not confident represents his thought. So you see I differ with you & Mitchel toto caelo. At the same time you utterly exaggerate my estimate of O'B. which never was, & is not, by any means what you suppose.[60]

O'Brien had gone up to Dublin immediately after a public dinner for Limerick's county and city Members, all four of them repealers, on 21 January. A week later, his eldest son, Edward, joined him *en route* to St Columba's College, a new Protestant school (it was founded in 1843) then situated at Stackallan in county Meath. O'Brien wanted an Irish education for his children and would later send Edward to Trinity College, Dublin. His second son, however, was sent to a special school for deaf and dumb children in Rugby, later in 1846. O'Brien wrote touchingly to Lucy about his sorrow 'that you have taken so much to heart the notion of parting with Willy' and his own doubts as to whether or not the Rugby school was 'a suitable place for a boy with imperfect articulation who is not deaf & dumb'.[61] Grace, his sister, reminisced, commenting that Edward and William were 'as old as you were when first you went off. Edward somewhat older. I do not remember what your previous attainments were. I only remember we used to get into scrapes together over a certain black catechism which was ... probably some dissenting production' – introduced, presumably, by their evangelistic mother. She also revealed that she and their brother-in-law, Charles Monsell, were turning towards repeal, although they could 'give no particular reason for the fact when we are asked why'.[62]

Association business kept O'Brien occupied for the next month, as he completed his Third Report (on the Irish measures of 1845) and attended the Parliamentary Committee and the Association's weekly meetings.[63] At one such meeting, on 26 January, he said that he feared the 'subtle influence' of a Whig administration more than the 'terrors' they were accustomed to from the Tories. He again advocated a

---

60 Papers of Charles Gavan Duffy, MS 5756, Pigot to Duffy, 23 January 1846. *Toto caelo*: As widely as the extent of the heavens; the greatest possible difference.   61 Smith O'Brien Papers, MS 8653 (21), O'Brien to Lucy O'Brien, 18 November 1845; (22), O'Brien to Lucy O'Brien, 12, 13, 16 April 1846. 62 Ibid., MS 436, f1506, Grace O'Brien to O'Brien, 9 February 1846.   63 Ibid., MS 454, Rough Diary, January-February 1846.

vigorous electoral effort to return a totally independent party of 60 to 70 MPs; he believed that this force could secure repeal, arguing quite reasonably that if Peel could abandon his principles on the corn laws the idea that a British leader might agree to repeal of the Union should not seem incredible. On the corn laws, he said 'let them fight it out among themselves'. He possibly disapproved of O'Connell's going over to support their repeal and immediately took advantage of the Liberator's departure with a major Association speech in favour of 'moderate protection'.[64] O'Brien's own departure was not long delayed, however. Ireland had seen an upsurge of agrarian violence since the onset of famine and this led to the Tory government's introduction in February of a coercion bill, the Protection of Life (Ireland) Bill, which included curfew and other emergency powers for the Lord Lieutenant. O'Brien had always been clear that there should be a return to Westminster if coercion was proposed; on 23 February he had the Association issue such a summons to the repeal MPs, and, after a short visit to Cahirmoyle, he crossed to England on 6 March.[65]

He quickly entered the fray in the Commons, speaking frequently and with a degree of passion that was commented upon by other Members. He warned that '100,000 of his fellow creatures were famishing' and mocked the 'miserable grants' voted by the Commons. Rejecting the idea of an appeal to England's 'generosity', he argued that Ireland could cope with the calamity from her own resources, advocating in particular the prohibition of grain exports ('the people were starving in the midst of plenty') and an absentee tax to retrieve some of the £4-5 million that absentees were 'squandering away' in London and elsewhere. The coercion bill would merely exasperate the starving peasantry and so increase crime, when the House should be devoting its time to measures to relieve suffering. Repeal of the corn laws, urged as it was by English manufacturers, he dismissed as 'a Bill for England, and not for Ireland'; he adhered to his preference for a degree of protection but did not vote in the corn laws divisions and so avoided siding against O'Connell. In a letter that was 'not written after conference with other Irish members ... or in their name, but upon my own sole responsibility', he told Lord George Bentinck that 'the people have been allowed to starve ... we shall have not only famine and pestilence but also a general convulsion'; he asked the protectionist leader to agree to a temporary suspension of the corn laws, to permit imports, a proposal Bentinck accepted but which Peel rejected in favour of full repeal.[66] O'Brien's efforts were acclaimed in Ireland. O'Connell made a brief return to the

---

64 *FJ*, 27 January, 3 February 1846.   65 *FJ*, 24 February 1846. Smith O'Brien Papers, MS 454, Rough Diary, February-March 1846.   66 *Hansard*, lxxxiv, 987-8, 1006, 13 March, 1048, 16 March, 1186-9, 18 March; lxxxv, 293-5, 361, 30 March, 372, 31 March, 403-6, 1 April, 609-10, 6 April, 703-10, 17 April, 980-4, 24 April 1846, O'Brien. Smith O'Brien Papers, MS 436, f1551, O'Brien to Bentinck, 19 April 1846. Norman Gash has written a flawed account of the Parliamentary activities of 'the Young Ireland group' of MPs – no such thing existed – and accepted an implausible report that O'Brien 'admitted in a private House of Commons conversation with Peel that he recognised the need for a coercion bill'. Norman Gash, *Sir Robert Peel: The Life of Sir Robert Peel after 1830* (London, New York, 1986), 586-7.

Association in mid-April and when he 'mentioned your name,' Martin Crean informed O'Brien, 'any thing to equal the enthusiastic cheers, the waving of hats and handkerchiefs, I never witnessed. The Liberator and the entire meeting stood up and the plaudits continued for several minutes.'[67]

O'Brien's hectoring tone was less appreciated, however, by the English Members, Peel commenting that the House had worked for weeks on relief measures only for O'Brien to turn up belatedly to pour scorn on English generosity.[68] O'Brien's tendency to righteous indignation was never his most attractive feature, and now, fuelled by the awful circumstances in Ireland, it permeated his every utterance. The House would soon have its revenge. With hundreds of railway bills to consider, the Commons resolved on 12 February that select committees of five Members would each consider a group of bills and that attendance at these committees would be compulsory. Previously, the House could vote to compel attendance if a Member defaulted, but now for the first time compulsion was provided for as a matter of course. Thomas Estcourt, the chairman of the Committee of Selection, informed O'Brien on 3 April that he might be selected. O'Brien replied, enclosing a copy of his June 1845 letter, that he would refuse to conduct any business that was not concerned with Irish interests. He was then selected to serve on the Committee on Railway Bills, Group 11, that is bills concerning railway construction in Scotland. He failed to attend on 27 April and again, despite a specific order by the House, on the following day. It was not a question of seeking martyrdom; he warned Lucy on several occasions during April that he might be imprisoned but he doubted if the House would 'proceed in a course so absurd'; as he confided to O'Connell on the 27th, he could not 'believe that the House will enter into a contention which must be attended with great inconvenience in regard to public business as well as to its results upon public feeling in Ireland'. He therefore expected 'that a motion will be made without parade to substitute another member in my place on the Committee'. Instead, Estcourt moved on 28 April that he was 'guilty of a contempt of this House'. When this was carried, it was resolved that O'Brien should be taken into custody by the Sergeant-at-Arms 'during the pleasure of the said House', and so, on 30 April, O'Brien was taken into custody.[69]

His prison, generally described as a cellar of the House of Commons, was actually a 'small and not cheerful' (O'Brien) ground-floor apartment, accessible through the Commons cellars, sparsely furnished and with one closely barred window. The *Freeman* claimed that it could be regarded as 'a good servant's room'. O'Brien was allowed long walks in nearby streets each day, with a keeper, and on at least one

---

67 Smith O'Brien Papers, MS 436, f1546, Crean to O'Brien, 13 April 1846.   68 *Hansard*, lxxxiv, 990, 13 March 1846, Peel.   69 Smith O'Brien Papers, MS 436, f1538, Estcourt to O'Brien, 6 April 1846; ibid., MS 8653 (22), O'Brien to Lucy O'Brien, 5, 12 April 1846; (23), O'Brien to Lucy O'Brien, 29 April 1846. M. O'Connell, *Correspondence of Daniel O'Connell*, viii, 3203, O'Brien to O'Connell [27] April 1846 [misdated 28 April]. *Hansard*, lxxxiii, 749-52, 12 February 1846, Resolutions; lxxxv, 840-4, 21 April 1846, O'Brien; lxxxv, 1071, 27 April 1846, Estcourt; lxxxv, 1153-60, 28 April 1846, Estcourt. *Nation*, 9 May 1846, O'Brien to the inhabitants of Limerick, 2 May 1846.

Sunday attended at St Margaret's, Westminster (the church in which Miss Wilton had had his first children baptised).[70] The real importance of this affair lies in its impact on O'Brien's relationship with O'Connell. O'Brien, as 'one who in everything could decide for himself' (O'Connell), had not consulted the Liberator. The latter was placed in a difficult position because John O'Connell had been attending a railway committee for several weeks. O'Connell also believed, as he told O'Neill Daunt, that it was 'a foolish thing to run amuck at the House of Commons'. So, in opposing Estcourt's motion, he debated the legal aspects of the case but did not give his approval to O'Brien's conduct or to the principle regarding an Irish MP's proper function. In fact, he effectively condemned his ally by saying that O'Brien 'had merely acted from a mistaken feeling of his duty'.[71] In Dublin, secretary Thomas Ray informed O'Connell, 'the better sense' of the General Committee 'certainly did not go with the prudence or the correctness' of O'Brien's conduct. While 'the young men' backed O'Brien, Tom Steele and others were critical. Ray wrote approvingly of one speaker who said 'that Ireland acknowledged you [O'Connell] only as Leader, that Mr O'B[rien] had not acted in unison with you but, on the contrary, took an opposite course ...' In the letter sent to Ray for reading in the Association, O'Connell merely said that O'Brien, 'having convinced himself that there is a great principle involved', would take a course that would not 'tarnish his high descent and patriotic values'. But he sent Edward Broderick a second letter that was read out in the privacy of the Committee. This one, according to Barry, expressed O'Connell's fear that the Association would court illegality by condemning a judicial decision of the House of Commons: it was 'of a most deprecatory character, full of terror lest the Association may be involved with the House ... and concluding with a sad representation of the state in which Ireland was placed by active enemies and rash friends, & a devout "God help us!" twice repeated'. The Association duly passed a vote of confidence in O'Brien (in his 'integrity, patriotism and personal courage') but did not express *approval* of his stand. Steele welcomed O'Connell's endorsement of this course. In the *Pilot*, the paper that always tried to reflect O'Connell's views, editor Richard Barrett regretted O'Brien's involvement in 'a miserable bye-battle' that, as John O'Connell's service on a committee proved, was not a matter of 'principle'.[72]

On 4 May, O'Brien wrote to Lucy that he was 'astonished to hear' that she felt 'anxiety' about his fate. 'You know how much I delight in excitement particularly when I have in my hands a winning game. Now I feel perfectly assured that I shall

---

70 Smith O'Brien Papers, MS 8653 (23), O'Brien to Lucy O'Brien, 4 May 1846; ibid., MS 454, Rough Diary, 3 May 1846 (St Margaret's). *FJ*, 2, 4, 9 May 1846. 71 *Hansard*, lxxxv, 1160-1, 1169-71, 28 April 1846, O'Connell, John O'Connell. Smith O'Brien Papers, MS 436, f1560, John O'Connell to O'Brien, 29 April 1846. Journal of O'Neill Daunt, MS 3040, f180, May 1846. W.J. O'Neill Daunt, *A Life Spent for Ireland, being Selections from the Journals of the late W.J. O'Neill Daunt* (London, 1896), 50. 72 M. O'Connell, *Correspondence of Daniel O'Connell*, viii, 3204, Ray to O'Connell, 30 April 1846; 3207a, Steele to O'Connell, 9 May 1846. Smith O'Brien Papers, MS 434, f1199a, Minutes taken by MacNevin, n.d.; ibid., MS 436, f1580, Barry to O'Brien, 9 May 1846. *Nation*, 2, 9 May 1846. *Pilot*, 1 May 1846.

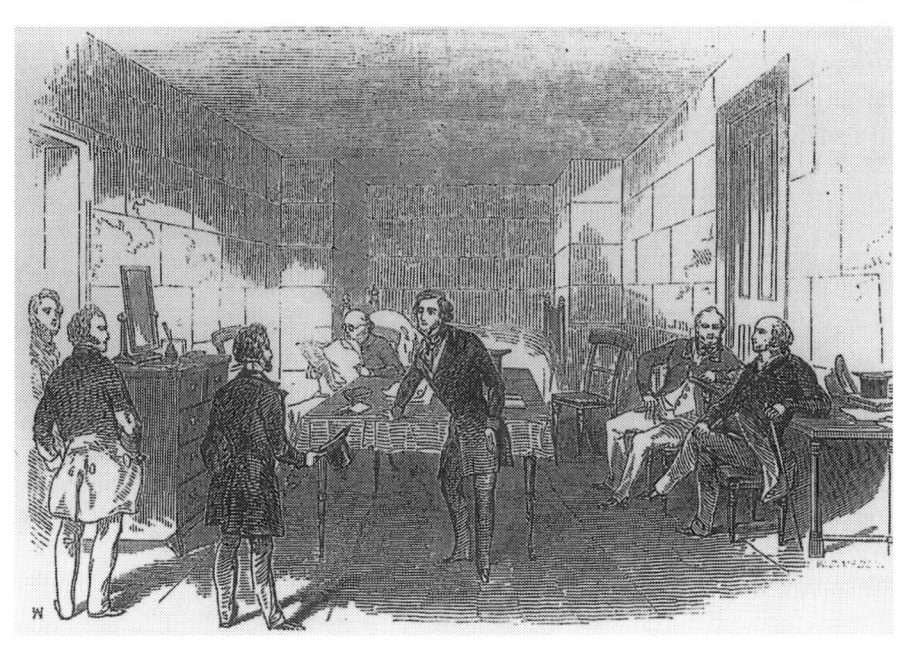

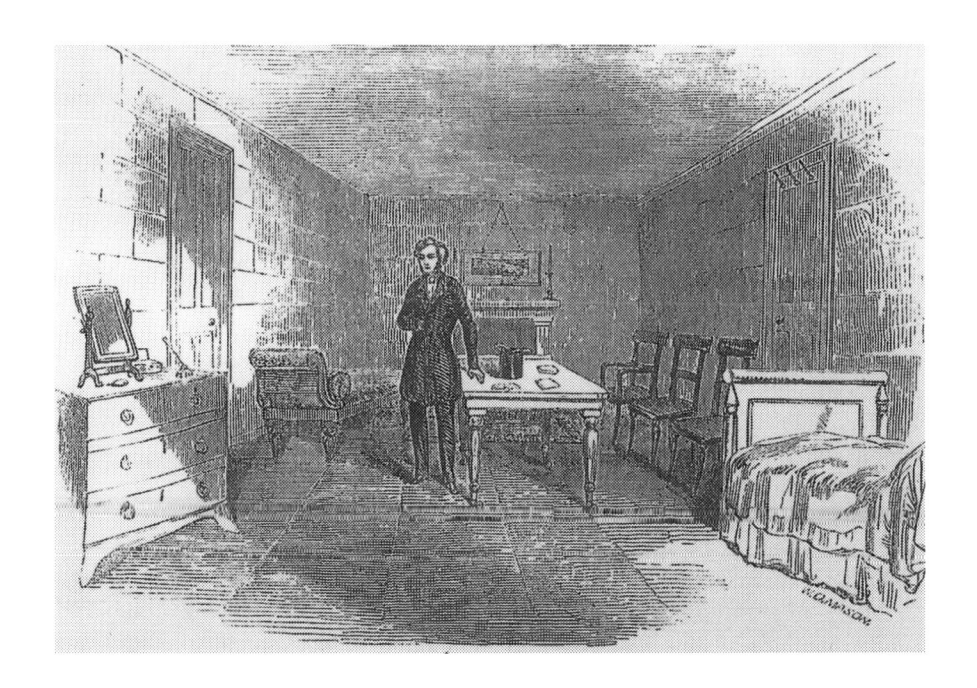

1 O'Brien's prison quarters – ante-room and private chamber

win the game which I am now playing.' He was reminded of 'the three weeks which elapsed after my vote on the Jamaica question' in 1839, when he went on to triumph, so he was 'in excellent spirits'. The fact that this almost jolly letter was written under the address 'Prison. Ho. Comm.' does not suggest great sensitivity to his wife's natural concern. He was 'prepared to remain here for four months' and happy, given the performance of other repealers, to 'show that I can fight the battle singlehanded'. From his prison chamber, he railed against his treacherous allies, telling Lucy on 30 April that he was 'most wretchedly defended by the Repeal MPs' and on 6 May that, 'I am in a "towering passion" this morning on reading the proceedings of the Association. The O'Connell *creatures* there have paralysed the expression of opinion so that the Association has withheld approval of my conduct.'[73] He told Duffy he was 'smitten at heart to find so little moral courage amongst those who claim for themselves the exalted title of *Patriots*'. O'Neill Daunt, visiting him in prison, found him 'extremely dissatisfied with O'Connell for not having espoused his cause more warmly when the subject was discussed in Parliament'. John Pigot, another visitor, noted that O'Brien was 'in a *bitterly* disappointed mood ... He feels *alone* & is evidently much disgusted. The Assoc. vote dissatisfied him too ... One thing is good. Even with his impression [*sic*] on Thursday there was no idea of surrender ... he spoke of being probably not supported (i.e. disavowed) by Limerick, & of consequent abandonment of his seat: but he spoke of this as an occasion *for doing more work at home than he could do in England.* This is a brave mood.'[74]

Declaring himself 'greatly disgusted', O'Brien wrote to Costelloe to say that he wished to resign his seat: 'If I had been firmly sustained by those whose views I have supported I should have been quite contented to encounter any personal hazard in giving effect to the resolve of the Irish nation. I have not been so sustained. I have been abandoned and disowned by the Repeal members in the House of Commons. The Repeal Association has withheld its approval of the step which I have taken. Even in that assembly some have been found to condemn my conduct – none openly to defend it.' However, the determination to resign was qualified: 'If my own constituents abandon me,' he told Duffy, 'as I have been abandoned in Parliament and in the Association I shall retire from the representation ...'[75] In the event, the Limerick repealers were strongly supportive; Costelloe deprecated the conduct of Steele and 'higher personages' (meaning O'Connell), organised two public meetings in O'Brien's favour and sent a deputation across to visit him in his prison. John Mitchel found him 'delighted with the conduct of the Limerick people', and the talk of resignation was short-lived.[76]

73 O'Brien Papers (AO), Letter Box, Bundle 3, O'Brien to Lucy O'Brien. n.d. Smith O'Brien Papers, MS 436, ff1569, 1575, O'Brien to Lucy O'Brien, 6, 8 May 1846; ibid., MS 8653 (23), O'Brien to Lucy O'Brien, 30 April, 4 May 1846.   74 Journal of O'Neill Daunt, MS 3040, f180, May 1846. W.J. O'Neill Daunt, *A Life Spent for Ireland*, 50. Papers of Charles Gavan Duffy, MS 2642, f3436, O'Brien to Duffy, 6 May 1846; ibid., MS 5756, f339, Pigot to Duffy, 9 May 1846.   75 Smith O'Brien Papers, MS 436, f1570, O'Brien to Costelloe, 6 May 1846. Papers of Charles Gavan Duffy, MS 2642, f3426, O'Brien to Duffy, 6 May 1846.   76 Smith O'Brien Papers, MS 436, f1579, Costelloe to O'Brien, 9 May 1846; ibid., MS 440, f2130, Costelloe to O'Brien, 16 May 1846; f2133, Griffin to O'Brien, n.d.; ibid., MS

Meetings in support of O'Brien were held in several southern towns, resulting in about 200 petitions to the Commons for his release, apparently at least some of them unwanted by a prisoner who discountenanced anything like a plea for mercy.[77] Nevertheless, the Lord Lieutenant celebrated the fact that, 'As a means of excitement, Mr O'Brien's folly and obstinacy have signally failed. The few meetings which have been held with the view of getting up addresses to this voluntary martyr have not only been ill-attended but have exhibited such a diversity of opinion amongst the Repealers as must have been anything but satisfactory to those who looked confidently to this new incident as the best chance of restoring unanimity and vigour to their councils.' Elizabeth Smith, the diarist, wrote that O'Brien was 'in a little room where he is locked up endeavouring to perform martyr in some nondescript cause, but as yet he is only laughed at ...'[78] Ray noted that the failure of the repeal rent to rise 'does not indicate much pocket sympathy with Mr O'Brien'.[79] One section of nationalist opinion did rally to O'Brien. In the Association, the *Nation*, the '82 Club, and their letters to O'Brien, Young Irelanders gave him their full support. O'Gorman, for example, was 'ashamed to think that of all the men we have sent from Ireland to represent Repeal opinions, only one has been found bold and true enough to do his duty ... *none now* hold a higher place than yourself in the opinion of the Irish people.' Duffy (in the *Nation*) lamented the 'faint and qualified sympathy' shown by repeal MPs and claimed that Ireland found the Association's response 'worthy only of condemnation or contempt'. Barry was disconcerted by the 'amount of intrigue and littleness' in the Association.[80] Thus emerged another source of difference between O'Connell and Young Ireland, with Tom Steele finding it 'truly afflicting that Smith O'Brien, a man with exalted qualities if well directed, should through the machinations of a perfidious clique, that sought (not caring one curse for him) to make him their plastic instrument, and through his own wayward personal impulses, which he mistook for majestic serene self-might [*sic*], bring himself into a position [? so] unenviable as his present one'. As an interpretation of O'Brien's relationship with Young Ireland and of how he came to be in a prison, this comment is hardly illuminating, but it says much about the rift in the Association. Proud of how he had opposed Young Ireland over O'Brien, Steele went on to say, 'I have long seen that matters *could not* go on as they were ... it was better that the matter should be *brought to a crisis, and a decisive one* ...'[81] In the rest of May, the O'Brien

---

454, Rough Diary, 25 May 1846. *Nation*, 16, 30 May 1846, O'Brien to his constituents, 25 May 1846. Duffy, *Life in Two Hemispheres*, i, 150-1, Mitchel to Duffy, 13 May 1846. 77 *Nation*, 16, 23 May 1846, M. O'Connell, *Correspondence of Daniel O'Connell*, viii, 3208, Ray to O'Connell, 11 May 1846. O'Connell Papers, MS 13646, Costelloe to Crean, 10 May 1846; ibid., Ray to Spillane, 13 May 1846. *Journals of the House of Commons*, ci, 703-767, May 1846. 78 Graham Papers, 30IR, Heytesbury to Graham, 24 May 1846; Graham to Heytesbury, 28 May 1846. David Thomson with Moyra McGusty (eds), *The Irish Journals of Elizabeth Smith, 1840-1850* (Oxford, 1980), 95, 5 May 1846. 79 M. O'Connell, *Correspondence of Daniel O'Connell*, viii, 3217, Ray to O'Connell, 20 May 1846. 80 *Nation*, 2, 9, 16 May 1846. Smith O'Brien Papers, MS 436, f1565, Doheny to O'Brien, 5 May 1846; f1566, O'Gorman to O'Brien, 5 May 1846; f1580, Barry to O'Brien, 9 May 1846; ibid., MS 441, ff2243, 2251, Duffy to O'Brien [May 1846]. 81 M. O'Connell, *Correspondence of Daniel O'Connell*, viii, 3207a, Steele to

issue festered in the Association and became the main focus of the contrast between the O'Connellite aversion to any suggestion of illegality and the bolder language of the Young Irelanders.[82]

O'Brien told Lucy that English public opinion was 'unanimous' in opposing him, a fact that he welcomed as an additional argument for repeal. In a public letter to Limerick's town clerk, O'Brien proclaimed that despite English hostility and the failure of other repealers to adhere to a 'principle of national policy', he was 'prepared to endure whatever indignities the injustice of a nation, the despotism of a senate, or the puny malice of individuals can inflict ... I am not prepared to compromise either my own opinions of the rights of the Irish nation.' Widening the constitutional issue, he believed that he had asserted 'the right of each Member of Parliament to exercise his own discretion with respect to the mode in which he may best apply his labours for the benefit of his country', against the 'dictation' of the majority, in a 'struggle which ought to command the support of every friend of representative institutions, and of every lover of constitutional liberty'. This was valid, both in principle and in the circumstance where Ireland's MPs were forced to divert their energies from the Famine to assist in 'adjusting gambling speculations on English Railways'. But an individual act of defiance could only be a futile gesture, especially when he failed to consult those from whom he expected unqualified support. The end result of a deepening of divisions – which O'Brien openly acknowledged in another public letter on 20 May – was hardly a vindication of the tactic. Barry's letter to O'Brien is especially interesting. Though critical of the O'Connellites, he also had to justify his own decision to endorse the lukewarm 'confidence' motion. He recalled that it was O'Brien who in the past had 'pressed prudential considerations on me as much as it was possible to do' and had 'often urged the necessity of preventing division'. The point was well made, but compromise had no place in O'Brien's thinking when he saw a question of principle. O'Brien was a better judge in other people's crises than he managed to be in his own.[83]

O'Brien's release was not easily achieved, for the honour of two ancient institutions – the House of Commons and (somewhat older) the name of O'Brien – had to be preserved. After three weeks, Frederick Shaw gave notice of a motion for his release. When O'Brien protested that the motion would damage his 'public character' and 'personal honour', Shaw persisted, believing as he did that he was doing 'a public duty, irrespective of, indeed, as it now appears, against your wishes'.[84] O'Brien asked O'Connell, having 'no hesitation ... in saying that I prefer to owe my discharge to you rather than to him [Shaw]', to present a procedural objection

---

O'Connell, 9 May 1846. 82 Ibid., 3215-7, 3221, Ray to O'Connell, 18, 19, 20, 25 May 1846. *Nation*, 23, 30 May 1846. 83 O'Brien Papers (AO), Letter Box, Bundle 3, O'Brien to Lucy O'Brien, n.d. Smith O'Brien Papers, MS 436, f1580, Barry to O'Brien, 9 May 1846; f1597, O'Brien to Raleigh, 15 May 1846 (also in *Limerick Examiner*, 20 May 1846). *Nation*, 30 May 1846, O'Brien to Meagher, 20 May 1846. 84 Papers of Charles Gavan Duffy, MS 2642, f3436, O'Brien to Duffy, 6 May 1846. Smith O'Brien Papers, MS 436, f1607, Shaw to O'Brien, 22 May 1846. *Nation*, 30 May 1846, O'Brien to Shaw, 21 May 1846; Shaw to O'Brien, 22 May 1846.

to his imprisonment: he believed that Estcourt's Committee of Selection had not been properly instituted. To O'Connell he opined that success in this tactic was 'of the utmost importance not to me alone but to "Ireland and Repeal" ... If I can be released without owing anything to the *indulgence* of the House our triumph would be great indeed ...' On 22 May, O'Connell's motion for O'Brien's discharge on the procedural point was defeated by 180 votes to 36. O'Connell then gave notice for 25 May of a straightforward motion for O'Brien's discharge. This led O'Brien to write to him protesting that his 'honour and reputation' would be undermined by such a motion. 'Suffering under an unjust and illegal imprisonment', he was opposed to anything like 'an appeal to the mercy of the House of Commons ... When half a million of my fellow-countrymen demand my release, not as a favour, but as a right, I shall leave you to exercise without interference your own discretion as to the propriety of protesting, in their name, against the wrong done to Ireland by the incarceration of one of her representatives.'[85]

On 25 May, Shaw moved for O'Brien's discharge, explaining that he thought his motion 'more likely to be adopted' than O'Connell's and that although O'Brien opposed his motion he thought the House should decide the question 'upon its own merits, and without reference to the peculiar views or personal feelings of Mr Smith O'Brien'. In the belief that 'the authority of the house had been sufficiently vindicated' (Peel), the motion was passed, amidst much laughter – the fact that another princess had just been born to Victoria gave rise to a hope that O'Brien, too, could be 'delivered' – that infuriated the *Nation* and cannot have improved O'Brien's disposition.[86] O'Brien paid the expenses fee (£41 6s. 8d.) on which his discharge was conditional and left his prison on 25 May, ending 25 days of incarceration. His objection to the fee had caused Woronzow Greig to hatch a plan to have O'Brien's 'friends' pay 'without William's knowledge and thereby *enforcing* his liberation'; it was knowledge of this, O'Brien subsequently informed Ray, that forced him to pay. O'Brien wrote the words 'Saxon robbery. Illegal exaction.' on the bill, and, on accepting the Association's offer (prompted by O'Connell) to reimburse him, his letter to Ray said that the fee was 'illegally extorted' by the House. Ray and Steele doubted if it would be 'safe' to have such a charge against the House of Commons feature in the Association's proceedings, so Steele had the word 'illegally' omitted from the letter that was read out and minuted. Steele expected that O'Brien 'will be greatly displeased; that is no affair of mine ...'[87]

At the end of May, O'Brien returned to a hero's welcome in Ireland, convincing him that the popular response to his adventure 'converted into a triumph that

---

85 Smith O'Brien Papers, MS 436, f1614, O'Brien to Lefevre, 21 May 1845 (also in *Nation*, 23 May 1846); f1617, O'Brien to O'Connell, 22 May 1846 (also in M. O'Connell, *Correspondence of Daniel O'Connell*, viii, 3220); MS 437, f1748, O'Brien to O'Connell [May 1846]. 86 *Hansard*, lxxxvi, 1198-9, 25 May 1846, Shaw, Peel. *Nation*, 30 May 1846. 87 Smith O'Brien Papers, MS 436, f1615, Discharge statement, 25 May 1846; f1618, Greig to Lady O'Brien, 23 May 1846; f1623, Ray to O'Brien, 31 May 1846. M. O'Connell, *Correspondence of Daniel O'Connell*, viii, 3224, Ray to O'Connell, 8 June 1846; 3224a, Steele to O'Connell [8 June 1846]. *Nation*, 13 June 1846, O'Brien to Ray, n.d.

which was intended as a disgrace'.[88] O'Connell, calling O'Brien 'my comrade, my colleague, and my co-equal in the struggle', led the Association in paying 'a tribute of national gratitude' and planning a banquet in Dublin in his honour. In a letter to Ray (marked 'not for publication'), O'Brien proposed that, instead of a banquet, there should be a great 'Festival of the Martyrs' every 6 September to celebrate the release of O'Connell and his fellow-prisoners in 1844; he had 'no objection to be included in the number of political martyrs although I have earned martyrdom *very cheaply* ...' He told Ray that if O'Connell and the Committee agreed he would write a public letter formally making the proposal, which he duly did on 20 June. This cannot have removed the impression in England that O'Brien wanted a share of the martyr's halo.[89] His release from the 'Saxon dungeon' was celebrated with his 'triumphal entry' into Limerick and a so-called 'monster soirée' there on 11 June. In accepting the mayor's invitation, O'Brien said he could 'probably' still get back to London in time to vote against the coercion bill. He may have intended a show of disdain for Parliament, but Steele thought the letter 'fatuity' and 'utterly suicidal of his public character. Accepting a pageant and a banquet; and leaving it a mere matter of probability!!! !!! !!! that he may perhaps be able to be in his place in Parliament, to vote on the second reading of the Irish Coercion Bill ...'[90] O'Connell's surviving correspondence does not give an indication of his private opinion of O'Brien at this time, but the fact that Steele, who would not have dreamed of displeasing O'Connell, felt free to use such language is possibly significant. The new coolness between the two men was public knowledge. One of the Limerick organisers tentatively asked O'Brien to assist the cause of reconciliation by proposing the toast to O'Connell. O'Brien in his speech acknowledged 'the undoubted leader of the Irish people' but repudiated O'Connell's 'over-zealous friends' – he 'was going to say false friends' – who said that some wished 'to overthrow his leadership'. He toasted the mayor of Limerick.[91]

The division in the Tory party over the corn laws meant that the days of Peel's government were numbered. Sir James Graham believed that O'Brien, 'not without reason', was 'afraid that O'Connell is ready to sell Repeal to the Whigs if they come into power', and a newspaper report that O'Connell told the Whigs in London that 'all he ever wanted was a real Union' prompted the *Nation* to launch a campaign against any accommodation with Whiggery.[92] O'Connell, probably seeing the *Nation*'s warnings as a questioning of his leadership, sent over a private letter for circulation among his '*friends*'. It is not extant, but the friends were 'delighted at

88 Journal of O'Neill Daunt, MS 3042, f1330, O'Brien to Daunt, 22 June 1846.   89 O'Brien Papers (AO), Book of Cuttings, O'Brien to Ray, 8 June 1846. *Nation*, 27 June 1846, O'Brien to Ray, 20 June 1846.   90 M. O'Connell, *Correspondence of Daniel O'Connell*, viii, 3223a, Steele to O'Connell, 6 June 1846. *Nation*, 6 June 1846, O'Brien to Ryan, 2 June 1846.   91 Smith O'Brien Papers, MS 436, ff1622, 1627, Lynch to O'Brien, 31 May, 8 June 1846. *Nation*, 13 June 1846.   92 Graham Papers, 30IR, Graham to Heytesbury, 28 May 1846. *Nation*, 6, 13 June 1846.

your determination to put down this most mischievous knot' (Crean). 'It has given your own Old-Ireland people joy beyond measure,' wrote Steele, 'that on your return you intend putting these scamps in their proper position.' They claimed that the Catholic clergy desired such action, Martin Crean citing a letter from a Clones priest who threatened to leave the Association if 'infidel' Young Ireland was not brought under control. Crean assured O'Connell there 'can be little doubt that Dr Magennis expresses the almost unanimous opinions of the clergy of Ireland'. O'Connell, so heavily dependent on the clergy's backing, cannot but have been affected by such information.[93]

The *Nation*'s articles against a Whig alliance provoked bitter arguments in the Association on 15 and 22 June, between Young Irelanders who joined in the sentiment and O'Connellites who believed that the *Nation* was attacking O'Connell. Emotions were heightened when Thomas Meagher's description of Davis as 'our prophet and our guide' led to Steele's objection that only O'Connell merited such elevation. O'Connell then joined in with an angry letter denouncing 'clap traps from juvenile orators'.[94] O'Brien had gone up to Dublin on 13 June to attend the Association, but, next day, 'news arrived' that there would be a division on the coercion bill on the 15th, so he 'went off by the 4 o'clock packet to London' on Sunday 14 June.[95] His absence from the Association delighted O'Connell's friends. Ray believed from 'the tone of his speeches at Limerick' – he would certainly have noted the reference to 'false friends' – that O'Brien 'would unquestionably have said something that could not be let to pass, and an open breach would have been inevitable'. Steele's opinion, commenting on O'Brien's departure, that 'Ray managed the affair with exquisite judgement' suggests that the secretary may even have tricked O'Brien into dashing across to London. The coercion vote did not, in the event, occur until 25 June. They were 'in great hopes that O'Brien may be detained beyond [in England] *until you* [O'Connell] *can be present* at the Association for we greatly fear that whenever he comes there will otherwise be something unpleasant ...'[96] Duffy and Barry, perhaps playing on his sense of honour, told O'Brien that, as the latter put it, 'the real grounds for attacking' the *Nation* was 'the position it assumed with respect to you in your late controversy with the House. This ... has created a hostility in O'Connell's mind towards the paper' and its Young Ireland writers.[97]

A secondary disagreement arose when Duffy was acquitted on his sedition charge (caused by Mitchel's railways article) on 18 June. O'Brien lauded the rousing nationalist speech of his defence barrister, Robert Holmes; it was 'an *event* in our national history ... I wish that we could hear such language in Conciliation Hall,' he wrote to Duffy, 'as Mr Holmes was not ashamed to utter in the Queen's Bench.' But

---

93 M. O'Connell, *Correspondence of Daniel O'Connell*, viii, 3227, Crean to O'Connell, 15 June 1846; 3228, Ray to O'Connell, 16 June 1846; 3228a, Steele to O'Connell, 16 June 1846.   94 *Nation*, 20, 27 June 1846, O'Connell to Ray, 18 June 1846.   95 O'Brien Papers (AO), Book of Cuttings, Handwritten note, 14 June 1846.   96 M. O'Connell, *Correspondence of Daniel O'Connell*, viii, 3228, Ray to O'Connell, 16 June 1846; 3228a, Steele to O'Connell, 16 June 1846.   97 Smith O'Brien Papers, MS 437, f1642, Barry to O'Brien, 25 June 1846; f1643, Duffy to O'Brien, 25 June 1846.

Steele and O'Connell, holding to the view that the *Nation* had been 'incendiary', refused to have the Holmes speech published by the Association and O'Connell gave notice that he intended 'separating the *Nation* from the Assn. and ceasing to circulate it' in the repeal reading rooms.[98] Also at this time, O'Connell displayed the extent of his antipathy to Young Ireland when he urged that Kilkenny, where a by-election was imminent, 'must return a Repealer, and I cannot possibly permit it to return either a Tory or Whig or an animal more mischievous than either of the others, called a Young Irelander'. He took particular exception to the proposal that Kilkenny might turn to Meagher, whose anti-Whig speech on 15 June O'Connell considered a 'base attack on me'. Meagher 'and his colleagues,' he warned, 'are actually ruining the Repeal cause. It will, I fear, become impossible to work the Repeal Association with them.'[99] He obviously intended to force their secession. Given all this, Peel's fall at the end of June – defeated on the Irish coercion bill by a combination of his Whig and liberal opponents, including O'Brien and O'Connell, with vengeful Tory protectionists – caused no celebration in the national movement. It would not be far behind the Tory party in breaking up.

O'Brien returned to Dublin and told the Association on 29 June that he had no confidence in the Whigs and that repealers should be put up against the 'Whig Placemen' – those Irish MPs who, because they were appointed to office, would have to resign their seats and stand again in by-elections – to 'prove to the country the importance of exhibiting ... an earnest and uncompromising fidelity to the principle of Repeal'. This, he expected, would mean challenging such 'able and excellent men' as Sheil, O'Ferrall, Somerville and Wyse (the latter two his old friends), but it was important to show 'that no concession has been made or will be made to any English party'.[100] He was encouraged in this by O'Connell, who urged the election of repealers wherever they stood a chance and told O'Brien that, 'You could not apply your admirable business talent to a more useful subject.'[101] On 6 July, however, O'Connell (in the Association) seemed to say he would support the Whigs in order to achieve 11 Irish measures – presented, Duffy later wrote, as 'a dainty dish to set before the people' to tempt them from repeal. In the by-elections, while he 'would go himself to Dungarvan' to ensure a repeal victory there, 'he would not sanction vexatious or bootless opposition'.[102] The ambiguity of this statement was obvious to the wary Young Irelanders. O'Brien, who went to Limerick earlier on the 6th, privately expressed disappointment that the Association did not adopt 'a firmer tone' on the subject and thought that if they could not persuade

---

98 Ibid., f1636, O'Loghlen to O'Brien, 23 June 1846; ibid., MS 437, f1643, Duffy to O'Brien, 25 June 1846. Papers of Charles Gavan Duffy, MS 2642, f3437, O'Brien to Duffy, 20 June 1846. M. O'Connell, *Correspondence of Daniel O'Connell*, viii, 3229a, Steele to O'Connell, 18 June 1846.   99 Ibid., 3234, 3235, O'Connell to Smithwick, 23, 25 June 1846.   100 *Nation*, 4 July 1846. Papers of Charles Gavan Duffy, MS 2642, f3439, O'Brien to Ray, 9 July 1846 (also in *Nation*, 18 July 1846).   101 Smith O'Brien Papers, MS 437, f1648, O'Connell to O'Brien, 30 June 1846 (also in M. O'Connell, *Correspondence of Daniel O'Connell*, viii, 3240).   102 *Nation*, 11 July 1846. Duffy, *Young Ireland: Four Years of Irish History*, 65.

electors to 'do their duty, they may as well cease to meet and to shout and record pledges and vows. We shall deserve nothing but the scorn and ridicule of mankind.'[103] In fact, if his own words can be believed, O'Connell's crime was worse than O'Brien could have imagined; he was 'glad to tell' David Pigot 'that I have stifled all opposition to Sheil in Dungarvan. The election will not cost him a shilling, and that is what he likes – among other things. I am also very glad to find that Wyse is in office again ...' He was also 'working in an under channel for Monahan' at Clonmel, that is to seat the Whigs' new Irish Solicitor General, James Henry Monahan.[104] Instead of Dungarvan being what the Young Irelanders hoped, a repetition of Clare in 1828, the new Lord of the Mint and very much a former repealer was allowed to resume his Dungarvan seat without a contest.[105]

O'Brien's absence from Dublin at this time was probably a deliberate attempt to avoid conflict. He went from Limerick to Kilkee in Clare on 7 July, in order to attend a meeting at nearby Kilrush on 15 July, and remained there until 24 July.[106] This was a very long stay. A diplomatic withdrawal is implied in Robert Potter's letter informing O'Brien about the Dungarvan decision: 'Some of your friends say the Committee would have come to a different conclusion had you remained in town, but I should say you acted wisely in the course you pursued.'[107] According to Duffy, 'there are angry complaints in the correspondence of the period that he evaded his proper responsibility'.[108] He himself sent O'Brien a strong rebuke. O'Brien's letter to Ray about the need to fight by-elections had been 'read and put aside without a word of comment. If it kept your character clear with the people, it certainly had no other practical effect. To have saved Dungarvan would have needed your personal presence in the Committee in the Assn. The contest for the honour of the cause and its safety (both being, I think, involved in the question of Dungarvan) was very unequally maintained when a few young men had to act themselves agst. all the venality, all the timidity and all the ... ignorance of the Assn.' O'Brien had expressed to Duffy the 'hope that all personal discussion at head quarters is at an end. I told Ray very plainly that if any motion not affecting equally other newspapers were made to separate the Association from the *Nation* ... I should be under the necessity of publicly expressing my dissent and that it would also lead to a fatal disruption of the elements of which the Association is composed.' This – a far cry from the patient mediation of earlier times – showed that O'Brien was 'not inattentive to your [Duffy's] wishes'. However, when O'Connell did not move immediately against the *Nation*, Duffy felt 'it would not be candid to you [O'Brien] to leave you under the impression that the men likely to be attacked attribute his silence to your remonstrance. One and all, they believe that, having got into this battle in your defence [in O'Brien's contest with the Commons], you left them,

---

103 Papers of Charles Gavan Duffy, MS 2642, f3438, O'Brien to Duffy, 9 July 1846.   104 M. O'Connell, *Correspondence of Daniel O'Connell*, viii, 3242, O'Connell to Pigot, 8 July 1846.   105 Smith O'Brien Papers, MS 437, f1664, Musgrave to O'Brien, 19 July 1846. Duffy, *Young Ireland: Four Years of Irish History*, 64-6.   106 Smith O'Brien Papers, MS 454, Rough Diary, July 1846.   107 Ibid., MS 437, f1656, Potter to O'Brien, 11 July 1846.   108 Duffy, *Young Ireland: Four Years of Irish History*, 66.

when a crisis came, to take care of themselves ... Nobody seems disposed to attribute any unworthy motive ... but we cannot reconcile the transaction to our preconception of the right and politic course ...'[109]

Duffy was also critical of O'Brien in letters to John Pigot in London, causing Pigot to reply that he 'saw nothing to be annoyed' about, that O'Brien's avoiding open conflict with O'Connell was 'prudent', and that he opposed 'any such intimate connection of our men with him as you [Duffy] so often seem to desire'. Later in life, Duffy still found it 'surprising', given O'Brien's 'proud and upright character', that he avoided a conflict 'by absenting himself when an important decision was to be made', but he acknowledged that as O'Brien was not yet a Young Irelander – he had a position 'resembling that of an umpire' – he 'wisely desired to avoid as long as it was possible, a controversy with O'Connell'.[110] O'Brien's reply to Duffy shows how, just days before the secession, he was still intent on avoiding a schism:

> With reference to the Nation party, I can truly say that I honour their motives, admire their abilities, feel obliged to them for their personal kindness, and am resolved to do all in my power to uphold them; but I am not prepared to identify myself with every opinion expressed by them, nor can I conceive any proceeding on my part more injurious to the cause of Repeal than that I should associate myself exclusively with any particular section of Repealers. The chief value of my present position is that I am enabled to cooperate with the various classes of Repealers, and to assist in keeping the machinery of the movement, which is but too much disjointed, from absolute disruption.[111]

In the General Committee on 9 July, O'Connell spoke about *Nation* articles which infringed the 'principle' of the Association that rejected entirely the use of physical force. The Young Irelanders had always accepted O'Connell's policy of moral force (that is, recourse only to peaceful and constitutional means) but did not exclude the possibility that physical force might at some time become necessary. The question arose in 1843, when O'Connell himself virtually threatened insurrection, and, of course, it was a central issue of his trial in 1844. The *Nation* article that caused Duffy's prosecution, and O'Brien's defiance of the Commons (which invited nationalists to court illegality by supporting him), kept the issue alive, and in June 1846 O'Connell secured the expulsion of a Liverpool repealer who seemed to contemplate a physical conflict. Duffy has argued that O'Connell's desire to support the Whig government – to gain control of Irish patronage for himself as well

---

[109] Papers of Charles Gavan Duffy, MS 2642, f3438, O'Brien to Duffy, 9 July 1846. Smith O'Brien Papers, MS 441, f2254, Duffy to O'Brien [13 July 1846]. Duffy, *Young Ireland: Four Years of Irish History*, 72. [110] Ibid., 66. Papers of Charles Gavan Duffy, MS 5756, ff375, 383, Pigot to Duffy, 18, 17 July 1846. [111] Duffy, *Young Ireland: Four Years of Irish History*, 74, O'Brien to Duffy, 16 July 1846.

as beneficial measures for Ireland – meant he had to 'silence, or exclude' the opponents of the Whig alliance. It is not clear that O'Connell acted against Young Ireland 'for this purpose alone' (Duffy), since the conflict had been building for several years and had many facets, but his decision to press the physical force question in July 1846 did reflect a determination 'to draw a marked line between Young Ireland and Old Ireland'; he said this in the Association on 13 July and warned that any dissentient would find him moving for 'his immediate expulsion'. In the Committee on 9 July, the adjourned meeting on 11 July, and the Association on 13 July, the Young Irelanders, with Barry, Meagher, Mitchel and O'Gorman to the fore, contested the issue. Mitchel, for example, was happy 'to disavow solemnly all intention of exciting our countrymen to insurrection', but he could not accept 'the abstract and universal principle' that use of force was wrong in every circumstance. O'Connell, however, insisted that 'the abstract principle of disclaiming physical force in any event must be held by all members of the Association' – excepting only acts of defence against 'unjust aggression on the part of a domestic government or a foreign enemy', a possible loophole that neither side had sufficient will to use to resolve the difference. O'Connell's so-called Peace Resolutions were carried in the Committee (Mitchel and Meagher voting against) and, on 13 July, in the full Association (with Meagher against).[112]

At his meeting at Kilrush on 15 July, O'Brien made a long speech that studiously avoided the controversies within the Association. However, another speaker, a relative of O'Connell (possibly the Charles O'Connell who played the mock priest at Ennis in 1831!) denounced the 'Young Ireland party' of 'young and beardless boys' who perpetually opposed the Liberator. O'Brien rose again to discountenance such abuse. Showing that he may have been stung by Duffy's criticism, he said that the young men had rallied to him over his arrest and had therefore 'some claims on him for defence'. On the physical force issue, he 'agreed with Mr Meagher': for 'the practical purposes of the Repeal agitation' only peaceful means would be used, but he could not subscribe to the doctrine, or remain in the Association if it required such subscription, 'that no phase of circumstance, no contingency could occur in a national history or in a nation's struggle for liberty in which a resort to physical force was justifiable'.[113] Thus, reluctantly, O'Brien came off the fence and sided with Young Ireland in a direct contradiction of the Liberator. Duffy thanked O'Brien for his 'most generous and most decided' intervention and dismissed their recent *contretemps*: 'We felt the value of your neutral position ... I, and all the friends I have seen, can and do freely say that any feelings of annoyance that existed for a minute have totally disappeared; and that they recognise and are must grateful for your generous defence of them at Kilrush.' Pigot was delighted to have his confidence in 'the depth of the man' vindicated; O'Brien '*will* do *all* that he thinks right when put to it, & will never shrink from his opinions when they appear to be called

---

112 Smith O'Brien Papers, MS 437, f1653, Crean to O'Brien, 9 July 1846; f1660, Report of General Committee meeting of 11 July, by Ray. *Nation*, 18 July 1846. Duffy, *Young Ireland: Four Years of Irish History*, 64.   113 *Nation*, 25 August 1846.

for from him. He has therefore done neither more nor less than I expected, and so I neither join in your [Duffy's] present exaltation nor in your former disappointment.'[114]

O'Connell almost certainly did not have news of the Kilrush speech when he wrote to O'Brien from London on 18 July. He considered it 'impossible for me to act with any of the avowed Young Irelanders unless they retract their physical force opinions altogether and submit to the resolutions of the Association'. He felt that he did not 'go too far in requiring the Young Irelanders candidly to adopt them [the resolutions] or to cease to cooperate with us ...'[115] If this implies that O'Connell assumed O'Brien would support him in the contest, he cannot have remained under this illusion for long. O'Brien's speech, along with a defiant editorial from Duffy, was discussed in the Association on 20 July. It must have been known to O'Connell when he sent Ray a letter on 24 July that came close to declaring an intention to have 'the physical force advocates' expelled from the Association on his return to Ireland.[116] O'Connell also sent over his son, John, for the Association meeting on 27 July, suggesting he had thought better of his 18 July request that O'Brien should represent him. The scene was set for the historic encounter whereby, in his absence, the movement that O'Connell had created would be all but destroyed.

According to Duffy, 'O'Brien endeavoured by private remonstrance with Mr John O'Connell to avert a crisis, but without success'. In the Association, O'Brien read O'Connell's letter and then gave a strong defence of his view that the avoidance of physical force (use of which would be 'madness and folly and wickedness' in 'present circumstances') could not be made a universal principle. He also attacked the Whigs and the decision on Dungarvan. John O'Connell's response made it clear that his father's Peace Resolutions had to be accepted by Young Ireland if they were to be allowed to remain in the Association. At the adjourned meeting on 28 July, the Young Ireland cause was led by Mitchel and Meagher, the latter producing his famous celebration of the sword, 'be it for the defence, or be it for the assertion, of a nation's liberty'. John O'Connell interrupted Meagher to say that it would be 'unsafe' to let him proceed and that 'he and his friends would retire' if the meeting approved of Meagher's views. O'Brien declared Meagher's argument 'perfectly fair and legitimate' and asked if the Association wished to vindicate its enemies 'by putting down the man who is endeavouring calmly and dispassionately to discuss a question to which he was invited – which he was compelled – to discuss'. When Meagher tried to resume, John O'Connell declared that if the members 'would not stand by the founder, let them adopt other resolutions and another leader'. Compromise was clearly impossible, so O'Brien walked out and was followed by most of the Young Irelanders.[117]

---

114 Smith O'Brien Papers, MS 441, f2250, Duffy to O'Brien [21 July 1846]. Papers of Charles Gavan Duffy, MS 5756, f383, Pigot to Duffy, 27 July 1846. Duffy, *Young Ireland: Four Years of Irish History*, 72, 74. 115 Smith O'Brien Papers, MS 437, f1663, O'Connell to O'Brien, 18 July 1846 (also in M. O'Connell, *Correspondence of Daniel O'Connell*, viii, 3248). 116 *Nation*, 25 July, 1 August 1846, O'Connell to Ray, 24 July 1846. 117 *Nation*, 1 August 1846. Journal of O'Neill Daunt, MS 3040, ff192-9, 1

The Road to Secession

It would be reasonable to attribute O'Brien's and Young Ireland's secession to the entire series of frustrations and disagreements since 1843. For O'Brien, however, the seminal event was his imprisonment in 1846. O'Connell and his acolytes betrayed him (he believed) on a matter of principle, while the Young Irelanders rallied to his defence. Duffy, perhaps unnecessarily, had reminded him of his debt. O'Neill Daunt, a repealer whose sympathies were divided, commented in terms that drive home the crucial importance of the imprisonment dispute:

> It is a curious inquiry how far personal jealousies may have influenced the recent quarrel. The crisis appears to have arisen upon O'Connell's denunciation of the *Nation* newspaper. Now, during O'Brien's imprisonment in London last May, it is notorious that the *Nation* covered him all over with praise for 'consistency', 'principle', and 'self devotion'. O'Connell at the same time took his friend's incarceration very quietly. O'Connell had doubtless this apology, that O'Brien had acted against his advice in the step that produced his imprisonment. But however this might be, O'Brien conceived himself abandoned, and he could not help contrasting the coldness of O'Connell with the fervid support he received from the writers in the *Nation*. Meanwhile O'Connell, who brooks no rival near his throne, not improbably regarded the immeasurable praise bestowed upon O'Brien as an attack by implication on himself. Again: O'Connell undoubtedly wishes that his son John should hereafter inherit his sceptre. Whereas the Young Irelanders, mindful that O'Connell's throne is elective, not hereditary, are fully resolved that whenever the Great Dan shall be removed from the scene O'Brien shall succeed him as leader of the agitation. These things rankled upon both sides. A spark was sufficient to explode the mine. The occasion of warfare was furnished by some eloquent rhapsody of Meagher's concerning the sword, and an article in the *Nation*. O'Connell denounced the military tone adopted by that journal. O'Brien, full of gratitude for the support he had received from it, considered himself bound to stand by it now that it had fallen under the ban of the great leader. John O'Connell, having doubtless received instructions from his father to make no concession, pushed the dispute to extremity; and the second day's talk, which is styled a 'debate', was thereupon ended by the sudden secession of O'Brien and his followers ...[118]

Of course, this was not an entire explanation of the schism, for questions of great moment were involved. Above all, when O'Connell seemed to weaken in his commitment to repeal, to look again to the Whigs, O'Brien and Young Ireland stood together on the ultimate question of principle, the difference between being gov-

---

August 1846. Duffy, *Young Ireland: Four Years of Irish History*, 82-86. Gwynn, *Young Ireland and 1848*, 74-8. 118 Journal of O'Neill Daunt, MS 3040, f194, 1 August 1946. See also ibid., Appendix, f1312, O'Loghlen to Daunt, 12 March 1848, on how 'John O'Connell became jealous of O'Brien'.

erned well (perhaps) and governing oneself. They believed that the so-called principle of moral force was pressed by once and future adherents of Whiggery in order to defeat the adherents of repeal. And what happened at Dungarvan – what O'Connell himself said happened at Dungarvan – suggests that O'Brien and Young Ireland were right.

7

Hard Times

After the schism in the repeal movement Young Ireland had to forge an independent way in politics. Now, as never before, the young men looked to O'Brien for leadership. They looked in vain. At times – and this is a strange thing to say of men of such stature in their country's history – they would sound like perplexed children whose parent ignored their pleas for help. O'Brien was often absent as his preference for life at Cahirmoyle became more evident than ever. Moreover, it turned out that he had none of the ambition and egotism of the would-be leader. He would give advice – sensible and realistic advice – but he had no more desire to dominate Young Ireland's thinking than he had been prepared to allow others to dominate his. Unfortunately, this was not good politics. The disarray into which Young Ireland later fell owed much to the abdication of their only natural leader. If O'Brien had any claim to greatness it was forfeited not in the tragic events of July 1848 but in his failure to give effective leadership during the two preceding years.

O'Brien's diary entry for 28 July 1846 was, 'Adjourned meeting at Conciliation Hall. Secession.'[1] He clearly knew it was more than an act of protest. O'Connell proceeded to use every Association meeting to denounce the Young Irelanders in the most vehement terms. They and their 'filthy partisans' were 'men of war' who would not be welcomed back until they accepted 'the great principle of moral force'. He did 'most heartily and bitterly regret' the loss of O'Brien, whose great 'ardour' and 'manliness' he lauded with typical hyperbole, but, even for O'Brien, he could not 'compromise one particle'. As well as abusing the Young Irelanders, he did nothing to minimise the differences. The physical force question was pressed relentlessly. On the Whigs, he declared his conviction 'that so much good for the country was never tendered by any government ... So long as the ministry does good for Ireland we will give them all the support in our power.'[2] The *Nation* was excluded from the Association's reading rooms. There was an escalation of the dispute in mid-August when secretary Ray, with O'Connell's support, informed a number of Young Irelanders that, by virtue of their refusal to accept its resolutions, they had ceased to be members of the Association.[3] The O'Connells knew that the

---

[1] Smith O'Brien Papers, MS 454, Rough Diary, 28 July 1846.   [2] *Nation*, 8 August 1846, *et seq.*   [3] Ibid.,

great majority of repealers (and the priests) had remained loyal to the Liberator and so they saw no need to use conciliatory language; John O'Connell assured his father that Young Ireland had not 'any real hold in the country, and we don't mind them'.[4]

O'Brien went to Cahirmoyle in mid-August and would remain there until January 1847. He habitually spent this time of year at home. However, it meant that at a crucial period, when the repeal movement was on the cusp, his political involvement was limited to correspondence. One of his reasons for staying down at Cahirmoyle in 1846 was to avoid being drawn into conflict with the O'Connells. His advice to Young Ireland, given principally in an important series of letters to Duffy, was dominated by the idea of forbearance. He urged the Young Irelanders to 'confine yourselves to self-defence' and trusted 'that nothing will be said or done which can tend to prevent the future reconstruction of the Repeal Party upon an honorable & independent basis'. He warned Duffy that 'the great mass of the Repealers will not tolerate systematic attacks upon Old Ireland'.[5] Unfortunately, he and Young Ireland found it difficult to defend their position in terms that were not critical of O'Connell. In a public letter to Ray on 12 August, O'Brien regretted O'Connell's hostile language and declared that, although he had no wish to 'widen the breach' between the two sides, he was not prepared to remain silent when he and his friends were 'unjustly assailed'. Thus, after protesting against the exclusion of the *Nation* (his reason for writing), he went on to repudiate the Peace Resolutions and warn that O'Connell's course 'seems to me calculated to defeat the consummation of our national hopes at the very moment when we were upon the eve of a final and glorious victory'.[6] Even as he advised forbearance, O'Brien admitted to Duffy on 1 September that he had 'not been allowed to preserve silence. A large body of people came here [Cahirmoyle] yesterday from Rathkeale & Newcastle animated with no inconsiderable amount of Young Irelandism … & I felt myself compelled to state at some length my reason for seceding from the Association …' The result was a speech which, as reported, assailed the Association's conduct over his imprisonment, Dungarvan and the Peace Resolutions. He again stated his commitment to peaceful agitation but, in terms that were as much a challenge to O'Connell as to Britain, he warned that if the government resorted to 'the use of the bayonet' the result would be a struggle in which the British might 'come off the worst'. Clearly infuriated by the conduct of the O'Connellites, he was not disposed to seek compromises with those whom he held responsible for the schism.[7]

By the end of September, he doubted if an 'early reconstitution of the elements of the Repeal Party' would be possible. The so-called 'Whig-Repealers' had shown

---

22, 29 August, 12 September 1846. Duffy, *Young Ireland: Four Years of Irish History*, 88-93, 104-6.   [4] M. O'Connell, *Correspondence of Daniel O'Connell*, viii, 3294, John O'Connell to O'Connell, 2 October 1846.   [5] Papers of Charles Gavan Duffy, MS 2642, f3441, O'Brien to Duffy, 1 September 1846.   [6] *Nation*, 22 August 1846, O'Brien to Ray, 11 August 1846.   [7] *Limerick Examiner*, 2 September 1846. O'Brien told Duffy he feared the speech would be 'subjected to misconstruction' by the only reporters present, from the hostile *Examiner*. Papers of Charles Gavan Duffy, MS 2642, f3441, O'Brien to Duffy, 1 September 1846. Duffy, *Young Ireland: Four Years of Irish History*, 102-3.

Hard Times

'no disposition to make any sort of concession to those whom they have driven out of the Association'. He went on to display not just a principled firmness of purpose but also the patience of the experienced politician who was prepared to allow events to unfold rather than seek a peace that would be 'derogatory to our honor & disadvantageous to the country':

> ... It is quite true that a reconstitution of the Repeal Party is the eventual object to which we ought to look – & with this view I think the articles in the Nation which hold out the olive branch are very judicious, but we must be careful not to purchase a reconciliation by concessions which would make it valueless. We stand very well at present. We keep in check the jobbers. We convince England & the world that there is a party in Ireland which will never compromise the Repeal [sic]. It seems to me that we ought not lightly to abandon so advantageous a position, at all events until we can obtain one more advantageous for the country. I prefer therefore to wait a little longer before we adopt a decided part. Let us fully understand the game which the present leaders of the Association intend to play. If they are really desirous to produce a repeal of the Union they must necessarily change their mode of treating the honest supporters of Repeal ... If on the other hand they exhibit a determination to undermine the Repeal Force ... we shall then be bound to throw aside all reserve & without any regard to personal considerations take such measures as shall appear best calculated to preserve our country from sinister influence.
>
> ... I shall not go [to] the Association until I think that I can promote the interests of Ireland by attendance there. This period will not arrive until the Whig alliance is abandoned. Until Repeal reassumes an ascendancy over Whiggery we could not work together harmoniously in a Committee representing Old & Young Ireland for 48 hours ... It is not improbable that before Christmas O'Connell may see reason to change his policy. We shall be prepared to regulate our course according to his movements – with or against him – according as he shall be with Ireland or with the Whigs.
>
> In the mean time let every man strive to do something by means of his pen or voice to promote the cause of Repeal, so that it may be seen that no party in Ireland is so zealous for the interests of their country as the 'Seceders' ...[8]

O'Brien was anxious to ensure that the seceders' views would be presented to the public. He wrote several times in October and November 1846 to urge Duffy to have the *Nation* deploy 'a trained band ... of men powerful in wielding the great weapons of truth & reason'. Such 'an intellectual "League" of Patriotic minds' would sustain the agitation for repeal at a time when O'Connell seemed ready to postpone it to work with the Whigs. His intention that the column should be entitled 'Young

---

8 Papers of Charles Gavan Duffy, MS 2642, f3443, O'Brien to Duffy, 28 September 1846.

Ireland' was set aside when he accepted M.J. Barry's objection that it was 'too sectarian', a symbol in itself of the division in the repeal movement. They decided to use the heading, 'The Irish Party', and the column, billed as 'Mr O'Brien's project', was launched on 28 November.[9] O'Brien also proposed that its writers should 'meet once a week or once a fortnight & partake of an ostentatious dinner at some hotel in Dublin', in order to 'promote union & social fellowship as well as to stimulate thought & exertion'. This 'Repeal Literary Club' should be 'kept quite private at first & very select ... its *tone* should be kept as high as possible especially at first. Men of refinement will not willingly throw themselves into associations in which they are liable to be assailed by such language as some gentlemen at Conciliation Hall whom it is not necessary to name know how to employ.'[10]

Such activity hardly offered the prospect of an immediate and telling impact, and O'Brien knew that they would be derided as 'nice young men for a tea party'.[11] Duffy later wrote that O'Brien's 'primary purpose' in proposing the new column 'was to avoid creating a rival Association'. His timidity tested the patience of the Young Irelanders. Duffy, O'Gorman and Meagher all urged that the '82 Club should be developed as a Young Ireland forum. 'I do not think mere writing will ever satisfy the people,' O'Gorman wrote. 'They like to have something picturesque to fill their fancies, and the '82 Club with its green and gold and fine speeches would be just the thing to show that we are alive and unremitting in our efforts ...' When O'Brien demurred, O'Gorman protested that 'surely forbearance must some time cease and give place to active work, or the Repeal cause, abandoned in the Repeal Association, and not actively supported by us, will die away in the hearts of men ...'[12] However, O'Brien counselled the need to be realistic about what was achievable. Activating the '82 Club threatened its 'virtual dissolution', for he doubted if there were '50 men out of the 250 of whom it is composed who would venture to act with the Club if it were denounced by O'Connell'. Any kind of public meeting 'would be turned into a bear garden' (that is, be disrupted), and he had 'not yet seen any exhibition of public opinion which would encourage nor any positive delinquency such as would justify the formation of a counter-organisation designed to supersede the Repeal Association'. In response to Duffy's desire for a public declaration on the physical force question, he warned 'that your party is not sufficiently numerous & influential to give to such a document as much weight as it ought to carry with it. You could not procure the signature of 100 names known to the public and it is not necessary to exhibit the apparent weakness of the Young Ireland Party.' He did not think the seceders could 'return a single member of Parliament, nor

9 Ibid., ff3443-9, 3451, 3454, 3455, O'Brien to Duffy, 28 September, 12, 15, 20, 29 October, 2, 5, 11, 19, 24 November 1846; ibid., MS 5758, f13, Duffy to O'Brien, n.d. Smith O'Brien Papers, MS 440, f2215, Duffy to O'Brien, n.d. *Nation*, 31 October, 7, 21, 28 November 1846, O'Brien to Duffy, 29 October, 5 November 1846. 10 Papers of Charles Gavan Duffy, MS 2642, ff3444, 3451, 3454, O'Brien to Duffy, 12 October, 11, 19 November 1846. 11 Ibid., f3454, O'Brien to Duffy, 19 November 1846. 12 Duffy, *Young Ireland: Four Years of Irish History*, 113. Smith O'Brien Papers, MS 437, ff1706, 1710, O'Gorman to O'Brien, 20, 27 November 1846; ibid., MS 440, f2208, Meagher to O'Brien [November 1846]; f2215, Duffy to O'Brien, n.d.

even a single corporator' in the municipalities. 'Of course,' he assured O'Gorman, 'our views will alter & our operations expand when "the Irish Party" becomes a synonym for the Irish nation. Such is not the case at present.'[13]

There was also a necessity for 'forbearance' if they were to achieve an eventual reunion of repealers. As O'Brien put it to Duffy on 5 November, 'Pray be cautious ... A rash word is not soon forgotten. Be bold, be bold, and every where be bold. Be *not too bold.*' When, on 16 November, the Catholic bishop of Elphin, Dr Browne, came to the Association and denounced the Young Irelanders as 'the enemies of religion', O'Brien advised that he 'ought to be *calmly* answered. Be very cautious however not to give offence to the clergy ... Let us avoid the formation of a Parti Pretre & of an Anti Priest Party. To say nothing of the social & religious effects of such a division it would be fatal to the cause of Repeal.'[14] In the end, O'Brien did concede that in January there might be 'a general meeting' of 'the unassociated Repealers'. Moreover, he envisaged forming '*a Council* of the Irish Party' to establish and lead a fully-fledged party. He urged Duffy to say nothing publicly about 'this embryo project. It was not my intention to have mentioned it for a few weeks, but perceiving (& rejoicing to perceive) that there is a good deal of impatience on the part of our friends to obtain some organisation I do not know why I should conceal from them what is passing in my mind.' He wondered, however, if they could find enough 'men of energy & activity' for the Council. 'Better do nothing than fail in any thing.' In fact, Duffy moved quickly to take advantage of this tentative proposition, planning a January meeting that 'the men here' believed could be the means by which 'such a Council of the Irish Party might be usefully appointed'.[15]

Even more striking than the forbearance he urged on others (and possibly just as frustrating) was the limited role that O'Brien himself was prepared to play. This owed much to the onset of famine in west Limerick; he told Duffy on several occasions that he was 'more required here than in Dublin'.[16] But there was more than this to O'Brien's staying away from Dublin. There was a deliberate withdrawal from politics. He expressed again the familiar preference for domestic life: 'For myself I enjoy beyond description the interval of tranquillity which recent circumstances have placed at my disposal – finding abundant occupation in my books which are too much neglected in the turmoil of agitation, & undescribable pleasure in the society of my family ...'[17] Regarding his idea of a Council, he wrote that, 'The foregoing project if carried into effect must be accomplished without my personal superintendence. I shall cheerfully give advice & assistance of every kind but I cannot undertake to superintend the proceedings of the Council as I did with respect to those of the Parl Comm.'[18] Moreover, he had no wish to act as the leader. At an

---

13 Papers of Charles Gavan Duffy, MS 2642, ff3444-5, 3447, 3455, O'Brien to Duffy, 12, 15, 29 October, 24 November 1846; f3458, O'Brien to O'Gorman, 28 November 1846.   14 Ibid., ff3449, 3454, O'Brien to Duffy, 5, 19 November 1846.   15 Ibid., f3456, O'Brien to Duffy, 26 November 1846. Smith O'Brien Papers, MS 441, f2262, Duffy to O'Brien [November 1846].   16 Papers of Charles Gavan Duffy, MS 2642, ff3443, 3445, 3449, O'Brien to Duffy, 28 September, 15 October, 5 November 1846.   17 Ibid., f3445, O'Brien to Duffy, 15 October 1846.   18 Ibid., f3456, O'Brien to Duffy, 26 November 1846.

early stage, on 28 September, he told Duffy that he did not 'claim any right to suggest to those with whom you are connected the course which they ought to pursue. I speak only for myself.'[19] Confident that the writers' meetings could become successful without his presence, he thought that, 'There has hitherto been too much disposition to rely upon leadership. For my own part when I recollect how much superior to me in natural talent are many of the men already on your list, I fear to call myself a leader of such a band, but if I were entitled to assume such a position I should be glad to see signs of *self reliance* before I placed myself amongst them.'[20] He deprecated 'the system which has prevailed of echoing with servility every opinion promulgated by O'Connell' and insisted that, 'Parties make leaders, not leaders parties. Every thing that I can do consistent with my sense of duty & my own conviction shall be done in concert with men who are honestly pursuing ends which I approve, but I neither claim for myself, nor will acknowledge on the part of others, the propriety of any thing like dictation.'[21] Much of this language is reminiscent of the independent Member of the 1830s. The leopard could not change its spots; O'Brien would not subsume his independence within a wider entity, even one he might lead.

The prospect of a reunion of repealers continued to dominate political debate. O'Neill Daunt and J.A. O'Neill, O'Connellites, privately urged O'Brien to work for reconciliation. The former wrote in his journal that he would 'heartily rejoice if Smith O'Brien, a man of honour, of talent, and of position, returns to the Association'; in his letter to O'Brien he acknowledged 'that there are various small scruples of delicacy, which are likely enough to create obstacles in a mind at once sensitive & honourable', but he was convinced that these 'should yield to the paramount consideration – viz. that your return would be of essential utility to the cause ...'[22] However, O'Brien, typically resistant to any thought of compromise, saw no point 'in endeavouring to act in concert with men who are pulling in a direction directly opposite to that in which we wish to go ... the present policy of Conciliation Hall is as widely separated from that which we deem right to pursue as humbug is from truth'. He deprecated 'hypocritical dissimulation' and the prospect of 'a fraternal embrace without the affection of a brother. No real reconciliation can take place until the Corn Exchangers throw overboard the Whigs, and virtually if not in terms [*sic*] rescind every thing which has been done at Conciliation Hall since the 1st of July.'[23] This meant withdrawal of the Peace Resolutions and, even more important for O'Brien – a real issue rather than a manufactured one – renunciation of any association with the Whigs. The floating of

19 Ibid., f3443, O'Brien to Duffy, 28 September 1846. 20 Ibid., f3451, O'Brien to Duffy, 11 November 1846. 21 Ibid., f3458, O'Brien to O'Gorman, 28 November 1846. 22 Journal of O'Neill Daunt, MS 3040, f244, 10 October 1846. Smith O'Brien Papers, MS 437, f1691, O'Neill Daunt to O'Brien, 14 October 1846; ff1695, 1705, O'Neill to O'Brien, 24 October, 20 November 1846. 23 Papers of Charles Gavan Duffy, MS 2642, f3458, O'Brien to O'Gorman, 28 November 1846.

the Council idea, which would, in effect, convert 'The Irish Party' from a newspaper column into a political party, meant that reunion was becoming a distant goal.

Nevertheless, December saw what might have been a genuine attempt to mend differences. In Dublin, on 2 December 1846, up to 2,000 repealers cheered as Richard O'Gorman denounced Conciliation Hall as 'the committee room of an English faction, a general advertising office for men in want of place'. Duffy believed that, 'The effect of the meeting was electric; men talked of nothing else from Kerry to Donegal'. O'Brien's correspondents celebrated a 'complete triumph': they were 'not now a crushed or silenced party'.[24] Perhaps apprehensive (for the first time) of a shift in opinion towards the seceders – it was said that on reading about the meeting he declared 'they are a powerful party, and we must have them back'[25] – O'Connell now proposed a reconciliation with Young Ireland. In the Association on 7 December, he suggested a private conference 'to discuss the points of difference between us'. He proposed that it should consist of himself and O'Brien and the barristers Sir Colman O'Loghlen, Thomas O'Hagan, James O'Hea and John Blake Dillon.[26] A succession of people, including O'Loghlen (a repealer but not attached to either of the two parties to the dispute), Duffy, O'Gorman and Robert Potter, urged O'Brien to return to Dublin to take part in Young Ireland's deliberations and, if it proceeded, the conference. Potter suspected that O'Connell hoped to put Young Ireland 'in the wrong before the public' and so felt all the more strongly that 'you [O'Brien] should be in town to guide your youthful adherents'.[27] Dillon, of all the Young Irelanders the most anxious to effect a reunion, warned O'Brien that the people were 'impatient for this reconciliation' and would blame Young Ireland if they did not give a quick and positive response. O'Brien, therefore, must return immediately. Dillon presented the latter as the wish of the Young Ireland leaders who had congregated in the offices of the *Nation* to discuss and, as it happened, to disagree about the answer to O'Connell: 'There are some of us really and honestly averse to reconciliation on any terms, while others consider that a reconciliation on good and honest terms is greatly to be desired ... There is talk of spending five years in "educating" the people ... but I have a strong notion that the five years might be better spent in getting a parliament ... P.S. One last word. It is my belief that we shall never have a conference if you do not come to town within a few days.'[28]

O'Brien's response to this tumult was a display of coolness under fire. He immediately made up his mind, against the torrent of impassioned advice, to remain at

---

24 *Nation*, 5 December 1846. Smith O'Brien Papers, MS 437, f1717, Bindon to O'Brien, 3 December 1846; ibid., ff1718, 1719, Lawlor to O'Brien, 3, 4 December 1846. Duffy, *Young Ireland: Four Years of Irish History*, 119-20. 25 Cavanagh, *Memoirs of Meagher*, 75. Gwynn, *Young Ireland and 1848*, 88. 26 *Nation*, 12 December 1846. *FJ*, 8 December 1846. 27 Smith O'Brien Papers, MS 437, f1721, O'Loghlen to O'Brien, 7 December 1846; f1722, Bindon to O'Brien, 8 December 1846; f1730, Potter to O'Brien, 13 December 1846; ibid., MS 441, ff2236, 2246, Duffy to O'Brien [December 1846]; ff2276, 2277, O'Gorman to O'Brien [December 1846]. 28 Ibid., MS 434, ff1298, 1299, Dillon to O'Brien, 10, 11 December 1846.

Cahirmoyle, telling Duffy that his absence 'will afford you a sufficient reason for delaying to give an immediate answer to questions which may require a good deal of consideration'. He thought that 'a prudent course is not I trust altogether an impossibility even to the "Young Gentlemen" of the "Physical Force Party"'.[29] The young men in Dublin were probably not gratified by such expressions of confidence when active leadership was sorely needed. Writing on 9 December, O'Brien urged Duffy to 'use the greatest possible forbearance in your next publication. The public are very desirous that a "reconciliation" should take place & great will be the responsibility of anyone who throws an unnecessary impediment in its way'. He showed no disposition, however, to compromise with O'Connell and sent up a list of 'propositions' to which O'Connell would have to agree. They described numerous organisational changes in the Association and opposed the acceptance of office and any sort of alliance with an English party. He thought them 'so reasonable in themselves that if they be rejected we cannot incur blame and if they be accepted we shall have attained all for which we ever contended'.[30] When O'Connell sent the Reverend Dr Miley to see him at Cahirmoyle, O'Brien refused to discuss 'the question of "the Forces"' because he believed 'that this controversy is nothing but a pretext – raised mainly for the purpose of excluding from the Association some men who were disposed to thwart the policy of Mr O'Connell with regard to a political connection with the Whigs'.[31] The Young Irelanders, apparently misunderstanding O'Brien's advice to the contrary, decided to send a deputation to O'Connell. O'Brien pressed them to state their 'terms' and 'take no less' and he stated his own determination to 'sign no pledges'. He had 'just as much right to exact from Mr O'Connell a pledge that he will not endeavour to make the Pope King of Ireland as he has to put a test to me respecting "the right of resistance"'. He went on to advise Duffy to 'put Mitchell [sic] into the conference. He is made of sterner stuff than some of our friends. I much fear the consequences of a *personal interview*. It will [do] no harm to have me to fall back upon as if so disposed the Young Irelanders can say at the conference that they will consent to no modification of the propositions (as finally agreed upon by us) without my concurrence.'[32]

If O'Brien was a difficult antagonist for O'Connell he was also a difficult ally for Young Ireland. He reserved the right to pursue an independent policy: 'I shall not commit myself to any particular conditions until I hear what are those upon which you have agreed. If I think them reasonable I shall make them mine also.'[33] His insistence on acting according to his own judgement was described in terms that must have made Duffy wonder if O'Brien could be relied on to work with others:

> I am exceedingly harassed by the difference of opinion which has arisen between our friends in Dublin & myself. They ask me to do that which my

---

29 Papers of Charles Gavan Duffy, MS 2642, f3460, O'Brien to Duffy, 8 December 1846.   30 Ibid., f3462, O'Brien to Duffy, 9 December 1846.   31 *Nation*, 19 December 1846, O'Brien to Miley, 16 December 1846.   32 Smith O'Brien Papers, MS 441, f2237, Duffy to O'Brien [December 1846]. Papers of Charles Gavan Duffy, MS 2642, f3463, O'Brien to Duffy, 13 December 1846.   33 Ibid.

own judgement condemns. From the first moment that I heard of O'C.'s proposal I begged that no step might be taken without our mutual concurrence. I do not complain or regret that Young Ireland shd have acted independently of me in approving of a conference at the very time when I was urging that we should proceed by way of resolutions, but I do somewhat complain that I should be asked to do that which I believe to be absolutely injurious to the interests of the party with whom I act ...

I shall be governed by the course of affairs & endeavour to accommodate my views as much as possible to those of your friends but if any degree of confidence be placed in my judgement I ought surely to be allowed to exercise it freely & act upon it accordingly.[34]

This was not leadership, and it was hardly consistent with any idea of solidarity. In the event, Duffy, Dillon, O'Gorman and James Haughton met O'Connell on 15 December. O'Connell insisted on retaining the Peace Resolutions and refused to discuss other matters until Young Ireland accepted them.[35] In other words, O'Connell sought to re-run the July 1846 attempt to force Young Ireland into submission. The delegates withdrew and the first attempt at reconciliation ended in acrimony. Most Young Irelanders, in private and through the *Nation*, accused O'Connell of acting in bad faith. Even Dillon seems to have concluded that O'Connell 'is *not* for reconciliation and that his conference was a humbug' designed to allow him to pose 'as a conciliator whose magnanimous and self-sacrificing offers were coldly and unworthily received'. The historian has as much difficulty reading O'Connell's mind as the Young Irelanders obviously had at the time, but it is probably fair to conclude that he was more interested in achieving a political victory (either Young Ireland's submission or their rejection of an attempt at peace) than reconciliation. O'Brien's caution was probably well judged. However, O'Loghlen accused O'Brien of missing a genuine opportunity, and Dillon was critical, albeit in terms that emphasised O'Brien's importance: 'If everything is not exactly as you would wish, remember that your absence has been a great source of embarrassment to us. We were most anxious that we should all be of one mind with you, but we were compelled sometimes to act without consulting you. This gave rise to apparent collision. However it may be all for the better, as Young Ireland boasts that it can think for itself in *non-essentials*.'[36] O'Brien's own assessment was more self-critical than his first protestations suggested. He acknowledged 'with the greatest satisfaction' that the young men in Dublin had been right to send the deputation to O'Connell and was glad that his advice had been 'so vague as to have been misunderstood'.[37] O'Connell was able to argue in the Association that he had sent Miley

---

[34] Ibid., f3464, O'Brien to Duffy, 15 December 1846. [35] Smith O'Brien Papers, MS 437, f1714, Dillon to O'Brien [15] December 1846. *Nation*, 19 December 1846. *FJ*, 17, 18, 19 December 1846. [36] Smith O'Brien Papers, MS 434, f1301, Dillon to O'Brien, 19 December 1846; ibid., MS 437, f1735, O'Loghlen to O'Brien, 16 December 1846. [37] Papers of Charles Gavan Duffy, MS 2642, f3466, O'Brien to Duffy, 18 December 1846.

as 'a messenger of peace' and read out a long letter in which the priest presented O'Brien as an obstinate opponent of reconciliation. 'I have had a triumph over him [O'Brien],' declared O'Connell. 'He has totally refused – he has refused in the most unpleasant terms.' O'Brien privately conceded that O'Connell had 'rather strengthened his position in public opinion by his late proposal' and admitted that 'the course taken by me has helped to produce *for a moment* this result ... Dr Miley took me at a great disadvantage for I believed him to be sincerely desirous to promote a reconciliation and disposed to deal fairly with me.'[38]

Behind O'Brien's show of modesty and self-reproach lay a reluctance to accept the responsibilities of leadership. Writing to Duffy on 18 December, he made this more obvious than ever before:

> Though I am somewhat *obstinate* in adhering to my own views when I am perfectly convinced of their soundness I always rejoice to witness the exercise of independent thought on the part of others ... I shall be always ready to give my advice and as my *concurrence* may sometimes be useful I shall not be sorry to be consulted, but as I cannot calculate upon spending more than a very short time in Dublin during each year you must rely upon yourselves for working out your views. So far from seeking for leadership nothing would give me so much satisfaction as to be convinced that there are 10 or 20 or 50 men resolute, judicious & experienced – capable of guiding the popular mind of Ireland in the right direction.
>
> You must now *train* several men to act together for this purpose. We want combination, not leadership, still less *dictatorship*. The habit of relying upon others is one which produces indolence & timidity. Teach self reliance to your friends. Let the public be accustomed to see such men as yourself, O'Gorman, Meagher, Dillon, &c acting together & they will soon recognise their right to lead. In this spirit I am disposed *earnestly* to dissuade you from inviting me to a public dinner after our January meeting. The effect of converting a public demonstration into a personal compliment is to exclude all those who do not think that the compliment is merited. I think it of much more importance that there should be a good meeting to advance national principles ...[39]

O'Connell, of course, had made tribute dinners a staple part of his political exertions for almost two decades and O'Brien was probably aware that ungenerous com-

---

38 Ibid., f3468, O'Brien to Duffy, 24 December 1846. *Nation*, 19, 26 December 1846, 2 January 1847. *FJ*, 15, 18, 19, 21, 28, 31 December 1846. These editions contained the recriminatory correspondence that O'Brien initiated with O'Connell and Miley. See also Smith O'Brien Papers, MS 437, f1744, O'Brien to Miley, 24 December 1846; f1746, Miley to O'Brien, 28 December 1846.   39 Papers of Charles Gavan Duffy, MS 2642, f3466, O'Brien to Duffy, 18 December 1846.

parisons would be made if he did likewise. However, there is no doubting his aversion to the principle of individual leadership and determination to avoid having the role of leader thrust upon him. His oft-repeated desire to stay with his family in Limerick was a factor. On 24 December, he wrote that Duffy 'must not rely upon me except as an *auxiliary* ready to give aid so long as your policy is straightforward & judicious. If it were in my power to remain permanently in Dublin I should not through weakness or false modesty abstain from acting as a sort of chief, but I must necessarily be absent & you must therefore bring forward other men ...' He urged Duffy to take on the role of leader: 'Allow me in candour to say that much depends *upon you* ... *you* are the man who ought to guide the party which you have been mainly instrumental in forming ... all entertain respect for your character & abilities ... Of the rest some are too young, others too fiery, others wanting in energy, others unequal ... in point of ability ... I have endeavoured to bring your name prominently before the public as one qualified to lead us. Am I justified in believing that you will not shrink from the task?'[40] Duffy's reply showed that O'Brien was valued for what he represented as well as his character and ability, but he was insistent on O'Brien's duty to provide the fledgling movement with leadership:

> As to the future our chance of effecting anything important depends on your continuing our recognised Leader. You seem to be providentially gifted with qualities and attributes for the time and place. The Protestants and the landed gentry must be won – and you [as] a man of property and family and a Protestant can, and will, win them. What chance of their listening to young men most of whom are Catholics and all of them springing directly from the trading classes. This is only one side of the question. You have already the trust and love of the public to an extent that no other man might win for years. If you will use this power, and devote *three months* of the year, chosen to suit your own convenience in weeks or months, to the practical working of the Irish party all will go well. There are a dozen men who will devote their entire time to it. But without your complete cooperation we would despair of our work.
>
> For myself I look to nothing else than habitual and daily labour at the national agitation till it has done its work. But I have neither capacity nor ambition for the task you would assign me ... Any other leadership than yours, none of us contemplate or would endure. Your character and position entitle you to lead ... if you shifted on any one else the responsibility of leadership nothing but evil would come of it.[41]

Commenting on his own letter the following day, Duffy wrote that, 'above all I desired to urge upon you that your continuing the recognised Leader of the Irish Party, and guiding it by your counsel (by letter when you could not be personally

---

40 Ibid., f3468, O'Brien to Duffy, 24 December 1846. 41 Smith O'Brien Papers, MS 434, f1303, Duffy to O'Brien, 26 December [1846].

present) was absolutely essential to its accomplishing anything effective. We have plenty of working men, but yours is a post we *cannot* fill.'[42] All this modesty and mutual respect, and O'Brien's desire to let bloom the young flowers of the national movement, were highly commendable in their own way. It stood in marked contrast to the strangulating hold that O'Connell had had on Irish liberalism, with his habit of stamping out independent thought and encouraging loyal mediocrities. However, for all that the Association had become rudderless, in that its nationalist principles were in doubt, everyone could recognise the figure at the helm. Young Ireland was about to launch a leaderless party in the naive hope that such a body could avoid division and give a clear direction to Irish nationalism.

Most people in Ireland had more pressing concerns during the dreadful winter of 1846-7. The 1845 failure of the potato was only partial, but that of 1846 was complete and the months that followed witnessed a terrible struggle for survival. It was at the start of September that O'Brien became fully conscious of the extent of the failure and of 'the danger to which we are liable. I fear,' he told Duffy, 'that there will be no potatoes available for food a month hence in this district – & as soon as the harvest work is over – that is in ten days or a fortnight – the population will not have the opportunity of earning money wherewith to buy meal. They are resolved however not to starve & probably will commence plunder. There are very few resident gentry in the country, public works are stopped, and cannot be [revived?] without taxing the sufferers. The farmers are protesting against payment of additional charges. In short nothing can be more gloomy than our prospects. Under these circumstances I have felt it to be my duty to address the Head of the Govt. on the subject ...'[43] This was a reference to his public letter of 9 September to Russell, in which he warned the Prime Minister of the 'awful magnitude' of the problem and the inadequacy of Parliament's provision of £50,000 towards public works. He urged the recall of Parliament, preferably to sit in Dublin, in order to pass relief measures. O'Brien made several proposals, including state grants and loans for employment-creating projects and older favourites like an absentee tax and a law to compensate tenants for improvements. There were several barbed comments in the midst of all this, including an accusation of 'gross breach of faith' by the Treasury, but it was generally a sober and constructive piece. Ray's opinion that it was 'very mischievous of him [O'Brien] to excite the discontent of the people at such a moment' seems inappropriate, not least when the comment was addressed to the great agitator himself.[44] O'Brien told his sister that, 'Thousands around us are beginning to want food. The potatoes which they are now eating are scarcely fit for pigs ... & I do not find that any adequate provision has been made to secure

---

[42] Ibid., MS 441, f2265, Duffy to O'Brien [27 December 1846].   [43] Papers of Charles Gavan Duffy, MS 2642, f3442, O'Brien to Duffy, 9 September 1846.   [44] *Nation*, 12 September 1846, O'Brien to Lord John Russell, 9 September 1846. M. O'Connell, *Correspondence of Daniel O'Connell*, viii, 3280, Ray to O'Connell, 12 September 1846.

employment or food.' He expected that the landlords, too, would struggle when rents dried up and they faced 'a thousand calls' on their benevolence. He asked her to persuade his absent mother 'that it is the duty of every proprietor to come to Ireland at present to assist in warding off the distress'.[45]

O'Brien himself remained at home to play his part. Very little is known about what was done on his own estate at Cahirmoyle. The fact that the land was mostly given over to grazing meant that O'Brien's tenants were not the potato-dependent cottiers who starved and died elsewhere in western Ireland. It was reported that the small number of men he employed were paid substantially less than the workers on nearby relief schemes, and that the cattle reared at Cahirmoyle were exported to England even during the worst of the Famine – but these were unsubstantiated claims by a British reporter who was hostile to both repeal and Irish landlords, with a particular dislike for the tendency of O'Brien and his ilk to 'misrepresent ... the generous exertions of the English government and the English public in behalf of the Irish people'.[46] (O'Connell, too, had been denounced as a bad landlord, in the *Times* in 1845, with allegations that W.E. Forster later found 'most unfair and untrue'.[47]) If O'Brien's conduct as a private individual is unclear, his role as a public figure is well documented. His rough diary shows a constant round of activity as he attended the Board of Guardians at Newcastle almost weekly, Road Sessions, Presentment Sessions, the Quarter Sessions and Relief Committees. In answer to the petition of 20 Limerick magistrates, in which it was hoped that his 'able advice & assistance' might be lent to their deliberations on the 'calamity', he was restored to the bench on 25 September by the Whig Lord Chancellor.[48] At the end of the month, he wrote to the Board of Works in Dublin in terms that reflected the nature of the emergency and the anxieties it caused in him:

> The labouring classes in the County of Limerick are upon the verge of starvation and are beginning to exhibit those symptoms of impatience which may naturally be expected on the part of a famishing population. It is my painful conviction that the peace of this district cannot be preserved for another fortnight unless immediate employment be afforded to those who are willing to work but unable to find employment. The magistrates & cess payers have done all that lies in their power, and henceforth the full responsibility of every contingency which may arise must rest with the Board of Works or with their agents.
>
> I trust that I shall be excused for using language so unreserved but really I should reproach myself with being guilty of criminal delusion if I were to

---

45 Smith O'Brien Papers, MS 18310 (2), O'Brien to Anne Martineau, 13 September 1846.   46 Alexander Somerville, *Letters from Ireland during the Famine of 1847*, edited by K.D.M. Snell (Dublin, 1994), 97, 131, 136-51, 162-5. Somerville's letters were for publication in the *Manchester Examiner*.   47 Charles Chenevix Trench, *The Great Dan: A Biography of Daniel O'Connell* (London, 1986), 288-9. Oliver MacDonagh, *The Emancipist: Daniel O'Connell, 1830-47* (London, 1989), 281-3.   48 Smith O'Brien Papers, MS 437, f1685, White to Brady, 20 September 1846; ff1686-7, Brady to O'Brien, 22, 25 September 1846; ibid., MS 440, f2132, Robert O'Brien to O'Brien [September 1846].

forbear from employing the strongest expressions which language can supply in my endeavours to impress upon the mind of the Commissioners of Public Works the necessity of exhibiting the utmost energy and celerity in regard to operations upon which depends the existence of so many thousands of my fellow creatures.

... I pen these few lines under feelings of the deepest anxiety.[49]

The Board of Works was overwhelmed by a deluge of applications and the secretary informed O'Brien that the law had established procedures which could not be laid aside.[50] The Whigs having withdrawn the Tory government's provision for half the cost of public works, the ratepayers, meeting in presentment sessions, were expected to bear the entire burden. O'Brien attended such sessions at Newcastle, Rathkeale and Shanagolden (all in west Limerick) and complained at the latter of the 'exceedingly disgraceful' delays that had forced 'starving' people to seek his assistance after being turned away from public works.[51] Explaining his inability to attend any meetings in Dublin, he told O'Gorman that, 'Upon my residence here at present may depend the lives of many hundreds. I am employed almost daily in endeavouring to secure employment & food for famishing thousands and without exaggerating my influence I really believe that I have been of considerable use in the district. Whenever I can do more good by going to Dublin than by remaining here I will go there but that period has not yet arrived.'[52]

In November and December 1846, O'Brien addressed eight long letters, which were published in the *Nation* and widely copied elsewhere, to the landed proprietors of Ireland. His purpose was to persuade them to press for practical measures in response to the 'national calamity'. He decried the continuing exportation of grain – 'English horses are now consuming provisions which would have afforded sustenance to our famishing population' – and the prospect of a crippling tax burden on Irish land to pay for largely useless public works. To stave off future crises, he wanted state investment, primarily in the form of repayable loans, in railways, drainage, reclamation of waste lands, harbours, model agriculture schools, and much more. Education, emigration, and an absentee tax were advanced again, and there was considerable focus on the need to compensate tenants for improvements. As Duffy noted, 'It is impossible to read his letters without respect for his practical ability and contempt for the Government which did nothing'.[53] Taken as a whole,

---

49 Ibid., MS 437, f1688, O'Brien to Board of Works, 29 September 1846. 50 Ibid., f1689, Board of Works to O'Brien, 2 October 1846. Cecil Woodham Smith, *The Great Hunger: Ireland 1845-9* (London, 1962), 78-80. 51 Smith O'Brien Papers, MS 454, Rough Diary, 18 September, 2, 6 October, 16, 27 November 1846. *Nation*, 21 November 1846. 52 Papers of Charles Gavan Duffy, MS 2642, f3458, O'Brien to O'Gorman, 28 November 1846. 53 *Nation*, 21, 28 November, 5, 12, 19, 26 December 1846, 2, 9 January 1847, O'Brien to the Landed Proprietors of Ireland, 17, 24 November, 1, 8, 15, 21, 29 December, 2 January 1847. William Smith O'Brien, *Reproductive Employment; a series of letters to the landed proprietors of Ireland: with a preliminary letter to Lord John Russell* (Dublin, 1847). Duffy, *Young Ireland: Four Years of Irish History*, 119, 128-9.

O'Brien's response to the crisis was as far different as one can imagine from that of those landlords who remained inactive and silent. If 'a multitude of the gentry stood apart, as if the transaction did not concern them' (Duffy), O'Brien was one of that heroic band whose intense activity and passionate advocacy compel admiration. He subsequently charged the British government with 'the crime of having wilfully allowed our people to perish' and argued that an attempt 'to purchase emancipation from British rule at a costly sacrifice of human life' was preferable to allowing a repetition of the horrors inflicted on Ireland by 'the incompetency or indifference of English statesmen'.[54] There is nothing to suggest that O'Brien contemplated any sort of violent protest in 1846-7 – the above words were written after the failed revolt in 1848 – but the Famine crisis clearly increased his opposition to British rule. His anger was surely justified. Historians continue to debate the rights and wrongs of Britain's policy, with many still attributing the Whigs' failure to intervene effectively to the *laissez-faire* spirit of the age. However, men like O'Brien ensured that ministers were fully aware of the possibility of alleviatory measures; the latter were part of contemporary political discourse, as was the idea that the British government simply lacked the will to relieve Irish suffering. The charge sheet is not drawn up from the anachronistic analysis of later nationalists.[55]

British politicians reviled Ireland's landlords as the authors of the crisis and proposed to throw on them the entire burden of relief. Aware of the possibility of political advantage, in his first landlords letter O'Brien argued the necessity of domestic legislation, telling the gentry that, 'In your hour of danger and difficulty you find yourselves abandoned by the power in which you trusted. The Premier taunts you with neglect of duty, and leaves you to your fate.'[56] Sensing again the prospect of Protestant converts, O'Brien told Duffy that he 'should not be at all surprised to find the landlords of Ireland placing themselves at the head of a Repeal movement'.[57] If this was to prove over-optimistic (yet again), it was true that politicians of all persuasions showed an unprecedented willingness to unite in opposition to the 'anti-Irish' spirit that seemed to prevail at Westminster. Many, including O'Brien in his public letters, urged that the Irish nobles and gentry should meet in Dublin in January 1847 to discuss relief measures and that, once in London, the Irish Members could then speak with 'the united strength of all' (O'Brien).[58] The idea of such an 'Irish Party' was promoted in the Tory *Evening Mail* and given a substantial boost when it was advocated by George A. Hamilton, one of the Tory Members for

---

54 Smith O'Brien Papers, MS 464, Draft Address of William Smith O'Brien, 1848, 23-7.   55 This point does scant justice to the complex issues. See Mary E. Daly, *The Famine in Ireland* (Dublin, 1986). Cormac O'Grada, *The Great Irish Famine* (London, 1989). Chris Morash and Richard Hayes, *'Fearful Realities': New Perspectives on the Famine* (Dublin, 1996). Christine Kinealy, *This Great Calamity: The Irish Famine, 1845-52* (Dublin, 1994).   56 *Nation*, 21 November 1846, O'Brien to the Landed Proprietors of Ireland, 17 November 1846.   57 Papers of Charles Gavan Duffy, MS 2642, ff3445, 3449, 3457, O'Brien to Duffy, 15 October, 5, 28 November 1846.   58 *Nation*, 21 November 1846, O'Brien to the Landed Proprietors of Ireland, 17 November 1846.

Dublin.[59] In mid-December, the Reproductive Works Committee was established to gather information and draw up resolutions for consideration at the projected meeting of the gentry. This committee included O'Connell, O'Loghlen, Frederick Shaw and Hamilton, and O'Brien attended seven of its sessions after going up to Dublin in January.[60] O'Brien, according to his own account, 'assisted in the arrangements' for the extraordinary meeting of nearly 1,000 Irish landlords in Dublin on 14 January, the first such 'aggregate' meeting since 1782-3. The resolutions adopted at the meeting resembled the practical measures that O'Brien (and others) had been espousing, with their emphasis on the need for state-assisted productive employment, but the most striking feature of the movement was the way in which men of all parties pledged themselves to 'joint and united action'. A declaration signed by 46 peers and 28 MPs urged that 'to make such an union binding and effective' the Irish Members should 'meet together' in London 'for the purpose of forming an Irish party, for the protection of Irish interests'. Hamilton said he hoped that the 'Irish party' would succeed in 'creating and infusing such a national feeling amongst Irishmen, in reference to Irish subjects, as will, I trust, ensure for Ireland her due and legitimate weight hereafter in the senate, and in the government of the country'. This, surely, was music to the ears of O'Brien. Seconding one of the resolutions, O'Brien welcomed the 'perfect unanimity' of the meeting and showed obvious delight in the prospect of an Irish party at Westminster:

> For many years I have sighed for the existence of an Irish party; and I rejoice that this important meeting holds out a prospect that we shall, indeed, have such a party working together cordially and earnestly for the good of our country. If we work together as we ought we cannot fail to obtain beneficial measures for Ireland; and the knowledge that we are determined to do so will, I believe, cause those measures to be the more readily granted. For my part, I shall most heartily co-operate with men whom I have long esteemed for their virtues and admired for their business habits, though we happened to sit on opposite sides of the house. I will go into council with them as if they participated in my opinions. And if the Irish Party wish to sit together as one body in the House of Commons I shall cheerfully give my consent to that arrangement and take my place beside my friend Mr Hamilton or Lord Bernard or any other political opponent ...[61]

It will be seen that these hopes were soon dashed. Of more lasting import was the secessionists' decision to establish the Irish Confederation. This occurred on 13

---

59 *FJ*, 5 January 1847, Hamilton to Osborne, 1 January 1847. Hamilton was one of those who alleged 'anti-Irish' views in Britain. 60 Smith O'Brien Papers, MS 437, ff1733, 1743, Foster to O'Brien, 14, 24 December 1846; f1735, O'Loghlen to O'Brien, 16 December 1846; ibid., MS 454, Rough Diary, 5, 6, 7, 8, 9, 11, 12 January 1847. *Nation*, 19 December 1846. *FJ*, 15 January 1847. 61 Smith O'Brien Papers, MS 449, f3399, Personal Memoranda, n.d. (private notes written soon after O'Brien's arrest in August 1848); ibid., MS 437, f1750, Sligo to O'Brien, 5 January 1847. *FJ*, 14, 15 January 1847. The resolution seconded by O'Brien commissioned the Reproductive Works Committee to continue meeting.

January, the day before the meeting of the gentry, and in the same building, the Rotundo. O'Brien saw a close connection between the two events, for he believed that with the landlords so 'thoroughly dispirited with England's management of Irish concerns' but still 'afraid of the ultra-democratic & ultra-Catholic tendencies of a portion of the Repeal Party' (the Association), the new body had a chance to win over 'a large portion of the Irish landed gentry'.[62] The decision was also an acknowledgement that the split in the repeal movement would not be quickly resolved. O'Brien, recognising the 'impatience' of Young Irelanders, had conceded the principle back in November, and the confused response to O'Connell's reconciliation proposal drove home the need to create a formal structure; as Shea Lawlor put it to O'Brien on 14 December, 'we are contending in *detachments* ... discussions are had at dinner, meetings held of individuals, yet no unity, no combination, no deliberative body having authority to bind & restrain individual opinions ... I know not myself with whom to communicate here, or when, or at what place ...'[63] O'Brien's role in the establishment of the Confederation was not entirely positive. He remained unwilling to become the leader. Moreover, there was a take-it-or-leave-it aspect to his planned movements – the founding meeting had to be held when he was stopping over in Dublin on his way to London – and he refused to commit himself to a public dinner on the grounds that 'circumstances vary so much from week to week ... A *splendid* martyr procession was arranged for Sept. 6 [in 1846]. It never took place ...' The projected dinner in Dublin was 'an excellent vision in prospect. I hope that it may not become a "splendid phantom".'[64]

This was hardly encouraging. On the other hand, O'Brien, writing on Christmas Eve and Christmas Day, gave Duffy elaborate instructions on how the new body should be established and organised. The pedantry of the natural bureaucrat is apparent in the elaborate detail of the specifications. The Young Irelanders closely followed O'Brien's advice: the Repeal Pledge of May 1845 was renewed; 'absolute independence of all English parties' was to be 'the basis & essence of the Irish Confederation'; the ruling Council had 39 members (O'Brien had suggested 50); the Council was to meet privately each week, but public meetings would occur only when specially called by the Council; a mass membership was hoped for but a network of local bodies was not attempted, O'Brien counselling against 'any extensive plan of organisation least [sic] we should fail to receive the support upon which we now calculate'. He went up to Dublin on 4 January and made the principal speech at the first meeting. Though denying that the Confederation was 'founded in antagonism to the Repeal Association', he declared that its purpose was to accommodate repealers who would not 'betray' their country 'for a mess of pottage' (place) and, pointedly, said it was not possible 'for any true Repealer to give his support to any government except that which favours Repeal'.[65]

62 Papers of Charles Gavan Duffy, MS 2642, f3468, O'Brien to Duffy, 24 December 1846. 63 Smith O'Brien Papers MS 434, f1306, Lawlor to O'Brien, 14 December [1846], from Dublin. 64 Papers of Charles Gavan Duffy, MS 2642, ff3466, 3468-9, O'Brien to Duffy, 18, 24, 25 December 1846. 65 Ibid. *FJ*, 14 January 1847. Dillon Papers, MS 6455, f22, Membership card of John Blake Dillon, with the

O'Brien played a very limited role in the early days of the Confederation. He went instead to London, having decided to 'take the field on the *Address* unless [the] Govt. greatly changes its mode of dealing with [the] Irish Famine'.[66] He was in his seat – 'on the Opposition benches', alongside the Conservative Members – for the opening of Parliament on 19 January 1847. In reply to the Queen's Speech, he attributed the loss of life to the government's passive reliance on the free market – he spoke scornfully of how deputations from Ireland were handed extracts from Adam Smith's *Wealth of Nations* – and urged ministers to 'ransack every part of the civilised world' for food. In the next ten weeks, O'Brien was constantly on his feet to press for relief measures. Rejecting the argument that the property of Ireland should sustain the poverty of Ireland, he said the Imperial Parliament had a duty 'to alleviate the misery of the inhabitants of one section of the united kingdom', and he contended that it was 'the business of political economy to teach the Government that a people subject to their care should not die of starvation ... it was the duty of government to interfere ...' The results were profoundly disappointing. The Tory protectionist leader Lord George Bentinck's bill to advance £16 million for railway building in Ireland was defeated on the second reading on 16 February. Government opposition ensured the loss of Sharman Crawford's bill to compensate improving tenants. The government's Poor Relief bill provided for outdoor relief, which O'Brien wanted, but the famous Gregory clause meant that it would be denied to anyone holding more than a quarter acre of land. As O'Brien put it, by this 'cruel enactment' a person might give up his land to 'receive relief for a few weeks', and in consequence would 'become a beggar for ever'; he was one of very few men who appreciated the considerable damage that would be wrought by this clause and his hostile amendment was duly lost by 117 votes to 7. He moved for an absentee tax that would compel landlords either to reside or to sell up; it was defeated by 70 votes to 19. On 9 March, a despairing O'Brien said he had to inform 'the civilised world' that 240,000 of his countrymen had been 'allowed to perish like vermin by that Legislature and by that Government.' Two days later, there was an angry confrontation when O'Brien supported an adjournment of the debate on Austria's repression of the Cracow Poles. Chief Secretary Labouchere accused him of obstructing progress on Irish business while on other occasions he brought 'the most serious charges' against Parliament's 'apathy towards Ireland'. O'Brien rose amidst cries of 'Spoke' and 'Explain'. He could hardly have expected sympathy from men who had imprisoned him a year earlier, but it would appear that his furious assault on their response to the Famine had excited more animosity towards him than compassion for Ireland.[67]

Fundamental Principles of the Irish Confederation, 13 January 1847. **66** Papers of Charles Gavan Duffy, MS 2642, f3466, O'Brien to Duffy, 18 December 1846. **67** *Hansard*, lxxxix, 76-84, 301, 453, 481, 635-44, 832-3, 916, 918, 928, 977-8, 1169-70, 1206-8, 1230, 19, 22, 25 January, 1, 4, 5, 8, 11, 12 February 1847, O'Brien; lxxxx, 123-6, 282-4, 445-6, 604, 624, 854-5, 1055, 1101-3, 1222-4, 1397-9, 16, 19, 24 February, 1, 4, 8, 9, 11, 15 March 1847, Division, O'Brien; lxxxxi,159-66, 399-400, 556-7, 587, 592-3, 593-4, 600, 18, 25, 29 March 1847, O'Brien, Divisions.

O'Brien's work was appreciated by the only Young Irelander who was in a position to observe his efforts. John Pigot, living in London, was 'very glad to be the means of clearing up any misapprehension about O'Brien' – possibly a reference to the growing feeling in Dublin that O'Brien was delaying his return unaccountably – 'I have seen a good deal of him this month back, and I believe no one could find any fault with what he has done. In truth I esteem him more & more when I see so many evidences of the disagreeable position of loneliness in which he has been placed here, and which is harder to support than one can easily imagine in the atmosphere of Dublin.'[68] His loneliness was political as well as social, and it is clear that the utter failure of the so-called Irish party added to O'Brien's frustration. An attempt at united action was certainly made. The *Mail* reported on 22 January that O'Brien, Hamilton and two others, acting for the Irish party, had taken 'apartments' in Palace Yard, Westminster, 'where the Irish Peers and members of the House of Commons will have an opportunity of consultation and conference'. O'Brien's rough diary records the first 'meeting of Irish Party', on 26 January, when almost 40 peers and MPs met, with a 'deputation to Lord J. Russell' the following day. The meetings, involving Whigs, Tories and repealers, continued into March.[69] However, differences soon emerged. Notably, whilst John O'Connell and several Irish Tories joined O'Brien on Bentinck's railways bill and the absentee tax, many Irish liberals voted against these initiatives, and the vast majority of Irish Members present, both liberal and Tory, supported the Gregory clause against O'Brien's amendment.[70] In a letter to a former Parliamentary colleague, Montague Chapman of Westmeath, O'Brien wrote that he was 'rendered exceedingly *desponding* [sic] by the manner in which Irish affairs are handled here. I regret also to say that "the Irish Party" promises nothing except to afford another proof of the impossibility of effecting *upon English soil* any successful combination to promote the interests of Ireland.' John Mitchel was informed that O'Brien had 'given up hope of doing much good by the Irish Party'.[71] Subsequently, in his Personal Memoranda, O'Brien gave a fuller picture of the experiment:

> Took an active part in the proceedings of the 'Irish Party' in London. Was present at the meeting [*on 2 February*] at which Lord G. Bentinck submitted his Railway scheme, & supported it in the House – intended to have spoken in the great debate but Speaker would not call me up.
>
> 'Irish Party', London.
> Protested against the Resolutions proposed in my absence by Lord Monteagle upon the subject of Poor Laws. [*This meeting, on 6 February, condemned the proposal to extend outdoor relief; O'Brien refused to sign the resolutions.*[72]] These

---

68 Dillon Papers, MS 6455, f28, Pigot to O'Hara, 25 March 1847.   69 Smith O'Brien Papers, MS 454, Rough Diary, 26, 27 January 1847. *DEM*, 29 January 1847 *et seq.*   70 *Hansard*, lxxxx, 123-6, 16 February; 91, 186-7, 592-3, 18, 29 March 1847, Divisions.   71 Smith O'Brien Papers, MS 8666, O'Brien to Chapman, 3 March 1847; ibid., MS 438, f1845, Mitchel to O'Brien, 19 March 1847.   72 *DEM*, 10, 12 February 1847.

>   resolutions were later attacked by the Cath. Clergy of the County of Cork and together with the conduct of many of the Irish Members in regard to the Railway proposal of Lord G. Bentinck tended very much to deprive the 'Irish Party' of popular confidence ...
>
>   1847. March 18
>   I brought forward a motion for the imposition of a Tax upon the absentees in Ireland. It was supported by a very feeble minority – 19 to 70.
>
>   Returned to Ireland disgusted with the mode in which Irish affairs were treated in Parliament – with the total disregard of the opinion of Ireland – with the contumely cast upon all classes of Irishmen – and with the conduct of the Irish Representatives.[73]

The *Nation* had warned 'Beware of the Whigs!', and O'Brien, commenting on the Irish party, said in the House that 'the influence of English party considerations ... too often enervated the patriotic purpose of Irish Members, as was evidenced in the discussion on the Railway Bill ... when a threat of resignation from the Minister induced some of them to forget their country and remember their party.'[74] Liberal Members favoured the Whigs and certainly did not want to bring down their administration. As for those who spoke for the Irish landlords, the priority was to avoid incurring the entire burden of the Famine. Their interest in long-term remedies was limited, and expectations that they would embrace measures like tenant compensation, outdoor relief and a tax on absentees were always likely to be disappointed.

The Young Irelanders now wanted O'Brien to remain in Ireland. Mitchel had urged that 'it will need all our energies *at home* to resist the deep & settled design of the English Government to uproot the Irish race from the soil ... *you are needed in Ireland*. And I have reason to know most of our Confederates are of that opinion too ... On the whole when you come over at Easter I do earnestly hope the result of our consultations will be that you will determine not to go back.'[75] Duffy wrote in similar vein, underlining O'Brien's importance to their movement:

>   I read your letter to O'Gorman with great satisfaction. I am convinced your return to Ireland, and your residence for some time in Dublin, would be the happiest and most effective measure that could be taken to forward the Confederation. You have made a sufficient demonstration in Parlt. and as you are unsupported [*and you*] effect nothing practical there, there is no objection on the score of neglecting business. On the other hand there is a manifest necessity for someone 'having authority' to concentrate and controul [*sic*] the operations of the Confederation ... If you were here two great operations could be carried on – missions and the election business. I am by

---

73 Smith O'Brien Papers, MS 449, f3399, Personal Memoranda, n.d.   74 *Nation*, 16 January 1847. *Hansard*, lxxxx, 1398, 15 March 1847, O'Brien.   75 Smith O'Brien Papers, MS 438, f1845, Mitchel to O'Brien, 19 March 1847.

no means without hope that an effective Parliamentary party could be formed at the next General Election, if it were seen to at once ... If you devoted the next three months to the Confederation instead of Parlt. all this might be done, and the Confed. would get a fair trial ...[76]

As O'Gorman put it, 'you are badly wanting here. There is indeed a perfect stagnation of political feeling. That cannot last long. The people must have some advice, leaders if you will, and that from some one of higher rank, authority, age and experience than any of us ...'[77] O'Brien finally left London for Dublin on 30 March, and on 21 April the Confederation resolved that he and 'the other Irish Members of all parties' should remain in Ireland.[78] In fact, O'Brien was now ready to give up on Parliament entirely. He 'became very anxious' to resign his seat, 'having totally lost all hope of serving Ireland in the British Legislature and being anxious to devote all my energies to the development of public opinion in Ireland itself ... [However] the friends whom I consulted urgently requested that I would postpone an actual resignation until the general election.'[79] These 'friends' possibly included Duffy and O'Gorman, with whom he dined on 4 and 5 April, respectively, and Sir Colman O'Loghlen told him to 'reconsider your proposed resolution ... *you* are the last man we can afford to lose ...'[80] The question would arise again, in the dramatic circumstances of the general election of August 1847.

The Council of the Confederation had taken offices in D'Olier Street and busied itself enrolling members, collecting subscriptions (which were voluntary) and registering electors, and in February many of the leaders went to Galway to fight a by-election that was seen as 'the Clare Election of the new Confederation'.[81] One candidate, Anthony O'Flaherty, had the support of both repeal factions but Dillon considered him 'as good a Young Irelander as any of us'.[82] Young Ireland's confidence that he could defeat the Whig Solicitor General, J.H. Monahan, was misplaced. The government man won by four votes (510-506) and the subsequent petition against the result, alleging bribery and intimidation, was unsuccessful. The repeal tide had waned long since. A pessimistic O'Gorman declared that repeal was 'starved out of the hearts of the people and corrupted out of the hearts of the other classes'.[83] Opposed by O'Connell and the Catholic clergy, the Confederation's prospects of winning popular support were even more gloomy. O'Gorman believed

---

76 Ibid., MS 441, f2257, Duffy to O'Brien [March 1847].   77 Ibid., MS 438, ff1856, 1867, O'Gorman to O'Brien, 24, 29 March 1847.   78 *Nation*, 24 April, 15 May (O'Brien) 1847. Hudson Papers, 12/0/17, 5th bundle, d, Minutes of Irish Confederation.   79 Smith O'Brien Papers, MS 449, f3399, Personal Memoranda, n.d.   80 Ibid., MS 434, f1871, O'Loghlen to O'Brien, 15 April 1847; ibid., MS 454, Rough Diary, 4, 5 April 1847.   81 Ibid., MS 440, f2222, Duffy to O'Brien, n.d.   82 Ibid., MS 437, f1774, O'Gorman to O'Brien, 3 February 1847; ibid., MS 440, f2109, Dillon to O'Brien, 3 February 1847.   83 Ibid., MS 441, f2273, O'Gorman to O'Brien, 15 March 1847. See also ibid., MS 438, f1838, Barry to O'Brien, 8 March 1847; f1845, Mitchel to O'Brien, 19 March 1847.

that the Confederation was 'working badly or rather not working at all' and doubted if their 'very elegant, eloquent, high toned sort of business' had much popular appeal. Duffy, with the benefit of hindsight, recognised that, for all the young men's efforts, 'the gentry only furnished a few stray volunteers, the bulk of the middle class stood apart, the Catholic clergy were unfriendly, and the people in their suffering and despair hardly knew what was going on ...'[84]

O'Brien attended the Confederation meeting of 7 April 1847 and spoke with a mixture of anger and 'deepest despondency' of the lamentable response of the government (and the 'Irish Party') to the famine. Referring to John O'Connell's recent speech in favour of a reunion of repealers, he issued a cold rebuff: the differences remained unresolved, above all the question of 'the Whig alliance ... We must know whether men are Whigs or Repealers'.[85] He spent the next four weeks down in Limerick, from where on 14 April he despatched a public letter which challenged John O'Connell to deny placehunting.[86] These were inauspicious circumstances for the reconciliation proposals made by Father McHugh of Meath and the liberal Lord Cloncurry. Echoing the difficulties of the previous December, O'Brien informed Pigot that he considered acceptance and refusal 'nearly equally injurious'. The Confederation's deputation met John O'Connell on 4 May. O'Brien, speaking for the Council, took a hard line, pressing for dissolution of both organisations and the creation of a new body based on such Young Ireland principles as repudiation of place-hunting, the exclusion of religious questions and publication of accounts. John O'Connell emphasised the physical force issue and refused to dissolve the Association. 'The attempt came to nothing,' wrote Duffy, who had favoured reconciliation, 'and the country was assured, in the few journals which adhered to the Association, that O'Brien had done all the mischief ...'[87] O'Brien seemed more anxious to build bridges in other directions. Deploring the government's apparent 'desire that Ireland should become a sheep farm for the English people and a charnel house for Irish paupers', he called on 13 May for a union of all classes in a national council. He secured the adhesion of a number of leading Protestants, including Isaac Butt and Samuel Ferguson, in establishing an 'Irish Council' that would continue the work of the moribund Reproductive Works Committee. 'Several meetings were held,' O'Brien later recalled, 'some Public and some Private, at which were [sic] discussed the Promotion of Irish manufactures, &c.' O'Brien's rough diary has him attending eight Irish Council sessions in May-June 1847 and he attended the body's three public meetings (on 1, 15 and 22 June). One of the men involved

---

84 Ibid., ff1856, 1867, O'Gorman to O'Brien, 24, 29 March 1847. Duffy, *Young Ireland: Four Years of Irish History*, 130.   85 *Nation*, 10 April 1847.   86 Ibid., 17 April 1847, O'Brien to *Freeman's Journal*, 14 April 1847.   87 Smith O'Brien Papers, MS 454, Rough Diary, April-May 1847. Ibid., MS 438, f1880, O'Gorman to O'Brien, 26 April 1847; ff1870, 1888, Pigot to O'Brien, n.d., 3 May 1847; f1889, Griffin to O'Brien, 6 May 1847; ibid., MS 440, f2191, Pigot to O'Brien, 10 May 1847. Journal of O'Neill Daunt, MS 3040, ff289, 290, 7, 12 April 1847. Dillon Papers, MS 6455, ff33, 33a, Pigot to O'Hara, 8, 15 May 1847. Hudson Papers, 12/0/17, 5th bundle, e, Minutes of Irish Confederation. Duffy, *Young Ireland: Four Years of Irish History*, 137-40. *Nation*, 8, 15 May 1847.

(Charles Monck) hoped that with the imminent demise of O'Connell 'the lion and the lamb of Protestantism and Popery' might be 'satisfied to lie quietly together'; but this initiative had more to do with devising practical Famine measures than stirring Protestant nationalism and there was little of the excited optimism that had flickered so briefly and brightly in January.[88]

These quiet endeavours were interrupted by the shocking news of O'Connell's death. Ill for several months, he had left for Rome in March, and it was in Genoa that he died on 17 May 1847. The news was announced in Dublin on 25 May. Even opponents were touched by his 'sad death so far from home' and ready to show 'due respect towards the memory of our greatest countryman'.[89] The *Nation*, black-bordered, paid tribute to the 'true king and father of his race' and O'Brien moved a resolution expressing the 'deep sorrow' of the Council.[90] O'Brien asked John O'Connell if the Confederates could go to the funeral, but the evasive reply (from Maurice O'Connell) forced him to infer that it was 'the wish of the family that he should not attend the funeral'.[91] The Liberator's death produced 'a revival of affection in which his mistakes and shortcomings were cheerfully put out of sight' (Duffy), and this could only damage the popular standing of those, O'Brien and the Young Irelanders, who had been his sternest critics. The *Pilot* accused Young Ireland of driving O'Connell to an early grave; their 'treason' had 'BURST HIS MIGHTY HEART'. Such anger against O'Connell's 'murderers' was compounded when Father John Kenyon of Templederry (in Tipperary), one of the Confederation's few clerical members, publicly dissented from O'Brien's resolution and the *Nation*'s panegyric; he denounced O'Connell as 'a mere time-serving politician – a huckster of expediencies', whose death was 'no loss whatever'. Then the funeral was delayed until August in a cynical attempt, Duffy suspected, to exploit the Liberator's memory in that month's general election. The death of O'Connell put paid to any chance the Confederation had of emerging as a serious electoral force in 1847.[92]

O'Brien left Dublin on 25 June, causing the Confederation's new secretary, Thomas D'Arcy McGee, to hope he would 'write to them [the Council] often, so long as you cannot personally be with them. I cannot but see that in addition to their old respect and esteem they have lately taken something like personal devotion to you.'[93]

88 Smith O'Brien Papers, MS 449, f3399, Personal Memoranda, n.d.; ibid., MS 438, f1872, Mitchel to O'Brien, 18 April 1847; f1877, Monck to O'Brien, 20 April 1847; f1894, Porter to O'Brien, 22 May 1847; ibid., MS 441, ff2033, 2240, Duffy to O'Brien, n.d. Duffy, *Young Ireland: Four Years of Irish History*, 140, 144-5. *Nation*, 15, 22 May, 5, 19, 26 June 1847. William John Fitzpatrick, *The Life, Times, and Cotemporaries of Lord Cloncurry* (Dublin, 1855), 508-10. W.J. McCormack, *Sheridan Le Fanu and Victorian Ireland* (Dublin, 1991), 101-2. 89 Smith O'Brien Papers, MS 438, f1899, Pigot to O'Brien, 27 May 1847; ibid., MS 440, f2198, Pigot to O'Brien, 1 June 1847. 90 *Nation*, 29 May 1847. See also ibid., 12 June 1847, O'Brien in Confederation on 10 June. 91 Smith O'Brien Papers, MS 438, f1905, O'Brien to John O'Connell, 7 June 1847; f1906, Maurice O'Connell to O'Brien, 7 June 1847; f1907, Minutes (in O'Brien's hand) of Council meeting of 7 June 1847. *Nation*, 12 June 1847. 92 Duffy, *Young Ireland: Four Years of Irish History*, 141, 145-6. *Nation*, 5 June 1847. *Pilot*, 28, 31 May, 9, 11 June 1847. 93 Smith O'Brien

Through an address issued by O'Brien, the Confederation called on the Irish voters to return only committed, anti-place repealers in the coming elections. Duffy later wrote of how Ireland required 70 such men as Smith O'Brien.[94] O'Brien initially played the part of a leader. In a preliminary skirmish, he went to Cork at the end of June to participate in the by-election caused by O'Connell's death. He induced Dr Maurice Power, the repealer, to take a pledge against place-hunting and was proud to claim later that he had 'reason to think that our support secured his election which would otherwise have been doubtful'.[95] At the beginning of July, responding to criticism of the Confederation's decision to oppose John O'Connell in Dublin, he argued in a public letter that it was 'utterly impossible for an individual to be at the same time a true Irish patriot and a time-serving dependent – a fawning sycophant – of an English Minister'; every repealer should 'shun the placehunter' and repudiate 'the crime of again selling our country to its hereditary oppressors'.[96] However, though seemingly as combative as ever, he had had enough of futile endeavours at Westminster. His decision in April had been to delay his resignation until the general election, and now he informed his 'political friends' in Limerick of his intention to retire. They 'earnestly entreated' him to continue 'and yielding to their wishes I consented to allow myself to be returned, if such were the general wish of the Freeholders' of Limerick.[97] His address to the electors was the most reluctant of appeals for men's votes: he dismissed the usefulness of sending MPs to Westminster and said he would 'prefer to labour for Ireland as a private individual'; he went forward only because he was told that it was the wish of the constituency. The impression of a tired and disillusioned man was compounded by his complaint that the other repeal MPs' 'subserviency' to the Whigs had been 'sanctioned rather than repudiated by the Repealers of Ireland' and the admission that he no longer wished to be 'an isolated Member of Parliament'.[98] He clearly held out little hope of Confederation success in the elections. His lack of interest in his own success was confirmed by the decision to return to Dublin on 26 July; he explained to Costelloe that he 'wish[ed] the County Club to take whatever course they may deem conducive to the public interest without the bias of any intervention upon my part'.[99]

In meetings on 20 and 27 July, the club adopted O'Brien and Caleb Powell as their candidates for the county, William Griffin reporting to O'Brien that 'your western friends attended in considerable number' to ensure his success. However, loyalty to O'Connell ran strong in Limerick. O'Brien had found on returning there that 'the feeling of the mob' was 'very adverse to the Confederation. The cry about

---

Papers, MS 438, f1917, McGee to O'Brien, 29 June 1847.   94 *Nation*, 26 June 1847, The Irish Confederation to the Parliamentary Electors of Ireland, n.d., By order, William S. O'Brien, Chairman of the Council. Duffy, *Young Ireland: Four Years of Irish History*, 147.   95 Smith O'Brien Papers, MS 449, f3399, Personal Memoranda, n.d. Ibid., MS 454, Rough Diary, 25, 28, 29 June 1847.   96 *FJ*, 6 July 1847, O'Brien to the Editor of the *Freeman's Journal*, 2 July 1847.   97 Smith O'Brien Papers, MS 449, f3399, Personal Memoranda, n.d.   98 *Limerick Chronicle*, 28 July 1847, O'Brien to the Electors of the County of Limerick, July 1847.   99 Ibid., 28 July 1847, O'Brien to Costelloe, 25 July 1847.

O'Connell's death, taken in connection with Mr Kenyon's letter, has done us much harm there. I am sorry that we didn't expose the injustice and falsehood of the cry at the time when it was first raised.' A city election meeting on 26 July saw disorderly scenes in which O'Brien and Young Ireland were abused as traitors and one man called out that O'Brien 'is a murderer – there is blood upon him'. Griffin considered those responsible 'a mere mob ... a set of blackguards', but O'Brien immediately wrote to Costelloe that reading a report of this meeting 'greatly augments my anxiety to retire from Parliament ... That such language ... should be allowed to pass without rebuke or protest is to me sufficient evidence that I am unfit to be [the] representative of such a people.'[100] A bitter contest was expected. William Monsell, put forward by the Limerick Tories, had attended the landlords' meeting in January and, more recently, the Irish Council, and he wrote to O'Brien of his dream that men could be 'neither Whig nor Tory nor repeal but simply Irish', 'happy concord' displacing the 'unhappy differences' of the past. Monsell had privately given 'one portion of his friends' (by which O'Brien, a relative, possibly meant himself) 'reason to believe that he was disposed to support the Question of Repeal'. This may have led O'Brien, always so interested in the prospect of landlord conversions to repeal, to have mixed feelings about opposing Monsell, but, as he later wrote, he 'could not support Mr Monsell because he had not avowed himself to be a Repealer'.[101]

O'Brien's objection to Powell was even stronger. His former ally, like many of the MP adherents to the Association, was no longer an active politician, and O'Brien complained to Costelloe about 'Mr Powell's neglect of the duties which belong to the function of a representative – duties which ought to be performed in Dublin if not discharged in London'. Above all, Powell, he declared, 'avows himself to be a place-hunter', who was therefore 'a more dangerous enemy to the independence of Ireland than either a Whig or a Tory ... , yet it is expected that I should make common cause with him at the approaching election. If such be the terms upon which support is offered, I must respectfully decline to receive it.' He concluded by telling Costelloe that 'if the electors of the County feel disposed to return me, without expecting that I should commit myself to the support of either of the other candidates, I shall continue to serve them as their representative to the best of my ability. If not, they ought to lose no time in providing a substitute. Plenty of candidates can be found who will send a five pound note to Conciliation Hall & swear fidelity to Repeal, with the intention of bartering the cause of their country for place whenever a suitable opportunity shall present itself.' He finished with a request that Costelloe should read the letter to the club and 'give it publicity'.[102] O'Brien's

---

100 Smith O'Brien Papers, MS 439, ff2043, 2068, Griffin to O'Brien [July 1847], 30 July [1847]. Duffy, *Young Ireland: Four Years of Irish History*, 144, O'Brien to Duffy [July 1847]. *Limerick Reporter*, 27 July 1847. *Limerick Chronicle*, 31 July 1847, O'Brien to Costelloe, 27 July 1847. Limerick City showed its colours again when it elected John O'Connell on 6 August.   101 Smith O'Brien Papers, MS 449, f3399, Personal Memoranda, n.d.; ibid., MS 440, f2160, Monsell to O'Brien, 31 October [1846].   102 *Limerick Chronicle*, 31 July 1847, O'Brien to Costelloe, 27 July 1847. See also Smith O'Brien Papers, MS 449,

distaste for Powell's conduct is not surprising, but it is not clear why it influenced his decision on standing for Parliament; he thought the club 'were disposed to expect that I should identify myself with him,'[103] but he could still, as with Fitzgibbon before 1841, have kept his distance. Of course, O'Brien's letter to Costelloe did not mean his resignation from the contest, but, in a private answer to an inquiry about 'the sum which you shall subscribe', he not only refused to contribute but also seemed to invite Costelloe to seek an alternative candidate:

> ... I wish the Electors of Limerick to hold themselves at liberty to dispose of my seat in case any candidate should appear to them more eligible or acceptable even at the last moment. I have nothing to add to what I said to you and other friends in Limerick and the events of each succeeding day tend more & more to confirm my opinion that I can be more useful out of Parliament than in it.[104]

Above all, on 29 July O'Brien sent Robert Potter a letter of resignation and 'deputed' him to read it in the club. He wrote that on further consideration he thought he 'should retire altogether from the approaching contest ... I therefore authorise you to offer my unequivocal resignation.'[105] It was on the basis of this letter that the club proceeded to find another candidate. Costelloe, despite past differences with O'Brien, seems to have acted entirely properly; he had not hesitated to advocate O'Brien's candidacy and, after the resignation, he supported the address in which many Limerick liberals deprecated the offensive remarks heard at the earlier meeting – even if in calling O'Brien 'the most pure, honorable, upright and faithful follower of the Father of his country' (that is, O'Connell) the priest was being economical with the truth.[106] The club now chose Costelloe's cousin, George John O'Connell, to stand alongside Powell.

And O'Brien went on holiday: 'I resolved to withdraw altogether from the election and in order that I might not be placed in circumstances which would tempt me to alter this decision I left Ireland and spent several days among the mountains of Cumberland. I thus cut myself off from all communication relative to the election and neither received nor sent letters to Ireland respecting it until after the election was over ...'[107] He left Dublin on 3 August, walked in the Lake District until the 9th, and then visited several places in northern Ireland on his way to a nine-day touring and walking holiday in Donegal; he finally returned to Dublin on 23 August.[108] That the party leader could take a holiday in the midst of a general elec-

---

f3399, Personal Memoranda, n.d.: 'I could not support Mr Powell consistently with the course which I had recommended in the Confederation and acted upon at Cork because Mr Powell would not pledge himself to abstain from solicitation of Place. His inefficiency had also been such as to afford just ground for complaint.' 103 Ibid. 104 Ibid., MS 439, f1938, Costelloe to O'Brien, 27 July 1847; f1939, O'Brien to Costelloe, 28 July 1847. 105 *Limerick Chronicle*, 31 July 1847, O'Brien to Potter, 29 July 1847. 106 Smith O'Brien Papers, MS 439, f2068, Griffin to O'Brien, 30 July [1847]. *Limerick Chronicle*, 21, 27 July, 4, 8, 11 August 1847. 107 Smith O'Brien Papers, MS 449, f3399, Personal Memoranda, n.d. 108 Ibid.,

tion must be considered rather surprising – even an abdication of responsibility – but it adds to the impression of a weary and demoralised man. Of course, the situation was quickly transformed by the sudden and unexpected intervention of a few of his Limerick friends. These 'came together almost by accident' (O'Donnell) and John Dowling (a Newcastle solicitor) nominated O'Brien without the latter's knowledge, arguing that the resignation had been 'accepted hastily and prematurely'. O'Brien, 'without a canvass, without preparation, organization, or money' (Dowling), was returned with 482 votes, 106 behind Monsell (588) but 24 ahead of Powell (458).[109] The defeated repealers were furious. Powell called O'Brien's resignation letter an 'electioneering squib to secure the return of his cousin', Monsell. That the contest had split the club and the Catholic priesthood, and that O'Brien's victory owed much to the landlords and the Protestant clergy – the Limerick Tories, in other words – added greatly to their anger. Costelloe wrote to the local *Examiner* asking if 'the boasted descendant of Brian Boroihme' would 'try snakingly to creep at Mr Monsell's tail ... into a place obtained by Tories'. He hoped O'Brien would refuse the seat. When O'Brien let him know that he felt 'honoured' by the result and considered that the voters in east Limerick 'took an ignoble part', Costelloe answered that he had secured only 142 liberal votes and was therefore 'the nominee of Tories, parsons and renegades from liberal principles'. Though unwilling 'to question your veracity or charge you with duplicity', he put it to O'Brien that 'a letter of advice from Mrs O'Brien' had been circulated by Potter on the eve of the election. He was filled with 'deep sorrow' by the 'truly disgraceful transactions'.[110] Given Lucy's lack of involvement in her husband's political life, as well as what is known of O'Brien's state of mind, the allegation regarding Potter is highly unlikely.

The Young Irelanders were delighted by the 'great triumph of your [O'Brien's] principles and your personal virtues' (McGee), with Dillon finding it 'quite delightful to see him after all in parliament, and scarcely less delightful to see that scamp Caleb Powell thrown out'. They begged him to accept the decision of his constituents.[111] Michael O'Shaughnessy, who acted for Monsell in the election and was no longer involved with the County Club, was also concerned about O'Brien's intentions and painted a revealing portrait of events: O'Brien had been elected by 'the really independent portion of the county', with votes garnered 'from all sections and parties ... The best portion of the Club, the western people anxiously and resolutely supported you [sic] ... I know no combination of circumstances which could place you in a prouder position. Even in relation to the county I am proud of it,

---

MS 454, Rough Diary, August 1847 109 *Limerick Chronicle*, 11, 14, 21 (Advertisement of John O'Donnell) August 1847. Smith O'Brien Papers, MS 439, ff1959, 1967, Dowling to O'Brien, 14, 19 August 1847. 110 Ibid., f1955, Costelloe to O'Hanlon and Mulcahy, 6 August 1847; f1972, Costelloe to O'Brien, 28 August 1847. *Limerick Chronicle*, 18 August 1847. See also *Limerick Reporter*, 10 September 1847, Costelloe in the County Club on 7 September 1847. 111 Smith O'Brien Papers, MS 439, f1958, Griffin to O'Brien, 9 August 1847; f1960, McGee to O'Brien, 14 August 1847; f1961, Pigot to O'Brien, 15 August 1847; f1966, Mitchel to O'Brien, 16 August 1847; ibid., MS 441, f2231, Duffy to O'Brien [August 1847]. Dillon Papers, MS 6455, f48, Dillon to Adelaide Hart [9 August 1847]. *Nation*, 14 August 1847.

for it exhibits a virtue which I scarcely expected. It puts this county in a position of Honor before the empire which I think you are bound to sustain ...'[112] There is no evidence that O'Brien was ever in doubt. As well as writing to Costelloe, he sent a public letter (from Donegal) to tell the voters he would not refuse to be 'a conscript in your service'. He later wrote, with evident pride, of how he 'had been returned by the active exertions of the Young Ireland Party and of the Cath. Clergy of the diocese of Limerick supported by all the Landed Gentry of the Country'. When a crowd of supporters went to Cahirmoyle on 27 August, he told them he considered the election 'the greatest triumph not only of his life, but that ever occurred in the history of Irish elections'.[113] The fact that he won with Protestant Tory votes probably delighted him as much as it horrified Costelloe.

If O'Brien's victory was not an unmixed success for nationalism, it was still one of few causes of celebration in the Confederation. Meagher, Duffy and the rest had not contested a single seat, lacking funds and knowing the futility of opposing the Association's candidates when the emotions generated by O'Connell's death ran so high. The borough of Youghal was won by Thomas Chisholm Anstey; an English lawyer who generally sympathised with Irish grievances, he was the author of a pamphlet backing O'Brien in the previous year's dispute with the Commons. Despite thinking 'that where fit Irishmen can be got to offer themselves they should be preferred' (Barry, describing O'Brien's opinion), O'Brien had encouraged Anstey's interest in an Irish constituency and supported his return for Youghal. Pigot was extremely upset that O'Brien pushed an Englishman on an Irish constituency, calling it 'a grievous & fundamental error likely to lead to disastrous confusion and ill consequences ... [It is] an admission of inferiority and a confession of incapacity for self government.' Anstey joined the Confederation later in August.[114] Several candidates took pledges against placehunting, causing the *Nation* to proclaim the election of 18 'Independent Repealers', but it is interesting that Barry believed the placehunting resolutions were adopted by the Cork liberals only because they were not advanced by known Confederates.[115] The fact is that out of 40 repeal MPs only two, O'Brien and Anstey, were Confederation men. In several places hostility to the Confederation had taken the form of violence. Richard O'Gorman and his father were attacked by an O'Connellite mob in Dublin, inducing a spirited defiance – 'we could easily beat the brains out of all that could come against us' – in O'Gorman but also deepening his despair at the Confederation's slow progress and his 'contempt' for a 'wretched people' who were 'not worth an honest man's efforts'.[116] A

112 Smith O'Brien Papers, MS 440, f2151, O'Shaughnessy to O'Brien [14 August 1847]. 113 *Limerick Chronicle*, 25 August 1847, O'Brien to the Electors of the County of Limerick, 17 August 1847. *Nation*, 4 September 1847. Smith O'Brien Papers, MS 449, f3399, Personal Memoranda, n.d. O'Brien's success with 'a large portion of the gentry of the county' certainly pleased his brother, Robert. The family could also celebrate Sir Lucius's election for Clare. Ibid., MS 439, f1964, Robert O'Brien to O'Brien, 15 August 1847. 114 Ibid., MS 438, f1919, Barry to O'Brien, 7 July 1847; f1922, Anstey to O'Brien, 10 July 1847; f1934, Doheny to O'Brien, 22 July 1847; ibid., MS 439, ff1937, 1941, Pigot to O'Brien, 24, 29 July 1847. *Nation*, 28 August 1847. 115 Smith O'Brien Papers, MS 438, f1936, Barry to O'Brien, 23 July 1847. *Nation*, 14, 21, 28 August 1847. 116 Smith O'Brien Papers, MS 438, ff1921, 1927, 1929, 1932, 1933,

year had passed since the secession and the story of that year is not an inspiring one. The oft-repeated expressions of optimism seem like whistling in the dark. The conclusion is inescapable: separated from O'Connell, O'Brien and Young Ireland had achieved virtually nothing.

After leaving Donegal, O'Brien spent only four days in Dublin, attending the Confederation meeting of 26 August and going on to Limerick the next day. Pigot told him he 'more & more look[ed] on it as vital to have you *permanently* within the immediate Dublin sphere', but O'Brien's appearances there would be more limited than ever in the coming months.[117] The prospects of the Confederation improved with the emergence of a number of political clubs during and after the general election. Duffy and Meagher saw them as the basis of a mass party, with the latter hopeful that they 'will distribute and localize our principles and spirit, and call the people into action'. Duffy, replying to O'Brien's rather surprising enthusiasm for reconciliation, considered that, 'A reunion of all the true Repealers is certainly the road to Repeal – but it must come when we are *strong*, to be useful. If it were possible now – and it is *not* for Con. Hall would spit upon us in the hour of their supposed triumph ... We must organize, and strengthen our hands on all sides ... we must have ranks, and many visible and formidable ones ... I have the firmest conviction that we will speedily array our friends in every district in Ireland and become the strongest party in the country ...' As chairman of the Committee of Organisation, he proposed the establishment of 'Confederate Clubs in every town and parish in Ireland', and his report, on O'Brien's motion, was adopted by the Confederation on 26 August. By this time, there were already five clubs in Dublin – peopled mostly by unenfranchised artisans – with such evocative names as the Grattan Club, the Swift Club and (the first) the Davis Club. It was decided that every local group of 20 members of the Confederation should form a club. McGee was able to tell the Confederation on 20 October that 12 clubs had been formed in Ireland and eight more in British cities like Manchester, Leeds and Glasgow.[118]

On 4 September, the Sarsfield Confederate Club was opened in Limerick, 'to cooperate with the Confederation in sustaining the pure principles of Repeal' (Doyle). O'Brien was elected its president, and his allies, notably the Griffin brothers and John O'Donnell, were well to the fore. By the end of the month it had 'at least 140 members' (O'Donnell), and William Griffin reported in mid-October that it 'has far outstripped my expectations ... winning adherents in all the small towns about, which will eventually give it the command of the County as well as the City. We already number nearly 200 ...'[119] O'Brien went to Cork on 20 September to

---

O'Gorman to O'Brien, 8, 16, 17, 19, 20 July 1847.   117 Ibid., MS 439, f1991, Pigot to O'Brien, 14 September 1847.   118 Ibid., ff1960, 1974, 1985, 1998, McGee to O'Brien, 14 August, 1, 9, 20 September 1847; f1966, Mitchel to O'Brien, 16 August 1847; ibid., MS 440, f2203, Meagher to O'Brien, [July 1847]; ibid., MS 441, f2231, Duffy to O'Brien [August 1847]. *Nation*, 21, 28 August, 23 October 1847.   119 Smith O'Brien Papers, MS 439, ff1979, 1988 [Clinehan?] to O'Brien, 4, 11 September 1847; f1995, Doyle

attend the first public meeting of the Desmond Club. The speakers were constantly interrupted from the gallery by such cries as 'O'Connell for ever' and (in Cork English) 'yerra hould your tongue, all of ye', and O'Brien had to sit down when the uproar drowned out his attempts to speak.[120] Griffin and Richard O'Gorman feared mob violence when the Sarsfield Club organised a similar meeting in Limerick, apprehending what O'Gorman called 'the triumph of a new and most odious despotism and the commencement of a new reign of terror'. On 20 October, O'Brien was 'obstructed and hooted' and some of his friends 'kicked and violently assaulted' by a 'large mob' outside the Limerick theatre. Nevertheless, the meeting proceeded and up to 2,000 people heard O'Brien say that while the club's name honoured an Irish warrior of the past the present called for peaceful methods.[121]

In November, O'Brien raised the Confederation standard in Belfast. He spent a couple of days at Crawford's home in Down – Crawford, issuing the invitation, called him 'a friend to whom I am sincerely attached' – and joined Meagher, Mitchel, McGee and John Martin in Belfast on 13 November. Crawford had warned O'Brien to 'be prepared' for Protestant opposition, but Duffy, who knew Belfast well, had assured him there was not 'the smallest danger of your mission to the north leading to any disturbance'.[122] In the event, the visit was ruined not by the Protestant unionists but by O'Connellite repealers. The first meeting on 15 November was much disrupted, with continual interruptions from part of the audience, windows broken, and blows exchanged. Mitchel recalled 'one of the most horrible scenes of uproar I have ever beheld in Ireland; shrieking, whistling, stamping, imprecations in the uncouth accentuations of Antrim county ...' As the mob gathered around the deputation, Meagher refused to leave 'except as a corpse', while O'Brien 'showed no excitement of any kind. He had thrown on his cloak, and stood with his arms folded in it, leaning upon a rail' and calmly reasoning with 'a very brutal looking butcher' who, drunk, seemed determined to show he was 'a better man' than O'Brien.[123] But it was the attempt to hold a second meeting on 18 November that saw the mob spin out of control. The others were apprehensive, but, Mitchel went on, 'No matter: O'Brien was, on that expedition, our acknowledged chief, captain and head centre; and where he chose to lead the way all would follow, being very sure that, though he might bring them into amusing situations, he could not bring them into any discreditable one.'[124] O'Brien's own description of his treatment by the Hercules Street butchers says much about his indomitable spirit:

to O'Brien, 18 September 1847; f2000, O'Donnell to O'Brien, 29 September 1847; ibid. MS 440, ff2088, 2184, Griffin to O'Brien, 7 September, 13 October 1847. *Limerick Reporter*, 7, 14 September 1847. **120** Smith O'Brien Papers, MS 439, f2004, Barry to O'Brien, 1 October 1847. *Cork Examiner*, 22 September 1847. **121** Smith O'Brien Papers, MS 439, f2005, O'Gorman to O'Brien, 2 October 1847; f2012, Griffin to O'Brien, 15 October 1847. *Limerick Reporter*, 22 October 1847. **122** Smith O'Brien Papers, MS 439, f1984, Crawford to O'Brien, 8 September 1847; ibid., MS 441, f2244, Duffy to O'Brien [October 1847]. **123** Gwynn, *Young Ireland and 1848*, 140-1, quoting from Mitchel's 1867 tribute to the recently deceased Thomas Meagher. See also M.J. MacManus (ed.), *Thomas Davis and Young Ireland* (Dublin, 1945), 78-83, 'Mitchel on Meagher'. **124** Gwynn, *Young Ireland and 1848*, 142.

A large mob was at this time collected round the theatre who threatened us with personal violence. I threw myself amongst them, discarded the aid of the police and declared that I would address them in Hercules St., the street in which the most violent of them resided. On my way thither I was accompanied by a large crowd vociferating in the most menacing language – and was struck in the cheek by a stone flung from the crowd. I proceeded however to Hercules St. but as I was advancing up the street a portion of the mob who appeared very anxious that I should not be personally injured although resolved that I should not be heard declared that they would not allow me to go further as my life would not be safe. They therefore forcibly carried me to the Hotel.

On the following day we made another effort to address the inhabitants of Belfast. Having secured the theatre upon this occasion we were not prevented by the magistrates from entering it, but we were left wholly unprotected to [sic] the mercy of the mob who forced an entrance and resolved to prevent us from speaking. After some expostulation I induced those who first entered to allow me to address them, but after I had spoken for about a quarter of an hour a reinforcement of men furnished with rattles &c arrived and all further efforts to procure a hearing became ineffectual. On returning to the Hotel we were again surrounded by a crowd vociferating as upon the previous day but were not injured in person.

It is due to the Orangemen of Belfast that I should record my belief that they were not in any way connected with these proceedings. They were altogether the operations of the dregs of the Old Ireland Repeal party at Belfast. Notwithstanding the failure of the main object of my visit I was much pleased with the excursion to Belfast as it enabled me to become acquainted with a considerable number of very intelligent men, to inspect the manufactories [and] public institutions and generally to acquire much information which I had long desired to obtain.[125]

Mitchel's account, even more dramatic, had O'Brien's companions in 'a loud outcry' against his declared intention to address his 'fellow countrymen' in Hercules Street, but he would not be dissuaded. The party was met by men 'with bloody hatchets in their hands', but O'Brien 'was still advancing as serene as a May morning' when supporters rushed forward to prevent a disaster: 'O'Brien was seized upon by two gentlemen, whose names I know not, lifted up from the ground, fairly carried back through the narrow defile into the open space, and Hercules Street was evacuated'. The mob followed, but, seeing that it was now 'in high good humour', O'Brien asked for a barrel or small cart from which to speak, and a butcher offered his shoulders; O'Brien was helped up and, 'balancing himself a moment, with an umbrella under his left arm', he delivered his address to an attentive audience. According to Mitchel, the crowd admired his 'pluck' but did not appreciate

---

125 Smith O'Brien Papers, MS 449, f3399, Personal Memoranda, n.d.

'the high civic virtue and courage which impelled that gallant spirit thus pertinaciously to insist upon his right to address the people of Belfast'.[126] O'Brien had put himself (and his friends) in considerable danger. William Griffin lamented the 'atrocious proceedings' but was hopeful that the 'whole adventure was one to claim attention and make an impression'. Another Limerick man, Lord Monteagle's son, mixed sympathy with admonition, telling O'Brien that if he had worked to put himself 'at the head of the gentlemen of Ireland, instead of seeking to lead the rabble that has betrayed you so foully, you would have been by this time one of the most powerful men in the united Empire'.[127] He did not attempt to substantiate this extraordinary claim. However, the implication that O'Brien was wasting himself in agitation hardly needed justifying. If there were signs of a better future, from the new clubs in particular, the butchers of Hercules Street showed that O'Connell was winning the political battle even from the grave. Their methods were especially forceful, but their verdict was the same as that of crowds in Dublin, Cork and Limerick and of voters all over Ireland. The prospect of O'Brien and the Confederation leading a national movement, or a national revolution, seemed as distant as ever.

---

126 Gwynn, *Young Ireland and 1848*, 142-3. *Northern Whig*, 20 November 1847. *Nation*, 20, 27 November 1847.   127 Smith O'Brien Papers, MS 439, f2022, Stephen Spring Rice to O'Brien, 26 November 1847; f2026, Griffin to O'Brien, 1 December 1847.

8

Springtime of Nations

O'Brien, undaunted, now took his struggle to a place that promised an opposition almost as fierce, in its own way, as that of Hercules Street, namely the British Parliament. Travelling to London from Belfast, his purpose in going over was to oppose the government's new Crime and Outrage bill. Agrarian crime had escalated as another bout of famine – caused on this occasion not by blight but by the failure of Irish farmers, left with too few seed potatoes, to plant anything like an adequate crop – reduced the Irish peasantry to a desperate state. In Limerick, Tipperary and other southern counties there had been a number of shocking murders. O'Brien's papers contain one striking response to this 'murderous system', when the (anonymous) secretary of 'a body of Protestants' warned the Catholic bishop of Limerick 'that for the life of every Protestant landlord, tenant or clergyman we will in retaliation take the life of the *Parish Priest* of that parish ... until the law is again respected and Priests and Popery trodden down under foot ... and we hope when we have made a few Parishes vacant that it will put a stop to this conspiracy which we well know the Priests are at the head of ...' O'Brien's brother, Robert, urged him to accept what he called 'the protection measure', contending that 'there is not a well disposed person who is not convinced that it was absolutely necessary to make some move to put an end to the terrorism of the country'.[1] All Irish politicians were entirely opposed to agrarian outrage, but the Confederates thought the bill draconian – the Lord Lieutenant acquired the power, for example, to disarm every man in a proclaimed county – and were furious that at a time of great distress it was the government's only measure for Ireland. O'Gorman, convinced that 'all classes are sinking into an abyss of utter ruin', deprecated the coercion bill's 'utter inefficiency for good and decided tendency to evil. If some better law than this be not soon passed to protect the people there ought to be a revolution.'[2]

O'Brien's opposition to the coercion bill was inhibited by a prolonged period of illness, to which his adventures in the streets of Belfast possibly contributed. He later noted: 'From Belfast I proceeded to London to attend Parliament. When I arrived there I was suffering under a very severe cold which assumed the form of

---

1 Smith O'Brien Papers, MS 439, f2027, Anonymous to Ryan, 1 December 1847; f2031, Robert O'Brien to O'Brien, 7 December 1847. 2 Ibid., MS 441, f2270, O'Gorman to O'Brien, n.d.

influenza then prevailing as a fatal epidemic in London. My strength became completely prostrated. I was confined to my room for about three weeks, and was unable to take any part in the earlier discussions on the Coercion Bill by which the government was authorised to disarm the population of Ireland. Though very unequal to such a task, being still very feeble, I attended the House for the purpose of opposing the third reading of this Bill – and spoke for nearly an hour against it.'[3] He told the House that the 'fearful outrages' in Ireland 'arose from the misgovernment of the country for many centuries' and that he could not consent to placing the Irish 'at the mercy and caprice' of the government. He was barely audible in the gallery and 'only isolated passages of his remarks reached the reporters'.[4] The Lord Lieutenant, Clarendon, denounced the Irish opponents of the bill as a 'knot of ruffians' who were 'abettors of murder'. However, several repeal Members failed to offer outright opposition. John O'Connell said he 'had expected a more severe measure' and therefore had conformed with the 'usual courtesy' of not opposing its being brought in. O'Gorman believed his conduct would 'go far to shake the confidence of his admirers'. Some behaved even worse, R.D. Browne, Henry Grattan and several other repealers supporting the second reading. Only 14 MPs (including Chisholm Anstey) joined O'Brien and John O'Connell in opposing the third reading.[5]

There was another lame display on 7 December, when Feargus O'Connor, once the repeal Member for Cork and now sitting for Nottingham as a Chartist, moved for a select committee to inquire into the effects of the Union. The debate was a sorry affair, with Henry Grattan feeling compelled to rebut O'Connor's preposterous claim that his illustrious father had been one of the rebels of 1798, and John Walter (the second Member for Nottingham) saying that 'judging from the specimens the House had had of their representatives' the Irish were 'about as fit for self-government as the blacks ... it was a curious fact that the blacks had a proverb that "if niggers were not niggers, Irishmen would be niggers"' The motion was lost by 255 votes to 23. O'Brien, too unwell to attend, deprecated the entire proceeding; he knew its futility and considered the debate 'wretchedly conducted'.[6] Michael Doheny, a Young Irelander, found O'Brien 'desponding and gloomy because of the late exhibition in the House. Pshaw! I have no patience with this sort of thing,' he told Duffy, 'I am glad of that failure!' He wrote to O'Brien that it merely demonstrated the contemptibility of Old Ireland: 'Surely it has only verified our predic-

---

3 Ibid., MS 449, f3399, Personal Memoranda, n.d. See also Papers of Charles Gavan Duffy, MS 5757, f71, O'Brien to Duffy, 13 December 1847. 4 *Hansard*, lxxxxv, 976-9, 13 December 1847, O'Brien. *Nation*, 18 December 1847. 5 *Hansard*, lxxxxv, 312-7, 364-5, 29 November 1847, John O'Connell, Division; lxxxxv, 720-6, 738-41, 748-50, 6 December 1847, Grattan, Browne, Division; lxxxxv, 990-1, 13 December 1847, Division. Clarendon Papers, Letterbook II, 20, 26, Clarendon to Grey, 9, 10 December 1847. Smith O'Brien Papers, MS 439, f2030, O'Gorman to O'Brien, 3 December 1847. 6 Ibid., MS 449, f3399, Personal Memoranda, n.d. *Hansard*, lxxxxv, 752-65 768-9, 792, 7 December 1847, O'Connor, Grattan, Walter. *Nation*, 24 December 1847. When John O'Connell accused Walter of 'buffoonery' it was he who was reprimanded by the Speaker. Chisholm Anstey tried to support the repeal motion but was 'shut out' from the division.

tions and sanctified our warning to the country against these men ...' O'Brien apparently told him that the Confederates must build up their '*Irish* strength', without which 'parliamentary efforts' were useless.⁷ There were signs, in fact, that the Confederation's support was now increasing. According to Clarendon, Old Ireland was 'sinking' and its 'exposure' in the Commons would be 'almost a finishing stroke'. On the other hand, 'Young Ireland is very popular, the people of Dublin are all for getting the wonderful advantages they have been so long promised by force, and if J. O'Connell had come over the day after the Crime Prevention Bill was introduced, he would have been murdered for having *sowld his Country*'.⁸

It was the question of 'force' that now disrupted the progress of the Confederation, as the coercion bill brought out differences that had developed during the course of 1847. James Fintan Lalor, the physically crippled son of a Queen's County gentleman – Doheny called him 'a poor distorted ill favoured humpbacked little creature' – and a member of the Council of the Confederation, had castigated Ireland's landlords in a series of letters published in the *Nation* from January. He advocated a general rent strike and wanted to 'repeal the Conquest' by restoring the land to the Irish peasantry. O'Brien, a landlord himself and committed to winning over the Protestant landlords to nationalism, wrote to John Mitchel in August arguing that the Confederation could not be associated with such ideas. Mitchel 'entirely agree[d]' regarding the Confederation but was determined himself to support Lalor's campaign in order to 'coerce' landlords 'into a fair settlement of the tenure question – the coercion to take the form of non payment to such landlords as hold out'. (He added that he deprecated the 'singular ideas' of Lalor and Kenyon 'about you [O'Brien] & your influence upon our councils ... if my feeling were not very widely different from theirs with respect to your public character you should not long be leader of mine [*sic*].') Duffy, alarmed by Lalor's radicalism and convinced that the peasantry were 'too broken by poverty and public works' to attempt any sort of rising, wrote to O'Brien about the need to continue pursuing the gentry: 'The sole security we have for keeping the Confed. from becoming firmly democratic is their junction. Every additional landlord that joins it will be an additional check upon movements such as you fear ...' He urged that if anyone sought to involve the Confederation with such dangerous ideas, 'you [O'Brien] should not hesitate to *stop them*. This is my *duty*, or the humblest man's in the Council, but how much more is it *yours* – the Leader of the movement. Men have made heavy sacrifices to join the Confed. You owe success to them, and success is only to be had by gathering all men we can influence into its ranks. If I were a landed proprietor, a member of Parlt. and the descendant of an Irish King so help me God I would repeal the Union – and I would begin with converting and enrolling my own class ...'⁹

---

7 Papers of Charles Gavan Duffy, MS 5757, f87, Doheny to Duffy, 24 December 1847. Smith O'Brien Papers, MS 439, f2041, Doheny to O'Brien, 31 December 1847.   8 Clarendon Papers, II, 33, Clarendon to Russell, 18 December 1847.   9 Smith O'Brien Papers, MS 439, ff1956, 1983, Mitchel to O'Brien, 8

Duffy, probably encouraged by O'Brien, set out to ensure that his less radical policy was preferred to Mitchel's. He persuaded the Council to order 'a plan to be prepared of the means and agencies by which we hoped to repeal the Union ... O'Brien was the leader, and we naturally wished him to undertake the task.' O'Brien duly wrote such a report at the beginning of September, but it merely advocated 'bringing up the public mind to a state of preparedness, and keeping it there, so as to be eager to seize any opportunity' and failed to spell out a coherent alternative to Lalor's bold strategy. Mitchel and Duffy both thought that the plan 'ought to be more *specific*' than O'Brien's report, which, Mitchel implied, was 'futile from vagueness' and fodder for 'the sneering enemy'. Duffy wanted a document 'as *exact* and comprehensive as one of Napoleon's plans of a campaign', one that would actually forestall Mitchel's preferred option of civil disobedience by specifying 'something more feasible'.[10] O'Brien, possibly anxious to avoid the dispute that a detailed plan would cause, refused to alter his course. His 'First Report upon the Principles and Policy of the Irish Confederation', unveiled at the Confederation's public meeting of 10 November 1847, defined the object of the movement (a separate legislature under the Crown), opposed physical force, and insisted on full independence of the British parties. Urging every effort to spread the repeal message, he preached the necessity of winning over Protestants in particular, but there was more emphasis on the need for 'moral courage' and 'boldness, fortitude, and perseverance' than anything like a plan of action. O'Brien did not even attend this Confederation meeting – it is possible he already had his feet under Crawford's table in Down – leaving O'Gorman the task of reading out the report. In the next issue of the *Nation*, Duffy, pointedly avoiding any reference to O'Brien's work, declared that, 'The people are now entitled to ask the Confederation for its policy, for the ways and means by which it intends to win Repeal'.[11]

The task of writing such a plan passed to Duffy, who would not present it for several months. In a letter to an American correspondent, O'Brien declared 'that there are few men who have a greater horror of bloodshed than I have, that there are none who value more highly the blessings of social order, none who would more anxiously deprecate a rash appeal to arms for the purpose of attempting (perhaps

---

August, 8 September 1847; f1980, Doheny to O'Brien, 7 September 1847; ibid., MS 441, ff2232, 2256, Duffy to O'Brien [September 1847]. See also Duffy, *Young Ireland: Four Years of Irish History*, 170-2. Even Duffy was occasionally prone to impatience; responding to O'Brien's complaint about an attack on landlords in the *Nation*, he wrote that 'if the landlords abandon the country may the country abandon them'. If they did not change their ways, he would 'wish God speed to their destruction. If they *will not* help Ireland, they are an impediment to her and hence to be got out of the way ... I am sick of pampering them in their long and dishonest neglect of their duties as Irishmen. Think of another year like the last – more deaths – more slavish whining – more ignorant despair, making us the laughing stock of Europe.' Smith O'Brien Papers, MS 440, f2224, Duffy to O'Brien, 6 October 1847. 10 Duffy, *Young Ireland: Four Years of Irish History*, 172-3, quoting Mitchel to O'Brien, 30 September 1847 and Duffy to O'Brien, n.d. Smith O'Brien Papers, MS 441, f2244, Duffy to O'Brien [October 1847]; ibid., MS 454, Rough Diary, 6 September 1847. Duffy, *Life in Two Hemispheres*, i, 240-1. 11 *Nation*, 13, 20 November 1847.

unsuccessfully) to accomplish results which may be obtained by peaceful exertion ...'[12] Regardless of O'Brien's views and clearly infuriated by the proposed coercion bill, Mitchel told a public meeting of the Confederation on 1 December that the disarming clauses were 'a direct invasion of the common rights and prerogatives of manhood. Every man has a right to bear arms.' He urged the formation of militia for 'mutual defence against aggression' by brigands: 'I say ... that farmers everywhere should not pile their arms at the nearest police station, but keep them safe and in good order, wear them and use them, that they should be formed into local militia, with their landlords at their head, or otherwise – [and] that they should be regimented and drilled ...' Duffy and McGee thought the speech 'very indiscreet', but O'Gorman approved, wanting a 'bold stand' against coercion, and he signed a set of resolutions, drawn up by Mitchel, in which the Swift Confederate Club proclaimed 'the indefeasible right of every citizen to bear arms' and stated 'that this right cannot be taken away under pretence of any law whatsoever, especially a law enacted in a foreign and hostile legislature'.[13]

The emerging conflict between Mitchel and Duffy made O'Gorman wonder if 'some wicked demon were lurking unseen to set us by the ears'; he saw 'symptoms of intended dictatorship on the part of Duffy and McGee, and that I for one won't stand'. He hoped O'Brien would soon return from London: 'I fear we shall want you in case of another secession'.[14] Duffy's letter to O'Brien revealed the full seriousness of the rift, which caused Mitchel and Devin Reilly to end their association with the *Nation*:

> I trust your influenza is gone. There was never more need of your being strong and ready, for sad things have been happening here. You know that at the last meeting of the Confed. Mitchel threatened the Govt. with 'secret societies' and warned the people not to obey the coercion bill – and O'Gorman pronounced the formidable dogma that after its enactment the Govt. would not be entitled to obedience. Walking home from that meeting, I had a serious conversation with Mitchel on the course he was taking, after our course had been determined on; and I told him that as far as the *Nation* was concerned I would not permit it to get any countenance for the future. He argued that the Coercion Bill justified his extreme courses. And, to come to the conclusion, on the Friday after he resigned all connexion with the *Nation*, and Reilly followed his example. His object in doing so, he assures me, is because he could not conscientiously rely on our policy or

---

12 Smith O'Brien Papers, MS 439, f2013, O'Brien to Gibbons, 23 October 1847. *Nation*, 30 October 1847.   13 Smith O'Brien Papers, MS 439, f2028, McGee to O'Brien, 2 December 1847; f2030, O'Gorman to O'Brien, 3 December 1847; ibid., MS 441, f2272, O'Gorman to O'Brien, 6 December 1847. *Nation*, 4, 11 December 1847, 8 January 1848, Mitchel to Duffy, 7 January 1848. The letters sent to O'Brien in December and January are the historian's principal source for the political turmoil of these months; Richard Davis's use of none of this correspondence is puzzling. Davis, *Revolutionary Imperialist*, 234-5.   14 Smith O'Brien Papers, MS 439, f2033, O'Gorman to O'Brien, 14 December 1847.

abandon his own – and he is one of the most resolute as well as the honestest and most disinterested of men.

... Now surely this threatens either ruin to the Confed. by frightening all moderate, and all clear sighted, men away from it, or a secession from the secession.

You must determine speedily what ought to be done in the matter or it may be too late ... if the Clubs be left without a definite policy they will inevitably fall into the extreme views. The fear of a new secession or of aimless violence ... have [sic] filled my mind with the desire for a reorganization of the entire Repeal party. If John O'Connell threw off the Brownes and Somerses & adopted the pledge against place-begging surely this would be possible. A requisition for an aggregate meeting of Repealers at Dublin ... would lay the foundation for it. I entreat of you to consider upon *some* adequate remedy against the national party falling into a set of factions and so the hope of Repeal being [quenched?] for this generation.

... When will you be in Dublin? I long greatly to see you at the Council again, before the Confed. is involved in a course from which there is no retreat and to which there is no success.[15]

The irony of one Young Irelander hoping to head off the physical force inclinations of another by seeking reconciliation with Old Ireland was probably not lost on Duffy. O'Brien's reply to Duffy on 13 December was unequivocally supportive. He was 'fully resolved' that he would not be '*compromised* by the reckless violence of men who care very little what is their [destiny?]. Neither if I can help it will I allow the Confederation to be *compromised*. If there be a new secession I trust it will not be a secession upon our part ... We ought to be able to carry the adoption of our principles & policy in any public discussion ... Still I cannot persuade myself that a breach is inevitable. I cannot believe that Mitchell [sic] is so [unmanageable?] as to plunge us into difficulties which will overthrow all hopes of doing good through the means of the Confederation ...'[16] His response to the despairing pleas for his presence in Dublin will come as no surprise. He arrived back in Dublin on 17 December and went on to Cahirmoyle the following day, being 'compelled to take care of myself as an invalid for some weeks' and feeling obliged to attend as a Grand Juror at the Special Commission established under the new coercion act to try agrarian crimes. So, he spent the Christmas period and almost all of January in Limerick. He had already told Duffy he could not return to Dublin for the anniversary meeting of the Confederation on 13 January. 'About the beginning of February' he would be there, 'before I go to London' for the resumption of Parliament. On 29 December, he again attempted to explain his predilection for this particular form of absenteeism:

---

15 Ibid., MS 441, f2235, Duffy to O'Brien, 11 December 1847. R.D. Browne and J.P. Somers were considered two of the more disreputable, place-hunting repeal MPs.   16 Papers of Charles Gavan Duffy, MS 5757, f71, O'Brien to Duffy, 13 December 1847.

> It is very unfortunate that my permanent residence is not established in Dublin. As however circumstances prevent this from being the case I am compelled to take into consideration the claims of duty arising out of my connection with & residence in the country as well as what I owe to my own family who have just reason to complain that I sacrifice them for the public. As I shall be under the necessity of absenting myself from here for several months after the first of February I cannot with propriety engage to return to Dublin until the end of January so that I cannot take part in the proceedings of the Confederation except by means of my pen during the interval. I regret exceedingly this necessity, but I cannot help repeating what I have felt during the whole of last year, that if there is not prudence sufficient to guide the movements of this body without my presence in Dublin it presents to the country but a very slender title to public confidence.[17]

A desire simply to reduce political involvement would be understandable. However, O'Brien's rationale in avoiding Dublin at a critical moment whilst planning to go over to Parliament 'for several months' is unfathomable – especially given his longstanding aversion to Parliament and the recent confirmation of the futility of action there. By the end of December, moreover, he appreciated that this was indeed a time of crisis in Dublin. Though not without hope 'that all parties will make mutual concessions and that differences in public may be avoided', he believed that Mitchel and his fellow 'mutineers' were attempting to take over the Confederation to make it an agent of physical force methods. He told Duffy that 'a few men have no right to endeavour to make the Confederation the *organ* of their peculiar views. They have no right to drag us into apparent acquiescence in opinions which we think tend not to national freedom but to anarchy followed by national slavery. I must say that I think this attempt has been made and sooner than that it should be successful I should prefer to witness the dissolution of the Confederation itself.'[18] O'Brien knew that the Confederation faced its first major trial, but he was inclined for several weeks to witness it from afar.

At the beginning of January, Thomas Meagher indicated to O'Brien the extent of his frustration with British rule and the fact that there was still no sign of a 'fine, generous national spirit' stirring amongst the Irish gentry. 'When I see all this,' he wrote in what has become a famous lament, 'my heart sinks under a weight of bitter thoughts, and I am almost driven to the conclusion that it would be better to risk all – to make one desperate effort – and *fix at once the fate of Ireland*.' Would patient waiting 'lead to anything *but despair and utter subjection*? And here is another ques-

---

17 Smith O'Brien Papers, MS 449, f3399, Personal Memoranda, n.d. Papers of Charles Gavan Duffy, MS 2642, f3473, O'Brien to Duffy, 29 December [1847]; ibid., MS 5757, f71, O'Brien to Duffy, 13 December 1847. 18 Ibid., MS 2642, f3473, O'Brien to Duffy, 29 December [1847].
19 Smith O'Brien Papers, MS 441, f2298, Meagher to O'Brien [January 1848].

tion, has any country ever suffered so much, ever had such terrible provocation, and been so jealous of the law, so anxious to keep it sacred? Would not God himself bless the boldest effort that could be made, and bless the sacrifice which it were better for a few to make ... ? Oh! That poor Davis could come to life, even for one short day, and beckon us, like a pillar of flame to some pathway in this wilderness – some sure track – so that we might be redeemed out of this uncertainty, this bewilderment, this despair, in which we now so feebly wander.' But even this future rebel, for all his anguish, acknowledged that 'an unconstitutional mode of action would *not* in present circumstances succeed. I am convinced that the only mode which we can adopt – the only policy which we can successfully conduct – is the constitutional policy advised by Duffy.'[19] Almost all of the leading Confederates, including O'Gorman, agreed, so that Mitchel and Reilly faced certain defeat when Duffy presented his report on the future policy of the Confederation. This directed the Confederation to concentrate its efforts on winning Parliamentary seats and securing control of such elective institutions as the corporations and poor law boards of guardians. When the Irish Members stopped 'the entire business of Parliament', their 'forcible expulsion' might ensue, in which case they would combine with delegates from the other institutions to form the Council of Three Hundred that O'Connell had first proposed in 1843. Such a body would demand repeal and, if necessary, 'clutch the justice which was refused', in other words issue a unilateral declaration of legislative independence. But this would be a last step, for 'nowhere has a popular movement succeeded that did not exhaust the resources of the Constitution first'. Duffy knew O'Brien would 'perhaps consider it too strong', but he believed that the 'sole security against the Confederation being drawn into the extreme courses of the "Mountaineers" is to take the boldest course compatible with our sense of right ...' In a series of votes during January 1848, the report was carried by large majorities in the Council.[20]

Mitchel, unwilling to 'submit to the majority of the Council', was determined to appeal for support to the wider membership of the Confederation.[21] The dispute became fully public when Duffy's intended editorial about their differences caused Mitchel to write to the *Nation* on 7 January. Mitchel argued that the country was 'actually in a state of war – a war of "property" against poverty – a war of "law" against life', and so men should refuse to be disarmed. The poor law was intended to ruin Irish farmers in order to 'uproot' them from the soil; 'ratepayers ought to offer steady and deliberate passive resistance to it'. He believed that 'parliamentary and constitutional agitation of all kinds' was 'merely throwing away time and strength, and ensuring our own perpetual defeat', that the *Nation* and the Confederation 'should rather employ themselves in promulgating sound instruction upon military affairs', with 'a deliberate study of the theory and practice of guerilla war-

---

20 Ibid., f2230, Duffy to O'Brien [January 1848]. Duffy, *Young Ireland: Four Years of Irish History*, 173-80. Duffy, *Life in Two Hemispheres*, i, 248-56. The 'Mountain' was the name given to the Jacobin members of the Convention during the French Revolution.   21 Smith O'Brien Papers, MS 441, f2347, Dillon to O'Brien, 3 January 1848.

fare'. Duffy's editorial warned that an attempt to rouse the peasantry risked 'the shambles of social anarchy'. It was Duffy who decided to publish the two pieces on 8 January. It 'had become indispensable. The *Nation* office was daily disturbed by persons arriving with reports ... that the men who would not adopt Mitchel's views were *betraying the cause*.' People 'must now choose with their eyes open ... We must not hold our next public meeting till you [O'Brien] come to town; and then and there we had better get rid of this question of anarchy. Under no circumstances will I be a party to a peasant war, or massacre.'[22]

It was expected that the Dublin clubmen, many of whom were influenced by Chartism, would support Mitchel. The anniversary meeting of the Confederation, held on 12 January, seemed to pass off without incident, Pigot calling it 'very good & on the whole calculated by its steadiness of tone to make up for late annoyances'.[23] McGee, as secretary, presented a picture of a healthy body with nearly 11,000 members and 27 associated clubs. O'Brien's letter to the meeting focused on the possibility of reconciliation with Old Ireland. This had been pressed by a familiar cast – O'Neill Daunt and Dillon – but O'Brien insisted that they could 'accept no terms' that infringed their 'principles'. In private, his exchanges with O'Neill Daunt foundered when the latter proposed a return to the Repeal Association and O'Brien, rejecting this 'humiliation', insisted that that body should be 'superseded by one purged from [*sic*] all the imputations of corruption, sectarianism, intolerance, financial embarrassment, &c to which the present association is liable ...'[24] O'Brien was proving as obdurate as ever and the dispute with Mitchel cannot be attributed to a wish to facilitate reconciliation with Old Ireland. At the meeting, Mitchel used strong words of solidarity with the Chartists against 'the common enemy', the British government, and predicted that both sets of oppressed people 'should find, before long, that we have rights, and are able to assert them'. Several representatives of the Confederate clubs in England promised that English workers would support repeal. John O'Connell was able to tell the Repeal Association that the English speakers were brought in because the Confederation's leaders were afraid to speak 'lest they would bite each other's noses off '.[25] He was right to surmise that, despite the public front, the split continued. The main business of the meeting was to choose a new Council. O'Brien had written to urge the removal of Mitchel, citing the latter's profession of a new policy in his *Nation* letter, but McGee had to reply that, 'Before your note arrived he [Mitchel] was put by the sub-committee on the new Council'. Mitchel pledged himself to leave the organisation if the lawyers decided that his letter compromised the Confederation; 'on his giving this pledge,'

---

22 *Nation*, 8 January 1848. Smith O'Brien Papers, MS 437, f1751, Duffy to O'Brien [11 January 1848]. 23 Ibid., MS 441, f2353, Pigot to O'Brien, 15 January 1848. 24 *Nation*, 15 January 1848, O'Brien to McGee, 10 January 1848. Smith O'Brien Papers, MS 434, f1302, Dillon to O'Brien, n.d.; ibid., MS 439, f2038, O'Neill Daunt to O'Brien, 26 December 1847; ibid., MS 441, f2347, Dillon to O'Brien, 3 January 1848; ff2348, 2352, O'Neill Daunt to O'Brien, 5, 14 January 1848; ibid., MS 10515 (4), O'Brien to O'Neill Daunt, 10 January 1848. Journal of O'Neill Daunt, MS 3042, Appendix, ff1332, 1335, O'Brien to O'Neill Daunt, 31 December 1847, 10 January 1848. 25 *Nation*, 15, 22 January 1848.

McGee reported, 'it was considered inadvisable to move his expulsion in public meeting'.[26]

O'Brien could not have been uninfluenced by the reaction of Sir Colman O'Loghlen, the eminent lawyer, who remained unattached to any repeal faction. A few days earlier, he had refused O'Brien's request that he should join the Confederation with the argument that 'I would rather live my life as a slave than wade through blood to freedom'. When O'Brien protested, he assured him that he should 'not for a moment imagine' that he attributed to O'Brien 'any agreement in the anarchical views propounded by Mitchell [sic] & Reilly'. But what, he asked, was he to conclude when he saw 'Mitchell the advocate of a guerilla war received with the loudest cheers in the Confederation, his seditious speech applauded to the very echo, his name put on the new Council, & he and Devin Reilly elected the Vice-presidents for the ensuing year of the Swift Confederate Club' in Dublin?[27] O'Gorman, 'wearied and disgusted' by the squabbles provoked by the 'extreme party' ('Infant Ireland'), and Pigot urged O'Brien to come to Dublin to oppose Mitchel; Pigot was 'strongly disposed to think your coming up or remaining away will determine the existence of the Confederation'.[28] O'Brien now decided that the future policy of the Confederation had to be settled and Mitchel's dangerous views openly rejected. He wrote to Duffy on 22 January that, 'The reappointment of Mitchell & Reilly on the Council, & the *Chartist* tone adopted by the English speakers, has I fear irretrievably damaged the Confederation. We have now no alternative but to gird ourselves for a full & [fair?] discussion – evading no longer any point in controversy.'[29] He went to Dublin at the end of January (no sooner than he had all along intended!) and pressed the issue so strongly that he brought about Mitchel's secession. As he later recalled,

> Mr Mitchell having endeavoured to make the Confederation an organ for the propagation of his views which appeared to me to be very dangerous in their character – both in regard to the interests of the repeal cause and in regard to the general well being of society – I felt it to be my duty to obtain from the Council of the Confederation a distinct disclaimer of participation in these views. I felt that I could not with propriety allow myself to be supposed by the public to acquiesce in the principles of Mr Mitchell and if they had been adopted by the Confederation I should have withdrawn from all further cooperation with that body. Accordingly in order to bring the matter to issue I submitted to the Council a series of resolutions condemnatory of the principles enunciated by Mr Mitchell as those which the Confederation ought to enforce. My resolutions having been adopted by a large majority

---

26 Smith O'Brien Papers, MS 441, f2354, McGee to O'Brien [12 January 1848]. See also ibid., f2353, Pigot to O'Brien, 15 January 1848. Duffy, *Young Ireland: Four Years of Irish History*, 181-2.   27 Smith O'Brien Papers, MS 441, ff2350-51, O'Loghlen to O'Brien, 10, 17 January 1848.   28 Ibid., ff2353, 2361, Pigot to O'Brien, 15, 25 January 1848; f2355, O'Gorman to O'Brien, 18 January 1848.   29 Papers of Charles Gavan Duffy, MS 2642, f3474, O'Brien to Duffy, 22 January 1848.

of the Council I subsequently proposed them at a meeting of the Confederation. An (evasive) amendment having been proposed by Mr Mitchell a discussion ensued which continued during three days. After a very spirited and well sustained debate a division took place on the third night at one o'clock when there appeared to be [*317*] in favor of the Resolutions and [*188*] in favor [*of*] the amendment. After this decision Mr Mitchell, Mr Reilly and Mr Martin retired from the Council of the Confederation and it was understood that the Policy of the Confederation should be governed by the Principles set forth in the resolutions.[30]

O'Brien's 10 resolutions were variations on a basic theme, that by its 'fundamental rule' the Confederation was established to obtain an Irish parliament by 'the combination of classes' and 'the force of opinion', engaged in 'constitutional action'. The public meeting that considered the issue was held in the Rotundo, beginning on 2 February and finishing, as O'Brien wrote, at one o'clock in the morning of 5 February. O'Brien argued in a long speech that there would be widespread starvation if the poor rate was withheld. Mitchel's ideas on arming the people would cause 'confusion, anarchy, and bloodshed' and invite repression and possibly 'a massacre'. The Confederation had to decide, he said, if it was to alter the principles which had been presented to the public with repeated denials, in answer to their opponents, that insurrection was planned. 'Their decision would determine whether he and others could continue to be members.' Mitchel contended that the prospect of united action had foundered on the self-seeking conduct of the landlords and, deploring the inadequacy of constitutional methods, said that only the opinion of an *armed* people could force England's hand. Thus did O'Brien and Mitchel rehearse the conflict between the constitutional and revolutionary brands of nationalism that was to persist into the next century. It was not in this instance a conflict between absolutes – O'Brien did not reject violent means in all circumstances, and Mitchel disclaimed any intention to start an insurrection – and such caveats make it difficult to pronounce unequivocally that one was right and the other wrong. O'Brien's own experience in July 1848 suggests he was more right than Mitchel. Almost all of the leaders thought so. They backed O'Brien in the debate, Meagher asking if a people Mitchel considered 'knaves, perjurers, cowards on the hustings' would be bold 'chevaliers, *sans peur et sans reproache*, within the trenches ... Without discipline, without arms, without food – beggared by the law, starved by the law, demoralised by the law – opposed to the might of England, they would have the weakness of a vapour.' Men who six months later would be in a state of rebellion – O'Brien, Meagher, O'Gorman, Doheny, Dillon – convinced the meeting that to contemplate force was madness. In another irony, men who 18 months before had been forced out of the Association by O'Connell's Peace Resolutions now led the

---

30 Smith O'Brien Papers, MS 449, f3399, Personal Memoranda, n.d. O'Brien's account omitted the voting figures; they have been taken from the *Nation*, 5 February 1848.

Confederation in supporting O'Brien's peace resolutions. The result, if not the intention, was similar. The defeated party withdrew, Mitchel, Reilly and John Martin resigning from the Council two days after the meeting.[31]

The new seceders remained members of the Confederation, however, and continued to build up their support among the clubs. Mitchel founded a new journal, the *United Irishman*, in which the radical nationalist view was propounded. O'Brien knew that there was 'much more sympathy with Mitchell as an individual than approval of his principles' and warned Duffy 'that an effort will be made to appeal to that sentiment by attacking you'.[32] Duffy urged 'an address' to the public about the dispute; O'Brien refused with the enigmatic comment that it was 'very difficult to realise the ideas of another man'.[33] There is just a suggestion in this that O'Brien did not wish to become (or be seen as) the ally of a particular individual in the movement, a possibility after his strong support for Duffy in the late contest. In another postscript, Aubrey de Vere congratulated O'Brien on his 'admirable tact & decision' in the debate and, with prophetic irony, predicted that Mitchel would find himself 'in sorrowful *Union* with Australia, & preaching to the kangaroos as St Antony did to the Fishes'.[34]

O'Brien crossed to London directly after the meeting. He felt 'no little hesitation in again undertaking, in obedience to the wishes of my constituents, to make one more effort in Parliament to obtain useful measures for the people of this country'.[35] If his making the effort is surprising, the outcome is not. On 15 February, Chief Secretary William Somerville brought in a tenants compensation bill. O'Brien opposed its cumbersome arbitration procedure and the numerous restrictions that made it inferior to the tenant-right of Ulster, a system, he charged, that the bill was 'calculated to undermine'. It was 'a sham manoeuvre to avoid popular obloquy', one that he later dismissed as a 'concession to agitation' that had been 'framed with great dexterity in such a manner as to excite universal condemnation'. The bill was subsequently referred to a committee and not reintroduced. The government's Franchise and Registration bill was quickly abandoned. O'Brien spoke and voted in favour of Colonel Dunne's motion for a committee of inquiry into the working of the Irish poor law. 61 Irish MPs – repealers, liberal-unionists and Tories – supported Dunne, 'and only 8 against it of whom 3 were officials. Nevertheless,' O'Brien recalled, 'though there appeared this concurrence of opinion amongst the Irish Members the Govt. set them at nought and overruled their opinion by the votes of English Members who were perfectly unconcerned with reference to the question under debate.' O'Brien 'daily felt more and more the inutility of exerting'

---

31 Ibid., 5, 12 February 1848. Smith O'Brien Papers, MS 441, f2369, Pigot to O'Brien, 7 February 1848. 32 Papers of Charles Gavan Duffy, MS 2642, f3475, O'Brien to Duffy, 2 February 1848. 33 Ibid., f3476, O'Brien to Duffy, 7 February 1848. 34 Smith O'Brien Papers, MS 441, f2370, Aubrey de Vere to O'Brien, 16 February 1848. Aubrey was the brother of Stephen de Vere and Ellen (wife of Robert) O'Brien. 35 *Nation*, 5 February 1848.

himself in Parliament. 'Upon this point the division on Colonel Dunne's motion was conclusive.'[36] A renewal of cross-party cooperation between the Irish Members yielded little of value. O'Brien attended several of their meetings and found 'perfectly good feeling' but 'a lamentable absence of manly spirit'. Even after the 'insulting division' on Dunne's motion 'they remained as tame as well beaten hounds and licked the hand which struck them'.[37]

At home, Thomas Meagher's attempt to win the Waterford by-election ended in failure. He 'won the *people*', as Dillon put it, but among the electors he trailed in a poor third behind a Whig and the Association's candidate.[38] This disappointment was eclipsed by the news of revolution in France. On 22 February, fighting broke out in Paris; within 48 hours, King Louis Philippe had fled and the Second French Republic was proclaimed from the Hôtel de Ville. Paris, the acknowledged home of revolution, had sneezed; the rest of Europe quickly caught cold as, in Vienna, Berlin, Milan and almost all the great cities, excited revolutionaries took to the streets and forced the surrender of their panicked rulers. As Alexander Herzen put it, 'All Europe took up its bed and walked'. O'Brien later recalled the 'electric sensation' caused by the events in France:

> Its opening scenes were characterised by alternations of moral grandeur and of moral beauty. Courage & resolution united with humanity and forbearance. A passionate enthusiasm for liberty was preserved from excess by a universal love of order. Liberty & equality appeared to be associated in reality as well as in name with the blessed principle of Fraternity. All Europe felt the electric sensation. Wherever oppression had been sustained by power, there the shock produced a convulsion. For the most part the energy communicated to the sufferer enabled him to cast off the chains by which he had been fettered. It is not surprising that Ireland should have felt & acknowledged the impulse. Why should this nation which has suffered more than any other in Europe be among the last to follow the example of those who have proved that the Power of the Tyrant lives only by the submission of the people whom he oppresses?[39]

Elsewhere he wrote that, 'The shock awakened mankind. Those who had believed themselves to be weak now felt themselves to be strong. Everywhere the oppressor trembled before his victim ...'[40] This accurately reflected the intoxicated enthusiasm

---

36 *Hansard*, lxxxxvi, 673-80, 697-8, 15 February 1848, Somerville, O'Brien, lxxxxvii, 23-5, 51-3, 63 3, 29 February 1848, Dunne, O'Brien, Division. Dillon Papers, MS 6455, f62, O'Brien to Dillon, 14 February 1848. Smith O'Brien Papers, MS 449, f3399, Personal Memoranda, n.d. See also Papers of Charles Gavan Duffy, MS 2642, f3451a, O'Brien to Duffy [1 March 1848]. 37 Smith O'Brien Papers, MS 449, f3399, Personal Memoranda, n.d. 38 Ibid., MS 438, f1788, Dillon to O'Brien, 11 February 1848; f1791, Smyth to O'Brien, 11 February 1848; f1803, O'Gorman to O'Brien, 18 February 1848; ibid., MS 439, f2072, Dillon to O'Brien [February 1848]; ibid., MS 440, f2178, Dillon to O'Brien [February 1848]. Papers of Charles Gavan Duffy, MS 5758, ff9, 86, Dillon to Adelaide Dillon [February 1848]. 39 Smith O'Brien Papers, MS 449, f3399, Personal Memoranda, n.d. 40 Ibid., MS 464, Draft Address by William Smith

felt by radicals almost everywhere, including Ireland. As in Paris, it was believed, a relatively bloodless revolution could be achieved in Ireland by a bold step forward. There was a remarkable transformation in the temper and language of Irish nationalists. On 2 March, Duffy proclaimed in the Confederation that the French revolution had created a historic opportunity and extolled the French tricolour 'that has so often waved over fields won for freedom'. In the *Nation* on 4 March, he declared that, 'A Republic means war with Europe; and war means Irish liberty. The new Government to a man desire to make France a Deliverer of the oppressed nations ... Ireland's opportunity – thank God, and France – has come at last! Its challenge rings in our ears like a call to battle ... If needs be, we must die, rather than let this providential hour pass over us unliberated.' He had no desire to see Dublin's streets filled with 'canals of blood – even though it were the blood of our oppressors. But if no other way is left us out of famine, bankruptcy, and disgrace than such a struggle, then may God give us the 'vantage ground and the victory.' These were bold words for the normally cautious Duffy. A week later, he urged the formation of a National Guard, the power of a people in arms having been shown by the revolt of the National Guardsmen in Paris. The Confederation meeting of 9 March approved O'Gorman's resolution that the people should proceed with 'organising and arming themselves'. It also adopted John Dillon's impassioned Address of the Council of the Irish Confederation to the People of Ireland. This hailed the efforts of the Italians and Poles to free themselves from foreign rule and asked, 'Shall Ireland alone remain buried in darkness, while her sisters are emerging into liberty and light?'[41] Dillon wrote to another Confederate that, 'We sail before the wind', echoing Duffy's opinion that the 'gust of revolution' had rekindled Irish nationalism.[42]

Thomas Meagher was even more agitated; his letter to Duffy at the beginning of March exulted in the prospect of a meeting to congratulate the French and declared, vaguely but ominously, that the time for 'action' had come:

> I write just a line about the French meeting, which I am in raptures about. We *must* have it – *bold strokes*, and nothing else! Every step must be a step out of the old road, for the future. A brilliant meeting – a meeting worthy of France – the tricolor displayed – a deputation to Paris – the 'surer sources' opened – Hurrah!
>
> With events, that speak like thunder-peals, breaking forth around us – every one of them a blow to England – I, for one, do think that the time for talk, &c is gone bye [sic], and the time for *new* and *decisive* action has arrived.

O'Brien, 1848, 29-31. 41 *Nation*, 4, 11 March 1848. The arming resolution moved by O'Gorman read, 'That we deem it expedient that the people of Ireland should follow the example of the English people, who are now generally organising and arming themselves, under the sanction of the authorities, for the defence of their country in any emergency which may arise'. According to Thomas Halpin, the new secretary, it was Dillon who drew up this resolution. Smith O'Brien Papers, MS 442, f2391, Halpin to O'Brien, 9 March 1848. 42 Dillon Papers, MS 6455, f61b, Dillon to O'Hara [March 1848]. Smith O'Brien Papers, MS 441, f2255, Duffy to O'Brien [March 1848].

He wrote to Dillon, 'Our time, I firmly believe, has at last come, and we should grasp it with a greedy and a wicked hand. Let us bring matters to a crisis – that's my advice ... I'm ready for *anything* and *everything*.'[43] On the other side, Clarendon, the Lord Lieutenant, was filled with alarm at 'this tremendous catastrophe', the French revolution: 'Heaven knows what will happen ... I quite tremble to think of the amount of disaster that may be oncoming ... The lower orders in Dublin are already somewhat excited and say now that the French have got their liberties they will come and help us get "repale".' In Clarendon's view, moreover, it was the Confederation that would gain most: 'The lower orders in Dublin are now all Young Irelanders. They repudiate Old Ireland & moral force & denounce the late O'Connell as the greatest robber & humbug that ever yet deceived them.'[44] All remembered that the French had gone on the march in 1792, exporting their revolution, and many (including Clarendon) were aware that Ledru Rollin, now a member of the Provisional Government in Paris, had shown his interest in repeal by attending the monster meeting at Tara in 1843. On 2 March, Lamartine, the new Foreign Minister, declared that, 'The treaties of 1815 exist no longer as law' but only as 'a *point de départ*', and that, 'If the hour of the reconstruction of some nationalities oppressed in Europe or elsewhere should appear to us to have sounded in the decrees of providence ... the French republic would believe itself entitled to arm itself in order to protect these legitimate movements ...' Although Lamartine also promised that the French Republic 'will not make war on any one', his expression of sympathy with oppressed nations stoked Clarendon's apprehension of 'a blaze' in Ireland.[45]

In his private letters, O'Brien showed that the new wave of optimism did not remove old doubts. He was 'fretting beyond measure' because divisions between repealers and 'the wretched and sordid spirit which has been manifested by some of them' (a reference to Old Ireland) meant they might 'lose the grand opportunity afforded by the events in France of taking up a great national position such as would make Ireland *arbiter* of the destinies of the Empire'. Although disgusted by the sight of Association MPs 'wallowing in the mire of Whiggery', he looked to 'the honest portion of the Old Irelanders' and encouraged Duffy to convene 'an aggregate meeting of all classes of repealers'. He also proposed 'an address to the Queen in favor of Repeal to be adopted if possible by a million or two' people and 'an address of congratulation to the French People – with a deputation to Paris to present it'.[46]

---

[43] Papers of Charles Gavan Duffy, MS 5757, f95, Meagher to Duffy [March 1848]. Dillon Papers, MS 6455, f83, Meagher to Dillon [March 1848]. It is not clear what Meagher meant by 'surer sources'. [44] Clarendon Papers, II, 132, 136, 137, 139, Clarendon to Grey, 26, 28, 29 February, 1 March 1848; 133, Clarendon to Russell, 27 February 1848; 134, Clarendon to Lansdowne, 27 February 1848. Charles Greville also found the French news 'astounding' and 'so awful and surprising ... that every mind has been kept in a restless whirl and tumult'. Lytton Strachey and Roger Fulford (eds), *The Greville Memoirs, 1814-1860* (London, 1938), vi, 20-4, entry for 28 February 1848. [45] Clarendon Papers, II, 150, Clarendon to Palmerston, 7 March 1848. *Nation*, 11 March 1848, Circular of the Minister of Foreign Affairs to the Diplomatic Agents of the French Republic, 2 March 1848. [46] Papers of Charles Gavan Duffy, MS 2642, ff3477, 3478, O'Brien to Duffy, 28, 29 February 1848.

Thus O'Brien set the Confederation's agenda in the coming weeks and initiated the attempt that would now be made to reunite the repeal movement. He wrote to Lord Cloncurry, who had proposed reconciliation in 1847, and 'invited him to undertake the reconstruction of the Repeal Party'.[47] He also told Duffy that, while he lamented the lost ardour of some, he feared the reckless passion of Mitchel and others:

> ... The events of the last year have destroyed all the confidence which I once felt in our national spirit. Nevertheless we ought to put it to the test. If we call a general meeting of Repealers of all sections by a requisition signed by even a portion of the non confederate Repealers we shall perhaps be enabled to take a lead and govern the mind of the country. At all events the experiment ought to be made.
>
> The Mitchellite difference is very unfortunate. There is no doubt that recent events in France will inflame the minds of all who are inclined to have recourse at once to extreme measures. If they should attempt any outbreak at present they will be put down, but circumstances may occur hereafter which will render a *sans culottes* revolution in Ireland a *possible* event. If it should take place we & probably Mitchell himself (who is not equal to such a strife) will be undoubtedly victimised. As for me I am prepared for any event. Neither the scaffold on the one hand nor an infuriated mob on the other shall deter me from pursuing the course which I deem conducive to the interests of Ireland. But one cannot help feeling regret that so grand an opportunity should be lost by the abject cowardice and selfishness of one body of our fellow countrymen and the precipitate rashness not to say criminal folly of another section.[48]

Duffy and Dillon, for all that they stoked the popular excitement, were also afraid of precipitate action and summoned O'Brien to Dublin to counter the revolutionary influence of Mitchel. Duffy informed O'Brien that, 'The French news has fallen like fire upon powder. There will be an outbreak sooner or later. Be sure of that. But unless *you* provide against it it will be a mere democratic one, which the English Govt. will extinguish in blood; or if by a miracle it succeeds, it will mean death and exile to the middle as well as the upper classes ... [and] you and I will meet on a Jacobin scaffold, ordered for execution as enemies of some new Marat or Robespierre ...' He wanted 'a peaceful revolution ... By peaceful, I mean without unnecessary or anarchical bloodshed. It may be won without a shot being fired ... but much depends on you. If you make such a juncture and return to Ireland we will probably have another '82 in 1849 ...'[49] O'Brien wrote later that he

---

[47] *Nation*, 11 March 1848, O'Brien to Cloncurry, 29 February 1848. See also Smith O'Brien Papers, MS 449, f3399, Personal Memoranda, n.d. [48] Papers of Charles Gavan Duffy, MS 2642, f3479, O'Brien to Duffy, 1 March 1848. [49] Smith O'Brien Papers, MS 439, f2042, Dillon to O'Brien [March 1848]; ibid., MS 440, f2225, Duffy to O'Brien [March 1848]; ibid., MS 441, f2255, Duffy to O'Brien [March 1848]; f2344, Duffy to O'Brien [March 1848].

had to return to stop the Confederation falling 'into the hands of men who were desirous to produce an immediate collision' for which the Irish people were 'wholly unprepared'. With the repealers divided and many people dependent on the government for food, 'an immediate blow' would lead only to 'an appalling extent of misery and starvation'.[50] On 9 March, O'Brien returned and, according to Duffy's later account, immediately 'urged patience ... No one was surprised at this advice, or misunderstood it. He was a man who ... advanced slowly and tentatively, but he never made a backward step ...'[51] Even O'Brien, however, could not remain untouched by the excitement of the moment. Two hours after landing in Dublin, he told the Confederation that the French soldiers had done 'that which the Irish soldiery would do under similar circumstances', namely 'fraternise with the people'. He defied anyone to declare now that no political change could ever be obtained 'by an appeal to arms'. The Lord Lieutenant wondered if O'Brien could be prosecuted for his part in a meeting which was 'as bad & violent as possible'.[52]

O'Brien fell foul of the law at the next Confederation meeting, on 15 March. In some respects, he was cautious. He warned that any revolt 'could be put down in a week' and described 'the utmost possible horror of engaging my countrymen in a fruitless and unsuccessful rebellion'. Confident that agitation would succeed, he said that a domestic parliament could be achieved 'within twelve months' – an expression painfully reminiscent of O'Connell's declaration of the 'repeal year' of 1843. Some impatience was shown, however, in the comment that his hopes regarding the Irish landlords had been 'miserably disappointed'. He now warned them, 'as their friend', that 'if any struggle should take place' and they were 'found acting against the Irish people', their estates could be 'sold as national property'. He said, contemplating the possibility that the government would use force to prevent the planned general meeting of repealers, that he would 'take the front place at that meeting and allow them to shoot me if they please'. He believed that, 'from what I can learn respecting the temper of the troops now stationed in Dublin, it is by no means improbable that if an order were given to them to fire upon a peaceable and unoffending multitude, the first person shot by the troops would be the officer who gave such an order ...'

> We must also be prepared to fraternise with the soldiery of the British army. Above one-third of the whole military force of Great Britain consists of Irishmen; and nothing will convince me that these gallant countrymen of ours would take part against their fathers and brothers in a struggle for the national rights of Ireland ... We ought also to fraternise with the police force ... [*who*] are Irishmen as well as ourselves; and, believe me, they will stand up for their country in her hour of need ... He recommended the formation of an Irish brigade in America, composed of Irish emigrants, which might,

---

50 Ibid., MS 449, f3399, Personal Memoranda, n.d.; ibid., MS 464, Draft Address of William Smith O'Brien, 1848, 31-3. 51 Duffy, *Young Ireland: Four Years of Irish History*, 195. 52 *Nation*, 11 March 1848. Clarendon Papers, II, 155, 156, Clarendon to Grey, 10, 12 March 1848.

hereafter, serve as the basis of an Irish army ... He had no hesitation in declaring that he thought that the minds of intelligent young men should be turned to the consideration of such questions as how strong places can be captured, and weak ones defended, how supplies of food and ammunition can be cut off from an enemy, and how they can be secured to a friendly force. The time was also come when every lover of his country should come forward openly and proclaim his willingness to be enrolled as a member of a National Guard.

He also called, regardless of the Convention Act, for the election of a 300-strong National Council, as proposed by O'Connell in 1843, to assemble in Dublin in May 'to consult for the common welfare' of Ireland. Recalling his warning to Macaulay in 1845, when he had raised the spectre of a French invasion, disturbances among the Irish in Britain, an armed intervention by Irish-Americans, and a mutiny among Irish soldiers in the army, he could now proclaim that the time when this would occur 'might not be far distant'. Finally, in an Address of the Irish Confederation to the Citizens of the French Republic, a document which O'Brien composed, he stated that they proposed 'to exhaust all the resources of constitutional action before we resort to other efforts for redress'. He hoped that the 'friendship' of France would increase the 'efficacy' of the Confederation's 'projects' and 'accelerate their success', and he reminded the French that the battle of Fontenoy in 1745 had seen 'the cheerful effusion of Irish blood in maintenance of the glory of France'. The meeting resolved that O'Brien and Meagher should lead a deputation to convey this address to Paris.[53] O'Brien's warning against insurrection was as strong as anything else in this remarkable speech. He was aware of how Emancipation had been exacted by the threat of violence – indeed, he had recently told the Commons that Peel then spoke of 'a cloud that was rising in the west'[54] – and, the example that many now recalled, of how the armed Volunteers of 1782 had achieved legislative independence. In both cases, Britain seemed to give way out of *fear* of an explosion. While he did not rule out the possibility of the latter, O'Brien believed that repeal could be achieved without violence, if the Irish would arm themselves and convince Britain that they had enough 'manly spirit' to fight for their 'national rights'.[55] Given the wave of revolutionary optimism then sweeping through Europe, this expectation was by no means surprising. It must be noted, however, that the over-confidence of European revolutionaries was the product of success, in that they overthrew their governments and therefore believed that victory was secured, whereas O'Brien's confidence looked forward to a success that would never materialise.

When O'Brien and Mitchel were prosecuted for sedition (see below), O'Brien's hostility to 'revolutionary views' was again brought out: 'The Government exhibited

---

[53] *Nation*, 18 March 1848. The third delegate was Edward Hollywood, a silk-weaver chosen according to the principle by which Albert, a worker, was placed in France's Provisional Government. Duffy, *Young Ireland: Four Years of Irish History*, 201.   [54] *Hansard*, lxxxxvi, 1356, 25 February 1848, O'Brien.   [55] Smith O'Brien Papers, MS 449, f3399, Personal Memoranda, n.d.

no little skill in directing against me a large amount of prejudice by coupling with me ... in this prosecution Mr Mitchell whose writings in the United Irishman had alienated from the cause of Repeal and from the Confederation an incalculable number of persons belonging to the higher & wealthier classes of society ... They now began to regard the agitation for Repeal as synonymous with a confiscation of property.'[56] On 24 March, he wrote that, while he did not want 'cowardice or hesitation', the violent language from Mitchel, who was regarded in London as a 'bloodthirsty villain', made him despair: 'I cannot without the deepest regret perceive the injury he has done & is daily doing to the cause of Repeal ... I greatly fear that his connection with the proposal for a National Guard will tend to defeat and disparage this suggestion which would otherwise have found favor with men of all classes ... "L'audacité, L'audacité" upon which these men [the Mitchelites] rely must be met by equal firmness & resolution.'[57] O'Brien's hope that 'all classes' would favour a National Guard suggests that he envisaged a body that, as in France, was dominated by men of property and was a force for order as well as a protagonist of the popular cause; indeed, he subsequently told the House of Commons that he was asking the people 'to arm now for the preservation of order, as well as for the purpose of acquiring their liberties'.[58] Even the likes of Duffy, according to his own account, moved more quickly than O'Brien towards revolution: by mid-March, Duffy, Dillon and other leaders wanted to 'procure funds and military aid from our countrymen in America', and they seriously entertained the idea that, if repeal was not conceded, they would 'unroll the green flag' and raise the country in rebellion after the autumn's harvest was in. However, O'Brien 'was unwilling to commence negotiations in America while there was still hope to gain the gentry', so a mission was delayed.[59]

A large meeting of repealers and Chartists took place in Manchester on 17 March. The revival of Chartism in England and the support which many of its Irish adherents gave to the repeal cause fuelled the optimism of the Confederates and the alarm of the government. John Saville has described how 'fraternal and political connections between the radical movements on both sides of the Irish Channel' were forged in the heat of the enthusiasm that followed events in Paris.[60] O'Brien, in his first speech back in the Confederation, had claimed that they had 'a garrison in England', in the form of 'from thirty to forty thousand Repealers' in Liverpool, 'some forty or fifty thousand Repealers' in Manchester, 'some hundred thousand Repealers' in London, and so on.[61] He wrote to Duffy that the Manchester meeting 'might if

---

56 Ibid.   57 Papers of Charles Gavan Duffy, MS 2642, f3480, O'Brien to Duffy, 24 March 1848, from London. Duffy, *Young Ireland; Four Years of Irish History*, 202.   58 *Hansard*, lxxxxviii, 77, 10 April 1848, O'Brien.   59 Duffy, *Young Ireland: Four Years of Irish History*, 196-7, 199-200. On the willingness of Irish Americans to assist a rising, see John Belchem, 'Republican spirit and military science: the "Irish brigade" and Irish-American nationalism in 1848', in *Irish Historical Studies*, xxix, no. 113 (May 1994), 44-64.   60 John Saville, *1848: The British State and the Chartist Movement* (Cambridge, 1987), 72-4.   61 *Nation*, 11 March 1848.

judiciously managed be a very important *diversion* in the very centre of the country of our opponents, and might be made the occasion of showing that if England has a garrison in Ireland we too have a garrison in England'. He was wary of any attempt 'to couple Chartism with Repeal', telling the Manchester organiser (who had invited him to attend) that he was 'not prepared to subscribe' to the Charter, with its democratic principles. Above all, he told Duffy, he was 'sorry to hear that Mitchell is going to attend the meeting. I fear that he will *spoil* its effect.' In the event, Mitchel did not go over and Clarendon's 'hope he may get his head broken' was not fulfilled.[62]

On 20 March, an open-air meeting of repealers was held near the North Wall in Dublin to adopt an address to the French people. Meetings embracing both Old and Young Ireland took place in several Irish towns (including Limerick) during March 1848 and the one in Dublin possibly began as a genuine initiative from below, when the tradesmen petitioned the Lord Mayor to convene a meeting. O'Brien told the Confederation on 9 March that he was happy to find the tradesmen acting in accordance with his views (as given to Duffy on 28 February).[63] Despite the widespread desire for reunion, John O'Connell was wary of the incendiary language of the Confederates; or, as Clarendon, who regarded Old Ireland as a spent force, put it, 'J. O'Connell has evidently no intention of being swamped as a politician or shot as a rioter'.[64] The road to reconciliation was destined to be long and difficult. However, O'Connell's opposition 'could not prevent the attendance of a great mass of people. Six months previously,' O'Brien observed, 'the lives of the speakers would not have been safe if they had attempted to convene a meeting in the open air. Upon this occasion the utmost popular enthusiasm was displayed and considering that the meeting was held upon a working day not upon a holiday the numbers present, not less than 10,000, formed a display of popular strength which was by no means insignificant.'[65] The *Freeman* estimated that 'at least' 10-12,000 – perhaps 15,000 during the lunch hour – attended; Clarendon's claims on this score – that the 'monster French meeting' was 'most contemptible. Between comers, goers and listeners there were never more than 300 persons on the ground' – raise questions about the reliability of his sources. 'Except Mitchell and Smith O'Brien none of the leaders spoke,' he went on, oblivious to Meagher, Duffy and O'Gorman. It was decided that the National Council should be established and, with regard to the National Guard, O'Brien said he would have 'an opportunity of consulting parties in France, who have been acquainted with such organisations'. He believed that its establishment 'could be effected in a manner perfectly constitutional'. This was not

---

62 Papers of Charles Gavan Duffy, MS 2642, f3479, O'Brien to Duffy, 1 March 1848. Smith O'Brien Papers, MS 442, f2376, Smyth to O'Brien, 25 February 1848; f2377, O'Brien to [Smyth], 26 February 1848. Clarendon Papers, II, 158, Clarendon to Grey, 14 March 1848. *Nation*, 25 March 1848. Meagher, Doheny and Feargus O'Connor were the principal speakers in Manchester. 63 Smith O'Brien Papers, MS 449, f3399, Personal Memoranda, n.d. *Nation*, 11 March 1848. 64 Clarendon Papers, II, 155, Clarendon to Grey, 10, 11 March 1848. *Nation*, 11 March 1848, Address from Mr John O'Connell, 10 March 1848. 65 Smith O'Brien Papers, MS 449, f3399, Personal Memoranda, n.d.

pie in the sky. Clarendon abhorred the idea that 'the Revolutionists' might create a National Guard but, he lamented, his advisers could not find any law to prevent its formation.[66]

Before leaving for France, O'Brien had to answer a summons on a charge of sedition. His speech on 15 March had 'developed views of a more warlike tendency than any which I had previously spoken'.[67] An angry Clarendon wrote that, 'W.S. O'Brien's speech is quite as seditious as Meagher's' and asked Home Secretary Grey if he could see any reason to treat them differently. 'There can be none that I know of except his being an MP & a man of family & station which in my opinion are grounds for not letting him off ...' It was 'disagreeable to gratify S. O'Brien's monomania for notoriety' and he would 'take care that he is treated in the Queen's Bench as the least important offender...' Grey, agreeing, saw 'not the slightest reason why S. O'Brien shd be let off' and considered him 'desirous of martyrdom'.[68] O'Brien certainly did not seek to avoid prosecution; he had known of the presence of a government reporter, and when the *Freeman*'s account of his speech omitted several passages, 'probably from prudential considerations', as O'Brien observed, he asked Duffy to publish it in full in the *Nation*.[69] The Irish government also decided to take action against Meagher, who had told the meeting that, if repeal were not conceded, 'then up with the barricades, and invoke the God of Battles!', and Mitchel was prosecuted at the same time for several articles in his *United Irishman*. The three men reported to the head-office of the Dublin police on 22 March to give bail on sedition charges. They were cheered through the streets and went to address the crowd from a window of the Confederation's offices in D'Olier Street, in what for O'Brien was probably an uncomfortable union. More promisingly, to Clarendon's annoyance, the Association denounced the prosecutions and John and Maurice O'Connell offered to bail O'Brien and Meagher.[70]

The North Wall meeting had adopted an address to the new French Republic and authorised O'Gorman and Dillon (who, in the event, was too ill to travel) to present it. So it was that O'Brien, Meagher, O'Gorman and several other Confederates made their way to France, O'Brien leaving on 22 March and, after a short stay in London, arriving in Paris on 28 March. Clarendon attributed the 'worst intentions' to 'these vile traitors' and feared that 'a well or ill founded hope of French assistance' would start a rising.[71] The government had no idea what O'Brien sought in

---

66 Clarendon Papers, II, 165-6, 174, Clarendon to Grey, 19, 20, 24 March 1848; 166, Clarendon to Russell, 19 March 1848. *FJ*, 21 March 1848. *Nation*, 25 March 1848. Elizabeth Smith noted that the North Wall meeting was attended by 'thousands of the merest rabble ...' Thomson and McGusty, *Irish Journals of Elizabeth Smith*, 174, 26 March 1848.   67 Smith O'Brien Papers, MS 449, f3399, Personal Memoranda, n.d.   68 Clarendon Papers, II, 163, 178, Clarendon to Grey, 18, 26 March 1848; Box 12, Grey to Clarendon, 20 March 1848.   69 *Nation*, 18 March 1848, O'Brien to Duffy, 16 March 1848.   70 Ibid., 25 March 1848. Clarendon Papers, II, 170, Clarendon to Grey, 22 March 1848.   71 Clarendon Papers, II, 170, 173, Clarendon to Grey, 22, 23 March 1848; 175, Clarendon to Russell, 25 March 1848.

Paris, but if they did not understand the Irish they certainly succeeded with their handling of the French. The Marquis of Normanby, the Lord Lieutenant in Ireland under Melbourne, was now the British ambassador to France. Urged on by Clarendon as well as Russell and Palmerston (the Foreign Secretary), Normanby pressed Lamartine constantly to ensure that the French gave not 'the slightest encouragement' to the Irish, persuading him that even an expression of sympathy would be an intervention in Britain's 'internal affairs' that would threaten 'the amicable relations between the two countries' (Normanby). Lamartine did not identify Ireland as one of the 'oppressed nationalities' in his famous Circular, and he apparently told Normanby on 13 March that, 'As to Ireland, ... I never can hear of Irish nationality in any other sense except as identical with English nationality'. Normanby, who went to see Lamartine almost daily in the week before O'Brien's arrival, attributed the mission to 'the most violent section of the Irish Repealers' and told the minister that it was disowned by 'all the more respectable portion of that party', meaning the Association, where 'loyal sentiments [were] expressed' and 'all idea of foreign interference in their concerns was repudiated'. He added that Lamartine 'would be surprised, perhaps, to learn that those two persons [O'Brien and Meagher] who would come here to announce themselves as slaves were, in every respect, as free as I was myself, and living under precisely the same laws. One was a member of Parliament for a county where his family had much influence from property. The other had, I believed, just been a candidate for a popular constituency, and had not been returned because his principles were not approved of.' Lamartine apparently told Normanby he was 'more ready ... to take *my* opinion upon the real state of Ireland than theirs' and promised he would be 'very firm' and would say 'that if they knew no nationalities but those which were established, still less would they enter into internal divisions between different parts of a friendly country ...'[72] At the end of March, Lamartine disappointed the Poles by saying that France would not fight for them; if Lamartine would not assist a nation for which he and all French liberals undoubtedly had sympathy, he was unlikely to help a nation he did not even recognise as such.[73]

So, the game was lost even before O'Brien arrived to play. Others in Paris might have been more responsive to the Irish, but it was the latter's misfortune that they had to deal with a Foreign Minister who was the epitome of cautious diplomacy and, in Normanby's opinion, 'the only one of these men who really likes England'. Even Ledru Rollin, seen by Clarendon as 'the man our traitors rely upon', though he privately advocated Ireland's 'independence' and expressed his 'deep satisfaction' at seeing 'the generous sons of Erin bearing their congratulations to our young commonwealth', wrote that 'with truth you [O'Brien] say that much caution must

---

[72] The Marquis of Normanby, *A Year of Revolution: From a Journal kept in Paris in 1848* (London, 1857), i, 193-5, 225-6, 241-6, 250-60, 272-7. Saville, *1848*, 82-7. D.N. Petler, 'Ireland and France in 1848', in *Irish Historical Studies*, xxiv, no. 96 (Nov. 1985), 496-501. Lawrence C. Jennings, *France and Europe in 1848: A Study of French Foreign Affairs in Time of Crisis* (Oxford, 1973), 6-23, 49-50.   [73] *Nation*, 1 April 1848.

be observed by the French provisional government in its relations with the government of England'.[74] O'Brien found Paris 'in a state of absolute intoxication from the excitement' and, writing later of trees of liberty, armed processions and the universal 'love of order', it is clear that the horrors to come, during the June Days, did not diminish his enthusiasm for the first fruits of France's revolution.[75] Normanby, in his journal, noted that 'the assumed superiority of Smith O'Brien offends the others'; this was probably untrue, for O'Brien's relations with Meagher and O'Gorman were always excellent, and Palmerston developed doubts about the reliability of the informant responsible for the story.[76] More seriously, and accurately, the ambassador heard of O'Brien's assertion that France, if asked, 'would be ready to send over 50,000 of her bravest citizens to fight' for Ireland. O'Brien, in a published reply to the address of the Paris United Irish Club, did indeed make this claim. He also said that an 'amicable settlement' between Ireland and England was still possible, 'but the best mode of attaining that desirable end will be to imitate the example which our fathers presented to us in 1782 by boldly contemplating an arbitrament of a sterner kind. We have already counselled our fellow-countrymen to prepare for the conflict by acquiring the possession and use of arms. We offer to you [the Irish who resided in Paris] the same advice ... Accustom yourselves to martial exercises and to military studies. Fraternise with the Irish officers of the French army ...'[77]

O'Brien insisted, however, that his purpose was to rouse French sympathy for the Irish cause and that he did not seek the armed assistance of France. This is entirely credible. For all the wildness of his public language, it is clear that O'Brien still looked to 1782 and not to Wolfe Tone, who was taken in 1798 in a French uniform. As Ledru Rollin's reply to his note suggested, O'Brien had a realistic view of France's need to avoid conflict with England. Of his contacts with the Provisional Government O'Brien's recollection is unequivocal:

> ... I must content myself with observing that in the conversations which I had with M. La Martine [*sic*], Monsieur Ledru Rollin and others I carefully abstained from soliciting armed succour from France. The address of the Confederation speaks for itself. The reply made to it by Lamartine or rather written in reply to it for the written answer differed materially from the speech made by M. Lamartine to the Irish deputation created an impression for which there really was no foundation that we had gone to France to seek

---

74 Normanby, *Journal*, i, 366. Russell Papers, PRO/30/22/7B, f168, Clarendon to Russell, 30 March 1848. Smith O'Brien Papers, MS 442, f2406, Ledru Rollin to O'Brien, 30 March 1848.   75 Ibid., MS 449, f3399, Personal Memoranda, n.d. See also ibid., Tasmanian Journal, Part VI, 27, entry for 20 April 1852. The description in his Tasmanian Journal is reproduced in full in Richard Davis (ed.), '*To Solitude Consigned': The Tasmanian Journal of William Smith O'Brien, 1849-1853* (Sydney, 1995), 315-23.   76 Normanby, *Journal*, i, 276-7. Petler, 'Ireland and France in 1848', 500, citing Normanby Papers, P/20/26, Palmerston to Normanby, 4 April 1848.   77 Normanby, *Journal*, i, 286. *Nation*, 8 April 1848, reply dated 31 March 1848 and signed by O'Brien and other delegates.

armed succour. His disclaimer of a wish on the part of France to interfere with the concerns of Ireland still less to incur the hostility of England by encouraging civil war has operated most unfairly and most injuriously upon the interests of our cause. So far from encouraging the idea that we had gone to France to seek armed assistance I stated to many who offered to embark in any enterprise which I should suggest that I hoped that our objects would be achieved without war – that we thought our countrymen ought to hold themselves in readiness to die for their country if necessary – that we were very desirous to cultivate the sympathies of the French, that in particular we wanted to be placed in friendly communication with the Irish officers in foreign service – but that we had no immediate intention of calling upon our fellow countrymen to appeal to arms [*sic*].[78]

This was by no means an entire rejection of physical force, a fact that makes his denial that he sought armed assistance from Lamartine all the more believable. Later in the year, Lamartine contradicted himself on the subject, announcing in the autumn that the Irish delegates came '*me demander des encouragements et des armes pour la guerre civile*' but writing in November that, '*J'ai eu en effet l'honneur de voir M. O'Brien à Paris, mais notre conversation a été entièrement extra-politique, et aucune demande ni promesse de secours n'a eu lieu*'. Then he claimed in his *History of the French Revolution of 1848* that 'the Irish agitators [*insurgés*]' came 'to demand succour and arms [*des encouragements et des armes*] from the French Republic'.[79] This, O'Brien wrote in 1852, was 'an inaccuracy ... which might possibly have cost me my life and which may still deprive me of my liberty for many years'. As 'the chief of the deputation and the only member of it who conversed personally with La Martine', he 'did not say anything that could justify his impression that we had come to seek armed succour from France'. He had hoped to 'engage the sympathies' of France and of 'revolutionised Europe' and America, so that they would 'cry Shame upon England for her treatment of my country, and hold themselves in readiness to assist Ireland in the event of a struggle, but I did not at that time contemplate the occurrence of an outbreak at any specified period. On the contrary my efforts were employed to restrain rather than to excite rebellion ...' When 'several enthusiastic Irishmen' serving as officers in the French army 'offered to engage at once in the organisation of a military force', he 'replied that the time had not arrived for an armed struggle' and 'that to enlist an armed force was not the object of my visit to Paris'. Although O'Brien acknowledged that Lamartine was 'influenced by no motives which could lead him to pervert the truth', the French minister clearly assumed the worst of those whom Normanby had presented as the dangerous enemies of his favoured ally.[80]

---

78 Smith O'Brien Papers, MS 449, f3399, Personal Memoranda, n.d. See also ibid., MS 464, Draft Address of William Smith O'Brien, 1848, 33-7.   79 Helen O'Donovan Johnstone, France and Ireland in 1848 (M.A., University College Galway, 1988), 138, 145. A. de Lamartine, *Histoire de la Révolution de 1848* (Paris, 1849), 266-7. Alphonse de Lamartine, *History of the French Revolution of 1848*, trans. (London, 1849), 427.   80 Smith O'Brien Papers, MS 449, Tasmanian Journal, Part VI, 23-5, 20 April

When the delegation was formally received at the Hôtel de Ville on 3 April, Lamartine, replying to the congratulatory address, repudiated 'intervention' in the 'internal disputes' of other countries. 'We are at peace' with Britain, he went on, and, recalling how Pitt had armed rebels against the first French republic, he said that 'this cause of dissension between Great Britain and us we will never renew by taking any similar course'. As Mitchel later wrote, 'foolish old Monsieur de Lamartine ... who, having previously made up his mind that the Irish repealers were coming to solicit armed aid from France against the English government, and having accordingly prepared his speech in reply to this address, did not hear one word of their actual address, and so responded to his imaginary one ...' A delighted Normanby noted that, 'In the material points of distinct discouragement of any idea of support or assistance from France to these disloyal men, Lamartine courageously and effectually kept his promise to me ...' ('Their allusion to Fontenoy,' he added, 'where their fathers fought as mercenaries in a French cause, showed they had no spark of that patriotic feeling which made their brothers the pride and glory of the British army in Spain and at Waterloo ...') O'Brien was subsequently permitted to dine with Lamartine at his official residence; Normanby's annoyance was mitigated by his sense that after the public 'rebuff' the delegates had suffered 'they cannot recover the confidence of their adherents by reporting subsequent private civilities'.[81] A few days earlier, Lamartine had publicly pledged 'the sword of France' to help the Italians; the fact that a notorious radical, Mazzini, achieved so much more than O'Brien (even if they were only words) highlights O'Brien's failure. For all that he was enthralled by the feverish atmosphere in Paris, O'Brien conceded that he was 'disappointed' by the outcome of the mission. Clarendon considered Lamartine's 'excellent' answer 'a blow to Young Ireland' and had it printed and posted to police stations for placarding throughout Ireland. The diarists Charles Greville and Elizabeth Smith reflected the general British delight at Lamartine's 'nobly liberal reply to those three crazy men' (Smith).[82]

O'Brien returned to London on 7 April, leaving behind O'Gorman and another Confederate (Eugene O'Reilly) because he 'wished them to learn in that great school of popular warfare the prompt discipline of new levies, and the rough-and-ready organisation of insurgent forces, and they applied themselves steadily to this task'. O'Gorman actually joined the National Guard to further his education and stayed in Paris for over a month.[83] In the Commons, the Home Secretary deprecated the

1852. 81 Lamartine, *Histoire*, 267-71. Lamartine, *History*, 427-9. MacManus, *Thomas Davis and Young Ireland*, 88-9, 'Mitchel on Meagher'. Normanby, *Journal*, i, 287-96, 300-1. 82 *Nation*, 1 April 1848 (on Mazzini). Smith O'Brien Papers, MS 449, Tasmanian Journal, VI, 26-7, 30-31, 20 April 1852. Clarendon Papers, II, 200, Clarendon to Grey, 6 April 1848. Strachey and Fulford, *Greville Memoirs*, vi, 48-9, 5 April 1848. Thomson and McGusty, *Irish Journals of Elizabeth Smith*, 175-6, 7, 9 April 1848. Duffy, *Young Ireland: Four Years of Irish History*, 203. 83 Duffy, *Young Ireland: Four Years of Irish History*, 203. Narratives of the Rising of 1848 by R. O'Gorman, T.B. MacManus and J. Kavanagh, 1848-1849,

delegation's 'direct treasonable appeal to a foreign country to aid them'. O'Brien told Duffy that Grey had quoted a misleading *Nation* report on the mission and complained that it had done him 'a good deal of harm in the opinion of many whose support is worth having ... Shall I ever escape from annoyances of this kind?'[84] He later recalled the 'great indignation' that his visit had caused in England and how it was against the advice of others that he went to the Commons on 10 April. His reception, on what was to be his last-ever appearance in the House, was extremely hostile. On rising, according to the *Freeman*, 'he was assailed with the most violent bursts of yelling which lasted fully ten minutes' and his speech was constantly interrupted with 'beastly bellowings'. Mitchel, typically colourful, wrote that 'never, since first Parliament met in Westminster, was heard such a chorus of frantic and obscene outcries. Honourable members crowed like cocks, lowed like cows, and brayed like jackasses.' O'Brien was at his most combative, even provocative. With regard to Grey's earlier speech, he said, 'I have been called a traitor. I do not profess disloyalty to the Queen of England. But if it is treason to profess disloyalty to this House, and to the government of Ireland by the Parliament of Great Britain – if that be treason, I avow the treason.' Denying that he had sought armed help in France, he claimed that if he had he 'should have come back accompanied by a tolerably large legion of troops'. He warned that the police and army would not fire on the Irish people and finished by telling Russell that if he behaved as Guizot and Metternich had done in France and Austria 'then I tell him it is not I but he and his colleagues that are traitors to the country, the Queen and the constitution'. Grey's reply described 'that indignation which all loyal subjects of this realm' felt in response to O'Brien's conduct.[85]

Clarendon congratulated Grey on giving O'Brien 'an excellent dressing for his speech on Monday which seems to have disgusted the House as it deserved to do', and he subsequently described a dejected O'Brien made 'sullen' by his reception in the House and 'brooding over the means of revenge'. In the *Nation*, on the other hand, O'Brien's speech was likened to 'the challenge which the knights of old flung to an enemy within his own strong walls'.[86] O'Brien had gone to the Commons to oppose the government's Crown and Government Security bill. This measure created a new offence, treason-felony, which broadened the scope of treason to encompass 'open and advised speaking' that would encourage rebellion and at the same time made convictions more likely by limiting the penalty to transportation, the normal sentence for a felony. 'Thus,' as Lord Campbell, whose idea the bill was,

---

MS 5886, Narrative by O'Gorman, 8-9. *Nation*, 22 April 1848 (O'Brien). 84 *Hansard*, lxxxxviii, 26-7, 7 April 1848, Grey. Papers of Charles Gavan Duffy, MS 2642, f3481, O'Brien to Duffy, 8 April 1848. *Nation*, 8 April 1848. 85 Smith O'Brien Papers, MS 449, f3399, Personal Memoranda, n.d. *FJ*, 12 April 1848. *Hansard*, lxxxxviii, 73-80, 80-83, 10 April 1848, O'Brien, Grey. John Mitchel, *The Last Conquest of Ireland (Perhaps)* (Glasgow, London, n.d.), 168. 86 Clarendon Papers, II, 208, Clarendon to Grey, 12 April 1848; 209, Clarendon to Russell, 13 April 1848. *Nation*, 15 April 1848. See also Strachey and Fulford, *Greville Memoirs*, vi, 53, 15 April 1848. Thomson and McGusty, *Irish Journals of Elizabeth Smith*, 177, 16 April 1848.

2 The battle of Limerick

put it to Russell, 'while you would have the glory of mitigating the severity of the penal code, you would be armed with the effectual means of sending Messrs Mitchell, Meagher and Smith O'Brien to Botany Bay'.[87] The bill made some forms of sedition, carrying a brief sentence, into treason that was punishable by transportation for life. It had an easy passage through Parliament. Chisholm Anstey spoke and voted for the second reading (which carried by 452 votes to 35), vindicating those who had questioned O'Brien's judgement in endorsing an English candidate for an Irish seat.[88]

Arguably more important than any of this, the Chartist demonstration in London on 10 April passed off peacefully, Feargus O'Connor refusing to challenge the ban imposed on a procession from the meeting place at Kennington Common, and the loyalty of the middle classes clearly demonstrated by the enrolment in the capital of about 85,000 special constables. Conservatives had braced themselves for a confrontation but instead were able to scoff at a contemptible display of weakness. O'Brien, that evening, still talked in the House of the 'aid which the Chartists are universally prepared to give' the Irish. However, although Chartist agitation was

---

[87] Russell Papers, PRO 30/22/7B, ff201, 272, Campbell to Russell [April 1848]. Kevin B. Nowlan, *The Politics of Repeal: A Study in the Relations between Great Britain and Ireland, 1841-50* (London, 1965), 199.   [88] *Hansard*, lxxxxviii, 103-4, 128-32, 10 April 1848, Anstey, Division.

far from spent, the prospect that Chartists would campaign effectively for repeal was undermined by the London failure, and it was now less likely that British soldiers would be withdrawn from Ireland to deal with disorder in England. A relieved Clarendon reported that, 'The rebels are dismayed just now by the total failure of their party in England, coming as it did upon the extinction of their hopes in France'. He found O'Brien 'very quiet since his arrival [in Dublin] & though he holds the same violent language in private he cannot conceal his dejection from his friends. I was told this by a man who dined with him yesterday.'[89] This was possibly a reference to John Donnellan Balfe. Balfe was a member of the Confederation's Council for several months from August 1847, but he was accused of being a spy by another member and, despite protesting his innocence in a letter to O'Brien in May 1848, he never retrieved his place in the Council. He displayed a fertile imagination in his reports to Clarendon, claiming that O'Brien was 'to be the future "president" if the struggle should be successful', that 'the O'Brienites' were 'delighted to have Mitchell transported', and that Duffy was a Machiavellian genius who controlled O'Brien. Clarendon believed most of this nonsense, sending it on to his superiors in London; it is doubtful if any other informer has ever achieved such dominion over the mind of the Queen's principal servant in Ireland. The result was that Clarendon had a distorted idea of what was happening in the country he supposedly governed.[90]

O'Brien would not be quiet for long. Two days after arriving back in Dublin on 13 April, he was the principal speaker at a soirée held to welcome the return of the Paris delegates. He congratulated 'the butcher's boys of Hercules-street' in Belfast on being 'infinitely more mannerly' than the so-called 'first assembly of gentlemen in the world', the House of Commons. He was given an original flag of the 3rd regiment of the Irish Volunteers of 1782 (and a banner inscribed 'William Smith O'Brien, MP, Ireland's Truest Patriot'), but the meeting is chiefly memorable for Meagher's presentation of the tricolour flag he had received in Paris. This was not the debut of the green, white and orange flag in Ireland – it was seen intermittently from 1830, and the delegation had worn these colours when they visited Lamartine – but it was now that it became one of the principal symbols of the national movement. As O'Brien said some days later, it signified the hope 'that the Protestants of the North and the Catholics of the South will unite in demanding the rights of their country'.[91] On 19 April, in the Council of the Confederation, O'Brien moved that all Irishmen should be invited to sign a declaration of readiness to serve in a National Guard 'for the purpose of preserving social order and of protecting this island against all foes, domestic and foreign'. He was the first signatory.[92] He then

---

89 Saville, *1848*, 109-20. Strachey and Fulford, *Greville Memoirs*, vi, 51-3, 13 April 1848. Hansard, lxxxxviii, 76, 10 April 1848, O'Brien. Clarendon Papers, II, 208, 210, 212, Clarendon to Grey, 12, 13, 14 April 1848.   90 Smith O'Brien Papers, MS 442, f2443, Balfe to O'Brien, 4 May 1848. Clarendon Papers, Box 53, Balfe's correspondence.   91 *Nation*, 22, 29 April 1848. G.A. Hayes-McCoy, *A History of Irish Flags from earliest times* (Dublin, 1979), 140-8. Hayes-McCoy believes that the 'truest patriot' banner is probably that which is now in the National Museum in Dublin; ibid., 136-7.   92 *Nation*, 22

embarked on 'an excursion to the country which was designed partly as a visit to my family, partly as a political tour', with secretary Thomas Halpin sending 'slips of the National Guard declaration' to the towns on his itinerary. Clarendon, alarmed, thought that O'Brien and other leaders headed off to Waterford and Limerick 'to do all the mischief in their power. They may perhaps try an outbreak in one of these cities as they find we are too strong for them in Dublin.'[93]

In fact, O'Brien's trip to Limerick ended only in an infamous riot. Before leaving Dublin, he had 'established an understanding with Mr Mitchell that he would not go to the south. I frankly told him that I differed so much with his views that I could not appear on the same platform with him without doing violence to my feelings.'[94] Mitchel had declared for a separate Irish republic in the Confederation on 23 March and, at more length, on 5 April, a policy running directly counter to the repealers' object of a domestic legislature under the Crown. The 'golden link of the Crown' was dismissed as 'humbug' in the *United Irishman*: 'I scorn and spit upon "Repeal of the Union"'. His denunciations of landlords ('Landlord Thugs') reflected a developing social radicalism – a concept of class struggle – that renounced O'Brien's aspiration to unite the Irish nation. Mitchel proclaimed that it was 'in flames and blood that Irish landlordism is to perish' and that, 'As for the Confederation "leaders", they must take their chance' in the 'democratic' revolution.[95] O'Brien believed that Mitchel gave the requested assurance. He went down to Limerick, where local nationalists proceeded to organise a soirée in honour of the three prosecuted leaders. A day before the event, having been out at Cahirmoyle for a week, he was surprised to learn that Mitchel had accepted an invitation to attend. O'Brien expected trouble from Old Irelanders who were outraged by an article in the *United Irishman* in which O'Connell was denounced as 'the great aider and abettor' of English 'plunderers' and 'the mortal enemy of the Irish working man, tiller and artificer'.[96] Against his better judgement, he was prevailed upon to let the meeting take place and turned up (with Meagher) expecting not 'actual collision' but 'some painful manifestations of adverse feeling'. A violent and painful (in more than one sense) collision did occur. An 'O'Connellite mob', as O'Brien described it, burnt an effigy of Mitchel, tried to set fire to the building, and battered the door until it was 'broken to pieces'. One intruder was shot in the thigh as he entered. O'Brien's account went on:

> From the first ... I had been very anxious to go out amongst the crowd and endeavour either to pacify them or offer myself to them as a victim, and I subsequently made repeated efforts to go out of the door but was retained by main force by my friends inside. Seeing now an aperture in the door ... I made a dash through it expecting to receive a blow immediately ... but not

April 1848. 93 Smith O'Brien Papers, MS 442, ff2420-1, Halpin to O'Brien, 24, 25 April 1848; ibid., MS 449, f3399, Personal Memoranda, n.d. Clarendon Papers, II, 222, Clarendon to Russell, 23 April 1848. 94 Smith O'Brien Papers, MS 449, f3399, Personal Memoranda, n.d. 95 *Nation*, 25 March, 8 April 1848. *United Irishman*, 1, 8, 22 April 1848. 96 Ibid., 22 April 1848.

convinced that the People would strike me as soon as they should recognise me ... I threw away a small deal stick which I had held in my hand on issuing from the building and with a view to show that I had not lost my confidence in the People I took off my hat & cried out 'a cheer for Repeal'. I was at this moment struck in the face but as soon as struck [sic] several persons rushed up & said do not injure Mr O'Brien. They threw their arms round me with a view to prevent me from falling. Whilst I was in this attitude, one of my arms being raised, I received a very severe blow in my side which incapacitated me from any further active exertion.[97]

He made his way home to George's Street, stopping at a shopkeeper's house to wash blood from his face. When he appeared in court two days later he was 'covered with wounds ... My face was greatly disfigured and I suffered acutely from pain arising from the blow which I had received in my side.' Not for the first time he was annoyed by the conduct of the citizens of Limerick. He was 'so much wounded in heart' by the attack he decided 'to withdraw altogether from Public Life', but, 'begged with great earnestness' by other leaders in Dublin, he relented on condition that Mitchel and Reilly should be required to retire from the Confederation.[98] Mitchel wrote to O'Brien on the morning after the affray, addressing him with a very formal 'My dear Sir'. Denying any 'breach of compact', he insisted that their agreement allowed him to go to any event to which he was 'specially invited', as had happened in this instance. 'Whether you exonerate me from this foul charge or not,' he went on, 'I declare that I am deeply grieved & ashamed at your having been so brutally treated in your own city on such an occasion. And that I wd far prefer to have suffered the disgrace & injury myself, or thrice as much ...'[99]

O'Brien's account shows, however, that he clung to the belief that Mitchel had 'broken faith' with him, and that he thought 'great injury' was done by Mitchel's ties with the Confederation, with his radical views attributed to the body as a whole. (Even Clarendon thought that 'the object of the Confederates now is not repeal but a Republic'.) For O'Brien, 'The proceedings at Limerick ... brought to an issue this question. My apparent connection with Mr Mitchell had nearly cost me my life and I felt that neither my public character nor the character of our movement could be preserved if Mr Mitchell continued a member of the Confederation.'[100] Any decision to divide a political movement can be criticised. Moreover, to disown Mitchel when state prosecutions were pending made it appear, as O'Brien was aware, 'that I was anxious to save myself by presenting him as a victim to the Government', and Mitchel privately thought that the reason the government 'pounced upon me with their "felony" was evidently because they imagined I was deprived of all sympathy on account of "the memory of O'Connell" and on account of being cut off

---

[97] Smith O'Brien Papers, MS 449, f3399, Personal Memoranda, n.d. *Limerick Reporter*, 2 May 1848. *Nation*, 6 May 1848. [98] Smith O'Brien Papers, MS 449, f3399, Personal Memoranda, n.d. [99] Ibid., MS 440, f2202, Mitchel to O'Brien [30 April 1848]. [100] Clarendon Papers, II, 193, Clarendon to Grey, 1 April 1848. Smith O'Brien Papers, MS 449, f3399, Personal Memoranda, n.d.

from the Confederation by the nonsense of Mr O'Brien'. It is clear, however, that Mitchel and the other Confederate leaders were on divergent paths and that a schism was almost inevitable. Indeed, Mitchel's explanation of the resignation, in his paper, emphasised their differences on a republic and landlordism ('the time for conciliation of the landlord class is past ... the national movement *must* become a class movement') and declared O'Brien's policy 'a very bad one'. O'Brien disagreed with Mitchel's representation of their agreement about meetings and was 'much annoyed with the invidious way in which he spoke of my opinions in contrast with his', but he was persuaded out of a public riposte by 'friends' who thought it 'would damage Mitchell at his approaching trial'.[101]

Clarendon, for all that his police had allowed a riot to take place, was delighted by 'the defeat of the confederates at Limerick'. It had made 'a great sensation' in Dublin and O'Brien's appearance in court 'with his crest fallen and his eyes blackened gave infinite satisfaction to the court and the public ...' The affray, he believed, was 'a heavy blow and a great discouragement to the Young Irelanders ... Both Old and Young Ireland are alarmed at losing so great a card as S. O'Brien and accordingly J. O'Connell yesterday [1 May] in the Association moved an address of sympathy & condolence to him upon his black eyes, and the Young Irelanders having persuaded him that the stone was meant for Mitchel and could only have been thrown by a Government spy he is going to withdraw his resignation of the County and you [Russell] may still have the benefit of his presence in Parliament ...'[102] Greville wrote of the 'great satisfaction' felt in England at the news that O'Brien, Mitchel and Meagher 'were near being killed by an O'Connellite mob ... Smith O'B. was severely beaten ... All these things have drawn both ridicule and contempt on these empty boasters, who began by blustering and swaggering, and who now crouch under the blows that are aimed at them.'[103] *Punch*, developing its Irish canon, featured a cartoon and a derisive ballad by Thackeray, both entitled 'The Battle of Limerick'; Thackeray's repertoire of mock-Irish English possibly did more to amuse than his unimaginative telling of the tale (' ... In his glory he arose, And he rush'd upon his foes, But they hit him on the nose ...').[104] In fact, in Ireland the assault provoked widespread sympathy, and anger. Meagher commanded, 'Don't be downhearted for one minute more – not one minute more! ... The most desperate indignation exists here [Cork], in every mind, against the Revd. Dr O'Brien and all his ruffians. They would kill him, in spite of his surplice, if he was to be found here ... Never fear, never doubt. Up! Up! And take heart ... So, dress the wound – and to the field once more!'[105] O'Brien's post-bag and scores of newspa-

---

101 Ibid. Mitchel to Downing, 16 May 1848, *Irish Monthly*, xvi (1888), 636. *United Irishman*, 6 May 1848. Papers of Charles Gavan Duffy, MS 2642, f3483, O'Brien to Duffy, 11 June 1848.   102 Clarendon Papers, II, 230, Clarendon to Grey, 1 May 1848; 231, Clarendon to Russell, 2 May 1848.   103 Strachey and Fulford, *Greville Memoirs*, vi, 59, 3, 5 May 1848.   104 W.M. Thackeray, *Ballads* (London, 1855), 120-3.   105 Smith O'Brien Papers, MS 440, f2209, Meagher to O'Brien, n.d. Dr O'Brien, 'a priest of highly O'Connellite type', was the leader of the anti-Mitchel demonstration; see MacManus, *Thomas Davis and Young Ireland*, 91, 'Mitchel on Meagher'.

per columns filled with equally supportive (if less spirited) messages. Old Ireland's embarrassment, combined with the fact of Mitchel's departure from the Confederation, meant that prospects for reconciliation were probably improved; O'Brien, John O'Connell and other prominent members of the two repeal bodies met at the beginning of May and published what the Lord Lieutenant called 'a long foolish document in favor of being united'.[106]

An indication of O'Brien's intentions, including his contemplation of the possibility of revolution, was given by his response to Duffy's statement of his political views, 'The Creed of The Nation', issued on 29 April 1848. Duffy wanted 'a settlement made by negotiation ... I would prefer it to a republic won by insurrection.' However, 'If we cannot save our country by peace, I am for war ... I love peace, I fear disorder – I hate anarchy; but the sudden and violent remedy of an hour, though it pain us to the quick, is better than the perpetual helplessness of disease. If this is our only resource, let it come.' O'Brien announced that he read this piece 'with extreme pleasure' and was 'fully prepared to hold myself responsible, both morally and legally, for the sentiments contained in that letter.' He subsequently wrote that he 'entirely concurred' with this description of 'national policy'.[107] The Confederation's leaders evidently wanted both repealers, who were becoming impatient and attracted to Mitchel's radical ideas, and the government, who showed no signs of weakening, to know that the moment of decision between peace and war would not be delayed indefinitely. Also at this time, O'Brien signed a Council 'proclamation' that countered (and mocked) the Lord Lieutenant's 'unlawful and unconstitutional' proclamation of the illegality of a National Guard and a Council of Three Hundred. The Council was so bold as to 'warn' all sheriffs, magistrates and constables that they had no legal power to obstruct the measures taken with regard to these matters. This caused O'Brien (as the signatory, though not the author) to be removed again from the magistracy, deprived by the same Whig Lord Chancellor, Maziere Brady, who had restored him in 1846.[108]

Awaiting trial and still feeling his 'bodily injury', O'Brien stayed for almost a fortnight with his wife 'in comparative quiet' at Killiney outside Dublin. Later, on his way into exile, he recalled this time of happiness, when he found 'an enjoyment which has of late years been rarely known to me'.[109] He recovered sufficiently to enable him 'to undergo tolerably well the fatigues of the trial'. On 15 May, 16 Dublin clubs escorted him through the streets to the Four Courts. The charge

---

106 Clarendon Papers, II, 236, 237, Clarendon to Russell, 5, 6 May 1848; 238, Clarendon to Grey, 6 May 1848. *Nation*, 6 May 1848.   107 Ibid., 29 April, 6 May 1848, O'Brien to Duffy, 2 May 1848. Smith O'Brien Papers, MS 464, Draft Address of William Smith O'Brien, 1848, 49.   108 Ibid., MS 442, f2434, Proclamation By the Council of the Irish Confederation, 3 May 1843; ff2446, 2451, Brady to O'Brien, 5, 9 May 1848; f2452, The Order of Supersedeas, 9 May 1848. Clarendon Papers, II, 236, Clarendon to Russell, 5 May 1848; 240, Clarendon to Grey, 10 May 1848. *Nation*, 6, 13 May 1848.   109 O'Brien Papers (AO), Journal for Mrs William S. O'Brien, 9 July 1849.

called him 'a wicked, turbulent, malicious and seditious person', and the Attorney General presented his 15 March speech as an attempt 'to excite the people to rise in rebellion against their lawful sovereign'. Isaac Butt, commissioned by the Council, made a famous speech in O'Brien's defence. O'Brien was probably guilty – indeed, Duffy would later despise a government that 'could not obtain a verdict for manifest sedition' – but one of the jurors (who included three Catholics and a Quaker) refused to convict and so the jury was discharged. On the following day, Meagher's trial ended in the same way, and Clarendon advised against retrials.[110] Mitchel would not be so fortunate. On 13 May he was arrested and charged with treason-felony (under the new law), instead of sedition. Given his unashamed advocacy of insurrection – in one of the cited passages he had called for the amassing of 'a hundred thousand pikes' to prevent the harvest from being exported and 'at one and the same blow [to] prostrate British dominion and landlordism together' – a conviction seemed likely, and the Council considered the feasibility of a rescue. Duffy recalled that a 'small minority' was in favour, but when the Confederates 'took stock' of their resources it was seen that, while there were 30 clubs in Dublin and 11 in Cork, there was only a smattering of clubs elsewhere and 'not one club' in rural Ireland, and that there was no money, no military leadership and not one arms depot. For weeks the *Nation* had run a column, 'The Irish Revolution', carrying reports of drilling, pike-making, shooting practice and the preparation of muskets and pistols. The *United Irishman* featured 'Our War Department', with detailed advice on military matters. The judgement now, however, was that little of genuine value had been achieved. Meagher and O'Gorman inspected the Dublin clubs and found, as O'Gorman put it, 'that the people were for all purposes of insurrection unprepared, unorganized, unarmed, and incapable of being even roughly disciplined for any military attempt'. Against this the government had 10,000 soldiers in Dublin and nearly 30,000 in the whole country, and the capacity to starve the people into submission by cutting off the food supplies from the warehouses.[111]

O'Brien's account showed his entire opposition to anything like a rising; under the heading 'Suppression of the proposed attempt to rescue Mr Mitchell', he wrote:

> I found that a party in Dublin (for the most part Confederates) were resolved to make an attempt to rescue Mr Mitchell in case he should be arrested and to make such rescue the signal of a general insurrection. Believing that any such attempt would be utterly abortive, believing that there was not such an amount of public sympathy with Mr Mitchell as would make such a movement universal, and believing also that if the movement were universal the

---

[110] Smith O'Brien Papers, MS 449, f3399, Personal Memoranda, n.d. Duffy, *Young Ireland: Four Years of Irish History*, 212. *Nation*, 20 May 1848. Clarendon Papers, II, 246, 250, Clarendon to Grey, 15, 17 May 1848; 247, 268, Clarendon to Russell, 16, 28 May 1848. Terence de Vere White, *The Road of Excess* (Dublin, 1945), 117-21.   [111] Duffy, *Young Ireland: Four Years of Irish History*, 213. Narrative by O'Gorman, MS 5886, 11-12. *Nation*, 3 June 1848. Saville, *1848*, 24.

resources of the country would not at that time allow the Irish People to sustain a conflict with the Power of England in consequence of their dependence for food upon supplies of foreign corn & Indian meal the stoppage of which for a fortnight would be followed by the starvation of large multitudes of the People – governed [*O'Brien initially wrote 'influenced' but changed it to the more imperative 'governed'*] by these and other considerations I used all the influence which I possessed with the leading members of the Confederation to induce them to put a stop to the contemplated proceeding. By great exertion they were enabled to prevent the execution of the designs contemplated. For myself, being unable to undertake any thing which required much physical exertion and being resolved to lend no countenance direct or indirect to the proceedings contemplated by the friends of Mr Mitchell, I went to the County of Wicklow with Mrs O'Brien and did not return until after the trial and removal of Mr Mitchell.[112]

The resolution adopted by the Council was moved by Dillon, but the rough draft that survives in O'Brien's papers was written in the older man's hand and includes his customary mis-spelling of Mitchel's name. It read,

That it is the fixed conviction of this Council that any outbreak or violation of the peace on the occasion of the Trial of Mr Mitchell would be in the highest degree mischievous if not fatal to the Repeal cause and that we therefore earnestly impress upon our fellow citizens the necessity of abstaining at this moment from any collision with the authorities.[113]

O'Brien must bear a large part of the blame for the movement's lack of military preparation, with so little achieved beyond the endless talk about a National Guard. Almost certainly, however, he was right to oppose any form of insurrection in May 1848. The clubs were not sufficiently well armed or organised and the military resources of the government were formidable. Although the question caused much concern, Clarendon and General Blakeney, the veteran commander in chief, were generally confident in the loyalty of their soldiers. In Dublin especially, where the army held the strategic points and discipline was ensured by despatching the unreliable 57th regiment northwards, an insurrection would have been stamped out quickly. Elsewhere in the country, resources were stretched and there was greater reliance on the police (discussed below), but the weakness of the Confederation in the rural areas meant that this was immaterial.[114] O'Brien's judgement was as sound in May as it was to prove disastrously unsound in July.

---

112 Smith O'Brien Papers, MS 449, f3399, Personal Memoranda, n.d. See also ibid., MS 464, Draft Address of William Smith O'Brien, 1848, 47. Papers of Charles Gavan Duffy, MS 2642, f3483, O'Brien to Duffy, 11 June 1848.   113 Smith O'Brien Papers, MS 440, f2156, Resolution of the Council [18 May 1848].   114 Clarendon Papers, II, 165-6, 181, 190, 193, 205-6, 208, 220-1, Clarendon to Grey, 19, 20, 28, 31 March, 1, 10, 11, 12, 21, 22 April 1848; 194, 209, 216, Clarendon to Russell, 2, 13, 18 April 1848.

Clarendon reported O'Brien's opposition to physical force and that he went to Wicklow pretending to be ill. In fact, O'Brien had relapsed 'into a state in which I was incapable of active bodily exertion'; as Clarendon did acknowledge (with a hint of malice) in a later letter, he was 'still suffering from the effects of his Limerick thrashing'.[115] But the story contained some truth: O'Brien disagreed with a Council decision to hold a demonstration against the Mitchel prosecution, fearing that, 'If an attempt to excite an outbreak should be made by rash and reckless men, or by emissaries of the Government, the Council would be deemed to have encouraged it if they invited the assemblage of a large multitude in the metropolis. As he was not prepared to take the responsibility of such a proceeding, and had remonstrated against the meeting in vain, he would leave town for a few days.'[116] The meeting proceeded on 21 May, with all the Confederation leaders except O'Brien. In essence, however, all but a couple of Council members agreed with O'Brien's opposition to a rising. The Council issued an address to the people of Dublin in which they were implored, 'Under no circumstances suffer yourselves to be provoked into a collision at this moment'. Halpin sent O'Brien reassuring news of the measures taken 'to state emphatically the opinion of this Council upon the perfect insanity of such a movement'.[117]

Mitchel's trial opened on 25 May. The Crown ensured by repeated challenges that every Catholic juror was set aside and so Mitchel was tried before an entirely Protestant and anti-repeal jury. He was found guilty and sentenced to 14 years' transportation. The trial caused a resurgence of agitation, with the press and public meetings furiously denouncing the packing of the jury, a rapid growth in club organisation, and Chartist sympathisers staging numerous demonstrations in English cities. O'Brien 'could not refrain from sharing the indignation created by the violation of all the principles of justice'. He later wrote that, despite his 'dissent from many of the doctrines of Mr Mitchell', he considered him 'an enthusiastic lover of Ireland, a warm friend ... pureminded and truthful, though wayward & capricious'. He had 'reason to believe' that Mitchel 'cherished towards me feelings of affection and respect'. In fact, Mitchel, on the warship that took him from Dublin, included critical comment on O'Brien in the first entry in his *Jail Journal*: 'O'Brien is bold and high-minded, but capricious, unaccountable, intractable; also, he is an aristocrat born and bred, and, being a genuine Irishman himself, he cannot be brought to see that his fellow-aristocrats are not Irish, but the irreconcilable enemies of Ireland.' Later, however, Mitchel, who could be the most vitriolic of writers (the *Jail Journal* was one of the most embittered and powerful denunciations of British imperialism ever written), was generally respectful towards O'Brien, not least in his comments (noticed below) on Ballingarry.[118]

---

115 Ibid., II, 260, 263-4, 275, Clarendon to Grey, 22, 25, 26, 31 May 1848. Smith O'Brien Papers, MS 449, f3399, Personal Memoranda, n.d.   116 Duffy, *Young Ireland: Four Years of Irish History*, 214.   117 Smith O'Brien Papers, MS 438, f1892, Halpin to O'Brien, 22 May 1848. *Nation*, 27 May 1848, Address of The Council of the Irish Confederation to the People of Dublin, 20 May 1848.   118 Smith O'Brien Papers, MS 449, f3399, Personal Memoranda, n.d.; ibid., MS 464, Draft Address of William Smith

At the beginning of May, Sir Lucius O'Brien had spoken to Chief Secretary Somerville about O'Brien's activities, causing Clarendon to comment to Grey that he did not 'wonder at the annoyance which Sir L. O'Brien feels about his brother who is every day sinking deeper in degradation ... It is to be regretted that some of O'Brien's family cannot induce him to see the folly of his ways.' Perhaps prompted by Grey, Lucius wrote to O'Brien about 'his present position ... It is useless to argue with him on the main question,' he reported to Clarendon, 'but it is easy to point out that he has been deceived in all his anticipations.' He had described to O'Brien the lack of unity and 'discretion' in his 'camp', the futility of expecting foreign or Chartist aid, 'the loyalty of the army & police', the hostility of the O'Connellites and the priests towards Young Ireland, and the continuing opposition not only of the gentry but also of the more prosperous farmers. 'Such are the topics I have urged, & it is the first time I have written on any political subject to him for many years.'[119] Lucius was not alone in his concern. On 14 April, 'overcome by the persevering entreaties' of his wife, O'Brien had signed a deed that made Lucius and Woronzow Greig trustees for half of his landed property. The trust, which was to be operated on Lucy's behalf, was created 'as a means of protecting my estate from forfeiture in case I should be found guilty of high treason'.[120] On 5 June Clarendon reported, just a little inaccurately, that O'Brien was in Limerick 'having it is said intended to go home [to Dromoland] but his mother would not receive him'. In fact, O'Brien went to Dromoland at the beginning of June and had 'a short & most painful interview', as he described it, with his mother.[121]

As Lucius suggested, the Confederation faced considerable difficulties. To continue the warlike words of the past months would eventually bring them to share the fate of Mitchel. The idea that the Confederation would launch a rising after the harvest was in, if repeal was not granted, had not been developed into a plan of action, but the growing realisation that the government would not yield made the leaders turn to it now with a new seriousness of purpose. The stock-taking exercise had shown that active exertions were required if they were to be in a position even to threaten a rising in August. When O'Brien was in Wicklow, Duffy, Dillon, Father Kenyon, Martin, Reilly and one other 'for the first time commenced a formal conspiracy' (Duffy). Kenyon's proposal to have a new Council elected, one that would be much smaller and more fit to organise a revolt, was adopted; it was elected by ballot at a Confederation meeting, Meagher and Kenyon leading the way with 31 votes apiece, O'Brien, Duffy, Dillon and O'Gorman each gaining 30. O'Brien later wrote to Duffy that he 'should have opposed this proposal' if he had been in Dublin, but he did not explain his doubts.[122] Clarendon's report on 28 May that O'Brien was

---

O'Brien, 1848, 45-7. John Mitchel, *Jail Journal* (Dublin, n.d.), 7, entry for 27 May 1848. **119** Clarendon Papers, II, 234, Clarendon to Grey, 4 May 1848; Box 12, Grey to Clarendon, 2 May 1848; Box 21, Sir Lucius O'Brien to Clarendon, 29 May 1848. **120** *Limerick Reporter*, 17, 21 January 1862, Memorandum of William Smith O'Brien, 6 January 1862 (in two parts). **121** Clarendon Papers, II, 287, Clarendon to Grey, 5 June 1848. Smith O'Brien Papers, MS 449, f3399, Personal Memoranda, n.d. **122** Papers of

Springtime of Nations 233

'still in Wicklow but has been *ordered* to go to Limerick & get up an immediate insurrection, which I hope will increase the disgust with which he already views the Confederates' was one of the Lord Lieutenant's flights of fancy, but he rightly identified a divergence between O'Brien and the 'war party'. He also described 'the abuse & contempt he [O'Brien] gets from the [Mitchelite] Clubs ... his vanity will probably lead him to retrieve his position & in that he will fail for the confederates who want a republic will always be in advance of him who only seeks Repeal.'[123]

At the end of May, just before leaving for Limerick, O'Brien wrote the Confederation's address to the Irish people on the subject of Mitchel's trial. His frustration, and possibly the impatience of his colleagues, showed up as he argued (or conceded) that hopes of a peaceful resolution were fading and that nationalists should 'prepare at once' for 'armed resistance':

> We will not conceal from you – we will not conceal from the government, that nothing but the most strenuous exertions of our Council prevented the outbreak of an insurrection last week ... We apprehended that under present circumstances an armed attempt to rescue him [*Mitchel*] and to free Ireland might have proved abortive. We therefore interposed, and with difficulty succeeded in preventing the fruitless effusion of blood.
>
> But whilst we hesitate not to avow that such has been our conduct, we do not feel at liberty to conceal from you that the recent indignities offered to the Irish nation have greatly tended to remove from our minds the hope which we have heretofore desired to cherish, that the question at issue between England and Ireland will be settled by amicable adjustment. We feel bound to tell you, without disguise, that these indignities and wrongs are rapidly bringing us to that period when armed resistance to the oppressors of our country will become a sacred obligation, enforced by the highest sanctions of public duty.
>
> Under these impressions we cannot shrink from the responsibility of advising you to prepare at once for the protection of your invaded liberties ... Learn to contemplate calmly and firmly the chances of a final struggle, and prepare for that struggle by furnishing yourselves with all such resources as may enable you to command success ...
>
> Signed on behalf of the Council,
> William Smith O'Brien, Chairman.[124]

The injunction to get ready for insurrection took on a new urgency with this address. The Lord Lieutenant commented that, 'The quiet phase in S. O'Brien,

---

Charles Gavan Duffy, MS 2642, f3482, O'Brien to Duffy, 8 June 1848. Duffy, *Young Ireland: Four Years of Irish History*, 217-8. The new Council had 21 members. **123** Clarendon Papers, II, 263, 275, Clarendon to Grey, 25, 31 May 1848; 267, Clarendon to Russell, 28 May 1848. **124** *Nation*, 3 June 1848, Address of the Council of the Irish Confederation to the Irish People, n.d. O'Brien 'avow[ed] the authorship' of this document in a public letter to Dillon. Ibid., 10 June 1848, O'Brien to Dillon, 31 May 1848.

brought on I suppose by his broken rib, has passed away & he has issued the abominable manifesto I enclose herewith. There were large placards of the same posted in the streets ... The violence of the Clubs has frightened the Council. S. O'Brien's proclamation is a proof of it ...'[125] O'Brien was apprehensive; in a revealing and frank letter to O'Loghlen, he wrote, 'I have a horror of *failure* in any design of an extreme nature which may be adopted – and though I am resolved to risk my liberty and my life rather than acquiesce in the continuance of the present state of things I am earnestly and sincerely desirous to prevent any rash or hasty proceedings on the part of my ardent companions ...'[126] The tensions within the movement were now considerable. Many did not share in O'Brien's fear of a failed uprising, and there was widespread discontent that the Confederation had failed to sustain the martyred leader, Mitchel.[127]

O'Brien's grip on events was loosened further by his return to Cahirmoyle at the start of June; the pain in his side had 'continued to increase' and he finally accepted his doctor's advice that he should 'remain in a state of perfect quiet until my strength should be perfectly restored. With this view I returned to Cahirmoyle' and stayed there 'for about a month'.[128] Duffy's description of the 'conspiracy' hatched in Dublin shows that O'Brien was being side-stepped:

> Measures were taken to obtain money, arms, and officers from abroad, to make a diversion in England, and procure the co-operation of the Irish resident there, and to prepare particular local men to expect the event ... It was deemed inadvisable to extend the area of responsibility ... O'Brien was at Cahirmoyle, and we refrained from asking him to share these hazardous enterprises. Danger we knew he disregarded, as far as it involved personal consequences; but he was nervously anxious about the safety of his class, and we foresaw that if he consented to decisive measures he would prepare them by deliberation so long and consultation so frequent that they would be quite fatal to promptness of action. It was a secret relief to men who loved him, and made full allowance for the peculiar difficulty of his position, that they could take this risk wholly on themselves. Enough was said, when he returned to Dublin, to keep good faith; not enough to create responsibility.[129]

That O'Brien's opposition to a general rising owed something to a horror of social disintegration, an aversion that he shared with most of his class, is undeniable, but it was also caused by a justified apprehension that a revolt would be a complete failure.

---

125 Clarendon Papers, II, 278, Clarendon to Grey, 2 June 1848.   126 O'Loghlen Papers, MS 13892, O'Brien to O'Loghlen, 1 June 1848, typescript.   127 Smith O'Brien Papers, MS 440, f2223, Duffy to O'Brien [10 June 1848]. Papers of Charles Gavan Duffy, MS 2642, f3483, O'Brien to Duffy, 11 June 1848.   128 Smith O'Brien Papers, MS 449, f3399, Personal Memoranda, n.d.   129 Duffy, *Young Ireland: Four Years of Irish History*, 217.

The excitement of the May trials was sustained and, in particular, June and July 1848 saw an astonishing proliferation of clubs. Duffy and O'Brien called for the establishment of 1,000, and Meagher, Dillon, Duffy, O'Gorman and others were deputed to visit towns all over the south to promote their organisation. Thomas Halpin claimed 34 in the Dublin area in mid-June and by the end of the month was trumpeting the achievement of a national (southern) network of clubs.[130] Clarendon reported that they were 'springing up like mushrooms' and he learnt from 'our General', his code-name for Balfe, 'that in & about Dublin they have 12,000 armed men' in 77 clubs, with the capital 'surrounded by a cordon of armed Clubbists', and 'in all Ireland [there were] about 170 [clubs] & upwards of 50,000 men enrolled. They expect,' he wrote on 27 June, 'that upwards of 200 new clubs will be formed in the course of this week ...'[131] Although he remained in close touch with Duffy and Halpin, O'Brien was little more than a passive observer of this bout of activity.

Also during O'Brien's absence at Cahirmoyle, the reunification of the repeal movement, which he had wanted for months and discussed with John O'Connell on 29 May, was finally achieved – after a fashion. The two existing bodies, the Confederation and the Association, were dissolved, as O'Brien had always insisted, and a new 'Irish League' was created out of them. O'Brien also ensured that the clubs were not affiliated to the League, for a connection would incur legal responsibility without securing control.[132] He told Duffy that he thought the Confederation 'wanted a good deal of *ballast* to prevent our gallant ship from being upset by squalls' and so was 'not at all sorry that we are to get an addition of heavy matter' in the form of Old Ireland, 'but whilst no one prizes more than I do *caution* & *prudence* I do not want cowardice or hesitation'. He was 'greatly afraid that we shall get a little too much *dead weight* by the junction'.[133] These doubts led to O'Brien's playing a role, inadvertently, in scuppering the enterprise. His purpose, as he wrote to Duffy, was 'to signify my concurrence in the arrangements', but his public letter on the subject, which appeared in the *Nation* on 17 June, showed too clearly the ambivalence he felt towards a union with men of straw and, importantly, his readiness to use physical force:

> All the principles for which the Confederates contended have in succession been conceded to us ... I should deeply regret the proposed union if I could persuade myself that it would tend to check the bold course of policy which has been adopted, after full deliberation, by the Irish Confederation ... These

---

130 *Nation*, 3, 17 June 1848, O'Brien to Halpin, 12 June 1848. Smith O'Brien Papers, MS 442, ff2473, 2475, 2480, 2484, 2486, Halpin to O'Brien, 12, 13, 20, 29 June, 1 July 1848. Duffy, *Young Ireland: Four Years of Irish History*, 218. 131 Clarendon Papers, II, 275, 278, 291, 296, Clarendon to Grey, 31 May, 2, 8, 10 June 1848; III, 11, 17, Clarendon to Russell, 20 June, 2 July 1848; 12, 15, Clarendon to Grey, 23, 27 June 1848; Box 53, Notes by Balfe [June 1848]. 132 *FJ*, 30 May 1848 (J. O'Connell). O'Loghlen Papers, MS 13892, O'Brien to O'Loghlen, 1 June 1848, typescript. 133 Papers of Charles Gavan Duffy, MS 2642, f3482, O'Brien to Duffy, 8 June 1848.

apprehensions have, however, been removed ... Both parties now admit that we stand upon the 'last plank' of the constitution. No one denies that Ireland is now ruled solely by military power. 'The Union' is now undeniably maintained – not by the bonds of affection and interest, but by a system of force, fraud, and corruption ... Events, events, not arguments, have cancelled the famous 'peace resolutions'. Our controversy will soon narrow itself into the single question, now often uttered with impatience – 'When shall the Irish nation strike?' Upon this question we ought to invite the deliberation of men who are cautious as well as resolute. In the language of one of your youthful poets –

'............... Your worst transgression
Were to strike, and strike in vain.'

The advocates of what is called 'moral force' tell us – and I believe them – that, if ever it should become necessary to vindicate the trampled rights of their country by an appeal to arms, they will be found amongst the foremost in the field. Shall we refuse to enter into confederacy with these men, for the purpose of considering how we can best concentrate the national energies in support of our national cause?[134]

This was highly ambiguous, seeming simultaneously to urge boldness and to warn against failure (striking in vain). But it was too much for John O'Connell. Some of the Catholic bishops had advised him against union with Young Ireland, long regarded as inimical to Catholicism. In a conference on 20 June, O'Connell proposed, unsuccessfully, to pledge the new League to views similar to the Peace Resolutions of 1846. He also objected to O'Brien's declaration of the death of these resolutions and to the warlike tone of O'Brien's letter and the *Nation*. He then announced his intention to retire from politics. Duffy's verdict that he was 'influenced by doubt and trepidation, for his mind was as unsteady as a quagmire', seems fair. Following O'Connell's example, none of the repeal MPs or the other Association leaders joined the League, which, although there were valuable gains like O'Loghlen and Doctor Gray of the *Freeman's Journal*, essentially remained the Confederation in all but name.[135]

The loss of so much 'dead weight' would not have been damaging in normal circumstances. However, John O'Connell's endorsement might have diminished the hostility of the priests, whose role in July was to be so crucial. Donal Kerr has shown how the clergy, 'almost without exception', had backed O'Connell and moral force against Young Ireland. The enthusiasm created by the French revolution induced

---

134 *Nation*, 17 June 1848, O'Brien to Halpin, 12 June 1848. Papers of Charles Gavan Duffy, MS 2642, f3482, O'Brien to Duffy, 8 June 1848.   135 Duffy, *Young Ireland: Four Years of Irish History*, 220-1. Smith O'Brien Papers, MS 442, f2481, O'Loghlen to O'Brien, 22 June 1848. *Nation*, 17, 24 June, 1 July 1848. In a public letter written after the conference, O'Connell said he 'should, perhaps, not have used the word "retirement", but rather that of "refusal" to join the *new League*. I trust to labour still for Ireland as a member of parliament, and at home by *writing*, where I am precluded from speaking.'

some priests to come forth with the sort of bold, conquer-or-die language usually heard on Confederation platforms. Kenyon was a conspicuous example, and Father James Birmingham of Borrisokane in Tipperary called on the people, 'First, make your peace with God ... Secondly – Arm quietly ...' Others were sympathetic, influenced, as Kerr put it, by 'the stimulus of the exciting events in France and Italy, where Catholicism and revolution appeared to go hand in hand'.[136] Archbishop Murray of Dublin made several attempts to restrain these priests, invoking 'the horrors of Civil War' and recalling the 'calamity' of 1798. Bishop Kennedy of Killaloe forced Birmingham into a public retraction of his dangerous language.[137] Clarendon reported that the bishops and older clergy were 'getting alarmed at the physical force movement and the socialist and irreligious principles of the Clubs, but the younger priests & the curates are all Young Irelanders & ready for a fight ...'[138] The balance of opinion in the priesthood now swung against Young Ireland. On 23 June, the workers of Paris rose up in the revolt that came to be known as the June Days. At least 1,000, possibly many times that, were killed and all of Europe had to observe a lesson in the horrors of popular insurrection. Among the victims, shot dead on 25 June, was the archbishop of Paris, Denys-Auguste Affre. The Lord Lieutenant wrote gleefully of 'the *salutary murder* of the Archbishop', who, 'poor man, never did a better thing in his life than getting himself murdered'. A Castle hireling had articles published in the *Dublin Evening Post* 'connecting the Clubs with infidelity and *proving*,' Clarendon enthused, 'that every Irish Priest must expect the fate of the Archbishop of Paris if the Irish leaders get the upper hand. The clergy are getting really frightened not for the state but for themselves and we may therefore with some degree of certainty reckon upon their support.'[139] Time would prove him right. A month before Ballingarry, the French, the original creators of all the excitement, had struck the first blow in the defeat of Ireland's revolution.

---

136 Donal A. Kerr, *'A Nation of Beggars'? Priests, People, and Politics in Famine Ireland, 1846-1852* (Oxford, 1994), 123-40. Donal Kerr, *The Catholic Church and the Famine* (Dublin, 1996), 64-5. *Nation*, 15 April 1848, Birmingham to Meagher, 12 April 1848.   137 Ibid., 29 April, 13 May 1848. Kerr, *Nation of Beggars*, 141-5.   138 Clarendon Papers, III, 16, Clarendon to Russell, 29 June 1848.   139 Ibid., III, 16, 24, 26, Clarendon to Grey, 30 June, 6, 8 July 1848; 23, Clarendon to Russell, 6 July 1848; c. 80, Clarendon to Bedford, 8 July 1848. Affre died whilst attempting to mediate at the barricades; it is not known if the shot was fired by a red-republican rebel or a government soldier.

9

Ballingarry

Duffy's new-found enthusiasm for rebellion prompted a call on O'Brien to take command: 'There is no half-way house for you,' he wrote in mid-June. 'You will be head of the movement, loyally obeyed; and the revolution will be conducted with order and clemency; or the mere anarchists will prevail with the people, and our revolution will be a bloody chaos ... I am perfectly well aware that you don't desire to lead or influence others; but I believe ... that that feeling which is a high personal and civic virtue, is a vice in revolutions ... If I were Smith O'Brien I would shape out in my own mind ... a definite course for the revolution, and labour incessantly to develop it that way ...' He regretted that, for want of a strong lead, O'Brien's plan to sign up volunteers for a National Guard had 'been permitted to fall into disuse ... The clubs, however, might take the place of the National Guard' if their expansion were 'vigorously and systematically carried out ... Forgive me for urging this so anxiously upon you; but I verily believe the hopes of the country depend upon the manner in which the next two months are used ...'[1] He knew O'Brien's instincts well enough to present revolution as an antidote to the prospect of 'bloody chaos'. But O'Brien was not so easily managed. He had frequently expressed his horror of failure, his fear that they might 'strike in vain', and he told Duffy on 11 June that he was 'not one of those who wish to plunge recklessly into the Lion's mouth'.[2] Events, not words, were destined to convert this reluctant revolutionary.

While the young men in Dublin dreamed and talked of revolution – it would become evident that they did little more – O'Brien was elsewhere, slowly regaining his health at Cahirmoyle. On 8 June he could not 'stoop or stretch without pain', and on the 15th he was 'not yet in speaking order', but by the 23rd he was claiming a 'perfect recovery'.[3] He readied himself to rejoin the fray, planning a major tour of the southern towns; he later claimed that he 'resolved to perambulate the whole

---

[1] John George Hodges, *Report of the Trial of William Smith O'Brien, for High Treason, at the Special Commission for the Co. Tipperary, held at Clonmel, September and October, 1848* (Dublin, 1849), 146-7, Duffy to O'Brien [17 June 1848]. [2] Papers of Charles Gavan Duffy, MS 2642, f3483, O'Brien to Duffy, 11 June 1848. [3] Ibid., ff3482, 3484, O'Brien to Duffy, 8, 15 June 1848. Smith O'Brien Papers, MS 442, f2482, O'Donnell to O'Brien, 25 June 1848.

kingdom of Ireland, not with a view to raise an immediate rebellion, but to marshal the Repealers of Ireland into such an attitude as would give the weight of physical force to the representation of their determination to rescue their country from the misrule of the British Parliament'. His meaning was made clearer when he remembered his tour in the journal he wrote for his wife in 1849: 'I endeavoured to impress upon both the English & Irish people [sic] a consciousness of the internal power of the Irish nation in such a manner as to secure the future happiness of Ireland under domestic legislation without a recurrence to the arbitrament of arms.'4 He held to his preference for the methods of 1782 over those of 1798.

He would begin, moreover, with a holiday in Kerry and west Cork, where he could indulge his 'love of nature in her wildest & most picturesque forms'.5 It was with 'a party of pleasure' that O'Brien began the month, July 1848, he would end as a fugitive rebel. As he journeyed through Kenmare, Castletown, Berehaven, Bantry and Macroom with two friends (Denis Shine Lawlor and John Shea Lawlor), O'Brien was 'everywhere welcomed with the utmost enthusiasm'. This tour, despite its pleasurable distractions, nudged him in the direction of revolt; he later wrote that he was 'led to believe that the country would sustain us in any effort which we might feel disposed to make for the Liberation of Ireland'. His comment to Lucy, understandably perhaps, given that she apparently expressed 'apprehensions' and 'anxieties', was more suggestive of a desire to avoid conflict: 'Throughout the whole of this excursion I have found the spirit of the people most enthusiastic in their disposition towards me and even too hot in regard to the country'.6 In Cork on 10 July, 'a very large number of respectable and intelligent men' attended a soirée and heard O'Brien laud the martial spirit of the people and declare that the Irish were 'fully justified in an appeal to arms'. He warned against any 'abortive effort', however: 'do not hazard a cause by placing it in jeopardy, or destroy the spirit of the country for a century by a perilous attempt that has not received the sanction of public opinion'. He argued that 'the true policy of this country is to place the Irish nation in such an attitude as that it shall be perfectly irresistible – that they shall forbear to strike until they can obtain full success. And my belief is that, when they are in that position, the chances are they will obtain all they want without striking a blow …' Making themselves irresistible meant, he said, union, more clubs and more arms. Restraint, patience and organisation, then, were his principal themes,

---

4 *Correspondence between John Martin and William Smith O'Brien relative to a French Invasion* (Dublin, 1861), 31. O'Brien Papers (AO), Journal for Mrs William S. O'Brien, 10 July 1849. Also in Smith O'Brien Papers, MS 3923 5 Ibid., MS 449, f.3399, Personal Memoranda, n.d. 6 Ibid.; ibid., MS 442, f.2490, O'Brien to Lucy O'Brien, 12 July 1848; ibid., MS 8653 (24), O'Brien to Lucy O'Brien [12 July 1848]. His reception at Bantry, where he was greeted by 'a flotilla of some hundreds of boats', is described in A.M. Sullivan, *New Ireland: Political Sketches and Personal Reminiscences* (London, 1878), i, 166-7. In his second letter on 12 July, O'Brien's anger at a Dublin arrest (under the law which forbade drilling) led him to risk involving his own family, and that of the judge who would soon preside in his trial, in political controversy: 'Ask Edward [his son] whether the son of Chief Justice Blackburne is drilled at Stackallan. I cannot reconcile to myself the transportation of a young boy for saying "stand at arms" &c. If he [Blackburne's son] is drilled the fact ought to be known.'

and the reference to awaiting the development of 'public opinion' suggests he was not easily deluded by the noise of cheering crowds.[7]

O'Brien's experience on the following evening made a substantial difference in this respect. Even if he was still a general who hoped that the threat of revolt would suffice, his willingness to use force seemed to be increased by the readiness of his men to fight:

> ... I signified a desire to inspect the Clubs and accordingly it was arranged that they should assemble in the evening in a yard from which all but the members of the Clubs could be excluded. Fifteen clubs consisting of upwards of 1500 ablebodied men the greater part of whom appeared to be of a very intelligent class took up their positions in a most orderly manner in the appointed place. An immense concourse of people who though not members of Clubs appeared to be animated by the same spirit having collected outside the building within which the Clubs were assembled I promised to address them in the city Park. Accordingly about nightfall by the light of a glorious moon the clubs marched in regular order to a convenient spot and took up a separate Position. There could not have been less than from 7000 to 10000 persons present. The scene was most animating. I left this meeting under the impression that the Population of Cork would be ready to act with the utmost vigour whenever their Country should demand their services.[8]

If O'Brien was at fault in misreading the martial spirit of the Irish people – and perhaps those who pledged their arms should share in any guilt involved there – his main error was in delaying too long a decision about what 'services' he would demand of them. Again, the account he sent Lucy is revealing. After describing the 'great enthusiasm & determination' of the Cork repealers, he said he was 'inclined to hope from the disposition evinced by the people here to take advice that we shall be able to make the whole of this power available for good purposes, but upon this point we must leave results to Providence. All that each of us can do is simply in a faithful spirit to do our duty.'[9] He was obviously resigned to the possibility of insurrection. Still, however, he shirked the decision, leaving it to Providence. In fact, it was the British government that would now take the initiative, commencing the struggle that showed which side was ready for war and which was not.

The Lord Lieutenant had vacillated since February between exaggerated fears and boundless confidence. The informer Balfe's reports usually stated that there would be no revolt before the harvest, but the spread of club organisation and

---

7 *Cork Examiner*, 12 July 1848. Smith O'Brien Papers, MS 449, f3399, Personal Memoranda, n.d.   8 Ibid. The *Examiner* put the number of clubmen, who lined up for O'Brien to inspect like an army officer, at 2-3,000, representing 15 clubs, and claimed a crowd of 10-12,000. *Cork Examiner*, 12 July 1848. The report of the 'review' that Russell related to Parliament had some colourful touches, including the unlikely story that when a woman called out 'Three cheers for the King of Munster' O'Brien replied, 'Not yet – not yet'. *Hansard*, c, 706-7, 22 July 1848, Russell.   9 Smith O'Brien Papers, MS 442, f2490, O'Brien to Lucy O'Brien, 12 July 1848.

arming during June, and the imminence of the harvest in August, induced a state of panic. Clarendon had urged legislation for the suspension of *Habeas Corpus* since March, despite Russell's doubts about his chances of carrying such a drastic measure through Parliament. By July, as the clubs proliferated and there was a prospect of rebellion after the prorogation of Parliament (in September), his pleas took on a new urgency; as he wrote to the Home Secretary on the 3rd, 'before Parliament is up the Government will have to determine whether they will ask for fresh powers or permit a regular organization for immediate civil war to remain unmolested'.[10] In the event, he acted first under the existing sedition and treason-felony laws. A letter from Balfe recommended the arrest of the Confederate leaders, a step that Clarendon 'had nearly decided upon', he informed Grey on the 8th, and that evening the sweep began.[11] The owners and editors of three newspapers – Duffy of the *Nation*, John Martin of the *Felon*, and Dalton Williams and Kevin O'Doherty of the *Tribune* – were arrested on 8-9 July. The *Felon* and the *Tribune* had been established to succeed the suppressed *United Irishman* and, following in Mitchel's footsteps, their incendiary language gave ample scope for charges of sedition (Martin) and treason-felony (Williams and O'Doherty). So, too, did Duffy's in the *Nation*. From mid-June his writing was increasingly violent, lending credence to the idea that he really did intend a revolt; among the articles in the seized 8 July edition, for example, was one headed 'How to Break Down a Bridge, or Blow One Up'. He was charged with treason-felony and, like the others, consigned to Dublin's Newgate prison. A few days later, Meagher, McGee and others were charged with sedition but released on bail.[12]

These developments made a considerable impact on O'Brien. He owned that the *Nation* had used 'much less prudent' language since the Mitchel trial: as he told Lucy on 16 July, it 'has done itself mischief by the character of some of its recent articles but upon the whole it is a journal which ought not to be put down with impunity'. He later wrote that he could not consistently with his 'sense of honor' allow Duffy to be 'sacrificed' without preparing himself 'to share his fate'. He decided 'if possible to prevent his transportation. What means I might possess for carrying into effect this determination would depend upon the feeling of the Country. Though still hoping that circumstances would render it unnecessary for me to call upon the Country to take up arms I yet felt that each new aggression on the part of the Government made it imperative upon me to place the Country in a condition to protect itself and its most valued and gifted children.' In the address he wrote to give at his trial, O'Brien described how he could not permit a repetition of such 'machinations' as were employed against Mitchel 'without an appeal to the manhood of Irishmen' on Duffy's behalf.[13] Clearly, O'Brien now took a sig-

---

10 Clarendon Papers, II, 188, 192, 285, 294, Clarendon to Russell, 31 March, 1 April, 4, 10 June 1848; 193, 285, Clarendon to Grey, 1 April, 3 June 1848; III, 16, 20, 25-6, Clarendon to Grey, 30 June, 3, 7, 8 July 1848; 21, 25, Clarendon to Russell, 4, 7 July 1848.   11 Ibid., 26, Clarendon to Grey, 8 July 1848.
12 *Nation*, 8, 15 July 1848. *FJ*, 10, 13 July 1848.   13 Smith O'Brien Papers, MS 8653 (24), O'Brien to Lucy O'Brien, 16 July 1848; ibid., MS 449, f3399, Personal Memoranda, n.d.; ibid., MS 464, Draft

nificant step towards rebellion, even if it was not irrevocable. He resolved to spend the time before Duffy's trial 'in efforts to rouse the Country and to place it in a state of preparation', with the clubs, he hoped, 'capable of being applied in each locality to operations of whatever character the circumstances of the country might suggest'. On the evening of Wednesday, 12 July, he returned to 'consult with our friends in Dublin'. He travelled by sea from Cork, the 'balminess of the air' inducing him to spend the night on deck, sleeping under his cloak.[14]

O'Brien stayed at Richard O'Gorman's house on Merchant's Quay and on 14 July went to assess the strength of the Dublin clubs. According to Duffy, 'O'Brien sat at the head of the table with a list of the metropolitan Clubs before him. When the secretary named a Club, the delegates came forward and reported the number of members, the quantity of arms ... and the state of opinion.' According to James Stevenson Dobbyn, a Dublin clubman (he claimed) who later gave evidence for the Crown, O'Brien stated his opinion 'that the organization was not perfect, at least he had not inspected Ireland to have proof positive', and declared 'that he would prefer ascending the gallows, rather than that one should lose his life on his account by a premature step'. He gave the same response, Dobbyn said, when 'all unanimously' announced their intention to rescue Duffy and the other journalists should they be convicted.[15] Clarendon produced an interesting if jaundiced account of this meeting:

> S. O'Brien arrived here from Cork on Thursday. He last night visited the Clubs, which are in good spirits and ready to act, he told them not to deceive him or themselves about their numbers but to state how many men could be relied upon to turn out instantly and armed, & it appeared there were 3,700 or rather more which just tallies with the information we have got. He is a brave determined man as well as half mad and under the guidance of Duffy who is not brave but who being in jail is desperate and can afford to give desperate advice which he will not have to act upon. These 3,700 don't constitute a formidable force but they might reckon upon a mob of at least 10,000 & in a very few hours the people might come pouring in from Wicklow and Meath to assist in the work of plunder ... The alarm and excitement in Dublin are considerable and it is beginning to be known that S. O'Brien is to *review the Clubs* tomorrow & let people learn their effective strength ...[16]

O'Brien cancelled this review out of fear of a 'collision' with the police.[17] Instead, Clarendon was informed, he received the presidents of the Dublin clubs on 16 July

---

Address of William Smith O'Brien, 1848, 49. **14** Ibid., MS 449, f3399, Personal Memoranda, n.d.; ibid., MS 8653 (24), O'Brien to Lucy O'Brien, 12, 16 July 1848. **15** Duffy, *Young Ireland: Four Years of Irish History*, 228. Hodges, *Report of the Trial of William Smith O'Brien*, 240-8, 261-70. **16** Clarendon Papers, III, 37, Clarendon to Grey, 15 July 1848. **17** Smith O'Brien Papers, MS 464, Draft Address of William Smith O'Brien, 1848, 53. See also Clarendon Papers, III, 41, Clarendon to Grey, 16 July 1848.

and 'each man saw S. O'Brien alone who gave him his instructions which they will not divulge. S. O'Brien is going to Drogheda this afternoon to review the Clubs there, as it is said, but probably to instruct them in the same way as he did here, he is then going to other places with the same object and Meagher is in the country upon a similar mission ...'[18]

On Monday, 17 July, O'Brien did embark on a short tour to inspect clubs and urge the people 'to hold themselves in readiness to cooperate in whatever national effort might be rendered necessary'. In Drogheda, he was 'received with the utmost enthusiasm' by a crowd that the *Nation* put at over 10,000, and the 500 clubmen who mustered in Navan appeared 'to be well organised and to be desirous of instant action'. The 'intimations' he gave 'that the day might not be far distant' when he would call upon his audience 'to afford sterner indications of Patriotism than mere cheers' were received with 'an enthusiasm which appeared to me significant of the most resolute determination'. A meeting on the hill at Tara provoked 'much emotion. The memories and traditions of the Royal Tara recalled the times when Ireland acknowledged no sway but that of her own Kings & Chiefs', the heir of Brian Boru recalled later. The ruined Norman fortifications at Trim reminded him of 'a time when the old Irish race were restrained from expelling from this island the English settlers only by fortifications of the strongest kind ... Is the spirit of that old Irish Race extinct? Heirs of their soil are we no longer heirs of their courage? To this question I was then disposed to give a very different answer from that which the experience of a few weeks would now compel me to dictate ...'[19]

On 19 July, O'Brien returned to Dublin for the second meeting of the League (having missed the first on 11 July). It was 'intensely crowded' and, again, there was a great display of 'enthusiasm' and willingness 'to follow me wherever I was disposed to lead them against the common enemy ... every allusion to the possibility of a collision was received with rapturous excitement.' In so describing his audiences, O'Brien was clearly anxious to excuse the fatal decision he was about to make – but there is no reason to doubt that the crowds were large and enthusiastic. Just before the meeting, the Catholic bishop of Derry, Dr Maginn, had promised O'Brien that he and his clergy would join the League 'upon the condition that its proceedings should be kept within the bounds of constitutional operation'. This and the presence of a 'large deputation of respectable but timid men' from Kilkenny made O'Brien quite guarded in his references to physical force, and he was 'fully resolved, if possible, not to bring myself within the operation of this new felony act'.[20] His call for 'self-restraint' – the same message that was propounded in Cork and Drogheda – stood in marked contrast to the approach taken in the *Nation*. On

---

18 Ibid., 42, Clarendon to Russell, 17 July 1848.   19 Smith O'Brien Papers, MS 449, f3399, Personal Memoranda, n.d.; ibid., MS 464, Draft Address of William Smith O'Brien, 1848, 51. *Nation*, 22 July 1848. The reference to 'the experience of a few weeks' is the clearest indication that the 'Personal Memoranda' was written when O'Brien was in prison that autumn.   20 Smith O'Brien Papers, MS 449, f3399, Personal Memoranda, n.d. See also ibid., MS 442, f2491, O'Brien to Lucy O'Brien, 20 July 1848. *FJ*, 20 July 1848. *Nation*, 22 July 1848.

22 July, it printed a long poem by O'Brien, a call for 'each arm to do its part, That Erin may be free'. Duffy, editing his paper from Newgate prison, introduced it as 'a marching song which five hundred Clubs, of a hundred thousand disciplined men, may tramp to the music of some summer morning. If the writer of it is at the head of them, he will be in the place men destine for him; and we accept this "prophet tone" as an omen of a success without stain – except the stain of patriot blood poured out in a joyful libation for the dear old land.' In fact, the poem was a romanticised vision that was nothing like the invocation to violence that Duffy represented it to be. Under the heading 'The Casus Belli', Duffy wrote an editorial that deprecated 'the fatal dry-rot of inaction' and summoned the Irish nation to 'the battle field ... we must strip our back for the lash, or strip our arms for the fight.' Another, unsigned column, entitled 'The Hour of Destiny', urged, 'Uplift your battle flag ... [for] a holy war ... Strike! Strike!'[21]

Earlier, on 18 July, the Lord Lieutenant announced the proclamation of Dublin (city and county), Drogheda, Cork and Waterford under the Crime and Outrage measure of 1847, thereby assuming the right to disarm everyone in these places. O'Brien later wrote angrily of this 'most unwarrantable stretch of power', by which legislation to suppress agrarian crimes was to be used to 'supersede the Bill of Rights by depriving the People of Ireland of their right to bear arms'.[22] In a private meeting held on 19 July to consider their reaction to this move, there was strong support among Dublin's club presidents for an immediate outbreak. Joseph Brennan of the Molyneux Club moved for this, arguing that they could not simply allow themselves to be disarmed. Dillon's amendment favoured 'passive resistance' to the proclamation and O'Brien said 'that a break out at this time would be premature'. The amendment was carried by 'a very small majority, and the minority were greatly dissatisfied'.[23] This was the version that Dobbyn gave in evidence against O'Brien. O'Brien denounced his 'perjuries', but his own account, in the address he wrote for his trial, was similar: he and the other Confederate leaders persuaded the club presidents that, while 'every possible obstruction should be thrown in the way of those deputed to search for arms', there should be 'no measure of active resistance'. This decision 'proved that we were desirous to avoid if possible a collision with the authorities'. He went on to state that even at this stage he 'had not formed any specific plan of insurrection, nor indeed did I consider it absolutely certain that a necessity would arise for actual collision with England'. He still intended 'not to throw the country into a state of actual insurrection but to place it in a condition to protect itself and to command by its intrinsic power the attainment of every object which it desired'.[24] Some years later, he claimed that he 'should probably have delayed for an indefinite period to summon the people to arms', had he not been

---

21 Ibid., 22 July 1848. 22 Smith O'Brien Papers, MS 464, Draft Address of William Smith O'Brien, 1848, 55. *FJ*, 19 July 1848. 23 Hodges, *Report of the Trial of William Smith O'Brien*, 248-50, 272-80. Clarendon Papers, Box 53, Balfe to Southern [July 1848]. See also Duffy, *Young Ireland: Four Years of Irish History*, 228. 24 Smith O'Brien Papers, MS 464, Draft Address of William Smith O'Brien, 1848, 53-59.

'compelled' by the suspension of *Habeas Corpus*.[25] However, immediately after his conviction, he wrote that, although the 'circumstances ... which gave occasion to the outbreak were in some measure unforeseen', he 'had previously formed a deliberate conviction that the time had come when it was the duty of every Irishman to be prepared to vindicate the rights of his country by force inasmuch as every effort of a peaceful nature had proved ineffectual'. He had decided that 'resistance to the English Government had become a duty and that the choice of a moment for the exercise of the right of resistance was a question to be determined solely by a calculation of the chances of success'.[26]

O'Brien told Lucy on 20 July that, 'The great danger now results from the trial of C.G. Duffy & others for felony. If an attempt be made to transport them nothing can prevent an insurrection.'[27] All of the leaders now accepted that a rising was a distinct possibility, even if O'Brien was less 'absolutely certain' than, say, Meagher, who was convinced that they 'would have to fight'. The unity of the leadership was evident when O'Brien dined with many of his young friends at O'Gorman's house on 21 July. Meagher recalled that while they thought it would be 'wiser' to delay a revolt until after the harvest, 'the time originally proposed', they also knew how the 'spirit and reputation' of the country 'would be affected by the loss of another leading man'. So, everyone was in full agreement that they would not allow any of the 'political prisoners' to be transported 'without an attempt being made to resist the execution of the sentence'.[28] After Mitchel's conviction by a packed jury, no-one could have entertained much hope that Duffy's acquittal would provide a way out. At another meeting later that evening (21 July), about 30 delegates from the Dublin clubs elected what Meagher, in a private memorandum, called the 'War Directory'. In his narrative, Meagher said it was to have 'the responsibility of giving the signal for insurrection, or withholding it, just as it appeared most fit'. It is possible that O'Brien's refusal to be involved – he did not attend the meeting and gave instructions that he should not be elected – reflected a reluctance to be embroiled in any rash proceeding. His only comment later was that he 'objected to its formation and refused to become a member of it not because I conceived it to be illegal but because I feared it would become a source of jealousy and be productive rather of weakness than of strength to our organisation'. Meagher explained to the delegates that O'Brien had 'conceived some objection' to the new body and so 'it would be useless to vote for him; the more particularly since he was to start in the morning for the South, where, for a few weeks, he would be engaged in the organisation and inspection of the Munster Clubs'. Dillon, Meagher, O'Gorman, McGee and Reilly were elected.[29]

---

25 *Correspondence between Martin and O'Brien*, 1861, 31.   26 Smith O'Brien Papers, MS 464, Draft Address of William Smith O'Brien, 1848, 9, 11, 51.   27 Ibid., MS 442, f2491, O'Brien to Lucy O'Brien, 20 July 1848.   28 Thomas Francis Meagher, Personal Recollections of the Insurrection, in *The Weekly News*, 3, 10 August 1867. See also *Nation*, 8, 15, 22 February, 1, 8 March 1851. Gwynn, *Young Ireland and 1848*, 276. Arthur Griffith (ed.), *Meagher of the Sword: Speeches of Thomas Francis Meagher, 1846-1848* (Dublin, 1916), 177. The *Weekly News* series, which ran from 3 August until 28 September 1867, is slightly more complete than the edited version that Gwynn and Griffith took from the *Nation*.   29 O'Loghlen Papers,

According to Meagher, the leaders – he specified 'O'Brien, O'Gorman, Dillon and the rest of us' – reckoned on having 'some three or four weeks more to devote to the organisation of the country'. O'Brien, 'in shaping out the course of his excursion through the country, fully calculated upon a month of uninterrupted agitation'.[30] He planned to follow a visit to Wexford with a League meeting in Kilkenny (where he would also take in the agricultural show), a 'short repose' at Cahirmoyle, and another 'repeal mission' to the north. 'Before the summer is over,' he told Lucy, 'I shall be tolerably well acquainted with this island, if left at large, and in regard to expense I do not think that I could employ £50 or £100 better than in making myself thoroughly acquainted with my own country. You would not grudge this amount for an excursion to Italy …' With Duffy and the others not due to appear in court until 8 August, and the likelihood that the trials would last at least a week, it would be mid-August before they would have to act.[31] On the morning of Saturday 22 July, O'Brien set out for Wexford. He went to stay with a former Parliamentary colleague, John Maher of Ballinkeele, near Enniscorthy, though he 'entertained no desire to compromise him [Maher] nor if I had foreseen what was about to happen would I have placed him in an equivocal position by allowing him to receive so dangerous a guest'.[32] He went, he claimed, with 'a bona fide intention of endeavouring to develop the public feeling of that county in a constitutional manner by adhesion to [the] League and by the establishment of local Clubs'.[33] O'Brien may have intended 'constitutional' speeches that did not break the law, but his intention was clearly to promote sufficient spirit and organisation among the people to intimidate the government and, if nothing was achieved in this way, to be ready to stage an insurrection.

In the event, the rebellion was induced – not caused – by the government's decision to have Parliament suspend the Act of *Habeas Corpus*. By this stage, Clarendon was stridently insisting that 'at any moment now there may be an outbreak' and complaining that the government was 'calmly looking on while every preparation for a bloody civil war was making before our faces'.[34] On 19 July, the Cabinet agreed that the clubs were 'seditious and treasonable associations' intended for rebellion and conceded that if 'an extensive system of organization for ulterior purposes dangerous to the peace of the community should be continued', the government would ask Parliament for 'additional powers'.[35] Clarendon was now pushing at an open door and

MS 13892, Meagher memorandum, n.d. Smith O'Brien Papers, MS 464, Draft Address of William Smith O'Brien, 1848, 57. Meagher, Personal Recollections, *Weekly News*, 10 August 1867. See also Hodges, *Report of the Trial of William Smith O'Brien*, 251-61, 280-4. Duffy, *Young Ireland: Four Years of Irish History*, 228-9. 30 Meagher, Personal Recollections, *Weekly News*, 3, 10 August 1867. 31 *Correspondence between Martin and O'Brien*, 1861, 33. Smith O'Brien Papers, MS 442, f2491, O'Brien to Lucy O'Brien, 20 July 1848. 32 Ibid., MS 464, Draft Address of William Smith O'Brien, 1848, 61. 33 Ibid., MS 449, f3399, Personal Memoranda, n.d. 34 Clarendon Papers, III, 33, 37, 41, 43, Clarendon to Grey, 11, 15, 16, 18 July 1848; 39, Clarendon to Lansdowne, 16 July 1848; 32, 38, 41, Clarendon to Russell, 11, 15, 16 July 1848. 35 Home Office Papers, HO 122/20/102, Grey to Clarendon, 19 July 1848.

so, on Friday 21 July, the Cabinet agreed to bring in a bill to suspend *Habeas Corpus*, by which Clarendon could detain persons until 1 March 1849. In a private note to Clarendon, Grey revealed that the measure omitted the customary clause respecting the privileges of Members of Parliament; this, he wrote, was to permit the arrest of O'Brien. Introducing the bill at a special, Saturday sitting of the Commons, the Prime Minister described the 'traitorous conspiracy', including O'Brien's trip to Paris and his review of the Cork clubs, and urged the measure as 'necessary for the purpose of preventing bloodshed ... , to stop an incipient insurrection'. One of O'Brien's former friends, Sir Denham Norreys, agreed that they must 'seize the heads of this conspiracy', the 'bad men' who exposed Ireland to the 'miseries of civil war'. Just eight Members voted against in the only division, and, with standing orders suspended, it was rushed through the Commons in a single day, 22 July. It passed through the Lords, unopposed, on 24 July. A delighted Clarendon hoped 'that the measure may be in time to save us from an outbreak'. He was also aware of the possibility that 'the announcement may produce one'. The charge that the government deliberately provoked a rebellion is a harsh one, for Clarendon's letters in July 1848 were filled with horror at the prospect, but the ministers did know that the new bill might prompt an insurrection. Indeed, Clarendon told Grey on 23 July that he had 'no doubt that whenever or wherever we arrest S. O'Brien & Meagher under the suspended Hab. Corp. Bill [*sic*] it will be the signal for rebellion'.[36]

Russell had given notice of the suspension bill on Friday 21 July and the news reached Dublin with unprecedented speed: the new 'electric telegraph' took it to the *Freeman's Journal*'s agent in Liverpool, it was carried to Dublin on the overnight mail, and it reached the paper's office early on Saturday. It was placarded and put in the *Weekly Freeman* of that day, with a (mistaken) report that a special warrant had been issued for O'Brien's arrest.[37] Meagher was stunned: 'Death itself could not have struck me more suddenly than this news'. With O'Gorman and O'Brien already departed (to Limerick and Wexford), and Duffy in Newgate, Meagher went looking for John Dillon and Devin Reilly. He came across Dillon in Merrion Square; Dillon proposed going to O'Brien in Wexford and that, if O'Brien 'conceived the time had come for making a stand', they should immediately begin a rebellion. They sent a man 'to procure a military intervention' from France – clearly showing how little appreciation they had of French politics in the wake of the June Days – and McGee went to Glasgow to raise an army from its Irish population and land it at Sligo or Killala in the west. After a series of manoeuvres designed to conceal their departure from the police, Dillon and Meagher boarded the night mail for Enniscorthy. Soon after five in the morning, they took a car to Ballinkeele, passing Vinegar Hill, scene of the principal battle of 1798, and an hour later were in Maher's house, where they found O'Brien still in bed.[38]

---

36 Clarendon Papers, III, 43, 49, Clarendon to Grey, 18, 21 July 1848; 44, 46, 50, Clarendon to Russell, 18, 20, 22 July 1848; Box 12, Grey to Clarendon, 21 July 1848. Hansard, c, 697-713, 731-2, 22 July 1848, Russell, Norreys.   37 *FJ*, 24 July 1848. Hodges, *Report of the Trial of William Smith O'Brien*, 688-92.   38 Meagher, Personal Recollections, *Weekly News*, 10, 17 August 1867. *Nation*, 8, 15 March 1851, McGee's

O'Brien told his junior counsel after his arrest that, when Meagher and Dillon proposed 'to raise the standard of revolt', he 'remonstrated with them on the hopelessness of such a struggle but they were satisfied the country was ready to fight and if he Smith O'Brien did not place himself at their head all the blame would rest on his head. After some hesitation O'Brien said if they were prepared to fight it shall never be said I was the cause of their failure.'[39] The reluctance to rebel and the suggestion that O'Brien's sense of honour was involved (exploited, even) ring true, although the idea that this most wilful of men capitulated so weakly comes as a surprise. The narratives left by O'Brien and Meagher did not reveal that O'Brien needed much persuading. Dillon put three courses to him. They could allow themselves to be imprisoned (they had told O'Brien he was to be 'immediately arrested'), they could try to escape, or they could begin an insurrection. 'O'Brien's answer', in favour of the third course, 'was just what we had expected', and Meagher 'told him we had come to the same conclusion previous to our leaving Dublin, and were prepared to take the field with him that day'.[40] As O'Brien later wrote, his own 'convenience or safety' suggested a different course. If arrested, he would have become 'an object of public sympathy', as a man imprisoned without being charged with a crime, and his incarceration would be brief. If he escaped to France or America, he would receive a warm welcome. However,

> It seemed to me that neither of these courses of action would have been either worthy of my own personal position or consistent with the character and interest of this country. So much had been said by the Party with which I was associated and by myself about the necessity of preparation for conflict, that we should have been exposed to ridicule and reproach if we had fled at the moment when all the contingencies which we had contemplated as justifying the use of force were realised. I had more than once proclaimed my opinion that armed resistance to the British Government had become a solemn duty and this new act of aggression upon the liberties of Ireland afforded a '*casus belli*', a motive and an occasion for a struggle such as no patriotic Irishman could question.[41]

Meagher had said before leaving Dublin, 'We are driven to it ... there is nothing for us now but to go out; we have not gone far enough to succeed, and yet, too far to retreat'. He felt 'we were aiming far beyond our strength ... I entertained no hope of success. I knew well the people were unprepared for a struggle', but the leaders, given all their defiant language, 'were bound to go out, and offer to the country the sword and banner of revolt', launching 'an enterprise which I felt convinced would fail'.[42] O'Brien's words to his counsel suggest that he shared these

---

Narrative of his Mission (also in Gwynn, *Young Ireland and 1848*, 318).   39 Young Ireland Papers of Michael R. O'Farrell, MS 9786, f27, Memoir of Michael O'Farrell, n.d.   40 Meagher, Personal Recollections, *Weekly News*, 24 August 1867.   41 Smith O'Brien Papers, MS 464, Draft Address of William Smith O'Brien, 1848, 63-5. See also *Correspondence between Martin and O'Brien*, 1861, 31-2.   42 Meagher,

fears, which were consistent with everything he had previously said on the subject, and that account continued with his asking Dillon and Meagher 'what arrangements they had made with the Clubs in Dublin before leaving. They had made none. He asked them what arrangements they made about money. They had only a few shillings between them, and thus equipped they took the field.' In the Draft Address, however, he wrote that 'a reasonable probability of success is an element of calculation upon which the moral responsibility of a rebellion mainly rests; and if I could have foreseen certain failure I should have been contented to submit even to personal ignominy rather than involve my country in a fruitless strife'. Seven million people, he believed, could not be held down by a military force of 40,000 men, not that the latter, with almost all the police and one-third of the soldiers Irishmen, would have remained loyal if the revolt achieved any degree of initial success. As for the people, he had recently met with 'large multitudes of men' who had shown their readiness to fight: 'It was therefore no presumptuous expectation to believe that upon the first call to arms one hundred thousand men would have appeared in the field …'[43] There is an element of recrimination in such comments, as in all of O'Brien's descriptions of how he was promised support that never materialised, and any attempt at self-justification – which the Draft Address certainly was – probably required him to demonstrate that he did not opt deliberately for 'fruitless strife'. Nevertheless, there is no reason to doubt that he did envisage a substantial uprising that stood a chance of success. He did not intend a hopeless and suicidal gesture.

Moreover, the battle plan he agreed with Meagher and Dillon was a good one. Clarendon's confidence that a rebellion could not succeed in Dublin was matched on the other side: Dillon informed Meagher that 'the leading men of the Dublin Clubs had determined', a few days before, 'upon not making Dublin the head-quarters of the insurrection; the garrison in the city – exceeding 11,000 men – being thought too formidable a body to contend with.' As Meagher put it, they could have made 'a desperate fight' in the streets of Dublin, but 'it would have been stifled in a pool of squandered blood'.[44] In continental Europe, revolutions had succeeded in the capital cities, but this was back in February and March, when the rulers were both unprepared and paralysed by panic. Six months of military preparations had ensured that the situation in Dublin was entirely different. On the other hand, Meagher believed, an outbreak in 'a thinly garrisoned district' might yield the success that would spark a national uprising. Kilkenny was the starting point chosen by Meagher and Dillon. At first, showing signs of the military ineptitude that would characterise his performance in the coming week, O'Brien 'was strongly in favour of going to New Ross' to invoke the spirit that Wexford had shown in 1798. However, Wexford contained relatively few Confederates and was 'hopelessly

---

Personal Recollections, *Weekly News*, 10, 24 August 1867. See also *FJ*, 8 January 1849, Dillon to McGee, 11 December 1848. 43 Young Ireland Papers of Michael R. O'Farrell, MS 9786, f27, Memoir of Michael O'Farrell, n.d. Smith O'Brien Papers, MS 464, Draft Address of William Smith O'Brien, 1848, 67-73, 93-5. 44 Clarendon Papers, III, 33, Clarendon to Grey, 11 July 1848; 42, Clarendon to Russell, 17 July 1848. Meagher, Personal Recollections, *Weekly News*, 17 August 1867.

exposed to the fire of the war-steamers then lying in the Barrow'. On the other hand, as Meagher later explained,

> Kilkenny was the very best place in which the insurrection could break out. Perfectly safe from all war-steamers, gunboats, floating batteries; standing on the frontiers of the three best fighting counties in Ireland – Waterford, Wexford and Tipperary – the peasantry of which could find no difficulty in pouring in to its relief; possessing from three to five thousand Confederates, the greater number of whom we understood to be armed; most of the streets being extremely narrow, and presenting, on this account, the greatest facility for the erection of barricades; the barracks lying outside the town, and the line of communication between the principal portions of the latter and the former being intercepted by the old bridge over the Nore, which might be easily defended, or, at the worst, very speedily demolished; no place, it appeared to us, could be better adapted for the first scene of the revolution than this, the ancient *'City of the Confederates'*.

The railway line from Dublin stopped 14 miles short of Kilkenny, at Bagenalstown (Muine Bheag), and the road thence to Kilkenny would be easily defended, with its many limestone walls, shrubberies and steep embankments to fire from; whole regiments could be 'surprised and cut to pieces'. The agricultural show about to start in Kilkenny would give the insurgents 'the choicest beef and mutton', and its noble patrons might be seized as hostages.[45] O'Brien quickly saw the merits of his comrades' arguments for Kilkenny: 'its occupation would have given us command over a large portion of the South East of Ireland.' Nearby lay Waterford (Meagher's town), Cork, Tipperary and Limerick, from all of which support could be expected.[46]

Although a plan was quickly settled, O'Brien was not yet fully decided on rebellion: 'In order to leave as little as possible to conjecture I resolved before I summoned the country to arms still further to test the disposition of the People' in a series of improvised meetings along the way.[47] The three men, having left Maher's after breakfast, that afternoon (Sunday, 23 July) addressed a gathering of about 500 people in Enniscorthy. There was another meeting at Graiguenamanagh a few hours later, when they visited and spoke from the doorway of 'General' Thomas Cloney, the aged veteran of '98, and a third, large meeting on Sunday evening in Kilkenny. O'Brien later described his experience of these and the following day's meetings in Tipperary:

> I addressed large masses of men ... , plainly telling them that the time for action had arrived, that the British Government had abrogated all law by subjecting to arbitrary imprisonment without charge and without trial every

---

45 Ibid., 17, 24, 31 August 1867. 46 Ibid., 24 August 1867. Smith O'Brien Papers, MS 464, Draft Address of William Smith O'Brien, 1848, 77. 47 Ibid., 75.

Ballingarry

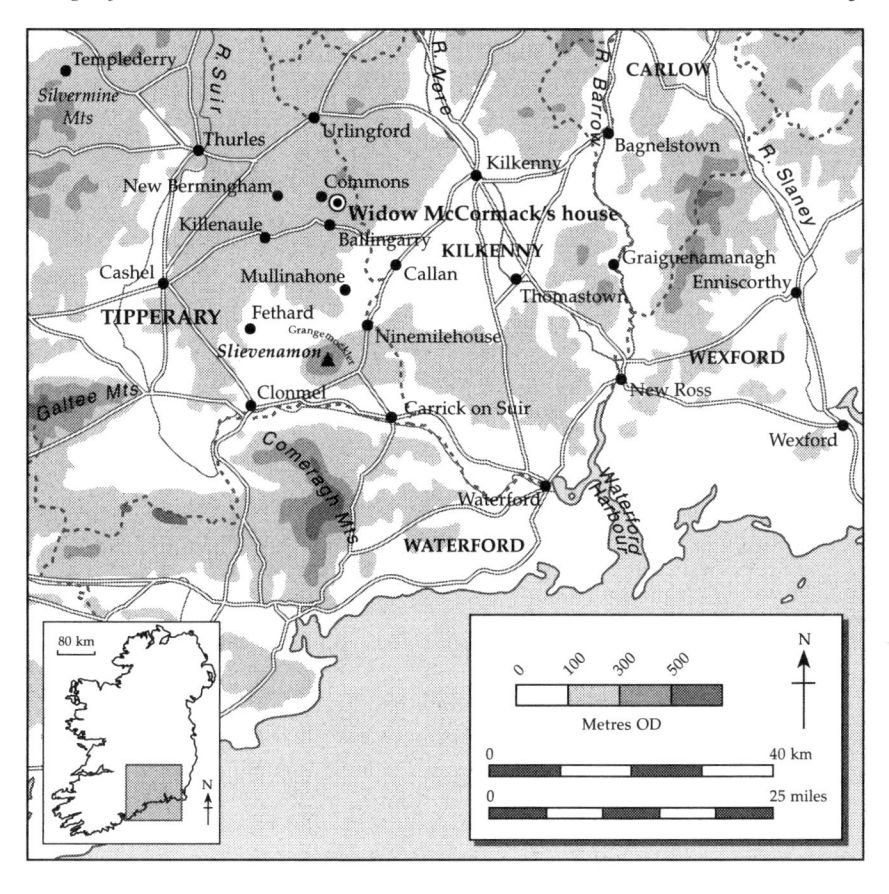

3 The geography of rebellion

man in Ireland whom they might think proper to seize and that it was my intention to set them at defiance provided I were supported by my fellow countrymen. I was every where counselled not to surrender and every where received the same pledge, that for the sake of our country as well as for my own sake I should be supported at the hazard of life and fortune whenever I thought proper to call for cooperation. Animated by such assurances and fully satisfied as to the Righteousness of our Cause, I resolved to take up arms ...

When the people were asked if they would allow O'Brien to be arrested, the answer was always a loud 'No', and when O'Brien said in Kilkenny that the time for insurrection was at hand the announcement was 'hailed with deafening cheers, and cries of: *"We'll stand to you; we'll die for you!"*'.[48] The response was not entirely positive, however. Meagher was disappointed to find 'but little inclination to welcome and support' a rising among people they met on the roadside. Clarendon, hardly well placed but passing comment that would be justified by events, reported that the party 'did not meet with the reception they hoped for. Their audiences were chiefly of the rabble class and the more respectable people abstained from attending. The priests also have in several places taken a more decided part against the Clubs.' Meagher's account includes his recollection of their meeting with Graiguenamanagh's Catholic curate. O'Brien told him of their intention to begin an armed uprising and voiced 'his apprehension, that unless the priests concurred with us, any attempt at insurrection, for the present, would prove abortive'. The curate's answer 'was of so indecisive a nature as to be somewhat discouraging. The most conclusive sentence we could elicit from him, was simply this – "that the whole affair was a very difficult subject to decide upon" ... During this interview, the people were waiting for us in the street, and anxiously expecting the result. Our looks conveyed it to them. The frank and merry smile upon every face before us changed in an instant – as though a black cloud were crossing it – into a dull, cold, sullen gloom.'[49]

If this was ominous, what happened in Kilkenny, where they arrived on Sunday evening, was a grave disappointment. The project to reunite the repeal movement had been particularly successful there, but this meant that Kilkenny's clubs were clubs of 'United Repealers' – men who in many cases were former adherents of the Repeal Association and, as such, wary of Young Ireland's physical force inclinations. O'Brien knew this; on 19 July he had had to tread softly with the 'respectable but timid' men who went up from Kilkenny to the second meeting of the League. Also, having been present on that occasion to hear Dr Robert Cane speak of Kilkenny's 1700 clubmen, it is unlikely that he was deceived by the *Evening Freeman*'s giving the figure as 17,000, which error was corrected in the next day's

---

48 Ibid., 75. Hodges, *Report of the Trial of William Smith O'Brien*, 290-3. Meagher, Personal Recollections, *Weekly News*, 31 August, 7 September 1867.   49 Ibid., 7 September 1867. Clarendon Papers, III, 56, Clarendon to Russell, 25 July 1848.

Journal. But he and his comrades were undoubtedly surprised when Cane, the leader of the town's Confederates, now told them that they could not begin in Kilkenny: the clubs 'were insufficiently armed, miserably so indeed. The club of which he was president, for instance, out of five hundred members, had but one hundred armed. For himself, he was obliged to leave Kilkenny in the morning, having been subpoenaed to attend an important trial at the Cork assizes' (Meagher). Of such law-abiding material are rebellions not made. Duffy was later told that, to confront a garrison of 1,000 infantry and two troops of cavalry, the town could barely muster 200 armed men. Six months of talk about arming had been accompanied by almost no effective action. Dillon and Meagher were keen to make an attempt, but the Kilkenny men 'did not consider themselves strong enough to encounter the garrison without the aid of auxiliary force' (O'Brien). It was agreed that O'Brien and his lieutenants should go into Tipperary to 'summon the people of those towns to arms; and, in three or four days, return to Kilkenny – at the head of an armed force, if possible – call out the clubs, barricade the streets and, from the Council Chamber of the Corporation, issue the first revolutionary edict to the country' (Meagher).[50]

Tipperary had certainly shown its enthusiasm in the cause. Michael Doheny had been tireless in organising the clubs around Cashel, Father Kenyon had his adherents in the west of the county, and Father Patrick Byrne and John O'Mahony (see below) had made Carrick-on-Suir a stronghold in the south. On 16 July, a meeting on Slievenamon mountain was attended, it was said, by 50,000 people; Doheny had intended that the requirement to climb a mountain would deter 'senseless and idle brawlers' and 'test the courage and sincerity of our followers', making the attendance all the more impressive. If it came to a fight in Tipperary, the rough and hilly terrain would be ideal for the 'simple operations of guerilla warfare' envisaged by O'Brien. Less promisingly, Tipperary was one of the counties proclaimed in December 1847 and thereby subjected to efforts to disarm the peasantry.[51] On Monday morning, Meagher and Dillon discussed 'a complete programme' of military arrangements with Kilkenny's club leaders, in anticipation of their return to the city, and they left, with O'Brien, at one o'clock. At Callan, in west Kilkenny, a large crowd issued a 'thrilling cheer' when they proclaimed their intention to rise and a party of Royal Irish Hussars stood by and, in Meagher's view, gave every sign of sympathy. At Ninemilehouse, on the way to Carrick, 20-odd people expressed their enthusiasm, but they had no weapons and, they said, 'as for priests – there was only an odd one or two up to the mark' and even these 'couldn't do much' because they were curates whose parish priests 'were agin them entirely'. A few 'fine young fellows' were told to go out to gather fighting men who would join the armed body that would shortly be marching back along the road; 'indeed it was absolutely necessary we should be reinforced at every town, village, and house along

---

50 Meagher, Personal Recollections, *Weekly News*, 7 August 1867. Smith O'Brien Papers, MS 464, Draft Address of William Smith O'Brien, 1848, 77-9. *Nation*, 22 February 1851 (Duffy). *FJ*, 20 July 1848.
51 Doheny, *Felon's Track*, 90. *FJ*, 18 July 1848. Smith O'Brien Papers, MS 464, Draft Address of William Smith O'Brien, 1848, 93-5.

the road ...' (Meagher) The three leaders changed their carriage and headed for Carrick. It was believed that this town had 2,000 clubmen, most of them armed, and that the garrison had only 200 men – almost the inverse of the position in Kilkenny. With these odds, Carrick could give the rebels the first victory that would have set all Ireland alight.[52]

About five miles from the town, they met John O'Mahony, a local landowner, president of his club, and a young man whose 'fine and soldierly appearance' and conviction that Tipperary's men would fight created what Meagher called 'the most joyous confidence ... He represented to us that the country all about Carrick, on towards Clonmel and along the Suir on the Tipperary side, was thoroughly alive and ready to take the field at once'. At Carrick, which they entered on Monday afternoon, they were met by a 'torrent of human beings ... , whirling in dizzy circles, and tossing up its dark waves, with sounds of wrath, vengeance, and defiance ... , eyes red with rage and desperation ... It was the Revolution, if we had accepted it,' Meagher thought, and, writing afterwards, he owned that he could not explain their failure to accept it – that is, to begin the battle there and then.[53] They addressed a large crowd in the main street (a Crown witness at O'Brien's trial estimated the attendance at 4-5,000), and O'Brien said, 'I will now test your courage ... by calling you at once to the field ... Are your hearts stout, and your arms nerved [sic], to stand by me in the coming struggle ... If you are ready, I for one am ready to strike the blow' and prepared 'to sacrifice my life'. Meagher asked, 'Are you ready to stand before the military ... Now is the time to strike the blow to make Ireland for her lovely sons.' Clarendon considered the speeches in Carrick 'unquestionable treason', involving 'incitement to levy war against the Crown' and duly signed warrants for the arrest of the 'traitors'.[54]

The Lord Lieutenant was increasingly concerned about the capacity of his forces to prevent a rising. However, behind the public enthusiasm of the Carrick people there was something less than steely resolve. O'Mahony, who had ridden in with O'Brien, later told Doheny of how the arrival of O'Brien and his companions was 'unexpected, sudden and startling', and that they made a peremptory and uninspiring demand that Carrick should protect them from arrest.[55] In his own account, O'Mahony recalled that they found the club officers in 'doubt and dismay ... They seemed confounded at the magnitude of the step they were called on to take, and a very manifest desire to get Mr O'Brien out of town appeared to sway the great majority of them. One man asked the gentlemen why they had come to that little town to commence the rising. Was Carrick able to fight the British Empire? Were they, the leaders, rejected by everywhere else?' O'Brien, showing 'evident disap-

---

52 Meagher, Personal Recollections, *Weekly News*, 7, 14, 21 September 1867. Hodges, *Report of the Trial of William Smith O'Brien*, 296-9. John O'Mahony, Personal Narrative of My Connection with the Attempted Rising of 1848, MS 868 (typescript), 2. 53 Meagher, Personal Recollections, *Weekly News*, 21, 28 September 1867. 54 Ibid. Hodges, *Report of the Trial of William Smith O'Brien*, 299-309. Clarendon Papers, III, 60, 63, Clarendon to Russell, 26 (x2) July 1848; 60, Clarendon to Grey, 26 July 1848; 62, Clarendon to Mackay, 26 July 1848. 55 Doheny, *Felon's Track*, 93.

pointment and disgust', told them he wanted Carrick to provide 600 armed men with 'sufficient means for self support to guard him and his companions while they were raising the country. For this no man was prepared, not anticipating any such demand.' O'Mahony reminded those who now asked why the three men had come to Carrick that, 'Our own boastings brought them to us'. Doheny wrote that, 'The great argument relied upon by every one was, why should Carrick be selected?' This view 'seems to have prevailed. Other arguments no doubt, were urged, such as want of provisions, want of arms, and want of ammunition. The moment of indecision is the harvest of evil passions – avarice, selfishness, cowardice cloud the intellect, and blast the destiny of man.' Thus the men of Carrick, 'with shrinking hand, marred their immortal lot'.[56] Meagher described a scene of utter confusion as each officer proclaimed his own plan of action:

> One was for commencing there and then. Another proposed that the night should be spent in preparation, and that the morning should be ushered in with the volleying of guns and the gleaming of the pikeheads. A third suggested – altogether overlooking the Suspension Act – that the elections for the Council of Three Hundred should take place with as little delay as possible, and that the delegates should proceed immediately upon their election to the Rotundo, each escorted by one thousand armed men, selected from the constituents of his electoral division. A fourth was in favour of a camp on Slievenamon. A fifth for taking to the loughs and glens of the Commeraha, and there holding out until the country had armed herself more formidably. There was a sixth proposition, too; and a seventh; and an eighth; and, for all I remember to the contrary, there may have been as many as the First Book of Euclid contains.
>
> Never did I behold so perplexing and bewildering a tumult! Never did there occur to me a scene less susceptible of repose, of guidance, of any clear, steady, intelligent control!
>
> Within, there was this confusion and uproar of tongues; without, there was the tossing and surging of the mighty throng, whose deep vibrations shook the walls of the house in which we were assembled. Add to this that hundreds were blocking up the stair-case; crowding and crushing on the landing-places; crowding and crushing round the table at which we sat; pressing down upon us in their hot anxiety to see and hear us; and, for this very reason, and urged on by this same vehement and generous passion, were overpowering every exertion we strove to make; drowning completely every word we uttered; exhausting our strength, and rendering us incapable of guiding with a firm hand the elements that swept and roared around us.[57]

Perhaps O'Brien could have been more effective in controlling this tumult, but it would appear that he knew what he wanted – 600 armed men – and encountered

56 O'Mahony, Personal Narrative, 3. Doheny, *Felon's Track*, 93-4. 57 Meagher, Personal Recollections, *Weekly News*, 28 September 1867.

club leaders who were more keen to argue and declaim than take the field 'to fight the British Empire'. Again, the failure to prepare is obvious. Carrick's clubs, 12 of which had been formed in the previous six weeks, lacked anything like the coherent organisation and leadership needed to launch a military campaign. O'Brien's low opinion of Carrick's men and his view that, lying as it did between two garrisoned towns (Waterford and Clonmel), Carrick was not defensible, made him decide to move on. Late on Monday, 'O'Brien and his comrades left the town deeply disappointed, if not in actual disgust and despair' (Doheny). O'Mahony (and Duffy) subsequently considered this decision a 'sad mistake', for he and other club leaders managed next day to raise a substantial force in the surrounding countryside. O'Mahony's own club sent 400 men with 80 guns and 'a goodly muster of pikes', and 1,000 came from Grangemockler; in all, O'Mahony reckoned, 12-15,000 men, 'enough surely to commence the revolution', were ready to march on Carrick, but they had to be stood down when it was found that O'Brien had left the area to travel to Cashel, almost 30 miles away. Even if his figures were not precise, O'Mahony, lamenting this lost opportunity, was probably right in his judgement that more men were ready to take the field that day, Tuesday 25 July, than at any subsequent point; thereafter, he believed, fear, doubts about the capacity of the leaders, and the opposition of the priests combined to ensure that so such muster could be repeated.[58]

Meagher, O'Mahony and Doheny all noted the absence of one man who might have given the lead that was necessary. In April, Father Patrick Byrne, one of Carrick's curates, had promised in a public letter that if a rising began 'the Irish priests shall be found amid the fight, invoking heaven's blessing upon it'. O'Mahony considered Byrne and the priests 'the originators of the [club] movement' in south Tipperary. Byrne told him in mid-July that, *'My heart, my heart is panting for that day'* when they would fight together.[59] Now O'Mahony was struck by the 'remarkable' fact that 'Father Byrne was not to be found. The day after which his heart panted had not come ...' Meagher, disappointed not to see 'the trusted guide and leader ... of the local clubs,' sent him a note 'earnestly begging of him to come over and give us the benefit of his honest and affectionate advice'. However, Byrne did not turn out.[60] The priests were soon actively discouraging involvement. Father Morrissey of Ballyneal (outside Carrick) dispersed a crowd of volunteers with the argument 'that he would put himself at the head of the people if they but waited three weeks' (Doheny). O'Mahony found on a subsequent visit to Carrick that Byrne and the priests were all against a rising, calling it 'premature' and arguing that 'it should be put off at least a *fortnight* until the harvest ripened. That O'Brien *must be mad.*' Meagher met Byrne on Wednesday morning, in Carrick, when the priest said that the country was not ready for a rising, and, a few days later, Byrne told

---

58 Doheny, *Felon's Track*, 94. O'Mahony, Personal Narrative, 4. Duffy, *Young Ireland: Four Years of Irish History*, 233-4.   59 *Nation*, 29 April 1848, Byrne to Conway, 21 April 1848. O'Mahony, Personal Narrative, 2.   60 Ibid., 3. Meagher, Personal Recollections, *Weekly News*, 28 September 1867. Doheny, *Felon's Track*, 94.

Michael Cavanagh that he thought O'Brien 'mad' and he could see only 'ultimate disaster to the devoted men who persevered in upholding what he believed to be a hopeless cause'. These priests, who it may be presumed had no intention of leading an insurrection at any time, may have defeated a national revolution, but they also averted a bloodbath, as they headed off an enterprise which (Doheny recalled) Byrne 'designated as rash, ill-designed, and fraught with ruin to the town'.[61]

The leaders arrived in Cashel at 2 o'clock on Tuesday morning. They went there to find Michael Doheny; unfortunately, the latter had gone to meet them in Carrick, not the last time that such mis-chances would befall the rebel leaders as they moved around Tipperary. 'My absence,' Doheny wrote, 'was used as an argument, sincere or pretended, against any effort in that town [Cashel]. Mr O'Brien, in ignorance of whom to apply to, took counsel with one man, at least, since accused of the darkest treachery. Others, from whom I had different hopes, shrunk from an encounter which, at other times, they seemed to long for as the dearest blessing Heaven could bestow.' Littleton, the club leader on whom they called, flatly refused to help in any way.[62] Discouraged by their reception in Cashel, the leaders decided to depart later on Tuesday morning. Meagher left for Waterford intending to collect 1,000 men from his own club there. He sent its president a letter summoning the men to meet him outside the city, but nobody came. Before the day was out he was back in Carrick with the news that his men would not march without the consent of Father Tracy. 'This Tracy, I afterwards understood, was the "Byrne" of Waterford' (O'Mahony). Michael Cavanagh discovered on Saturday, 29 July, that there were many in Waterford who expressed their 'willingness to follow him [Meagher] to death' and said they were 'both amazed and sorely disappointed at not having received any orders from him'; Cavanagh believed that Meagher was 'deceived', and the '*sacred cause* betrayed, by a few pusillanimous wretches' who had misrepresented Tracy. It is impossible to know if what Cavanagh heard was anything more than the sort of bluster that was the constant refrain of 1848. Equally, his being told by a soldier outside Waterford that two-thirds of his regiment 'were true Irishmen – and ready to prove it – *when called upon*' may have signified everything – or nothing.[63]

O'Brien and Dillon left Cashel with a new set of young companions, Patrick O'Donohoe and James Cantwell from Dublin, and James Stephens of Kilkenny. Stephens, a 24-year-old employee of the Limerick and Waterford Railway Company, recalled how at Doheny's house he had 'stepped over to Smith O'Brien and asked him if he were actually in the field, "for if you be," I observed, "I would wish to

---

61 Ibid. O'Mahony, Personal Narrative, 5. The Rev. Philip Fitzgerald, *A Narrative of the Proceedings of the Confederates of '48, from the suspension of the Habeas Corpus Act, to their final dispersion at Ballingarry* (Dublin, 1868), 19. Cavanagh, *Memoirs of Meagher*, 275-6.   62 Doheny, *Felon's Track*, 96. Fitzgerald, *Narrative of the Proceedings of the Confederates*, 9.   63 O'Mahony, Personal Narrative, 5. Cavanagh, *Memoirs of Meagher*, 276-9. Fitzgerald, *Narrative of the Proceedings of the Confederates*, 14-17.

remain by your side as long as the struggle continues". He replied in the affirmative, and told me that as he had given over [sic] all hope of constitutional agitation, he saw no other recourse for Ireland than an appeal to arms.'[64] O'Brien appointed him 'his *aide-de-camp*'. Travelling in two cars, the party headed east out of Cashel, into the hills, having 'resolved as a final resource to take up their position in the most inaccessible part of the country' (Doheny). So, the initial hope that Carrick and Cashel, sizeable towns, would provide an army was given up, and they fell back on rural districts where there had been virtually no club organisation. At the first village, Killenaule, 12 miles from Cashel, O'Brien addressed an enthusiastic crowd in front of the police barracks. 'Several Police were present,' O'Donohoe recalled, 'and seemed to smile approbation at the sentiments uttered.'[65] They travelled on to another village, Mullinahone. Anticipating his arrival there, Charles Kickham had already had a pike made according to instructions given in the *Nation*; he thought it 'the first pike made in that part of Tipperary since '98', a belief which, if true, provides further evidence of lack of preparedness. Moreover, Kickham had to tell his visitors that the local club had only three members. O'Brien seemed to Kickham 'to be like a man in a dream'. However, he was well received as he moved up and down the streets of Mullinahone for several hours. According to the Crown witnesses at his trial, he led 200 men 'marching' through the town, 'two deep', and carried 'a pistol in his left side' pocket. He told the people 'to get their arms, that he might see the strength of them'. About 5,000 men gathered, many of them armed with 'guns, pikes, and old swords, pitchforks, and scythes', and, according to O'Donohoe, 'all offering to stand to the death by Smith O'Brien'. The blacksmith's was besieged by men who wanted pikes and, in its own way a sign of revolutionary fervour, Kickham's was stolen.[66]

O'Brien called on the crowd not to permit his arrest, but he also urged 'in the strongest terms the necessity of preserving the rights of property and cautioned them against infringing on vested rights of any kind'.[67] When some men began to build barricades, he 'forbade the felling of trees across the roads without the permission of the owners of the estate upon which they grew'.[68] As will be seen more fully below, O'Brien was a most conservative revolutionary. He distributed bread at his own expense but warned that the people would have to provide for themselves in future because 'he had no means of doing so, and [he] did not mean to offer violence to any one's person or property'. Father Philip Fitzgerald of Ballingarry, who related this story, thought that, 'This announcement gave a death-blow to the entire movement. Those poor fellows returned home late in the evening

[64] Personal Recollections of '48, by James Stephens, chapter IV, *The Irishman*, 18 February 1882. [65] Ibid., ch. V, *Irishman*, 25 February 1882. Doheny, *Felon's Track*, 96-7. O'Donoghue MSS, MS 770, P. O'Donohoe, Incidents connected with political disturbances in Ireland in 1848: origin, progress and failure of the movement (dated 28 August 1848), 12. [66] James Maher (ed.), *The Valley Near Slievenamon: A Kickham Anthology* (n.p., 1942), 182-5. Hodges, *Report of the Trial of William Smith O'Brien*, 310-5, 320-3. O'Donoghue MSS, MS 770, 14. Duffy, *Young Ireland: Four Years of Irish History*, 236-7. [67] O'Donoghue MSS, MS 770, 14-15. [68] Duffy, *Young Ireland: Four Years of Irish History*, 237, quoting Charles Kickham.

faint with hunger, resolved not to expose themselves a second time to the same privations'.[69] O'Brien 'continued to drill the men who thronged about him until 3 o'clock next morning'. The Attorney General claimed that it was in Mullinahone that O'Brien began what 'amounted to an actual commencement of levying war' as he drew up his supporters in 'military array'.[70]

However impressive this might have been, O'Brien was undermined by the opposition of the Catholic clergy. Soon after their arrival in Mullinahone, the curate, William Cahill, had 'entered into a long disquisition with Messrs. O'Brien and Dillon on their policy and the imprudence of any disturbances on the part of [the] people, alleging principally as his reasons that it was premature, that the harvest was unripe, and that the people would be starved – he also urged the great power of the British Army & Navy, and our want of organization'.[71] Doheny described how the village's two priests, Cahill and Corcoran (the parish priest), sowed 'discussion and disunion', and O'Brien later complained of how the prize had been snatched away:

> ... if it had not been for the interference of the Roman Catholic Clergymen of that Parish [Mullinahone] I should have found myself in command of a large armed force which might in a few days have been rendered available either for such a movement as I contemplated [a march on Kilkenny] or for any of the operations of guerilla warfare. Upon the evening of my first appearance in arms at Mullinahone I was surrounded by a body of men the number of whom has been estimated at from 2,000 to 5,000 men by the witnesses for the Prosecution. These men were all animated with the best spirit, and if left to themselves would have cheerfully encountered privation and danger in fighting for their country. But they were completely paralysed by the operation of spiritual influences. The same men who had shewed the utmost ardour in the evening were upon the following morning, after listening to the exhortations of the Priest [Corcoran], if not indisposed at least utterly unfit for action.[72]

O'Brien had appointed a guard to ensure that he would not be arrested and slept a few hours at the home of a young, Protestant student called Wright. He awoke next morning to discover that most of his followers had gone home. Kickham believed they went because they saw that there was 'no fighting to be done', and they wanted their breakfast, but most accounts, echoing O'Brien, blamed the priests. Stephens wrote of how the leaders were 'expectant and elated' as they went to bed, 'but when morning came, and hour after hour slipped by, we fell into a despondent mood, for not a man, I believe, of those who pledged their words to come,

---

69 Rev. P. Fitzgerald, P.P., *Personal Recollections of the Insurrection at Ballingarry in July, 1848* (Dublin, 1861), 13-14.   70 O'Donoghue MSS, MS 770, 15. Hodges, *Report of the Trial of William Smith O'Brien*, 135-6.   71 O'Donoghue MSS, MS 770, 14.   72 Smith O'Brien Papers, MS 464, Draft Address of William Smith O'Brien, 1848, 79-81. Doheny, *Felon's Track*, 97.

did come'. He it was who told O'Brien that 'it would have a bad effect on the people if we don't take' the village's police barracks. As O'Brien put it, 'Finding that the presence of the Police in this village served as a pretext for the change of feeling which had taken place I resolved to remove this impediment. With this view I visited the Police in their barrack accompanied by two armed companions and by a few unarmed spectators who remained outside the building.' This took place at about 8 o'clock on Wednesday 26 July. He wore the cap of the '82 Club, green with a gold band and a peak, and was armed: according to O'Donohoe, he had two pistols, but the police said he carried a pike (it was probably a stick) in his left hand and a pistol in his right hand, and that three pistols could be seen protruding from his coat pockets. O'Donohoe and Stephens, his 'body-guard', also carried firearms. Stephens recalled how O'Brien, as if to prove that Clare men came from the wild west, 'drew his revolver from his pocket, and, raising the muzzle in the coolest and most deliberate manner possible, spoke bluntly to the sergeant, saying – "You are our prisoners"'. He called on the seven constables, one of whom fainted, to surrender their arms. Some of them later described their defiant response ('I would be unworthy the name of an Irishman if I gave up my arms'), but O'Brien, Stephens and O'Donohoe all contended that the police 'professed to us entire sympathy with our proceedings', asked O'Brien to bring enough men to *compel* them to give up their arms, and even promised to join the rebellion. O'Brien 'pitied' the constables and, suggesting a certain naivety, told them 'that he did not wish to spill blood, that he wished to redress the wrongs of the Irish people without loss of life or property'. He offered them time to consider and withdrew; the constables, apart from the one who was 'so weak from the nervous fright' (Stephens), then sneaked out of town.

Afterwards, O'Brien threw a positive light on this, arguing that the 'departure of the Police from this village as well as from all the other stations of the district afforded great facilities for preparation. By the concentration of the Police we were enabled to move without interruption in armed bodies throughout the whole space lying between Thurles and Carrick and between Clonmel and Kilkenny.' This was true, but the episode would have been a genuine (and much needed) success had the Mullinahone constables not been permitted to depart with their weapons. O'Mahony was possibly the Carrick club leader who later told Duffy that O'Brien's retiring without the weapons 'filled him with despair, as indicating a dangerous ignorance of the population with which he had to deal'. The people would shun the rebels if they showed they lacked the capacity to prevail. Stephens, 'discontented' but unwilling to criticise O'Brien, claimed that, 'The success we gained at Mullinahone raised us very much in the estimation of its inhabitants. The feat we performed – however imperfect it might have been – proved to them that we meant real work. The capture of the enemy's citadel was the talk of the town ... our hopes were once more high.'[73]

[73] Smith O'Brien Papers, MS 464, Draft Address of William Smith O'Brien, 1848, 81-3. Personal Recollections of Stephens, ch. V, *Irishman*, 25 February 1882. O'Donoghue MSS, MS 770, 16-17.

Clarendon reported that O'Brien's conduct in the station constituted 'openly levying war and treason. I have therefore proclaimed Mr O'Brien as a traitor and offered £500 for his apprehension and £300 each for his companions Meagher and Dillon.' He ordered his forces not to rest 'until O'Brien's army is dispersed and destroyed and he himself with his officers taken or shot'.[74] O'Brien's Rubicon was crossed when he went over the threshold of Mullinahone's police station. For the moment, however, the law was not his most active enemy. Father Corcoran arrived and 'urged very strongly the imprudence of Mr O'Brien's course, stating the poverty of the people, the danger of defeat, and that no hope of success could be entertained until the harvest was over. Upon which Mr O'Brien expressed his readiness to surrender that instant if the Revd. Gentleman so desired – to which the latter replied that he would shed his heart's blood to save him, Mr O'Brien, from arrest. This ended the interview.'[75] If Corcoran's conduct was not entirely priestly, O'Brien's, with his offer to surrender, was even less soldierly. Corcoran and Cahill proceeded to use all their influence to stop the villagers leaving with O'Brien. 'They tried every means, entreaty, expostulation, remonstrance, menace', despite which O'Brien left Mullinahone with several hundred would-be fighters.[76]

Two men had come to Mullinahone and invited O'Brien to the nearby village of Ballingarry, saying it had 500 men in arms.[77] It was decided, on the journey from Mullinahone, 'that a *ruse* should be made to test the courage' of their followers. Some 'tried friends' were sent ahead with orders to return 'and report that the enemy was coming on against us at no great distance'. This 'simulated alarm' produced not 'the least dismay,' Stephens recalled. 'Not a man blanched with fear. All was determination, all was courage. They seemed to be impregnated, if I may so speak, with an ardour and bravery that no opposition could break down.' However, hunger could do what fear could not. O'Brien issued 'commands ... to the effect that nothing should be taken on the way without its exact value being immediately returned'. This policy meant that, as Stephens put it, they 'passed by the demesnes of landlords, whose mansions and properties would have furnished us with the necessaries of life; but the order was given that they were not to be touched ... Discouragement became rife in the ranks' and the order 'so disheartened the peasants that many of them took advantage of every occasion that presented itself to abandon us, while those who remained suffered the pangs of hunger in the midst of plenty'.[78] The aristocratic landowner in O'Brien had no wish to unleash a rampaging, looting mob. He hoped that hostilities would 'derange' ordinary life as little as possible, that they would not 'destroy public credit or interfere with the occupations of life', and that he could 'establish confidence by discouraging pillage and

---

Hodges, *Report of the Trial of William Smith O'Brien*, 137-8, 316-7, 323-31. Doheny, *Felon's Track*, 97. Duffy, *Young Ireland: Four Years of Irish History*, 237-8.   **74** Clarendon Papers, III, 65, Clarendon to Grey, 27 July 1848; 68, Clarendon to Russell, 28 July 1848.   **75** O'Donoghue MSS, MS 770, 18.   **76** Doheny, *Felon's Track*, 97. Hodges, *Report of the Trial of William Smith O'Brien*, 138. Personal Recollections of Stephens, ch. VI, *Irishman*, 4 March 1882.   **77** Fitzgerald, *Narrative of the Proceedings of the Confederates*, 14.   **78** Personal Recollections of Stephens, ch. VI, *Irishman*, 4 March 1882.

wanton destruction of life'. He seemed to believe that 'the laws of honourable warfare' required that 'the lives and properties of all who remained neutral' had to be respected. Finally, while some form of 'equitable assessment upon property', with compensation paid out at a later date, would have been 'ultimately necessary', O'Brien proposed to raise 'bodies of men sufficiently independent in their circumstances to be able to maintain themselves for a short time upon their own resources'.[79] Unfortunately, the men who rallied in Tipperary were impoverished peasants and colliers. O'Donohoe wrote frankly about O'Brien's lack of appreciation of the needs and wants of his followers:

> He was unceasing in enforcing morality, sobriety, absence of all crime and above all to touch no man's property and infringe not private rights of any kind. This doctrine was wholly unsuited to the class of men he addressed it to in the mountain fastnesses of Tipperary, impoverished, famished and thirsting for food and revenge on those whom they conceive have so long oppressed them. Therefore such admonitions were distasteful and disgusting and invariably had the effect of driving the people away grumbling with disappointment. It was truly ridiculous to hear the leader of a revolution, which to be successful should have sanctioned all the wild and savage passions of the hordes of oppressed wretches who followed its standard, inculcating those virtues which are practised in the best-ordered communities. Such inconsistency was discernable [sic] to the meanest of his followers. They could not reconcile such [a] doctrine with the notions they entertained of that course of licentiousness which the flood of revolution was about to open to them. Hence the rapid desertions which invariably followed his harangues, on his first appearance in every village and hamlet he was hailed with ecstasy as a deliverer and men, women and children would have followed him to death in wild delight. But the moment he spoke their visions of future happiness vanished and they shrunk from his standard in despair and dismay.[80]

Stephens had to temper his 'esteem and admiration' for O'Brien's character with a repudiation of his 'over scrupulous' adherence to 'strictly honourable' tactics; the leader of the 'national army' should 'place the whole property of the nation' under his control, whereas 'to tell a poor insurgent people that they must not take a cow, a horse, or a sack of corn, or potatoes, without paying for them on the spot, is most assuredly not alone to discourage, but also to demoralise and break up their forces'.[81] At a conference of leaders that evening in Ballingarry, Doheny (just arrived, with Devin Reilly) annoyed O'Brien with the suggestion that they might take the money from the bank in Carrick if they managed to capture that town. O'Brien was 'quite horrified' and asked if Doheny 'wanted to uproot social order and destroy the char-

---

[79] Smith O'Brien Papers, MS 464, Draft Address of William Smith O'Brien, 1848, 89-91. See also *Correspondence between Martin and O'Brien*, 1861, 34.   [80] O'Donoghue MSS, MS 770, 27.   [81] Personal Recollections of Stephens, ch. VI, *Irishman*, 4 March 1882.

Ballingarry 263

4 Ballingarry, with distant view of Slievenamon

acter of the movement. He went on to say that the revolution he wished to achieve should be done without injury to property, that otherwise all the good and virtuous portions of the community would condemn and stigmatize us as plunderers, that he was desirous that all men should pursue their callings as usual.'[82] Someone, possibly Dillon, suggested 'that a proclamation should forthwith be published confiscating the landed property of the country and offering it as the gage of battle and reward of victory, and another proclamation directing the people to live at the expense of the enemy'. Doheny recalled that a majority (which no doubt included O'Brien) rejected this as 'an act of mere plunder'.[83] In an earlier age, George Washington, no mean general, had given similar instructions regarding property rights, but his rebellion did not depend on raising and sustaining a famished peasantry.

Late on Wednesday morning (26 July), the Mullinahone men were allowed to turn back when others came out from Ballingarry and 'assumed the duty of his [O'Brien's] escort and, if need be, of his defence' (Doheny). Charles Kickham shook hands with Stephens, who appeared 'cheerful and hopeful', and with O'Brien, 'who looked happy and dreamy, smoking a cigar'. O'Donohoe described a party of about 600 with 'guns, pistols, pitchforks and pikes ... marching in good order and singing merrily'. Ballingarry's parish priest, probably the only one who openly backed the rising, 'was in a gig at their head and was after giving them benediction. Nothing could exceed the enthusiasm of the country people. Men, women and children

---

82 O'Donoghue MSS, MS 770, 20.   83 Doheny, *Felon's Track*, 98. See also Fitzgerald, *Narrative of the Proceedings of the Confederates*, 24-5.

shouted joyously.'[84] In fact, the priest was the senile Father Edmund Prendergast, 'a P.P. only in name', being 'of weak mind', according to Philip Fitzgerald, then the acting parish priest (administrator).[85] O'Brien reached Ballingarry around lunchtime, his first visit to the place that would be associated with his name in shameful memory. People gathered round in response to the ringing of the chapel bell, and O'Brien gave a 20-minute speech:

> He strictly enjoined respect for property and cautioned all persons against joining him who would not preserve the rights of property inviolate. He desired all married men who had families to remain at home, and all poor labouring men to continue at their labour, and stated he desired no man to join him who could not bring with him three days provisions of bread or biscuit. That he desired society to be preserved and concluded by desiring all present to go home except twenty men whom he selected to guard him from arrest during the night. Mr Dillon also addressed the people much to the same effect.[86]

Some of this, the turning away of married men, is barely believable. And the expectation that the men, given the Famine, could have found three days' provisions was not realistic. In Fitzgerald's account, he asked them to return in the morning 'with provisions for at least four days: the quality of provisions which he would recommend was oatmeal, bread and hard eggs'; unfortunately, most men there 'were prompted to join the movement solely in the hope of being fed. Indeed to any one it must have appeared little less than solemn mockery of their wants, to tell a people living on a daily allowance of a pound of Indian meal to return on the following day bringing ... four days' provisions.' The invocation to respect property – Fitzgerald had him saying that 'he would punish with death any one of his followers who would injure the property of any man' – was a common theme, and the remark about labourers staying at their work was probably related to the danger of pillage. As a result of O'Brien's words, 'The people dispersed downcast and dispirited, and from this day forward never again came together in such numbers.'[87] The mood was dampened further, Stephens recalled, when 'the elements themselves declared against us – the rain coming down in torrents, and drenching us to the very skin'.[88]

After a tea of mutton chops (which O'Donohoe made a point of recalling), the afore-mentioned conference of leaders took place that evening. It was a sombre

---

84 Doheny, *Felon's Track*, 97. Duffy, *Young Ireland: Four Years of Irish History*, 237. O'Donoghue MSS, MS 770, 19. 85 Fitzgerald, *Narrative of the Proceedings of the Confederates*, 22, 114. Fitzgerald later succeeded Prendergast in the parish. 86 O'Donoghue MSS, MS 770, 19-20. 87 Fitzgerald, *Narrative of the Proceedings of the Confederates*, 22-3. The reference to the death penalty lends some support to an otherwise unlikely and uncorroborated tale, reported by Clarendon, about O'Brien's 'ordering a man to be taken *to the rear & shot* for having stolen something as he said he was determined to repress plunder & to disprove the charges brought against those who were in arms for their country. His order of course was not obeyed.' Clarendon Papers, III, 98, Clarendon to Russell, 9 August 1848. 88 Personal Recollections of Stephens, ch. VI, *Irishman*, 4 March 1882.

affair: 'one thing seemed quite clear,' Doheny believed, 'namely, that the country demanded a delay of at least a month'. It was proposed 'that we should scatter, and take shelter individually as best we could until harvest time. But Mr O'Brien refused to hear counsel which involved, as its first principle, the idea of becoming fugitives.' They decided to continue raising the countryside and preparing men 'for active service'. Safe in the knowledge that the government had concentrated its forces in the towns, 'the idea of maintaining our position for a few weeks seemed not at all improbable'. The factor that many used to explain their reluctance to act, 'the apprehension of starvation', would be removed when the harvest was in. The impression of aimlessness and procrastination was already evident, however, and this new strategy seemed certain to baffle and frustrate all who were zealous for action. Doheny had found that the people of Ballingarry 'seemed incapable of appreciating' O'Brien's object, given his failure to 'propose any plan of immediate offensive operations' and general lack of clarity about the way ahead. Most of the Ballingarry crowd retired to their home districts for the night. O'Brien slept in the house of a Ballingarry shopkeeper, Kavanagh, a man whose obstinate refusal to admit knowing O'Brien would bring a few moments of absurdity to the latter's trial.[89]

O'Mahony arrived next morning, Thursday 27 July. He was sent by Meagher to bring O'Brien to Slievenamon, 'where he either could be more safely concealed for a time, or a last desperate effort could be made under better auspices'.[90] O'Mahony found 100 well-armed men at the two barricades (built on O'Brien's orders) on the edge of Ballingarry, but the rest of the town was quiet:

> Having come from the Carrick side of the hills, where I left all the forges in full work [*making weapons*], and with the midnight ring of the anvil ... , the stillness and apathy of Ballingarry convinced me that O'Brien had come to the wrong place. I told him so and urged him to come to me at once ... He said I was mistaken, that the people had gone home to rest after their day's drill. That all the previous day he was attended by some 2,000 stout Ballingarry men ... Bells were rung. Men came slowly out of their lairs. All the ragamuffins of the town appeared armed – some with straightened reaping-hooks stuck on poles, some with old scythes, and I saw more than one or two with knives and – if my eyes did not deceive me – forks stuck on hand-staves ...

Some in Ballingarry said they feared it was 'a mock O'Brien' sent to 'entrap' them, they would 'stay at home until more certain'. Stephens (and Fitzgerald) blamed O'Brien's 'indiscreet conduct' in relation to seizing property, and this is also suggested by the comment of another new arrival, Terence Bellew MacManus, a

---

89 O'Donoghue MSS, MS 770, 20. Hodges, *Report of the Trial of William Smith O'Brien*, 339-45. Doheny, *Felon's Track*, 97-8.   90 Ibid., 99. Fitzgerald, *Narrative of the Proceedings of the Confederates*, 27.

Liverpool-based Monaghan man, that the people had been 'sent home by O'B. – with (I believe) orders to appear next day, provisioned for two days. This was *never done*.' Eventually 'about 400 good men' came in from the country, with 'a pretty fair scattering of guns', but they had no good pikes and O'Mahony could only lament that the months of talk about pike-making had produced nothing even in a town with half-a-dozen blacksmiths. All in all, 'Mr O'Brien could not have commenced in a much worse place.' It was at this point in his account that O'Mahony, undoubtedly one of the more vigorous and effective of the leaders who emerged in Tipperary, began to denounce 'the great men that the country looked up to for light and guidance', chief among them O'Brien, of course. They 'seemed themselves completely at fault, and stunned by the magnitude of their attempt. Destroying the country's hopes, and making a farse [*sic*] of its struggle by their – yes, it must come out – *absolute imbecility*.[91] O'Brien, still bearing his pistols, 'drilled the gunmen in hedge and street firing and the pikemen in charging'. He sent the men with guns dashing into houses and gardens from which they brought their weapons to bear 'as if to shoot any thing on the road'. MacManus was appointed to 'the light cavalry command, which consisted of myself & a horse when I could get one'.[92] O'Brien's military qualifications rested on the presumption that martial skills were inherent in men of his class; he also had some knowledge of the history of war and, at least as important, the confidence that went naturally with an intimate knowledge of the history of the O'Briens.

The rest of the country saw even less progress. Before he left Dublin, Meagher had asked Thomas Halpin to inform the imprisoned journalists of the intention to raise the south and to have the Dublin clubmen prepare to take up arms 'and barricade the streets, when the news of our being in the field should reach them'. Halpin apparently said nothing of this to the prisoners, who on Monday sent him 'to ascertain from O'Brien what was about to be done' in Tipperary. According to O'Mahony, Halpin arrived in Carrick on Tuesday (25 July) in search of 'instructions for the Dublin clubmen, who were completely at fault on account of the sudden dispersion of the leaders, who had left town without leaving a word of instructions for their guidance, or any means of communicating with their missing chief'. He subsequently met Meagher and was told to go and get Dublin 'ready for action'; he returned and published an inflammatory letter that led to his arrest. During all his time, Duffy complained, 'the Prisoners never received a word from Mr Halpin', and 'the want of precise information threw the Clubs into complete confusion'.[93] Michael Cavanagh was one of the frustrated Dublin Confederates (before he took the initiative and headed south, ending up looking for O'Brien in New Ross!); he lamented the fact that the great Dublin club movement was 'per-

---

[91] O'Mahony, Personal Narrative, 6-7. Personal Recollections of Stephens, ch. VI, *Irishman*, 4 March 1882. Narrative by MacManus (for Duffy, written in August 1848), MS 5886, 1. [92] Ibid., 2. O'Donoghue MSS, MS 770, 21-2. Hodges, *Report of the Trial of William Smith O'Brien*, 335-9, 352-65. [93] O'Mahony, Personal Narrative, 5. *Nation*, 15 February 1851 (Duffy). Duffy, *Young Ireland: Four Years of Irish History*, 234-5. Fitzgerald, *Narrative of the Proceedings of the Confederates*, 20-1.

mitted to lie idle', its members 'doomed to remain passive spectators of the drama', while the leaders threw themselves on 'the unorganized peasantry'. O'Brien made at least one attempt to stir rebellion elsewhere – on Tuesday morning, he sent P.J. Smyth with 'instructions to Dublin as well as to other parts of the kingdom directing that a general rising should simultaneously take place' (O'Brien) – to no apparent effect. The messengers may have performed inadequately, and the failure to strike a decisive blow in Tipperary meant that there was nothing to spark action elsewhere. With General Blakeney refusing to despatch a regiment out of Dublin, the military stranglehold on the capital remained intact. Dublin stayed quiet, its clubmen 'frightened hares' albeit 'sullen and angry' (Clarendon). Eugene O'Reilly's attempted rising in Meath was a fiasco and O'Gorman delayed making a serious effort in Limerick until O'Brien's main rising gave a lead. Thus, it was left to the men in Tipperary to fight alone.[94]

Early in the afternoon of Thursday 27 July, O'Brien, riding on 'a mule's car', led over 100 men – 'all in high glee' (MacManus) – out of Ballingarry. He now intended marching to Slievenamon (the mountain in southern Tipperary) to join Meagher. This involved passing through Mullinahone, where MacManus was ordered to buy bread for the entire contingent and so, plausibly, could claim to know the precise number of men in the party; he 'paid for 160 and had about 15 men's shares left'. The men 'were halted in the village and during their hasty meal the *British allies* were not idle. Unseen by us the Parish Priest got among them …'[95] Stephens recalled how the clergy 'ordered all the peasants to abandon us, which command, if they had the temerity to disobey, hell's fires would consume them in the world beyond the grave', and Doheny heard that the priests now 'had recourse to threats, and even blows'. In consequence, MacManus wrote, 'when, in half an hour, we were ready to march, we found at least one third of our men disaffected, and in a few minutes they dispersed'. The march was resumed, but 'we found as we went along desertion at every opportunity', until 'we had not more than a score' left. Stephens, 'seeing our body dwindle away to a mere nothing', remonstrated with the men, one of whom raised his rifle to him, but he could do nothing as the 'poor fellows, before whose mental visions the torments devils can inflict flitted wildly and loathsomely, hid their haggard faces in their hands, bowed their heads, and followed their clergymen back into the unholy serfdom that has ever been their sad,

94 Cavanagh, *Memoirs of Meagher*, 253-8. Smith O'Brien Papers, MS 464, Draft Address of William Smith O'Brien, 1848, 83. Clarendon Papers, III, 60, Clarendon to Grey, 26 July 1848; 63, 68, Clarendon to Russell, 26, 28 July 1848. Narrative by O'Gorman, MS 5886, 14-6. Duffy, *Young Ireland: Four Years of Irish History*, 241-3. **95** Narrative by MacManus (for Duffy), MS 5886, 2. In his published accounts, Duffy tended to make small alterations when reproducing material. The MacManus narratives (he wrote another for Dillon, which Duffy also used) were subjected to very substantial changes, however, a fact that is particularly unfortunate because historians have relied so much on the Duffy transcriptions. In this case, he omitted the striking reference to 'the British allies'. Duffy, *Young Ireland: Four Years of Irish History*, 238.

sad lot'. 'Under those circumstances,' MacManus wrote, 'we gave up the descent on Slievenamon' and dismissed the remaining followers 'with orders to hold themselves in readiness for the next or day after.' O'Donohoe, more dramatically, recalled that 'the entire body of men deserted us', leaving O'Brien, Dillon, MacManus, Stephens and O'Donohoe himself 'alone on the high road'. O'Brien 'seemed to despair' and asked the others what each wanted to do 'as all hope was over'. He said he would 'go to Cahirmoyle and throw himself on his tenantry who would save him from arrest'. Everyone was 'very gloomy'. Stephens, describing O'Brien's tear-filled distress, was clear that his leader's qualities far outweighed the merits of those who, in their 'dire apathy', failed to respond to his call to arms:

> What Smith O'Brien felt, and suffered, that day the great God Himself only knows. We were all seated on a grassy slope by the roadside, many taking advantage of the moment to woo 'tired nature's sweet restorer, balmy sleep'. I was reclining side by side with my leader. He threw himself on his back, drawing his hat over those proud eyes of his from which I saw the hot tears trickling rapidly down. Ah! how my soul was stirred to its very depths by this harrowing spectacle. Once or twice I thought to break in on that silent grief he was trying to conceal, but, on after consideration, I restrained my impetuosity, and left him to his sacred sorrow. I knew well why it was he wept. That noble, pure, undaunted man, brave as a lion and as bold, had imagined a few days previously that he had only to unfurl the standard of revolt and he would be joined by thousands and tens of thousands of his compatriots. But now he knew what a dire apathy paralysed a race that would make no effort to save itself, but preferred the doom of a starved dog to the glorious deaths of freedom-worshippers. Smith O'Brien must have had bitter communings with himself on that dreary day ...

Duffy described how O'Brien sat 'on a bank, while silent tears of shame and despair ran down his cheeks, because the people had let the warning of a young man fresh from college [the priest] outweigh his years of service and sacrifice'. It was probably of this occasion that Dillon later wrote, 'I remember poor O'B. (after a priest one day had succeeded in driving our ragged army away from us) turning round to me and saying, "Dillon I believe after all there is some truth in what those bigots say. A religious change must precede the social."' A neighbouring farmer provided his 'genial hospitality', which 'thawed' the 'despondent mood' (Stephens). Some of the group sat with the farmer and, rather incongruously, discussed the merits of Livy, Tacitus, Horace and other classical writers, while Stephens and others went out and 'exercised our accuracy of aim by a series of rifle shots at certain fixed marks'. They then took a car to Killenaule and, 'wearied for want of rest or proper food', arrived at Thomas Walsh's hotel after midnight.[96]

---

[96] Personal Recollections of Stephens, chs. VI, VII, *Irishman*, 4, 11 March 1882. Narrative by MacManus (for Duffy), MS 5886, 2-3. O'Donoghue MSS, MS 770, 22-3. Duffy, *Young Ireland: Four Years of Irish*

In southern Tipperary, Doheny, on returning to Carrick, discovered that 'delay and indecision', and a host of 'contradictory and false' rumours about O'Brien, had undermined morale: 'at each step we found the difficulties of our position and the weakness of public confidence fearfully increased'. It was now that Doheny heard of Meagher's disappointing news from Waterford, ending the hope that assistance from there would 'restore unanimity and confidence.' Meagher, on failing to get news of O'Brien, 'must have been persuaded ... that Mr O'Brien had been driven from his position, or perhaps captured', leading (in Doheny's view) to his decision to set out for Father Kenyon's at Templederry, far to the north. Doheny, to whom it 'was then apparent that our position had become desperate', went looking for O'Mahony. The latter, as agreed at the Ballingarry conference, was supposed to collect men from Carrick and Grangemockler to join up with O'Brien's force and march to Slievenamon. News of the damaging influence of the Mullinahone priest reached Carrick before O'Mahony, and he was told 'that not a man could be had *without Father Byrne's permission*'. Then, at Grangemockler, when he sent for the 100 men who had promised him to be ready, only one turned up. This man said that Fathers Morrissey and Comerford 'had been from house to house through the parish on that day [Thursday], and had told the people not to stir *without their especial* orders. That Smith O'Brien was *mad*, and we all either fools or traitors [*sic*]. *That no more was to be made for a fortnight, until the harvest was ripe*. That when the proper time came they, Morrissy [*sic*] and Comerford, would be their leaders. This chat I heard before in other parishes ...' The priests had been clever enough not to forbid rebellion, instead urging men to wait a fortnight until the harvest was in; this cry 'met our friends everywhere' in Waterford, Tipperary and Kilkenny. Also, O'Mahony was 'much disheartened' by Meagher's departure to Templederry; he thought that Meagher's absence would 'prevent a sufficiently imposing force from assembling. O'Brien's personal prestige was gone. Ballingarry and Mullinahone killed him, and men believed the priests when they said he was mad ...' When he met up with Doheny and Reilly and heard their news that 'madness, treachery and the wildest folly were imputed to us' by the priests, O'Mahony actually agreed that it was a fair description of 'the acting leaders'. And his description of O'Brien's performance in Ballingarry led Reilly to respond that 'O'Brien ought to be shot!' The three malcontents set out to find O'Brien to urge 'the necessity of some decisive course'.[97]

O'Brien's decision to go to Killenaule meant turning away from Slievenamon, presumably intending to raise another force to bring there to join up with Meagher. On Tuesday, he had been well received on passing through Killenaule, like Ballin-

---

History, 238. Doheny, *Felon's Track*, 99-100. Dillon Papers, MS 6455, f88, Dillon to Adelaide Dillon, n.d. Fitzgerald, *Narrative of the Proceedings of the Confederates*, 33-6. Hodges, *Report of the Trial of William Smith O'Brien*, 139, 316-9, 355-6, 365, 372.   97 Doheny, *Felon's Track*, 98-9. O'Mahony, Personal Narrative, 7-9.

garry a village inhabited by a number of colliers from Tipperary's extensive coalfield. On the morning of Friday 28 July, O'Brien instructed O'Donohoe and MacManus to 'arrest' and take as a 'hostage' a judge who was expected to pass near Killenaule on his way to Clonmel. MacManus 'was seized with a fit of cold shivering from the wet and fatigue' of the previous day – O'Donohoe called it a 'nervous fever' – and the idea was given up anyway in the excitement of the morning's events. A crowd gathered, summoned by the chapel bell; they were, 'as usual in that quarter, miserably armed. But they were enthusiastic, and the Catholic priests did not interfere' (Doheny). Then word came that a body of soldiers was about to arrive in the village. Carts of turf and other items were seized and several barricades hastily constructed. The troop consisted of 45 cavalrymen of the 8th Royal Irish Hussars, under a Captain Longmore. One of the soldiers in the advance party claimed, in evidence, that someone at the main barricade warned him that 'if I did not halt he would blow my brains out', and that the people were crying 'kill all the bloody soldiers'. O'Donohoe gave a leading role on the barricade to a pistol-waving O'Brien, but most accounts state that he was not there and MacManus wrote of how, fearing that the soldiers had come to seize O'Brien, the others insisted on his 'retiring to some distance from the scene, which they got him to do with some difficulty'. Stephens, glad of the encounter after their demoralising experience of 'running over the country like hunted hares', covered Longmore with a rifle, while Dillon announced that they would not allow O'Brien to be taken and asked if the officer had a warrant for O'Brien's arrest. Longmore gave his 'word of honour as a soldier' that he had no such warrant and, according to MacManus, said that 'if allowed to pass quietly through the town he should neither molest or arrest him or anybody else. After some consideration Dillon allowed them to pass *one by one* through the barricade, and the soldiers being Irish, and evidently not hostile, the people gave them a cheer as the last man passed through.' Dillon led the captain's horse through the town and the troop continued on its way to Thurles, having been delayed for only 10 minutes.

The rebels 'exulted' in their 'victory', Doheny learnt that evening. MacManus would write proudly that 'by those who witnessed it and were not concerned in it, it is designated as "one of the most daring and reckless acts of bravery ever witnessed"', and O'Brien believed that a few 'resolute men' and a 'motley crowd' of badly armed peasants had 'arrest[ed] the progress of a troop of cavalry'. However, MacManus knew that some might 'sneer and call this a ridiculous and paltry affair', and Doheny sided with those who 'mourned over the escape of the military'. O'Mahony commented that Stephens, 'perhaps, had the fate of the struggle at the end of his rifle, had he been allowed to fire', and O'Brien himself claimed that 'if an actual conflict had taken place the result would probably have been favourable to the insurgents'. Any assessment must take account of the possibility (which Stephens thought considerable) that the soldiers would have joined the rebellion. Otherwise, the Hussars would surely have routed the untrained and poorly armed crowd. O'Donohoe's report that passage was given because O'Brien 'did not wish to spill blood unnecessarily' begs questions about his leader's intentions. At times the whole rising looked more like an effort to resist arrest than a genuine attempt at revolution.[98]

They gathered in their men; only 50 had arms and, 'not finding this a sufficient force' (MacManus), they decided to turn to the collieries of the surrounding countryside. The revolutionaries paid their hotel bill – 13 shillings – and at noon left town in a hired car. Travelling around, they 'met with every demonstration of support as far as the people could offer,' wrote MacManus, 'but then they were without arms, and seemed to a great extent to have had much of their physical courage starved out of them. They were all Hero Worshippers, & O'B. was their Idol.' O'Donohoe's recollection, slightly different, was that, 'The people flocked round us in all directions', and, sheltering from the rain in a hut, O'Brien 'addressed about 150 colliers all of whom stated they had guns and ammunition and were ready to fight'. However, O'Mahony, following in O'Brien's tracks, found that the people 'looked upon us as traitors'. He blamed the priests for such opinions and for the effect on O'Brien: 'ignorant, I believe, of the real nature of the Irish peasant, [he] seemed to despair when forsaken by the clerical revolutionists' and, uncertain how to proceed, was driven to procrastinate with 'meaningless armed meetings, his drillings', which only left the people 'tired out and disgusted' – clear evidence of 'O'Brien's obstinate mismanagement'.[99] A mine superintendent, John Pemberty, was warned by O'Brien that, if the mining company suspended production because the colliers supported him, 'he would take possession of the collieries'. O'Brien also 'said that he would have Ireland rescued from the British Government in less than a week ... They were all ready in the towns, and so far as he had travelled in the country he found every one of the same mind.' At least O'Brien had the good sense to affect an image of ruthlessness and strength, even if he probably had no intention to confiscate property and none of the boasted confidence in imminent victory. He cannot have helped his cause, however, by adding that 'if he was caught he would be hanged'.[100]

Along the road they were found by most of the other leaders who had been active in Tipperary. Meagher later gave an evocative description of his own arrival:

> Approaching still nearer, a shout was given – another, and then a third – the pikes, scythes, and bayonets being thrust upward in the murky air, amid the waving of hats and green branches, and the discharge of pistols. The next moment I recognised Smith O'Brien, John Dillon, and O'Donohue [sic].

---

[98] O'Donoghue MSS, MS 770, 23-4. Narrative by MacManus (for Duffy), MS 5886, 3-6. Doheny, *Felon's Track*, 100-1. O'Mahony, Personal Narrative, 10. Personal Recollections of Stephens, ch. VII, *Irishman*, 11 March 1882. Smith O'Brien Papers, MS 464, Draft Address of William Smith O'Brien, 1848, 85. Fitzgerald, *Narrative of the Proceedings of the Confederates*, 36-8. Hodges, *Report of the Trial of William Smith O'Brien*, 378-86. See also Mitchel, *Last Conquest of Ireland*, 199-200. [99] Hodges, *Report of the Trial of William Smith O'Brien*, 374-6, 386. Narrative by MacManus (for Duffy), MS 5886, 6. O'Donoghue MSS, MS 770, 25. O'Mahony, Personal Narrative, 10. [100] Hodges, *Report of the Trial of William Smith O'Brien*, 394-5.

Smith O'Brien stood with folded arms a little in advance of the crowd, looking as immutable and serene as usual. Dillon, with a large blue military cloak thrown over his shoulders, smiled quietly and picturesquely alongside of him, his mild, dark, handsome features contrasting with the plainer and sterner aspect of O'Brien. With a thick, black fur cap – something like a Grenadier's *razeed* – drawn over his ears and down to his eyebrows, with a little black cape hooked round his neck and a musket hugged to his cheek, O'Donohue peered through the front rank of the guerrillas, his sharp black eyes darting in sparks of fire from him the wild delight excited by the scene and the prospect of a fight ...[101]

Meagher had come from seeing Father Kenyon. Having been suspended from his duties by his bishop (Kennedy of Killaloe), Kenyon was newly restored on condition that he desisted from radical politics. He now told Meagher and James Cantwell (who had gone with a letter from O'Brien) that he 'dissented entirely from Mr O'Brien's policy' (O'Donohoe) and that he 'could foresee nothing but disaster and defeat' (Fitzgerald) coming from it. O'Mahony commented bitterly that 'Father Kenyon held the same opinion of our proceedings as his reverend confreres ... he must have known that it was in his power to turn the scale in our favour ...' Apparently under pressure from his worried comrades, O'Brien agreed to 'hold a council at once and hear all our opinions' (O'Mahony). They went that evening to the Commons, known variously as the Commons of Boulagh and the Commons of Ballingarry, a small village built around the local colliery. In an upstairs room of Thomas Sullivan's public house, there was a full council of war, involving O'Brien, Meagher, Dillon, O'Mahony, Doheny, Reilly, O'Donohoe, MacManus, Cantwell, Stephens and four others. According to Stephens, 'Dejection reigned' as each man struggled against 'an overwhelming despair'. 'The debate,' Doheny wrote, 'was long and warm ... It has been said that the discussion was acrimonious and the separation final. The truth is, there was not one word even of an angry tone ...' However, O'Mahony recalled that, 'Having reviewed our position, O'Brien asked us separately for our opinions. Nearly all, if not all, dis-approved of the course he was pursuing. Some even considered that the game had gone quite against us and that we were clearly rejected by the country.'

Someone advocated seizing all requisite supplies and paying for them with 'drafts on a future National Government'. The offering of rent-free farms to all volunteer fighters and the confiscation of the estates of opponents were also proposed. O'Brien 'would not consent; and this decision starved the insurrection' (Duffy). Several – Stephens attributed the proposal to Doheny, and he and MacManus reckoned a majority agreed – advocated waiting for the harvest, and 'concealing themselves meantime'. (Duffy later commented, scathingly, that 'to hide gentlemen among a population of peasants was about as feasible as to hide gold-fish in a duck pond'.) It was also suggested (by Dillon) that O'Brien should try to raise Limerick; he was

---

101 Duffy, *Young Ireland, Four Years of Irish History*, 239.

merely damaging the cause in Tipperary, 'where his reputation for capability was then completely used up. One week had sufficed for this.' (O'Mahony, who wrote this, had not seen the 'Hero Worshippers' noticed by MacManus.) O'Brien was unwilling to contemplate a flight to Limerick: 'I won't hide,' Stephens quoted him as saying, 'I won't be a fugitive where my forefathers reigned; I won't go to Limerick; I will continue to appeal to the people as I have been doing, till we gather enough support to enable us to take the field.' As O'Mahony put it, O'Brien 'said he trusted fully in the people of his present district ... That he would, and he thought he could, hold that district for a fortnight, until the priests' stipulated time had elapsed ...' It is hard to believe that he thought the priests would support him after the harvest, and that he expected the authorities to allow him to wait untroubled. None of his comrades agreed that O'Brien's plan could work; he was bound to be arrested. However, he 'remained stern and resolute, despite all opposition' (Stephens), his views assuming their 'most rigid sternness as his fortunes became clouded by a deeper gloom. He was averse to everything which bore the stamp of desperation, or could possibly imply a shrinking from fate' and he clung to his ideas 'the more steadfastly in proportion as ruin became more inevitable' (Doheny). Thus did O'Brien's ideas of duty and honour, the mainstays of his existence, lead him on to disaster.

After a little over an hour, the party agreed to split up to explore a range of possibilities. By being active in various places, the others could prevent a concentrated effort against O'Brien and, 'if strong enough, act on our own responsibilities and according to our own principles' (Doheny). O'Brien asked Stephens (who called this 'one of the proudest moments in my whole existence') and MacManus to remain with him in the area of the collieries. Meagher, O'Mahony, O'Donohoe and Maurice Leyne were to attempt to raise Waterford, Doheny to return to Slievenamon, and Dillon to try in his native Mayo and Roscommon. MacManus and O'Mahony, in their accounts, wondered if this was a fatal error; MacManus could not 'help thinking that had we *all stuck together* that night ... we might have done some thing more respectable. I think we would at all events have left our *mark some place* ...' Some years later, O'Brien seemed to harbour a sense of grievance against the men who left, writing of 'a failure which might never have occurred if they had like myself kept the field as long as a shadow of support, or a hope of success remained for the Cause'.[102]

A crowd having gathered, a public meeting followed outside Sullivan's. The Crown witnesses later gave rather confused evidence about what was said. One had Meagher urging them 'to drive the Saxon from the soil', while for another it was Dillon who told them to 'hunt every English b—r or beggar to his own side, and

---

[102] O'Donoghue MSS, MS 770, 25. O'Mahony, Personal Narrative, 10-12. Doheny, *Felon's Track*, 100-2. Personal Recollections of Stephens, chs. VII, VIII, *Irishman*, 11, 18 March 1882. Narrative by MacManus (for Duffy), MS 5886, 6-7. Narrative by MacManus (for Dillon, dated 25 January 1849), MS 5886, 7. Duffy, *Young Ireland: Four Years of Irish History*, 239-40. *Correspondence between Martin and O'Brien*, 1861, 31. Fitzgerald, *Narrative of the Proceedings of the Confederates*, 28-32, 38-40.

let him live there'. O'Brien apparently said that 'if they would protect him and arm, that Ireland would be free in a fortnight' (and 'that stones were very good weapons if they had no other arms'). According to one witness, Meagher asked them 'to be in readiness in three weeks, when the wisp would be lit over the hills', but another had him saying that if they defended O'Brien 'they would have Ireland free in a fortnight'. The latter witness then said that Dillon promised 'that if they would arm and protect Mr O'Brien, they would have Ireland free in six months'.[103] This sort of confusion was typical of the evidence given against O'Brien, but it must be wondered if the speakers were less than clear in their own minds, as well as their words, when Ireland would be 'free'.

Late on Friday evening, the leaders split up and started for their various destinations, leaving O'Brien, Stephens and MacManus at the Commons. O'Brien asked a mine employee for the key of the small police barrack provided by the mining company; it was now empty and O'Brien wanted to use it to station some men. He also requested the use ('for a night') of a colliery horse that he spotted. The man later claimed, 'I said I could not give him either, that I was only the company's servant; and he at once admitted the justice of my refusal, and said he would not take either.' Next morning, O'Brien, allegedly with a pistol in hand and 'a small boy walking after him', entered the colliery yard and asked again for the key. He also wanted the 'carts and boxes' that lay around, 'to help to throw up a barricade across the road'. When the supervisor declined, 'He said he would take them by force ... He ordered a man who was standing by to wheel away the cart, but he refused', and O'Brien 'commenced to wheel the cart himself' but went 'not more than a few yards'. Such was the evidence of Crown witnesses, questionable sources, but the stories, with their suggestion of shambling inadequacy, ring true. A guard of 30 men was organised. The three leaders spent Friday night in the house of Mrs Ellen Lacken (whom they duly paid). MacManus, according to Stephens, had difficulty sleeping as he contemplated the prospect of 'death on the field for the cause of Ireland'. Next morning, MacManus 'bought all the bread in the village and gave the men their breakfast'. O'Brien rose early and wrote a letter to the directors of the Mining Company of Ireland, which owned the local colliery. Aware that many of the men who had marched with him, in Mullinahone, Ballingarry and Killenaule, were colliers, he feared that the Company would, as he now wrote, 'endeavour to destroy the people by withholding wages and other means'. So, he threatened, if the wages were withheld, he would 'instruct the colliers to occupy and work the mines on their own account, and in case the Irish revolution should succeed, the property of the Mining Company will be confiscated as national property'. On the other hand, if the Company observed 'a strict and honourable neutrality' their property would be 'protected to the utmost extent' of his power. This warning, essentially the same as that given to Pemberty the previous day, suggests greater radicalism than was usually evident in O'Brien; it reflected his genuine concern for the men, who stood to suffer 'in consequence of the noble and courageous protection'

---

103 Hodges, *Report of the Trial of William Smith O'Brien*, 391-2, 398-9.

they had given him. The letter would be used by the Attorney General to prove O'Brien's leadership of a 'revolution'.[104]

On the morning of Saturday 29 July, MacManus reviewed the rebel army and found that they had only 18 'very rude' pikes and 20 guns and pistols 'with about one charge of powder each'. Some men went home to collect guns (they said), 'but few of these returned'. Having heard that the nearby village of Urlingford had 'a large number ready to join us', and a curate who 'would put himself at their head', he persuaded O'Brien that they should march to meet up with that force. According to MacManus, they planned an attack on the police station at New Birmingham, and then they would either retreat to a 'commanding position' or proceed to 'march on Carrick, Clonmel, or Kilkenny'. Hope sprang eternal. Unfortunately, their departure was delayed by O'Brien's reception of 'deputations of country farmers who were suggesting all modes of action into any which [sic] none of them had the slightest idea of entering themselves ...' Soon after noon, when they were 'just getting the men in motion', a man came on horseback with the news that 'a large body of police were advancing on us from Ballingarry'.[105] The messenger, John Kavanagh, later wrote that, on being taken to O'Brien, he 'never saw him in better spirits; his eyes fairly sparkled' when Kavanagh told him of stirrings in Kilkenny. The news of the approach of the police produced a flurry of interest: 'Instantly we were surrounded by two or three hundred women, boys and lazy scoundrels who evidently came with their hands in their pockets to be spectators ...' This 'mob' were 'yelling like savages, one shouting to do this another do that a third something else and it was fully a quarter of an hour before the butts of our rifles could even get us as much room as that we three could act together' (MacManus). The crowd consisted 'of all ages and both sexes,' but with women 'more numerous than the men'; only 22 had guns, according to Kavanagh, and two-thirds of those present held no weapon of any kind.[106] The leaders decided to defend the village – 'To march towards Urlingford would be to retreat before them [the police] and get us the name of cowards' (MacManus) – and a barricade was constructed. When the enemy drew near, O'Brien, again wearing his '82 Club cap, 'jumped over the barricade and stood in front of it, exposed to the fire of the enemy. As a matter of course,' Stephens noted, 'I followed my chief, and we remained together side by side ...' MacManus's account leaves no doubt that a battle was intended, with pike and pitchfork men

---

[104] Ibid., 148-9, 389-90, 397-412. Personal Recollections of Stephens, ch. VIII, *Irishman*, 18 March 1848. Narrative by MacManus (for Duffy), MS 5886, 8. Narrative by MacManus (for Dillon), MS 5886, 7. According to MacManus, O'Brien also wrote 'a long despatch regarding the Killenaule affair'; it is not extant. [105] Narrative by MacManus (for Duffy), MS 5886, 9. Narrative by MacManus (for Dillon), MS 5886, 8. [106] Narrative by MacManus (for Duffy), MS 5886, 9-10. Narrative by MacManus (for Dillon), MS 5886, 9-10. Narrative by Kavanagh, MS 5886, 5-6. Doheny, *Felon's Track*, 102-3. Duffy judiciously omitted MacManus's description of 'a mob yelling like savages'. The rifle butts were probably used by MacManus and Stephens, who, unlike O'Brien, carried rifles. Duffy, *Young Ireland: Four Years of Irish History*, 245-6.

prepared to charge, 'gun men' deployed in the nearby houses to fire as the police arrived, and a body of 80 men and women ready to spring out, 'yelling like devils', to 'give them a volley of stones and close on them'.[107]

Almost all of the 13,000-strong Royal Irish Constabulary was Irish, but it was also predominantly Protestant and, as Saville has shown, cut off from sympathy and contact with the people by virtue of its role in the struggle against agrarian crime.[108] Few constables who had experience of the recent atrocities in the midland counties could identify with the Catholic peasantry and nationalist politics – as O'Brien was soon to discover. The troop that now approached the Commons had been sent there, from Callan, to arrest O'Brien. It was led by Sub-Inspector Thomas Trant (an anti-Catholic zealot, as his later writings showed) and comprised a total of 47 men. A number of people followed the police from Ballingarry. Two miles out of that village, soon after one o'clock, Trant saw the 'great crowds' ahead at the Commons. He estimated 'five or six hundred, or more'; this was far above the figure suggested by MacManus and Kavanagh, while O'Brien later claimed that he led 'a few hundred colliers of whom not more than sixty or seventy were armed'.[109] At Scott's Cross, the police could turn right up a lane and escape encirclement. When they did this it is possible that (as MacManus wrote) the police started to run: 'The moment the people saw this, without waiting [for] orders they broke up and with a yell dashed' forward across the fields, intent on cutting off the apparent retreat. 'All was now confusion and unfortunately O'B. instead of trying to keep back the mob was carried away in the front of it.' Kavanagh described the scene in similar terms, but Stephens, who was beside O'Brien, wrote that 'O'Brien gave an order to pursue' the police.[110]

By the time the police approached a house one mile up the side-road, the people were outflanking them, and just as he ordered his men to break for the house one of the crowd fired a shot, Trant claimed. The dwelling, in the townland of Farrinrory, belonged to a widow, Mrs McCormack; she was not present, but five of her young children were, and these Trant, with more care for self-preservation than the rule of law, decided to use as 'hostages'.[111] The house was typical of the better sort of Irish farm-house: a large, stone, almost 'square' building, two stories high; at the front, there were three windows in the top storey and two in the lower, with a door in the centre; the gable ends also had windows and at the back there were one or two windows and another door. A stone garden wall, about five feet high, ran around the whole, joining up with a set of outhouses at the back to create a yard. By the time MacManus got to the house, the windows were either bristling with

---

107 Narrative by MacManus (for Dillon), MS 5886, 9-10. Narrative by MacManus (for Duffy), MS 5886, 10. Personal Recollections of Stephens, ch. VIII, *Irishman*, 18 March 1882.   108 Saville, *1848*, 33-4, 40-4.   109 Hodges, *Report of the Trial of William Smith O'Brien*, 412-3, 415. Smith O'Brien Papers, MS 464, Draft Address of William Smith O'Brien, 1848, 85.   110 Narrative by MacManus (for Dillon), MS 5886, 10-11. Narrative by MacManus (for Duffy), MS 5886, 11. Narrative by Kavanagh, MS 5886, 6-7. Personal Recollections of Stephens, ch. VIII, *Irishman*, 18 March 1882.   111 Hodges, *Report of the Trial of William Smith O'Brien*, 413-4, 420.

5 The affray at Widow McCormack's

rifles or barricaded with furniture (or a combination of the two). He told O'Brien that the building 'could not be taken without a piece of artillery, but O'B. was certain they would surrender and that we must attack. I then asked leave to lead it and stated that we had but one way, and that was by "smoking them out".' O'Brien 'gave his permission', and MacManus put hay against the back door and, having no 'light', fired his gun into it to create the sparks that would start a fire; the hay was just beginning to smoke 'when O'Brien appeared and ordered us to desist, saying – "Here is the Widow McCormack and she has been sent round by the police to say they will make terms"'.[112] Trant denied having any contact with the widow until after the affray. Doheny (who was not there, of course) claimed that when the police saw the preparations to burn them out they seized the children 'and held them up to the windows to terrify or appease the people', while Father Fitzgerald understood that the widow had upbraided O'Brien 'in no very polite language'.[113]

O'Brien, MacManus and Mrs McCormack entered the front garden – Clarendon heard an improbable tale that the 'coward', O'Brien, 'bravely seized the *widow McCormack* ... and pushed her before him to save himself from being shot' – and went to the parlour window to the left of the front door (as one faces the building). O'Brien, because the bottom part of the window was barricaded, stood on the window sill a couple of feet off the ground; he put in his hand and 'shook hands with the police and said it was not their lives but their arms we wanted' (MacManus). According to Constable Cornelius Mahony (and other policemen reported in similar terms), O'Brien 'said that he was an Irishman and a soldier ... and asked us to give up our arms, and he would protect our lives ...' Stephens, slightly different,

---

112 Narrative by MacManus (for Dillon), MS 5886, 11-3. Narrative by MacManus (for Duffy), MS 5886, 11-2.   113 Doheny, *Felon's Track*, 103. Fitzgerald, *Personal Recollections of the Insurrection*, 23.

described how his leader, 'advancing from our ranks, pistol in hand, went up to one of the windows, and in a loud tone of voice cried out – "Surrender!"' The police apparently refused and sent for Trant, who had placed himself in an upstairs room. O'Brien jumped down and allegedly said, 'Slash away, boys, and slaughter the whole of them'. Several policemen declared this at O'Brien's trial. O'Brien angrily interrupted the first time he heard the claim (from Constable John Moran): 'Don't you know you are swearing falsely when you are swearing that?' Many things are surprising about O'Brien's conduct in July 1848, but the idea that he used such words (in his English public school accent) is literally incredible. The *Freeman* called it 'an order in sentiment and in language as unlike anything that could emanate from Smith O'Brien as it is to the phraseology of Timbuctoo'.[114]

After this, the firing began immediately (or two minutes later, depending on which policeman lied least). The police insisted that the first shooting came from the crowd; Trant claimed that he heard a 'crash of stones and shots' and gave the order to fire. According to MacManus, some men 'commenced from under cover of the walls throwing stones at the gable end of the house ... and perhaps about eight or ten of them struck the windows, when all at once a volley from about forty carbines was discharged at us ...' Father Fitzgerald, arriving on the scene, found the people angry that the police, 'without provocation', had begun the firing, and Doheny wrote that it was the throwing of stones which prompted Trant to order his men to fire, a 'black lie' that Trant specifically denied in his pamphlet answer to Fitzgerald and in a hand-written comment on the first edition of *The Felon's Track*. Clarendon's version is interesting; although probably based on police information, it says that a policeman began the shooting when he shot at O'Brien: he 'fired at him (S. O'B.) but missed him and the insurgents who were nearly all armed then fired upon the house. The constabulary returned the fire vigorously ...'[115] None of the evidence can be trusted fully, but, whoever fired first, the insurgents now took a pasting. Two of O'Brien's men were shot dead, and Kavanagh (badly), MacManus and several others were injured, while not a single casualty was inflicted on the defenders. The firepower of the police was far superior. They had more guns and bullets, while the crowd, with women to the fore, relied largely on stones. O'Brien's defence counsel made much of the subsequent failure of the police to find more than a few bullet marks on the house and one spent bullet.

114 Narrative by MacManus (for Dillon), MS 5886, 13. Narrative by MacManus (for Duffy), MS 5886, 12. Clarendon Papers, III, 80, Clarendon to Grey, 2 August 1848. Personal Recollections of Stephens, ch. VIII, *Irishman*, 18 March 1882. Hodges, *Report of the Trial of William Smith O'Brien*, 424-51, 494. *FJ*, 4 October 1848. 115 Hodges, *Report of the Trial of William Smith O'Brien*, 415. Personal Recollections of Stephens, ch. VIII, *Irishman*, 18 March 1882. Narrative by MacManus (for Dillon), MS 5886, 13. Narrative by MacManus (for Duffy), MS 5886, 13. Duffy, *Young Ireland: Four Years of Irish History*, 246. Fitzgerald, *Personal Recollections of the Insurrection*, 25. Doheny, *Felon's Track*, 103. Thomas Trant, *1848. Reply to Father Fitzgerald's Pamphlet, entitled His 'Personal Recollections on the Insurrection at Ballingarry in July, 1848'. With Remarks on Irish Constabulary, and Hints to all Officials* (Dublin, 1862), 13. Hand-written Account by [Thomas] Trant on [Michael] Doheny's *The Felon's Track*, MS 4325, n.d. Clarendon Papers, III, 74, Clarendon to Russell, 30 July 1848.

The serious fighting lasted about 15 minutes; there were occasional shots for another half-hour; towards the end, the police were firing without reply. MacManus, at an early stage, joined O'Brien and 'insisted on calling the men off as they had expended all their ammunition and on our falling back on the village and make [*sic*] a rally, but he declared he would never leave the spot, that an "O'Brien never turned his back on the enemy". In fact, he became desperately determined, and stood in the midst of the fire without any purpose.' Stephens, whose account included an eloquent tribute to O'Brien's 'splendid bravery' and readiness for martyrdom, found him standing 'at his post of danger alone and unprotected' and urged withdrawal. O'Brien 'raised his form to its full height, and replied to me in his calm, but proud and resolute way – "I shall never retreat, sir, from the fields where my forefathers reigned as kings!"' Eventually, MacManus and Stephens simply forced him off the ground: MacManus, in another passage omitted by Duffy, told of how he and Stephens 'got our rifles across his breast and drove him before us, all the men but six having retired. When we got him off in this manner for about 30 yards he then consented to go but on condition that he would be allowed to walk, to which of course we assented. All the time the bullets were tearing the earth up about us' and 'whistling about our ears. He [O'Brien] was the last man who left.' MacManus was later infuriated by newspaper reports that O'Brien 'crept out of the garden on all fours. This is, simply, a falsehood ... On the contrary all thro' he exposed himself almost unnecessarily to danger and, I may add, for the week previous he endured more hardships, more fatigue and showed more self denial than any man with him ...'[116]

Fathers Fitzgerald and Maher, having followed their parishioners up from Ballingarry, found O'Brien and most of the people on or near the road, just out of sight of the house. The crowd, Fitzgerald wrote, was 'anxious to go up again to the house. I was asked if I would go with them, and when I refused, Mr O'Brien asked what would I advise them to do, and said that he would act as I would recommend.' This was not the belligerent O'Brien described by MacManus and Stephens, but the failure to give a strong lead is recognisable. O'Brien allegedly said he 'would be satisfied if they would give up their arms' and asked Fitzgerald to deliver this message. The priest duly rode to the house, saw one dead man and gave the last sacraments to another who was dying, and went to speak to Trant. The officer later described Fitzgerald's attempt to induce his surrender, how, for example, the priest warned that the insurgents would burn the house (to which Trant replied that he had 'five hostages'). Trant believed that the exchange was 'suppressed' – excluded from O'Brien's trial – by a Whig government which, anxious to conciliate the Catholic clergy, had no wish to expose the priest's questionable conduct. Fitzgerald, his approach rejected, withdrew; he found the people still 'greatly incensed' and 'anxious to return', and 'again Mr O'Brien asked my advice, which was the same as before, to give up that notion and postpone hostilities to some future time. No one could appear more calm or recollected [*sic*]. He at once assented to my desire

---

116 Narrative by MacManus (for Dillon), MS 5886, 13-5. Narrative by MacManus (for Duffy), MS 5886, 13-4, 16. Personal Recollections of Stephens, ch. IX, *Irishman*, 25 March 1882.

of not proceeding farther at present, but, being taken aside and differently advised by other officers who surrounded him, he seemed disposed to listen to them.' Fitzgerald also worked on the people; Stephens wrote of his 'haranguing them in a violent fashion, fulminating ecclesiastical curses on the [their] heads' and accusing them of 'endeavouring "to tear up the roots of society itself, and establish a reign of anarchy in the island"'.

O'Brien 'made a speech and tried to rally them' (MacManus); according to the evidence of Constable John Carroll (see below), he claimed 'that he could take the place where Mr Trant was in an hour'. O'Brien later insisted, perhaps confusing the order of events slightly, 'that if the Police had not been saved by the intervention of two priests they might have been compelled to surrender by the application of fire to the building which they occupied'. As a result of Fitzgerald's efforts, some 'went away and abandoned us'. Stephens was 'proud to see that the majority remained firm and undaunted', but MacManus was clear that damage had been done: when O'Brien spoke after the priest 'they would not respond. In fact *the spell was on them*.' He put O'Brien on a policeman's horse 'with a view of taking him off the ground but the moment I let go the rein he again returned and again addressed them [the people], but with a similar result. I saw clearly from the cold, stern ... indifference of this well fed, well clothed & well mounted clerical functionary [Fitzgerald] that we had no chance there, and I again implored of O'B. to fall back on either the Collieries or Ballingarry and rally our men ... Again I turned his horse's head, & putting a man at each side of the bridle moved towards the village. When some distance down I took a short cut across the fields; but to my mortification on looking round I again beheld him returning to where the young priest and the mob were standing ...' News of the imminent arrival of police reinforcements came around five o'clock; most of the people dispersed and Stephens called on O'Brien to ride off 'or else you'll be taken ... This was accordingly done.' O'Brien was no longer there when the new detachment of police arrived. There was a small and one-sided skirmish with this force, when Stephens received several injuries. The battle of Ballingarry was over.[117]

MacManus gave the impression that O'Brien was in a daze; he was frog-marched off the field, had his horse turned for him, and eluded his guide at the first opportunity. O'Brien's curious encounter with Constable John Carroll also raises questions about his state of mind. Carroll had met Fitzgerald and the other priest just before the first fighting began; he carried a message for Trant, that he should not engage with O'Brien as police could not be sent from Kilkenny, and it is quite possible (as Trant later charged) that he colluded with Fitzgerald to bring an end to hostilities by giving this discouraging news to Trant. Having delivered the letter, he

---

117 Fitzgerald, *Personal Recollections of the Insurrection*, 28-30. Trant, *Reply to Father Fitzgerald's Pamphlet*, 3-4, 5-7, 15. Narrative by MacManus (for Dillon), MS 5886, 15. Narrative by MacManus (for Duffy), MS 5886, 14. Personal Recollections of Stephens, chs. IX, X, *Irishman*, 25 March, 1 April 1882. Smith O'Brien Papers, MS 464, Draft Address of William Smith O'Brien, 1848, 85. Hodges, *Report of the Trial of William Smith O'Brien*, 458-9. Stephens claimed that Fitzgerald's surprising decision to cut short his intervention and go home was caused by his convincing the priest he would be 'shot down' if he stayed.

joined the crowd on the road – a baffling decision – and was almost shot as a spy by Stephens. It was Carroll's horse that either Stephens or MacManus took (both claimed the feat) and gave to O'Brien. Carroll, released just before the police reinforcements arrived, was walking towards Ballingarry when he met O'Brien again. The latter was still on the sequestered horse, but now with a 'common hat' as opposed to the '82 Club cap he wore during the affray; Stephens had induced O'Brien to make a swap because 'the green-and-gold cap ... would be a target for the peelers'. According to Carroll's evidence, O'Brien 'pulled out a pistol and said it was his life or mine; was I going to arrest him. I said I was not, that I had no arms, and that he might shoot me if he liked ... He said it was beneath him to do so, or to fire on an unprotected man ... He said that I should go back with him along the road' towards the Commons. On the way, Carroll allegedly told him that his cause was hopeless, 'particularly as the Roman Catholic clergy, as he had seen that day, were against him. How could he expect to meet troops ... He said that for twenty years he had worked for his country, and that his country could redeem itself if it liked, or something to that effect ... he said also that he wanted no blood ... He gave me my horse immediately after that' and walked on towards the Commons. Thus, this remarkably frank exchange with a perfect stranger, a policeman, ended with his returning the man's horse just as he (O'Brien) was about to flee.[118]

In the course of the next few days, the embers of rebellion expired. Soldiers flooded the county and 20 'poor foolish peasants' and colliers, 'the rank & file of O'Brien's army' (Clarendon), were arrested and taken to Dublin. Around Carrick, O'Mahony encountered men who wanted a lead from someone like Meagher or Dillon ('O'Brien's name I found completely useless'). He – and Stephens (in Urlingford) – found men in high excitement as news came through of the glorious victory at the Commons. But the truth was soon known everywhere and the priests, busily 'rebuking their flocks for their folly' (Clarendon), ensured that men returned quietly to their homes. O'Gorman's efforts in Limerick fizzled out and McGee, who arrived in Sligo on 2 August, without a Scottish army, found that the enthusiasm for rebellion dissipated when the failure in Tipperary was proven. As early as 2 August, Balfe informed Clarendon that 'the *rebellion is over*', and on 3 August Ireland's governor duly reported to Russell, '*The Rebellion is over*'. Almost two months later, O'Mahony led a muster of the peasantry in the hills of south Tipperary and north Waterford (the so-called 'September rising'); they staged a number of 'rash, ill-advised, and ill-arranged' (Doheny) attacks that effected nothing.[119]

---

118 Hodges, *Report of the Trial of William Smith O'Brien*, 453-63. Fitzgerald, *Personal Recollections of the Insurrection*, 28, 31, 48. Trant, *Reply to Father Fitzgerald's Pamphlet*, 4, 16-7, 20-25. Personal Recollections of Stephens, chs. IX, X, *Irishman*, 25 March, 1 April 1848. *FJ*, 15 November 1848, Fitzgerald to the Editor of the Freeman, 13 November 1848. 119 Personal Recollections of Stephens, ch. IX, *Irishman*, 25 March 1882. O'Mahony, Personal Narrative, 12-5. Clarendon Papers, III, 84, Clarendon to Russell, 3 August 1848; 88, Clarendon to Grey, 4 August 1848; Box 53, Balfe to Southern, 2 [3]August 1848. *Nation*, 15 March 1851, McGee's Narrative of his Mission. Duffy, *Young Ireland: Four Years of Irish History*, 243-4. Doheny,

6 Arrest of O'Brien at Thurles

It is not possible to trace O'Brien's movements during the week after Ballingarry, for the two chroniclers, MacManus and Stephens, who described his conduct at Farrinrory separated from him towards the end of the battle. Stephens fled northwards and MacManus looked in vain for his leader at Ballingarry and Slievenamon.[120] O'Brien revealed only that he 'remained in concealment for a few days

---

Felon's Track, 104-6, 157-9. Cavanagh, *Memoirs of Meagher*, 276, 287-9, 315-6. *FJ*, 2, 5, 7, 8 August 1848.
120 Personal Recollections of Stephens, ch. IX, *Irishman*, 25 March 1882. Narrative by MacManus (for Dillon), MS 5886 16. Narrative by MacManus (for Duffy), MS 5886, 15.

amongst a peasantry who were too much intimidated to protect me, but who, to their eternal honor, declined to avail themselves of the opportunity of acquiring a large sum of money (£500) by betraying me'.[121] Alexander Sullivan, who may have received his information from O'Brien, later wrote that, 'Ere the evening [of 29 July] fell, O'Brien, accompanied by two or three faithful adherents, was a fugitive in the defiles of the Kilnamanagh mountains' in western Tipperary.[122] On Monday, Clarendon triumphantly proclaimed that, 'Smith O'Brien within a day or two will be a prisoner or a corpse or a wandering outcast ... The people are getting afraid of harbouring him partly because they know him to be a proclaimed traitor and partly because they think him mad ...' To add further discouragement, he announced 'that all who harbour persons accused of treason render themselves liable to capital punishment. This will not assist them in getting lodgings.' In fact, the people did harbour O'Brien, as he disappeared almost without trace for a week. Clarendon reported on 4 August that he 'is nowhere to be found. His clothes & a shirt with his name in full have been found in a peasant's house where he put on a disguise ... the whole country from Kilkenny to Galway is on the alert to catch him.' Some imaginative rumours filled the newspapers, but, in truth, his precise movements are unknown – almost as much a mystery to the historian as they were to a Lord Lieutenant who sent Grey two letters on 1 August, one saying that 'O'Brien was seen galloping in the direction of Kilkenny' to the east, the other that he was heading west to Cahirmoyle. The fact that he was apprehended at nearby Thurles suggests he did not move far from central Tipperary.[123]

The *coup de grace* was delivered around eight o'clock in the evening of 5 August, when O'Brien was arrested at Thurles railway station. Although 'the people would not betray them', wrote Duffy, indicating that O'Brien had not been alone, 'they were alarmed and distressed, and the situation became intolerable. He determined to go straight home where the police would be sure to find him.' Dillon's brother-in-law, Charles Hart, was told that 'when S. O'B. went into Thurles police who knew him *well* took opportunities of passing him close & whispering "for God's sake Sir why do you expose yourself so?"'[124] On arriving at the station, O'Brien bought a second-class ticket to Limerick and, according to newspaper accounts, was sufficiently flustered to leave his change. A railway guard, an Englishman called Hulme, recognised him and informed a policeman in plain clothes; the latter drew a pistol and, assisted by other officers who gathered quickly, duly made the arrest. Balfe – who, incredibly, had gone to Tipperary to help in the search for O'Brien and was at the station to witness everything – claimed he was unarmed, but most reports said he carried a loaded pistol but did not seek to use it or in any way to resist arrest. The *Freeman* carried the story that two constables 'dragged him by the collar, as if he were a pickpocket, or petty thief', and that his only words were,

---

121 *Correspondence between Martin and O'Brien*, 1861, 33.   122 Sullivan, *New Ireland*, i, 192.   123 Clarendon Papers, III, 77, Clarendon to Russell, 31 July 1848; 79, 88, Clarendon to Grey, 1 (x2), 4 August 1848. *FJ*, 2 August 1848.   124 Duffy, *Young Ireland: Four Years of Irish History*, 250-1. Journal of Charles Hart, MS 6464, Part 1, 27, 4 October 1848.

'Easy – take me easy'. He was 'well dressed, [in] a short cloak with collar turned up' (Balfe) and he carried a large black stick. 'His appearance was that of a person wearied and tired,' one trial witness said, 'as if he had undergone great fatigue.' He had £10 16s. 2d. in his purse. In the middle of the night of 5 August, the prisoner was taken by a specially commissioned train to Dublin, to Kilmainham gaol. He was soon joined there by Meagher, O'Donohoe, Leyne and MacManus. A surprising number of leaders escaped into exile, among them Stephens, Dillon, Doheny and McGee, all of whom made their way to France or the United States.[125]

Responses to the rising and O'Brien's part in it naturally varied enormously. O'Neill Daunt wrote of the 'disastrous news' that O'Brien had 'engaged in a driftless and unaccountable affray with the police ... My heart bleeds for him! I have intense confidence in his honour and in his devotion to Ireland ...' O'Brien, he believed, was 'certain at least of transportation and fortunate if he escapes a rope. Such is the evil fortune that has befallen one of the purest, truest, noblest spirits in Ireland ...'[126] Sir Denham Norreys's brother-in-law was probably right in his assessment on 8 August that 'the sympathy for Smith O'Brien's fate is very general, from the impression of his being considered insane which his whole conduct has so fully proved ...' Old friends like Sir Denham, Sir David Roche and William Monsell were sufficiently sympathetic to appear as defence witnesses, in due course, to show that O'Brien had long been an advocate of constitutional means and a loyal subject of the Queen.[127] Thackeray probably spoke for most people in England when he gave 'thanks that the deplorable revolution and rebellion which everybody anticipated ... has been averted in so singular, I may say unprecedented, a manner. How pitiful is the Figure cut by Mr Smith O'Brien, and indeed by Popery altogether.'[128] Charles Greville called the revolt 'a disgraceful hoax' which, after 'all the swaggering and boasting', had 'shrunk into nothing ... The whole thing is suddenly so contemptible as to be almost ridiculous.' O'Brien 'is a good-for-nothing, conceited, contemptible fellow, who has done a great deal of mischief and deserves to be hung ...'[129]

Clarendon, convinced of his antagonist's 'selfish' motives, wrote that O'Brien 'thought he should be king of Ireland or President of the Republic'. He initially held that O'Brien 'must be mad' – 'No brain could long stand the pressure of so much conceit, obstinacy & spurious ambition' – a view he delighted in attributing to the Irish people, but he (and Russell) quickly decided otherwise when the ques-

---

125 Clarendon Papers, III, 92, Clarendon to Russell, 6 August 1848; Box 53, Balfe to Southern [5] August 1848. Hodges, *Report of the Trial of William Smith O'Brien*, 208, 586. *FJ*, 7, 8 August 1848. *Illustrated London News*, 12 August 1848. 126 Journal of O'Neill Daunt, MS 3040, ff316, 317, 28 July, 6 August 1848. W.J. O'Neill Daunt, *A Life Spent for Ireland*, 67-8. 127 Hodges, *Report of the Trial of William Smith O'Brien*, 700-4. Jephson, *Anglo-Irish Miscellany*, 231, Franks to Norreys, 10 August 1848. On O'Brien's gratitude for Norreys's 'act of friendship', see ibid., 232-3, O'Brien to Norreys, 9 November 1848. 128 Gordon N. Ray (ed.), *The Letters and Private Papers of William Makepeace Thackeray* (London, 1945), ii, 414, Thackeray to Mrs Brookfield, August 1848. 129 Strachey and Fulford, *Greville Memoirs*, vi, 93-5, 99, 31 July, 8 August 1848.

tion of legal responsibility arose: 'There is no reason to think O'Brien mad. He has committed acts of gross folly but there is nothing in the state of his mind to prevent his being made responsible for them.'[130] Ridicule proved the most devastating of weapons. The *Times* claimed that 'a handful of constabulary have put down a rebellion' and, referring to O'Brien's tame surrender at Thurles, that 'he has allowed himself to be picked up like a £500 note in the gutter'. Mocking the idea of 'the King of Munster', it contrasted King Charles II, who hid in the oak, with 'King O'Brien', who allegedly hid among the cabbages that Mrs McCormack grew outside her garden wall. The *Times* poured scorn on 'the contemptible figure of Smith O'Brien crouching amidst Widow Cormack's cabbages' – hence the popular sobriquet, 'the cabbage-patch revolt', and O'Brien's fame as 'the Hero of the Cabbage garden'.[131]

Importantly, for all that they had not approved of his conduct of the campaign, the subsequent comments of other leaders were remarkably positive and sympathetic. When Doheny (an exception) tried 'to fasten some charge of rashness upon O'Brien', Dillon railed, 'Nothing can be baser than this. It is both false and ungenerous and I am resolved when a proper time arrives to vindicate O'Brien's character.'[132] An opportunity arose when the Dublin correspondent of the *New York Nation* newspaper had the temerity to criticise O'Brien's military capacity and suggest that 'the result would have been quite different if O'B. had acted with more decision'. Writing to his wife from America, Dillon found it 'disgusting to hear those ruffians talk about him [O'Brien] now who would not lift a hand to help him'. He decried the impression in both Ireland and America 'that *he* was not equal to the occasion', in particular 'that the failure of the movement was owing to his having opposed some bold counsels recommended by the rest of us'. He privately blamed the 'false, boastful and cowardly' men of Ireland – 'a more shocking exhibition of national cowardice was never made' – and despised especially those clubmen who 'would hear of nothing but *blood*, and threatened to assassinate anyone who spoke a moderate word, and when the hour came they hid themselves in their houses'. He believed that the 'basest portion of their conduct is their endeavouring to fix upon poor O'Brien the blame of the failure'. Dillon despatched a public letter containing a vigorous defence of O'Brien: in the circumstances of clerical opposition, popular apathy and lack of arms, neither Hannibal nor Napoleon, he claimed, 'could have achieved any more respectable result'. Rather more credibly, Dillon declared that 'of all that party which acknowledged him for its head, he [O'Brien] was ever the most reluctant to commit his country to the perils of a civil war – and that,

---

130 Clarendon Papers, III, 78, 80, Clarendon to Grey, 31 July, 2 August 1848; 84, 93, 98, 99, Clarendon to Russell, 3, 6, 9, 10 August 1848; Box 43, Russell to Clarendon, 8 August 1848.   131 *Times*, 8, 11, 12 August 1848. *Correspondence between Martin and O'Brien*, 1861, 30. The chief proprietor of the *Times* was John Walter, the MP who denigrated the Irish in December 1847.   132 Dillon Papers, MS 6455, f86b, Dillon to Adelaide Dillon [1848]. Dillon subsequently deprecated Doheny's practice of telling 'ludicrous stories' around New York 'about his having seen no less than twenty thousand pikes in one day and 'the women sharpening them on the road-side with their babies sitting by their side...' Ibid., f94, Dillon to Adelaide Dillon, 3 March 1849.

once driven to resistance, he was, of all, the firmest and most fearless in maintaining the position he had assumed and the last to abandon it ...' He fully deserved that which his critics would undermine, 'the reputation of a brave and true man'.[133]

Later, in 1849, Dillon accused McGee (the editor of the *New York Nation*) of continuing to comment unjustly on the efforts of 'a man whose great sacrifices and disinterested heroism go far to rescue his country from that contempt which the conduct of others is calculated to call down upon it'. Writing to Duffy, Dillon called O'Brien 'that man whose character I regard as a sacred trust deposited in my hands'.[134] Duffy himself acknowledged that 'O'Brien did all that an honourable man could do to overcome intractable difficulties ...'[135] For O'Donohoe he possessed 'the most rigid virtue, the purest courage and reckless bravery', and Meagher proclaimed that the 'reckless libellers of our race' could find no military favourite who could ever 'boast of having braved death more resolutely or with such unaffected and conscientious courage' as O'Brien did at Ballingarry. Stephens, throughout his account far more devoted to O'Brien's person than he was critical of his tactics, knew 'what a fund of nobility, what a depth of chivalry, that no enemy could question, that no influence could buy, adorned the character and fixed the soul of this man ... I admired him then, as I cherish his memory still.'[136] Coming from the founder and leader of the Fenians, this tribute must carry weight when O'Brien's failures are contrasted with the achievements of later, more radical nationalists. The same may be said of John Mitchel's sympathy for 'O'Brien and those brave men who sought in his company for an honourable chance of throwing their lives away'. In his *Jail Journal*, Mitchel could only despise the 'poor extemporised abortion of a rising in Tipperary', but he did not blame its 'estimable and worthy' leader, 'poor O'Brien', for the failure. When he met O'Brien in Van Diemen's Land he found it 'sad to look upon this noblest of Irishmen, thrust in here among the off-scourings of England's gaols ... He is a rare and noble sight to see: a man who cannot be crushed, bowed, or broken ...'[137]

These comments, though often qualified, as they had to be, by references to his mistakes, recognised that O'Brien was not the only cause of failure. The revolt stood little chance of success. Britain could deploy impressive resources, military and police (not to speak of the Protestant yeomanry), and it is difficult to envisage any rebellion succeeding when British forces were not distracted by a foreign war. The Irish people were unwilling to risk a repeat of the dreadful scenes of '98, which claimed 30,000 lives and visited a reign of terror on much of the peasantry. Dillon obviously felt contempt for their lack of heart; he had travelled with O'Brien almost

---

133 Ibid., ff75-6, Dillon to Adelaide Dillon, 12, 19 December 1848. *FJ*, 8 January 1849, Dillon to McGee, 11 December 1848. Charles Hart also commented on Doheny's 'unhandsome & false insinuations & statements about S. O'B.'. Journal of Charles Hart, MS 6464, Part 1, 47, 4 November 1848. 134 Dillon Papers, MS 6455, f106a, Dillon to Duffy, 19 May 1849; f107a, Dillon to McGee, 22 May 1849. 135 Duffy, *Young Ireland: Four Years of Irish History*, 248. 136 O'Donoghue MSS MS 770, 28. *Limerick Chronicle*, 11 August 1864, Meagher to Smith, 16 July 1864. Personal Recollections of Stephens, ch. III, *Irishman*, 11 February 1882. 137 Mitchel, *Last Conquest of Ireland*, 196, 200-5. Mitchel, *Jail Journal*, 72, 146-7, 156, 266-7.

to the bitter end and heard thousands loudly pledge their arms before melting away. O'Gorman felt 'woefully deceived' by a people who 'did not want to fight', and Meagher said on 4 August, just before his arrest, that 'we have found that the people are not up to the mark'. O'Brien himself betrayed such feelings, writing in 1861 that, 'Every man of the fifty thousand who had incited me to take up arms was as much bound as myself to expose his life and fortunes to danger in the cause of Ireland.' He wondered what would have happened 'had even a portion of those who professed their readiness to fight taken the field ... , what might have been done if every man pledged to the Cause had thrown himself into the conflict with unhesitating devotion ...' Few of the more prosperous farmers were prepared to risk all in revolution, and among the lower orders, as Meagher appreciated, 'hunger and disease' had sapped both physical and mental resources. Famine, he believed, had eaten its way 'into the soul itself', destroying the instinct which teaches every being 'to turn upon the foot by which its humble life is perilled'.[138] The fact that the suspension of *Habeas Corpus* sparked an uprising before the harvest exacerbated this; nobody who depended on government food stocks would act so as to cause supplies to be cut off, as O'Brien himself had always warned.

The government strike also made them begin the rebellion before preparations were completed – 'forcing the rebels into action a month before they were ready'.[139] This was the 'fatal inadvertance' that had made Meagher so pessimistic, and he concluded that, 'Owing to it, we were routed without a struggle ...' And O'Brien, after his arrest, was said to have told Tipperary's sheriff 'that they had been driven into their present course too soon, that 6 weeks later they should have been certain of success ...'[140] O'Donohoe, in describing what he considered the 'three concurring causes' of their 'total failure', began with an exasperated complaint against the leaders' 'ill-considered and premature conduct' in rushing into battle after hearing of the suspension of *Habeas Corpus* and the supposed arrest warrant for O'Brien. They had no 'properly preconceived plan ... and even then only a few of them resolved upon this course leaving the other leaders of the Dublin Club men in total ignorance of their intentions'.[141] The decision to take to the countryside was a military necessity, but it was made and pursued so precipitately that the thousands of clubmen in Dublin were effectively excluded from the struggle and the fate of the movement came to rest on the backs of unorganised, unarmed and half-starving peasants.

Above all, the role of the priests was crucial. Their importance in discouraging rebellion was fully acknowledged by the British – not least Clarendon and Grey[142]

---

138 Fitzgerald, *Narrative of the Proceedings of the Confederates*, 98, Meagher quoted in the diary of Father O'Carroll, 4 August 1848. Narrative by O'Gorman, MS 5886, 19. Smith O'Brien Papers, MS 464, Draft Address of William Smith O'Brien, 1848, 83. *Correspondence between Martin and O'Brien*, 1861, 34. Meagher, Personal Recollections, *Weekly News*, 31 August 1867.   139 Clarendon Papers, III, 78, Clarendon to Grey, 31 July 1848.   140 Meagher, Personal Recollections, *Weekly News*, 10 August 1867. Clarendon Papers, III, 92, Clarendon to Russell, 6 August 1848.   141 O'Donoghue MSS, MS 770, 27.
142 Clarendon Papers, III, 78, Clarendon to Grey, 31 July 1848; 84, 93, 99, 109, Clarendon to Russell, 3, 6, 10, 13 August 1848. Home Office Papers, HO 122/20/123, Grey to Clarendon, 5 August 1848.

– and greatly resented by every leader of the rising. Immediately after his arrest, his brother found that, 'William ascribes his defeat entirely to the Priests, who he says thwarted him at every step ...'[143] Some weeks later, in his Draft Address, O'Brien expressed his 'sincere belief that it was through the instrumentality of the superior order of the Catholic Clergy that the insurrection was suppressed. For my own part I feel convinced that we were defeated ... by the influences brought into action by the Catholic Clergy.'[144] He who had once advocated bringing priests into dependence on the state was defeated by their refusal to levy war against that state. During their prison-island encounter in 1851, Mitchel found that O'Brien remained full of resentment on this subject:

> We wandered several hours, talking of '48. He gave me a more minute account than I had heard before of his own movements in Tipperary; and [*he*] attributed his failure, in great part, to the behaviour (what shall I call it? – the cowardice, the treachery, or the mere priestliness) of the priests. Priests hovered round him everywhere; and, on two or three occasions, when the people seemed to be gathering in force, they came whispering round, and melted off the crowd like a silent thaw. He described to me old grey-haired men coming up to him with tears streaming down their faces, telling him they would follow him so gladly to the world's end – that they had long been praying for that day – and God knows it was not life they valued: but *there* was his reverence, and he said that if they shed blood they would lose their immortal souls; and what could they do? ...[145]

In 1861, the stance of the priests was the factor to which O'Brien attributed his failure, although he 'never concurred in the reproaches which have been lavished upon them' and understood that they 'conscientiously believed' it was their duty to prevent their flocks from incurring the penalties of a failed revolt.[146] All of the main chroniclers – Stephens, O'Mahony, O'Donohoe, Doheny and Meagher – faulted the conduct of the priests, as shown above. O'Donohoe gave their denunciation of the rebels' 'schemes of revolution and anarchy' as the second of the main causes of failure, and Dillon declared that Catholicism 'must be a religion for *men* as well as *women*'. In 1850, Meagher 'firmly believe[d] that, had the Catholic Priests of Ireland preached the Revolution from their altars – had they blessed the arms and banners of the people – had they gone out, like the Sicilian Priests, or the Archbishop of Milan, and borne the Cross in front of the insurgent ranks – had this been the case, I firmly believe that there would have been a young Nation, crowned with glory, standing proudly up by the side of England at this hour'. Duffy

---

143 Papers relating to William Smith O'Brien, TCD MS 10610/4, Robert O'Brien to Ellen O'Brien, 9 August 1848. See also Grania O'Brien, *These My Friends and Forebears*, 135. **144** Smith O'Brien Papers, MS 464, Draft Address of William Smith O'Brien, 1848, 85-7. **145** Mitchel, *Jail Journal*, 267, entry for 15 October 1851. See also Mitchel, *Last Conquest of Ireland*, 197-8: 'the clergy, as a body, were found on the side of the enemy'. **146** *Correspondence between Martin and O'Brien*, 1861, 33.

despised the likes of Kenyon and 'the handful of priests who stimulated the insurrection' and then 'behaved shamefully' in repudiating it. Like O'Brien, Meagher and Duffy refused to accuse the priests of acting 'treacherously'. For the most part, they 'only did their duty' in stopping a movement that they believed 'had no chance of success' (Duffy). As one man said to Doheny, the clergy were obliged to prevent 'a useless wreck and slaughter'. However, the priests ensured the complete collapse of a rising that, as Duffy wrote (with, typically, more caution and less flamboyance than Meagher), 'had they helped it cordially ... would have been widespread and protracted, and perhaps successful'.[147]

So, the entire blame for failure cannot be heaped on O'Brien. Having said this, it must be acknowledged that Irish nationalism could not have had a worse leader in 1848. He failed, in the final analysis, to estimate the clamour of the previous months for what it was worth, in terms of real willingness to fight. The lack of preparation, in relation to arms especially, was aggravated but not caused by the need to act weeks earlier than expected. It was primarily the result of six months of bluster and inaction – by all nationalists, of course, from those whose 'boastings' brought O'Brien to Tipperary to the leaders who in May-June decided to organise a rebellion but achieved nothing – but it was the dead hand of the reluctant general that did untold damage. He later argued that many European revolutions had succeeded 'without previous preparation', but the fact remained that he had a chance to arm his people and failed to take it. O'Brien knew that in 1782 the apprehension of rebellion had been decisive, but he was wrong to think that that easy success could be repeated when Britain was strong and at peace. He discovered too late – in the field – that the threat of war had not forged pikes. Nothing could be less like the meticulous preparations that went into the rebellion of 1916. Indeed the only meticulous preparation undertaken in 1848 was that of General Blakeney and the army in Dublin. Revolutionaries discovered throughout Europe in 1848-9 that in the struggle between the phrase-gusher and the soldier the latter was bound to prevail, and in Ireland at least this owed a great deal to the fact that the soldier anticipated war while the politician anticipated victory. Perhaps even more important, however, was O'Brien's conduct during the rebellion. O'Donohoe blamed 'Mr Smith O'Brien's scrupulous and conscientious behaviour respecting the rights of property'. He loyally saw it as 'the triumph of virtue over vice', of O'Brien's 'ennobling instincts of humanity ... He scorned success when to obtain it would create rapine and crime ...' O'Donohoe clearly had more respect for O'Brien's principles than for the 'servile and mean passions' he attributed to the people. But he still considered this factor 'the great and paramount cause of failure beyond all question'.[148]

147 O'Donoghue MSS, MS 770, 27. Dillon Papers, MS 6455, f88, Dillon to Adelaide Dillon, n.d. *Nation*, 3 August 1850, Meagher to Duffy, 16 February 1850. Cavanagh, *Memoirs of Meagher*, 284-5. Duffy, *Young Ireland: Four Years of Irish History*, 249. Doheny, *Felon's Track*, 94. Kerr, *Nation of Beggars*, 152-64. 148 *Correspondence between Martin and O'Brien*, 1861, 34. O'Donoghue MSS, MS 770, 27-8. Duffy, *Young Ireland: Four Years of Irish History*, 248. See also Griffith, *Meagher of the Sword*, xiv.

An early success 'would have given confidence to those who were waiting for encouragement,' as O'Brien wrote afterwards. Had that happened, it was 'impossible to say what might have been the results of our undertaking'.[149] Everyone knew that 'the smallest victory' was needed to stimulate the country, 'tempting it to still more daring exploits'.[150] Equally, soldiers and policemen required more to inspire them to mutiny than reminders that they were Irishmen. Mitchel commented that O'Brien 'might have made, at least, a fight'[151] – might have made the all-or-nothing effort that would have given the revolt a chance. Instead, O'Brien spent a week moving to and fro and achieving nothing more inspiring than clearing out a little police station and allowing a troop of dragoons to proceed on their way. Then, on 29 July, came the decisive confrontation. 'Had the policemen been taken or slain,' O'Mahony mused, 'the cause and the country would have been saved.' Instead there was the half-hearted attack on Trant's force, what O'Mahony called 'the mimic war of the Collieries'.[152] If the building had been burned out, a victory was achievable, and if O'Brien was deterred by the thought of sacrificing five small children this meant he was a decent human being but an ineffective rebel. So, no news of victory came to send shock waves through Ireland. Indeed, until the whole business was over, there was little awareness elsewhere that a revolt had begun. In Dublin, the *Freeman's Journal* carried only sketchy reports of O'Brien's movements and gave the Kilkenny cattle show more coverage than Ireland's revolution. Of course, the people might not have responded even to a victory. Or, if many did rebel, the slaughter of '98 might have been repeated. In all probability the completeness of O'Brien's failure prevented a bloody war which Irish nationalism did not have the strength to win. Such thoughts can only be speculation. What is certain, looking at the events that did occur, is that O'Brien's integrity, bravery and humanity – in sum his *character*, which made Dillon and the others revere him – were not enough. The situation in 1848 required qualities of judgement and ruthlessness that he did not possess, and the result was a humiliating fiasco.

---

149 Smith O'Brien Papers, MS 464, Draft Address of William Smith O'Brien, 1848, 83. **150** Meagher, Personal Recollections, *Weekly News*, 17 August 1867. **151** Mitchel, *Last Conquest of Ireland*, 201. **152** O'Mahony, Personal Narrative, 12, 16.

Epilogue

O'Brien was charged with high treason and held at Kilmainham until two days before his trial began at Clonmel (Tipperary) on 21 September 1848. He immediately sent for his brother, Robert, and Lucy, who was asked to bring 'one or two of the children' and instructed (again) to 'sell the horse'. Lucy, with the children, took lodgings near Kilmainham and stood 'very heroically' (Grace O'Brien) by her husband's side. She was pregnant with their seventh and last child. O'Brien also decided that their eldest son, Edward, 'is not to go back to school at present as William is to teach him' in the gaol; O'Brien, perhaps realising that one way or another they were likely to be parted, 'set his heart on having Edward to teach for some time'.[1] O'Brien's mother – he professed 'greater anxiety upon her account than for any other individual, however dear to me'[2] – and brothers and sisters flocked to Dublin. Robert's first impression was that although he did 'not think there is any ground for the allegation of insanity yet he is in a high state of excitement and bitterness against every thing English'.[3] On 21 August, O'Brien signed an indenture by which the rest of his property, including that which he stood to inherit on his mother's death, was put into the protective trust established in April.[4] Before leaving London, Lucius saw the Home Secretary and asked for an assurance 'that his [O'Brien's] life wd be spared, adding that he thought he ought to be shut up for life'. O'Brien apparently agreed to Lucius's acting as a mediator who would negotiate 'terms' consistent with 'the honor and high principles of his Brother!' (Clarendon) According to Lucius, O'Brien insisted that any agreement 'should embrace all parties', that is, include his fellow-prisoners, and indicated 'that he was quite ready to quit Ireland' and go to live in Europe. It is not clear how much

---

[1] Smith O'Brien Papers, MS 441, f.300, Grace O'Brien to Anne Martineau, 29 August 1848; ibid., MS 8653 (24), O'Brien to Lucy O'Brien, 22 August 1848. Papers relating to William Smith O'Brien, TCD MS 10610/2, 13, Robert O'Brien to Ellen (Elinor) O'Brien, 7 [15] August 1848; ibid., 35, O'Brien to Robert O'Brien, 7 August 1848. Lucy decided against exposing young William to the sight of his father in prison and sent him back to school in England. Ibid., 1, Robert O'Brien to Ellen O'Brien, n.d. Grania O'Brien, *These My Friends and Forebears*, 135. [2] Smith O'Brien Papers, MS 8653 (24), O'Brien to Lucy O'Brien, 22 August 1848. [3] Papers relating to William Smith O'Brien, TCD MS 10610/4, Robert O'Brien to Ellen O'Brien, 9 August 1848. [4] *Limerick Reporter*, 21 January 1862, Memorandum of William Smith O'Brien, 6 January 1862.

7 O'Brien (seated) with Meagher (middle) in Kilmainham, the daguerreotype by Leon Gluckman

Epilogue

8 O'Brien's trial at Clonmel

O'Brien knew of the terms his brother presented, namely that he should 'live in France for 3 or possibly for 5 years', keep his property and have his income remitted, and retain his seat in Parliament. Clarendon thought that, 'Even from the King of Munster to Queen Victoria I think this *un peu fort.*' He sent for Lucius 'and explained what *high treason was*' and that they would 'deal with all traitors as they deserved'. Lucius then commented that O'Brien 'must prepare for a voyage'.[5]

Robert and Grace O'Brien developed considerable sympathy for the 'noble spirit' that had induced their brother to rebel, Robert complaining rather preciously that among the people who ran out to see his mother near Clonmel 'no man touched his hat & no woman curtseyed or said God speed. Such are the persons for whom a man of honour has sacrificed life, property, wife, children, friends and all that are near and dear.'[6] Robert persuaded O'Brien to have the redoubtable James Whiteside hired to lead his defence, which also included O'Loghlen, Francis Fitzgerald and Robert Potter.[7] Whiteside's strategy was to contend that the whole business had been no more than an attempt to evade arrest, an approach that tended to degrade the struggle for national liberation. O'Brien later described the 'humiliation' that this caused him, how he wished he could have 'avowed' and 'justified' all he had

---

[5] Clarendon Papers, III, 141, Clarendon to Grey, 7 September 1848; Box 12, Grey to Clarendon, 12 August 1848; Box 21, Sir Lucius O'Brien to Clarendon, 3 September 1848. [6] Papers relating to William Smith O'Brien, TCD MS 10610/1, 20, 22, Robert O'Brien to Ellen O'Brien, n.d., 24 September, 1 October 1848; ibid., 36, Grace O'Brien to Ellen O'Brien, n.d. Grania O'Brien, *These My Friends and Forebears*, 137. [7] Papers relating to William Smith O'Brien, TCD MS 10610/8, 11, Robert O'Brien to Ellen O'Brien, 12, 15 August 1848.

done. Instead he yielded 'most reluctantly to the unanimous wishes of all my friends' and to the need to avoid making statements that might incriminate those whose trials would follow.[8] O'Brien's reference to 'revolution' in his letter to the Mining Company put paid to Whiteside's argument, and on 7 October, the 13th day of the trial, the jury duly pronounced him guilty of high treason. Many of the witnesses perjured themselves and the jury was entirely Protestant. Chief Justice Blackburne made a number of dubious decisions that were not in O'Brien's favour and his charge to the jury, Robert claimed, 'slurred over what had been said in defence'. O'Brien's mother, who attended, thought the trial 'was conducted in a vindictive, persecuting spirit ... You [O'Brien] have come out of it with credit & honor, notwithstanding the verdict of the jury.' She expressed her *'righteous indignation against conduct which was not either just, generous or true ...'* However, in his planned address, O'Brien acknowledged that 'the principal facts alleged in the indictment have been proved beyond doubt'. Robert knew that O'Brien 'said and did things ... that showed that he desired to make the attempt to arrest him an occasion for a general insurrection ... I am prepared to maintain that the trial was fair & the verdict just ...' Robert went on to show that it was only during the trial that O'Brien himself was brought to see the truth of his position:

> Poor fellow, he says he had made up his mind to the result since he heard the Solicitor General's speech. He felt he had brought himself within the compass of the law of High Treason which he did not before believe & that he did not realise to himself the consequences. He has borne the whole with manly firmness & does not regret the trial as it has put his whole conduct clearly before the public. He is much delighted that he has been relieved from the charge that [*he*] said those words at the widow Cormack's which so many swore against him. He now feels also that had he pleaded guilty as [*he*] had at first intended & justified himself he would have implicated so many others. I saw him this evening, he was not cast down but seemed grateful for all that had been done for him ... Poor Lucy bore up wonderfully & perhaps for her the certainty is better than the dreadful state she was in during the last 10 days. We are all going to a service in the gaol & Henry [O'Brien] is to read for us. When shall we all meet again? Never I fear on this side of the grave as years must roll over before William can be allowed at large in this kingdom. Sad indeed is the contemplation of what a person may be driven to by allowing his mind continually to foster a feeling of discontent with every thing about him.[9]

---

8 Smith O'Brien Papers, MS 449, Tasmanian Journal, Journal II, Part II, 16, entry for 6 August 1850. Davis, *To Solitude Consigned: The Tasmanian Journal*, 139.   9 Papers relating to William Smith O'Brien, TCD MS 10610/32, Robert O'Brien to Ellen O'Brien [7/8] October 1848. O'Brien Papers (AO), Lady O'Brien to O'Brien, 15 December 1848. Smith O'Brien Papers, MS 464, Draft Address of William Smith O'Brien, 1848, 9. Grania O'Brien, *These My Friends and Forebears*, 139-40. Saville, *1848*, 187-93. Davis, *Revolutionary Imperialist*, 280-7.

O'Brien refrained from delivering his address lest it compromised the prisoners still to be tried. It was an unapologetic defence of the decision to rebel. In fact, it was unapologetic in every respect, for he (and all the other leaders) tended to blame others – the priests, the people in Tipperary, the British who had provoked the rising – for their failure. He could acknowledge that his revolt was 'feeble' and 'contemptible', but his declared acceptance of responsibility was partly ritual – what is expected of the honourable leader – and partly a matter of saying that his fault lay in mistaking the weakness of others:

> I am compelled to admit that our escapade – it does not deserve the name of an insurrection – was in a supreme degree contemptible as the result of a great national movement in which many an idle boast and many a futile menace had been employed. I am compelled to charge myself with having totally miscalculated the energies of the Irish People. I cannot disavow my responsibility for this disastrous failure and therefore will not now shrink from the reproach which it involves. Nor am I ashamed to confess that I entertain deep and sincere grief for the sufferings occasioned to individuals by this abortive attempt. Above all do I regret with bitterness that these events have strengthened the hands of our enemies, discouraged the hearts of our friends, and dimmed for a time the hopes which led us to believe that an era was approaching fraught with national happiness and national glory.[10]

On 9 October, O'Brien was sentenced to be drawn, hanged until dead and then beheaded and quartered, with the four quarters 'dispersed as Her Majesty shall think fit'. He declared himself reconciled to the prospect that he would be executed: 'Having failed, I know that my life is forfeited ... For Ireland I shall cheerfully surrender Life itself.'[11] In what he called 'Lines written upon my birthday for my dear wife while I was lying under sentence of death in Clonmel Gaol, Oct. 17, 1848', he hoped that his memory would be treasured by his wife and family and that, 'Ireland too will not forget, The son who strove her ills to heal ..., And died a victim ... , Farewell, Farewell.'[12] Grace noted in mid-October that 'William eats, drinks & sleeps well'; he felt 'no real anxiety about his fate' and did 'not seek the usual consolation of a Christian'. From the time of the sentence, there was a considerable popular movement against execution. Grace observed that 'thousands take an interest in him now who never thought about him before ... he is the great champion of Anti Humbug ...' Dillon, embittered, despised 'the cowards around him [O'Brien] sobbing like women or running to beg that his life might be spared'.[13] In fact, as Lucius and Robert expected, the government had no intention of enforcing the death penalty.

---

10 Smith O'Brien Papers, MS 464, Draft Address of William Smith O'Brien, 1848, 87-9.   11 Ibid., 101, 103, 105.   12 O'Brien Papers (AO), Letter Box, Bundle 3. In Tasmania he wrote that he had been 'prepared cheerfully' to face the death penalty. Smith O'Brien Papers, MS 449, Tasmanian Journal, Journal II, Part II, 15, entry for 6 August 1850. Davis, *To Solitude Consigned: The Tasmanian Journal*, 138.   13 Smith O'Brien Papers, MS 441, f2304, Grace O'Brien to Anne Martineau, 18 October 1848. Dillon Papers, MS 6455, f69a, Dillon to Adelaide Dillon, 30 October 1848. *FJ*, 12-28 October 1848.

Grey knew it would be 'a good thing if we can avoid hanging him without proclaiming impunity to future rebels, as the less we do to exalt him to the rank of a martyr the better', and Clarendon took account of O'Brien's 'foolishness bordering on insanity' and 'his manifest abhorrence of bloodshed & plunder & the fact that no person in the Queen's service was killed or even hurt ...' The 'great stir' in favour of mercy, with 'a monster memorial' signed by 25,000 in Dublin and other petitions 'coming in by dozens', confirmed Clarendon's view that the punishment should be commuted to transportation for life. He insisted that it should be for life, 'for it would otherwise appear to the public that we are treating the crime with undue leniency because the criminal happened to be a gentleman'. Clarendon showed genuine sympathy for O'Brien's mother: when the defence moved a writ of error, on technical grounds, he commented that the expense of this 'is no object to his unfortunate mother who is distressed with grief & who will hope to keep her son a short time longer in the country'. The writ meant a delay in announcing a commutation, so, on hearing that 'his mother was very unhappy at not feeling sure', on 18 October, months before a formal announcement, Clarendon told Chief Secretary Somerville to give the family a private 'assurance' on the matter.[14]

Meagher, MacManus and O'Donohoe were also convicted of high treason and, on 23 October, duly sentenced to death; that evening they held a party and toasted the health of O'Brien.[15] Among the peasants and colliers in the prison, there was 'not a man,' Grace found, 'that grumbles over his sentence, I mean among the poor, I mean grumbles at Wm'. In fact, these men, who numbered no more than 20, were never brought to trial; they were freed during November 1848, a relieved O'Brien noting that, 'The poor Ballingarry men have I believe been all liberated'.[16] Writs of error sent the cases of the four condemned men into an appeal court, the Court of Queen's Bench. The prisoners were returned to Kilmainham on 16 November but moved to Richmond Bridewell after a few days, and here they remained for eight months of what O'Brien called 'monotonous though not disagreeable residence'. He told Anne (O'Brien) Martineau that his time in prison 'would have been as agreeable as any that I have passed for many years if it were not for the funereal looks of those whom I love – which picture [sic] a mental anxiety to which I have myself been a stranger. I place great confidence in Providence ... In proportion also as I have been freed from responsibility I have been relieved from care ...' O'Brien had sustained a remarkably intense political involvement since 1843, the months leading up to the revolt brought an immense burden of responsibility, and what he

---

14 Clarendon Papers, III, 98-9, 160, 171-2, 175-6, 178, Clarendon to Russell, 9, 10 August, 30 September, 8, 10, 12, 14, 16, 18 October 1848; 170, 173, Clarendon to Grey, 8, 12 October 1848; Box 12, Grey to Clarendon, 12 August 1848; Box 43, Russell to Clarendon, 12 October 1848. 15 *FJ*, 24 October 1848. Griffith, *Meagher of the Sword*, 334-5. 16 Smith O'Brien Papers, MS 441, f2323, Grace O'Brien to Anne Martineau, 24 October 1848; ibid., MS 18310 (2), O'Brien to Anne Martineau, 30 November 1848. *FJ*, 11, 13 November 1848.

underwent in Tipperary must have been nearly as traumatic as anything that a politician has experienced in modern Irish history. Not surprisingly, he was tired and partly relieved that his future would be decided by others. The 'load of painful responsibility' which had 'weighed upon' him for several years was no more. He was surrounded by his family and visited constantly by friends. He was able to read and to write poetry; he sent verses to many people, commenting to Anne that, 'It is rather late in life for me to discover that I am a poet'. In 1850, he called this 'one of the happiest periods of my life'.[17] His physical comfort, too, was considerable, despite a severe attack of lumbago in November. He was 'remarkably comfortably located' in an apartment in the governor's house, 'quite a handsome establishment,' Grace noted, 'in fact it is not like being in gaol'. Richmond's governor had 'a taste for good furniture, so that in reality he has the use of much better rooms, china, &c. than he had at home'. Meagher reported to Dillon, by this time safely in New York, that, 'O'Brien resides in the Governor's house, and (one would imagine) fancies himself in Cahirmoyle, so calmly does he smoke his diurnal cigar, and allude, each morning, to the state of the weather.'[18]

The appeal court found against the prisoners in January 1849 and the writs of error were then taken to the House of Lords. As for the journalists in Newgate, Martin and O'Doherty had already been convicted and sentenced to be transported, Williams was acquitted, and Duffy's prosecution was finally abandoned in April. One feature of Duffy's several trials famously involved O'Brien, who proved almost as dangerous a comrade behind bars as he had been in war. He had taken a leather-covered portmanteau down to Wicklow on 22 July and a few days later left it with Michael Doheny's wife in Cashel. While still in Thurles, immediately after his arrest, O'Brien was asked by General McDonald 'if there was anything that he could do for me that would contribute to my comfort', and, believing he was 'in the hands of a gentleman', O'Brien asked that the portmanteau should be brought as he 'had been for some days without a change of dress'.[19] Instead, it was taken to the Under Secretary, Thomas Redington (a Catholic Whig), in Dublin and, after having the lock broken, this functionary searched among the various papers inside and found the June letter in which Duffy had urged O'Brien to put himself at the head of 'our revolution' (see above). O'Brien, perhaps foolishly, 'could not have believed it possible' that a general, who had obtained the portmanteau 'not by way of capture, but upon an honorable understanding, would have allowed it to be rifled by state detectives of any grade whatsoever'. He was especially angry with Redington, who had 'ransacked' the portmanteau and sifted through his personal belongings; his

---

17 Smith O'Brien Papers, MS 8653 (24), O'Brien to Lucy O'Brien, 5 November 1848; ibid., MS 18310 (2), O'Brien to Anne Martineau, 29 October 1848; ibid., MS 449, Tasmanian Journal, Journal II, Part II, 16-7, entry for 6 August 1850. O'Brien Papers (AO), Journal for Mrs William S. O'Brien, 9, 16 July 1849. 18 Smith O'Brien Papers, MS 441, ff2302, 2306, 2307, Grace O'Brien to Anne Martineau [November 1848], 24 November 1848. Dillon Papers, MS 6455, f96, Meagher to Dillon, 12 March 1849. 19 Dillon Papers, MS 6456, f328, O'Brien to O'Flaherty, 21 July 1857. *Nation*, 1 August 1857. Hodges, *Report of the Trial of William Smith O'Brien*, 207-9.

public exposure of the story and questioning how far Redington's conduct 'was or was not consistent with the character of an *Irish gentleman*' may have prevented the scoundrel's standing for Galway in 1857.[20] Duffy's letter was used, to little apparent effect, in O'Brien's trial, but it was the basis of a new charge against Duffy, that he had incited O'Brien to make war on the Queen. O'Brien 'suffered much pain of mind ... from self-reproach for having through my confiding inadvertence compromised the safety of a friend'. However, he also hoped that his 'act of indiscretion' might assist Duffy, given that the letter showed the editor's aversion to anarchy and chaos, and the attempt to implicate Duffy in a revolt that occurred when he was under lock and key may have alienated some jurors; the jury, split down the middle, failed to agree and he was set free.[21]

The appeals by O'Brien and his three fellow-prisoners were rejected by the Lords in May 1849 and O'Brien was expelled from Parliament as a convicted traitor. The government decided to proceed with commuting the death sentences to transportation for life. Lucius, informed of this on 30 May, 'expressed himself grateful for the course taken' but warned that his brother might refuse to accept clemency. Although Grey called this an 'absurd' course, Lucius reminded him that 'we had to do with a very brave & obstinate man & that his object would be to force the Government to shock public opinion'.[22] O'Brien was horrified by the thought of perpetual banishment and considered it anything but an act of mercy; he wrote (for Lucy) that from the moment he realised that transportation was his destiny he 'lamented' that he 'was not executed at Clonmel'. It 'surely would have been more merciful to have put me to death at Clonmel than to have sent me to a colony distant 16,000 miles from all whom I love ...' O'Brien probably appreciated that his standing (and the national cause) would be best served by his becoming a martyr, but what he wanted was imprisonment at home, not death. His lawyers said that the Crown could not alter the original death sentence to transportation without his consent; he expected, therefore, that the outcome would be 'a protracted imprisonment in the United Kingdom – a lot,' he later commented, 'which I contemplated without repining', with the prospect 'of being encircled by my family and friends'.[23] Early in June, the Lord Lieutenant sent the prisoners his decision to commute their sentences to transportation for life and they responded by challenging the legality of the change. However, a new law, controversially *ex post facto*, was rushed through Parliament to confirm the legal position.

---

20 Ibid. This was the 'retribution' described in Brendan O'Cathaoir, 'Smith O'Brien's Retribution', in *North Munster Antiquarian Journal*, xxvii (1985), 70. Grace O'Brien noted her brother's 'fit of excitement about bringing up his Portmanteau'. Smith O'Brien Papers, MS 441, f2304, Grace O'Brien to Anne Martineau, 18 October 1848. *Correspondence between Martin and O'Brien*, 1861, 32. **21** Duffy, *Young Ireland: Four Years of Irish History*, 251-4, 260-74, including O'Brien to Duffy, 10 February 1849. Duffy, *Life in Two Hemispheres*, i, 296-7, 322-35. **22** Home Office Papers, HO 79/9, Grey to Clarendon, 31 May 1849. **23** O'Brien Papers (AO), Journal for Mrs William S. O'Brien, 9 July 1849. Also in Smith O'Brien Papers, MS 3923. Ibid., MS 449, Tasmanian Journal, Part II, 19; Journal II, Part II, 17, entries for 23 November 1849, 6 August 1850. Davis, *To Solitude Consigned: The Tasmanian Journal*, 60, 140.

Epilogue

9 O'Brien, in chains, and Lucy: pottery figures at Mallow Castle in Cork

On 9 July, the four men were taken from their prison and despatched on the long journey to Van Diemen's Land (Tasmania). Lucy and the children were at Richmond for the sad parting. O'Brien wrote a plaintive poem for Lucy, in which he could not 'speak the word "Farewell", ... For something still my heart doth tell, That we shall meet again.'[24] Meagher recalled, referring to O'Brien, that,

> ... as the door of that vile vehicle in which we were hurried from our prison to the sloop-of-war was shut upon us, I saw that the face which had never quivered in any danger, and on which an unconquerable will had stamped the defiance of death in iron characters, was bathed in tears. It was but a moment before he had embraced his wife and children, and bade them goodbye – it might be for ever! This was the thought which ruled him then – and it ruled him as though he were the tenderest child that ever laid an aching head upon a mother's lap. His country should have witnessed that scene to know the depth of his love for Ireland, and what it cost him to be true to her. It gave me the measure of his severe greatness as a patriot and his sweet goodness as a man ...[25]

---

24 Papers relating to William Smith O'Brien, TCD MS 10611/2, Lucy and William: A Dialogue, written on 4 July 1849. **25** *Limerick Chronicle*, 11 August 1864, Meagher to Smith, 16 July 1864. See also Duffy, *Young Ireland: Four Years of Irish History*, 275.

After boarding the *Swift* at Kingstown (Dun Laoghaire), O'Brien asked Michael O'Farrell, a junior counsel, to take his 'last words to Lucy and [he] wrote five words in an envelope which I duly delivered'. In his journal he wrote of 'sorrows which cannot be soothed' and 'a deep undercurrent of bitter grief'. The *Swift* headed south and O'Brien noted, 'In the evening of this day we lost sight of Ireland. Shall I ever see it again?'[26]

O'Brien was obviously distressed by the thought of separation from his family, but his feelings about his country were more mixed. In his journal he lamented,

> Hope and exultation are converted into despondency & humiliation, so converted I fear through the precipitation of myself and my friends. Had we been contented still a little longer to brave the animadversions of those who imputed to us sluggishness and timidity. Had we been contented to allow ourselves to be carried to Prison under the suspension of the Habeas Corpus act instead of making an appeal to the country for which it was not prepared we should probably have been at this moment masters of the public opinion of Ireland instead of being exiles whose imprudence is condemned even by many who are attached to us and our cause. Yet the past ought not to be judged solely by the events which time developes [sic]. We did that which the nation at large ought to have done, or at all events which those who had professed our principles and goaded us forward ought to have sustained us in doing. We did that which a sense of our duty to our country enjoined. If therefore we failed in our attempt we have less reason to complain of indiscretion in ourselves than of excess of discretion in others ...

He regretted the 'want of union, energy & truth' of the people, 'their subserviency to a power which inflicts upon them wrongs & insults innumerable', and he expressed a desire to return only when Ireland was free of 'the disastrous life-destroying authority of the British Parliament'. He accepted that Ballingarry had a 'discouraging' impact, but he also mused upon the possibility that the 'trials' of the moment might work 'to refine and ennoble the character of Irish Patriotism rather than to extinguish it ... our sufferings will tend to strengthen the aspirations after nationality, to make future compromise impossible, to prove that the leaders were sincere and deemed Ireland's well being a prize worthy of great sacrifices & our example will generate an imitation which will one day be crowned with a happier success'.[27]

---

26 O'Brien Papers (AO), Journal for Mrs William S. O'Brien, 9, 10 July 1849. Young Ireland Papers of Michael R. O'Farrell, MS 9786, f27, Memoir of Michael O'Farrell, n.d. See also Clarendon Papers, Letterbook IV, Clarendon to Grey, 9 July 1849. 27 O'Brien Papers (AO), Journal for Mrs William S. O'Brien, 9, 10 July 1849. For similar, retrospective comment – including scornful remarks about those 'who when the moment for action arrived found it expedient to retreat rather than to fight' (to Dillon), and the claim that 'the fault was not mine but that of others' (Journal) – see Dillon Papers, MS 6456, f220, O'Brien to Dillon, 23 November 1852. Smith O'Brien Papers, MS 449, Tasmanian Journal, Journal II, Part II, 15-18, entry for 6 August 1850. Davis, *To Solitude Consigned: The Tasmanian Journal*, 138-41. *Correspondence between Martin and O'Brien*, 1861, 35.

On 27 October, O'Brien and the others reached Van Diemen's Land, the destination of about 500 Irish convicts each year and the setting for the new career of J.D. Balfe, rewarded for his services with the post of Assistant Comptroller of Convicts in Van Diemen's Land.[28] O'Brien's experiences there lie outside the remit of this study; that aspect of his story has, in any case, received plenty of attention from recent historians.[29] MacManus (1851), Meagher (1852), O'Donohoe (1852) and Mitchel (1853) all escaped to the United States. In 1850, O'Brien made an escape attempt, which failed, and he remained in Van Diemen's Land, distressed by the separation from home and family and occasionally troubled by bad health, until 1854. The British government then gave him (and Martin and O'Doherty) a conditional pardon; he could travel anywhere except to the United Kingdom, and he chose to live in Brussels. In 1856, Palmerston conceded a free pardon and O'Brien returned to Ireland. In his absence, Irish nationalism, demoralised by Ballingarry and deprived of its leaders, had ceased to exist as an effective force in Ireland. Peel's famous judgement that O'Brien had rendered a valuable service 'by making rebellion ridiculous' had some validity – even his old friend and fellow-repealer, Henry Grattan, had told the Commons that 'a vote of thanks should be passed to Mr Smith O'Brien, because, by his nonsensical exhibition and burlesque insurrection, he had made that species of high treason vulgar' – and the damaging impact of '48 extended to the repeal movement as a whole. English power and Irish weakness had been displayed with such clarity that few relished continuing the struggle. The campaign for tenant right dominated the politics of the 1850s and, as O'Brien observed, 'all parties' apparently 'agreed to lay aside for a time at least the agitation of the Repeal of the Union and the claims of a class now supersede the claims of a nation'.[30]

However, many of the Young Irelanders were bloodied but unbowed and they made the United States the new centre of anti-British campaigning. Among these men the failure of '48 bred not despair and abandonment but a determination to make rebellion work next time. Mitchel was publishing his powerful polemical works from 1854. In 1858, Stephens, who returned to Ireland two years before, established the Irish Republican Brotherhood in Dublin. O'Mahony and Doheny led its American equivalent, the Fenian Brotherhood, and 'Fenians' soon became the generic name for revolutionaries on both sides of the Atlantic. So, O'Brien's comrades, through Fenianism, continued to give a violent response to British rule. The long-term result was 1916. O'Brien's only role in this lay in the lessons he had provided in what should not be done. The Fenians certainly did not seek 'an imita-

---

28 Duffy, *Young Ireland: Four Years of Irish History*, 257 Cavanagh, *Memoirs of Meagher*, 197 Davis, *To Solitude Consigned: The Tasmanian Journal*, 17. 29 See Blanche M. Touhill, *William Smith O'Brien and His Irish Revolutionary Companions in Penal Exile* (Columbia, London, 1981). Richard Davis, *William Smith O'Brien: Ireland – 1848 – Tasmania* (Dublin, 1989). Davis, *To Solitude Consigned: The Tasmanian Journal*. Davis, *Revolutionary Imperialist*, 296-320. J.H. Cullen, *Young Ireland in Exile: The Story of the Men of '48 in Tasmania* (Dublin, Cork, 1928), 9-38. Thomas Keneally, *The Great Shame: A Story of the Irish in the Old World and the New* (London, 1998), 199-283. 30 *Hansard*, cvi, 393-4, 18 June 1849, Grattan. Smith O'Brien Papers, MS 449, Tasmanian Journal, Journal II, Part V, 22, entry for 31 March 1851. Davis, *To Solitude Consigned: The Tasmanian Journal*, 225.

tion' of his rising, instead working to create a secret revolutionary movement, organising in the army and police, avoiding dependence on the (hostile) Catholic clergy, acquiring aid from America, and aiming at a completely separate republic. Nor did his memory prove an inspiration. His failure was too complete and ignominious and he was denied the martyrdom that made Robert Emmet, author of a fiasco to rank with O'Brien's, a venerated figure. The Fenian flag captured at the Battle of Tallaght in 1867 said 'Remember Emmet'. By 1916 O'Brien was virtually forgotten. Irish nationalism did not disregard its failures – witness the veneration of Tone, Emmet and the Fenians – but O'Brien and his rising had no heroic aspect that could be recalled. O'Brien was in the blind spot that every movement, especially a national one, must use to hide its embarrassments.

Had O'Brien joined in reviving the national movement upon his return, his standing might have been a little different. Instead, he played only a peripheral role, showing reluctance to work with others. He refused to join 'any political associations in this country', having 'lost all confidence in public men'; he had known many who 'were brought into prominence by the part which they took in the advocacy of questions which they utterly abandoned as soon as they had satisfied the cravings of their own personal ambition or cupidity'. He 'resolved to confine my future efforts to the occasional publication of my own *individual* opinions'.[31] In other words, he restricted himself to writing public letters. He was invited in 1856 to stand as the Parliamentary candidate for Tipperary, scene of his desperate adventure, but family pressures and political disillusionment made him refuse. Having had a lesson in their futility, he opposed violent methods: in 1858 he rejected Fenianism and in 1861 derided Martin's enthusiasm for a French invasion, although he still advocated repeal and was bitterly hostile to Britain. In 1862, he challenged Sir Robert Peel to a duel after the former Prime Minister's son referred scathingly to 'the cabbage garden heroes of 1848'.[32] He travelled widely, to the United States, where he was received by President Buchanan and both Houses of Congress and welcomed by Irish Americans 'not as a failed revolutionary leader living in retirement, but as a major world statesman' (R. Davis), and to Canada, Spain, France, Austria, Hungary, Italy, Greece, Turkey and Poland. Lucy died in 1861, and a dispute over the trusteeship into which O'Brien had put Cahirmoyle in 1848 created acrimony with Lucius and Woronzow Greig, and possibly with his eldest son, Edward, so his final years were lonely and unhappy. He died at Bangor, in north Wales, on 18 June 1864. Although thousands turned out for his funeral, his family's opposition prevented a repetition of the massive political demonstration that nation-

---

31 O'Brien Papers (AO), Letter Box, Bundle 4, O'Brien to Moore, 25 December 1856, 10 January 1857.
32 O'Brien called Peel 'a *bully*' and 'too much of a *coward* by nature to expose yourself to personal hazard in support of your insolent language ... I shall be prepared in any part of Europe which you may select to determine the question whether or not you shall continue to insult with impunity my country and my fellow countrymen.' Smith O'Brien Papers, MS 447, f3262, O'Brien to Peel, 22 February 1862 (also in Dillon Papers, MS 6456, f337). Peel did not take up the challenge. *DEM*, 4, 5, 6, 8, 11 March 1862.

alists made of the return of MacManus's body to Ireland in 1861. He was buried beside Lucy in a quiet church graveyard at Kilronan, near Cahirmoyle.[33]

Apart from the small mausoleum at Kilronan, the physical reminders of O'Brien's life are few and far between. Cahirmoyle was rebuilt in the 1870s and (like Dromoland) is no longer in the family's hands. In Tasmania, two of the cottages O'Brien inhabited have been preserved and that at Port Arthur is a Smith O'Brien museum. In 1989, Cardinal O'Fiaich unveiled the National Flag monument at the Commons and Widow McCormack's, known locally as the 'Warhouse', was declared a national monument. The house lies in a state of disrepair and until recently the only visible indication of its importance was the sign above the door, saying 'Remember 48'. Taoiseach Bertie Ahern unveiled a plaque on the gable on 30 July 1998 and announced that the house would be purchased by the nation and made the site of a permanent exhibition to commemorate the events of 1848. A statue of O'Brien was erected before the Carlisle Building in D'Olier Street in 1870. It now stands in O'Connell Street, between the much grander monuments to the two undisputed giants of 19th century Ireland, O'Connell and Parnell. The relative dimensions are entirely appropriate. O'Brien could only be the victim and never the master of circumstance. He did not have the political stature to dictate the political agenda, and he lacked the flexibility and finesse to excel as an opportunist. His unbending disposition was evident from the early days of his political career, but it was only in 1848 that it became a fatal liability. His blind faith in the methods of 1782 caused the failure to prepare for revolution, his decision to take the field owed more to ideas of duty and honour than any realistic assessment of the position, and his actions in Tipperary have become a byword for incompetence. There was also much to admire, however. O'Brien was the most noble, honourable, principled and patriotic politician of his age. There were times when he provided all the qualities that O'Connell lacked; he was a truer nationalist than O'Connell even if he was a less effective national leader. But for 1848, he might have been remembered as a fine parliamentarian and public servant, and one of the more respected leaders of a formidable national movement. In 1848, he showed he was a better man than those who stood idly by. O'Brien deserves his statue in O'Connell Street. He should certainly be honoured as one of the brave men who spent themselves in the struggle for Irish freedom.

---

33 Davis, *To Solitude Consigned: The Tasmanian Journal*, 428-35.

Bibliography

MANUSCRIPTS

National Library of Ireland, Dublin
Bourke Papers
Thomas Davis Papers
Papers of Charles Gavan Duffy
Graham Papers (microfilm)
James Grattan's Notebooks and Personal Journals of Proceedings in Parliament
Hatherton Papers (microfilm)
Inchiquin Papers
Larcom Papers
Monteagle Papers
O'Connell Papers
O'Donoghue MSS
Narratives of the Rising of 1848 by R. O'Gorman, T.B. MacManus and J. Kavanagh
O'Loghlen Papers
Personal Narrative of John O'Mahony (typescript)
Journal of O'Neill Daunt
Smith O'Brien Papers
Thomas Trant's notes on Doheny
Wyse Papers
Young Ireland Papers of Michael R. O'Farrell

Royal Irish Academy, Dublin
Hudson Papers
Correspondence of R.R. Madden

Trinity College, Dublin
Dillon Papers
Journal of Charles Hart
Papers relating to William Smith O'Brien

O'Brien Papers in possession of Anthony O'Brien of Dublin

Bodleian Library, Oxford
Clarendon Papers

British Library, London
Peel Papers

Liverpool Record Office
Derby Papers

Public Record Office, London
Home Office Papers
Russell Papers
Wellington Papers

University of Southampton
Broadlands MSS

NEWSPAPERS

Clare Journal
Cork Examiner
Cork Standard
Dublin Evening Mail
Dublin Evening Post
Dublin Monitor
Freeman's Journal
Illustrated London News
Irishman
Irish Monthly
Irish Times
Limerick Chronicle
Limerick and Clare Examiner

Limerick Evening Post and Clare Sentinel
Limerick Reporter and Tipperary Vindicator
Limerick Standard
Limerick Star and Evening Post
Limerick Times
Munster News
Nation
Northern Whig
Pilot
Punch
The Times
United Irishman
Weekly News

CONTEMPORARY WORKS

Correspondence between John Martin and William Smith O'Brien relative to a French Invasion (Dublin, 1861).
Reports of the Parliamentary Committee of the Loyal National Repeal Association of Ireland (Dublin 1844).
Third General Report of the Parliamentary Committee of the Loyal National Repeal Association (Dublin, 1846).
T. Chisholme Anstey, *Case as to the legality of the arrest and imprisonment of William Smith O'Brien, Esquire, Member of Parliament for the County of Limerick, for disobeying an order of the House of Commons, with the opinion of counsel thereon* (London, 1846).
Valentine Lord Cloncurry, *Personal Recollections of the Life and Times, with Extracts from the Correspondence of Valentine Lord Cloncurry* (Dublin, 1849).
William Sharman Crawford, *The expediency and necessity of a local legislative body in Ireland, supported by a reference to facts and principles* (Newry, 1833).
—, *Observations on the Irish Tithe Bill passed by the House of Commons in the last session of the Imperial Parliament, submitted to the consideration of the Electors of Dundalk, in letters addressed to William Brett* (Dundalk, 1835).
Thomas Davis, *Report of the Parliamentary Committee of the Loyal National Repeal on the Tenants' Compensation Bill* (Dublin, 1845).
Rev. Philip Fitzgerald, *A Narrative of the Proceedings of the Confederates of '48, from the suspension of the Habeas Corpus Act, to their final dispersion at Ballingarry* (Dublin, 1868).
Rev. P. Fitzgerald, P.P., *Personal Recollections of the Insurrection at Ballingarry in July, 1848* (Dublin, 1861).
John George Hodges, *Report of the Trial of William Smith O'Brien, for High Treason, at the Special Commission for the Co. Tipperary, held at Clonmel, September and October, 1848* (Dublin, 1849).
D.O. Madden, *Ireland and its rulers since 1829* (London, 1843), 3 vols.
John Mitchel, *Jail Journal* (Dublin, n.d.).
—, *The Last Conquest of Ireland (Perhaps)* (Glasgow, London, n.d.).
William Smith O'Brien, *Considerations relative to the renewal of the East-India Company's Charter* (London, 1830).
—, *Education in Ireland* (London, 1839).
—, *Emigration. Speech by Mr William Smith O'Brien, M.P., on moving resolutions relative to emigration in the House of Commons on Tuesday the 2d of June 1840* (London, 1840).
—, *A Letter of William Smith O'Brien, Esq., M.P., in reply to the Letter of the Rev. T. O'Malley* (Dublin, 1844).
—, *Plan for the Relief of the Poor in Ireland, with observations on the English and Scotch Poor Laws, addressed to the landed proprietors of Ireland* (London, 1830).

—, *Reproductive Employment; a series of letters to the landed proprietors of Ireland: with a preliminary letter to Lord John Russell* (Dublin, 1847).
—, *Speech of William Smith O'Brien Esq MP on the Causes of Discontent in Ireland, delivered in the House of Commons, on the 4th July 1843* (Dublin, 1843).
—, *Thoughts upon Ecclesiastical Reform and Suggestions for the Conciliatory Adjustment of the Tithe Question* (Limerick, 1833).
John O'Connell, *Recollections and Experiences During a Parliamentary Career from 1833 to 1848* (London, 1849), 2 vols.
Thomas Trant, *1848. Reply to Father Fitzgerald's Pamphlet, entitled His 'Personal Recollections on the Insurrection at Ballingarry in July, 1848'. With Remarks on Irish Constabulary, and Hints to all Officials* (Dublin, 1862).
Thomas Wyse, *Education Reform; or, the Necessity of a National System of Education* (London, 1836), i, 2nd vol. not published.
—, *Historical Sketch of the Late Catholic Association of Ireland* (London, 1829), 2 vols.
—, *Speech on the extension and improvement of academical, collegiate, and university education in Ireland; at the meeting held for that purpose, at Cork, November 13, 1844. With notes* (Cork, 1845).
—, *Speech of Thomas Wyse, Esq., MP, on seconding the motion of W. S. O'Brien, Esq., MP, for Redress of Grievances (Ireland), in the House of Commons, on Tuesday July 4th, 1843* (Dublin, 1843).

OTHER WORKS

Patsy Adam-Smith, *Heart of Exile: Ireland, 1848* (Melbourne, 1986).
D.H. Akenson, *The Church of Ireland: Ecclesiastical Reform and Revolution, 1800-1885* (New Haven, London, 1971).
—, *The Irish Education Experiment* (London, Toronto, 1970).
Peter Allen, *The Cambridge Apostles: The Early Years* (Cambridge, 1978).
The Marquess of Anglesey, *One-Leg: The Life and Letters of Henry William Paget, first Marquess of Anglesey, K.G., 1768-1854* (London, 1961).
A. Aspinall (ed.), *Three Early Nineteenth Century Diaries* (London, 1952).
N. Atkinson, *Irish Education: A History Of Educational Institutions* (Dublin, 1969).
J.J. Auchmuty, *Irish Education: A Historical Survey* (Dublin, London, 1937).
—, *Sir Thomas Wyse, 1791-1862: The Life and Career of an Educator and Diplomat* (London, 1939).
Richard P.J. Batterberry, 'Sir Thomas Wyse and Mixed Education', in *Irish Ecclesiastical Record*, 5th Series, liii (June 1939), 561; liv (July 1939), 21.
—, *Sir Thomas Wyse, 1791-1862: An Advocate of a 'Mixed Education' Policy over Ireland* (Dublin, Belfast, Cork, 1939).
John Belchem, 'Republican spirit and military science: the "Irish brigade" and Irish-American nationalism in 1848', in *Irish Historical Studies*, xxix, no. 113 (May 1994), 44-64.
R.D. Collison Black, *Economic Thought and the Irish Question, 1817-1870* (Cambridge, 1960).
Edward Blackburne, *Life of the Rt. Hon. Francis Blackburne, late Lord Chancellor of Ireland* (London, 1874).
Sir Henry Blackhall and J. H. Whyte, 'Correspondence on O'Connell and the repeal party', in *Irish Historical Studies*, xii, no. 46 (Sept. 1960), 139-43.

W.J. Bradley, 'Sir Thomas Wyse, Irish Pioneer in Education Reform' (Ph.D., Trinity College Dublin, 1945).
G. Broeker, *Rural Disorder and Police Reform in Ireland, 1812-36* (London, 1970).
Lord Brougham, *The Life and Times of Henry Lord Brougham, written by himself* (Edinburgh, London, 1871), 3 vols.
E.P. Brynn, 'A Political History of the Church of Ireland, 1801-1845' (M. Litt., Trinity College Dublin, 1968).
David N. Buckley, *James Fintan Lalor: Radical* (Cork, 1990).
H.L. Bulwer, *The Life and Times of Henry John Temple, Viscount Palmerston: with selections from his diaries and correspondence* (London, 1870, 1874), 3 vols.
Michael Cavanagh, *Memoirs of Gen. Thomas Francis Meagher* (Worcester, Mass., 1892).
G. Kitson Clark, *Peel and the Conservative Party: a study in party politics, 1832-1841* (London, 1964).
Randall Clarke, 'The Relations between O'Connell and the Young Irelanders', in *Irish Historical Studies*, iii, no. 9 (March 1942), 18-30.
D. Close, 'The formation of a two-party alignment in the House of Commons between 1832 and 1841', in *English Historical Review*, lxxxiv (April 1969), 257-77.
R.V. Comerford, *Charles J. Kickham. A Study in Irish nationalism and literature* (Dublin, 1979).
—, *The Fenians in Context: Irish Politics and Society 1848-82* (Dublin, 1985).
M.D. Condon, 'The Irish Church and the Reform Ministries', in *Journal of British Studies*, iii, no. 2 (May 1964), 120-42.
Nuala Costello, *John MacHale, Archbishop of Tuam* (Dublin, London, 1939).
Percy Cradock, *Recollections of the Cambridge Union, 1815-1939* (Cambridge, 1953).
J.H. Cullen, *Young Ireland in Exile: The Story of the Men of '48 in Tasmania* (Dublin, Cork, 1928), 9-38.
Mary E. Daly, *The Famine in Ireland* (Dublin, 1986).
Richard Davis, *Revolutionary Imperialist: William Smith O'Brien 1803-1864* (Dublin, Darlinghurst, 1998).
— (ed.), *'To Solitude Consigned': The Tasmanian Journal of William Smith O'Brien, 1849-1853* (Sydney, 1995).
—, *William Smith O'Brien: Ireland – 1848 – Tasmania* (Dublin, 1989).
—, *The Young Ireland Movement* (Dublin, 1987).
Richard and Marianne Davis (eds.), *The Rebel in his Family: Selected Papers of William Smith O'Brien* (Cork, 1998).
Richard Deacon, *The Cambridge Apostles* (London, 1985).
John Devoy, *Recollections of an Irish Rebel* (Shannon, 1969).
Charles R. Dod, *Electoral Facts, from 1832 to 1852* (London, 1852).
Michael Doheny, *The Felon's Track* (Dublin, 1914).
Sir Charles Gavan Duffy, *My Life in Two Hemispheres* (London, 1898), 2 vols.
—, *Thomas Davis: The Memoirs of an Irish Patriot, 1840-1846* (London, 1890).
—, *Young Ireland* (London, 1880).
—, *Young Ireland: A Fragment of Irish History, 1840-1845* (Dublin, 1884).
—, *Young Ireland, Part II: Four Years of Irish History, 1845-1849* (Dublin, 1887).
R.D. Edwards and T.D. Williams (eds.), *The Great Famine: Studies in Irish History, 1845-52* (Dublin, 1956).
W.J. Fitzpatrick (ed.), *Correspondence of Daniel O'Connell, The Liberator, edited with notices of his life and times* (London, 1888), 2 vols.

W.J. Fitzpatrick, *The Life, Times, and Correspondence of the Right Rev. Dr Doyle, Bishop of Kildare and Leighlin* (Dublin, 1890), 2 vols.

—, *The Life, Times, and Cotemporaries of Lord Cloncurry* (Dublin, 1855).

—, *Memoirs of Richard Whately, Archbishop of Dublin, with a Glance at his Cotemporaries and Times* (London, 1864), 2 vols.

R.F. Foster, *Modern Ireland, 1600-1972* (London, 1988)

—, *Paddy and Mr Punch: Connections in Irish and English History* (London, 1993).

Norman Gash, *Sir Robert Peel: The Life of Sir Robert Peel after 1830* (London, New York, 1986).

G.P. Gooch (ed.), *The Later Correspondence of Lord John Russell, 1840-1878* (London, 1925), 2 vols.

A.H. Graham, 'The Lichfield House Compact, 1835', in *Irish Historical Studies*, xii, no. 47 (March 1961), 209-25.

Arthur Griffith (ed.), *Meagher of the Sword: Speeches of Thomas Francis Meagher in Ireland, 1846-1848* (Dublin, 1916).

Denis Gwynn, 'O'Connell, Davis and the Colleges Bill', in *Irish Ecclesiastical Record*, lxix (1947), 561, 668, 767, 957, 1051; lxx (1948), 17.

—, *O'Connell, Davis and the Colleges Bill* (Cork, 1948).

—, *The O'Gorman Mahon: Duellist, Adventurer and Politician* (London, 1934).

—, 'William Smith O'Brien', in *Studies*, xxxv (Dec. 1946), 448-58.

—, 'Smith O'Brien and Young Ireland', in *Studies*, xxxvi (March 1947), 29-39.

—, 'Smith O'Brien and the "Secession"', in *Studies*, xxxvi (June 1947), 129-40.

—, 'The Rising of 1848', in *Studies*, xxxvii (March 1948), 7-17.

—, 'The Rising of 1848', in *Studies*, xxxvii (June 1948), 149-60.

—, *Young Ireland and 1848* (Cork, 1949).

G.A. Hayes-McCoy, *A History of Irish Flags from earliest times* (Dublin, 1979).

J.M. Hone, 'William Smith O'Brien', in *Dublin Magazine*, xii, no. 3 (July-Sept. 1937), 37-46.

K.T. Hoppen, *Elections, Politics and Society in Ireland, 1832-1885* (Oxford, 1984).

—, 'Landlords, Society and Electoral Politics in Mid-Nineteenth Century Ireland', in *Past and Present*, no. 75 (May 1977), 62-93.

—, 'Politics, the Law, and the nature of the Irish electorate, 1832-50', in *English Historical Review*, lxxxxii, no. 365 (Oct., 1977), 746-76.

—, 'Roads to Democracy: Electioneering and Corruption in Nineteenth-Century England and Ireland', in *History*, lxxxi, no. 264 (October, 1996).

The Earl of Ilchester (ed.), *Elizabeth, Lady Holland to her son, 1821-1845* (London, 1946).

Lawrence C. Jennings, *France and Europe in 1848: A Study of French Foreign Affairs in Time of Crisis* (Oxford, 1973).

Maurice Denham Jephson, *An Anglo-Irish Miscellany: Some Records of the Jephsons of Mallow* (Dublin, 1964).

Helen O'Donovan Johnstone, 'France and Ireland in 1848' (M.A., University College Galway, 1988).

John Francis Kavanagh, 'William Smith O'Brien and Young Ireland, 1843-1848' (Ph.D., University of Maine, 1973).

Robert Kee, *The Green Flag: The Most Distressful Country* (London, 1972).

James Kelly, *That Damned Thing Called Honour: Duelling in Ireland, 1570-1860* (Cork, 1995).

Thomas Keneally, *The Great Shame: A Story of the Irish in the Old World and the New* (London, 1998).

Donal A. Kerr, *'A Nation of Beggars'? Priests, People, and Politics in Famine Ireland, 1846-1852* (Oxford, 1994).
—, *Peel, Priests and Politics* (Oxford, 1982).
—, *The Catholic Church and the Famine* (Dublin, 1996).
Colm Kerrigan, *Father Mathew and the Irish temperance movement* (Cork, 1992).
Christine Kinealy, *This Great Calamity: The Irish Famine, 1845-52* (Dublin, 1994).
A.D. Kriegel (ed.), *The Holland House Diaries, 1831-1840* (London, 1977).
A. de Lamartine, *Histoire de la Révolution de 1848* (Paris, 1849).
Alphonse de Lamartine, *History of the French Revolution of 1848*, trans. (London, 1849).
D. Large, 'The House of Lords and Ireland in the age of Peel, 1832-50', in *Irish Historical Studies*, ix, no. 36 (Sept. 1955), 367-99.
G. Lyne, 'The General Association of Ireland, 1836-7' (M.A., University College Dublin, 1968).
F.S.L. Lyons and R.A. J. Hawkins (eds.), *Ireland under the Union: Varieties of Tension. Essays in Honour of T.W. Moody* (Oxford, 1980).
Thomas G. McAllister, *Terence Bellew McManus, 1811(?)-1861. A Short Biography* (Maynooth, 1972).
L.J. McCaffrey, *Daniel O'Connell and the Repeal Year* (Lexington, 1966).
W.J. McCormack, *Sheridan Le Fanu and Victorian Ireland* (Dublin, 1991).
Oliver MacDonagh, *The Emancipist: Daniel O'Connell, 1830-47* (London, 1989).
—, *Ireland: the Union and its aftermath* (London, 1977).
—, 'The Politicization of the Irish Catholic Bishops, 1800-1850', in *Historical Journal*, xviii, no. 1 (1975), 37-53.
R.B. McDowell, *Public Opinion and Government Policy in Ireland, 1801-1846* (London, 1952).
Angus MacIntryre, *The Liberator: Daniel O'Connell and the Irish Party, 1830-1847* (London, 1965).
J.F. McLennan, *Memoir of Thomas Drummond, Under Secretary to the Lord Lieutenant of Ireland, 1835 to 1840* (Edinburgh, 1867).
M.J. MacManus (ed.), *Thomas Davis and Young Ireland* (Dublin, 1945).
James Maher (ed.), *The Valley near Slievenamon: A Kickham Anthology* (n.p., 1942).
Sir Herbert Maxwell, *The Life and Letters of George William Frederick, fourth Earl of Clarendon* (London, 1913), 2 vols.
John N. Molony, *A Soul Came into Ireland. Thomas Davis, 1814-1845: A Biography* (Dublin, 1995).
T.W. Moody, 'The Irish University Question of the Nineteenth Century', in *History*, xliii (1958), 90-109.
Chris Morash and Richard Hayes (eds.), *'Fearful Realities': New Perspectives on the Famine* (Dublin, 1996).
John Morisy, *A Wreath for the O'Brien Statue* (Dublin, 1871).
George Nicholls, *A History of the Irish Poor Law* (London, 1856).
E.R. Norman, 'The Maynooth Question of 1845', in *Irish Historical Studies*, xv, no. 60 (Sept. 1967), 407-37.
The Marquis of Normanby, *A Year of Revolution: from a Journal kept in Paris in 1848* (London, 1857), 2 vols.
Kevin B. Nowlan, *The Politics of Repeal: A Study in the Relations between Great Britain and Ireland, 1841-50* (London, 1965).
Donough O'Brien, *History of the O'Briens from Brian Boroimhe, AD 1000 to AD 1945* (London, 1949).

Grania R. O'Brien, *These My Friends and Forebears: The O'Briens of Dromoland* (Whitegate, Co. Clare, 1991).
Ivar O'Brien, *O'Brien of Thomond: The O'Briens in Irish History, 1500-1865* (Chichester, 1986).
R.B. O'Brien, *Fifty Years of Concessions to Ireland, 1831-1881* (London, 1883-5), 2 vols.
—, *Thomas Drummond, Under-Secretary in Ireland, 1835-40: Life and Letters* (London, 1889).
Leon O'Broin, *Charles Gavan Duffy: Patriot and Statesman. The Story of Charles Gavan Duffy, 1816-1903* (Dublin, 1967).
Brendan O'Cathaoir, *John Blake Dillon, Young Irelander* (Dublin, 1990).
—, 'Smith O'Brien's Retribution', in *North Munster Antiquarian Journal*, xxvii (1985), 70.
Maurice R. O'Connell (ed.), *The Correspondence of Daniel O'Connell* (Dublin, 1972-80), 8 vols.
— (ed.), *Education, Church and State* (Dublin, 1992).
P. O'Donoghue, 'Causes of the Opposition to Tithes, 1830-38', in *Studia Hibernica*, no. 5 (1965), 7-28.
—, 'Opposition to Tithe Payment in 1830-31', in *Studia Hibernica*, no. 6 (1966), 69-98.
—, 'Opposition to Tithe Payment in 1832-33', in *Studia Hibernica*, no. 12 (1972), 77-108.
—, 'The Tithe War, 1830-1833' (M.A., University College Dublin, 1961).
Cormac O'Grada, *The Great Irish Famine* (London, 1989).
John O'Leary, *Recollections of Fenians and Fenianism* (London, 1896), 2 vols.
W.J. O'Neill Daunt, *Eighty-five Years of Irish History, 1800-1885* (London, 1888).
—, *A Life Spent for Ireland, being Selections from the Journals of the late W. J. O'Neill Daunt, edited by his daughter* (London, 1896).
Bernard O'Reilly, *John Mac Hale, Archbishop of Tuam, His Life, Times, and Correspondence* (New York, Cincinnati, 1890), 2 vols.
Peter O'Shaughnessy (ed.), *The Gardens of Hell: John Mitchel in Van Diemen's Land, 1850-1853* (Kenthurst, 1988).
T.F. O'Sullivan, *The Young Irelanders* (Tralee, 1944).
G. O'Tuathaigh, *Ireland before the Famine, 1798-1848* (Dublin, 1972).
Stanley H. Palmer, *Police and Protest in England and Ireland 1780-1850* (Cambridge, 1988).
C.S. Parker (ed.), *Life and Letters of Sir James Graham, second Baronet of Netherby, 1792-1861* (London, 1907), 2 vols.
—, *Sir Robert Peel, from his private papers* (London, 1891-99), 3 vols.
Cyril Pearl, *The Three Lives of Gavan Duffy* (Kensington, New South Wales, 1979).
D.N. Petler, 'Ireland and France in 1848', in *Irish Historical Studies*, xxiv, no. 96 (Nov. 1985).
John M. Prest, *Lord John Russell* (London, 1972).
Gordon N. Ray (ed.), *The Letters and Private Papers of William Makepeace Thackeray* (London, 1945).
Rollo Russell (ed.), *Early Correspondence of Lord John Russell, 1805-40* (London, 1913), 2 vols.
Desmond Ryan, *The Fenian Chief: A Biography of James Stephens* (Dublin, 1967).
L.C. Sanders (ed.), *Lord Melbourne's Papers* (London, 1889).
John Saville, *1848: The British State and the Chartist Movement* (Cambridge, 1987).
Ellen Shannon-Mangan, *James Clarence Mangan: A Biography* (Dublin, 1996).
Kieran Sheedy, *The Clare Elections* (Dublin, 1993).
Robert Sloan, 'O'Connell's liberal rivals in 1843', in *Irish Historical Studies*, xxx, no. 117 (May 1996).

R.C. Sloan, 'Irish issues and Unionist MPs, 1832-1846' (Ph.D., University of Glasgow, 1982).
Alexander Somerville, *Letters from Ireland during the Famine of 1847*, edited by K.D.M. Snell (Dublin, 1994).
Lytton Strachey and Roger Fulford (eds.), *The Greville Memoirs, 1814-1860* (London, 1938), 7 vols.
A.M. Sullivan, *New Ireland: Political Sketches and Personal Reminiscences* (London, 1878), 2 vols.
W.M. Thackeray, *Ballads* (London, 1855).
David Thomson with Moyra McGusty (eds.), *The Irish Journals of Elizabeth Smith, 1840-1850* (Oxford, 1980).
Blanche M. Touhill, *William Smith O'Brien and His Irish Revolutionary Companions in Penal Exile* (Columbia, London, 1981).
Charles Chenevix Trench, *The Great Dan: A Biography of Daniel O'Connell* (London, 1986).
Glyndon G. Van Deusen, *The Jacksonian Era: 1828-1848* (New York, 1959).
W.E. Vaughan (ed.), *A New History of Ireland: V – Ireland under the Union, 1, 1801-70* (Oxford, 1989).
Aubrey de Vere, *Recollections of Aubrey de Vere* (New York, London, 1897).
Terence de Vere White, *The Road of Excess* (Dublin, 1945).
Terence de Vere White, *The Story of the Royal Dublin Society* (Tralee, 1955).
Hugh Weir, *O'Brien People and Places* (Whitegate, Co. Clare, 1988).
—, 'William Smith O'Brien's Secret Family', in *The Other Clare*, xx (April 1996), 55-6.
E.J. Whateley, *Life and Correspondence of Richard Whateley, D.D., late Archbishop of Dublin* (London, 1866), 2 vols.
J.H. Whyte, 'Daniel O'Connell and the repeal party', in *Irish Historical Studies*, xi, no. 44 (Sept. 1959), 297-316.
Cecil Woodham Smith, *The Great Hunger: Ireland 1845-9* (London, 1962).
Winifrede M. Wyse, *Notes on Education Reform in Ireland during the first half of the 19th century: compiled from speeches, letters, &c, contained in the Unpublished Memoirs of the Rt. Hon. Sir Thomas Wyse, KCB* (Waterford, 1901).
Phillip Ziegler, *Melbourne: A biography of William Lamb, 2nd Viscount Melbourne* (London, 1976).

Index

absentee landlords, 40, 45, 148, 176, 178, 182, 183, 184
Adam-Smith, Patsy, 81
Affre, Archbishop Denys-Auguste, 237
Agricultural Society, 117n48
Ahern, Bertie, 9, 303
Albert, Alexandre Martin, 214n53
Albert (Prince), 103
Allen, Peter, 15
Althorp, Lord, 26
Anstey, Thomas Chisholm, 192, 198, 223
Anti-Tory Association, 39-41, 43
Antrim, 194
Apostles, 14-5
arms bill (1843), 85-6, 93-5, 105, 108
Ashley, Lord, 67n107
Australia, 75, 208
Austria, 222, 302

Bagenalstown (Muine Bheag), 250
Balfe, John Donnellan, 224, 235, 240, 241, 281, 283-4, 301
Ballingarry, 9, 237, 258, 261-6, 267- 82 *passim*, 286, 296, 300, 301
Ballinkeele, 246, 247
Ballyneal, 256
Bangor, 302
Barrett, Edward, 57
Barrett, Richard, 54, 103, 150
Barrow (river), 250
Barry, Michael John, 114, 120, 121; and O'Brien's imprisonment in 1846, 150, 153, 154; 157, 161, 168, 192
Belfast, 63, 79, 118, 119, 128, 137; visit of Confederates in 1847, 194-6; 197, 224
Belgium, 103, 108
Bentham, Jeremy, 76
Bentinck, Lord George, 148, 182, 183, 184
Berlin, 209
Bernal, Ralph, 98
Bernard, Lord, 180
Birmingham, Father James, 237
Blackburne, Francis, 239n6, 294

Blakeney, Sir Edward, 230, 267, 289
Board of Works, 177-8
Bonaparte, Napoleon, 200, 285
Borrisokane, 237
Boru, Brian, 11, 105, 130, 191, 199, 243
Botany Bay, 223
Boulagh, see Commons
Bourgoin, Eugene, 23
Bourgoin, Madame, 23
Bourke, Sir Richard, 86
Brady, Maziere, 177, 228
Brennan, Joseph, 244
Brew, Jane, 23, 53
Brignot, Madame, 23
Bristol, 72, 138
British Legion in Spain, 54
Broderick, Edward, 150
Browne, Bishop George Joseph, 169
Browne, Robert Dillon, 116-17, 128, 198, 202
Brussels, 301
Buchanan, James, 302
Buckland, William, 84
Burdett, Sir Francis, 18
Butt, Isaac, 186, 229
Byrne, Father Patrick, 253, 256-7, 269

Cahill, Father William, 259, 261
Cahirmoyle, 12, 14, 23; possession taken in 1832, 33-5, 39; 47, 53, 54, 58-9, 63, 70, 72, 76, 81, 89, 104, 107, 109, 110, 116, 123, 129, 142, 143, 148; in 1846, 165-6, 172, 177; 192, 202-3, 225; refuge in 1848, 234, 235, 238; 246, 268, 283, 297, 302, 303
Callan, 253, 276
Campbell, Lord, 222
Canada, 35, 67, 75, 76-7, 87, 302
Cane, Robert, 252-3
Cantwell, James, 257, 272
Cantwell, Bishop John, 128
Carew, Robert, 100
Carlisle Building, 303
Caroline, 76-7
Carrick-on-Suir, 253-69 *passim*, 275, 281

312

Index

Carroll, John, 280-1
Cashel, 43, 253, 256-7, 297
Castletown, 239
Cambridge Union, 29
Catholic Association, 17, 18, 19
Catholic clergy, state payment, 27, 29, 37, 38, 40, 45, 46, 50-1, 54, 61, 70
Catholic Emancipation, 14,17, 18, 19, 20, 25, 29, 31, 43, 214
Caulfield, Henry, 118
Cavanagh, Michael, 257, 266-7
Central Society of Education, 62-3, 73
Chandos, Lord, 26, 30
Chapman, Benjamin, 95n92
Chapman, Montague, 183
charitable bequests, 116-18, 128
Charlemont, Lord, 118
Charles II, 285
Chartism, 73-4, 198, 205-6, 215-6, 223-4, 231, 232
Chiswick, 71
Christian Brothers, 62
Church of Ireland, 13, 14; O'Brien's reform proposals, 35-9; 44, 46, 48-50, 52, 60, 61, 90, 92, 96, 99, 101
Citizens Club, Limerick, 75-6
Clare, 11, 16, 17, 18-21, 26, 28, 29, 32, 33, 34, 38, 39, 40, 44, 50-1, 88, 159, 185, 192n113
Clare Journal, 16, 20-1
Clare, Lord, 57
Clarendon, Lord, 197, 198; and revolution in France, 211, 213, 216, 217-18, 221; 222, 224, 225, 226-8, 229-31, 232-4, 235, 237; decision to coerce, 240-1, 242, 244, 246-7; 249, 252, 254, 261, 264n87, 267, 277, 278, 281; arrest and trial of O'Brien, 283, 284-5, 287, 291, 293, 296, 298
Clements, Lord, 94-5, 100-1
Cloncurry, Lord, 69, 70, 186, 212
Cloney, Thomas, 250
Clonmel, 159, 238, 254, 256, 260, 270, 275, 291, 293, 295, 298
Clontarf, 11, 104, 105, 111, 115, 130
clubs, 193-4, 196, 202, 205, 208, 228, 229, 230; growth in May-July 1848, 231, 233, 234, 235, 237, 238; 239, 240, 241, 242-3, 244, 245, 246, 247, 249, 252-3; in Carrick, 254-6; 257, 258, 266-7, 287
Cochrane, A.D.W.R.B., 97n97
coercion in 1846 (Protection of Life bill), 148, 156, 157, 158
coercion in 1847-8 (Crime and Outrage bill), 197-8, 201, 202, 244, 253
coercion in 1848 (Crown and Government Security bill), 222-3, 229
coercion in 1848 (Habeas Corpus suspension bill), 246-7
Coll, Father Thomas, 71
colleges, 44, 63-5, 91, 124, 127-31, 134-7, 139-40, 142-3, 146

Colonial Society, 73
Colquhoun, J.C., 135
Comeragh mountains, 255
Comerford, Father Richard, 269
Commons, The, 272, 274, 280, 281, 303
Conciliation Hall, 105, 108, 123, 124, 125, 135, 144, 157, 165, 168, 170, 171, 189, 193
Confederation, *see* Irish Confederation
Convention Act, 214
Conway, George, 131
Coote, Chidley, 57
Corcoran, Father Daniel, 259, 261, 267-8
Cork, 30, 63-5, 72, 113, 118, 128-9, 133, 134, 137, 184; in 1847, 188, 192, 193-4, 196; 198, 227, 229; O'Brien's visit in 1848, 239-40, 242, 243; 244, 247, 250, 253, 299
Cork Examiner, 240n8
Corn Exchange, 113n31, 170
corn laws, 66-7, 133, 142, 143-4, 145, 148, 156
Corofin, 33
Costelloe, Father Thomas O'Brien, 45, 50, 52, 56; 1839 crisis, 68-71; 81, 103, 152; Limerick election in 1847, 188-92
Council of Three Hundred, 204, 214, 216, 228, 255
County Club, Limerick, 41, 45, 50, 52, 56; 1839 crisis, 69-71; 77-8; Limerick election in 1847, 188-91
Cracow uprising, 182
Crawford, William Sharman, 49, 52, 90, 118, 121, 182, 194, 200
Crean, Martin, 149, 157
Creed of *The Nation*, 228
Cumberland, the Lake District, 190

D'Arcy, Burton, 32
Davis Club, 193
Davis, Richard, 52, 85n45, 114, 201n13, 302
Davis, Thomas, 9, 111, 114, 115-23, 125, 126; the colleges dispute of 1845, 128-32, 133-7, 138; 139-42, 143, 157, 204
Dawson, George Robert, 80
de la Beche, Henry Thomas, 84
de Vere, Aubrey, 208
de Vere, Stephen, 80, 208n34
Deacon, Richard, 15
Derrynane, 142
Desmond Club, 194
D'Esterre, John, 20n45
Devon Commission, 126
Dillon, John Blake, 139, 171, 173, 174, 185, 191, 205, 207, 209; Address to People of Ireland, 210-1; 212, 215, 217, 230, 232, 233n124, 235, 244, 245-6; the decision to rebel, 247-50; 253, 254-8, 259, 261, 263, 264, 267n95, 268; at Killenaule, 270-1; at the Commons, 272-4; 281, 283, 284; defends O'Brien, 285-7; 288, 290, 295, 297, 301
Dobbyn, James Stevenson, 242, 244

Doheny, Michael, 115, 198-9, 207, 216n62; the rising, 253, 254-5, 256, 257, 258, 259, 262-3, 265, 267, 269, 270; at the Commons, 272-3; 277, 278, 281, 284, 285, 288-9, 297
D'Olier Street, 185, 217
Donegal, 171, 190, 192, 193
Dowling, John, 191
Down, 125, 194, 200
Doyle, Daniel, 193
Doyle, Bishop James, 35, 36, 38, 63
Drogheda, 243, 244
Dromoland, 11, 12, 14, 20, 23, 28-9, 33, 34, 39, 40, 47, 52, 58, 79, 81, 89, 106, 107, 124, 232, 303
Dublin Evening Mail, 84n43, 87, 88-9, 141, 145, 179, 183
Dublin Evening Post, 95, 237
Dublin Monitor, 80-1, 118
Duffy, Charles Gavan, 48n20, 102, 111, 113, 115, 120-1, 122, 131-2, 141, 143-4, 146-7, 152; O'Brien's ally against O'Connell (1846-7), 153, 157, 158, 159-63, 166-75, 176, 178-9, 181, 184-5, 186, 187, 188, 192, 193, 194, 198; physical force split in 1848, 210-18; 222, 224, 228, 229, 232, 234, 235, 236; advocate of revolution, 238-68, 272, 275n106, 279, 283, 286, 288-9, 297-8
Dundalk, 49, 52
Dungarvan, 158-9, 162, 164, 166
Dunne, Francis Plunket, 208-9
Dunraven, Lord, 35
East India Company, 24
education, 27, 29-30, 39, 44, 62-5, 73, 77, 90-1, 92, 124, 127-31, 137, 178
'82 Club, 125, 129, 153, 168, 260, 281
Eliot, Lord, 80-1, 85
Ellenborough, Lord, 80
Elphin, 169
emigration, 35, 39, 55, 57, 178
Emmet, Robert, 9, 11, 302
Ennis, 16-18, 19, 26, 27, 28-9, 30, 31-3, 39, 72, 79, 161
Enniscorthy, 246, 247, 250
Erne, Lord, 117
Estcourt, Thomas, 149-50, 155
Evening Freeman, 252
Ewart, William, 77

Famine, 142, 143, 148-9, 154, 169; O'Brien's activities, 176-9; 182, 184, 187, 197
Farrinrory, 276, 282
federalism, 118-21, 125
Felon, 241
Fenian Brotherhood, 286, 301-2
Fergus (river), 11, 28, 29, 32
Ferguson, Sir Robert, 79-80
Ferguson, Samuel, 186
Fermanagh, 125
Ffrench, Lord, 87
Fitzgerald, Francis, 293

Fitzgerald, James, 26
Fitzgerald, Father Philip, 258, 264, 265, 272, 277, 278, 279-80
Fitzgerald, R.A., 123

Fitzgerald, Vesey, 17, 19, 20, 28, 31
Fitzgibbon, Richard, 25, 41, 42, 56-8, 78, 190
Fontenoy, 214, 221
Forster, W.E., 177
Fox, S. Lane, 85-6, 95
France, 39, 127, 142; France in 1848, 209-10, 211, 212, 214, 216, 217-21, 222, 224, 236-7, 247; 248, 284, 293, 302
Franklin, Benjamin, 102
Freeman's Journal, 86, 111, 123, 149, 216, 217, 222, 236, 247, 252-3, 278, 283, 290

Gabbett, Joseph, 33-5
Galway, 128-9, 137, 185, 283, 298
Gascoyne, Isaac, 27, 28
Gash, Norman, 148n66
General Association, 49, 54, 56
general election, 1832, 43
general election, 1835, 41-2, 45
general election, 1837, 55-8
general election, 1841, 77-8
general election, 1847, 187, 188-93
Geological Society, 84
George's Street, 35, 226
Germany, 103
Gibbons, James, 200
Gladstone, William E., 96
Glasgow, 193, 247
Globe and Traveller, 20
Gluckman, Leon, 292
Gort, Lord, 39
Graham, Sir James, 87-8, 93-4, 96, 97, 103, 127, 128, 141, 156
Graiguenamanagh, 250, 252
Grand Jury reform, 30, 32, 37, 92
Grangemockler, 256, 269
Grattan Club, 193
Grattan, Henry, 11, 126, 198
Grattan, Henry (jnr.), 43, 102, 198, 301
Grattan, James, 27, 43, 60-1, 62, 67, 68
Gray, John, 86, 123, 236
Great Harborough, 12
Greece, 302
Greenough, George Bellas, 84
Gregory (William) clause, 182, 183
Greig, Woronzow, 20-1, 28, 73, 81, 104n121, 155, 232, 302
Greville, Charles, 211n44, 221, 227, 284
Grey, Sir George, 217, 221-2, 232, 241, 247, 283, 287, 291, 296, 298
Griffin, William, 69-71, 135, 188-9, 193-4, 196
Grote, George, 50, 54
Guizot, François, 76, 222
Gwynn, Denis, 245n28

Index 315

Habeas Corpus, 241, 245, 246-7, 255, 287, 300
Halpin, Thomas M., 210n41, 225, 231, 235, 266
Hamburg, 104
Hamilton, George A., 179-80, 183
Hancock, John, 102
Hannibal, 285
Hansard, 73, 94
Hardinge, Sir Henry, 54
Harris, Charles, 84
Harris, Jenny, 138
Harrow School, 12
Hart (Dillon), Adelaide, 285
Hart, Charles, 283, 286n133
Haughton, James, 173
Hayes-McCoy, G.A., 224n91
Haymarket theatre, 78
Helps, Sir Arthur, 15
Henderson, Edward, 48
Henry VIII, 11
Hercules Street, 194-7, 224
Herzen, Alexander, 209
Heytesbury, Lord, 127, 153
Hill, Lord Arthur Edwin, 125
Hodder, Joseph, 81-2
Hogan, John, 142
Hogan, Father Maurice, 71
Holland, 108
Hollywood, Edward, 214n53
Holmes, Robert, 157-8
Hull, 104
Hulme, ——, 283
Hume, Joseph, 68, 124-5, 138
Hungarian Diet, 104
Hungary, 302
Hutt, William, 57

Inchiquin, Lord, 11
income tax, 80
Inglis, Sir Robert, 128
Irish Confederation, 169, 180-2, 184-7, 188, 192-4, 196; physical force split in 1848, 199-208; and French Revolution of 1848, 210-7; 224, 225, 226-7, 228, 229-34, 235-7
Irish Council, 186-7, 189
Irish language, 125
Irish League, 235-6, 243, 246, 252
Irish Party (1846), 168-9, 171
Irish Party (1847), 179-80, 183-4, 186
Irish Republican Brotherhood, 301
Isabella, queen of Spain, 54
Italians, the, 221
Italy, 237, 246, 302

Jackson, Joseph, D., 59, 79
Jail Journal, 231, 286
Jamaica, 53, 67-8, 71, 112, 145, 152
Jephson (Norreys), Denham, 51, 90, 106, 247, 284
June Days (Paris), 219, 237, 247

Kavanagh, John, 275-6, 278
Kavanagh (of Ballingarry), John, 265
Keevan, Bridget, 23, 53
Kemble, J.M., 14
Kenmare, 239
Kennedy, Bishop Patrick, 237, 272
Kennington Common, 223
Kensington Gardens, 101
Kenyon, Father John, 187, 189, 199, 232, 237, 253, 269, 272, 289
Kerr, Donal A., 236-7
Kerry, 142, 171, 239
Kickham, Charles, 258-9, 263
Kildare Place Society, 27, 29
Kilburn, 20-1
Kilkee, 159
Kilkenny, 36, 64, 68, 89, 243, 246; unready to rebel, 249-54; 257, 259, 260, 269, 275, 280, 283, 290
Killala, 247
Killaloe, 237, 272
Killarney, 142, 158
Killenaule, 258, 268-71, 274, 275n104
Killiney, 228
Kilmainham, 284, 291-2, 296
Kilnamanagh mountains, 283
Kilronan, 303
Kilrush, 159, 161, 162
King's County, 80
King's Inns, Dublin, 14
King's Island, 39
Kingstown (Dun Laoghaire), 300

Labouchere, Henry, 144, 182
Lacken, Ellen, 274
Lalor, James Fintan, 199-200
Lamartine, Alphonse de, 211, 218-21, 224
land question, 82, 90, 92, 99-100, 110; in 1845, 125, 126; 176, 178, 182, 184, 199, 208, 225, 227, 301
Lane, Denny, 134
Lascelles, William, 61, 97n97
Lawless, Edward, 69
Lawlor, Denis Shine, 239
Lawlor, John Shea, 181, 239
Leader, Nicholas Philpot, 27
Ledru Rollin, Alexandre, 211, 218-19
Leeds, 193
Lefroy, Thomas, 79-80
Lewis, Franklyn, 17
Leyne, Maurice, 273, 284
Lichfield House, 44
Limerick, 9, 12, 25, 27, 33-5, 39; O'Brien first elected, 40-2; 43-4, 46-7, 48; O'Brien's 1837 dispute with O'Connell, 49-52; 54, 56-8; college question, 63-5; 66; 1839 crisis, 69-71; 72, 75, 76, 77-8, 81, 82, 86, 88, 97, 104, 105, 106, 128-9, 135, 137, 138, 147, 152, 154, 156, 157, 158-9, 169, 175; Famine, 177-8; 186; 1847 election,

Limerick (*continued*)
  188-92; 193-4, 196, 197, 202, 216; riot in 1848, 225-8; 232, 233, 247, 250, 267, 272-3, 281, 283
Limerick Chronicle, 56-7
Limerick Examiner, 166n7, 191
Limerick Star, 41, 45, 56-7
Littleton, —, 257
Littleton, Edward John, 36
Liverpool, 72, 104, 160, 215, 247, 266
Londonderry, 64, 79
Longford, 67
Longmore, Captain, 270
Lorton, Lord, 67, 141
Louis Philippe (King of France), 209
Lucas, Edward, 79
Lyell, Charles, 84
Lynch, —, 156
Lyndhurst, Lord, 49

McCormack, the widow, 276-7, 285, 294, 303
McDonald, General, 297
MacDonnell, John, 28, 81-2
McGee, Thomas D'Arcy, 187, 191, 193, 194, 201, 205-6, 241, 245, 247, 281, 284, 286
MacHale, Archbishop John, 62, 116, 117, 120, 128
McHugh, Father, 186
MacIntyre, Angus, 58, 95
McLeod, Alexander, 76-7
MacManus, Terence B., 265-6, 267-8, 270-1; at the Commons, 272-6; at widow McCormack's, 276-81; 282, 284, 296, 301, 303
MacNevin, Thomas, 122, 133-4
Macaulay, Thomas Babington, 14, 127, 138, 214
Machiavelli, Niccolo, 224
Macroom, 239
Madden, Daniel Owen, 122
Magennis, Father Francis, 157
Maginn, Bishop Edward, 243
Maher, John, 246, 247, 250
Maher (Meagher), Father Patrick, 279-80
Mahon, The O'Gorman (James Patrick), 20-1, 28
Mahon, William, 28
Mahony, Cornelius, 277
Mahony, Pierce, 19, 119-20
Maine, 76
Mallow, 51, 299
Manchester, 193, 215-16
Manchester Examiner, 177n46
Manners, Lord John, 97n97
Mansion House Committee, 142
Marat, Jean Paul, 212
Martin, John, 194, 207-8, 232, 241, 297, 301, 302
Martineau, Arthur, 80
Marylebone, 97
Mathew, Father Theobald, 72, 79, 112
Maynooth, 54, 124, 126-7, 133, 141
Mayo, 273
Mazzini, Giuseppe, 221

Meagher, Thomas Francis, 108n10, 111n22, 157-8, 161, 162, 163, 168, 174, 192, 193, 194; physical force split in 1848, 203-4, 207; 209, 210-11, 214, 216; to Paris in 1848, 217, 219, 223, 224; 225, 227, 229, 232, 235, 241, 243, 245-6, 247; the decision to rebel, 247-50; 252, 253; at Carrick, 254-7; 261, 265, 266, 267, 269; at the Commons, 271-4; 281, 284, 286, 287, 288-9, 292, 296, 297, 299, 301
Meath, 147, 242, 267
medical charities, 48
Mehemet Ali, 76
Melbourne, Lord, 48, 61, 68, 218
Merrion Square, 104, 247
Metternich, Clemens, Prince von, 222
Milan, 209, 288
Miley, Father John, 172, 173-4
Milltown Malbay, 34
Mining Company of Ireland, 271, 274, 294
Mitchel, John, 146-7, 152, 161, 162, 172, 183, 184, 194-6; physical force split in 1848, 199-208; 212, 214-15, 216, 217, 221, 222, 223, 224; Limerick riot in 1848, 225-8; conviction, 229-31; 232, 233, 234, 241, 245, 286, 288, 290, 301
Molyneux Club, 244
Monaghan, 266
Monahan, James Henry, 159, 185, 275
Monck, Charles, 186-7
Monsell, Charles, 147
Monsell, William, 189, 191, 284
Monteagle, *see* Spring Rice, Thomas
Moran, John, 278
Morpeth, Lord, 47, 48, 71, 79, 80
Morrissey, Father Patrick, 256, 269
Mountain (Jacobin), The, 204
Mulgrave (Normanby), Lord, 49, 54; ambassador to France in 1848, 218-21
Mullinahone, 258-61, 263, 265, 267, 269, 274
municipal corporations, 39, 41, 46, 47, 49, 55, 59-61, 63, 74, 82, 99, 140-1
Munster, 64, 240n8, 245, 285, 293
Murphy, Francis S., 95, 118
Murray, Archbishop Daniel, 48, 237
Musgrave, Sir Richard, 45

Nagle, Richard, 122
Nation, 102, 112, 114, 115, 116, 120, 121, 122, 130, 131-2, 140, 144, 146, 153, 155, 156-8, 159, 160, 163, 165-8, 171, 173, 178, 184, 187, 192, 200, 201, 204-5, 210, 217, 222, 229, 235, 236, 241, 243-4, 245n28, 258
National Colonisation Society, 75
National Education System, 29-30, 44, 62, 65
National Guard, 210, 214, 215, 216-17, 224-5, 228, 230
National Museum, Dublin, 224n91
Navan, 133, 243
New Birmingham, 275
New Ross, 249, 266

Index 317

New York, 76, 297
New York Nation, 285-6
Newcastle (Limerick), 65, 70, 71, 76, 79, 81, 166, 177-8, 191
Newgate, 241, 244, 247, 297
Newport rising, 73
Newport, Sir John, 36-7
Newry, 146
Nicholls, George, 55, 65, 79
Ninemilehouse, 253
Nore (river), 250
Normanby, *see* Mulgrave
Norreys, Denham, *see* Jephson, Denham
North Wall meeting, 216, 217
Nottingham, 198

O'Brien (Martineau), Anne (WSO's sister), 21-2, 24, 80n33, 103-4, 176-7, 296-7
O'Brien, Anthony, 72n2
O'Brien, Augustus Stafford, 57
O' Brien (Harris), Catherine (WSO's sister), 138
O'Brien, Charles Murrough (WSO's son), 291
O'Brien, Lady Charlotte (WSO's mother), 12, 14, 15, 18, 23, 29, 33-4, 39, 40-1, 52, 53, 58-9, 82, 89; on O'Brien's conversion to repeal, 106-7; 113n29, 138, 147, 177, 232, 291, 293, 294, 296
O'Brien, Charlotte Grace (WSO's daughter), 142
O'Brien, Donough, 11
O'Brien, Donough (WSO's uncle), 19-20
O'Brien, Sir Edward, 4th baronet (WSO's father), 11-12, 14, 15, 16, 17-18, 19, 21-3, 24-5, 26, 27, 28-9, 32; on O'Brien's marriage, 33-4; 38-9, 40-1, 51, 53, 59
O'Brien, Edward (WSO's brother), 15, 21-2, 41, 53, 76
O'Brien, Edward (WSO's son), 53-4, 78, 147, 239n6, 291, 302
O'Brien, Ellen (wife of Robert), 208n34
O'Brien, Grace (WSO's sister), 14, 21, 78, 124, 138, 147, 291, 293, 295, 296-7, 298n20
O'Brien, Grania R., 28n27
O'Brien, Henry (WSO's brother), 294
O'Brien, Ivar, 23
O'Brien, James, 13
O'Brien, James Bronterre, 74
O'Brien, John, 118
O'Brien, Sir Lucius, 3rd baronet (WSO's grandfather), 11, 12
O'Brien, Sir Lucius, 5th baronet (WSO's brother), 12, 14, 15, 16, 17, 18, 19-20, 21-2, 25, 28, 32, 33, 34, 40, 88-9, 107, 192n113, 232; O'Brien's trial, 291, 293, 295, 298; 302
O'Brien, Lucius (WSO's uncle), 15
O'Brien, Lucius Henry (WSO's son), 81, 87n58
O'Brien, Lucy, 23, 33-5, 39, 40, 52, 53-4, 58-9, 63, 72-3, 76, 78-9, 81-2; the repeal crisis of 1843, 82-4, 86-7, 89-90, 92, 94, 96, 104, 107; 109-10, 111, 112, 113n29, 116, 123, 124, 142, 147; O'Brien's imprisonment in 1846, 149, 150-1, 154; 191, 228, 230, 232, 239, 240, 241, 245, 246; O'Brien's trial and transportation, 291, 294, 295, 298, 299-300; 302-3
O'Brien, Mary Wilton, 22-3
O'Brien, Father Michael, 227
O'Brien, Robert (WSO's brother), 34, 80n33, 192n113, 197, 208n34, 288, 291, 293, 294, 295
O'Brien, Robert Donough (WSO's son), 123
O'Brien, William (Wilton), 21-3
O'Brien, William (WSO's son), 65, 147, 291n1
O'Brien, William Smith
  birth, 11
  family history, 11-12, 20
  father, 11-2, 14, 15, 16, 17-18, 19, 21-3, 24-5, 26, 27, 28-9, 32, 33-4, 38-9, 40-1, 51, 53, 59
  mother, 12, 14, 15, 18, 23, 29, 33-4, 39, 40-1, 52, 53, 58-9
  school and university, 12, 13, 14-15
  religion, 12-13, 14, 24, 73, 78, 86n54, 113, 295
  first entry into Parliament, 16, 17-18
  early Toryism, 9, 16, 18, 19, 25-6
  Catholic Emancipation, 17, 18, 19, 25
  Clare by-election of 1828, 18-20, 38, 51, 159
  duels, 19-21, 23, 28
  children, 21-3, 53, 65, 76, 78, 81, 89, 107, 123, 142, 291, 299
  and Daniel O'Connell, 1828-43, 9, 17, 18-21, 25, 30-2, 35, 38, 40-1, 43-4, 45, 46-7, 49-52, 54-5, 56, 57, 58, 59, 65-6, 67-71, 76, 80, 82, 88, 96, 97, 103, 104; 1843-7, 105, 108, 109, 112-14, 115-23, 124-5, 128-32, 134-7, 138-40, 142, 143-7, 148-9, 150-6, 157-64, 165-7, 170-4
  conversion to liberalism, 26-7, 29-30, 35, 38, 39-41
  repeal, 1831-43, 9, 26, 29-30, 31-2, 33, 37-8, 42, 47, 49, 54, 74, 76, 81, 82-3, 84, 85-8, 89-90, 92-3, 95-6, 97, 99, 101-4; 1843-8, 108, 110, 111-12, 118-21, 127, 133, 139, 143-5, 158, 163-4, 166, 200
  poor law, 27, 29, 35, 37-8, 39, 40, 44-5, 46, 47, 49, 51, 55, 63, 65, 75, 76, 79, 84, 85-6, 208
  education, 27, 29-30, 39, 44, 62-5, 73, 77, 124, 127-31, 135, 137
  state payment of Catholic clergy, 27, 29, 37, 38, 40, 45, 46, 50-1, 54, 61, 70
  wife (Lucy) 23, 33-5, 39, 40, 52, 53-4, 58-9, 63, 72-3, 76, 78-9, 81-4, 86-7, 89-90, 92, 94, 96, 104, 107, 109-10, 111, 112, 113n29, 116, 123, 124, 142, 147, 149, 150-1, 154, 191, 228, 230, 232, 239, 240, 241, 245, 246, 291, 294, 295, 298, 299-300, 302-3
  Cahirmoyle, 12, 14, 23, 33-5, 39, 47, 53, 54, 58-9, 63, 70, 72, 76, 81, 89, 104, 107, 109, 110, 116, 123, 129, 142, 143, 148, 165-6, 172, 177, 192, 202-3, 225, 234, 235, 238, 246, 268, 283, 297, 302, 303
  emigration, 35, 39, 55, 57, 65, 72, 73, 75, 79, 84
  Church of Ireland, 35-9, 41, 44, 46, 48-50, 60, 61, 63, 139

O'Brien, William Smith (*continued*)
  municipal reform, 39, 41, 46, 47, 49, 59-61, 63, 74
  general election, 1835, 41-2, 45
  general election, 1837, 55-8
  general election, 1841, 77-8
  general election, 1847, 187, 188-93
  patronage, 45-6, 48-9, 56, 81
  annual reports, 46, 48, 49, 50, 63, 66, 66, 72
  finances, 23, 34, 52, 54, 58-9, 77, 81
  corn laws, 66-7, 80, 87
  crisis of 1839, 65, 67-72, 112, 145
  arms bill (1843), 85-6, 93-5
  state of Ireland debate (July 1843), 95-7
  Remonstrance of 1843, 90-2, 98-102, 104
  Young Ireland, 71, 112, 114-23, 132, 136-7, 143, 145, 146-7, 150, 153-4, 157, 159-64, 165, 168, 169-76, 181, 183, 184-5, 187, 191
  federalism, 91-2
  Irish language, 125
  physical force, 89-90, 110, 127, 130-1, 146, 160-4, 166, 168, 172, 194, 199-208, 212-15, 219-21, 228, 229-31, 233-4, 235-6, 238 *et seq.*
  Famine, 142, 148-9, 154, 169, 176-9, 182
  absentee landlords, 40, 45, 148, 176, 178, 182, 183, 184
  imprisonment in 1846, 149-56, 163, 166
  secession of 1846, 162-4, 165-7, 170
  leadership, 165, 169-70, 172-6, 181, 188, 190-1, 203
  Paris in 1848, 217-21
  Limerick riot in 1848, 225-8
  trial for sedition, 228-9
  the decision to rebel, 247-50
  at Carrick, 254-7
  at Mullinahone, 258-61
  at Ballingarry and Killenaule, 262-71
  at the Commons, 272-6
  at widow McCormack's, 276-81
  on trial, 293-5
  exile, 299-301
  death, 302
O'Callaghan, J.C., 130
O'Connell, Charles, 161
O'Connell, Daniel, 9, 17, 18-21, 24, 25, 28, 30-2, 35, 38, 39, 40-1, 43-4, 45, 46-7; 1837 dispute with O'Brien, 49-52; 54-5, 56, 57, 58, 59, 60-1; 1839 dispute with O'Brien, 65-6, 67-71; 74-5, 76, 78, 80; the repeal year of 1843, 82, 85, 87, 88, 89, 90, 92, 94, 96, 100-1, 102, 104, 105; 108, 109, 110, 111; leader and deputy, 112-14, 115-23, 124-5, 126, 127, 128-32; 133-7, 138-40, 142, 143-7, 148-9; estrangement from O'Brien, 149-64, 165-8, 170-4; 176, 177, 180, 181, 185; death in 1847, 187; 188-9, 190, 192, 193, 194, 196, 204, 207, 211, 225, 226, 303
O'Connell, Daniel (jnr.), 116, 123
O'Connell, Edward, 46, 56, 70

O'Connell, George John, 190
O'Connell, John, 71, 97, 105, 110; a difficult ally, 114, 117-18, 119, 121, 125, 128, 129, 131, 134, 136, 137, 138-40, 142-3, 146, 150; and the seceders, 162, 163, 166; 183, 186, 187, 188, 198, 202; in 1848, 205, 216, 217, 227, 228, 235-6
O'Connell, Maurice, 28, 113, 135, 136-7, 142, 146, 187, 217
O'Connell, Morgan John, 98
O'Connor, Denis, The O'Conor Don, 100-1
O'Connor, Feargus, 198, 216n62, 223
O'Doherty, Kevin, 241, 297, 301
O'Donnell, John, 191, 193
O'Donohoe, Patrick, 257-8, 261, 262, 263, 264, 268, 270-1; at the Commons, 272-3; 284, 286, 287, 288, 289, 296, 301
O'Farrell, Michael R., 248, 300
O'Ferrall, Richard More, 93-4, 98, 100-1, 102, 158
O'Fiaich, Cardinal Tomas, 303
O'Flaherty, Anthony, 185
O'Gorman, Richard, 114; the rift with O'Connell, 134, 146, 153, 161, 168-9, 171, 173, 174; 178, 184-6, 192, 194, 197, 198, 200; the physical force split in 1848, 201, 204, 206, 207; 210, 216; to Paris with O'Brien, 217, 219, 221; 229, 232, 235, 242; preparations for rebellion, 245-6; 247, 267, 281, 287
O'Grady, Standish, 35, 41, 42
O'Hagan, John, 143
O'Hagan, Thomas, 171
O'Hea, James, 171
O'Loghlen, Sir Colman, 130, 133, 138, 144, 146, 171, 173, 180, 185; the physical force split in 1848, 206; 234, 236, 293
O'Mahony, John, 253; at Carrick, 254-5, 256, 257; 260, 265-6, 269, 270-1; at the Commons, 272-3; 281, 288, 290, 301
O'Malley, Father Thaddeus, 51
O'Mara, Thomas, 57
O'Neill, J.A., 170
O'Neill Daunt, W.J., 121, 136, 150, 152, 163, 170, 205, 284
Orange Order, 30, 90
O'Reilly, Eugene, 221, 267
O'Shaughnessy, Michael, 41, 45, 50, 51, 56, 58, 66, 69, 97, 191
Oxford and Cambridge Club, 73

Palmerston, Lord, 54, 71, 76, 83, 106, 218, 219, 301
Papal States, 122
Paris, 15; in 1848, 209-10, 211, 214, 215, 217-21, 224, 237, 247
Paris United Irish Club, 219
Parliamentary Committee (Repeal Association), 110-11, 114, 117-18, 123-4, 126, 139, 146, 147, 169
Parliamentary Reform, 25-6, 27, 28-9, 30-1, 44, 73-4, 90, 92, 99, 110

Index

Parnell, Charles Stewart, 9, 95, 105, 145, 303
Peel, Sir Robert, 19, 24, 25, 26, 43, 44, 47, 51, 59-60, 65, 68, 75; as Prime Minister, 79-80, 81, 82, 86, 90, 94, 97, 104, 116, 124, 125, 126, 127, 128, 133, 140-1, 143-4, 148-9, 155, 156, 158; 214, 301
Peel, Sir Robert (jnr.), 302
Pemberty, John, 271
Perceval, Alexander, 80
Perrin, Louis, 43
Philipstown murder, 80-1
Pigot, David, 94, 103, 144, 159
Pigot, John, 125, 143, 144n52, 147, 152; and secession in 1846, 160-2; 183, 186, 192, 193, 205, 206
Pilot, 54, 150, 187
Pitt, William, 221
Poland, 302
Poles, The, 218
Political Union, Limerick, 41, 42
poor law, 27, 29, 35, 37-8, 39, 40, 44-5, 46, 47, 49, 51; carried in 1838, 55; 59-60, 63, 65, 75, 82, 84, 85-6, 100, 101, 204, 208
Poor Relief Bill (1847), 182, 183-4
Port Arthur, 303
Porter, John Grey, 125-6
Potter, Robert, 45, 70-1, 143, 159, 171, 190, 191, 293
Powell, Caleb, 69-71, 78, 79, 111, 123; 1847 Limerick election, 188, 189-91
Power, Maurice, 188
Prendergast, Father Edmund, 263-4
Pressburg (Bratislava), 104
Protestant repeal, 113, 114, 120, 125-6, 127, 140-1, 179, 181, 187, 189, 199, 200, 224
Provincial Bank, 29
Punch, 227

Queen's County, 199
Queen's University, 137

railways, 142, 149, 154, 178, 182, 183, 184
Raleigh, John F., 154
Rathkeale (Limerick), 70, 71, 166, 178
Ray, Thomas, 89, 98, 104, 109, 129; and O'Brien's imprisonment in 1846, 150, 153, 155-6; 157, 159, 162, 165, 166, 176
Redington, Thomas, 90-1, 297-8
Reform Club, 61, 98, 108
Reform Registry Association, 49
registration of voters, 65-6, 74-5, 208
Reilly, Devon, 201, 204, 206, 207-8, 226, 232, 245, 247, 262, 269, 272
Remonstrance of 1843, 90-2, 98-102, 104, 105, 106, 108
repeal, 1831-43, 9, 26, 29-30, 31-2, 33, 37-8, 42, 43, 47, 49, 54, 74, 76, 78, 80-99 *passim*, 101-4; in 1843-8, 108, 110, 111-12, 118-21, 133, 148, 158, 163-4, 166, 185, 198, 200, 204, 301
Repeal Association, 9, 76, 88, 97, 103, 104, 105; O'Brien's early days, 108, 109, 110-12; 114, 115, 116; federalism controversy, 118, 119, 120, 121; 122, 123, 124, 125, 126, 127; colleges dispute, 128-32, 134-8; 138-40, 142-4, 145-6, 147-9; and O'Brien's imprisonment, 150-6; 157-8, 159; the seceders, 160-2, 165-73; 176, 181, 186, 189, 192; in 1848, 205, 209, 211, 216, 217, 218, 228, 235-6, 252
Repeal Literary Club, 168, 170
Reproductive Works Committee, 180, 186
Richmond Bridewell, 113, 118, 296-7, 299
Robespierre, Maximilien, 212
Roche, Dir David, 102, 284
Roche, James, 64
Roden, Lord, 67
Roebuck, John Arthur, 135
Rome, 187
Romilly, Sir Samuel, 76
Ronayne, Dominick, 40
Roscommon, 62, 273
Ross, D.R., 90-1, 98, 118
Rotundo, 133, 181, 207, 255
Rous, Henry John, 97n97
Rousseau, Jean-Jacques, 76
Royal Dublin Society, 48
Royal Irish Constabulary, 276
Royal Irish Hussars, 253, 270
Russell, Lord John, 55, 60-1, 67, 75, 81; in 1843, 91, 93, 97-8; 105, 143-5; as Prime Minister, 176, 179, 183, 218, 222, 223, 227, 240n8, 241, 247, 281, 284
Ryan, Bishop John, 197
Ryan, Michael, 156

St Antony, 208
St Columba's College, 147
St Margaret's Church, Westminster, 23, 150
Sarsfield Club, 193-4
Saville, John, 215, 276
Scotland, 149
Scott's Cross, Ballingarry, 276
Scott, Percy, 12, 13, 14
Second French Republic, 209, 211, 214, 217
secession of 1846, 162-4, 165-7, 170
secret ballot, 30, 50-1, 54, 57, 71, 74, 138-9
Shanagolden (Limerick), 178
Shaw, Frederick, 127, 140-1, 154-5, 180
Sheedy, Kieran, 17
Sheil, Richard L., 60, 81, 100-1, 102, 158-9
Sicily, 288
Sinn Féin, 145
Skague Fort, 142
Slievenamon mountain, 253, 255, 263, 265, 267-8, 269, 273, 282
Sligo, 247, 281
Smith, Adam, 182
Smith, Elizabeth, 153, 217n66, 221
Smith, Thomas, 23, 53
Smith, William, 12, 23, 34, 53

Smyth, Patrick J., 267
Smythe, George P.S., 97n97
Society for the Diffusion of Useful Knowledge, 62, 73, 111
Somers, John Patrick, 202
Somerville, Alexander, 177
Somerville, Sir William, 100, 158, 208, 232
Spain, 221, 302
Spottiswode conspiracy, 58
Spring Rice, Stephen, 196
Spring Rice, Thomas (Lord Monteagle), 62, 106, 126, 183, 196
Stackallan, 147
Stanley, E.J., 45
Stanley, Lord, 26-7, 29-30, 36, 37, 47, 66, 74-5, 97, 126
state of Ireland debate (July 1843), 95-7
Statistical Society, 73
Staunton, Michael, 84
Steele, Tom, 18-21, 103, 130; and O'Brien's imprisonment in 1846, 150, 152, 153, 155-6; 157-8
Stephens, James, 257-8, 259-60, 261, 262; at Ballingarry and Killenaule, 263, 264, 265, 267-8, 270; at the Commons, 272-3, 274-6; at widow McCormack's, 276-81; 282, 284, 286, 288, 301
Stockdale, John Joseph, 73
Stuart, Villiers, 27, 35, 60, 98, 99, 100
sugar duties, 77
Sugden, Sir Edward, 79-80, 87-8
Suir (river), 254
Sullivan, Alexander M., 283
Sullivan, Thomas, 272, 273
Swift, 300
Swift Club, 193, 201, 206
Switzerland, 39

Tallaght, 302
Tara, 211, 243
Tasmania, *see* Van Diemen's Land
Templederry, 187, 269
Tennyson, Alfred, Lord, 14
Thackeray, William M., 227, 284
Thomond, 11
Thucydides, 76
Thurles, 260, 270, 282-3, 285, 297
Times, 107, 177, 285
Tipperary, 123, 187, 197, 237, 238, 250; the rising, 253-81; 283, 286, 287, 288, 289, 291, 295, 297, 302, 303
tithes, 36-8, 40, 41, 44, 46, 48-50, 52, 55, 61, 63, 82
Tone, Theobald Wolfe, 9, 114, 219, 302
Tracy, Father Patrick, 257
Trant, Thomas, 276-81, 290
Tribune, 241
Trim, 243
Trinity College, Cambridge, 12, 14-15
Trinity College, Dublin, 63-5, 129, 131, 135, 147
Tuam, 62, 116, 117

Turkey, 302

Ulster custom, 126, 208
United Irishman, 208, 215, 217, 225, 229, 241
United States, 76-7, 83, 127, 213, 215, 220, 248, 284, 285, 301-2
Urlingford, 275, 281

Van Diemen's Land (Tasmania), 82, 286, 299, 301, 303
Vandeleur, Crofton, 88
Victoria (Queen), 56, 68, 103, 155, 211, 293
Vienna, 209
Villiers, Charles, 80
Vinegar Hill, 247
Volunteers of 1782, 214, 224

Wakefield, E.G., 75
Wales, 302
Walsh, Thomas, 268
Walter, John, 198, 285
War Directory, 245
Ward, Henry George, 101
Washington, George, 263
Waterford, 43, 72, 137, 138, 209, 225; and the rising in 1848, 244, 250, 256, 257, 269, 273, 281
Waterloo, 221
Wealth of Nations, 182
Weekly Freeman, 247
Weekly News, 245n28
Weir, Hugh W.L., 23
Welling, 12
Wellington, Duke of, 25, 68, 89, 96
West Indies, 53, 67
Wexford, 36, 246, 247, 249-50
Whately, Archbishop Richard, 62
Whiteside, James, 293-4
Wicklow, 131, 230-1, 232-3, 242, 297
William IV, 55
Williams, Dalton, 241, 297
Wilton, Mary Ann, 21-3, 25, 150
Wiltshire, 30
Wood, Charles, 98
Wright, Thomas, 259
Wyse, George, 85, 90, 94
Wyse, Thomas, 30-1, 36-7, 43, 44, 46, 57, 60, 62-5, 74, 80, 82; the Parliamentary campaign of 1843, 85, 88, 90-103, 104; 105-6, 108-9, 110, 118; the colleges question in 1845, 124, 128-9, 137; 158-9

Youghal, 58, 192
Young England, 97n97
Young Ireland, 71, 112; relations with O'Brien in 1844; 114-23, 125, 126, 128, 130, 131-2, 134, 136-7, 138, 143, 145-7; and O'Brien's imprisonment in 1846, 150, 153-4; 156-8; seceders, 159-64, 165-76; the Confederation, 181, 185-7, 189, 191-3, 211, 221, 227, 232, 236; 237, 238, 245-6, 252, 301